PINSON
ON
REVENUE LAW

AUSTRALIA
The Law Book Company Ltd.
Sydney : Melbourne : Brisbane

CANADA AND U.S.A.
The Carswell Company Ltd.
Agincourt, Ontario

INDIA
N. M. Tripathi Private Ltd.
Bombay
and
Eastern Law House Private Ltd.
Calcutta
M.P.P. House
Bangalore

ISRAEL
Steimatzky's Agency Ltd.
Jerusalem : Tel Aviv : Haifa

MALAYSIA : SINGAPORE : BRUNEI
Malayan Law Journal (Pte.) Ltd.
Singapore

NEW ZEALAND
Sweet & Maxwell (N.Z.) Ltd.
Wellington

PAKISTAN
Pakistan Law House
Karachi

PREFACE

THIS book is offered as an introduction to the study of revenue law for the reader who already has some knowledge of basic legal principles. The subject is presented in a form which enables the book to be used as a textbook for examinations, but I hope that it will also be of value to the practising lawyer or accountant, not otherwise an expert in this field, who wishes to have at least a sufficient working knowledge of the principles of taxation to sense when a problem exists. Many lawyers and accountants have said of previous editions that they have found the book to be a useful starting-off point on a journey of advanced research. I hope that it will continue to fulfil this role.

Because this is an introductory book, the main object has been to state the principles of revenue law in as readable and intelligible a form as the subject-matter allows. No attempt has been made to be exhaustive but I have not hesitated to express views on controversial or difficult subjects.

The legislation enacted since the publication of the first edition in 1962 has added enormously to the complexities of the tax system and it is becoming increasingly difficult to state the effect of legislation concisely and in a form which is both accurate and intelligible. The task of the writer who seeks to encompass the principles of revenue law within a few hundred pages is very much more difficult than that of the writer of the practitioners' book, who feels under no such constraint; for the latter does not experience the difficulties involved in having continually to decide what to leave out. One is reminded of the letter of Pascale[1]: " Je n'ai fait celle-ci plus longue que parceque je n'ai pas en le loisir de la faire plus courte." (" I have made this letter longer than usual because I lack the time to make it short.")

The book is in five parts. Part 1 deals with taxes on income and on capital gains. This part is in four divisions dealing with A. the taxation of the income of non-corporate bodies; B. the taxation of companies; C. the taxation of capital gains, and development land tax; and D. administration, assessments and back duty respectively. Part 2 is on capital transfer tax. Part 3 states the principles of the law relating to stamp duties as briefly as the subject allows. Part 4 deals with value added tax, and Part 5, entitled " Tax Planning," offers the reader no more than a glimpse of the kinds of problems which commonly arise in practice in connection with gifts, settlements, arrangements on divorce and separation, wills, pension schemes, golden handshakes, etc.

This edition incorporates the changes in revenue law made by the Finance Act 1978 and by regulations and judicial decisions of the past year. The Finance Act, containing 80 sections and 13 Schedules, has made numerous changes in almost all branches of revenue law, including some concessions designed to assist " small businesses."

---

[1] Pascale, *Lettres Provinciales* (1657), xvi.

In this edition I have made substantial alterations to Chapter 16 (capital gains tax), on which subject there have been a number of important judicial decisions, and to Chapter 17 (on administration, assessments and back duty). A number of sections of the text have been rewritten and, hopefully, improved.

I am indebted to Mr. John Gardiner who has updated the sections of the book on value added tax and development land tax (which he contributed). My thanks are once again due to the many readers who have contributed by their criticism to the improvement of the book and to the editorial staff of Sweet & Maxwell who have assisted in its production.

The law is stated as at September 1, 1978

11 New Square,
Lincoln's Inn
London WC2A 3QB   BARRY PINSON

CONTENTS

PART 1: TAXES ON INCOME AND CAPITAL GAINS

DIVISION A: THE TAXATION OF THE INCOME OF NON-CORPORATE BODIES

PART 3: STAMP DUTIES

PART 5: TAX PLANNING

TABLE OF CASES

XV

TABLE OF STATUTES

WORKS CITED

THE following works and periodicals are cited by the means of abbreviations which appear in the left-hand column:

B.T.E.   *British Tax Encyclopedia,* General Editor: Philip Lawton. (Sweet & Maxwell Limited.)

Simon   Simon's *Taxes,* 3rd. edition. (Butterworths.)

Alpe   Alpe's *Law of Stamp Duties,* 25th edition, by Peter E. Whitworth and James Mackenzie, M.B.E. (Jordan & Sons.)

Sergeant   *Sergeant and Sims on Stamp Duties,* 7th edition, by B. J. and Sims   Sims, LL.B., F.T.I.I., Solicitor assisted by A. K. Tavaré, LL.B., Solicitor. (Butterworths.)

B.T.R.   The *British Tax Review,* edited by Philip Lawton and John Avery Jones. This is published six times a year and deals with all aspects of taxation. It contains a section entitled Current Tax Intelligence which is invaluable for keeping up to date. (Sweet & Maxwell Limited.)

S.T.C.   Simon's *Tax Cases.*

S.T.I.   Simon's *Tax Intelligence.*

Other books are cited but without abbreviations.

PART 1

TAXES ON INCOME AND
CAPITAL GAINS

DIVISION A

THE TAXATION OF THE INCOME OF
NON-CORPORATE BODIES

CHAPTER 1

INTRODUCTION

1. PREFATORY

Sources

1-01   The principal Act charging income tax and corporation tax is the Income and Corporation Taxes Act 1970. Matters of administration and procedure are dealt with in the Taxes Management Act 1970. Capital allowances are dealt with in the Capital Allowances Act 1968 and in the Finance Act 1971. The Acts of 1970 and 1968 are consolidating statutes, consolidating the statute law formerly contained in the Income Tax Act 1952 and in numerous later Finance Acts. The consolidation does not extend to capital gains tax, except in relation to companies' capital gains (which are chargeable to corporation tax and are dealt with in the Income and Corporation Taxes Act 1970) and matters of administration; so reference has to be made principally to the capital gains provisions in the Finance Act 1965 which continues in operation, amended to take account of the repeals made necessary by the 1970 consolidation.

It should be noted that the Acts of 1970 are consolidating and not codifying statutes. It is therefore necessary to refer to decided cases for many of the fundamental principles of income taxation. Tax cases are reported in the official *Law Reports* published by the Council of Law Reporting and also in the *Reports of Tax Cases* (cited as T.C.) published by the Stationery Office under the directions of the Board of Inland Revenue. Where there is a discrepancy between the official reports and the *Tax Cases*, the former are to be preferred.[1]

There are a number of extra-statutory concessions which are applied in practice.[2] The Revenue produce a number of explanatory booklets[3] and have recently announced their intention to publish Statements of Practice.[3a]

Annual nature of tax

1-02   All taxes on income are annual taxes which are renewed each year by Act of Parliament. Proposals made by the Chancellor of the Exchequer in his Budget speech are at once agreed to by resolution of the House of Commons: and because such a resolution would otherwise lack the force of law, the Provisional Collection of Taxes Act 1968 provides that resolutions which vary an existing tax or renew a tax shall have limited statutory force

---

[1] *Fairman v. Perpetual Investment Building Society* [1923] A.C. 74 at pp. 78–79; [1931] W.N. 121. The official *Law Reports* include summaries of the arguments of counsel which are often of some value and which are not in the *Tax Cases*. On the other hand, the *Tax Cases* usually include the case stated by the Commissioners. It is the practice not to report a case in the *Tax Cases* until it is disposed of by the final court to which appeal is made: this causes considerable delay in publication. In proceedings in the House of Lords the *Law Reports* should be cited in preference to the *Tax Cases: Practice Note* [1970] 1 W.L.R. 1400. In *Murphy v. Ingram* [1973] Ch. 434 at p. 438; [1973] S.T.C. at p. 314, Megarry J. expressed the view (giving reasons) that the *Law Reports* should generally be cited, not only in the House of Lords. The actual decision in that case was reversed on appeal: [1974] Ch. 363; 49 T.C. 410.

[2] See Revenue Booklet I.R.I. (1976) entitled *Extra-Statutory Concessions in operation at September 30, 1977,* reproduced in [1977] S.T.I. 114.   [3] See list in [1978] S.T.I. 154–155.

[3a] [1978] S.T.I. 349. These will be designated SP1/78 *et seq.*

until the Finance Act embodying the resolutions is passed.[4] This Act must be passed within about four months of the resolution and, in practice, the Finance Act usually receives the Royal Assent on about July 31. Changes made by the Act may be retrospective to Budget Day or to some other date specified in the Act.

The annual nature of tax is reflected in the method by which individuals and companies are assessed to tax. For individuals the tax year commences on April 6 in one year and ends on April 5 in the following year and such a year is termed a " year of assessment " [5]; for companies liable to corporation tax, the year commences on April 1 in one year and ends on March 31 in the following year and such a year is termed a " financial year." [6] The term " assessment " describes the administrative act by which income is made liable to tax and every such assessment is made for a year of assessment (or a financial year, as the case may be) irrespective of the period for which the taxpayer renders accounts.

2. The Six Schedules

1-03 The general scheme of the Income Tax Acts [7] is to charge tax according to the source from which income arises. Thus section 1 of the Income and Corporation Taxes Act 1970 charges tax for each year of assessment in respect of " all property, profits or gains " described or comprised in Schedules A, B, C, D, E and F of the Act and in accordance with the provisions applicable to those Schedules. Schedules D and E are further subdivided into Cases.

1-04 The following table shows how " income " is classified by reference to the source from which it arises, and how the basis on which the amount of taxable income is measured or computed differs as between the Schedules. References to sections are (unless otherwise stated) to those of the Income and Corporation Taxes Act 1970.

		Tax is charged on:	*Basis on which income is computed:*
1-05	SCHEDULE A (s. 67)	Annual profits or gains arising in respect of certain rents or receipts from land in the United Kingdom.	The rents or receipts to which the taxpayer becomes entitled in the year of assessment *less* the deductions authorised by the Act.
		Note: Schedule A was originally Case VIII of Schedule D and was introduced as such by the Finance Act 1963. Before 1963, Schedule A existed in a different form.	
1-06	SCHEDULE B (s. 91)	Income from the occupation of woodlands in the United Kingdom managed on a commercial basis and with a view to the realisation of profits.	One-third of the G.A.V. for the current year of assessment.

---

[4] There are similar provisions relating to stamp duty which have permanent statutory effect until repealed or varied: F.A. 1973, s. 50.

[5] See the definition of " year of assessment " and " the year 1970–71 " in I.C.T.A. 1970, s. 526 (5).

[6] I.C.T.A. 1970, ss. 238 (1), 527 (1).

[7] " The Income Tax Acts " means, except in so far as the context otherwise requires, all enactments relating to income tax, including the provisions of the Corporation Tax Acts which relate to income tax: I.C.T.A. 1970, s. 526 (1) (*b*).

	Tax is charged on:	*Basis on which income is computed:*
1-07 SCHEDULE C (s. 93)	Profits arising from public revenue dividends payable in the United Kingdom; or payable in the Republic of Ireland, being dividends on Government stock registered or inscribed in the books of the Bank of Ireland in Dublin; and overseas public revenue dividends payable through a banker or other person in the United Kingdom, if paid by means of coupons.	The income of the current year of assessment.

Schedule C thus applies to interest payable on certain securities of the United Kingdom and of foreign governments, where the interest is paid in the United Kingdom. The tax is assessed on the paying authority and is deducted from the interest which is paid.

1-08 SCHEDULE D (ss. 108–109)		Normal Basis: the profits of the taxpayer's accounting year ending in the preceding year of assessment.
CASE I	Profits of a trade.	
CASE II	Profits of a profession or vocation.	Special rules for opening and closing years (ss. 115–118).

Example: Brown, a solicitor, prepares annual accounts made up to December 31 each year. The profits of the accounting year ended December 31, 1975, constitute the statutory income (Case II) of the year of assessment 1976–77.

CASE III	Interest, annuities or other annual payments; discounts; small maintenance payments, etc.	Normal Basis: the income arising in the preceding year of assessment. Special rules for opening and closing years (ss. 119–121).
CASE IV	Income arising from securities out of the United Kingdom not charged under Schedule C.	Normal Basis: the income arising in the preceding year of assessment.
CASE V	Income arising from possessions out of the United Kingdom.	Special rules for opening and closing years (ss. 122–124).

Income arising under Cases IV and V is assessable only if the taxpayer is resident in the United Kingdom. In some cases, tax is payable only on the income which is received in the United Kingdom.

CASE VI	Any annual profits or gains not falling under any other Schedule or Case; and certain income specifically directed to be charged under Case VI.	The profits of the current year of assessment (s. 125).

	Tax is charged on:	*Basis on which income is computed:*
1-09 SCHEDULE E (s. 181)	Income arising from offices, employments and pensions; and certain income specifically directed to be charged under Schedule E, *e.g.* social security benefits (s. 219).	The emoluments or other income of the current year of assessment.
	Schedule E is divided into three Cases, of which Cases II and III apply where there is a foreign element.	
1-10 SCHEDULE F (s. 232) [8]	Dividends and other distributions made by companies resident in the United Kingdom.	The dividends etc. of the year of assessment.

1-11   Capital gains tax is, as its name implies, a tax on gains of a capital (not income) nature; and such gains are not taxed as income.

1-12   It will be observed from the table that there are, broadly speaking, six sources of income:

(1) income from the ownership or occupation of land (Schedules A and B);

(2) profits of a trade, profession or vocation (Schedule D, Cases I and II) and other profits brought into charge (Schedule D, Case VI);

(3) emoluments of an office or employment (Schedule E, Case I);

(4) " pure income " comprising interest, annuities and other annual payments (Schedule D, Case III);

(5) foreign income (Schedule C; Schedule D, Cases IV and V; Schedule E, Cases II and III);

(6) dividends and other distributions made by United Kingdom companies (Schedule F).

Corporation tax is merely a tax levied on the profits of certain companies from the sources above referred to. Before 1965 both companies and individuals were charged to income tax. Since the Finance Act 1965 companies have been separately charged to corporation tax in order that changes in the rates of company taxation can be made without affecting individuals, and vice versa.

Where a taxpayer has numerous sources of income falling under different Schedules, it is necessary to aggregate the statutory income computed under each Schedule for the purpose of determining his income in the year of assessment. Under some Schedules (*e.g.* Schedule E) the statutory income of a year of assessment is the income of that year; whereas under all the Cases of Schedule D (other than Case VI) statutory income is measured by reference to the profits or income of a preceding period. It follows that income as computed for the purposes of the Income Tax Acts for a year of assessment may bear no relation to the taxpayer's real income in that year.

---

[8] For the year 1973–74 and subsequent years of assessment, this means I.C.T.A. 1970, s. 232, as substituted by F.A. 1972, s. 87.

Relationship between the Schedules

1-13   The six Schedules are mutually exclusive so the Revenue cannot charge under one Schedule income which properly falls under another.

> Thus in *Fry* v. *Salisbury House Estate Ltd.*[9] a company formed to acquire, manage and deal with a building let out the rooms as unfurnished offices. The company provided a staff of lift-operators and porters and also certain services at an additional charge. It was held that the income from rents was assessable only under Schedule A and not (as the Revenue contended) under Schedule D. Profits made on services supplied to tenants were assessable under Schedule D.

In *Mitchell and Edon* v. *Ross* [10] specialists holding part-time appointments under the National Health Service (Schedule E) also engaged in private practice (Schedule D, Case II). A claim was made to set against the Schedule D receipts certain expenses incurred in connection with the Schedule E appointments which were not allowable under the rules applicable to Schedule E. The House of Lords rejected the claim and Lord Radcliffe said this:

> " Generally speaking, the . . . schedules of taxable categories are distinguished from each other by distinctions as to the nature of the source from which the chargeable profit arises. The source may be property in the ordinary sense such as land, securities, copyright, office, or it may be an activity sufficiently coherent, trade or profession, for example, to be regarded as itself the stock upon which profits grow. That is not an exhaustive account, but it is, I think, a sufficient general introduction. Before you can assess a profit to tax you must be sure that you have properly identified its source or other description according to the correct schedule: but, once you have done that, it is obligatory that it should be charged, if at all, under that schedule and strictly in accordance with the rules that are there laid down for assessments under it. It is a necessary consequence of this conception that the sources of profit in the different schedules are mutually exclusive."

Whereas the Revenue have no choice as between Schedules, where income falls under more than one Case of the same Schedule the Revenue may elect the Case under which to make the assessment. [11]

Profits not chargeable to tax

1-14   A profit or gain which does not fall within the charging provisions escapes tax. Suppose, for example, that Adam sells his house at a profit. If Adam is a property dealer and the house is part of his trading stock, the profit is assessable under Case I of Schedule D; otherwise the profit is a " capital profit " which escapes tax, unless the capital gains tax applies. It will be apparent from this example that the taxable quality of a payment must be determined by reference to the circumstances surrounding the payment. Where Adam is not trading with the house, there is no " source " which the Acts recognise as income-producing; but the possibility of a taxable capital gain must be considered.

" [1930] A.C. 432; 15 T.C. 266 (H.L.). At this time Schedule A was a tax on the net annual value of the building. In consequence of this decision, statute provided for the assessment of " excess rents " under Case VI of Schedule D. Now rents are assessed under Schedule A.

[10] [1962] A.C. 814; 40 T.C. 11 (H.L.).

[11] *Liverpool & London & Globe Insurance Co.* v. *Bennett* [1913] A.C. 610; 6 T.C. 327 (H.L.). Where the Revenue make an assessment under the wrong Case of Schedule D, *e.g.* Case VII and not Case I, the court has a discretion to deal with the assessment under the right Case: see T.M.A. 1970, s. 56 (6) applied in *Bath and West Counties Property Trust Ltd.* v. *Thomas* [1978] S.T.C. 30.

A profit or gain which clearly falls within one of the Schedules may nevertheless escape tax if the source from which it comes does not exist in the year when the profit arises.[12] Thus when a trader or professional man dies or retires and sums are later received for goods supplied or services rendered during the course of the trade or profession, such receipts are not chargeable to tax in the year of receipt,[13] except where statute otherwise provides.[14] Similarly, payments made to an employee after his employment has terminated escape tax, unless they are deferred remuneration or statute imposes a charge to tax.[15]

3. THE SCOPE OF THE INCOME TAX ACTS

1-15 The Income Tax Acts apply to the United Kingdom: that is, to England, Wales, Scotland and Northern Ireland, but not to the Channel Islands or the Isle of Man. The territorial sea of the United Kingdom is deemed to be part of the United Kingdom and there are provisions to ensure that profits arising from the exploitation of the natural resources of the United Kingdom part of the Continental Shelf shall be charged to United Kingdom tax.[16]

Broadly speaking, all income which arises in the United Kingdom is liable to United Kingdom income tax, irrespective of the nationality, domicile or residence of the recipient; and foreign income is assessable to tax only if the recipient is resident in the United Kingdom. Where income is liable to double taxation (*e.g.* in the country where it arises and in the country where the recipient resides), relief may be available.[17]

Exemptions from tax

1-16 The following income is exempt from income tax:
  (1) Scholarship and similar income.[18]
  (2) Certain social security benefits and payments of child benefit.[19]
  (3) Accumulated interest and any terminal bonus or other sum payable in respect of United Kingdom savings certificates.[20]
  (4) Interest on post-war credits.[21]
  (5) Interest on tax reserve certificates.[22]
  (6) The first £70 interest on ordinary (but not investments) deposits with the National Savings Bank and ordinary deposits with a trustee savings bank. The £70 exemption applies to both husband and wife, *i.e.* the exemption is £140 on a joint account or £70 each on separate accounts.[23]
  (7) Dividends and interest paid by a Building Society, if the society

---

[12] On the doctrine of " the source " see *Brown* v. *National Provident Institution* [1921] 2 A.C. 222; 8 T.C. 57 (H.L.).
[13] *Bennett* v. *Ogston* (1930) 15 T.C. 374; *Carson* v. *Cheyney's Executors* [1959] A.C. 412; 38 T.C. 240.
[14] See *post*, §§ 2-88 *et seq.*
[15] *Post*, §§ 3-24 *et seq.*   [16] F.A. 1970, s. 38.
[17] *Post*, § 7-25.   [18] I.C.T.A. 1970, s. 375.
[19] *Ibid.* s. 219 as amended by F.A. 1977, s. 23, and F.A. 1978, s. 20 (4). See § 8-45A.
[20] *Ibid.* s. 95.   [21] Income Tax (Repayment of Post-War Credits) Act 1959, s. 2 (4).
[22] I.C.T.A. 1970, s. 98. These were at one time issued by the Treasury as a means by which money could be invested to meet liability for tax. Tax reserve certificates have now been replaced by Certificates of Tax Deposit, the interest on which is taxable: see [1975] S.T.I. 348; [1976] S.T.I. 107; [1978] S.T.I. 154.
[23] *Ibid.* s. 414 amended by F.A. 1977, s. 26.

has an arrangement with the Revenue.[24] (This exemption applies only to income tax at the basic rate.)

    (8) Terminal bonuses under certified contractual saving schemes (*e.g.* S.A.Y.E.).[25]

    (9) Interest on damages for personal injuries.[26]

   (10) The first £50 of war widow's pension.[27]

   (11) Payments under job release schemes under the the Job Release Act 1977.[28]

Interest from certain United Kingdom Government securities belonging to persons not ordinarily resident in the United Kingdom is exempt from tax.[29]

The Crown

1-17   Generally, all persons having a source of income which is chargeable to tax are liable to tax, irrespective of personal incapacity. The Crown is not liable to tax unless statute otherwise provides. By section 524 of the Income and Corporation Taxes Act 1970, the provisions of the Income Tax Acts relating to the assessment, charge, deduction and payment of income tax are made to apply in relation to public offices and departments of the Crown, except in so far that these provisions would require the payment of any tax which would be ultimately payable by the Crown. The section enables public offices and departments of the Crown to deduct tax from annual payments etc. made by them and enables the Revenue to recover the tax so deducted.[30]

Charities

1-18   Bodies of persons established for charitable purposes enjoy the following main exemptions from tax [31]:

    (a) exemption from tax under Schedules A and D in respect of the rents and profits of any lands, etc., if applied to charitable purposes only;

    (b) exemption from tax under Schedule B in respect of any lands occupied by a charity;

    (c) exemption from tax on interest, annuities, dividends, etc., if applied to charitable purposes only [32];

    (d) profits of a trade carried on by a charity are exempt from tax under Schedule D if the profits are applied solely to the purposes of the charity *and* either (i) the trade is exercised in the course of the actual carrying out of a primary purpose of the charity; or (ii) the work in connection with the trade is mainly carried on by beneficiaries of the charity.

---

[24] I.C.T.A. 1970, s. 343.
[25] *Ibid*. s. 415.
[26] I.C.T.A. 1970, s. 375A.
[27] F.A. 1976, s. 31.
[28] F.A. 1977, s. 30.
[29] I.C.T.A. 1970, s. 99 (1).
[30] See *post*, §§ 5-30 *et seq*.
[31] I.C.T.A. 1970, s. 360.
[32] Thus a charity is able to recover basic rate income tax on payments made under " seven year covenants." If tax rates go down, a charity recovers less (but see the transitional relief in F.A. 1973, s. 52).

For other exemptions from tax, reference should be made to sections 360–377 of the Income and Corporation Taxes Act 1970 and to standard works on income tax.

4. THE UNIFIED SYSTEM OF PERSONAL TAXATION

1-19 Sections 32 to 39 of the Finance Act 1971 introduced a new method of charging tax on the income of individuals which applies in the year 1973–74 and in subsequent years of assessment. This has been called the " unified system " of direct personal taxation. The significance of the term " unified " will appear from the following comparison between the unified system and the system in operation in years up to and including the year 1972–73.

The pre-1973 system

Before the year 1973–74, the individuals were subject to income tax and in some cases surtax. Each Finance Act contained a section charging income tax for the appropriate year of assessment at a rate which was termed " the standard rate." Thus section 62 of the Finance Act 1972 charged income tax for the year 1972–73 at the standard rate of 38·75 per cent. An individual's entire income was not taxed at the standard rate for he was entitled to personal reliefs and allowances which increased in amount with the number of his dependants and which had the effect of relieving altogether a portion of his income from tax. Only a proportion of an individual's earned income was subject to income tax by reason of the earned income relief available to earned but not unearned (such as investment) income. Hence the pre-1973 system discriminated against unearned income by taxing it (in effect) at higher rates, thereby discouraging saving.

Where the total income of an individual exceeded a certain amount, he was liable to surtax in addition to income tax. Surtax was a progressive tax the rate of which increased with each successive slice of the taxpayer's income above the figure at which liability began. The rates of surtax were fixed each year by the Finance Act. Section 10 of the Finance Act 1973, for example, fixed the surtax rates for 1972–73. Each Finance Act fixed the rates of surtax for the preceding fiscal year; surtax was technically a deferred instalment of income tax.

Assume, for example, that a trader's accounting period ends on March 31 in each year. His profits for the year ended March 31, 1970, would form his statutory income for the year of assessment 1970–71: see the example in § 1-08. Income tax would be payable at the standard rate with the benefit of the personal reliefs and allowances fixed by the Finance Act 1970, the income tax being payable in two instalments during the year 1971. Surtax on the profits for the year ended March 31, 1970, would be payable in 1972 at rates fixed by the Finance Act 1971. This dual system of income tax and surtax therefore involved some complication.

The post-1973 unified system

The unified system of personal taxation involves the abolition of earned income relief as such and the abolition of surtax as such. For the year

1973–74 and subsequent years of assessment there is a single tax on all income, namely, income tax. The concept of a " standard rate " of tax disappears in favour of a new concept of " basic rate " to be fixed annually by Parliament. Section 66 of the Finance Act 1972 fixed the basic rate of income tax for 1973–74 at 30 per cent. This rate of 30 per cent. corresponded roughly to tax at the standard rate of 38·75 per cent. less earned income relief; earned income relief disappears and instead all income (including unearned or investment income) is taxed at the lower rate formerly applicable only to earned income. The object of the new system is therefore to remove the discrimination against unearned income and to simplify personal taxation by removing the separate charge of surtax.

Not all income is taxed only at the basic rate, for when the total income of an individual exceeds a certain figure, income tax at higher rates is payable. A table showing the higher rates of income tax is in § 8-04.

The discrimination against unearned income does not wholly disappear, however, for section 32 of the Finance Act 1971 provides that where an individual's total income includes investment income and that investment income exceeds such amount as Parliament may determine, income tax shall also be charged in respect of the excess at such additional rate or rates as Parliament may determine.

Section 13 of the Finance Act 1978 charges income tax for the year 1978–79 at the basic rate of 33 per cent. and at the higher rate(s) shown in the table in § 8-04. Investment income is taxed at additional rates as shown in the table in § 8-05. The additional rate tax on investment income may be termed the investment income surcharge. Computation A in § 8-69 shows how income is taxed under the unified system.

Persons other than individuals—such as trustees—are not liable to higher rate income tax or to the investment income surcharge. Hence the income of trustees will normally be subject only to basic rate income tax, but there is an exception in the case of accumulated income.[33] The unified system is discussed in Chapter 8.

Husband and wife

1-20   A husband and wife living together are treated as one unit for tax purposes. Their separate incomes are therefore added together and income tax (including surtax in years up to and including the years 1972–73) is charged on the total joint income, as if it were the income of one person.[34] This principle of aggregation may cause hardship where each spouse has a substantial income, and the principle is subject to some modification in the case of a wife's earned income.[35]

Parent and child

1-21   The income of a minor is treated as his income and not that of his parent (subject to an exception in the case of income paid to or for the benefit of a minor under a settlement made on him by his parent: see §§ 10-23 and

---

[33] F.A. 1973, s. 16, *post*, § 9-02.
[34] For details, see *post*, §§ 8-23 *et seq.*
[35] See § 8-29.

10-35). In March 1974 the Labour Government announced its intention to aggregate a minor's income with that of his parents but this proposal has, for the moment, been deferred.[36]

Companies

1-22   Companies are subject to corporation tax, not income tax; hence the new unified system of taxation does not affect companies as such. The manner in which companies are taxed is discussed in Chapter 14.

5. COLLECTION OF TAX

1-23   The Income Tax Acts provide two principal methods of collecting tax on income:

(1) *By direct assessment*. Tax which is due under, for example, Schedule D, Cases I and II, is collected by direct assessment. After the amount of tax which is due has been determined by the Inspector, a formal assessment is made which (unless appealed against) becomes final; and the tax is collected by the Collector of Taxes. The investment income surcharge is so collected under the unified system of personal taxation.

(2) *By deduction at source*. A high proportion of income tax is collected by the Revenue at the source where the income arises. In the case of the employee, for example, tax is deducted from his salary under the Pay As You Earn system (P.A.Y.E.) and the employer is made accountable to the Revenue for the tax so deducted. The necessity for assessing the employee is therefore removed and the administrative work of the Revenue is reduced. Income tax at the basic rate is collected at the source in the case of annuities and other annual payments [37] and is treated as so collected in the case of dividends.[38]

The following illustration shows how the system of collection operates:

A (who has £5,000 a year) covenants to pay B £800 a year for the joint lives of A and B. This covenant gives B a new source of income falling under Case III of Schedule D and reduces A's total income by £800. A is nevertheless assessed to tax on £5,000, for no deduction is allowed in respect of the payment to B. Under the collection machinery of section 52 of the Income and Corporation Taxes Act 1970 A is entitled to deduct tax at the basic rate when making the payment to B, who is then said to have " suffered tax by deduction at the source." A has to account to the Revenue for the tax which he deducts. Thus A acts as a collector for the Revenue of the basic rate tax on B's income.

This system is explored in Chapters 5 and 8.

Date of payment [39]

1-24   Income tax is generally payable on January 1 in the year of assessment to which the tax relates. But in the case of earned income of an individual it is

---

[36] See § 8-30.
[37] See §§ 5-30 *et seq.*
[38] See § 14-01B.
[39] I.C.T.A. 1970, s. 4.

payable in two equal instalments on January 1 and the following July 1. Generally, income tax charged at a rate other than the basic rate on income from which tax has been deducted before its receipt is payable on or by July 6 following the end of the year for which it is assessed. Interest is payable on overdue tax. [40]

---

[40] T.M.A. 1970, s. 86, as amended by F. (No. 2) A. 1975, s. 46. The rate of interest is normally 9 per cent. per annum: Income Tax (Interest on Unpaid Tax) Order 1974.

CHAPTER 2

SCHEDULE D CASES I AND II:
PROFITS OF A TRADE,
PROFESSION OR VOCATION

1. THE SCOPE OF THE CHARGE

2-01 TAX under Schedule D is charged on the profits of a trade (Case I), profession or vocation (Case II) carried on wholly or partly in the United Kingdom.[1] Trades, professions and vocations carried on outside the United Kingdom are considered later.[2]

Trade is defined in section 526 (5) of the Income and Corporation Taxes Act 1970, to include " every trade, manufacture, adventure or concern in the nature of trade."

Profession is not defined in the Act but has been said to " involve the idea of an occupation requiring either purely intellectual skill, or manual skill controlled by the intellectual skill of the operator "[3] (*e.g.* barrister, solicitor, surgeon).

Vocation means " the way a person passes his life "[4] (*e.g.* author).

The method of computing profits and losses under Cases I and II of Schedule D is similar and generally no practical importance attaches to the distinction between a trade, on the one hand, and a profession or vocation on the other. The important distinction is that between the activity which constitutes the carrying on of a trade, profession or vocation (the profits or losses from which are dealt with under income tax rules) and the activity which does not (the gains or losses from which are dealt with under capital gains tax rules). Trading profits of an individual are subject to income tax (at the basic and higher rates) whereas capital gains are subject to capital gains tax. In this chapter, the terms " trade " and " trading " should be read as including professions and vocations, unless otherwise stated.

2. WHAT CONSTITUTES TRADING

2-02 The term " trade " is not precisely defined in the Tax Acts. Section 526 (5) merely extends its ordinary meaning to include " every trade, manufacture, adventure or concern in the nature of trade." It was said in one case that the words " in the nature of trade " govern only the word " concern " but this is of doubtful authority.[5]

Whether or not an activity is a trade in this extended sense is a mixed question of law and fact. A person does not trade if he simply procures others to trade: he must be involved in the buying and selling or rendering

---

[1] I.C.T.A. 1970, ss. 108, 109.
[2] *Post*, §§ 7-02 *et seq.*
[3] *Per* Scrutton L.J. in *I.R.C.* v. *Maxse* [1919] 1 K.B. 647; 12 T.C. 41 (C.A.).
[4] *Partridge* v. *Mallandaine* (1886) 18 Q.B.D. 276 at p. 278; 2 T.C. 179 at p. 180 (bookmaker). *Cf.* *Graham* v. *Green* [1925] 2 K.B. 37; 9 T.C. 309 (where a person whose sole means of livelihood was betting on horses at starting prices was held not to be carrying on a vocation).
[5] See, generally, *Johnston* v. *Heath* (1970) 46 T.C. 463 at pp. 469–470.

of services.[6] If there is regular buying or selling or rendering of services, this is clearly trading and the annual profits or gains thereof are assessable to tax; but an isolated or casual transaction may be " an adventure or concern in the nature of trade " if it is of a commercial nature. In *Erichsen* v. *Last,*[7] the Master of the Rolls said:

> " There is not, I think, any principle of law which lays down what carrying on trade is. There are a multitude of things which together make up the carrying on of trade, but I know no one distinguishing incident, for it is a compound fact made up of a variety of things."

Appeals to the High Court

2-03 The question whether a profit is the result of trading is decided initially by the Inspector of Taxes. If he decides that it is, an assessment is made against which the taxpayer may appeal to the Commissioners. From the Commissioners an appeal lies to the High Court, but only by way of case stated on a point of law.[8] The High Court has no jurisdiction to rehear the case and shows a marked reluctance to interfere with the findings of the Commissioners if there was evidence before the Commissioners to justify those findings. Lord Denning remarked in one case [9] that:

> " the powers of the High Court on an appeal are very limited. The judge cannot reverse the Commissioners on their findings of fact. He can only reverse their decision if it is ' erroneous in point of law.' Now here the primary facts were all found by the Commissioners. They were stated in the case. They cannot be disputed. What is disputed is their conclusion from them. And it is now well settled, as well as anything can be, that their conclusion cannot be challenged unless it was unreasonable, so unreasonable that it can be dismissed as one which could not reasonably be entertained by them. It is not sufficient that the judge would himself have come to a different conclusion."

In the case from which this extract is taken, the Commissioners had found that a dividend-stripping transaction carried out by the taxpayer was not an adventure or concern in the nature of trade and Lord Denning's remarks were directed to the decision of the Commissioners on that issue. Appellate courts show a marked reluctance to interfere with decisions of the Commissioners where the issue is essentially one of fact, and this reluctance must always be kept in mind when considering decisions of the courts in such cases. But while paying proper regard to the facts found by the Commissioners and to the inferences drawn by them from those facts, the court will itself decide questions of law, such as whether receipts are capital or income receipts or whether expenditure is incurred on capital or revenue account, and questions of construction of statutes, including the question as to the meaning of " trade " in the Tax Acts.[10] The duty of the court when hearing appeals from Commissioners in tax cases was stated by Lord Radcliffe in *Edwards* v. *Bairstow and Harrison* [11] as follows:

---

[6] *Ransom* v. *Higgs* (1974) 50 T.C. 1; [1974] S.T.C. 539 (H.L.).

[7] (1881) 8 Q.B.D. 414 at p. 416; *cf.* 4 T.C. 422 at p. 423 (C.A.), where the text differs.

[8] T.M.A. 1970, s. 56.

[9] *J. P. Harrison (Watford) Ltd.* v. *Griffiths* (1962) 40 T.C. 281 at pp. 298–299 (a dissenting judgment).

[10] See generally *Edwards* v. *Bairstow and Harrison* [1956] A.C. 14 (H.L.); 36 T.C. 207; *Jeffrey* v. *Rolls-Royce Ltd.* (1962) 40 T.C. 443, *per* Viscount Simonds at p. 490.

[11] [1956] A.C. 14 at p. 35; 36 T.C. 207 at p. 229. See also *Ransom* v. *Higgs* (1974) 50 T.C. 1 (H.L.), *per* Lord Simon at pp. 95–96.

> " I think that the true position of the Court in all these cases can be shortly stated. If a party to a hearing before Commissioners expresses dissatisfaction with their determination as being erroneous in point of law, it is for them to state a Case and in the body of it to set out the facts that they have found as well as their determination. I do not think that inferences drawn from other facts are incapable of being themselves findings of fact, although there is value in the distinction between primary facts and inferences drawn from them. When the Case comes before the Court, it is its duty to examine the determination having regard to its knowledge of the relevant law. If the Case contains anything *ex facie* which is bad law and which bears upon the determination, it is, obviously, erroneous in point of law. But, without any such misconception appearing *ex facie*, it may be that the facts found are such that no person acting judicially and properly instructed as to the relevant law could have come to the determination under appeal. In those circumstances, too, the Court must intervene. It has no option but to assume that there has been some misconception of the law and that this has been responsible for the determination. So there, too, there has been error in point of law. I do not think that it much matters whether this state of affairs is described as one in which there is no evidence to support the determination or as one in which the evidence is inconsistent with and contradictory of the determination or as one in which the true and only reasonable conclusion contradicts the determination. Rightly understood, each phrase propounds the same test. For my part, I prefer the last of the three, since I think that it is rather misleading to speak of there being no evidence to support a conclusion when in cases such as these many of the facts are likely to be neutral in themselves and only to take their colour from the combination of circumstances in which they are found to occur."

Thus if the court is satisfied that the only reasonable conclusion to which the Commissioners could come on the facts found by them is that a trade was (or was not) carried on, it will set aside any determination of the Commissioners to the contrary.

Judicial Decisions

2-04   The *Law Reports* abound in decisions on the question whether an activity constitutes trading. Only by study of these cases can one come to recognise the incidents which distinguish the trading from the non-trading activity. Some of these incidents are now considered.

The single speculation

2-05   It is wrong to suppose that the profit on a transaction escapes tax because the transaction is " isolated." Numerous decisions show that a single speculation or deal may constitute a " concern in the nature of trade."

Thus in *Martin* v. *Lowry* [12] an agricultural machinery merchant who had had no previous connection with the linen trade purchased from the Government its entire surplus stock of aeroplane linen amounting to some 44 million yards. Failing to sell the linen outright to manufacturers, he set up an organisation to facilitate its disposal to the public: he advertised extensively, rented offices and engaged a manager and staff. By this means he disposed of the linen over a period of about 12 months and realised a profit of about £1,900,000. It was held that, although there was a single purchase and the taxpayer envisaged a " single gigantic speculation," the operations constituted trading.

---

[12] [1927] A.C. 312; 11 T.C. 320 (H.L.).

Martin v. *Lowry* was a case of a single purchase and of disposal through a selling organisation over a considerable period. But a single purchase followed by a single immediate sale may likewise constitute trading.

> Thus in *Rutledge* v. *I.R.C.* [13] the taxpayer, while on business in Berlin for a cinema company in which he was interested, accepted an offer to purchase 1 million rolls of toilet paper for £1,000. Within a short time after his return to England he sold the entire consignment to one person at a profit of over £10,000. It was held that this was an adventure in the nature of trade.

2-06   This case, and the preceding case, illustrate that the commercial nature of a transaction can be deduced from the nature and quantity of the subject-matter. A person who purchases a vast consignment of linen or toilet paper must be taken to have intended to resell it and thus to be engaged in a commercial speculation. Where the property purchased is income-producing or has some value as an investment or some other intrinsic value (*e.g.* a work of art), its subsequent realisation at a profit may not constitute trading.

> Thus in *I.R.C.* v. *Reinhold,* [14] the taxpayer (a director of a company carrying on the business of warehousemen) bought four houses. He admitted that he bought them for resale and that he had once before engaged in a property deal. The Court of Session held that the fact that property was purchased with a view to resale did not of itself establish that the transaction was an adventure in the nature of trade, and that the Commissioners were justified in treating the profit as not assessable.

Lord Keith stated the position as follows:

> " It is not enough for the Revenue to show that the subjects were purchased with the intention of realising them some day at a profit. This is the expectation of most, if not all, people who make investments. Heritable property is a not uncommon subject of investment and generally has the feature, expected of investments, of yielding an income while it is being held. In the present case the property yielded an income from rents. . . . The intention to resell some day at a profit is not *per se* sufficient in this case to attract tax."

When the owner of an ordinary investment chooses to realise it, and obtains a greater price than he paid for it, the enhanced price is not profit assessable to income tax. [15]

Adaptations

2-07   The trading (as distinct from the investment) nature of a transaction may in some cases be deduced from the method of handling or treating its subject-matter.

> Thus in *Cape Brandy Syndicate* v. *I.R.C.,* [16] three individuals in the wine trade formed a syndicate (independently of their firms) and acquired a quantity of

---

[13] (1929) 14 T.C. 490. See also *I.R.C.* v. *Fraser* (1942) 24 T.C. 498: woodcutter buys whisky in bond, does not take delivery, resells at a profit: held to be trading; and *J. P. Harrison (Watford) Ltd.* v. *Griffiths* (1962) 40 T.C. 281 at p. 303. *Cf. Wisdom* v. *Chamberlain* (1969) 45 T.C. 92 (C.A.) (silver bullion purchased with borrowed money as hedge against devaluation: profit on sale *held* taxable).

[14] (1953) 34 T.C. 389. *Cf. Cooke* v. *Haddock* (1960) 39 T.C. 64 where the interest on moneys borrowed to purchase land exceeded the net income from the land; this is not consistent with normal investment policy. See also *Turner* v. *Last* (1965) 42 T.C. 517; *Johnston* v. *Heath* (1970) 46 T.C. 463.

[15] *Californian Copper Syndicate Ltd.* v. *Harris* (1905) 5 T.C. 159 at p. 165. But there may be liability to capital gains tax.

[16] [1921] 2 K.B. 403 (C.A.); 12 T.C. 358.

Cape brandy. This was shipped to the United Kingdom, blended with French brandy, recasked and sold in lots to different purchasers over a period of about 18 months. It was held that the resultant profit was assessable as profit of a trade.

" This case," said Rowlatt J., " presents some curious features. It is quite clear that these gentlemen did far more than simply buy an article which they thought was going cheap, and resell it. They bought it with a view to transport it, with a view to modify its character by skilful manipulation, by blending, with a view to alter, not only the amounts by which it could be sold as a man might split up an estate, but by altering the character in the way it was done up so that it could be sold in smaller quantities. They employed experts—and were experts themselves—to dispose of it over a long period of time. . . . They did not buy it and put it away, they never intended to buy it and put it away and keep it. They bought it to turn over at once obviously and to turn over advantageously by means of the operations which I have indicated." [17]

Similarly in *I.R.C.* v. *Livingston,* [18] three men (only one of whom was in the ship business) purchased as a joint venture a cargo vessel with a view to converting it into a steam drifter and selling it. They had never previously done this. They sold the converted ship at a profit, which was held assessable as the profit of an adventure in the nature of trade.

The test (said Lord President Clyde at p. 542) is " whether the operations involved in it are of the same kind, and carried on in the same way, as those which are characteristic of ordinary trading in the line of business in which the venture was made." All the operations carried on by the three men were characteristic of those carried on by professional ship-repairers.

Repetition

2-08   An important factor in deciding whether or not a trade (as distinct from an adventure or concern in the nature of trade) is carried on is whether the taxpayer has engaged in repeated transactions of the same kind.

Thus in *Pickford* v. *Quirke* [19] the taxpayer was one of a syndicate who purchased the shares of a mill-owning company, liquidated the company, and sold its assets (at a profit) to another company formed for the purpose. The taxpayer had engaged in four transactions of this nature, each resulting in a profit to him. It was held that although the transactions, considered separately, were capital transactions, they together constituted the carrying on of a trade.

It follows that if there are successive purchases and resales of property over a period of time, the repetitious nature of the transactions is evidence of trading.

Profit motive

2-09   The fact that the taxpayer does not intend to make a profit or carries on activities which are not directed primarily to profit-making does not preclude the assessment of a profit which in fact emerges. The question

---

[17] In (1921) 12 T.C. at p. 364. Not reported on this point in the *Law Reports.*
[18] (1927) 11 T.C. 538.
[19] (1927) 13 T.C. 251 (C.A.) (an Excess Profits Duty case). See also *I.R.C.* v. *Rolls-Royce Ltd.* (1962) 40 T.C. 443 (H.L.).

whether there is trading must be determined objectively. If commercial methods are used, this points to trading.[20] Moreover, the fact that the taxpayer is bound by statute or otherwise to apply a profit for a particular purpose is irrelevant to the question whether the profit is the consequence of trading.[21]

Transactions designed to secure fiscal advantages

2-10   In a number of cases the question has arisen whether a loss on the purchase and resale of shares arose in the ordinary course of the trade of dealing in shares, where the transaction was a device to secure some fiscal advantage, as by dividend stripping. The principles may be summarised as follows. A share dealing which is clearly part of a trade of dealing in shares will not cease to be so merely by virtue of the dealer's intention to obtain a fiscal advantage [22]; but what is in reality merely a device to secure a fiscal advantage will not become part of a trade of dealing in shares because it is given the trappings normally associated with a share dealing within the trade of dealing in shares.[23]

Business knowledge

2-11   The business knowledge of the taxpayer or of his associates [24] may indicate the commercial nature of a transaction. In the *Cape Brandy* [25] case, Rowlatt J. referred to the expert knowledge of the members of the syndicate; and in *I.R.C.* v. *Fraser,* [26] Lord Normand said that, " It is in general more easy to hold that a single transaction entered into by an individual in the line of his own trade (although not part and parcel of his ordinary business) is an adventure in the nature of trade than to hold that a transaction entered into by an individual outside the line of his own trade or occupation is an adventure in the nature of trade."

Mere realisation

2-11A   The mere act of selling property does not constitute trading. The concept of trading generally implies purchasing property with the object at the time of purchase of resale at a profit, although the cases establish that the taxpayer's object at the time of purchase is a matter to be determined objectively in the light of all surrounding circumstances including, for example, the nature of the commodity purchased: see §§ 2-05 *et seq.* Where property is purchased as an investment (*e.g.* income-producing land or shares) or to be used or enjoyed (*e.g.* a private residence or an old master), a surplus which emerges on a subsequent sale is not a trading profit even if steps have been taken (*e.g.* the obtaining of planning permission in respect

---

[20] *Grove* v. *Y.M.C.A.* (1903) 4 T.C. 613: restaurant carried on by Y.M.C.A. held to be a trading activity. *Cf. Religious Tract and Book Society* v. *Forbes* (1896) 3 T.C. 415: colportage business held not to be a trade.

[21] *Mersey Docks and Harbour Board* v. *Lucas* (1883) 8 App.Cas. 891; 2 T.C. 25.

[22] *Griffiths* v. *J. P. Harrison (Watford) Ltd.* [1963] A.C. 1; 40 T.C. 281 (H.L.).

[23] *Lupton* v. *F.A. & A.B. Ltd.* [1972] A.C. 634; 47 T.C. 580 (H.L.); *Thomson* v. *Gurneville Securities Ltd.* [1972] A.C. 661 (H.L.); 47 T.C. 633; *Finsbury Securities Ltd.* v. *Bishop* (1966) 43 T.C. 591 (H.L.). For an article on the cases in this and the preceding note, see [1972] B.T.R. 6.

[24] *Burrell, Webber, Magness, Austin and Austin* v. *Davis* (1958) 38 T.C. 307.

[25] [1921] 2 K.B. 403; 12 T.C. 358 (C.A.); *ante,* § 2-07.

[26] (1942) 24 T.C. 498: see note 13, *supra*.

of land or the restoration of an old master) to obtain the best possible price on resale. Where a landowner lays out part of his estate with roads and sewers and sells it in lots for building, he does this as a landowner and not as a speculator or trader.[27] Similarly, if land is purchased as an investment and the landowner, realising that his investment is no longer a sound one, decides to sell off the land, this is not trading.[28]

Property not originally purchased for resale in the course of trade may be " appropriated " to trading stock. An established trader in old masters might, for example, elect to deal with a painting acquired by inheritance by exhibiting it for sale in his gallery in the ordinary course of his trade; or a non-trader, wishing to embark on a trade of *buying and selling* paintings, might initiate the trade by using assets acquired by inheritance as opening stock-in-trade. In such cases the paintings are said to be appropriated to trading stock with the consequences (i) that there is a notional disposal of the assets for capital gains tax purposes at their market value at the time of appropriation[29] and (ii) that the assets are brought into trading stock at their market value at that time.[30]

> Thus in *Pilkington* v. *Randall*[31] the taxpayer purchased his sister's share of inherited land with a view to making a profit by resale after development, and it was found as a fact that he appropriated his own inherited share to trading stock at the same time.

Although an established trader may appropriate non-trading assets to trading stock, assets purchased by a non-trader for an admitted non-trading purpose do not subsequently become trading stock where the purchaser does nothing more than take steps to realise the assets to the greatest advantage, having no intention of making any further purchases.[32]

Where land which is acquired with a non-trading purpose is subsequently developed with the sole or main object of realising a gain from disposing of the land when developed, any gain of a capital nature which is obtained from the disposal of the land, so far as attributable to the period after the intention to develop was formed, is chargeable to income tax under Case VI of Schedule D under provisions contained in section 488 of the Income and Corporation Taxes Act 1970.[33] Where a charge to development land tax accrues on the commencement of a development (see § 16-107), the tax payable is deductible in computing the gain which is chargeable under section 488.

Company transactions

2-12   A company formed to hold land or other property as an investment and having a constitution appropriate for this purpose is commonly known as

---

[27] *Hudson's Bay Co. Ltd.* v. *Stevens* (1909) 5 T.C. 424, *per* Farwell L.J. at p. 437; *Rand* v. *Alberni Land Co. Ltd.* (1920) 7 T.C. 629. *Cf. Alabama Coal etc. Co. Ltd.* v. *Mylam* (1926) 11 T.C. 232.
[28] *West* v. *Phillips* (1958) 38 T.C. 203; *Simmons* v. *I.R.C.* [1978] S.T.C. 344.
[29] F.A. 1965, Sched. 7, para. 1, discussed *post*, § 16-11.
[30] See *post*, § 2-48. Thus any profit which arises before appropriation bears capital gains tax and only the subsequent profit (if any) is taxed as a trading profit.
[31] (1966) 42 T.C. 662 (C.A.). But see *McClelland* v. *Australia Taxation Commissioner* [1971] 1 W.L.R. 191 (P.C.).
[32] *Taylor* v. *Good* (1974) 49 T.C. 277; [1974] S.T.C. 148 (C.A.).
[33] See *post*, §§ 40-16 *et seq.*

an " investment company." It is distinguished from the " property dealing " or " finance " company which trades in land or securities. If a company makes a profit by trading, that profit is assessable notwithstanding that the company is described as an investment company. Thus in *I.R.C.* v. *Hyndland Investment Co. Ltd.,*[34] the Lord President (at p. 699) said:

> " The first point that strikes one is that the company in its memorandum of association describes its objects as being the acquisition of land and other heritable property, and the holding of the same as an investment, and the division of the income thereof. That is not, however, conclusive, because the question is not what business does the taxpayer *profess* to carry on, but what business does he *actually* carry on."

The professed objects of the company are, however, relevant to the consideration of the nature of transactions engaged in by the company.[35] The fact that a company has always been treated by the Revenue as an investment company does not preclude the Revenue from treating a sale as in the nature of trade. " The Revenue are free to revise the position."[36]

Share transactions

2-13   If the shares of a company are sold at a profit, the share-vendor's profit is not assessable under Case I of Schedule D unless he can be shown to be a dealer in shares. This was the basis of a common device for avoiding tax until, by the Finance Act 1960, profits on the sale of shares in land-owning companies were made assessable under Case VI of Schedule D as if the shareholders had themselves bought and sold the land.[37]

In one case a company (A Limited) owned certain land. To procure the development of the land and turn it to account, another company (B Limited) was formed with capital subscribed equally by A Limited and C, an individual. A Limited and C provided capital to finance the purchase of the land by B Limited from A Limited and its development. On completion of the development A Limited sold its shares in B Limited to C. It was held that the profit made by A Limited was taxable as a trading profit: A Limited had employed this device as a special method of dealing with land in which, in reality, it continued to retain an interest.[38]

Share exchanges etc.

2-13A   Where shares which are held as trading stock are exchanged for other shares or securities, *e.g.* on a takeover, the shares acquired on the exchange have to be valued and any profit on the transaction is taxable under Case I of Schedule D. Section 46 of the Finance Act 1977 now affords a measure of

---

[34] (1929) 14 T.C. 694. And see *W. M. Robb Ltd.* v. *Page* (1971) 47 T.C. 465: factory built by trading company in course of its trade but shown as fixed capital in accounts: profit on sale held a trading receipt.
[35] *Balgownie Land Trust Ltd.* v. *I.R.C.* (1929) 14 T.C. 684 at p. 692.
[36] *Rellim Ltd.* v. *Vise* (1951) 32 T.C. 254 at p. 257.
[37] See now I.C.T.A. 1970, ss. 488–489 discussed *post*, §§ 40-16 *et seq.*
[38] *Associated London Properties Ltd.* v. *Henriksen* (1944) 26 T.C. 46. *Cf. Fundfarms Developments Ltd.* v. *Parsons* (1969) 45 T.C. 707 in which a property development company purchased shares in a land-owning company as an indirect means of acquiring the land and subsequently realised a loss on the liquidation of the company so acquired. *Held*, not a trading loss; the transaction, though of a trading or commercial character, did not form part of the normal business of the company.

relief where, if the shares had been held as fixed capital, roll over relief would have been available under the capital gains tax rules in paragraphs 4–7 of Schedule 7 to the Finance Act 1965: see §§ 40-28 *et seq*. Thus, if a bank holds as trading stock 30 per cent. of the shares of Company A (called " the original holding ") which it transfers in exchange for an issue of shares or debentures (called " the new holding ") in Company B, the bank incurs no tax liability under Case I of Schedule D until it sells the new holding in Company B. Section 46 (3) of the Finance Act 1977 provides that in making any computation in accordance with the provisions of the Taxes Act applicable to Case I of Schedule D of the profits or losses of the business, the transaction shall be treated as not involving any disposal of the original holding, and the new holding shall be treated as the same asset as the original holding. The section applies where the securities comprised in the new holding are issued after April 19, 1977.

Illegal trading

2-14   Once it is established that an activity constitutes trading, any profits thereof which are illegally obtained are nevertheless assessable to tax.[39] The trader cannot rely on the incidental illegality to avoid tax.[40] For this reason, profits derived from *ultra vires* trading are taxable.[41] It is doubtful if systematic crime can itself constitute a trade.[42]

Trading after discontinuance

2-15   The mere realisation of assets *after* the permanent discontinuance of a trade, *e.g.* by a liquidator in the course of winding up a company or by personal representatives in the course of administration, is not trading if it is incidental to the liquidation or administration.[43]

> Thus in *I.R.C.* v. *Nelson*[44] a whisky broker was compelled through ill-health to close his business. He closed his bank account, instructed his accountant to wind up the business, and notified creditors and customers. Within a few days, one of his customers purchased the business including a stock of whisky which was its principal asset. *Held,* that this was not a sale in the course of trade, but after the cessation of the business, and that the profit on the sale was not assessable to tax as a profit of trading.

If a trader decides to sell off his stock with a view to discontinuing business he will be treated as realising assets in the course of trade until the stock is finally sold off.[45]

If the liquidator or personal representative does something more than merely realise assets, *e.g.* if he also makes purchases, he may be held to be

---

[39]   *Mann* v. *Nash* [1932] 1 K.B. 752; 16 T.C. 523 (diddler machines); *Southern* v. *A.B.* [1933] 1 K.B. 713; 18 T.C. 59.

[40]   *Minister of Finance* v. *Smith* [1927] A.C. 193 (J.C.).

[41]   See *Lewis Emanuel* v. *White* (1965) 42 T.C. 369.

[42]   In *Partridge* v. *Mallandaine* (1886) 2 T.C. 179 at p. 181, Denman J. expressed the view that the profits of systematic crime were assessable; but the report in (1886) 18 Q.B.D. 276 has been considerably revised. In *Lindsay* v. *I.R.C.* (1933) 18 T.C. 43 at p. 55, Lord Clyde expressed a contrary view; so also Lord Denning in *J. P. Harrison (Watford) Ltd.* v. *Griffiths* (1962) 40 T.C. 281 at p. 299. See also *I.R.C.* v. *Alexander von Glehn & Co. Ltd.* [1920] 2 K.B. 553; 12 T.C. 232, especially Scrutton L.J.

[43]   *Cohan's Executors* v. *I.R.C.* (1924) 12 T.C. 602 (C.A.).

[44]   (1938) 22 T.C. 716.

[45]   *O'Kane & Co.* v. *I.R.C.* (1922) 12 T.C. 303 (H.L.).

trading,[46] unless such purchases were necessary to facilitate the disposal of the existing assets.[47]

If the deceased trader was one of a number of partners, the participation of his personal representatives in the trading activities of the continuing partners will not necessarily constitute trading.[48]

Mutual trading

2-16   Where a number of persons contribute to a common fund for their mutual benefit, as in the case of a mutual insurance body,[49] a municipal undertaking or a members club,[50] any surplus received by the members on the division of the fund is tax free. " As the common fund is composed of sums provided by the contributors out of their own moneys, any surplus arising after satisfying claims obviously remains their own money. Such a surplus resulting from miscalculation or unexpected immunity cannot in any sense be regarded as taxable profit. This was clearly laid down in the case of *New York Life Insurance Co.* v. *Styles.* "[51]

> " The cardinal requirement is that all the contributors to the common fund must be entitled to participate in the surplus and that all the participators in the surplus must be contributors to the common fund; in other words, there must be complete identity between the contributors and the participators. If this requirement is satisfied, the particular form which the association takes is immaterial." [52]

Thus the principle applies if the association is carried on through the medium or machinery of an incorporated company. The cardinal requirement referred to is satisfied if, at any given time, the contributors comprise the same group of persons as those who are entitled to participate in a surplus: it matters not that the group is a fluctuating body with a changing membership.[53] The mutual principle can be usefully employed by farmers, fruit growers and others who wish to form a " Co-operative " Society for the purpose of acquiring and holding equipment to be used in common by the members.

2-17   If a mutual association trades with outsiders, the profits of that trade are taxable. Thus in *Carlisle and Silloth Golf Club* v. *Smith,*[54] profits on green fees charged by a golf club to outsiders were held to be taxable; and in

---

[46] *Weisberg's Executrices* v. *I.R.C.* (1933) 17 T.C. 696.

[47] *I.R.C.* v. *Old Bushmills Distillery Co. Ltd.* (1928) 12 T.C. 1148; liquidator purchased spirit to blend with the company's stock of whisky; also bottles and casks to facilitate sale. *Held*, not trading. *Cf. Alabama Coal* v. *Mylam* (1926) 11 T.C. 232.

[48] *Marshall and Hood's Executors and Rogers* v. *Joly* (1936) 20 T.C. 256; *cf. Newbarns Syndicate* v. *Hay* (1939) 22 T.C. 461 (C.A.).

[49] *New York Life Insurance Co.* v. *Styles* (1889) 14 App.Cas. 381; 2 T.C. 460 (H.L.).

[50] *I.R.C.* v. *The Eccentric Club Ltd.* [1924] 1 K.B. 390; 12 T.C. 657 (H.L.).

[51] (1889) 14 App.Cas. 381; 2 T.C. 460 (H.L.). The recent decision of the Judicial Committee in *Fletcher* v. *Income Tax Commissioner* [1972] A.C. 414 (J.C.) merits study. For a useful article see Robert Burgess " The Mutuality Principle " [1976] B.T.R. 361.

[52] *Municipal Mutual Insurance Ltd.* v. *Hills* (1932) 16 T.C. 430, *per* Lord Macmillan at p. 448 (H.L.); see also *Jones* v. *South-West Lancashire Coal Owners' Association Ltd.* [1927] A.C. 827; 11 T.C. 790 (H.L.).

[53] *Faulconbridge* v. *National Employers' Mutual General Insurance Association Ltd.* (1952) 33 T.C. 103.

[54] [1913] 3 K.B. 75; 6 T.C. 198. See also *Fletcher* v. *Income Tax Commissioner* [1972] A.C. 414 (J.C.), where the " outsiders " (hotel guests) came to enjoy club facilities through " hotel membership " and the mutual principle was held not to apply.

N.A.L.G.O. v. *Watkins,*[55] profits derived from the admission of non-members of a trade union to a holiday camp established for union members were held to be taxable. Where such profits are derived from a trade or adventure or concern in the nature of trade, tax will be charged under Case I of Schedule D. In other cases, liability will fall under Case VI of Schedule D.

2-18   The mutual trading doctrine has presented opportunities for the avoidance of tax.

> Thus in *Brogan* v. *Stafford Coal & Iron Co. Ltd.*[56] the appellant company and a number of other colliery companies were members of a mutual indemnity company formed to insure their members against accident claims. The mutual company insured only its own members and its only source of income was premiums paid by the members, such premiums being deductible as trading expenses of the member-companies.[57] On the nationalisation of the collieries, the mutual company ceased to carry on business and a substantial surplus was received on the liquidation of the mutual insurance company by the appellant company. The House of Lords held that this surplus was not taxable, notwithstanding that the premiums were deductible.

The decision in *Brogan's* case was nullified by section 21 of the Finance Act 1964 (now s. 347 of the Income and Corporation Taxes Act 1970), under which the surpluses received in similar cases are now taxable. The provisions of the Corporation Tax Acts relating to distributions apply in some cases to distributions by a mutual concern.[58]

Farming etc.

2-18A   All farming and market gardening in the United Kingdom is treated as the carrying on of a trade within Case I of Schedule D; so also is any occupation of land in the United Kingdom where the land is managed on a commercial basis with a view to the realisation of profits.[59] See also *post*, § 6-04.

3. THE COMPUTATION OF PROFITS

A. General Matters

2-19   Tax under Schedule D Cases I and II is charged on the " annual profits or gains " of the trade, profession or vocation.[60] The word " annual " in this context means that only profits of an income nature (as distinct from capital profits) are chargeable to tax; the word does not mean that profits are chargeable only if they are recurrent.[61] Thus the profits of an isolated transaction in the nature of trade are " annual profits." [62] The Tax Acts do not prescribe general rules as to the manner in which annual profits or gains should be determined for tax purposes. The Acts assume that the

---

[55] (1934) 18 T.C. 499.

[56] (1963) 41 T.C. 305 (H.L.).

[57] *Thomas* v. *Richard Evans & Co. Ltd.* [1927] 1 K.B. 33; 11 T.C. 790 (C.A.).

[58] I.C.T.A. 1970, s. 346.

[59] I.C.T.A. 1970, s. 110.

[60] I.C.T.A. 1970, ss. 108–109.

[61] *Scottish Provident Institution* v. *Farmer* (1912) 6 T.C. 34; *Ryall* v. *Hoare* [1923] 2 K.B. 447 at p. 454; 8 T.C. 521 at p. 526.

[62] *Martin* v. *Lowry* [1926] 1 K.B. 550 at pp. 556, 558; 11 T.C. 297 at pp. 310, 311, 312; affirmed [1927] A.C. 312; 11 T.C. 320.

trader will prepare an account showing his profit or loss for the accounting period and that this account will be prepared in accordance with correct principles of commercial accountancy. The profit or loss disclosed by this account will be the profit or loss for the purposes of Case I or II of Schedule D, as appropriate, subject to any adjustments which may be required by the Tax Acts or may be needed to comply with established principles of revenue law.

> " . . . first, . . . the ordinary principles of commercial accounting must, as far as practicable, be observed, and, secondly, . . . the law relating to income tax must not be violated . . . that is to say, by one means or another the full amount of the profits or gains must be determined." [63]

2-19A   The role of the evidence of accountants in the determination of profit has been considered by the courts in a number of recent cases. In *Odeon Associated Theatres Ltd.* v. *Jones* [64] the Special Commissioners found as a fact on the basis of expert evidence from accountants that, in accordance with the principles of sound commercial accounting at the relevant time, the disputed expenditure [on deferred repairs] would be dealt with as a charge to revenue in the purchasers' accounts. The court could find no reason in law for dissenting from this finding of fact and the expenditure was accordingly allowed as a deduction for tax purposes. The *Odeon* case led some commentators to suppose that the question whether expenditure was of a capital or revenue nature was a matter for accountancy evidence alone, but in *Heather* v. *P-E Consulting Group Ltd.* [65] it was held that the question of capital or revenue was a question of law for the court to decide. In the *Odeon* case Buckley L.J. said:

> " As Lord Reid observed in *Regent Oil Co.* v. *Strick* [66]: ' The question [whether a particular outlay can be set against income or must be regarded as a capital outlay] is ultimately a question of law for the court, but it is a question which must be answered in light of all the circumstances which it is reasonable to take into account, and the weight which must be given to a particular circumstance in a particular case must depend rather on common sense than on strict application of any single legal principle.' In answering that question of law it is right that the court should pay regard to the ordinary principles of commercial accounting so far as applicable. Accountants are, after all, the persons best qualified by training and practical experience to suggest answers to the many difficult problems that can arise in this field. Nevertheless, the question remains ultimately a question of law."

The principle has recently been re-affirmed by the House of Lords in *Willingale* v. *International Commercial Bank Ltd.,* which is discussed in § 2-21A.

Cash or earnings basis

2-20   As a general rule, the profits of the trade must be computed for tax purposes by crediting sums *earned* in the accounting period and not merely sums actually received. If a trader contracts to sell goods in year 1 for

---

[63] *Duple Motors Ltd.* v. *I.R.C.* (1961) 39 T.C. 537, *per* Lord Simonds at p. 566.
[64] (1971) 48 T.C. 257 (C.A.). For the facts, see § 2-62. See also *Pitt* v. *Castle Hill Warehousing Co. Ltd.* (1974) 49 T.C. 638; *E.C.C. Quarries Ltd.* v. *Watkis* [1975] S.T.C. 578.
[65] [1973] Ch. 189; 48 T.C. 293 (C.A.). For the facts, see § 2-53, note 55.
[66] [1966] A.C. 295 at p. 313; 43 T.C. 1 at p. 29 (H.L.).

delivery in year 2, payment to be due on delivery, the amount due should be credited as a trading receipt of year 2 because, by delivery, the trader will have fulfilled the condition entitling him to payment.[67] The goods in such a case are replaced in the trader's books by a debt and so the profit (if any) has been " earned " or " realised." If the contract in such a case provided for delivery to be made in year 2 but for payment to be made in (say) year 3, the trader should nevertheless bring in the price as a trading receipt of year 2. If the position were otherwise, a trader who purchased goods for £500 and sold them for £600 in the same accounting period on the terms that the price should be paid in a later period or periods, would show (in respect of that transaction) a trading loss whereas, on normal accounting principles, he would have earned a profit of £100. Lord Simon stated the principle as follows in *I.R.C.* v. *Gardner, Mountain and D'Ambrumenil Ltd.*[68]:

> " In calculating the taxable profit of a business on income tax principles . . . goods supplied, which are not to be paid for until a subsequent year, cannot, generally speaking, be dealt with by treating the taxpayer's outlay as pure loss in the year in which it was incurred and bringing in the remuneration as pure profit in the subsequent year in which it is paid, or is due to be paid. In making an assessment to income tax under Schedule D the net result of the transaction, setting expenses on the one side and a figure for remuneration on the other side, ought to appear (as it would appear in a proper system of accountancy) in the same year's profit and loss account, and that year will be the year when the . . . goods were delivered . . . this may involve in some instances, an estimate of what the future remuneration will amount to. . . ."[69]

The principle applies only where the trader has fulfilled *all* the conditions entitling him to payment; and it applies not only to a contract of sale but also to a contract for the supply of services. In one case a company was refused planning consent in year 1. On selling the land in year 5 the company became entitled to compensation in respect of the earlier refusal. It was held that since the compensation was payable only when the company sold the land, it should be credited as a trade receipt of year 5.[70]

If the trader receives payment in money's worth, this must be brought in at market value, subject to the statutory exception in § 2-13A.[71]

> In *Emery & Sons* v. *I.R.C.*[72] a firm of builders sold freehold houses for a cash payment and a rentcharge reserved out of the land. It was held that the realisable value of the rentcharge should be added to the cash payment in computing the receipts of the firm.

2-21 In the case of professions and vocations, the Revenue may allow profits to be calculated by reference to actual cash received in the accounting period, no account being taken during any accounting period of uncollected fees.

[67] *J. P. Hall & Co.* v. *I.R.C.* [1921] 3 K.B. 152; 12 T.C. 382 (C.A.); *New Conveyor Co. Ltd.* v. *Dodd* (1945) 27 T.C. 11.

[68] (1947) 29 T.C. 69 at p. 93 (H.L.). See also Whiteman and Wheatcroft, §§ 9-03 *et seq.* For a case in which trade expenses were " bunched " into a single year and partially disallowed, see § 2-70, note 6.

[69] A trader who failed to recover the sum earned would be entitled to bad debt relief: see *post*, § 2-68.

[70] *Johnson* v. *W. S. Try Ltd.* (1946) 27 T.C. 167 (C.A.).

[71] *Gold Coast Selection Trust Ltd.* v. *Humphrey* [1948] A.C. 459; 30 T.C. 209. In *Varty* v. *British South Africa Company* (1965) 42 T.C. 406 (H.L.) a company had an option to acquire shares at 20s. each which it exercised when the shares were worth 43s. 6d. It was held that the exercise of the option was not a realisation: no trading profit or loss would arise until the shares were sold.

[72] [1937] A.C. 91; 20 T.C. 213. When a builder sells leasehold houses for a premium and a ground rent, only the premium is brought in as a Case I trading receipt: *Hughes* v. *Utting* [1940] A.C. 463. The ground rent remains part of the builder's stock-in-trade and must be brought in at cost price (see *post*, §§ 2-34 *et seq.*). If the ground rents are sold, the proceeds of sale must be brought in as Case I trading receipts of the accounting period when the sale occurs.

The accounts of barristers and authors are often rendered on this " cash " (or " receipts ") basis but there is no rule of law to prevent them rendering accounts on an earnings basis if they choose to do so. In the case of other professions (*e.g.* solicitors) the Revenue may allow accounts to be submitted on a cash basis, except in the early years when the earnings basis is usually obligatory. Thereafter, the Revenue may allow a change to a cash basis (usually only on the taxpayer giving an undertaking to render bills promptly), but no deduction is allowed from the profits computed on a cash basis in respect of fees already brought into charge on an earnings basis.[73] Such fees may thus be taxed twice.[74] Once an assessment has been made on a cash basis for any year, it is not open to the Revenue to make additional assessments on an earnings basis for that year; but the Revenue can make original assessments for other years on an earnings basis.[75]

Profits not yet earned

2-21A   The converse of the principle stated in § 2-20 is that a trader who is assessed on the " earnings basis " cannot be taxed on profits which have not yet been earned. The question whether a profit had been earned arose recently in *Willingale* v. *International Commercial Bank Ltd.*[76] in relation to bills purchased by a bank at a discount. A typical transaction was as follows. In 1970 the bank purchased, for £1,000, a bill having a face value of £1,500 which was due to mature in 1975. From the date of purchase onwards the bill's market value increased as the maturity date drew nearer and, in its accounts for each year, the bank credited a fractional part of the profit which the bank expected to make assuming the bills were held to maturity. There was accountancy evidence that this was an appropriate method of applying the principles of commercial accountancy, consistent with that adopted by the clearing banks, since it gave a fair and realistic picture of the position from year to year. There was also evidence that it would have been equally appropriate as a matter of accountancy treatment to bring in any profit only when a bill either matured or was sold.

The Revenue contended that the bank should be treated as having earned the profit attributable to the bill in each of the five years, *i.e.* that the accountancy treatment actually adopted by the bank should be applied for tax purposes. The bank contended that the profit on the bill was not " earned " or " realised " until the year in which the bill matured or was sold prior to maturity. (The Revenue did not contend that the profit realised in year 5 should be related back to the earlier years.)

The House of Lords (by a majority), affirming the decision (by a majority) of the Court of Appeal, decided as follows. First, it affirmed the principle stated in § 2-19A that the principles of commercial accountancy must yield to the overriding principles of tax law where there is any conflict between the two. Secondly, the court held that it was an established principle of tax law that a profit cannot be taxed until it is " earned " or

---

[73] *I.R.C.* v. *Morrison* (1932) 17 T.C. 325.
[74] This apparent inequity was at one time compensated by the immunity from tax (now abolished) of post-cessation receipts: *post,* §§ 2-88 *et seq.*
[75] *Rankine* v. *I.R.C.* (1952) 32 T.C. 520; *Wetton Page & Co.* v. *Attwooll* (1962) 40 T.C. 619.
[76] [1977] S.T.C. 183 (C.A.); [1978] S.T.C. 75 (H.L.). The example of a " typical transaction " in the text is oversimplified. Whether or not the value of a bill would " increase " with time would depend on interest trends and, in the case of non-sterling bills, changes in the value of the foreign currency relative to sterling.

" realised." A trader cannot be taxed on " contingent profits." Put in another way, neither profit nor loss may be " anticipated," save in the exceptional case of stock-in-trade: see § 2-35. (There was an alternative contention by the bank that the bills were stock-in-trade but, in the absence of any finding by the Commissioners to this effect, this contention was not dealt with by the court.) Thirdly, the court held that no profit was earned by the bank until the bank was entitled to receive payment on the bill, whether by reason of its maturity or on sale prior to maturity. As Ormerod L.J. said:

> " I am unable to see how it can be argued that the bank becomes legally entitled as a matter of contract to these separate increments in each of the five accounting years. The obligation of the person signing the bill is simply to pay £1,500 in five years time to the then holder of the bill. This seems to be an obligation which is different in kind from the contract to borrow money at an annual interest even if the interest is not payable until the end of the five year period. The argument for the Crown is ultimately reduced to the proposition that just as the money earns interest in the latter case, so in the former it earns discount. This is like saying that because two roads run A to B, they are the same road. Money ' earns ' interest because the lender becomes legally entitled to it during the year of account; in the instant case the bill appreciates in value in the bank's safe, very much as stock-in-trade may increase in value in the trader's stores. The bank holds a single large debt, not a succession of five small ones."

Post-cessation receipts

2-22   The term " post-cessation receipts " describes sums which are received after the permanent discontinuance of a trade, profession or vocation for work done, or services rendered, before discontinuance. The liability of such receipts to tax under special provisions contained in the Tax Acts depends upon whether a cash or earnings basis was adopted.[77]

B. Trading Receipts

2-23   Once it is established that an activity constitutes trading, the annual profits or gains thereof are assessable under Case I of Schedule D. But not *all* profits are so assessable, for some may be of a capital nature. Capital profits are not taxed as income but may fall within the scope of the tax on capital gains, discussed later in this book.

> If a manufacturer acquires a new factory and disposes of his old factory at a profit, such profit is not assessable under Schedule D, for it is an accretion to capital.

This conclusion can be reached by saying that the factory forms part of the *fixed* capital of the manufacturer and that a sum realised on the disposal of fixed capital does not have to be brought into the computation of the profits for income tax purposes: it is a capital receipt, not a revenue receipt. Alternatively, it can be said that it is excluded because it is not a receipt *of the trade*. In *Mallet* v. *Staveley Coal & Iron Co. Ltd.*[78] Lord Hanworth M.R. distinguished fixed and circulating capital:

> " I think one has to keep clear in one's mind that in dealing with any business there are two kinds of capital, one the fixed capital, which is laid out in the

---

[77] This subject is considered, *post*, §§ 2-88 *et seq.*
[78] [1928] 2 K.B. 405 at p. 413; 13 T.C. 772 at p. 780 (C.A.)

fixed plant, whereby the opportunity of making profits or gains is secured, and the other the circulating capital, which is turned over and over in the course of the business which is carried on.''

It is not always easy, however, to determine whether an asset belongs to one category or the other, and little or no assistance can be obtained by examining the nature of the asset itself. This difficulty is referred to by Romer L.J. in *Golden Horse Shoe (New) Ltd.* v. *Thurgood* [79]:

> '' Land may in certain circumstances be circulating capital. A chattel or chose in action may be fixed capital. *The determining factor must be the nature of the trade in which the asset is employed.* The land upon which a manufacturer carries on his business is part of his fixed capital. The land with which a dealer in real estate carries on his business is part of his circulating capital. The machinery with which a manufacturer makes the articles that he sells is part of his fixed capital. The machinery that a dealer in machinery buys and sells is part of his circulating capital, as is the coal that a coal merchant buys and sells in the course of his trade.''

Again, the character of an asset may change in the course of business: thus land originally acquired as an investment may later become part of the owner's circulating capital or stock-in-trade. Indeed, the value of the distinction between fixed and circulating capital as a criterion for determining the nature of a receipt may be questioned; but it is thought that the distinction has some value if it is recognised that the character of the asset is but one of a number of factors which are material. Where a receipt comes from the sale of ordinary trading stock or from the rendering of services, it will be brought into the computation of the annual profits or gains for tax purposes. A sum realised on the sale of a fixed asset may be a trading receipt. If, for example, the asset is sold on terms which secure to the vendor a right to future commission on sales by the purchaser the commission thus received is a trading receipt of the vendor.[80] The question in such cases is whether there is a sale of an asset providing for the payment of capital sums by instalments or a sale coupled with a collateral bargain for the sharing of commission.[81]

2-24   A sum received by a trader for undertaking *not* to carry on some trading activity may not be a receipt of the trade.

> Thus in *Higgs* v. *Olivier*,[82] following the production of the film Henry V and to assist in its promotion, Sir Laurence Olivier entered into a covenant under which he received £15,000 in consideration of an undertaking by him to appear in no other film for any company other than the covenantee company for a period of 18 months.

It was held that the sum was not taxable. It did not come to the recipient as income of his vocation; it came to him for refraining from carrying on one facet of his vocation, namely '' that part of it which showed him as an actor on the celluloid stage.'' It should be observed that there was a finding of the Special Commissioners in that case that the covenant formed no part of the agreement under which the appellant made the film. Where, however, a

---

[79] [1934] 1 K.B. 548 at p. 563; 18 T.C. 280 at p. 300 (C.A.).
[80] *Orchard Wine and Spirit Company* v. *Loynes* (1952) 33 T.C. 97.
[81] *Lamport & Holt Line Ltd.* v. *Langwell* (1958) 38 T.C. 193 (C.A.).
[82] [1952] Ch. 311; 33 T.C. 136. *Cf.* payments made to employees for restrictive covenants: *Beak* v. *Robson* [1943] A.C. 352; 25 T.C. 33; *post,* § 3-05.

trader agrees to some restriction on his trading activities as part of an arrangement to obtain supplies of raw material, the sums receivable by him are trading receipts.

> Thus in *Thompson* v. *Magnesium Elektron Ltd.,*[83] the respondent company entered into two agreements with I.C.I.:
> (i) an agreement for the purchase of chlorine at a stated price per ton; and
> (ii) an agreement not to manufacture chlorine or caustic soda (its by-product), in consideration of a payment of £x for each ton of caustic soda which the respondent company would have produced if it had manufactured its own chlorine, for which latter purpose it was to be treated as having produced an agreed number of tons for each ton of chlorine purchased from I.C.I.

It was held that the two agreements should be read together as an arrangement for the supply of chlorine and that the sums received under agreement (ii) were taxable.

There are many cases where the problem of distinguishing an income from a capital receipt presents great difficulty and, as Lord Macmillan said in one such case, " the task of assigning it to income or capital is one of much refinement." Some of these cases must now be considered.

(1) *The compensation cases*

2-25   The problems now to be considered arise where a trader is deprived of some profitable asset and receives compensation by way of damages or otherwise for loss suffered or anticipated. It should be kept in mind that the cases discussed below preceded the introduction of the tax on capital gains and that compensation payments are often taxable as capital gains: see § 16-08.

2-26   *Compensation for sterilisation of assets.* The leading case is *Glenboig Union Fireclay Co. Ltd.* v. *I.R.C.,*[84] where the facts were as follows:

> The appellants manufactured fireclay goods and sold raw fireclay. They were lessees of fireclay fields in the neighbourhood of the Caledonian Railway and a dispute arose with the railway company as to their right to work the fireclay under the railway. An action by the railway company to restrain the appellants was eventually unsuccessful, but during its pendency the appellants were restrained from working the fields (but incurred expense in keeping them open). When the House of Lords decided against the railway company, that company exercised its statutory powers to require part of the fireclay to be left unworked on payment of compensation. *Held,* that the amount received for compensation was a capital receipt, not subject to tax.

Lord Wrenbury stated the principle (at p. 465) as follows:

> " Was that compensation profit? The answer may be supplied, I think, by the answer to the following question: Is a sum profit which is paid to an owner of property on the terms that he shall not use his property so as to make a profit? The answer must be in the negative. The whole point is that he is not to make a profit and is paid for abstaining from seeking to make a profit. . . . It was the price paid for sterilising the asset from which otherwise profit might have been obtained."

It must not be supposed, however, that *all* payments for sterilisation of assets are capital receipts. In the *Glenboig* case, the asset of which the appellants were deprived was a capital asset (*i.e.* fixed capital); moreover,

---

[83] (1944) 26 T.C. 1 (C.A.).
[84] (1921) 12 T.C. 427 (H.L.).

sterilisation was complete. If the appellants had been dealers in fireclay beds (which would then be circulating capital or stock-in-trade), or if the asset had been only partially sterilised or sterilised in the last year of its effective life, the payment might be regarded as of an income nature. The real test, it seems, is whether the thing in respect of which the taxpayer has recovered compensation is the depreciation of one of the capital assets of his trading enterprise or a mere restriction of his trading opportunities. The *Glenboig*
2-27 case should be contrasted with *Burmah Steam Ship Co. Ltd.* v. *I.R.C.*[85] where the facts were as follows:

> Repairers of a vessel exceeded the time stipulated by contract for the completion of an overhaul and damages were paid in compromise of a claim for loss of profit. The payment was held to be a trading receipt.

The character of a payment for sterilisation of assets is not determined by the manner in which the compensation payment is calculated. In the *Glenboig* case, for example, the compensation was estimated on the basis of the profits lost to the appellants; yet the payment was held to be a capital receipt.

> " There is no relation," said Lord Buckmaster, " between the measure that is used for the purpose of calculating a particular result and the quality of the figure that is arrived at by means of the application of that test."

2-28 *Compensation for cancellation of business contracts.* In *Van den Berghs Ltd.* v. *Clark* [86] an English company manufacturing margarine and other butter substitutes had a Dutch company as its principal trade rival. In 1908 and 1913 certain " pooling agreements " were entered into between the companies under which each company retained its separate identity but agreed to conduct business on certain agreed lines to the mutual advantage of both companies. After some years these agreements became unworkable and it was agreed that they should be rescinded and that the Dutch company should pay the English company £450,000 " as damages." It was held that this was a capital receipt. The following passage in Lord Macmillan's judgment [87] is frequently cited:

> " The three agreements which the appellants consented to cancel were not ordinary commercial contracts made in the course of carrying on their trade; they were not contracts for the disposal of their products, or for the engagement of agents or other employees necessary for the conduct of their business; nor were they merely agreements as to how their trading profits when earned should be distributed as between the contracting parties. On the contrary *the cancelled agreements related to the whole structure of the appellant's profit-making apparatus.* They regulated the appellants' activities, defined what they might and what they might not do, and affected the whole conduct of their business. I have difficulty in seeing how money laid out to secure, or money received for the cancellation of so fundamental an organisation of a trader's activities can be regarded as an income disbursement or an income receipt. . . . It is not the largeness of the sum that is important but the nature of the asset that was surrendered."

[85] (1931) 16 T.C. 67 (Ct. of Sess.).
[86] [1935] A.C. 431; 19 T.C. 390. See also *Barr, Crombie & Co. Ltd.* v. *I.R.C.* (1945) 26 T.C. 406; *I.R.C.* v. *Fleming & Co. (Machinery)* (1951) 33 T.C. 57; *Wiseburgh* v. *Domville* (1956) 36 T.C. 527 (C.A.); *Keir & Cawder Ltd.* v. *I.R.C.* (1958) 38 T.C. 23; *Sabine* v. *Lookers Ltd.* (1958) 38 T.C. 120 (C.A.).
[87] [1935] A.C. 431 at pp. 442–443; 19 T.C. 390 at pp. 431–432.

This passage is the foundation of the distinction, often made, between payments for the cancellation of ordinary trading contracts (which are taxable as income under Case I of Schedule D) and payments for the cancellation of contracts affecting the structure of the taxpayer's profit-making apparatus (which are not).

2-29   In contrast to the decision in the *Van den Berghs* case is *Kelsall Parsons & Co.* v. *I.R.C.*[88] The appellants were manufacturers' agents; that is, they had contracts with a number of manufacturers whose products they sold on a commission basis. They had sold Ellison products for some time under agency contracts which had occasionally been varied, and the agreement in force in 1934 was due to expire on September 30, 1935. In May 1934, however, Ellisons requested that the agency agreement should be terminated and, in due course, £1,500 was paid as compensation for the premature determination. This amount was held to be a taxable receipt.

The *Kelsall Parsons* case can be distinguished from the *Van den Berghs* case in the following respects:

(a) In the *Kelsall Parsons* case, the taxpayer was a manufacturers' agent, so the acquisition and loss of an agency was a normal incident of the business.

" The agency agreements," said Lord Normand at p. 621, " so far from being a fixed framework, are rather to be regarded as temporary and variable elements of the . . . profit-making enterprise."

(b) In the *Kelsall Parsons* case, the abandoned agreement had only one year to run (a factor to which importance was attached) and the compensation was " really a surrogatum for one year's profits." In the *Van den Berghs* case, however, the cancelled agreements had 13 years to run.

There are numerous reported cases in which the courts have been called on to decide whether a payment is taxable as income, within the *Kelsall Parsons* principle, or escapes tax as income under the *Van den Berghs* principle.[89]

(2) *Unclaimed balances and released debts*

2-30   In *Morley* v. *Tattersall*,[90] a firm of bloodstock auctioneers received sums from sales for which they were liable to account to the vendors, their clients. These sums were not trade receipts; they were the clients' money. Substantial sums were never collected by the clients and remained in the firm's hands as " unclaimed balances "; and, in due course, when such balances seemed unlikely ever to be claimed, they were transferred to the credit of the individual partners. It was held that these sums were not trading receipts of the firm. The following passage from the judgment of Sir Wilfrid Greene M.R. (at p. 65) shows clearly the basis of the decision:

---

[88] (1938) 21 T.C. 608 (Ct. of Sess.). See also *Elson* v. *James G. Johnston Ltd.* (1965) 42 T.C. 545; *Fleming* v. *Bellow Machine Co. Ltd.* (1965) 42 T.C. 308.

[89] Some of these cases are cited *ante*, § 2-28 in note 86. See *London & Thames Haven Oil Wharves Ltd.* v. *Attwooll* (1966) 42 T.C. 491 (C.A.); *Rajas Commercial College* v. *Gian Singh* [1977] A.C. 312; [1976] S.T.C. 282 (J.C.).

[90] (1938) 22 T.C. 51 (C.A.).

" I invited Mr. Hills to point to any authority which in any way supported the proposition that a receipt which at the time of its receipt was not a trading receipt could by some subsequent operation *ex post facto* be turned into a trading receipt, not, be it observed, as at the date of receipt, but as at the date of the subsequent operation. It seems to me, with all respect to that argument, that it is based on a complete misapprehension of what is meant by a trading receipt in income tax law. . . . It seems to me that the quality and nature of a receipt for income tax purposes is fixed once and for all when it is received."

2-31 This case was distinguished in *Jay's the Jewellers Ltd.* v. *I.R.C.*,[91] where a company of pawnbrokers had unclaimed balances representing the proceeds of sale of unredeemed pledges. Some of these balances became the property of the pawnbroker after a period of time by virtue of the Pawnbrokers Act 1872, and these were held to have become trade receipts when they became the pawnbroker's property. The statute had changed the character of the balances. Other unclaimed balances were outside the Pawnbrokers Act but they became statute-barred after six years under the Statutes of Limitation. Atkinson J. decided that these also became trade receipts of the pawnbroker. It is not clear from the report whether this part of the case was fully argued but, in the author's view, this part of the decision cannot be reconciled with the decision of the Court of Appeal in *Tattersall's* case.[92]

2-32 In *Elson* v. *Prices Tailors Ltd.*,[93] the defendant tailors took " deposits " from customers who ordered garments. Where garments were not collected, the deposits were eventually transferred to an " Unclaimed Deposits Account " and would ordinarily be returned to dissatisfied customers. It was held:

> (i) that the payments were true deposits and were therefore strictly irrecoverable by the customers;
> (ii) that they were trading receipts because they were paid to the defendant company subject to the consequence that they would be used in the company's business, and they were receipts of the year when the payments were made (following *Smart* v. *Lincolnshire Sugar Co.*[94]).

Morley v. *Tattersall* and *Jay's the Jewellers Ltd.* v. *I.R.C.* were distinguished because in those cases the balances in the traders' hands were originally their clients' property and they were not receipts of the trade.

2-33 *Released, remitted or forgiven debts.* In *British Mexican Petroleum Co. Ltd.* v. *I.R.C.*,[95] it was held that where a trade debt is incurred in an accounting period and the creditor later releases or forgives the debt (or part of it) (a) the accounts for the earlier period cannot be reopened and (b) no assessment can be made in the year of release, for there is then no trade

---

[91] (1947) 29 T.C. 274.

[92] Although the debts in *Tattersall's* case might not have been technically statute-barred, it is not thought that this is a sufficient ground of distinction.

[93] (1962) 40 T.C. 671.

[94] (1937) 20 T.C. 643 (H.L.); where Government advances to sugar manufacturing companies were repayable in certain contingencies and it was held that they became trade receipts in the year of payment and not in the year when the contingency of repayment ceased. What was decisive was that these payments were made in order that the money might be used in the business: Lord Macmillan at p. 670.

[95] (1932) 16 T.C. 570 (H.L.).

receipt. This decision was nullified by section 36 of the Finance Act 1960 (now s. 136 of the Income and Corporation Taxes Act 1970), as respects releases effected after April 5, 1960. Now, where a deduction has been allowed for any debt incurred for the purposes of a trade and the whole or part of that debt is thereafter released, the amount released is treated as a trading receipt of the period in which the release is effected.[96] The section does not apply to debts incurred on capital account which are later released.

(3) *Trading stock*

2-34   In computing the profits of a trade, profession or vocation, it is necessary to bring into account the value of the stock-in-trade at the beginning and end of the accounting period. The following account shows the relevance of stock valuation in the ascertainment of profits:

	£		£
Opening stock	1,000	Sales during the year	15,000
Purchases during the		Closing stock	1,300
year	12,000		
Gross profit	3,300		
	£16,300		£16,300

The trader in this example begins the year with £1,000's worth of stock. During the year he purchases a further £12,000 of stock. He takes £15,000 in sales. Note that the stock must be again valued at the close of the year before the gross profit can be ascertained. The closing stock becomes the figure for opening stock in the next accounting period.

2-35   The trader values his stock, item by item, at the close of each accounting period. The higher the figure for closing stock, the higher the gross profit; the lower the figure, the lower the profit. In *I.R.C.* v. *Cock, Russell & Co. Ltd.,*[97] judicial approval was given to the rule of accounting that, when valuing stock, the trader may value each item at its cost price or its market price whichever is the lower. He may value one item at cost and another at market price: thus he may " pick and choose." Market price means the best price obtainable in the market in which the trader sells.[98] The practical effect of the rule is that where an item of stock increases in value during the accounting period, such increase does not enter into the computation of profits; yet if an item of stock decreases in value, so that a loss may be anticipated,[99] the decrease will be taken into account.[100] This is an exception to the general principle of tax law, under which neither profits nor losses may be " anticipated " (see § 2-21A).

---

[96] This can have important repercussions when shares of a tax-loss company are purchased. It is not uncommon in such a case for trade creditors who are associated with the company to release their debts in order to facilitate the sale of the shares to outsiders. s. 136 might have the effect of extinguishing the losses.

[97] (1949) 29 T.C. 387.

[98] *B.S.C. Footwear Ltd.* v. *Ridgway* [1972] A.C. 544; 47 T.C. 495 (H.L.): thus in the case of the retail trade, it means the retail market.

[99] In the case cited in note 98 Lord Pearson said *obiter* that goods should not be written down below cost price unless there really is a loss, actual or prospective. They should not be written down where a reduced profit only is anticipated.

[100] Generally tax law permits no relief for unrealised losses on (for example) future contracts: the rule applicable to stock is a departure from the general rule: *Naval Colliery Co. Ltd.* v. *I.R.C.* (1928) 12 T.C. 1017, *per* Lord Warrington. *Whimster & Co.* v. *I.R.C.* (1925) 12 T.C. 813.

2-35A   *Relief for increase in stock values.* It will be seen from the above that, in
periods of inflation, increases in the cost of replacing stock lead to a higher
charge to tax. Section 18 of the Finance Act 1975 and section 54 of and
Schedule 10 to the Finance (No. 2) Act 1975 introduced a temporary system
of stock relief. Section 37 of and Schedule 5 to the Finance Act 1976
introduce a new temporary system. Broadly, the increase in stock value over
the period of account has to be calculated. From this is deducted 15 per
cent. of the trading income *after* deducting capital allowances. The
resultant figure is the amount of stock relief. (The greater the investment in
plant or machinery, etc., the greater the capital allowances and the greater
the stock relief.) The relief is treated as a trade expense in the case of
companies and as a deduction in charging profits in the case of an
individual. The Chancellor announced in his April 1978 Budget Statement
that the present stock relief scheme would continue indefinitely and gave an
assurance that, if no permanent scheme had been devised within a year,
legislation would be introduced to limit the build-up of deferred tax
liabilities. [1]

2-36   *The Emery Formula.* Where a builder or developer erects houses on plots
of land owned by him and grants leases for lump sum payments (premiums)
and rents reserved out of the land (ground rents), the freehold reversions
which the builder retains form part of his stock-in-trade and must be
brought into account at the lower of cost or market price. [2] The formula for
ascertaining cost in such cases was determined by the Special
Commissioners in *John Emery & Sons* v. *I.R.C.* [3] The effect of the formula
is that part of the building costs which goes to improve the ground rent
which the builder retains must be eliminated in computing his building
profits. [4]

2-37   *Work in Progress.* There are in many trades, at the end of each
accounting period, unfinished products in hand, such as goods in process of
manufacture or houses in course of erection. Each unit of " work in
progress " may be valued in the same way as stock-in-trade [5] that is, at the
lower of cost or market price. In arriving at a figure for the cost of a
product, however, some account must be taken of the cost of production
and for this purpose a distinction is made between *direct costs* (which are
readily attributable to a given item, such as the wages of a person engaged in
making the product) and *indirect costs* (which, though part of the total cost
of production, cannot be attributed to any one item, *e.g.* general
overheads). Where the value of work in progress is computed by the
" direct cost " method, only direct costs are taken into account; whereas,
where the " on-cost " method is used, a proportion of indirect costs is
added to the direct costs. There is no rule of law requiring one method to be

---

[1] See [1978] S.T.I. at pp. 161–162.   [2] *Utting* v. *Hughes* (1940) 23 T.C. 174 (H.L.).
[3] (1937) 20 T.C. 213. This aspect of the case is not reported in [1937] A.C. 91. The formula is sometimes
referred to as the " Macnaghten formula " because of Macnaghten J.'s reference to it in *Heather* v.
Redfern (1944) 26 T.C. 119 at p. 124. The formula, he said is a simple rule of three sum: As A, the
premiums, plus B, the selling value of the ground rents, is to B, so is C, the total expenses of the builder, to
D, the cost of the ground rents or reversions.
[4] *McMillan* v. *I.R.C.* (1942) 24 T.C. 417 (Ct. of Sess.).
[5] Trading stock is defined in I.C.T.A. 1970, s. 137 (4), to mean property such as is sold in the ordinary
course of the trade or would be so sold if it were mature or if its manufacture, preparation or construction
were complete. It thus includes work in progress.

used rather than another.[6] The relief for the rise in the cost of replacement of stock [7] also applies to work in progress.

2-38 *Valuation of stock on discontinuance of a trade.* It has been observed that the mere realisation of assets after the permanent discontinuance of a trade does not constitute trading.[8] Any tax advantages which could hitherto be gained by this rule (*e.g.* by a company purchasing an appreciating asset, such as whisky, and going into liquidation when the whisky reached maturity) were nullified by provisions now in section 137 of the Income and Corporation Taxes Act 1970. This section requires that, on the discontinuance of a trade, any trading stock (including work in progress) then belonging to the trader must be valued at the amount realisable on a sale in the open market at the date of discontinuance. Any latent profit is thereby brought into account in the final chargeable period.

2-39 Section 137 does not apply:
(1) If the stock is sold or transferred for valuable consideration to a person who carries on or intends to carry on [9] a trade in the United Kingdom so that the cost thereof is a deductible expense in computing his (the purchaser's) profits. In this case, the vendor brings into account the actual consideration for the transfer.
(2) If the discontinuance is caused by the death of a sole proprietor.[10] In this case the figure for closing stock remains undisturbed.

Where (1) applies the Revenue lose nothing, for the profit will eventually come into charge when the purchaser sells the stock in the course of his trade. The explanation of (2) is that section 137 is an anti-avoidance section and is designed to prevent tax avoidance by " artificial cessations " when stock figures are low and market values high. Section 137 applies where the discontinuance of trading and the sale are simultaneous.[11]

2-40 *Valuation of work in progress on discontinuance of a profession or vocation.* Section 137 of the Income and Corporation Taxes Act 1970 applies only to discontinued trades. Section 138 of the Income and Corporation Taxes Act 1970 contains similar provisions which apply to work in progress on the discontinuance of a profession or vocation. Subsection (1) provides that where, on such a discontinuance, a valuation is taken of the work of the profession or vocation in progress at the discontinuance, that work shall be valued as follows:
(a) if the work is transferred for money or other valuable consideration to a person who carries on or intends to carry on a profession or vocation in the United Kingdom, and the cost of the work may be deducted by that person as an expense in computing for any such purpose the profits or gains of that profession or vocation, the value of the work shall be taken to be the amount paid or other consideration given for the transfer;

---

[6] *Duple Motor Bodies Ltd.* v. *Ostime* (1961) 39 T.C. 537 (H.L.).
[7] *Ante,* § 2-35A.   [8] *Ante,* § 2-15.
[9] I.C.T.A. 1970, s. 137 (1) (*a*). Thus where a partnership is " converted " into a company and stock is sold to the company, the exception applies.
[10] I.C.T.A. 1970, s. 137 (3). But where a business passes on death to the trader's husband or wife who has been living with him or her, the discontinuance provisions are not enforced unless claimed. See Concession No. A8.   [11] *Moore* v. *R. J. Mackenzie & Sons Ltd.* (1971) 48 T.C. 196.

(b) if the work does not fall to be valued under (a), its value shall be taken to be the amount which would have been paid for a transfer thereof on the date of the discontinuance as between parties at arm's length.

2-41 It should be observed that the subsection imposes no obligation to value work in progress: it provides that *if* a valuation of work in progress is taken, it shall be made in accordance with the section. The subsection applies only if accounts have been rendered in such a form that normal accountancy practice demands a valuation of work in progress; thus if accounts have been rendered on a cash basis (*i.e.* crediting only sums actually received) no adjustment to those accounts is required by section 138 of the Income and Corporation Taxes Act 1970 on the discontinuance of the profession or vocation. Where accounts have been rendered on a cash basis and there is a discontinuance, the Revenue might require accounts to be rendered on an earnings basis in respect of the final accounting period [12] (assuming that accounts have not already been accepted on a cash basis prior to the date of discontinuance). Work in progress would then have to be brought in at the time of discontinuance, valued in accordance with section 138 of the Income and Corporation Taxes Act 1970, but the taxpayer would be entitled to bring in the value of work in progress as at the beginning of that accounting period. [13] Thus only the increase in value of the work in progress in the final accounting period would be brought into charge under section 138.

2-42 Work in progress is defined for the purposes of section 138 (5) as including:

(a) any services performed in the ordinary course of the profession or vocation, the performance of which was wholly or partly completed at the time of the discontinuance and for which it would be reasonable to expect that a charge would have been made on their completion if the profession or vocation had not been discontinued; and

(b) any article produced, and any such material as is used, in the performance of any such services.

The definition thus includes completed but unbilled work as well as uncompleted or partly completed work.

(4) *Section 485 and the rule in Sharkey* v. *Wernher* [14]

2-43 Generally, a trader is free to dispose of his stock on any terms he pleases and is entitled, for example, to sell at an under-value for the purpose of

---

[12] As in *Rankine* v. *I.R.C.* (1952) 32 T.C. 520, *ante*, § 2-21.

[13] *Bombay Commissioner of Income Tax* v. *Ahmedabad New Cotton Mills Co. Ltd.* (1929) 8 A.T.C. 575. But see *Pearce* v. *Woodall Duckham Ltd.* [1978] S.T.C. 372 (C.A.) where the Court of Appeal held that a sum thrown up in consequence of a change in the method of valuing work in progress was a profit of the year of change. *Quaere* if this decision is correct. See the accountancy treatment agreed with the Inland Revenue: [1978] S.T.I. 216.

[14] [1956] A.C. 58; 36 T.C. 275 (H.L.).

avoiding liability to income tax. There is no rule of law which demands that a trader shall realise the maximum profit; nor can tax be levied on a profit which is forgone. This general rule is subject to some important exceptions which must now be considered:

2-44   (a) *Section 485 of the Income and Corporation Taxes Act 1970.* Where on a sale between " associated persons " property is sold at a price less than the price which it might have been expected to fetch if the parties to the transaction had been independent persons dealing at arm's length, then, in computing the income, profits or losses of the seller for tax purposes, the like consequences are to ensue as would have ensued if the property had been sold for the price it would have fetched if the transaction had been between independent persons dealing at arm's length.[15] There is an important exception where the buyer is resident in the United Kingdom and is carrying on a trade therein, where the price of the property has to be taken into account as a deduction in computing the profits or gains or losses of that trade for income tax purposes.[16]

> Thus if a trading company sells property at an under-value to an associated investment company, the receipts of the trading company will be adjusted in accordance with section 485 on a direction being made by the Board.

The section contains similar provisions for adjustment of the profits or losses of the buyer where property is sold in excess of its arm's length value.[17]

Persons are " associated " for the purpose of section 485 if the buyer is a body of persons (including a partnership)[18] over whom the seller has control, or vice versa, or both seller and buyer are bodies of persons over whom some other person has control.

2-45   " Control " has the meaning ascribed to it in section 534 of the Income and Corporation Taxes Act 1970, which, in relation to a body corporate, means the power of a person to secure:

> " (a) by means of the holding of shares or the possession of voting power in or in relation to that or any other body corporate, or
> (b) by virtue of any powers conferred by the articles of association or other document regulating that or any other body corporate,
>
> that the affairs of the first-mentioned body corporate are conducted in accordance with the wishes of that person, and, in relation to a partnership, means the right to a share of more than one-half of the assets, or of more than one half of the income, of the partnership."

In applying this test a person is deemed to possess all the rights and powers of any nominee for him or of any person who is connected [19] with him.[20] There are similar provisions for the adjustment of the consideration in the case of " lettings and hirings of property, grants and transfers of rights,

---

[15] I.C.T.A. 1970, s. 485 (1).
[16] *Ibid.* s. 485 (1), proviso.
[17] *Ibid.* s. 485 (2).
[18] *Ibid.* s. 485 (5).
[19] The definition of " connected persons " is found in I.C.T.A. 1970, s. 533: see § 16-18A.
[20] F.A. 1975, s. 17 (1) enacting a new I.C.T.A. 1970, s. 485 (5A).

interests or licences and the giving of business facilities of whatever kind,"
where the parties to the transaction are associated. [21]

The Commissioners are given extensive powers to obtain information for
the purpose of this provision, in particular, as regards any related
transaction which may have a bearing on market value. The powers include
the right of a properly authorised person to enter premises and inspect
documents. [22]

2-46   (b) *The Rule in Sharkey* v. *Wernher.* [23] The rule is that where a trader
disposes of part of his stock-in-trade not by way of sale in the course of
trade but for his own use, enjoyment or recreation, he must bring into his
trading account for tax purposes as a receipt the market value of that stock
at the time of such disposition. The facts of the case were as follows:

> Lady Wernher owned a stud farm, which was a trade assessed under Case I of
> Schedule D. She also owned racing stables where horses were trained and this
> activity was admitted to be merely recreational. Lady Wernher transferred five
> horses from the farm to the stables, having debited in the stud farm accounts
> the cost of breeding the horses. Some figure (it was admitted) had to be brought
> into the stud farm accounts as a receipt. *Held*, that the figure to be brought in
> was the market value of the horses.

This case shows that a person can make a taxable profit by trading with
himself; and that unrealised profits may be assessable to tax. The practical
consequence of the decision is that a farmer or grocer who (for example)
takes his own produce or stock for domestic consumption must credit his
account as if he had sold it in the normal course of trade, at the retail
market value. The same problem arises (said Viscount Simonds)

> " whether the owner of a stud farm diverts the produce of his farm to his own
> enjoyment or a diamond merchant, neglecting profitable sales, uses his
> choicest jewels for the adornment of his wife, or a caterer provides lavish
> entertainment for a daughter's wedding breakfast. Are the horses, the jewels,
> the cakes and ale to be treated for the purpose of income tax as disposed of for
> nothing or for their market value or for the cost of their production? " [24]

The answer given by the House of Lords (Lord Oaksey dissenting) was their
market value.

2-47   It should be observed that the rule applies only to dispositions of
stock-in-trade [25]: property which never becomes part of the trader's stock is
outside the rule. The rule applies in all cases where a trader disposes of his
stock otherwise than in the normal course of trade. Thus a sale at an undervalue to secure some tax advantage is subject to review by the Revenue, even
in cases to which section 485 of the Income and Corporation Taxes Act 1970
does not apply.

---

[21] I.C.T.A. 1970, s. 485 (6).
[22] See generally F.A. 1975, s. 17.
[23] [1956] A.C. 58; 36 T.C. 275 (H.L.).
[24] [1956] A.C. 58 at pp. 69–70; 36 T.C. 275 at p. 297.
[25] In *Mason* v. *Innes* [1967] Ch. 1079; 44 T.C. 326 (C.A.) the Revenue contended unsuccessfully that the
rule applied to a gift by an author of his rights in an unpublished novel. Such a gift would now attract
capital gains tax.

In *Petrotim Securities Ltd.* v. *Ayres,*[26] Petrotim (a company dealing in securities) purchased War Loan which it sold four days later at less than one-tenth of its cost and of its realisable market value at the date of sale. It was held that neither the purchase nor the sale was a trading transaction and that both should therefore be expunged from the company's accounts. Petrotim also sold for £205,000 securities forming part of its trading stock which it acquired some time previously for £478,573, and which had a market value of £835,505. It was held that the sale was not a trading transaction. It was further held in *Petrotim Securities Ltd.* v. *Ayres*[27] that the principle in *Sharkey* v. *Wernher*[28] applied and that a figure equal to the market value of the securities at the date of disposal should be brought in as a receipt. These decisions were affirmed by the Court of Appeal.[29] In one case it was held that a sale of land at an under-value by a land-dealing company to its parent company was a sale otherwise than in the ordinary course of trade.[30]

2-48   If a trader starts a business with stock provided gratuitously, he may bring in the stock at its market value at that time: he will not be taxed on the basis that the value of the opening stock is nil.[31] But this principle was held not to apply in a case in which the Commissioners had held that the acquisition of the stock was " a commercial acquisition."[32]

(5) *Interest, etc.*

2-49   Interest earned by a trader whose stock-in-trade is money and who earns the interest by the use of that money, as by borrowing at one rate and lending at a higher rate, is a trading receipt and will be brought into the profit and loss account. But, for tax purposes, a distinction is drawn between interest from which income tax is deducted before its receipt by the trader (which has to be excluded from the receipts in the tax computation[33]) and interest paid in full without deduction (which is not so excluded). This distinction is said to be based on the proposition that, if interest taxed by deduction were treated as a trade receipt for tax purposes, it would be taxed twice because there is no provision for giving relief for tax already suffered by deduction in the Case I assessment: see the discussion in § 5-23.

(6) *Know-how*

2-50   In *Evans Medical Supplies Ltd.* v. *Moriarty*[34] the House of Lords held that a sum received by a trading company on the sale of know-how was not

[26] (1963) 41 T.C. 389.
[27] *Ibid.* at p. 402.
[28] [1956] A.C. 58; 36 T.C. 275 (H.L.).
[29] *Ibid.* at p. 406 (C.A.).
[30] *Skinner* v. *Berry Head Lands Ltd.* (1970) 46 T.C. 377.
[31] *Ridge Securities* v. *I.R.C.* (1963) 44 T.C. 373 at p. 392.
[32] *Jacgilden (Weston Hall) Ltd.* v. *Castle* [1971] Ch. 408; 45 T.C. 685, where R, having agreed to buy land for £72,000 and paid a deposit, directed the vendor to convey the land to the appellant company by which time the land was worth £150,000. *Held*, the company could deduct only the price actually paid. " The *Sharkey* v. *Wernher* line of authority has never . . . been applied to a case where the price at which property passed had been negotiated at a fair and proper price . . ." (*ibid.* at p. 700).
[33] See *F. S. Securities Ltd.* v. *I.R.C.* (1964) 41 T.C. 666 (H.L.) which related to the taxation of dividends payable under deduction of tax; but the same principle has been held to apply to interest and other sums paid under deduction: *Bucks* v. *Bowers* (1969) 46 T.C. 267: see § 8-08.
[34] (1957) 37 T.C. 540.

taxable as a trading receipt. In *Jeffrey* v. *Rolls-Royce Ltd.,*[35] the House of Lords held that a sum received for imparting know-how was taxable. Section 21 of the Finance Act 1968 clarified the position in provisions now contained in section 386 of the Income and Corporation Taxes Act 1970.

Where after March 19, 1968, a person disposes of know-how which has been used in a trade carried on by him, and continues to carry on the trade after the disposal, the amount or value of any consideration received by him for the disposal will, so far as not chargeable to tax as a revenue or income receipt, be treated for all purposes as a trading receipt[36]; but this provision does not apply to know-how which is an element in a business sold by the vendor (see below).[37] Where the consideration for the sale is in kind, such as shares in the purchasing company, the shares must be valued for the purpose of determining the vendor's tax liability.[38] The expression " know-how " is defined[39] for the purposes of section 386 as meaning

> " Any industrial information and techniques likely to assist in the manufacture or processing of goods or materials, or in the working of mine, oilwell or other source of mineral deposits (including the searching for, discovery, or testing of deposits or the winning of access thereto), or in the carrying out of any agricultural, forestry or fishing operations."

Where in connection with any disposal of know-how a person gives an undertaking (whether absolute or qualified, and whether legally valid or not) the tenor or effect of which is to restrict his or another's activities in any way, any consideration received in respect of the giving of the undertaking or its total or partial fulfilment is to be treated for the purposes of section 386 as consideration received for the disposal of know-how.[40]

Where after March 19, 1968, a person disposes of a trade or part of a trade and, together therewith, of know-how used therein, any consideration received by him for the know-how is to be dealt with in relation both to him and to the person acquiring the know-how, if that person provided the consideration, as a payment for goodwill.[41] Hence an individual in such circumstances may become liable to capital gains tax. Know-how which is chargeable to tax under neither of the provisions referred to above will generally be treated as a profit or gain chargeable to tax under Case VI of Schedule D.[42]

For writing down allowances as regards know-how, see § 13-22.

(7) *Voluntary payments*

2-50A   A voluntary payment of an income character may be a trading receipt, as is illustrated by the case of *British Commonwealth International Newsfilm*

---

[35] (1962) 40 T.C. 443. See also *Musker* v. *English Electric Co. Ltd.* (1964) 41 T.C. 556 (H.L.); *Coalite & Chemical Products Ltd.* v. *Treeby* (1971) 48 T.C. 171; *Sturge Ltd.* v. *Hessel* [1975] S.T.C. 573 (C.A.); *Thomsons (Carron) Ltd.* v. *I.R.C.* [1976] S.T.C. 317.

[36] I.C.T.A. 1970, s. 386 (2); there is, however, no charge where one party to the transaction is controlled by the other: *ibid.* s. 386 (6).

[37] *Ibid.* s. 386 (3).

[38] *Gold Coast Selection Trust* v. *Humphrey* [1948] A.C. 459; 30 T.C. 209 (H.L.).

[39] *Ibid.* s. 386 (7).

[40] I.C.T.A. 1970, s. 386 (8).

[41] *Ibid.* s. 386 (3).

[42] *Ibid.* s. 386 (4).

Agency v. *Mahany*,[43] discussed in § 5-18. But not all voluntary payments are of an income nature.

In *Walker* v. *Carnaby Harrower, Barnham & Pykett* [44] the taxpayers, a firm of accountants, had for many years acted as auditors to a group of companies. As a result of a group re-organisation the taxpayers were asked if, after completing the 1962 audit, they would not seek re-appointment. Their charges of £2,567 for the 1962 audit were duly paid and later the taxpayers, as a firm, received an unsolicited *ex gratia* payment, also of £2,567, as compensation for the loss of their office as auditors. It was held that the payment was not taxable. Pennycuick J. said:

> " . . . [the taxpayers] were carrying on the business of chartered accountants, which consists in rendering services of a certain professional character in return for reward. They rendered those services to these six companies over a number of years and duly received their reward for so doing. At the end of their final term of office they had no legal claim of any description to receive any further payment from the companies. The companies then proceeded to make the wholly voluntary payment to the respondent firm. It is, I think, irrelevant that the companies elected to make that payment in an amount identical to a penny with the fees paid to the firm during their last year of office. It seems to me that a gift of that kind made by a former client cannot reasonably be treated as a receipt of a business which consists in rendering professional services. The subject matter of the assessment under Cases I and II is the full amount of the profits or gains of the trade or profession. Those profits have to be computed, it is well established, upon ordinary commercial principles. It does not seem to me that ordinary commercial principles require that bringing into account of this sort of voluntary payment, not made as the consideration for any services rendered by the firm, but by way of recognition of past services or by way of consolation for the termination of a contract. . . ."

A similar point arose in *Simpson* v. *John Reynolds & Co. (Insurances) Ltd.*[45] where a voluntary payment was made to a firm of insurance brokers by a client company which, following its takeover by a public company, was no longer able to place its business with the brokers. The payment was held not to be taxable as a trading receipt. Russell L.J. said the following:

> " First, this was a wholly unexpected and unsolicited gift. Secondly, it was made after the business connection had ceased. Thirdly, the gift was in recognition of past services rendered to the client company over a long period, though not because those past services were considered to have been inadequately remunerated. Fourthly, the gift was made as a consolation for the fact that those remunerative services were no longer to be performed by the taxpayer for the donor; and, fifthly, there is no suggestion that at a future date the business connection might be renewed."

The Crown had contended that the fact that a payment was made without legal obligation did not *per se* elude the fiscal grasp. Russell L.J. said (at p. 712F):

> " This is true. Gifts made or promised during the relevant connection may well be caught. It was also pointed out that the fact that payments are made after the connection has ceased does not *per se* elude the fiscal grasp. This also is true: for it may be part of the connection that such payments after its

---

[43] (1962) 40 T.C. 550. And see the case in note 45.   [44] (1969) 46 T.C. 561.
[45] (1975) 49 T.C. 693 (C.A.). See also *Murray* v. *Goodhews* [1978] S.T.C. 207 (C.A.).

determination are to be expected. But that does not in my view lead to the suggested conclusion that when both of those circumstances are present—that is to say, where the gift is wholly voluntary and made unexpectedly after the business connection has come to an end—the payment is within the statutory language. The Crown contended, as I understand it, as a general proposition, that in the case of a business connection that was a trade connection, and the trade of the donee as a whole continued with persons other than the donee, a gift made for the reasons given in the present case *must* be caught: for it was not made merely out of personal affection or regard. Or, the Crown submitted, that viewed as a whole the circumstances of this case showed that this sum did accrue or arise from the trade. For my part, I am unable to accept this. The impact of the argument would, it seems to me, be very wide indeed. A legacy to a doctor or a solicitor expressed to be in gratitude for his professional services to the testator or the testator's late spouse (*ex hypothesi* operative after the connection had ceased) would apparently, according to the Crown's argument . . . be liable to income tax, granted that the solicitor or the doctor had not at the time of the death retired from practice. That is a suggestion I have certainly never met.''

By contrast, in *I.R.C.* v. *Falkirk Ice Rink Ltd.*[46] a donation to a trading company which operated an ice rink on a commercial basis made in order to supplement its trading revenue from curling and to ensure the continuation of its ability to continue to provide curling facilities in the future was held to be a trading receipt. It was a supplement to its trading revenue.

C. Trading Expenses

2-51 Not all expenses incurred in the course of trading are deductible in computing the annual profits or gains for tax purposes. Section 130 of the Income and Corporation Taxes Act 1970 contains a list of prohibited deductions which are followed, in some cases, by words of exception. There is no enumeration of permitted deductions. Thus section 130 (*a*) does not provide that money wholly and exclusively laid out or expended for the purposes of a trade may be deducted, but that no sum shall be deducted in respect of any disbursements or expenses not being money wholly and exclusively laid out or expended for the purposes of the trade. It is, however, obvious that if no deduction of expenses from gross receipts was allowed, it would be impossible to arrive at the balance of the profits and gains of a trade on which tax under Case I of Schedule D is to be assessed. Accordingly, it has long been well settled that the effect of the provisions now contained in section 130 is that the balance of the profits and gains of a trade must be ascertained in accordance with the ordinary principles of commercial accounting, by deducting from the gross receipts all expenditure properly deductible from them on those principles, save in so far as any amount so deducted falls within any of the statutory prohibitions contained in section 130, in which case the amount disallowed must be added back.[47] Generally, any expenditure which is justified by commercial expediency and is incurred for the purpose of enabling a person to carry on and earn profits in the trade is deductible, even if those profits may arise *in*

---

[46] [1975] S.T.C. 434. *Cf.* the *British Commonwealth* case in § 5-18.
[47] See the remarks of Lord Sumner in *Usher's Wiltshire Brewery Ltd.* v. *Bruce* [1915] A.C. 433 at p. 467; 6 T.C. 399 at p. 436.

futuro.[48] The principles of commercial accounting can be determined by the court on the evidence before it: see § 2-19.

2-52 Expenditure in earning profits must be distinguished from the application of profits after they have been earned.[49] The payment of income tax is an application of profits after they have been earned: it is not an expense of earning profits.[50]

Two conditions must be satisfied before an item of expenditure is deductible:

(1) It must be revenue and not capital expenditure.
(2) The expenditure must be incurred wholly and exclusively for the purposes of the trade.[51]

Hence the cost of fixed assets (*e.g.* business premises) is not deductible,[52] even if paid by instalments [53]; nor is a sum set aside to cover depreciation of capital assets.[54] Expenditure incurred in anticipation of the commencement of trading (*e.g.* the cost of forming a company) is not deductible.[55] Capital expenditure is dealt with in the provisions relating to capital allowances (Chap. 13) and capital gains tax (Chap. 17).

(1) *Capital and revenue expenditure distinguished*

2-53 In *Vallambrosa Rubber Co. Ltd.* v. *Farmer,*[56] Lord Dunedin suggested that expenditure which is made once and for all is normally capital expenditure, whereas recurrent expenditure (or expenditure which is likely to recur) is revenue expenditure. In *British Insulated and Helsby Cables Ltd.* v. *Atherton,*[57] Lord Cave carried the matter a stage further:

> " When an expenditure is made, not only once and for all, but with a view to bringing into existence an asset or an advantage for the enduring benefit of a trade, I think that there is very good reason . . . for treating such an expenditure as properly attributable not to revenue but to capital."

Whether an item of expenditure is capital or revenue expenditure is ultimately a question of law for the court; and in one case [58] Lord Greene M.R. remarked that " in many cases it is almost true to say that the spin of a coin would decide the matter almost as satisfactorily as an attempt to find reasons." The procedure by coin-spinning has not as yet commended itself to the Commissioners, however, so the quest for legal principles must continue.

---

[48] *Vallambrosa Rubber Co. Ltd.* v. *Farmer* (1910) 5 T.C. 529.
[49] *Mersey Docks and Harbour Board* v. *Lucas* (1883) 2 T.C. 25 (H.L.); *Racecourse Betting Control Board* v. *Young* (1959) 38 T.C. 426 (H.L.).
[50] *Ashton Gas Co.* v. *Att.-Gen.* [1906] A.C. 10 (H.L.).
[51] I.C.T.A. 1970, s. 130 (*a*).
[52] *Watney* v. *Musgrave* (1880) 5 Ex.D. 241; 1 T.C. 272 (premium for lease); *European Investment Trust Co. Ltd.* v. *Jackson* (1932) 18 T.C. 1 (C.A.).
[53] *Green* v. *Favourite Cinemas Ltd.* (1930) 15 T.C. 390.
[54] But capital allowances may be claimed: see Chap. 13.
[55] *Royal Insurance Co.* v. *Watson* [1897] A.C. 1; 3 T.C. 500.
[56] (1910) 5 T.C. 529 (Ct. of Sess.).
[57] [1926] A.C. 205 at p. 214; 10 T.C. 155 at p. 192. *Cf. Heather* v. *P-E Consulting Group Ltd.* [1973] Ch. 189; 48 T.C. 293 (C.A.), in which annual payments made by a company to establish a fund to acquire shares for the benefit of the employees were held to be of a revenue nature and deductible in computing profits (C.A.). See also *Strick* v. *Regent Oil Co. Ltd.* (1965) 43 T.C. 1 (H.L.).
[58] *British Salmson Aero Engines Ltd.* v. *I.R.C.* [1938] 2 K.B. 482; 22 T.C. 29 (C.A.).

2-54 The cost of an item from the resale of which a trader makes his profit is generally deductible: the item is part of the trader's " circulating capital." There is, however, an important distinction between the purchase of the raw material of a trade (revenue expenditure) and the purchase of an asset from which the trader obtains his raw material (capital expenditure).

> Thus in *Stow Bardolph Gravel Co. Ltd.* v. *Poole,*[59] the company who were dealers in sand and gravel claimed as a deduction the cost of a contract giving them the exclusive right to excavate gravel. The contract was unlimited in time and imposed no obligation on the company to excavate the gravel; the price was not related to the quantity of gravel excavated; and there were options to acquire other reserves of gravel. *Held* to be capital expenditure.

This distinction was maintained in *H. J. Rorke Ltd.* v. *I.R.C.,*[60] notwithstanding evidence that the payments in that case were a normal and recurrent incident of the trade and that, since the purchaser had a lease for one year only, no " enduring benefit " was obtained. " They were not payments made for the purchase of coal but payments to put the company into the position to get coal."

2-55
> In *Mitchell* v. *B. W. Noble Ltd.*[61] a lump sum was paid to a director who, though liable to dismissal, agreed to retire to avoid undesirable publicity. *Held* to be deductible: " . . . a payment to get rid of a servant in the interests of the trade is a proper deduction " (*per* Rowlatt J.).
>
> Similarly in *Anglo-Persian Oil Co. Ltd.* v. *Dale*[62] a lump sum paid by a principal to his agent for the cancellation of an onerous agreement, the payment being in the course of a change in the principal's business methods and to effect an economy in the business, was allowed as a deduction.
>
> In *Southern* v. *Borax Consolidated Ltd.*[63] costs incurred by a company in defending its title to certain land were allowed as a deduction.
>
> In *I.R.C.* v. *Carron Company*[64] the cost of obtaining a new charter which provided a better administrative structure for the company was held to be deductible " . . . what matters is the nature of the advantage for which the money was spent. This money was spent to remove restrictions which were preventing profits from being earned. It created no new asset. It did not even open new fields of trading which had previously been closed to the Company ": Lord Reid at p. 68.

2-56 These cases may be contrasted with the following:

> *Mallet* v. *Staveley Coal and Iron Co. Ltd.,*[65] where a colliery company with long-term mining leases found that some of the seams of coal it had contracted to work were unprofitable. The lessor agreed to release the company from its obligations under the leases on payment of a lump sum. *Held*, this was not deductible. The company was " getting rid of a permanent disadvantage or onerous burden, arising with regard to the lease which was a permanent asset of the business ": *per* Sargant L.J.
>
> *Associated Portland Cement Manufacturers Ltd.* v. *Kerr,*[66] where lump sum payments to retiring directors in consideration of covenants that they would not thereafter carry on a similar business were held to be capital expenditure.

[59] (1954) 35 T.C. 459 (C.A.); see also *Golden Horse Shoe (New) Ltd.* v. *Thurgood* [1934] 1 K.B. 548; 18 T.C. 280 (C.A.); *Saunders* v. *Pilcher* (1949) 31 T.C. 314 (C.A.); *Hopwood* v. *C. N. Spencer Ltd.* (1964) 42 T.C. 169.
[60] (1960) 39 T.C. 194.
[61] [1927] 1 K.B. 719; 11 T.C. 372 (C.A.).
[62] [1932] 1 K.B. 124; 16 T.C. 253 (C.A.).
[63] [1941] 1 K.B. 111; 23 T.C. 597.
[64] (1968) 45 T.C. 18 (H.L.).
[65] [1928] 2 K.B. 405; 13 T.C. 772 (C.A.).
[66] (1945) 27 T.C. 103 (C.A.).

(2) *Wholly and exclusively for the purposes of the trade*

2-57   Section 130 (*a*) of the Income and Corporation Taxes Act 1970 disallows any disbursements or expenses, not being money wholly and exclusively laid out or expended for the purposes of the trade, profession or vocation. Section 130 (*b*) disallows any disbursements or expenses of maintenance of the parties, their families or establishments, or any sums expended for any other domestic or private purposes distinct from the purposes of a trade, profession or vocation.

> In *Bentleys, Stokes & Lowless* v. *Beeson* [67] the appellants, a firm of solicitors, had incurred expenses in entertaining clients. The question arose whether such expenses were wholly and exclusively incurred for professional purposes. The Crown contended that the expenses could not be wholly divorced from the relationship of host and guest and that the " wholly and exclusively " test was not satisfied. The Court of Appeal allowed the expenses.

The sole question for the consideration of the court was whether the expenditure in question was " exclusively " laid out for business purposes having regard to the fact that entertaining inevitably involves the characteristic of hospitality. Romer L.J. said (at p. 504):

> " . . . it is quite clear that the [business] purpose must be the sole purpose. The paragraph says so in clear terms. If the activity be undertaken with the object both of promoting business and also with some other purpose, for example, with the object of indulging an independent wish of entertaining a friend or stranger or of supporting a charitable or benevolent object, then the paragraph is not satisfied although in the mind of the actor the business motive may predominate. For the statute so prescribes. *Per contra*, if in truth the sole object is business promotion, the expenditure is not disqualified because the nature of the activity necessarily involves some other result, or the attainment or furtherance of some other objective, since the latter result or objective is necessarily inherent in the act."

2-58   The court held that the primary purpose of the expenditure was a business purpose and so allowed the deduction.[68] It follows from the principle enunciated by Romer L.J. that where expenditure is incurred for a dual purpose, one a business purpose and one not, no part of the expenditure is deductible.[69] Logically, where the taxpayer admits some degree of non-business purpose by claiming a percentage deduction for private use from total expenditure, disallowance of the whole should follow; but the Revenue do not in all cases so apply the law. The *Bentleys* case may be contrasted with *Norman* v. *Golder* [70] where a sick shorthand-writer unsuccessfully claimed as a deduction expenses involved in getting well. Lord Greene M.R. said:

---

[67] (1952) 33 T.C. 491 (C.A.). Business entertaining expenses are now disallowed by statute: see *post*, §§ 2-71 *et seq.*

[68] See *Usher's Wiltshire Brewery* v. *Bruce* (1914) 6 T.C. 399 at p. 469 (Lord Sumner); *Morgan* v. *Tate & Lyle Ltd.* (1954) 35 T.C. 367 at p. 417 (Lord Reid).

[69] *Bowden* v. *Russell and Russell* (1965) 42 T.C. 301: a solicitor combining attendance at foreign law conference with holiday; no deduction allowed.

[70] (1944) 26 T.C. 293 (C.A.). See also *Murgatroyd* v. *Evans-Jackson* (1966) 43 T.C. 581 (professional man entered nursing home to enjoy facility of private room, telephone, etc., which he could use as office; cost not deductible); *Prince* v. *Mapp* (1969) 46 T.C. 169 (guitar player played professionally and as hobby—cost of operation on finger not allowable expense); *Knight* v. *Parry* (1972) 48 T.C. 580; [1973] S.T.C. 56 (expenses of solicitor in refuting allegations of professional misconduct disallowed); *Kilmorie (Aldridge) Ltd.* v. *Dickinson* (1974) 50 T.C. 1; *Caillebotte* v. *Quinn* [1975] 50 T.C. 222; S.T.C. 265 (self-employed carpenter incurring extra costs on meals when away from home—held not allowable).

" It is quite impossible to argue that doctors' bills represent money wholly and exclusively laid out for the purposes of a trade, profession, employment or vocation of the patient. True it is that if you do not get yourself well and so incur expenses to doctors you cannot carry on your trade or profession and if you do not carry on your trade or profession you will not earn an income, and if you do not earn an income the Revenue will not get any tax. The same thing applies to the food you eat and the clothes that you wear. But expenses of that kind are not wholly and lusively laid out for the purposes of trade, profession or vocation. They are laid out in part for the advantage and benefit of the taxpayer as a living human being."

If Company A incurs expenditure to sustain the trade of Company B, the expenditure is not deductible unless the trades are interlinked and it can be shown that the expenditure was incurred to ensure the prosperity of Company A's trade.[71]

2-59 It appears that the word " wholly " in the phrase " wholly and exclusively " relates to *quantum*. Thus if an employee is paid a salary which is excessive having regard to the services he renders, the excess may be disallowed as a deduction[72]; and the same rule applies to excessive pensions.[73]

Specific Items of Expenditure

2-60 *Rent and premiums for business premises.* Rent paid for business premises is deductible in computing trading rofits, even if the premises are temporarily out of use.[74] If premises are used partly for business and partly for domestic purposes, the Revenue allow a deduction in respect of such part of the rent as is attributable to the business but disallow the remainder.[75] A deduction is allowed to a trader who pays a premium for (or a sum on the assignment of) business premises which is chargeable on the recipient.[76] When a capital asset is acquired by means of payment of " rent," the payment will be disallowed.[77]

2-61 *Sale and lease-back transactions.* A trader who sells his business premises, whether freehold or leasehold, for a capital sum and takes from the purchaser a lease or sub-lease at a rent is generally entitled to deduct the whole of the rent as an expense of his trade. Any chargeable gain accruing on the transaction is subject to capital gains tax. This general principle is subject to two statutory exceptions:

First, if the rent under the lease is in excess of a commercial rent, the excess will be disallowed as a deduction, under section 491 of the Income and Corporation Taxes Act 1970.

Secondly, where a lease with not more than 50 years to run (called " the original lease ") is assigned or surrendered in consideration of a capital sum

---

[71] *Milnes* v. *J. Beam Group Ltd.* [1975] S.T.C. 487 (where Company A guaranteed loans to an associated company and it was not established that a sum paid by Company A in discharging its liability was made wholly and exclusively for the purpose of the trade of Company A); *cf. Morley* v. *Lawford* (1928) 14 T.C. 229.

[72] *Copeman* v. *Flood* [1941] 1 K.B. 202; 24 T.C. 53: but *quaere* if this decision can be reconciled with the principle enunciated by Romer L.J. in the *Bentleys* case, above.

[73] An agreement to provide a pension may be *ultra vires* and void: see *Re W. & M. Roith Ltd.* [1967] 1 W.L.R. 432.

[74] *I.R.C.* v. *The Falkirk Iron Company Ltd.* (1g33) 17 T.C. 625. The position is the same where the premises have been sub-let: *Hyett* v. *Lennard* (1940) 23 T.C. 346.

[75] I.C.T.A. 1970, s. 130 (c).

[76] *Ibid.* s. 134, as amended by F.A. 1978, s. 32. For the taxation of premiums, see *post*, §§ 6-16 *et seq.*

[77] *Littlewoods Mail Order Stores Ltd.* v. *McGregor* (1969) 45 T.C. 519 (C.A.); *I.R.C.* v. *Land Securities Investment Trust Ltd.* (1969) 45 T.C. 495 (H.L.).

and the lessee [78] takes a lease back at a rent, the lease back (called " the new lease ") being for a term not exceeding 15 years, [79] a proportion of the capital sum is taxable as income under section 80 of the Finance Act 1972. The rent will be allowed as a deduction, subject to the provisions of section 491 (above). The proportion of the capital sum which is taxable as income is found by applying the formula $\frac{16-n}{15}$ where " n " is the term of the new lease expressed in years. [80]

> Thus if the new lease is for a term of 15 years, one-fifteenth of the capital sum is taxable; if for a term of one year, the whole of the capital sum is taxable.

" Top slicing " relief is available to prevent the capital sum being treated as income of a single year of assessment. [81] That part of the capital sum which is chargeable as income is outside the charge to capital gains tax. [82]

Section 80 of the Finance Act 1972 applies only where the new lease is " a lease . . . of or including the whole or any part of the land which was the subject of the original lease." [83] Difficulties in applying this provision may arise in practice in cases where, for example, the original lease is surrendered to a landlord who demolishes the existing premises, rebuilds a tower block on the site of the old premises, and grants to the original lessee a lease of a floor which was airspace before the rebuilding. Section 80 (4) of the Finance Act 1972 provides that where the property which is the subject of the new lease does not include the *whole* of the property which was the subject of the original lease, the consideration received by the lessee should be treated as reduced to that portion thereof which is reasonably attributable to such part of the property which was the subject of the original lease as consists of, or is included in, the property which is the subject of the new lease.

> Thus if one-third of the property included in the original lease is included in the new lease, only one-third of the capital sum is taken into account in applying the section.

2-62   *Repairs and improvements.* A deduction is allowed for the sum actually expended on repairs to business assets, [84] provided the expenditure is revenue and not capital expenditure.

> In *Law Shipping Co. Limited* v. *I.R.C.* [85] a trader purchased a ship in a state of disrepair. After the completion of the voyage on which it was then embarked, repairs were necessary to obtain the Lloyd's certificate which was essential if the ship was to remain a profit-earning asset. The Revenue claimed that the cost of the repairs was capital expenditure to the extent that it was attributable to the state of disrepair of the ship at the time of purchase. The Court of Session upheld the Revenue's claim and disallowed the expenditure. (Part of the cost of the repairs was attributable to deterioration during the last voyage when the ship was in the appellant's ownership: this was conceded to be revenue expenditure.)

---

[78]   Defined to include a partner or associate of the original lessee: see F.A. 1972, s. 80 (7).
[79]   There are anti-avoidance provisions which cause the section to apply when the term of the new lease is " artificially " extended beyond 15 years: see F.A. 1972, s. 80 (2).
[80]   F.A. 1972, s. 80 (3).
[81]   *Ibid.* s. 80 (5).
[82]   *Post*, § 16-19.
[83]   *Ibid.* s. 80 (1) (*a*).
[84]   I.C.T.A. 1970, s. 130 (*d*).
[85]   (1924) 12 T.C. 621. See also *I.R.C.* v. *Granite City Steamship Co. Ltd.* (1927) 13 T.C. 1.

In another case where a trader acquired business premises in a state of dilapidation, the cost of reinstating the premises was disallowed.[86]

> In *Odeon Associated Theatres Limited* v. *Jones* [87] the taxpayer purchased a cinema in 1945 which, owing to war time restrictions on building, had not been kept in repair. Some years later the taxpayer carried out repairs which were outstanding at the time when the cinema was purchased. There was no element of improvement in the repairs and the price paid for the cinema was not diminished on their account. The Special Commissioners found as a fact that, on the principles of sound commercial accounting, the deferred repairs would be dealt with as a charge to revenue in the taxpayer's accounts. The Court of Appeal held that the cost of the repairs was deductible as revenue expenditure.

The *Law Shipping* [88] case was distinguished on the grounds (i) that in that case there was no evidence of accountancy practice [89]; (ii) that the cinema was a profit-earning asset even though in a state of disrepair; and (iii) that the purchase price for the cinema was unaffected by the state of disrepair.[90]

2-63   The cost of improvements (as distinct from repairs) is not deductible for income tax or corporation tax purposes,[91] although the cost may be deductible for the purposes of capital gains tax (as explained in § 16-30). The terms " repair " and " improvement " are not defined in the Taxing Acts but the following passage from the judgment of Buckley L.J., in *Lurcott* v. *Wakely & Wheeler,* [92] in which he contrasts the terms " repair " and " renew," is frequently cited in tax cases as indicating the difference between repair and improvement:

> " ' Repair ' and ' renew ' are not words expressive of a clear contrast. Repair always involves renewal; renewal of a part; of a subordinate part. A skylight leaks; repair is effected by hacking out the putties, putting in new ones, and renewing the paint. A roof falls out of repair; the necessary work is to replace the decayed timbers by sound wood; to substitute sound tiles or slates for those which are cracked, broken, or missing; to make good the flashings, and the like. Part of a garden wall tumbles down; repair is effected by building it up again with new mortar, and, so far as necessary, new bricks or stone. Repair is restoration by renewal or replacement of subsidiary parts of a whole. Renewal, as distinguished from repair, is reconstruction of the entirety, meaning by the entirety not necessarily the whole but substantially the whole subject matter under discussion."

The judge refers in this extract to *the entirety* and in many cases it becomes material to determine what constitutes the entirety. If, for example, a factory chimney falls into disrepair and is rebuilt, the question may arise whether the entirety was the factory (a subsidiary part of which was rebuilt—this would be " repair ") or the chimney (the whole of which

---

[86] *Jackson* v. *Laskers Home Furnishers Ltd.* (1957) 37 T.C. 69. See also *Bidwell* v. *Gardiner* (1960) 39 T.C. 31.

[87] (1971) 48 T.C. 257 (C.A.).

[88] (1924) 12 T.C. 621.

[89] As to the weight to be given to evidence of accountancy practice, see *Heather* v. *P-E Consulting Group Ltd.* [1973] Ch. 189; 48 T.C. 293 (C.A.) and the discussion in § 2-19A.

[90] Other points of contrast are discussed in a Note in [1972] B.T.R. at p. 51.

[91] I.C.T.A. 1970, s. 130 (*g*).

[92] [1911] 1 K.B. 905 (C.A.). See *Morcom* v. *Campbell-Johnson* [1956] 1 Q.B. 106.

was renewed—this would be " improvement ").[93] In some cases the Crown has contended that the question whether expenditure on (say) rebuilding is to be regarded as capital or revenue expenditure is a different question from the question whether the expenditure is on improvements or repairs. The author doubts whether these can properly be regarded as separate questions.[94]

2-64   *Damages and losses.* No sum can be deducted in respect of " any loss not connected with or arising out of " the trade.[95] In *Strong & Co. Ltd.* v. *Woodifield,*[96] damages paid to an hotel guest for injury sustained in the hotel when part of the building collapsed were disallowed. The basis of this decision appears to be that the loss was not sufficiently incidental to the trade of *hotel keeper* to be outside the specific prohibition quoted above. Damages paid to a guest who is injured, *e.g.* by bad food served in the hotel, would apparently be deductible.

2-65   Penalties incurred by a trader for breaches of the law committed in the course of trading are not allowable.[97]

If money is lent by a trader and the loan is not repaid, a deduction is allowed only if the trade is, or includes, moneylending.[98]

2-66   *Compensation payments.* A payment made by a company to get rid of a director or employee is an allowable expense if the payment is made in the interests of the company's trade [99]; but a payment which is made on the occasion of the acquisition of the company's shares by outsiders will often be disallowed. In *James Snook & Co. Ltd.* v. *Blasdale,*[1] Donovan J. said in such a case:

> " The mere circumstance that compensation to retiring directors is paid on a change of shareholding control does not of itself involve the consequence that such compensation can never be a deductible trading expense. But it is essential that the company should prove to the Commissioners' satisfaction that it considered the question of payment wholly untrammelled by the terms of the bargain its shareholders had struck with those who were to buy their shares and came to a decision to pay solely in the interests of its trade."

[93] *O'Grady* v. *Bullcroft Main Collieries Ltd.* (1932) 17 T.C. 93: " If you replace in entirety, it is having a new one and it is not repairing an old one "; *Margrett* v. *Lowestoft Water and Gas Co.* (1935) 19 T.C. 481; *Samuel Jones and Company (Devonvale) Ltd.* v. *I.R.C.* (1951) 32 T.C. 513; *William P. Lawrie* v. *I.R.C.* (1952) 34 T.C. 20; *Thomas Wilson (Keighley) Ltd.* v. *Emmerson* (1960) 39 T.C. 360; *Wynne-Jones* v. *Bedale Auction Ltd.* [1977] S.T.C. 50.

[94] *Cf. Phillips* v. *Whieldon Sanitary Potteries Ltd.* (1952) 33 T.C. 213; *Conn* v. *Robins Brothers Ltd.* (1966) 43 T.C. 266; *Hodgins* v. *Plunder & Pollack* [1957] I.R. 58.

[95] I.C.T.A. 1970, s. 130 (*e*). And see *Allen* v. *Farquharson Bros. & Co.* (1932) 17 T.C. 59, 64 where Finlay J. distinguishes " disbursements " in s. 130 (*a*) from " loss " in s. 130 (*e*).

[96] [1906] A.C. 448; 5 T.C. 215. See also *Fairrie* v. *Hall* (1948) 28 T.C. 200: damages for libel held not deductible as a trading expense of a sugar broker.

[97] *I.R.C.* v. *Alexander von Glehn & Co. Ltd.* [1920] 2 K.B. 553; 12 T.C. 232 (C.A.) (fines are not paid for the purpose of earning profits; they are unfortunate incidents which follow after the profits have been earned: Scrutton L.J.).

[98] *Hagart and Burn-Murdoch* v. *I.R.C.* [1929] A.C. 386; 14 T.C. 433; *Rutherford* v. *I.R.C.* (1939) 23 T.C. 8; and *Bury and Walkers* v. *Phillips* (1951) 32 T.C. 198. And see *Reid's Brewery Co.* v. *Male* [1891] 2 Q.B. 1; 3 T.C. 279, where a loss on loans to clients was allowed. See also *Jennings* v. *Barfield & Barfield* (1962) 40 T.C. 365.

[99] *Mitchell* v. *B. W. Noble Ltd.* [1927] 1 K.B. 719; 11 T.C. 372 (C.A.), *ante,* § 2-55.

[1] (1952) 33 T.C. 244 at p. 251; *Godden* v. *Wilson's Stores (Holdings) Ltd.* (1962) 40 T.C. 161 (C.A.); *George Peters & Co. Ltd.* v. *Smith* (1963) 41 T.C. 264. *Cf. I.R.C.* v. *Patrick Thomson Ltd.* (1956) 37 T.C. 145.

'' Golden handshakes '' which are tax free in the hands of the recipient are in some cases disallowed as sums not incurred wholly and exclusively for the purposes of the payer's trade.

2-67 *Tax.* In one case it was held that the Argentine '' substitute tax '' for which the appellant was liable was deductible as expenditure incurred wholly and exclusively for the purposes of the appellant's trade. [2]

2-68 *Bad debts.* An amount to which a trader is entitled, *e.g.* for goods supplied by him, enters into the computation of his profits in the period when the sum falls due. [3] If, later, the trader is able to prove that the debt is a bad or doubtful debt, the Revenue allow a deduction—in the latter case, to the extent that the debt is estimated to be a bad debt. [4] A debt may be a bad debt even though the debtor continues to trade. [5] If an allowance is given and the debt is later paid, the amount must be brought in as a trading receipt of the year when it is paid. [6]

2-69 *Defalcations.* In *Curtis* v. *Oldfield,* [7] the managing director of a company had taken moneys from the company's bank account for his own purposes. It was held that this could not be treated by the company as a bad debt. In this connection, the remarks of Rowlatt J. are important:

> '' If you have a business . . . in the course of which you have to employ subordinates, and owing to the negligence or the dishonesty *of the subordinates*, some of the receipts of the business do not find their way into the till, or some of the bills are not collected at all, or something of that sort, that may be an expense connected with and arising out of the trade in the most complete sense of the word.''

2-70 *Legal and other professional charges.* The costs of a tax appeal arising out of a disputed assessment of trading profits are not allowable. [8] In practice, the fees paid to an accountant in agreeing tax computations with the Inspector are allowed; so also are fees paid in seeking advice on liability to tax. Legal expenses incurred in the course of a trade, *e.g.* in recovering debts, in settling disputes and in the preparation of service agreements are allowed; but the costs of acquiring premises or a lease thereof will normally be disallowed as capital expenses. The cost of renewing a short lease is usually allowed. [9]

---

[2] *Harrods (Buenos Aires) Ltd.* v. *Taylor-Gooby* (1964) 41 T.C. 450 (C.A.). As regards the deduction of VAT, see Chap. 35.

[3] *Ante,* § 2-20.   [4] I.C.T.A. 1970, s. 130 (*i*).

[5] *Dinshaw* v. *Income Tax Commissioners (Bombay)* (1934) 50 T.L.R. 527 (J.C.).

[6] *Bristow* v. *Dickinson* [1946] K.B. 321; 27 T.C. 157 (C.A.). If the trade has been discontinued at the date of payment, the sum will be assessed as a post-cessation receipt under the I.C.T.A. 1970, s. 143; *post,* §§ 2-88 *et seq.*

[7] (1925) 9 T.C. 319. In *Bamford* v. *A. T. A. Advertising Ltd.* (1972) 48 T.C. 359, sum fraudulently misappropriated by a director and sums paid as director's PAYE tax were disallowed as deductions in computing trading profits.

[8] *Smith's Potato Estates Ltd.* v. *Bolland* [1948] A.C. 508; 30 T.C. 267 (H.L.). See also *Meredith* v. *Roberts* (1968) 44 T.C. 559.

[9] In *Stephenson* v. *Payne, Stone, Fraser & Co.* (1968) 44 T.C. 507, a firm of accountants formed a service company to provide them with all their administrative requirements, and in the first year the charge made to the firm exceeded the cost by £15,000. *Held,* that the £15,000 was not an allowable expense of the year. And see § 2-20.

2-71   *Business entertaining expenses*. The rules which apply to Cases I and II of Schedule D allow the deduction of entertaining expenses incurred for the purposes of a trade [10]; but section 411 of the Income and Corporation Taxes Act 1970 disallows as a deduction all expenses incurred in providing business entertainment, including expenses allowances made for that purpose. " Business entertainment " is defined as meaning

> " entertainment (including hospitality of any kind [11]) provided by a person, or by a member of his staff,[12] in connection with a trade carried on by that person, but does not include anything provided by him for bona fide members of his staff unless its provision for them is incidental to its provision also for others."

2-72   There is an exception in the case of expenses incurred by a United Kingdom trader in the entertainment of an " overseas customer," meaning

(1) Any person who is not ordinarily resident nor carrying on a trade in the United Kingdom and who avails himself, or may be expected to avail himself, in the course of a trade carried on by him outside the United Kingdom, of any goods, services or facilities which it is the trade of the United Kingdom trader to provide; and

(2) any person who is not ordinarily resident in the United Kingdom and is acting, in relation to such goods, services or facilities, on behalf of an overseas customer within (1) or on behalf of any government or public authority of a country outside the United Kingdom. [13]

Expenditure incurred by a publisher of newspapers in giving hospitality to informants, contributors and other contacts, in order to gather material, has been disallowed. [14]

2-72A   *Business travelling expenses*. The cost of travelling on business is a deductible expense. In *Horton* v. *Young* [15] it was held on the facts that a self-employed bricklayer's home was his " base of operations " and that the expense he incurred in travelling between his home and building sites was an allowable deduction in computing his profits under Case I of Schedule D. This may be contrasted with *Newsom* v. *Robertson* [16] where it was held that a Chancery barrister's chambers in Lincoln's Inn were his base, and that the home in which he did a large part of his work was not. It is thought that the principle in *Horton* v. *Young* would apply to the case of a barrister who practised on circuit, who seldom visited his chambers, and who used his home as a base; the costs of travelling between home and the courts in which he practised (as well as the costs of travelling between courts) would be allowed as a deduction. Expenses of travelling which are " necessarily " expended for professional purposes may nevertheless be disallowed as not being " wholly and exclusively " so expended. [17]

---

[10] *Bentleys, Stokes and Lowless* v. *Beeson* (1952) 33 T.C. 491 (C.A.); *ante*, § 2-57.
[11] Gifts are included, with an exception for certain small gifts bearing advertisements for the donor.
[12] This means employees and directors: I.C.T.A. 1970, s. 411 (7).
[13] See I.C.T.A. 1970, s. 411 (6).
[14] *Fleming* v. *Associated Newspapers Ltd.* [1973] A.C. 628; 48 T.C. 382 (H.L.).
[15] [1972] 1 Ch. 157; 47 T.C. 60 (C.A.).
[16] [1953] Ch. 7; 33 T.C. 452 (C.A.).
[17] *Sargent* v. *Barnes* [1978] S.T.C. 322.

2-73   *Annual payments.* No deduction can be made *in computing* profits in respect of any annuity or other annual payment (other than interest) payable out of the profits or gains.[18] The types of payment which fall within this prohibition are discussed *post*, §§ 5-04 *et seq.* The prohibition applies only to payments which are charged on the profits: it does not apply to payments which are made in earning profits.[19] Many annuities and annual payments are a charge on income and are deductible as such: see § 8-31 (individuals) and § 14-08 (companies).

2-74   *Patent royalties.* No deduction is allowed for any royalty or other sum paid in respect of the user of a patent.[20] Expenses of obtaining a patent may be allowed.[21]

2-75   *Interest.* Interest paid as a business expense, whether short interest or yearly interest, is deductible [22] except in the case of companies where yearly interest (other than bank interest) is not deductible as a business expense but is a charge on income.[23] Other provisions relating to interest are discussed *post*, §§ 8-57 *et seq.*

2-76   *Betterment levy and development land tax.* Where land forms part of the trading stock of a trader, betterment levy paid in respect of that land is clearly an expense of a revenue nature incurred wholly and exclusively for the purposes of the trade and is therefore deductible in computing trading profit. This will apply whether the levy is payable on a disposal of the land or on the grant of a lease (under Cases A or B) or on the commencement of a project of material development (under Case C) prior to disposal.[24] Development land tax, as such, is not deductible in computing profits under Case I but provisions exist, subject to certain limitations, whereby the development value on which development land tax is charged is excluded in computing Case I profits: see § 16-166.

2-77   *Pensions.* Pensions paid by employers are deductible in computing profits if the expenditure is incurred wholly and exclusively for the purposes of the trade. A pension which is paid voluntarily may fulfil this condition.[25] A pension which is excessive may be disallowed as expenditure incurred not wholly and exclusively for the purposes of the payer's trade.[26]

2-78   *Payments to provide pensions.*[27] An employer who wishes to provide his employee or employees with a pension may do so in one of the following ways:

---

[18] I.C.T.A. 1970, s. 130 (*l*).

[19] *Gresham Life Assurance Society* v. *Styles* [1892] A.C. 309; 3 T.C. 185; annuities paid by a society whose business it was to grant annuities; *held* to be deductible.

[20] I.C.T.A. 1970, s. 130 (*n*).

[21] See *ibid.* s. 132 for details.

[22] *Ibid.* s. 130 (*l*).

[23] I.C.T.A. 1970, s. 251 (2), (3) and s. 248: see *post*, §§ 14-08 *et seq.*

[24] Betterment levy (which has now been abolished) was discussed in the 4th ed. of this book in Chaps. 31 and 32.

[25] *Smith* v. *Incorporated Council of Law Reporting* [1914] 3 K.B. 674; 6 T.C. 477.

[26] See *ante*, § 2-59.

[27] See also *post*, §§ 39-08 *et seq.*

(1) By contributing to a pension fund established for the purpose. An initial contribution made by an employer to establish a pension fund is not deductible,[28] unless the pension scheme is an " exempt approved " scheme. Ordinary annual contributions are usually deductible.[29]

(2) By purchase of an annuity from an insurance company. The cost of purchasing an annuity for an employee in substitution for a pension already awarded is deductible.[30]

(3) By paying premiums on a policy assuring retirement benefits. The premiums are deductible if the policy moneys are held upon trust for the employees [31] and the arrangement is approved by the Revenue or if the premiums are a proper business expense.[32]

If the employer makes contributions to a pension fund which is not an " exempt approved scheme " within section 21 of the Finance Act 1970, any relief in respect of those contributions will be governed by section 130 of the Taxes Act 1970. To qualify for relief the payment must not be of a capital nature [28] and must be wholly and exclusively for the purposes of the employer's trade.

4. THE BASIS OF ASSESSING PROFITS [33]

A. The Normal Basis

2-79 The normal basis on which profits arising under Cases I and II of Schedule D are assessed is the " preceding year basis "; that is, in each year of assessment, the assessment is based on the profits of the accounting period ending in the preceding year of assessment.

> *Example*: A trader prepares yearly accounts to December 31 each year. In 1962–63, he is assessed on the profits of the year ended December 31, 1961. (The accounting year to December 31, 1961, is described as the " basis period " for the year 1962–63.)

B. Rules for Opening Years

2-80 The normal preceding year basis cannot, of course, be applied in the opening year of a business. Accordingly, sections 115–117 of the Income and Corporation Taxes Act 1970 contain special provisions which apply from the date when a trade, profession or vocation has been set up and commenced. These " commencement provisions " are as follows:

---

[28] *British Insulated and Helsby Cables Ltd.* v. *Atherton* [1926] A.C. 205; 10 T.C. 155.
[29] *Morgan Crucible Co. Ltd.* v. *I.R.C.* [1932] 2 K.B. 185; 17 T.C. 311. And see *Southern Railway of Peru Ltd.* v. *Owen* [1957] A.C. 334; 36 T.C. 634. See also F.A. 1970, s. 21.
[30] *Hancock* v. *General Reversionary and Investment Co. Ltd.* [1919] 1 K.B. 25; 7 T.C. 358. *Cf. Morgan Crucible Co. Ltd.* v. *I.R.C.* [1932] 2 K.B. 185; 17 T.C. 311: sum paid by company in purchasing annuity out of which the company could itself pay voluntary pensions; *held*, not deductible.
[31] See n. 29, *ante.*
[32] *Dracup & Sons Ltd.* v. *Dakin* (1957) 37 T.C. 377.
[33] The basis of assessing profits in the case of companies chargeable to corporation tax is discussed in Chap. 14.

Basis of Assessment

First tax year   The profits from the date of commencement to the
s. 116 (1)   following April 5. If the first accounting period covers one
                  year not ending on or about April 5, such profits must be
                  computed by apportioning the profits of the accounting
                  period on a time basis.

Thus if a trader commences business on January 1, 1962, and his first
accounts, prepared to December 31, 1962, show a profit of £1,200, the first tax
year is 1961/62 (because the business started in that year) and the assessment is
3/12ths of £1,200 = £300.

Second tax year   The profits for one year from the date of commencement
s. 116 (2)   of the business.

Thus if the first accounts cover a period of one year, the profits of that period
form the basis of assessment. If the first accounts cover a period of less than a
year, the assessment for the second tax year must be computed by apportioning
the profits shown by the accounts of the first two years. (See *Example* in
§ 2-81.)

Third tax year   Generally, the normal preceding year basis.
s. 115.

Election for actual basis: s. 117

2-81   The taxpayer has an option with regard to the second and third tax year
(but not for one without the other) to have the assessments based on the
actual profits of the tax years themselves, *i.e.* from April 6 to the following
April 5 in each of those years. Such profits are computed by apportioning
on a time basis the profits disclosed by the accounts which overlap the two
tax years. The option is exercisable by notice to the Inspector within seven
years from the end of the second tax year and can be revoked during that
time.

Example: A trader starts business on December 6, 1967. His trading
         profits for the first three years are as follows:

                                                                    £

Accounting year ended December 5, 1968 1,200
        ,,   ,,   ,,   ,,   ,, 1969 1,800
        ,,   ,,   ,,   ,,   ,, 1970 2,400

Assessments are as follows:
1967–68 4/12ths of the actual profits in year ended
        December 5, 1968 400
1968–69 Actual profits to December 5, 1968 ... 1,200
1969–70   ,,   ,,   ,,   ,,   ,, 1968 ... 1,200
1970–71   ,,   ,,   ,,   ,,   ,, 1969 ... 1,800
1971–72   ,,   ,,   ,,   ,,   ,, 1970 ... 2,400

Alternative assessments for the second and third years if
the taxpayer elects for the " actual basis " are as follows
(other years being unaffected by the exercise of the
option):

Basis of Assessment

1968–69	April 6, 1968—December 5, 1968: 8/12ths × 1,200 = 800 December 6, 1968—April 5, 1969: 4/12ths × 1,800 = 600	1,400
1969–70	April 6, 1969—December 5, 1969: 8/12ths × 1,800 = 1,200 December 6, 1969—April 5, 1970: 4/12ths × 2,400 = 800	2,000

Note. Where the profits of the trade are rising, as in this example, the option would not normally be exercised. If, however, the profits of the first three accounting years had been £1,200, £900 and £600 the assessments for the second and third years would have been respectively £1,200 and £1,200 (on the normal basis) or £1,100 and £800 (on the alternative basis) and the option would be exercised.

2-82   The method of computing profits in the opening years of a business is highly artificial and may often result in assessable profits being substantially more or less than actual profits during the same period. Generally, the profits for the first accounting period should be kept as low as possible,[34] and in the case of trades with fluctuating profits the greatest care should be taken in selecting the closing date of the first accounting period.[35]

C. Rules for Closing Years

2-83   When a trade, profession or vocation is permanently discontinued, section 118 of the Income and Corporation Taxes Act 1970 applies. This section contains special provisions (called the " cessation provisions ") which govern the assessment of profits in the tax year in which the trade, etc., is discontinued and in the two previous tax years. These provisions are as follows:

Basis of Assessment

Final tax year s. 118 (1) (*a*)	Actual profits from April 6 to the date of discontinuance.
Penultimate tax year s. 118 (1) (*b*) and Pre-penultimate tax year s. 118 (1) (*b*)	Assessments for these years will have already been made on the normal preceding year basis. If the aggregate of the *actual* profits of these two years exceeds the aggregate of the profits computed on the normal preceding year basis, the profits of these two years must be computed on the actual basis and any further assessment or adjustment made. No reduction in the assessments will be allowed if the aggregate of the actual profits is less than the aggregate of the profits as assessed on the normal preceding year basis. " Actual profit " is found by apportioning the profits of the accounting periods which overlap the penultimate tax year.[36]

---

[34]   See *Stephenson* v. *Payne, Stone, Fraser & Co.* (1968) 44 T.C. 507; *ante*, § 2-70.
[35]   For the practice of the Board of Inland Revenue when there is a change of accounting date, see the Notes published by the Board and printed in B.T.E., para. 6-148.
[36]   *Wesley* v. *Manson* [1932] A.C. 635; 16 T.C. 654 (H.L.).

Example of the cessation provisions

2-84 The trading profits in the final years of a business (up to March 5, 1975, when the business was permanently discontinued) are as follows:

£

Accounting year ending December 5, 1971 2,400

,,   ,,   ,,   ,,   ,, 1972 2,100

,,   ,,   ,,   ,,   ,, 1973 3,000

,,   ,,   ,,   ,,   ,, 1974 3,600

Period from December 6, 1974 to March 5, 1975 900

Assessments are as follows:

Basis of Assessment

Final year   Actual Profits April 6, 1974 to March
                      5, 1975

                      April 6, 1974—December 5, 1974:
1974–75   8/12ths × 3,600 = 2,400   3,300
                      December 6, 1974—March 5, 1975:
                                         = 900

Penultimate
year 1973–74

                      Normal basis:
                      Actual profits to December 5, 1972   .. 2,100
                      Actual year basis:

                      April 6, 1973—December 5, 1973:
                          8/12ths × 3,000 = 2,000   3,200
                      December 6, 1973—April 5, 1974:
                          4/12ths × 3,600 = 1,200

Pre-penultimate
year 1972–73

                      Normal basis:
                      Actual profits to December 5, 1971   .. 2,400
                      Actual year basis:
                      April 6, 1972—December 5, 1972:
                          8/12ths × 2,100 = 1,400   2,400
                      December 6, 1972—April 5, 1973
                          4/12ths × 3,000 = 1,000

For the penultimate and pre-penultimate years, assessments on the normal basis (£2,100 + £2,400) will have already been made when the business ceases. The Revenue have the power to make a further assessment for 1963–64 on £1,100, *i.e.* the amount by which assessment on the actual basis exceeds assessment on the normal basis. If, in the example, the assessed profits had been £2,100 + £2,400 and the actual profits £3,200 + £2,300, there would be a further assessment of £1,100 for the first year and a £100 reduction of the assessment for the second year.

A cessation may result in a saving of income tax. In this example the trading profits from December 6, 1970 to the date of cessation are £12,000; whereas the assessable profits are £8,900. There are provisions designed to prevent avoidance of tax by artificial cessation.[37]

Farming and market gardening

2-84A There are special provisions which apply in and from 1977–78 for averaging over a two-year period the fluctuating profits of a person (or partnership) carrying on the trade of farming or market gardening.[38]

---

[37] See I.C.T.A. 1970, ss. 483–484.   [38] See F.A. 1978, s. 28.

D. The Application of the Rules on changes of Ownership

2-85   The new business provisions apply when in any year of assessment a trade, profession or vocation has been " set up and commenced " [39]; the cessation provisions apply when it is " permanently discontinued." [40] It is often a difficult question of fact whether a new business has been set up. [41] Where, for example, a new branch is opened, it may be contended that this is an extension of an existing trade rather than a setting up of a new trade. Where a trader discontinues one of several *distinct* trades carried on by him, the cessation provisions apply to the discontinued trade. If, on the other hand, part of a *single* trade is discontinued (as where a department in a store is closed), the cessation provisions do not apply. It is often a difficult question of fact, especially where the trading activities are diverse but are controlled under a single organisation, to decide whether the discontinuance of one activity constitutes the discontinuance of a separate trade or the discontinuance of a mere department of a trade.

Changes in ownership of trade, etc.

2-86   By section 154 (1) of the Income and Corporation Taxes Act 1970, where there is a change in the *persons* engaged in carrying on a trade, profession or vocation,

> the amount of the profits or gains of the trade, profession or vocation, on which tax is chargeable and the persons on whom it is chargeable, must be determined as if the trade, profession or vocation, had been permanently discontinued at the date of the change and a new trade, profession or vocation, had been then set up and commenced.

If, therefore, on October 5, 1973, A sells his business as a going concern to B, A is assessed as if his trade were discontinued on that date (so the cessation provisions apply); and B is assessed as if he had set up a new business (so the commencement provisions apply).

2-87   The commencement provisions apply to the new owner by virtue of section 154 only if, notwithstanding the change of ownership, the trade itself continues. [42] The new owner must *succeed* to the former trade. Whether a " succession " has taken place is a question of fact, [43] but the following propositions may be advanced:

(1) If a person takes over the whole of a trade as a going concern, he succeeds to that trade, even if he already has a trade of the same nature and the newly acquired trade is merged with it. [44]

The new owner must produce accounts (i) for the existing trade, on the normal preceding year basis; and (ii) for the new trade, on the " new

---

[39] I.C.T.A. 1970, s. 116 (1).   [40] *Ibid.* s. 118 (1).
[41] See *Merchiston Steamship Co. Ltd.* v. *Turner* (1910) 5 T.C. 520; *Kirk and Randall Ltd.* v. *Dunn* (1924) 8 T.C. 663; *H. and G. Kinemas Ltd.* v. *Cook* (1933) 18 T.C. 116.
[42] *I.R.C.* v. *Barr* (1954) 35 T.C. 293 (H.L.).
[43] *Alexander Ferguson & Co. Ltd.* v. *Aikin* (1898) 4 T.C. 36. For succession generally, see B.T.E. (I.T.), § 6-10. The terms " succeed " and " succession " are not used in s. 154, but the terms were used in the earlier legislation and it is assumed that this requirement exists under the present law. *Cf.* § 13-19A (capital allowances).
[44] *Bell* v. *National Provincial Bank* [1904] 1 K.B. 149; 5 T.C. 1 (C.A.); *Briton Ferry Steel Co. Ltd.* v. *Barry* [1940] 1 K.B. 463; 23 T.C. 414. *Cf. Laycock* v. *Freeman, Hardy & Willis* [1939] 2 K.B. 1; 22 T.C. 288 (C.A.).

business '' basis, *i.e.* he must treat them as separate trades for tax purposes even though they may be managed as a single trade. This may cause inconvenience and difficulty. Further, if the profits of the acquired trade are high in the first accounting period, these will form the basis of its tax liability for three years.

(2) If a person merely takes over the assets of a trade, with no intention of taking over the business as a going concern, there is no succession.[45]

The new owner's existing trade absorbs the acquired assets and the basis on which profits were assessed remains the same.

If the new owner has acquired only part of a trade carried on by the vendor, it may be a difficult question of fact for the Commissioners to decide if a succession has occurred.

5. POST-CESSATION RECEIPTS

2-88 The term '' post-cessation receipts '' describes sums which are received after the permanent discontinuance of a trade, profession or vocation for work done, or services rendered, before discontinuance. The position before the Finance Act 1960 was as follows:

(1) If the pre-cessation profits were assessed on an *earnings* basis, post-cessation receipts were not assessable as such because the sums received would normally have already been brought into account while the trading was continuing. In the case of a receipt which had not previously been brought in, the Revenue could reopen the account for the period to which the sum related and raise an additional assessment.[46]

(2) If the pre-cessation profits were assessed otherwise than by reference to earnings, as in the case of a professional man assessed on a *cash* basis, post-cessation receipts escaped tax. They were not taxable under Case II, because the profession had ceased; and attempts by the Revenue to tax them under other Cases of Schedule D failed.[47]

2-89 The Finance Act 1960 brought into charge to tax some post-cessation receipts of a trade, profession or vocation which previously escaped tax, and the Finance Act 1968 closed a number of gaps left by the 1960 Act. These enactments have now been consolidated in sections 143–151 of the Income and Corporation Taxes Act 1970.

Earnings and conventional basis distinguished

2-90 The enactments charging tax on post-cessation receipts distinguish the case where the pre-cessation profits were computed '' by reference to earnings '' from the case where they were computed '' on a conventional basis (that is to say, were computed otherwise than by reference to earnings).''

---

[45] *Watson Bros.* v. *Lothian* (1902) 4 T.C. 441; *Reynolds, Sons & Co. Ltd.* v. *Ogston* (1930) 15 T.C. 501.
[46] As in *Severne* v. *Dadswell* (1954) 35 T.C. 649.
[47] *Stainer's Executors* v. *Purchase* [1952] A.C. 280; 32 T.C. 367 (H.L.); *Carson* v. *Cheyney's Executors* [1959] A.C. 412; 38 T.C. 240 (H.L.). See also *Hume* v. *Asquith* (1968) 45 T.C. 251: royalties paid to legatee of deceased author held not chargeable to tax.

The profits or gains of a trade, profession or vocation in any period are to be treated as computed by reference to earnings where all credits and liabilities accruing during that period as a consequence of the carrying on of the trade, profession or vocation, are brought into account in computing those profits or gains for tax purposes.[48] This is termed the " earnings basis."

The expression " conventional basis " is used to describe any method of computing profits otherwise than by reference to earnings,[49] such as the " cash basis." If profits are computed on a " bills delivered " basis, work in progress being disregarded, or if a figure is brought in for completed but unbilled work, partly completed work being disregarded, profits are computed on a conventional basis.

Receipts after discontinuance

2-91   The following sums arising from the carrying on of a trade, profession or vocation during any period before the discontinuance are chargeable to tax under Case VI of Schedule D, if not otherwise chargeable to tax:

(1) Where the profits or gains for that period were computed by reference to earnings, all such sums in so far as their value was not brought into account in computing the profits or gains for any period before the discontinuance [50];

(2) Where those profits or gains were computed on a conventional basis, any sums which, if those profits or gains had been computed by reference to earnings, would *not* have been brought into the computation for any period before the discontinuance because either (i) the date on which they became due, or (ii) the date on which the amount due in respect thereof was ascertained, fell after the discontinuance.[51]

2-92   *Exceptions.*[52] Some post-cessation receipts are expressly excepted from these provisions, namely:

(a) sums received by or on behalf of a person not resident in the United Kingdom representing income arising outside the United Kingdom; and

(b) a lump sum paid to the personal representatives of an author as consideration for the assignment by them of the copyright in the author's work [53]; and

(c) sums realised by the transfer of trading stock belonging to a trade on its discontinuance, or by the transfer of the work of a profession or vocation in progress on discontinuance.[54]

Further, the provisions do not apply to the post-cessation receipts of a partnership resident outside and not trading within the United Kingdom,

[48] I.C.T.A. 1970, s. 151 (2).
[49] *Ibid.* s. 151 (3).
[50] *Ibid.* s. 143 (1), (2) (*a*).
[51] *Ibid.* s. 143 (1), (2) (*b*).
[52] *Ibid.* s. 143 (3).
[53] See *post*, §§ 5-62 *et seq.*
[54] See *ante*, §§ 2-38 to 2-42.

because the profits of such a partnership would not be chargeable to tax under Case I or Case II of Schedule D.

2-93   *Released debts.* We have seen that where a deduction has been allowed for any debt incurred for the purposes of a trade, profession or vocation and the whole or any part of the debt is subsequently released, a sum equal to the amount released is treated as a receipt of the chargeable period in which the release is effected.[55] Where the trade, profession or vocation has been permanently discontinued before the release was effected, the sum referred to is treated as a post-cessation receipt.[56]

2-94   *Bad debts.* Where relief is given under section 130 (*i*) of the Income and Corporation Taxes Act 1970 in respect of a bad debt and the debt is subsequently paid, a sum equal to the amount paid is treated as a trading receipt of the chargeable period in which payment is made.[57] Where the trade, profession or vocation has been permanently discontinued before payment is made, the sum paid is treated as a post-cessation receipt.[58]

Other receipts after discontinuance or change of basis

2-95   The provisions in paragraphs (1) and (2) in § 2-91 were introduced by the Finance Act 1960 in order to nullify the decision of the House of Lords in the *Cheyney*[59] case. As regards paragraph (2), it will be observed that sums which would have been brought into the computation on a hypothetical earnings basis escaped tax, such as the post-cessation receipts of a professional man assessed on a cash basis; so also sums which would not have been brought in for some reason other than (i) or (ii). The Finance Act 1968 contained provisions designed to tax post-cessation receipts which escaped tax under the Act of 1960 and generally to prevent avoidance of tax on a change in the basis of computing profits. To illustrate this last-mentioned point: suppose that a professional man was assessed on a cash basis in years 1, 2 and 3. In year 4 his profits were computed by reference to earnings. Profits earned in years 1, 2 and 3 which were received in year 4 would escape tax in year 4 because they were not earned in that year and the Revenue could not (having accepted accounts on a cash basis for years 1, 2 and 3) reopen the assessments for those years.[60]

2-96   The Act of 1968—in provisions now contained in Chapter V of Part VI of the Income and Corporation Taxes Act 1970—provided:

(1) that all sums received after discontinuance arising from the carrying on of a trade, profession or vocation during any period before the discontinuance, including sums received as consideration for the transfer of work in progress on the discontinuance of a profession or vocation,[61] should if not otherwise chargeable to tax (*e.g.* under the

[55] *Ante,* § 2-33.
[56] I.C.T.A. 1970, s. 143 (4).
[57] *Ante,* § 2-68.
[58] I.C.T.A. 1970, s. 143 (5).
[59] [1959] A.C. 412; 38 T.C. 240 (H.L.).
[60] See *ante,* § 2-21.
[61] I.C.T.A. 1970, s. 144 (3).

provisions in § 2-91), be chargeable under Case VI of Schedule D on being received [62]:

> Thus the post-cessation receipts of a professional man previously assessed on a cash basis (including the proceeds of sale of work in progress) are now taxable under section 144 (1), subject to the relief mentioned in § 2-100, *post*;

(2) that sums which dropped out of the computation or otherwise escaped assessment on a change of basis should be charged under Case VI of Schedule D when received after the change and before discontinuance [63]:

> See the illustration in § 2-95. The profits received in year 4 which would previously have escaped tax are taxed under section 144 (2).

(3) that work in progress which escaped assessment on a change of basis should likewise be charged under Case VI. [64]

Where relevant the exceptions mentioned in § 2-92 also apply to these charging provisions.

Permanent discontinuance

2-97   For the purposes of the above provisions, any reference to the permanent discontinuance of a trade, profession or vocation includes a reference to the occurring of any event which, under section 154 or 251 (1) of the Income and Corporation Taxes Act 1970, is to be treated as equivalent to the permanent discontinuance of a trade, profession or vocation. [65]

Method of charge

2-98   A sum which is chargeable under section 143 or 144 of the Income and Corporation Taxes Act 1970 is assessable under Case VI of Schedule D in the year of assessment in which the sum is received, except that if the sum is received not later than six years after the discontinuance or, as the case may be, a change of basis, by the person by whom the trade, profession or vocation was carried on before the discontinuance or change (or by his personal representatives), the recipient may, by notice in writing sent to the Inspector within two years after that year of assessment, elect that the tax chargeable shall be charged as if the sum in question were received on the date on which the discontinuance took place or, as the case may be, on the last day of the period at the end of which the change of basis took place. [66]

2-99   Sums assessable under sections 143 to 144, above, are treated as earned income if the profits of the trade, profession or vocation were so treated [67] and there are provisions for deducting from the assessable sum certain

---

[62] I.C.T.A. 1970, s. 144 (1).
[63] *Ibid.* s. 144 (2).
[64] *Ibid.* s. 144 (4).
[65] *Ibid.* s. 146. See *ante*, § 2-86.
[66] *Ibid.* s. 149.
[67] *Ibid.* s. 148.

expenses, unrelieved losses and unabsorbed capital allowances which would have been deductible before the discontinuance or change of basis.[68]

Reliefs for individuals [69]

2-100   Some relief is given to individuals from the charge imposed by section 144 of the Income and Corporation Taxes Act 1970. The relief is available only to individuals born before April 6, 1917. Briefly, an individual aged 65 or more on April 6, 1968, is taxed on 5/20ths of his post-cessation receipts; if he was aged 64, he is taxed on 6/20ths of his post-cessation receipts—and so on; so that an individual aged 51 on April 6, 1968, would be taxed on 19/20ths of his post-cessation receipts, while an individual who was aged 50 or less would be taxed on the whole of the receipts without any relief.

---

[68] *Ibid.* s. 145.
[69] *Ibid.* s. 150.

CHAPTER 3

THE TAXATION OF EMOLUMENTS: SCHEDULE E

1. THE SCOPE OF THE CHARGE

3-01 UNDER the Income Tax Act 1918, tax under Schedule E was charged only " in respect of every public office or employment of profit." Income from other employments was charged under Schedule D. The Finance Act 1922 transferred to Schedule E the emoluments which were previously charged under Schedule D, other than foreign emoluments which continued to be charged under Case V of Schedule D as income from a foreign possession. The Finance Act 1956 which applied for years from and including 1956–57, brought all emoluments of all employments into charge under Schedule E and removed the distinction which hitherto existed between public offices and employments of profit and other offices and employments. This distinction must nevertheless be kept in mind when reading cases relating to years before 1956–57. The rules of Schedule E are now contained in Part VIII of the Income and Corporation Taxes Act 1970 as amended and extended by later legislation.

3-02 Tax is charged under Schedule E on the emoluments of the offices and employments which fall under one of the three Cases into which the Schedule is divided.[1] Case I applies to the emoluments of a chargeable period [2] in which the person holding the office or employment is resident and ordinarily resident in the United Kingdom, subject to a deduction or exception if he performs the duties of the office or employment wholly outside the United Kingdom or the emoluments are foreign emoluments. Cases II and III apply where some foreign element is involved. Cases in which a foreign element is present, including the Case I deductions or exceptions, are discussed in Chapter 7. It should be assumed that the discussion in the present chapter is directed to Case I of Schedule E. Social security benefits (if not exempt) are specifically brought into charge under Schedule E: I.C.T.A. 1970, s. 219.

Tax is chargeable under Schedule E only if the following three conditions are satisfied:

(1) *There must be an " office " or " employment "*

3-03 The term " office " is not defined in the Income and Corporation Taxes Act 1970, but has been judicially described as a subsisting, permanent, substantive position which has an existence independent of the person who fills it, which goes on and is filled in succession by successive holders.[3] A

---

[1] I.C.T.A. 1970, s. 181 (1), para. 1.
[2] " Chargeable period " means an accounting period of a company or a year of assessment: *ibid.* s. 526 (5).
[3] Rowlatt J. in *Great Western Railway Co.* v. *Bater* [1920] 3 K.B. 266 at p. 274; approved in *McMillan* v. *Guest* [1942] A.C. 561 at p. 564; 24 T.C. 190 at p. 201.

director of a company holds an office [4]; so also do consultants with part-time appointments under the National Health Service [5]; so also do trustees and executors. [6] An auditorship is an office. [7] The term " employment " signifies something in the nature of a " post.'' Where a person works for more than one employer it is often a difficult question whether there are a number of separate employments (each chargeable under Schedule E) or whether the employments are mere engagements undertaken in the course of exercising a single profession or vocation (Schedule D). Where the activities of the taxpayer do not consist of obtaining a post and staying in it but consist of a series of engagements and moving from one to the other, as in the case of an actor, he may be treated as carrying on a profession. [8] In *Fall* v. *Hitchin* [9] it was held that the word " employment " in Schedule E is coterminous with the words " contract of service " and that income derived by a ballet dancer from a contract with Sadler's Wells having the attributes of a contract of service was taxable under Schedule E notwithstanding the fact that the dancer carried on a profession as such and entered into the contract in the normal course of carrying on that profession. This decision narrows the scope of *Davies* v. *Braithwaite* [10] to contracts entered upon in the course of carrying on a profession which are contracts for services. The two cases are, however, difficult to reconcile since the modern cases [11] show that the test for distinguishing a contract of service from a contract for services is whether the propositus carries on business on his own account, and *ex hypothesi* a person who carries on a profession does so. It is interesting to note that the Solicitor-General, arguing the case for the Crown in *Davies* v. *Braithwaite*, contended that the Schedule E rules were not applicable to a person who carries on a profession whether or not the profit arises under a contract for services or a contract of service. [12]

An individual may hold an office or employment and carry on a profession at the same time, [13] in which case the rules of Schedule E apply to the office or employment.

> Thus in *I.R.C.* v. *Brander & Cruickshank* [14] a firm of advocates in Scotland, although not holding themselves out as professional registrars, acted as secretaries and registrars for companies and performed the duties imposed on the holders of such offices by the Companies Acts. The registrarships were acquired in the ordinary course of the firm's practice as advocates. It was held that the registrarships were offices and that a payment of £2,500 on the termination of a registrarship was a payment to which the Schedule E rules applied, and being less than £5,000 was accordingly exempt from tax: see § 3-25.

---

[4] *McMillan* v. *Guest, supra.*

[5] *Mitchell and Edon* v. *Ross* [1960] Ch. 498; 40 T.C. 11 (C.A.) (on this point).

[6] *Att.-Gen.* v. *Eyres* [1909] 1 K.B. 723.

[7] *Ellis* v. *Lucas* (1966) 43 T.C. 276; followed in *I.R.C.* v. *Brander & Cruickshank* (1971) 46 T.C. 574 (H.L.).

[8] *Davies* v. *Braithwaite* [1931] 2 K.B. 628; 18 T.C. 198 (an actress).

[9] (1972) 49 T.C. 433; [1973] S.T.C. 66.

[10] See n. 8, above.

[11] *Ready Mixed Concrete (South-East) Ltd.* v. *Minister of Pensions and National Insurance* [1968] 2 Q.B. 487; *Market Investigations Ltd.* v. *Minister of Social Security* [1969] 2 Q.B. 173; *Global Plant Ltd.* v. *Secretary of State for Social Services* [1972] 1 Q.B. 139.

[12] See [1931] 2 K.B. at pp. 631-632.

[13] See, *e.g.* the case in n. 5, *supra*, summarised *ante*, § 1-13.

[14] (1971) 46 T.C. 574 (H.L.) (H.L.Sc.). See also *Ellis* v. *Lucas, supra. Cf. Walker* v. *Carnaby Harrower, Barnham & Pykett* (1969) 46 T.C. 561 in § 2-50A.

In practice, and as a matter of convenience, receipts from offices held by persons carrying on a profession are often treated as receipts of the profession. Hence accountants bring in their fees from auditorships in computing profits chargeable under Case II of Schedule D. A strict application of the law would require that each auditorship should be treated as a separate office in respect of which a separate claim for expenses should be made in accordance with the Schedule E expenses rules discussed in § 3-35; moreover, in the case of partners, since a partnership is not treated as a separate legal entity in England and there is no provision for joint Schedule E assessments in the partnership name,[15] the Schedule E rules ought strictly to be applied to each partner's share of the Schedule E income. The cases cited in note 14 show that the Schedule E rules are applied to terminal payments[16] notwithstanding the practice of convenience above referred to. In one case[17] a company trading as merchant bankers (Schedule D) entered into agreements with other companies to provide managerial and secretarial services for fees which the Crown conceded were properly chargeable under Schedule E; nevertheless, it was held that compensation received by the banking company on the termination of one of its Schedule E agreements was chargeable under Case I of Schedule D on the ground that the banking company acquired the Schedule E source of income in the course of its trade. The terminal payment was so linked to the trade as to be identified as one of its products; but this conclusion could be reached only in a case in which there was a clear finding that the trader sought the office as part of his profession.[18] In *Brander & Cruickshank*[19] the office was acquired incidentally in the course of carrying on the profession of advocates. There are statutory provisions which apply Schedule E to payments made to workers supplied to clients by agencies. Thus if a secretary (S) is supplied to a client by an agency and S is subject to, or to the right of, supervision, direction or control as to the manner in which she renders those services, remuneration received by S under her contract with the agency is chargeable to income tax under Schedule E (if not so chargeable apart from the statute).[20]

(2) *There must be " emoluments "*

3-04   Emoluments are defined as including salaries, fees, wages, perquisites and profits whatsoever.[21] Examples of emoluments are given in §§ 3-09 *et seq.*

(3) *The emoluments must derive from the office or employment*

3-05   Not every payment made to an employee is made to him as a profit arising from his employment: " the payment must be made in reference to the services the employee renders by virtue of his office, and it must be

---

[15] See §§ 11-03 *et seq.* A partnership is treated as a separate legal entity in Scotland.
[16] Discussed *post*, §§ 3-24 *et seq.*
[17] *Blackburn* v. *Close Brothers Ltd.* (1960) 39 T.C. 164.
[18] See Lord Donovan in *I.R.C.* v. *Brander & Cruickshank* (1971) 46 T.C. 574 at p. 595.
[19] See n. 14, above.
[20] F. (No. 2) A. 1975, s. 38.
[21] I.C.T.A. 1970, s. 183 (1).

something in the nature of a reward for services, past, present or future." [22] The office or employment must be the *source* of the payment. [23]

> In *Hochstrasser* v. *Mayes* [24] the I.C.I. established a housing scheme to assist those of their married male employees whose jobs demanded mobility. If the employee sold his house at a loss, the I.C.I. (subject to certain options reserved to the I.C.I.) guaranteed him against the loss. *Held*, that a sum paid to an employee in respect of such a loss was not an emolument from the employment.

This case shows that, to render a benefit chargeable to tax, the office or employment must be the *causa causans* of the benefit; it is not sufficient that it is the *causa sine qua non*. In another case an employee was required, as a condition of entering upon his employment to enter into a restrictive covenant with his employer which was to take effect on leaving his employer's service; and it was held that a lump sum paid in consideration for such a restrictive covenant was not an emolument from the employment. [25] " It is quite true that, if he had not entered into the agreement to serve as a director and manager, he would not have received £7,000. But that is not the same thing as saying that the £7,000 is profit from his office of director so as to attract tax under Schedule E." [26] Another illustration of the principle under discussion is given by Lord Denning M.R. in his judgment in *Jarrold* v. *Boustead* [27]:

> " Suppose there was a man who was an expert organist but was very fond of playing golf on Sundays. He is asked to become the organist of the parish church for the ensuing seven months at a salary of £10 a month for the seven months, but it is expressly stipulated by this strange parish council that, if he takes up the post, he is to give up Sunday golf for the rest of his life. Thereupon he says that, if he is to give up golf, he wants an extra £500 and they agree to pay it. In such a case the £500 is not a payment for his services as an organist for seven months. It is a payment for relinquishing what he considered to be an advantage to him."

An employee may receive a present in such circumstances that the employment is not its source. [28]

---

[22] *Hochstrasser* v. *Mayes* [1960] A.C. 376, *per* Viscount Simonds at p. 388; 38 T.C. 673 at p. 705, quoting with approval from the judgment of Upjohn J. in [1959] Ch. 22 at p. 33. See also *Laidler* v. *Perry* (1965) 42 T.C. 351 (H.L.), where Christmas gift vouchers given to employees were held to be assessable emoluments: the vouchers were a reward for services notwithstanding that they were given to all members of staff alike. In *Holland* v. *Geoghegan* (1972) 48 T.C. 482, refuse collectors' compensation for loss of salvage was held to be an emolument of the employment: ". . . the main purpose of the Borough was to get the respondent back to work, and the money when received by him was a form of substituted remuneration for his former rights to share in the proceeds of sale of the salvage " (p. 492H). And see *Tyrer* v. *Smart* [1968] S.T.C. 141 (C.A.), where employees of a group of companies with at least 5 years' service were given a right to subscribe for shares on preferential terms on the occasion of the group going public. *Held* not an assessable emolument: the employees who subscribed for shares did so as private investors.

[23] In *Pritchard* v. *Arundale* (1972) 47 T.C. 680, a transfer of shares to a former partner in a firm of accountants, in consideration of his undertaking to serve a company, was held not to be an assessable emolument. It was an inducement to him to give up an established position and status and not a reward for future services. But *semble* the transferee could have been assessed under Case VI of Schedule D: see §§ 4-02 *et seq.*   [24] See n. 22, above.

[25] *Beak* v. *Robson* [1943] A.C. 352; 25 T.C. 33 (H.L.). The position is the same where the covenant is to take effect during the currency of the agreement: *Hose* v. *Warwick* (1946) 27 T.C. 459. Payments for restrictive covenants are chargeable to higher rate income tax under I.C.T.A. 1970, s. 34; *post*, § 3-24, para. (4).   [26] *Beak* v. *Robson, supra; per* Viscount Simon L.C. at pp. 355 and 41, respectively.

[27] (1964) 41 T.C. 701 at p. 729. In this case, signing-on fees paid to Rugby League players on relinquishing amateur status were held not to be taxable. As to surtax and its equivalent under the unified system of tax, see *post*, § 3-24 (4).   [28] *Post*, §§ 3-09 *et seq.*

When a director wrongly directs moneys from a company into his own pocket and, by virtue of his fiduciary obligation to the company to preserve its assets, holds those moneys as trustee for the company, such moneys are not received as an emolument of the office.[29]

Basis of charge

3-06   Tax under Schedule E is charged on the full amount of the emoluments falling under the appropriate Case, subject to such deductions only as are authorised by the Tax Acts.[30] The permissible deductions are considered later.[31]

It seems that emoluments are not chargeable to tax unless they are received by or credited to or otherwise placed at the disposal of the employee. If an employee assigns his right to emoluments to a third person, they will be treated as having been received by the employee.[32] If the emoluments, when received, relate to services rendered in the past, they must be treated as income of the years in which the services were rendered.[33]

> Thus in *Heasman* v. *Jordan,*[33] a special bonus paid to an employee in 1945 for overtime during the war years (it being understood that the overtime would not be " overlooked ") was held to be taxable as an emolument of the years when the services were rendered.

Where emoluments otherwise chargeable under Schedule E are formally waived or repaid before any assessment has become final and conclusive, it seems to be the Revenue's practice not to claim Schedule E tax, provided the employer's profits or losses are adjusted so as to make no deduction in respect of such emoluments.[34]

3-07   Payments made to an employee after his employment has ceased are not chargeable under Schedule E [35] unless they are remuneration for past services or are expressly charged to tax, *e.g.* pensions [36] and " golden handshakes." [37] Tax under Schedule E is charged on the emoluments of the current year of assessment, *e.g.* the statutory income for the year 1978–79 includes the total of the emoluments of that year. Income tax is collected under the Pay As You Earn system (*post,* § 3-53). Where the tax collected under P.A.Y.E. is the same in amount as would be payable under a Schedule E assessment, the need for such an assessment is dispensed with unless required by the taxpayer.[38]

Annual payments

3-08   The remuneration of executors and trustees by annual payments is discussed later.[39]

---

[29] *Rose* v. *Humbles* (1971) 48 T.C. 103, *per* Buckley J. at p. 117H.
[30] I.C.T.A. 1970, s. 183 (1).   [31] *Post,* §§ 3-35 *et seq.*
[32] *Smyth* v. *Stretton* (1904) 5 T.C. 36; *cf. Edwards* v. *Roberts* (1935) 19 T.C. 618 (C.A.); *Hibbert* v. *Fysh* (1962) 40 T.C. 305 (earnings of undischarged bankrupt).
[33] *Heasman* v. *Jordan* [1954] Ch. 744; 35 T.C. 518. As to the time limit for assessments in such cases, see T.M.A. 1970, s. 35. *Quaere* if remuneration paid some years in advance can be " spread forward."
[34] See § 15-19A. As to capital transfer tax, see § 18-04A.
[35] See, *e.g. Cowan* v. *Seymour* [1920] 1 K.B. 500; 7 T.C. 372; *post,* § 3-09.
[36] I.C.T.A. 1970, ss. 181–182.   [37] I.C.T.A. 1970, s. 187; *post,* §§ 3-24 *et seq.*
[38] I.C.T.A. 1970, s. 205.   [39] See *post,* § 5-22.

2. TAXABLE EMOLUMENTS

Gifts and other voluntary payments

3-09   Gifts are not, as such, chargeable to income tax for they are not " income." [40] If however, a gift is made to an employee by virtue of his employment, its taxable quality differs and it is chargeable under Schedule E. [41] A gift which is attributable to the personal qualities of the employee or to his relationship to the donor is not made by virtue of the employment [42]: it is a " mere present." [43]

> In *Cowan* v. *Seymour,* [44] the appellant acted without remuneration as the secretary of a company from the date of its incorporation until he was appointed its liquidator. On completion of the liquidation there remained a sum in hand which under the Memorandum of Association was divisible among the ordinary shareholders; but they, by unanimous resolution, voted this sum to the chairman and the appellant in equal shares. *Held*, that the sum was not assessable under Schedule E.

Sterndale M.R. was influenced by two considerations: (i) that the payment was made by the shareholders and not by the employer; and (ii) that the employment had already terminated before the payment was voted. [45] It is more difficult in practice to prove that payments made by the employer are not assessable emoluments than those made by a third person. Other considerations which affect the taxable quality of a gift or similar payment are illustrated by the following cases:

3-10   (a) *Tips.* In *Calvert* v. *Wainwright,* [46] the tips of a taxi-driver were held to be taxable emoluments; but Atkinson J. remarked that an especially large tip given on a special occasion (such as Christmas) by a regular customer might escape tax as a mere present.

3-11   (b) *Easter offerings.* In *Blakiston* v. *Cooper* [47] the Easter " freewill offerings " of an incumbent, most of which were raised by collections on Easter Sunday, were held to be taxable.

> " It was suggested," said Lord Ashbourne, " that the offerings were made as personal gifts to the vicar as marks of esteem and respect. Such reasons

---

[40] R. v. *Supplementary Benefits Commission, ex p. Singer* [1973] 1 W.L.R. 713 (D.C.). Gifts are not assessable under Case VI of Schedule D: *post*, § 4-01. Gifts are disposals for purposes of the taxation of capital gains (*post*, § 15-18): and may involve the donor in liability to stamp duty (*post*, Chap. 30). Gifts made on or after March 26, 1974, may attract capital transfer tax.

[41] Collins M.R. in *Herbert* v. *McQuade* [1902] 2 K.B. 631 at p. 649; 4 T.C. 489 at p. 500 (C.A.).

[42] See, *e.g. Bridges* v. *Hewitt* (1957) 37 T.C. 289 (C.A.).

[43] *Blakiston* v. *Cooper* [1909] A.C. 104 at p. 107; 5 T.C. 347 at p. 355. For a recent case in which all the authorities are reviewed, see *I.R.C.* v. *Morris* (1967) 44 T.C. 685 (Ct. of Sess.): employee of Atomic Energy Authority seconded to Scottish Electricity Board received £1,000 from Board as a mark of appreciation after his employment with the Board had terminated: *held*, not an assessable emolument. And see *Ball* v. *Johnson* (1971) 47 T.C. 155; award to bank clerk for passing examinations *held* not to be remuneration for services, upholding the decision of General Commissioners; *Moore* v. *Griffiths* (1972) 48 T.C. 338: bonus and prizes paid to World Cup footballer *held* to be a testimonial and not a reward for services.

[44] [1920] 1 K.B. 500; 7 T.C. 372 (C.A.).

[45] But Sterndale M.R. was not prepared to hold that all voluntary payments made after an employment has terminated are not assessable. It is thought that the payment in *Cowan* v. *Seymour* would now be assessable under I.C.T.A. 1970, s. 187: *post*, § 3-25.

[46] [1947] K.B. 526; 27 T.C. 475. See also *Wright* v. *Boyce* (1958) 38 T.C. 160 (C.A.), where Christmas presents of cash received by a huntsman from followers of the hunt were held to be assessable even though (i) the gifts were spontaneous and there was no organised collection and (ii) his contract of service conferred no right to the gifts (*cf.* the " benefit " matches). The payments were made pursuant to a custom and the expectation of receiving Christmas presents went with the office.

[47] See n. 43, above.

no doubt played their part in obtaining and increasing the amount of the offerings, but I cannot doubt that *they were given to the vicar as vicar*, and that they formed part of the profits accruing by reason of his office."

3-12   (c) *Benefit matches.* In *Moorhouse* v. *Dooland* [48] moneys collected for a professional cricketer for meritorious performances at matches were held to be assessable, where the cricketer had a contractual right to talent money. In *Seymour* v. *Reed*, [49] on the other hand, where a benefit match was held for a professional cricketer on the occasion of his retirement following a lifetime's service to cricket, the gate money was held not to be taxable.

" Its purpose," said Lord Cave, " is not to encourage the cricketer to further exertions, but to express the gratitude of his employers and of the cricket-loving public for what he has already done, and their appreciation of his personal qualities."

3-13   (d) *Bonuses.* The ordinary bonus paid by an employer at his discretion in addition to salary is taxable [50]; so also are long service payments. [51] Moreover, the employee's tax liability is not avoided by the employer's declaration that he did not intend the payment to be remuneration or that he intended it to be a gift. [52]

Money's worth: benefits in kind and fringe benefits

3-14   The term emoluments includes not only money payments but also " substantial things of money value . . . capable of being turned into money." [53] This brings within the charge under Schedule E a variety of " fringe benefits " or " benefits in kind." It should be observed that the words of Lord Halsbury distinguish two types of benefit:

(1) Benefits not convertible into money, such as free travel, free board and lodging, [54] free meals, free uniform or free education; and

(2) benefits convertible into money.

Benefits of the first type are not assessable (subject to the exception hereinafter mentioned and the special legislation affecting directors and certain employees [55]) even if their value was taken into account in determining the employee's remuneration; whereas convertible benefits are assessable, although it is not the practice of the Revenue to tax all such benefits. [56] A cash payment in lieu of any of the benefits referred to in (1) would be assessable. [57] Meal vouchers are by concession exempt from tax if

---

[48] [1955] Ch. 284; 36 T.C. 1 (C.A.). See especially the judgment of Jenkins L.J.

[49] [1927] A.C. 554; 11 T.C. 625.

[50] *Denny* v. *Reed* (1933) 18 T.C. 254.

[51] But see the concessions in [1973] S.T.I. 324 and [1977] S.T.I. 52 (Concession No. A24).

[52] *Weston* v. *Hearn* (1943) 25 T.C. 425; *Radcliffe* v. *Holt* (1927) 11 T.C. 621. See also *Davis* v. *Harrison* (1927) 11 T.C. 707; *Corbett* v. *Duff* (1941) 23 T.C. 763.

[53] *Per* Lord Halsbury in *Tennant* v. *Smith* [1892] A.C. 150, 156; 3 T.C. 158, 164. Lord Watson used the words " that which can be turned to pecuniary account."

[54] *Daly* v. *I.R.C.* (1934) 18 T.C. 641 (free maintenance of a priest in a communal presbytery house).

[55] See *post*, §§ 3-40 *et seq.*

[56] Thus in *Wright* v. *Boyce* (1958) 38 T.C. 160 (C.A.), only gifts in cash appear to have been assessed.

[57] *Corry* v. *Robinson* (1933) 18 T.C. 411 (C.A.): colonial allowance of civil servant; *Sanderson* v. *Durbridge* (1955) 36 T.C. 239: allowance for meals on overtime; *Evans* v. *Richardson* (1957) 37 T.C. 178; army lodging allowance.

they are (a) non-transferable and used for meals only; (b) available to lower paid staff if their issue is restricted; (c) limited to a value of 15p for each working day.[58]

3-15

Examples: (i) In *Machon* v. *McLoughlin* [59] a male attendant at an asylum was paid a salary out of which he was bound to pay 10s. a week for board, lodging, etc. *Held*, that he was taxable on his gross salary. " If a person is paid a wage with some advantage thrown in, you cannot add the advantage to the wage for the purpose of taxation unless that advantage can be turned into money. That is one proposition. But when you have a person paid a wage with the necessity—the contractual necessity if you like—to expend that wage in a particular way, then he must pay tax upon the gross wage and no question of alienability or inalienability arises."

(ii) In *Weight* v. *Salmon* [60] the directors by resolution each year gave S. the privilege of subscribing for unissued shares of the company at par value, which was below market value. *Held*, that the difference between the two values was assessable to tax.

(iii) In *Heaton* v. *Bell* [61] B was employed by a company which introduced a voluntary car loan scheme for employees who earned less than £2,000 per annum and were not directors. The company purchased the car and paid tax and insurance. B applied to join the scheme and an agreed amount was deducted from his weekly wage. An employee joining the scheme could withdraw on 14 days' notice, when the weekly deduction would cease. B was assessed under Schedule E on the weekly wage without any deduction in respect of the amount paid under the scheme. *Held*, (i) (Lord Reid dissenting) that the true effect of the contractual arrangements was that the emoluments of an employee who joined the scheme remained unaltered, so the assessment was correctly made. *Cf.* Lord Reid, who held that the employee had agreed to accept a reduced wage plus the free use of a car; (ii) (Lord Hodson and Lord Upjohn dissenting) that even if Lord Reid's view of the effect of the agreement was right, the assessment was correctly made because B could convert his free use of the car into money by withdrawing from the scheme and no longer suffering any reduction in salary.

(iv) In *Clayton* v. *Gothorp* [62] the discharge of an obligation to repay a loan was held to give rise to an assessable emolument.

Medical insurance

3-15A   Section 68 of the Finance Act 1976 treats as emoluments of an employment, and accordingly as chargeable to tax under Schedule E, an amount equal to the expense incurred by the employer or others, and not made good by the employee, in connection with the provision for the employee, and for others being members of his family or household [63] of insurance against the cost of medical treatment (defined so as to include, *inter alia*, procedures for diagnosing any physical or mental ailment, infirmity or defect). The section applies only where the provision is made by reason of the employment,[64] and only where the provision is not otherwise chargeable as income. The section applies in and from the year 1976–77. In the case of group insurance schemes there are provisions for apportioning

---

[58] Concession No. A3.
[59] (1926) 11 T.C. 83 (C.A.).
[60] (1935) 19 T.C. 174 (H.L.). And see F.A. 1976, s. 67 in § 3-47.
[61] [1970] A.C. 728; 46 T.C. 211 (H.L.).
[62] (1971) 47 T.C. 168; and see F.A. 1976, s. 66 (3) in § 3-50.
[63] References to members of a person's family or household are to his spouse, his sons and daughters and their spouses, his parents and his servants, dependants and guests: F.A. 1976, s. 72 (4).
[64] See definitions in F.A. 1976, s. 72. See § 3-43.

the expense incurred between the group members. There is excepted from the operation of the section expense incurred against the cost of medical treatment outside the United Kingdom, the need for which arises while the employee is outside the United Kingdom for the purpose of performing the duties of his employment.

Discharging obligations of employee

3-16   If an employer discharges out of his own resources some obligation which his employee has incurred to a third person, otherwise than in performing the duties of the employment, the sum paid by the employer is a taxable emolument: it is " money's worth." [65] Thus if an employer pays his employee's income tax or pays a salary expressed to be free of tax, the tax must be added to the salary for the purpose of determining the gross emoluments of the employee. [66]

> In *Barclays Bank Ltd.* v. *Naylor*, [67] a liability incurred by the employee in respect of his child's school fees was settled not by the employer, but (at the request of the employee) by trustees out of a fund established by the employer for the purpose, the income whereof was payable to the employee's child. *Held*, this was not income of the employee: " the way in which the employer contributed to the education expenses . . . was not by paying the school bills . . . out of own money, but by providing the child with an income out of which the bills . . . could be met " (p. 268).

3-17   Where an employer discharges an obligation incurred by his employee to a third person, the measure of the taxable emolument is the cost to the employer of discharging the obligation. Where, however, the employer purchases something which he then gives to his employee, the measure of the taxable emolument is the value of the benefit to the employee. [68]

> In *Wilkins* v. *Rogerson*, [69] a company decided to give certain employees a suit, overcoat or raincoat as a Christmas present. The tailor was instructed to give each employee a fitting and send the account to the company. There was no contractual relationship between the tailor and the employee. *Held*, that this was a " perquisite or profit " of the employment and that the measure of the emolument was the value of the suit to the employee, *i.e.* its second-hand value. [If the employer had paid for a suit previously ordered by the employee, the measure of the emolument would have been the cost of the suit.]

If, however, an employer provides a voucher, stamp or similar document, other than a cash voucher, [69] capable of being exchanged for money, goods or services the employee is taxed on the cost incurred by the employer and not the value of the goods or services ultimately acquired by the employee with the voucher. [70] Where no vouchers are involved but there is a supply of goods or services as in *Wilkins* v. *Rogerson*, the principle in that case

---

[65] *Nicoll* v. *Austin* (1935) 19 T.C. 531 (company paid sums for rates, light, heat, telephone and upkeep of gardens of directors' residence: *held* that the amount so paid was an assessable emolument).
[66] *Hartland* v. *Diggines* [1926] A.C. 289; 10 T.C. 247 (H.L.).
[67] [1961] Ch. 7; 39 T.C. 256.
[68] *Wilkins* v. *Rogerson* [1961] Ch. 133; 39 T.C. 344 (C.A.). Contrast § 3-46.
[69] A cash voucher is defined by F. (No. 2) A. 1975, s. 37 (3) as one which can be exchanged for an amount of money not substantially less than the cost of providing it. The employee is taxed on the amount for which it can be exchanged and tax must be deducted under the P.A.Y.E. system: *ibid.* s. 37 (1) applicable in and from 1977–78: see F.A. 1976, s. 71.
[70] See F. (No. 2) A. 1975, s. 36.

applies. Likewise it seems that if property is directly given to an employee for his actual use (without the interposition of a voucher) and that property is subject to some restriction affecting its transferability (*e.g.* a non-transferable season ticket) the restriction may be taken into account in determining the value of the benefit.[71]

Share options: non-approved schemes

3-18 In *Abbott* v. *Philbin* [72] the facts were that an employee accepted an offer from his employing company in year one to acquire for £20 a 10-year non-assignable option to purchase up to 2,000 shares at 68s. 6d., their then market price. In year two he exercised the option as regards 250 shares, then worth 82s. each. It was held that the benefit, namely the value of the option less the cost of acquiring it, arose in year one. The effect of this decision was that liability under Schedule E arose in the *grant* of an option on the then value of the right conferred on the director or employee; no Schedule E liability arose on the *exercise* of the option. In practice, the tax liability on the grant of the option was often small because of the difficulty of putting more than a nominal value on the option rights at that time. The director or employee might, of course, be liable to capital gains tax on the transfer of the shares or the assignment of the option rights.

3-19 The tax position was altered by section 25 of the Finance Act 1966 which, on the 1970 consolidation, was re-enacted in section 186 of the Taxes Act 1970. Section 186 provides that where, on or after May 3, 1966, a person realises a gain by the exercise, or by the assignment or release, of a right to acquire shares in a body corporate obtained by that person as a director or employee of that or any other body corporate, he is chargeable to income tax under Schedule E on an amount equal to the amount of his gain as computed in accordance with the section.[73] In such a case no tax is charged on the *grant* of the option.[74] Where an option is exercised in respect of shares, the gain is the difference between (i) the amount a person might reasonably expect to obtain from a sale in the open market of such shares at the time the option is exercised and (ii) the amount or value of the consideration given whether for the shares or for the grant of the option right, the value of any services to be performed by the director or employee being disregarded in computing the consideration. The gain is treated as earned income and is deductible for the purposes of capital gains tax if the shares are later sold.[75]

> *Example.* X is granted an option to purchase 100 shares at £1 each, the cost of the option being £10. X later exercises the option when the shares are worth £250. X is assessed under s. 186 on £250 less £110 = £140. X later sells the shares for £300. The chargeable gain is £300 less (£110 + £140) = £50.

Similarly, where the option rights are assigned or released, the gain is the difference between (i) the amount or value of the consideration for the

---

[71] See *Ede* v. *Wilson* (1945) 26 T.C. 381.
[72] [1961] A.C. 352; 39 T.C. 82 (H.L.).
[73] I.C.T.A. 1970, s. 186 (1).
[74] *Ibid.* s. 186 (2). But see the exception in § 3-19A.
[75] *Ibid.* s. 186 (12).

assignment or release and (ii) the amount or value of the consideration given for the grant of the option right. By way of exception to these general rules, where the option right is granted before May 3, 1966, the gain is not to exceed the difference between the market value of the shares at the time of the realisation of the gain and their market value on May 3, 1966.[76]

3-19A If an option obtained on or after April 11, 1972, is capable of being exercised later than seven years thereafter and the amount payable to exercise it is less than the market value of the equivalent shares when the option is obtained, a Schedule E assessment can be raised on the *grant* of the option on the difference between these two amounts.[77] When a Schedule E charge is so raised, the tax payable will be deducted from tax charged under section 186 on the exercise or assignment of the right.[77]

3-20 Section 186 of the Taxes Act 1970 applies only if the right is obtained by a person as a director or employee of a body corporate; and a right to acquire shares is treated as obtained by a person as a director or employee of a body corporate—

(a) if it is granted to him by reason of his office or employment as a director or employee of the body corporate who is chargeable to tax in respect of that office or employment under Case I of Schedule E, or

(b) if the right is assigned to him and was granted by reason of any such office or employment of his to some other person,

and paragraph (a) applies to a right granted by reason of a person's office or employment after he has ceased to hold it if it would apply to a right so granted in the last year of assessment in which he did hold it.[78]

Share options: approved schemes

3-20A Section 78 of the Finance Act 1972 introduced the " approved share option scheme " and Schedule 12 to that Act set out the conditions which had to be satisfied for a scheme to secure the approval of the Board of Inland Revenue. Where a scheme was approved and the director or employee satisfied certain conditions, section 186 of the Taxes Act 1970 (*ante*, § 3-19) did not apply to any gain realised by the exercise of an option granted in the circumstances mentioned in § 3-19 nor was tax chargeable under any other provision of the Tax Acts in respect of the receipt of the right.[79] Section 20 of the Finance Act 1974 provided that section 78 of the Finance Act 1972 should cease to have effect except in its application to cases where the option was exercised before March 27, 1974. Consequently any option now granted by reason of office or employment falls to be taxed under section 186 of the Taxes Act 1970.

---

[76] I.C.T.A. 1970, s. 186 (8). Subject to this subsection, s. 186 applies to an option right whenever granted.

[77] F.A. 1972, s. 77. See *Abbott* v. *Philbin* in § 3-18.

[78] I.C.T.A. 1970, s. 186 (9).

[79] F.A. 1972, s. 78 (1). This subsection applied if the option was exercised on or after April 6, 1972, even if the right was granted before that date, provided the scheme was approved under Sched. 12 (whether before or after the right was obtained or exercised) and the director or employee satisfies certain conditions.

Share incentive schemes

3-20B The legislation summarised in § 3-19 applied to share option schemes, *i.e.* when the director or employee was granted and subsequently exercised an *option* to acquire shares. It did not apply if a director or employee subscribed for shares to which certain restrictions were attached for a prescribed period (*e.g.* restrictions as to voting and the right to receive dividends so long as a loan to the subscriber remained outstanding) and those shares became more valuable on the lifting of the restrictions; except that a Schedule E liability would arise if the amount subscribed was less than the value of the shares at the time of subscription.[80] Section 79 of the Finance Act 1972 accordingly extended the charge under Schedule E to such share incentive schemes. The section applies where a person, on or after April 6, 1972, acquires shares or an interest in shares in a body corporate in pursuance of a right conferred on him or opportunity offered to him as a director or employee of that or any other body corporate and not in pursuance of an offer to the public.[81] Section 186 (9) of the Taxes Act 1970, summarised in § 3-20, applies for the purpose of determining whether a person acquires a right or opportunity " as a director or employee." [82] There are two separate charges to tax under section 79:

(1) *The tax on appreciation in value*

3-20C Where the market value of the shares at the end of a prescribed period exceeds their market value at the time of the acquisition, the acquirer is chargeable to tax under Schedule E for the year of assessment in which the prescribed period ends on an amount equal to the excess, the amount chargeable being treated as earned income.[83] Hence the director or employee is taxed on any unrealised appreciation in the value of his shares or interest in shares. If the acquirer has an interest less than full beneficial ownership, *e.g.* if he is entitled only to a share in a trust fund made up of the company's shares, he is taxed only on such part of the appreciation in value as corresponds to his interest.[83] There are provisions for a reduction in the amount chargeable where, in accordance with the terms on which the acquisition of the shares was made, the consideration for the acquisition is subsequently increased (*e.g.* on the acquirer leaving the company's service prematurely) or the shares are disposed of for a consideration which is less than their market value at the time of the disposal.[84] In such cases the increase in market value over the prescribed period would not provide a proper measure of the benefit received.

3-20D The prescribed period referred to above is a period ending at the earliest of the following times:

(a) the expiration of seven years from the acquisition of the shares or interest in the shares;

---

[80] See *Weight* v. *Salmon* (1935) 19 T.C. 174 (H.L.) in § 3-15.

[81] *Ibid.* s. 79 (1). And see s. 79 (10) as to offers to connected persons. As to the furnishing of information, see *ibid.* Sched. 12, Pt. VII, paras. 3–5.

[82] *Ibid.* Sched. 12, Pt. VII, para. 7.

[83] *Ibid.* s. 79 (4). The charge to tax on the appreciation in the value of shares is excluded in the case of approved profit-sharing schemes: see § 3-56.   [84] *Ibid.* s. 79 (5).

(b) the time when the acquirer ceases to have any beneficial interest in the shares; and

(c) in relation only to a person who acquires shares (*i.e.* not merely an *interest* in shares), the time when the shares cease to be subject to restrictions specified in section 79 (2A). [85]

The assessment is made for the year in which the period ends. [86] A person whose beneficial interest in shares is reduced is treated as ceasing to have an interest in such a part of the shares as is proportionate to the reduction. [87] A person who disposes of shares or an interest in shares otherwise than by a bargain at arm's length with a person who is not connected with him is deemed not to cease to have a beneficial interest in the shares. [88] But a Schedule E charge will arise on a gift of shares to a connected person, including a transfer by way of gift to trustees of a settlement made by the transferor. Increases in market value chargeable under section 79 of the Finance Act 1972 are deductible for capital gains tax purposes on the occasion of the first disposal of the shares after their acquisition. [89]

3-20E   The charge discussed in § 3-20C does not apply [90] if:

(a) the acquisition was made before March 27, 1974, in pursuance of a scheme approved (whether before or after the acquisition) under Schedule 12 to the Act and the person making the acquisition satisfied the conditions specified in Part V of that Schedule [91]; or

(b) the acquisition was made in pursuance of arrangements under which employees of a body corporate receive as part of their emoluments shares or interests in shares of that body or of a body controlling it to an extent determined in advance by reference to the profits of either body [92]; or

Thus ordinary profit-sharing schemes are excluded. The shares or interest in shares in such cases will be assessable emoluments under the general rules of Schedule E. [93]

(c) the acquisition was of shares which immediately after the acquisition were subject to none of the specified restrictions (see § 3-20 EE), and were not exchangeable for shares subject to such restrictions, where the majority of the available shares of the same class was acquired otherwise than in pursuance of a right conferred or opportunity offered to a director or employee of the company. Shares are " available shares " if they are not held by or for the benefit of an associated company of the body; and

---

[85] F.A. 1972, s. 79 (6), as amended by F.A. 1973, s. 19 and Sched. 8, para. 4 (c).

[86] *Ibid.* s. 79 (4). See § 3-20 EE.

[87] See n. 85, above.

[88] *Ibid.* s. 79 (11). For the meaning of " connected person," see I.C.T.A. 1970, s. 533, *post*, § 16-18A.

[89] *Ibid.* s. 79 (9).

[90] *Ibid.* s. 79 (1) (2) (8).

[91] Approval of share incentive schemes has been removed by s. 20 of the F.A. 1974, except where the acquisition was made before March 27, 1974.

[92] *Ibid.* s. 79 (8), to be read subject to F.A. 1973, s. 19 and Sched. 8 (Part I), in the case of arrangements made or modified after March 22, 1973. Control is defined in I.C.T.A. 1970, s. 534.

[93] See *Brumby* v. *Milner* [1975] S.T.C. 534 (H.L.) where it was held that the distribution of capital on the termination of a profit-sharing scheme was taxable in the year of distribution.

shares are exchangeable for other shares if (whether by one
transaction or a series of transactions) they can be exchanged for
or converted into other shares.[94]

(i) Thus if X, a director of P Limited, is offered shares in P
Limited and the majority of the shares in P Limited are owned by
(say) the public, section 79 will not apply provided the conditions as
to the absence of restrictions, etc., are satisfied.

(ii) Assume, however, that P Limited in example (i) forms a
subsidiary company, S Limited, and subscribes for 90 per cent. of its
shares. X then obtains the remaining 10 per cent. by virtue of his
office or employment with P Limited, or S Limited. Section 79
applies because the shares held by P Limited in S Limited are not
" available shares." Of the available shares, all will be held by X;
i.e. the majority of available shares will not be acquired otherwise
than through rights conferred on directors, etc.

(d) the acquisition was of shares which immediately after the acquisition were not subject to specified restrictions (see § 3-20 EE) and
not exchangeable for shares subject to such restrictions, where the
majority of the available shares of the same class were acquired by
persons who were or had been employees or directors of or of a
body controlled by, the body in which they were shares and who
were together able as holders of the shares to control that body.[95]

Thus, if P Limited forms a subsidiary company, S Limited, and,
later, directors or employees of P Limited acquire the majority of
the shares in S Limited (excluding those owned by P Limited), so
that S Limited is a director/employee-controlled company, section
79 does not apply provided the shares are unrestricted, as required
by the section.

3-20 EE   *Specified restrictions.* The restrictions which are referred to in paragraphs
(c) and (d) in § 3-20 E are:

(i) Restrictions not attaching to all shares of the same class; or

(ii) restrictions ceasing or liable to cease some time after the acquisition;
or

(iii) restrictions depending on the shares being or ceasing to be held by
directors or employees of any body corporate (other than such
restrictions imposed by a company's articles of association as require
shares to be disposed of on ceasing to be so held).[96]

The exemption in paragraph (c) requires that the shares are not subject to
any such restrictions. The exemption in paragraph (d) above is not,
however, lost if the shares are subject to the restriction in (iii). This is an
exemption which applies to a director- or employee-controlled company
and it is not fatal that the holding of shares is made conditional on
continuation in office or employment.

There is treated as a restriction attaching to shares any contract,
agreement, arrangement or condition by which the owner's freedom to
dispose of the shares or any interest in them or to exercise any right
conferred by them is restricted, or by which such a disposal or exercise may

---

[94] F.A. 1972, s. 79 (2) (c) (i).
[95] *Ibid.* s. 79 (2) (c) (ii). Control has the meaning given in T.A. 1970, s. 534.
[96] *Ibid.* s. 79 (2A).

result in any disadvantage to him or a person connected with him, except where the restriction is imposed as a condition of a loan which is not a related loan.[97]

(2) *The tax on special benefits*

3-20F   Some share incentive schemes provide for participants to receive, in their capacity as holders of incentive shares, benefits not received by shareholders generally. Accordingly it is provided that where the person making the acquisition referred to in § 3-20B receives, by virtue of his ownership of or interest in the shares, any benefit not received by the majority of ordinary shareholders who acquired their shares otherwise than pursuant to a share incentive scheme, he is chargeable to tax under Schedule E for the year of assessment in which he receives the benefit on an amount equal to the value of the benefit, the amount so chargeable being treated as earned income.[98]

3-20G   This charge does not apply [99] if:

    (a) the acquisition was made before March 27, 1974, and the benefit mentioned was received in pursuance of a scheme approved (whether before or after the acquisition or receipt) under Schedule 12 to the Act [1]; or

    (b) the acquisition was made under such arrangements as are mentioned in paragraph (b) in § 3-20E above.

3-20H   Where any amount is chargeable to tax under section 79 on a person acquiring any shares or interest in shares, the amount so chargeable is deductible in computing any chargeable gain on the first disposal of the shares, whether by that or another person.[2]

Provision of living accommodation

3-21   *History.* Before the year 1977–78, an employee was not assessable to tax under Schedule E on the value of accommodation which he was *required* to occupy for the more efficient performance of his duties.[3] This was because the employee was regarded as a " representative occupier," occupying the accommodation on behalf of his employer.[4] An employee who was *entitled* (but not *required*) to occupy accommodation provided by his employer was formerly assessed on its annual value under Schedule A but not under Schedule E. When the Schedule A charge was abolished in 1963–64, a Schedule E charge was introduced by what became section 185 of the Income and Corporation Taxes Act 1970. Section 185 proved unsatisfactory

---

[97] See F.A. 1973, s. 19 and Sched. 8, paras. 5–7, where " related loan " is defined.
[98] F.A. 1972, s. 79 (7).
[99] *Ibid.* s. 79 (1) (3).
[1] See n. 91, above.
[2] *Ibid.* s. 79 (9).
[3] *Langley* v. *Appleby* [1976] S.T.C. 368 (police officer required by the express terms of his contract to occupy particular premises, such occupation enabling him to perform his duties more effectively).
[4] In *Tennant* v. *Smith* [1892] A.C. 150; 3 T.C. 158, it was thought that this rule applied only if the benefit was non-convertible, *e.g.* if the employee had no power to sell or lease the accommodation; but this view was rejected in *I.R.C.* v. *Miller* [1930] A.C. 222; 15 T.C. 25 (H.L.).

in many respects [5] and was repealed in and from the year 1977–78, and replaced by new provisions contained in section 33 of the Finance Act 1977.

3-21A   *Position from 1977–78 onwards.* Section 33 of the Finance Act 1977 states that where living accommodation is provided for a person in any period *by reason of his employment* (see § 3-22), and is not otherwise made the subject of any charge to him by way of income tax, he is to be treated for Schedule E purposes as being in receipt of emoluments of an amount equal to the value to him of the accommodation for the period, less so much as is properly attributable to that provision of any sum made good by him to those at whose cost the accommodation is provided. The value of the accommodation to the employee in any period is the rent which would have been payable for the period if the premises had been let to him at an annual rent equal to their annual value as ascertained under section 531 of the Taxes Act. " Annual value " is there defined as the rent which might reasonably be expected to be obtained on a letting from year to year if the tenant undertakes to pay all usual tenant's rates and taxes, and if the landlord undertakes to bear the costs of the repairs and insurance and the other expenses, if any, necessary for maintaining the subject of the valuation in a state to command that rent.[6] For any period, however, in which those at whose cost the accommodation is provided pay rent at an annual value greater than the annual value so ascertained under section 531, the value of the accommodation to the employee is an amount equal to the rent payable by them for the period. From any amount which is treated as emoluments under section 33, the employee can deduct as a Schedule E expense such amounts (if any) as would have been so deductible if the accommodation had been paid for by the employee out of his emoluments. As to the expenses which are so allowable, see §§ 3-35 *et seq.*

3-21B   *Exceptions.* There are a number of cases where accommodation provided for the employee gives rise to no assessable emolument. These cases are as follows [7]:

(a) Where it is necessary for the proper performance of the employee's duties that he should reside in the accommodation;

(b) where the accommodation is provided for the better performance of the duties of his employment, and his is one of the kinds of employment in the case of which it is customary for employers to provide living accommodation for employees;

This may apply, for example, to accommodation provided for police officers or fire officers.

(c) where the accommodation is provided for him as the holder of an office or employment under the Crown and the Secretary of State certifies that there exists a special threat to his security and, accordingly, that special security arrangements are in force.

---

[5] A working party was set up in July 1976 to undertake a review of the tax treatment of representative occupation, and to make recommendations.

[6] *Ibid.* s. 531. This definition of annual value corresponds with the definition of " gross value " for rating purposes in England: see General Rate Act 1967, s. 19 (6). Rates are differently assessed in Northern Ireland but the Taxing Acts apply there also.

[7] F.A. 1977, s. 33 (4).

In these cases there is no charge to tax under Schedule E either by virtue of section 33 of the Finance Act 1977 or section 183 of the Taxes Act 1970 (§ 3-06) or otherwise in respect of a liability for rates on the premises being discharged for or on behalf of the employee or the employee being reimbursed for the discharge of that liability. These exceptions are wider and more precise in their scope than the old exception for the " representative occupier." [8]

3-21C   Exceptions (a) and (b) do not apply (and there may be a tax liability under section 33) if the accommodation is provided by a company and the employee is a director of the company or of an associated company unless, for each employment of his which is employment as director of the company or an associated company, the following conditions are fulfilled, that is:

(a) he has no material interest in the company; and
(b) either his employment is as a full-time working director or the company is non-profit making (meaning that neither does it carry on a trade, nor do its functions consist wholly or mainly in the holding of investments or other property) or is established for charitable purposes only. [9]

Accommodation provided for the employee's family or household

3-22   If by reason of a person's employment accommodation is provided for others being members of his family or household, he is to be treated as if it were accommodation provided for him. [10] Living accommodation provided for an employee, or for members of his family or household, by his employer, is deemed to be provided by reason of his employment unless:

(a) the employer is an individual, and it can be shown that he makes the provision in the normal course of his domestic, family or personal relationships; or
(b) the accommodation is provided by a local authority for an employee of theirs, and it can be shown that the terms on which it is provided are no more favourable than those on which similar accommodation is provided by the authority for persons who are not their employees but are otherwise similarly circumstanced. [11]

Special rules apply where the provision of living accommodation gives rise to a charge to tax under section 33 of the Finance Act 1977 (§ 3-21B) where the person is employed in director's or higher-paid employment. This is discussed in § 3-47.

Expenses allowances

3-23   If an employer reimburses his employee for expenses which he has incurred wholly, exclusively and necessarily in the performance of his

---

[8] See the case cited in n. 3, above.
[9] *Ibid.* s. 33 (5). For definitions, see F.A. 1976, s. 72.
[10] *Ibid.* s. 33 (6).
[11] *Ibid.* s. 33 (7).

duties, the amount paid does not form part of the employee's emoluments.[12] If a lump sum is paid to an employee as an expenses allowance, it is not in practice treated as an emolument if it is of a reasonable amount.[13] There are special provisions affecting expenses allowances paid to directors and employees remunerated at the rate of £7,500 a year or more (£8,500 in and from 1979–80).[14]

3. TERMINAL PAYMENTS

3-24 Before 1960, a sum paid to an employee or office-holder on the termination of his office or employment or in consideration of a variation of its terms was dealt with as follows:

(1) If there was a previous arrangement that the sum would be paid (such as a provision in articles of association), the sum was treated as deferred remuneration and taxed under Schedule E.[15]

(2) If the payment was in anticipation of future services, it was treated as advance remuneration and taxed under Schedule E.[16]

(3) If the payment was not related to services rendered or to be rendered but was paid as consideration for the release of the employers' obligations under the service agreement, it escaped tax.

Thus in *Chibbett* v. *Robinson*,[17] payments by way of compensation for loss of office voted by shareholders on the liquidation of a company were held not to be taxable.

In *Hunter* v. *Dewhurst* [18] a company director was paid £10,000 as compensation for loss of office on ceasing to be chairman of the company. " It seems to me," said Lord Atkin, " that a sum of money paid to obtain a release from a contingent liability under a contract of employment, cannot be said to be received ' under ' the contract of employment, is not remuneration for services rendered or to be rendered under the contract of employment, and is not received ' from ' the contract of employment."

In *Tilley* v. *Wales* [19] a lump sum paid to commute a pension was held not to be taxable because it was " in the nature of a capital payment which is substituted for a series of recurrent and periodic sums which partake of the nature of income " (*per* Viscount Simon L.C.).

(4) A payment made in consideration of the employee entering into a restrictive covenant was not chargeable to income tax.[20] Such

---

[12] *Pook* v. *Owen* [1970] A.C. 244; 45 T.C. 571 (H.L.).
[13] But see *McLeish* v. *I.R.C.* (1958) 38 T.C. 1, where the allowance was found excessive. *Cf. Napier* v. *National Business Agency* [1951] 2 All E.R. 264; 30 A.T.C. 180 (C.A.) where N was employed at a salary of £13 a week plus £6 a week for expenses. Both the employer and N knew N's expenses could not exceed £1 a week. N was dismissed and sued on the basis that his weekly salary was £13. *Held*, the service agreement was unenforceable as being contrary to public policy, it being intended to mislead the Revenue. The provisions relating to salaries were not severable from the rest of the agreement and could not be enforced.
[14] *Post*, §§ 3-40 *et seq.*
[15] *Henry* v. *Foster* (1932) 16 T.C. 605 (H.L.); *Dale* v. *De Soissons* (1950) 32 T.C. 118 (C.A.); *cf. Henley* v. *Murray* (1950) 31 T.C. 351 (C.A.).
[16] *Cameron* v. *Prendergast* [1940] A.C. 549; 23 T.C. 122; *Tilley* v. *Wales* [1943] A.C. 386; 25 T.C. 136.
[17] (1924) 9 T.C. 48. See also *Clayton* v. *Lavender* (1965) 42 T.C. 607 and *Comptroller-General of Inland Revenue* v. *Knight* [1973] A.C. 428, J.C.
[18] (1932) 16 T.C. 605 (H.L.).
[19] [1943] A.C. 386; 25 T.C. 136.
[20] *Beak* v. *Robson* [1943] A.C. 352; 25 T.C. 33 (*ante*, § 3-05). Such a payment is not deductible in computing the employer's profits under Schedule D: *Associated Portland Cement Manufacturers Ltd.* v. *Kerr* (1945) 27 T.C. 103 (C.A.): *ante*, § 2-56.

payments were, however, chargeable to surtax, for which purpose the amount paid was grossed up at the standard rate.[21] For 1973–74 and subsequent years, the payment is treated as a net amount of income received after deduction of income tax at the basic rate; the tax notionally deducted is not repayable; where the recipient is assessed at higher rates, the notional tax is allowed as a credit; and the income is treated in the recipient's hands as income not brought into charge to income tax for the purposes of sections 52 and 53 of the Taxes Act 1970.[22]

The Finance Act 1960 provided for the assessment under Schedule E of payments which hitherto escaped tax under paragraph (3), above. Payments already taxable under paragraphs (1) and (2) were unaffected by the Act; and the payments referred to in paragraph (4) were expressly excluded. These statutory provisions are now in sections 187–188 of the Income and Corporation Taxes Act 1970.

Income and Corporation Taxes Act 1970, ss. 187–188

3-25   Section 187 charges tax under Schedule E on any payment to which the section applies which is made to the holder or past holder of any office or employment, or to his personal representatives, whether the payment is made by the employer or by any other person. Payments made to the spouse or any relative or dependant of the employee, or on his behalf or by his direction, are treated as made to him; and any valuable consideration other than money must be treated as a payment of money equal to the value of the consideration at the date of the gift. There is a statutory obligation on the employer to deliver particulars of the payment to the Inspector within 14 days after the end of the year of assessment in which the payment is made. Personal representatives can be assessed in respect of payments made to the deceased. There is an exemption from tax on a payment not exceeding £10,000; and where a payment exceeds this amount only the excess over £10,000 is taxable.[23] Section 187 applies

" to any payment (not otherwise chargeable to tax [24]) which is made, whether in pursuance of any legal obligation or not, either directly or indirectly in consideration or in consequence of, or otherwise in connection with, the termination of the holding of the office or employment or any change in its functions or emoluments, including any payment in commutation of annual or periodical payments (whether chargeable to tax or not) which would otherwise have been made as aforesaid." [25]

---

[21] I.C.T.A. 1970, s. 34. This section applies to any undertaking " the tenor or effect of which is to restrict [the individual] as to his conduct or activities ": this would seem sufficiently wide to cover an undertaking of the kind imposed on the organist in Lord Denning's illustration in *Jarrold* v. *Boustead, ante*, § 3-05.

[22] I.C.T.A. 1970, s. 34 (1) as amended by F.A. 1971, Sched. 6, para. 15. And see *post*, §§ 5-30 *et seq.*

[23] I.C.T.A. 1970, s. 188 (3), which also contains provisions to prevent avoidance by payments made by associated employers. The question whether payments of compensation are deductible as a trading expense is referred to *ante*, § 2-65. The tax free sum of up to £10,000 is not chargeable to capital gains tax: *post*, § 16-29. Figure increased from £5,000 by F.A. 1978, s. 24.

[24] Thus a payment which was a distribution within Schedule F would fall outside s. 187 and the exemption and rulings in § 3-26 would not apply.

[25] I.C.T.A. 1970, s. 187 (2). Payments made before April 6, 1960, are outside the charge; so also are payments made after that date in respect of obligations incurred or employments terminating before that date: *ibid.* s. 187 (6).

The types of payment referred to in (3) in § 3-24 are within this section. Payments which are chargeable under Schedule E apart from the section continue to be so chargeable, and do not attract the £10,000 exemption and the other reliefs which apply to payments which are chargeable under the Act. It should be observed that section 187 is not confined to payments by way of compensation for loss of office; it applies also to those retirement gratuities which would otherwise escape tax.

Exemptions and reliefs

3-26 Section 188 of the Income and Corporation Taxes Act 1970 contains a list of payments to which section 187 (above) does not apply including:

(a) any payment made in connection with the termination of the holding of an office or employment by the death of the holder, or made on account of injury to or disability of the holder of an office or employment [26];

(b) any sum paid in consideration of the employee entering into a restrictive covenant and chargeable to tax under section 34 of the Income and Corporation Taxes Act 1970 [27];

(c) payments under approved retirement benefit schemes. [28]

The taxation of terminal payments in cases where a foreign element is involved is considered later. [29]

Methods of assessing terminal payments

3-27 A payment which is chargeable to tax under section 187 of the Income and Corporation Taxes Act 1970 is treated as earned income and as received (a) in the case of a payment in commutation of annual or other periodical payments, on the date when the commutation is effected; and (b) in the case of any other payment, on the date of the termination or charge in respect of which the payment is made. [30] Relief may be available by virtue of section 188 (3) of the Act (which exempts from tax under section 187 the first £10,000 of the terminal payments) and under Schedule 8. [31] The P.A.Y.E. Regulations apply to payments chargeable to tax under section 187 and the appropriate amount of tax must be deducted by the payer. If the payer fails to deduct tax he cannot recover the amount overpaid from the recipient (for

---

[26] I.C.T.A. 1970, s. 188 (1) (a).
[27] Ibid. s. 188 (1) (b); see ante, § 3-24, para. (4).
[28] Ibid. s. 188 (1) (c); see post, § 3-34.
[29] Post, § 7-16.
[30] Ibid. s. 187 (4).
[31] The relieving provisions are of extreme complexity. Briefly, payments which are chargeable under s. 187 are divided into two overlapping categories: (1) *Payments which are not by way of compensation for loss of office*, as defined in para. 13 of Sched. 8 (e.g. a retirement gratuity). If an office-holder or employee is paid less than his " standard capital superannuation benefit "—roughly the average emoluments during the last three years of the employment, divided by 20 and multiplied by the number of years of service, less any non-taxable lump sum received under a retirement benefit scheme—the sum paid is not taxable. If he is paid more than the " standard capital superannuation benefit," only the excess is taxable under s. 187; except that if the " standard capital superannuation benefit " is less than £10,000, only the excess of the payment over £10,000 is taxable. (See Sched. 8, paras. 3–6.) (2) *All payments chargeable under s. 187, whether by way of retirement gratuity or compensation for loss of office or otherwise*. It has been seen that any payment chargeable under s. 187 is to be treated as received on one date and thus forms part of the emoluments of a single year of assessment. Sched. 8, paras. 7–11, provide a form of relief, called " top-slicing," which prevents the payment being swallowed in higher rate income tax in a single year.

this is a case of money paid under a mistake of law [32]) save in exceptional cases referred to in the Regulations. [33]

4. PENSIONS

3-28 It is usual for employers to offer pension schemes for the benefit of their employees. There are many different types of scheme but the tax problems, so far as employees are concerned, are as follows:

(1) *Whether contributions made by the employee are deductible in computing his emoluments*

3-29 The employee's contributions may take the form of payments (usually by deduction from salary) into a pension fund established by the employer, or of payments to an insurance company which has made arrangements with the employer to provide pensions. In either case, the contributions are not deductible in computing the employee's emoluments, unless the pension scheme is an " exempt approved " scheme within the meaning of section 21 of the Finance Act 1970: the contributions are treated as an application of income, not as expenditure incurred in earning the income. [34] The types and conditions of approval are considered later. [35] In some cases, contributions qualify for life assurance relief. [36]

(2) *Whether contributions made by the employer are to be treated as additional emoluments of the employee*

3-30 Under most types of pension scheme, contributions are made by the employer in respect of each employee in his service. By virtue of section 23 of the Finance Act 1970, where any sum is paid pursuant to a scheme (called a " retirement benefits scheme " [37]) for the provision of relevant benefits for any employee, the sum so paid, if not otherwise chargeable to income tax as income of the employer, is deemed to be income of the employee assessable under Schedule E for the year of assessment in which the sum is paid. The section applies whether the sum paid is a contribution to a pension fund established by the employer or a premium on a life policy. " Relevant benefits " means, [37]

3-31 " any pension, lump sum, gratuity or other like benefit given or to be given on retirement, or on death or in anticipation of retirement, or in connection with past service, after retirement, or death or to be given on or in anticipation of or in connection with any change in the nature of the service of the employee in question . . ."

It includes benefits payable to the employee's wife or widow, children, dependants or personal representatives. [38] It does not include any benefit which is to be offered solely by reason of the disablement by accident of a person occurring during his service or of his death by accident so occurring

[32] *Bernard & Shaw Ltd.* v. *Shaw* (1951) 30 A.T.C. 187.
[33] See Income Tax (Employments) Regulations 1973 (S.I. 1973 No. 334), para. 26 (3) and (4).
[34] *Smyth* v. *Stretton* (1904) 5 T.C. 36.
[35] *Post*, §§ 39-08 *et seq.*   [36] *Post*, § 8-68.
[37] F.A. 1970, s. 25 (1) defines " retirement benefits scheme " and F.A. 1970, s. 26 (1) defines " relevant benefits."
[38] F.A. 1970, s. 23 (5).

and for no other reason.[39] The section applies not only to the case where the employer pays a contribution towards the provision of the employee's retirement or other benefits; it applies where there is an agreement between employer and employee for the provision of future retirement or other benefits, such as a service contract with a director under which he is entitled to a pension on retirement. In such a case, an estimate has to be made of the annual cost to the employer of securing the benefits under a contract with a third person, such as an insurance company, and the annual cost so estimated is treated as an emolument of the employee and taxed accordingly.[40] It should be noted that a service agreement between a company and a single employee may be a " retirement benefits scheme ": the word " scheme " is deceptive. The provisions of section 23 should be kept in mind when negotiating service agreements for directors and employees. A director or employee who feels disheartened by the amount of tax payable on a proposed increase in salary may wish to forgo the increase in return for increased benefits after retirement. Section 23 may treat as " emoluments " the actual or estimated cost of providing those benefits.

Exemption from the consequences of section 23

3-32   Section 24 of the Finance Act 1970 provides that certain schemes are to be exempt from the provisions of section 23 of that Act. The main exemption is for approved schemes, but statutory schemes and those set up by a foreign government for its own employees are also exempt. It is further provided that employees who are resident and working overseas will not be liable to a Schedule E charge under section 23 if they are not liable to United Kingdom tax on their earnings.[41]

[The next paragraph is 3-34.]

(3) *Whether pensions are taxable*

3-34   All pensions paid under any scheme which is approved or being considered for approval are chargeable to tax under Schedule E and P.A.Y.E. should be operated on the payment.[42] Pensions paid by a person outside the United Kingdom to a resident of the United Kingdom are chargeable under Case V of Schedule D (*post*, § 7-07). Pensions are ordinarily treated as earned income and not as investment income.[43] There are provisions for excluding from the charge under Schedule E lump sum benefits paid on retirement pursuant to approved schemes.[44]

5. EXPENSES ALLOWABLE UNDER SCHEDULE E

3-35   Section 189 (1) of the Income and Corporation Taxes Act 1970 provides that:

---

[39] See *ibid.* s. 26 (1), defining " relevant benefits."   [40] See *ibid.* s. 23 (2) and (3).
[41] F.A. 1970, s. 24 (2) as substituted by F.A. 1974, s. 21 (7).
[42] F.A. 1970, Sched. 5, Pt. II, para. 1. It seems that no specific case of Schedule E applies.
[43] See *post*, § 8-07.
[44] See F.A. 1973, s. 14; but see F.A. 1972, s. 73 and F.A. 1971, Sched. 3, para. 9.

" If the holder of an office or employment is necessarily obliged to incur and defray out of the emoluments thereof the expenses of travelling in the performance of the duties of the office or employment, or of keeping and maintaining a horse to enable him to perform the same, or otherwise to expend money wholly, exclusively and necessarily in the performance of the said duties, there may be deducted from the emoluments to be assessed the expenses so necessarily incurred and defrayed."

Two conditions must exist before an expense is allowable:

3-36   (1) The expense must be incurred in the performance of the duties of the office or employment. Expenditure which is incurred merely to enable a person to perform the duties, or to perform them more efficiently, does not satisfy this test.

In *Simpson* v. *Tate*,[45] a county medical officer of health joined certain medical and scientific societies so that he might keep up to date on matters affecting public health. A claim to deduct the subscriptions paid to the societies was refused on the ground that the expense was incurred not in the performance of the duties but so that the officer might keep himself fit to perform them.

A deduction was similarly refused in *Blackwell* v. *Mills* [46] where the taxpayer was bound as a condition of his employment to incur the expenses. " The test," said Donovan L.J. in another case, " is not whether the employer imposes the expense but whether the duties do, in the sense that, irrespective of what the employer may prescribe, the duties cannot be performed without incurring the particular outlay." [47]

3-37   (2) The expense must be necessary to the office or employment in the sense that the job must generate the need for the expenditure.

In *Roskams* v. *Bennett*,[48] B (who was district manager of an insurance company) was unable, through defective eyesight, to drive a car and found it necessary to maintain an office at home. A claim in respect of the additional household expenses was refused.

3-38   It follows that the cost of travelling from the place where the employee lives to the place where he is employed is not deductible; and that the expense incurred by a person who practises a profession in one place of travelling to another place where he is employed is not deductible.[49]

(i) In *Ricketts* v. *Colquhoun*,[50] the Recorder of a provincial borough who was a barrister residing and practising in London claimed to deduct from his emoluments as Recorder the travelling expenses between London and the borough and hotel expenses in the borough. *Held*, that the travelling expenses

---

[45] [1925] 2 K.B. 214; 9 T.C. 314. Certain fees and subscriptions are deductible under I.C.T.A. 1970, s. 192.

[46] (1945) 26 T.C. 468. See also *Lupton* v. *Potts* (1969) 45 T.C. 643: examination fees paid to Law Society by solicitor's articled clerk held not deductible. The clerk paid the fees " not to benefit or fulfil an obligation to an employer but to benefit himself because he wanted to become a solicitor."

[47] *Brown* v. *Bullock* (1961) 40 T.C. 1 at p. 10 (C.A.). *Cf. Elwood* v. *Utitz* (1965) 42 T.C. 482 (C.A.N.I.). The sum must be defrayed " in doing the work of the office ": *Nolder* v. *Walters* (1930) 15 T.C. 380 at p. 387. See also *McKie* v. *Warner* (1961) 40 T.C. 65. *Owen* v. *Burden* (1971) 47 T.C. 476 (C.A.).

[48] (1950) 32 T.C. 129. See also *Marsden* v. *I.R.C.* (1965) 42 T.C. 326 (car expenses of Inland Revenue investigator).

[49] In *Mitchell and Edon* v. *Ross* [1962] A.C. 814; 40 T.C. 11 (H.L.), an unsuccessful attempt was made by consultants holding appointments under the National Health Service (Schedule E) and also carrying on private practice (Schedule D) to offset certain Schedule E expenses against the Schedule D receipts on the basis that they in fact practised a single profession. See *ante*, § 1-13.   [50] [1926] A.C. 1; 10 T.C. 118.

were attributable to the Recorder's own choice of residence and were not necessary to the office as such; nor were any of the expenses incurred " in the performance of " his duties as Recorder.

(ii) In *Pook* v. *Owen* [51] O., a general medical practitioner in Fishguard, also held two part-time hospital appointments as obstetrician and anaesthetist 15 miles away in Haverfordwest. Under the appointments O. was on stand-by duty to deal with emergency cases and was required to be available by telephone. His responsibility for the patient began from the moment he received a call, but not every call resulted in a visit to the hospital. Under his appointment O. was paid travelling expenses at a fixed rate per mile up to a single journey of 10 miles. O. bore the cost of travelling the additional five miles of the journey from Fishguard. *Held*, (i) distinguishing *Ricketts* v. *Colquhoun* (Lord Donovan and Lord Pearson dissenting), that the duties of O.'s office were performed in two places, namely, in the hospital and in the place where he received the telephone call and that the travelling expenses from one place to the other were incurred in the performance of the duties; and (ii) (Lord Pearson dissenting and Lord Wilberforce doubting) that the travelling allowance paid by the hospital was a reimbursement for actual expenditure incurred by O., and was not an assessable emolument. [52]

In the past it has often been supposed that the Schedule E expenses rule should be applied " objectively " without taking account of the duties imposed on the taxpayer by the express terms of his office or employment. This approach may be wrong.

In *Taylor* v. *Provan* [53] T, who lived and worked in Canada and the Bahamas and who was not resident in the United Kingdom, accepted a special assignment to advise certain United Kingdom companies on terms that he should be free to perform the bulk of his duties outside the United Kingdom and should be reimbursed expenses of travelling to and from the United Kingdom. A majority of the House of Lords held on the special facts of the case that, although T chose to live and work outside the United Kingdom, the expenses of travelling were nevertheless incurred in the performance of the duties.

This case shows that travelling expenses from home to work, where the terms of employment contemplate that home shall be a place of work, may in some cases be deductible.

3-39   The prohibition against the deduction of business entertainment expenses and the exception in the case of the " overseas customer," which has already been mentioned with regard to Schedule D, [54] also applies to Schedule E. The Rules of Schedule E relating to allowable expenses have been the subject of much comment and criticism. [55]

6. LEGISLATION AFFECTING DIRECTORS AND CERTAIN EMPLOYEES [56]

3-40   It has been observed that many expenses allowances and benefits in kind escape tax under the ordinary rules applicable to Schedule E. There are, however, special provisions (now contained in sections 60 to 72 of the Finance Act 1976, as amended), which apply to persons in " director's or

---

[51] [1970] A.C. 244; 45 T.C. 571 (H.L.). See also *Taylor* v. *Provan* [1975] A.C. 194; 49 T.C. 579 (H.L.).

[52] *Semble* the principle in (ii) applies not only to expenditure incurred in performing the duties of the office or employment but also to expenditure to put the person in a position to perform such duties. *Cf.* § 3-42.

[53] [1975] A.C. 194; 49 T.C. 579 (H.L.). See also the concessions in S.T.I. (1976) 7: Concession No. A30.

[54] *Ante*, § 2-71.   [55] See Cmd. 9474, paras. 118–143.

[56] See I.R. Booklet No. 480: *Notes on Expenses Payments and Benefits for Directors and Certain Employees* (with 1978 Supplement).

higher-paid employment '' (as defined) under which, with some exceptions, all expense allowances and the cash equivalent of all benefits in kind provided for them are treated as taxable emoluments, subject to the right to claim a deduction under section 189 (*ante*, § 3-35) for money expended wholly, exclusively and necessarily in performing the duties of the office or employment or under section 192 in respect of fees, contributions or subscriptions falling within that section. These provisions in the Finance Act 1976 apply in and from 1977–78 and supersede provisions (now repealed) in sections 195–203 of the Income and Corporation Taxes Act 1970.

3-41   These special provisions in sections 60 to 72 of the Finance Act 1976 ('' the special provisions '') apply only to persons in '' director's or higher-paid employment.'' [57]

Directors. The special provisions apply to a person employed as a director of a company and the word '' director '' is widely defined in section 72 (8) of the Finance Act 1976 to include *inter alia* any person in accordance with whose directions or instructions the directors of a company are accustomed to act, excluding a person giving advice in a professional capacity. The special provisions do not apply to a director with no material interest in the company if either (a) his employment is as a full-time working director or (b) the company is non-profit making (meaning that neither does it carry on trade, nor do its functions consist wholly or mainly in the holding of investments or other property) or is established for charitable purposes only. [58] '' Full-time working director '' means a director who is required to devote substantially the whole of his time to the service of the company in a managerial or technical capacity. [59] A person has a material interest if (broadly) he controls, directly or indirectly, more than 5 per cent. of the company's ordinary share capital. [60] Directors who are so excluded from the special provisions will be caught by them if their emoluments are such that the next paragraph applies.

Other employees. The special provisions apply to all persons in employment with emoluments at the rate of £7,500 a year or more in and from 1978–79 (£8,500 in and from 1979–80). [61] The figure of £7,500 (or £8,500) has to be calculated on the assumption that the special provisions apply and on the further assumption that all benefits in respect of medical insurance (§ 3-15A) and cash vouchers (§ 3-17) are included. [62] The special provisions apply whether the employer is a company, firm or an individual. Separate employments with the same employer are treated as one employment; so also are separate employments with employers under common control. [63]

The effect of the special provisions is as follows:

---

[57] F.A. 1976, s. 69 (1) and (3); (substituted by F.A. 1978, s. 23).
[58] F.A. 1976, s. 69 (5).
[59] *Ibid*. s. 72 (9).
[60] *Ibid*. s. 72 (10).
[61] F.A. 1976, s. 69 (1) and (3), substituted by F.A. 1978, s. 23.
[62] F.A. 1976, s. 69 (2).
[63] *Ibid*. s. 69 (3), (4).

(1) *Expenses allowances* [64]

3-42   Any sum paid in respect of expenses (whether by way of reimbursement of expenses actually incurred or " round sum allowances " or otherwise) to a person in director's or higher-paid employment is, if not otherwise chargeable to tax as his income, treated as emoluments of the employment and accordingly chargeable to income tax under Schedule E. If the director or employee is able to show that the allowance was expended wholly, exclusively and necessarily in the performance of the duties of the office or employment, a claim for a deduction under section 189 (*ante*, § 3-35) may be made. The onus of showing that the conditions of section 189 of the Income and Corporation Taxes Act 1970 have been satisfied is thus thrown on the director or employee.

(2) *Benefits in kind*

3-43   There is legislation in section 33 of the Finance Act 1977 which deals with the provision of living accommodation, whether for a director or other employee. This has been discussed in §§ 3-21A *et seq*. Subject to this legislation, section 61 of the Finance Act 1976 (which applies in and from 1977–78) treats as the emolument of an employment and accordingly as chargeable to income tax under Schedule E an amount equal to the " cash equivalent " of certain benefits provided for a person who is in director's or higher-paid employment (see § 3-41) where the benefit is provided by reason of his employment. The persons providing a benefit are those at whose cost the provision is made. The section applies whether the benefit is provided for the director or employee or for others who are members of his family or household,[65] except that where the employer is an individual the section does not apply to payments or provisions which can be shown to have been made in the normal course of the individual's domestic, family or personal relationships. Section 61 (2) provides as follows [66]:

> " The benefits to which [section 61] applies are accommodation (other than living accommodation), entertainment, domestic or other services, and other benefits and facilities of whatsoever nature (whether or not similar to any of those mentioned above in this subsection), excluding however those taxable under sections 64 to 68 below in this chapter, and subject to the exceptions provided for by the next following section." [67]

The section does not apply where the cost of providing the benefit is chargeable under the ordinary rules of Schedule E apart from the special provisions applicable to persons in director's or higher-paid employment. Thus if an employer discharges an obligation which his employee has incurred to pay £x to a third person and the £x is chargeable under Schedule E under the principle in *Nicoll* v. *Austin* (see § 3-16), section 61 of the Finance Act 1976 is not needed and does not apply.

---

[64] F.A. 1976, s. 60.

[65] References to members of a person's family or household are to his spouse, his sons and daughters and their spouses, his parents and his servants, dependants and guests: F.A. 1976, s. 72 (4).

[66] *Ibid.* s. 72 (3).

[67] F.A. 1976, ss. 64 and 65 (cars): § 3-48; s. 66 (beneficial loan arrangements): § 3-45; s. 67 (employee shareholdings): § 3-47; s. 68 (medical insurance): § 3-15A.

In *Rendell* v. *Went* [68] the company which employed the appellant met the legal costs involved in defending the appellant on a charge of causing the death of a pedestrian by reckless or dangerous driving. If the charge had been proved the appellant would have been liable to be imprisoned and the company did not wish to be deprived of his services. *Held*, that the expense incurred by the company was a benefit or facility giving rise to a charge to tax.

3-44   Section 61 of the Finance Act 1976 applies only to benefits provided for a director or employee *by reason of his employment.* [69] Section 72 (3) provides that all sums paid to an employee by his employer in respect of expenses, and all such provision as is mentioned in the chapter of which section 72 forms part which is made for an employee, or for members of his family or household, by his employer, shall be deemed to be paid to or made for him or them by reason of his employment; but this does not apply to any such payment or provision made by the employer, being an individual, as can be shown to have been made in the normal course of his domestic, family or personal relationships. Section 61 may apply to scholarship schemes for an employee's children. [70]

3-45   Section 61 does not apply to a benefit consisting in the provision by the employee's employer for the employee himself, or for the spouse, children or dependants of the employee, of any pension, annuity, lump sum, gratuity or other like benefit to be given on the employee's death or retirement [71]; nor does section 61 apply to a benefit consisting in the provision by the employee's employer of meals in any canteen in which meals are provided for the staff generally. [72] Section 61 does not apply to accommodation in the employer's premises, or to supplies or services, used by the employee solely in performing the duties of his employment. [73]

The measure of the charge under section 61

3-46   Where tax is charged under section 61 on a benefit, the measure of the charge under Schedule E is " an amount equal to whatever is the *cash equivalent* of the benefit." [74] This means an amount equal to the *cost* of the benefit, less so much (if any) of it as is made good by the employee to those providing the benefit. [75] Generally, the cost of a benefit is the amount of any expense incurred in or in connection with its provision including a proper proportion of any expense relating partly to the benefit and partly to other matters. [76]

This represents a radical departure from the normal Schedule E rule under which tax on many benefits in kind is charged on the value of the benefit to the employee. In *Wilkins* v. *Rogerson*, for example (see § 3-17), the taxable emolument was an amount equal to the secondhand value of the suit provided for the employee. If in such a case the employee were in

---

[68] (1964) 41 T.C. 641 (H.L.) (a case under the law before 1977–78).
[69] F.A. 1976, s. 61 (1).
[70] See Inland Revenue Press Releases in [1978] S.T.I. 276, 303.
[71] *Ibid.* s. 62 (6).
[72] *Ibid.* s. 62 (7).
[73] *Ibid.* s. 62 (3).
[74] *Ibid.* s. 61 (1).
[75] *Ibid.* s. 63 (1).
[76] *Ibid.* s. 63 (2).

director's or higher-paid employment, the tax charge in and from 1977–78 would be on an amount equal to the cost of the suit.

Where the benefit consists in the transfer of an asset by any person, and since that person acquired or produced the asset it has been used or has depreciated, the cost of the benefit is deemed to be the market value of the asset at the time of transfer.[77] Where the employer retains the asset and places it at the employee's disposal, or at the disposal of others being members of his family or household, tax is levied on the cost of the benefit in any year, which is deemed to be the *annual value* of the use of the asset plus the total of any expense incurred in or in connection with the provision of the benefit (excluding however the expense of acquiring or producing it incurred by the person to whom the asset belongs).[78] The annual value of the use of the asset [79]:

(a) in the case of land, is its annual value being the rent which might reasonably be expected to be obtained on a letting from year to year if the tenant undertakes to pay all usual tenant's rates and taxes, and if the landlord undertakes to bear the costs of the repairs and insurance, and the other expenses, if any, necessary for maintaining the subject of the valuation in a state to command that rent; and

(b) in any other case, is 10 per cent. of the market value of the asset at the time when it was first applied (by those providing the benefit in question) in the provision of any benefit for a person, or for members of his family or household, by reason of his employment. There are special provisions which apply to cars (see § 3-48) and to assets hired or rented to the employer and then put at the employee's disposal.[80]

Expense connected with living accommodation: representative occupiers

3-47   We have seen in § 3-21A that all employees, whether or not in director's or higher-paid employment, are taxable under section 33 of the Finance Act 1977 on the annual value of living accommodation provided for them, subject only to three exceptions in § 3-21C where there is no tax either on the annual value or on any liability for rates which the employer discharges. Two of these exceptions remove any tax charge in respect of the emoluments of representative occupiers. Where there would be a tax charge under section 33 but for these exceptions, section 63A of the Finance Act 1976 [81] prevents persons in director's or higher-paid employment being taxed (as a benefit in kind) on the full amount of expenditure incurred in providing one or more of the following:

(a) heating, lighting, or cleaning the premises concerned;

(b) repairs (other than structural repairs) to the premises, their maintenance or decoration;

---

[77] *Ibid.* s. 63 (3).
[78] *Ibid.* s. 63 (4).
[79] *Ibid.* s. 63 (5).
[80] *Ibid.* s. 63 (6).
[81] Inserted by F.A. 1977, s. 34.

(c) the provision in the premises of furniture, or other appurtenances or effects which are normal for domestic occupation.

The tax charge under section 61 of the Finance Act 1976 is limited in the case of such expenditure to 10 per cent. of the net amount of the emoluments of the employment for the year (for which purpose the expenditure falling into categories (a)–(c) is left out of account) plus capital allowances and certain pension contributions.

> Thus if X is employed as a teacher at a boarding school at a salary of £8,000 a year and is required to live in a house provided by the school, the cash equivalent of any benefits in categories (a)–(c) is taxable under section 61 of the Finance Act 1976, subject to the 10 per cent. limit.

There are provisions which prevent tax being avoided by dividing an employment between different associated employers.

Cars and benefits associated with cars

3-48   The special legislation applicable to persons in director's or higher-paid employment applies to benefits in kind in the form of cars which are available for private use; but the legislation distinguishes three separate cases. The measure of the tax charge differs in each case.

(1) *No business or insubstantial business travel* [82]: This is the case where a car is used wholly for private purposes or where its use for business travel is insubstantial compared with private use. The word " insubstantial " is not defined. An Inland Revenue Press Release states that " its application must depend on the facts of each case and be determined, if necessary, on appeal. But, in response to questions which have been raised about the interpretation of the subsection, the Inland Revenue wishes it to be known that in practice Inspectors of Taxes will be concentrating their attention on cases in which two or more cars are provided for the use of a director or employee or of their families, or where a car appears to be provided as a recognition of his status with the employer rather than for business use. The business use of a car will not be regarded as ' insubstantial ' for purposes of section 62 (1) of the Finance Act 1976 if that use exceeds 10 per cent. of its total use in the tax year." [83] Where there is no business or insubstantial business travel (in this sense), section 61 of the Finance Act 1976 applies and all benefits in connection with the car are taxable as emoluments (§ 3-43). Where the car is retained by the employer but put at the employee's use, tax is levied on the annual value of the use of the car, which is 20 per cent. of its original market value or 10 per cent. if at the end of the year its age exceeds four years. [84] Any other expenses incurred by the employer in running the car *e.g.* the cost of licensing or insuring or repairing the car are chargeable under section 61 as provided in § 3-46.

---

[82] F.A. 1976, s. 62 (1) and (2). Business travel means travelling which a person is necessarily obliged to do in the performance of the duties of his employment: *ibid.* s. 72 (5) (*c*). Private use is use otherwise than for business travel: *ibid.* s. 72 (5) (*f*).

[83] [1976] S.T.I. 396.

[84] F.A. 1976, s. 63 (5) (*b*).

(2) *Substantial business travel.* In this case section 61 of the Finance Act 1976 applies only to benefits in connection with the provision of a driver for the car.[85] The annual value test in section 63 (5) (see § 3-46) does not apply but, instead, section 64 of the Finance Act 1976 imposes an elaborate charge on the cash equivalent of the benefit of the car which has to be reckoned by applying Tables A, B and C (as appropriate) in Schedule 7 to the Act.[86] Tables A and B apply in the case of cars with an original market value up to £8,000. Table C applies in the case of cars with an original market value more than that amount. The amount which is assessed varies according to the cost of the car, its cylinder capacity and its age (reckoned from the date of its first registration) at the end of the year of assessment.

> Thus if a car has an original market value of £4,000 and a cylinder capacity of 1,800 ccs., and is under four years old, the taxable amount is £250. This covers all benefits.
> The taxable amount in this example is reduced by half if the employee travels at least 25,000 miles a year on business travel.

(3) *Pooled cars.*[87] Broadly, cars which are included in a car pool for a number of employees, which are kept overnight on the employer's premises, and where any private use is merely incidental to the employee's other use of the car during the year, attract no tax charge under either section 61 or 64 of the Finance Act 1976.

Beneficial loan arrangements

3-49   (1) *Loans.* Beneficial loans are not caught by the tax charge on " benefits in kind " (see § 3-43) because, generally, no expense is incurred by the employer in providing the loan; and they are generally not taxable as emoluments under Schedule E because the benefit of the loan is not convertible into money (see § 3-14).

Section 66 (1) of the Finance Act 1976, which takes effect in and from the year 1977–78, provides that where a person employed in director's or higher-paid employment (§ 3-41) has the benefit of a loan which is obtained by reason of his employment, being a loan which is interest-free or at a rate less than the official rate (as defined),[88] the cash equivalent of the benefit (as defined)[89] shall be treated as emoluments of the employment. The section applies whether the loan is to the employee or to a relative of his except that no tax charge arises in the case of a loan to a relative where the employee is able to show that he derived no benefit from the loan. There is no charge to tax if the cash equivalent does not exceed £50; and there are provisions for excluding the section where the interest on the loan would be eligible for relief under section 75 of the Finance Act 1972 (see §§ 8-57 *et seq.*). The section takes effect in and from 1977–78 with a reduced tax charge for the two years 1977–78 and 1978–79. Loans which give rise to a charge to income tax under section 66 (1), above, are not chargeable to

---

[85] *Ibid.* s. 62 (2).
[86] New Tables were substituted with effect from April 6, 1978, by the Income Tax (Cash Equivalents of Car Benefits) Order 1978 in [1978] S.T.I. 150. The figure of £8,000 was increased from £6,000.
[87] *Ibid.* s. 65.
[88] *Ibid.* s. 66 (9). The official rate as from April 6, 1978, is 9 per cent. per annum: see [1978] S.T.I. 36.
[89] *Ibid.* s. 66 (8) and Sched. 8, Pt. II.

capital transfer tax under section 115 of the Finance Act 1976 (*post*, § 21-09).[90]

3-50   (2) *Loans released or written off.* In many cases the act of releasing or writing off a loan made to an employee will give rise to an assessable emolument under the ordinary rules of Schedule E.[91] However, section 66 (3) of the Finance Act 1976 (which generally applies for the year 1976–77 and subsequent years) provides that where in the case of a person employed in director's or higher-paid employment (as defined) [92] there is in any year released or written off the whole or part of a loan (whether to the employee himself or to a relative of his and whether or not such a loan as is mentioned in § 3-49), the benefit of which was obtained by reason of his employment, an amount equal to that which is released or written off shall be treated as emoluments of the employment chargeable to income tax under Schedule E. Section 66 (3) does not apply in the case of a loan to a relative if the employee shows he derived no benefit from it. Further, section 66 (3) does not apply to amounts otherwise chargeable to income tax as income of the employee, except that it applies to amounts chargeable only under section 187 of the Taxes Act: thus sums released or written off on the occasion of the termination of a director's or higher-paid employment are taxed without the benefit of the £10,000 exemption (see § 3-25). Section 66 (3) cannot be avoided by the employer deferring the release or writing off of the loan until after the director's or higher-paid employment has terminated, except that no charge arises where the release or writing off takes effect on or after the employee's death.

Employee's shareholdings acquired at an undervalue: treatment as notional loan

3-51   Section 67 of the Finance Act 1976 applies where, after April 6, 1976, a person employed or about to be employed in director's or higher-paid employment (" the employee "), or a person connected with him, acquires shares in a company (whether the employing company or not) and the shares are acquired at an undervalue (as defined) in pursuance of a right or opportunity available by reason of the employment. The section applies for 1976–77 and subsequent years and has the effect of treating the undervalue as if the employee had the benefit of an interest-free loan of an equivalent amount (called " the notional loan ") within section 66 (1) of the Act (see § 3-49). The tax charge imposed by section 67 does not apply to the extent that the acquisition at an undervalue gives rise to a Schedule E emolument apart from that section, *e.g.* under the principle in *Weight* v. *Salmon* referred to in § 3-15. Payments or further payments for the shares go to reduce the amount outstanding of the notional loan but, subject thereto, the loan is treated as outstanding until (a) the whole amount outstanding is made good, or (b) the debt is released, or (c) the beneficial interest in the shares is disposed of, or (d) the employee dies. In case (a) the tax charge

---

[90] F.A. 1976, s. 115 (8).
[91] See *Clayton* v. *Gothorp, ante,* § 3-15.
[92] F.A. 1976, s. 69.

under section 66 (1) comes to an end. In cases (b) and (c) the employee is taxed under section 66 (3) (see § 3-46) as if an amount equal to the outstanding loan had been released or written off. In case (d) there is no Schedule E charge but the shares will form part of the employee's estate for the purposes of capital transfer tax. In cases (a)–(c) the tax charge arises notwithstanding the cessation of the employment.

3-52   *Sale of shares acquired by employees.* Where after April 6, 1976, shares are acquired as mentioned in § 3-51 (but whether or not at an undervalue) and those shares are subsequently disposed of by surrender or otherwise so that neither the employee nor any person connected with him any longer has a beneficial interest in them and the disposal is for a consideration which exceeds the then market value of the shares, the amount of the excess is treated as an emolument of the employee's employment and is accordingly chargeable to income tax under Schedule E for the year in which the disposal is effected. The charge to tax arises even if the employment has ceased but it does not apply to a disposal effected after the employee's death.

7. THE PAY AS YOU EARN SYSTEM [93]

3-53   It would be out of place in a book dealing with the principles of Revenue Law to consider in any detail the administrative machinery by which the tax due from directors and employees in respect of their emoluments is collected. Briefly, every person liable to assessment under Schedule E and who earns more than £15·50 weekly and £68 monthly [94] (below which figures the P.A.Y.E. system does not have to be operated) has a code number allocated to him by the Revenue. The code number is determined by the total of reliefs and allowances due to the taxpayer. The employer is supplied with tax tables by reference to which he is able to calculate the amount of tax to be deducted from the salary, the object of these tables being to secure that the tax payable for the year of assessment is spread over the year. Where reliefs or allowances change during the year (*e.g.* through marriage or the birth of a child), the code number is revised and an adjustment follows in the amount of tax deducted. The employer is bound to account to the Collector of Taxes within 14 days from the end of each month for the tax which he ought to have deducted from the employee's emoluments.

Surtax was not deductible under the P.A.Y.E. system but was charged by direct assessment. Under the unified system, operative for 1973–74 and subsequent years, the P.A.Y.E. system applies to income tax at the basic and other rates and the tables have been reconstructed to achieve this.

8. APPROVED PROFIT SHARING SCHEMES

3-54   The Finance Act 1978 [95] has introduced elaborate provisions which enable employers to establish trusts and provide funds to enable the trustees to buy

---

[93] See I.C.T.A. 1970, s. 204, and the Income Tax (Employment) Regulations 1973 (S.I. 1973 No. 334). These are printed in Simon, Volume G, pp. 448–473. The system is explained in detail in the Employer's Guide to Pay As You Earn (April 1977) issued by the Board of Inland Revenue under reference P7.
[94] [1977] S.T.I. 96.
[95] F.A. 1978, ss. 53–61 and Sched. 9.

ordinary shares in the employing company and appropriate and hold them on trust for individual employees of the company. Such profit sharing schemes, if approved by the Revenue, enjoy certain tax advantages. The provisions take effect as respects schemes approved after April 5, 1979, but the Board of Inland Revenue has already announced its willingness to accept applications for approval and, where possible, to give an informal opinion in advance of a formal application, provided that full particulars of the proposed scheme and the relevant documentation are provided. There is a right of appeal to the Special Commissioners against refusal or withdrawal of approval. Only a brief outline of the relevant provisions is given in this edition.

Conditions for approval

3-55   The scheme must provide for the establishment of a body of trustees resident in the United Kingdom who, out of moneys paid to them by the company, will acquire shares (e.g. by purchase or subscription) and appropriate the shares so acquired to eligible individuals. The initial market value of the shares appropriated to any one participant in a year of assessment must not exceed £500 but such appropriations may be made year-by-year. Generally, every full-time employee or director of the company concerned who has been such during a qualifying period not exceeding five years must be eligible to participate in the scheme on similar terms. The shares purchased must be shares in the employing company or in a company which has control of it or of a member of a consortium which has control of it; and the shares must be either shares of a class quoted on a recognised Stock Exchange or shares in a company which is not under the control of another company. Thus employees of a subsidiary company cannot be given an interest in the shares of that company (unless its shares are quoted) but must take an interest in shares in the parent company. The shares in question must be fully paid up and not redeemable, and they must be subject to no restrictions, other than restrictions which attach to all shares of the same class. There are a number of conditions as to the individuals eligible to participate. For example, an individual is not eligible unless, at the time of appropriation or within 18 months previously, he was a director or employee of the company concerned or, where the scheme is a group scheme, of a participating company. Individuals with a material interest (as defined) in a close company whose shares are appropriated are ineligible.

It is a condition of approval that every participant in the scheme will be bound to permit his shares to remain in the hands of the trustees during the " period of retention " and that he will be bound not to assign, charge or otherwise dispose of his beneficial interest in the shares during that period. The *period of retention* in relation to any participant's shares means the period from the date on which they are appropriated to him and ending on the fifth anniversary of that date or, if sooner, the date on which the participant ceases to be an employee or director of the company by reason of injury, disability or dismissal through redundancy (as defined) or the date on which the participant reaches pensionable age (as defined) or the date of the participant's death. A participant can direct the trustees to transfer the shares appropriated to him at any time after the period of retention but if the direction is given within 10 years from the date of appropriation, the transfer must be by way of sale at the best price obtainable. After 10 years the participant can deal with the shares as he pleases. He can, if he wishes, sell his interest to the trustees.

Tax treatment

3-56   On the appropriation of shares to a participant under an approved profit sharing scheme no charge arises under Schedule E (§ 3-02) or under section 67 of the Finance Act 1976 (§ 3-57); nor does any charge arise on the appreciation in value of the shares under section 69 of the Finance Act 1972 (§ 3-20C). The full benefit of the exemption from income tax is obtained only if the participant holds his shares until the *release date* or until his death, if sooner. The release date in relation to a participant's shares means the tenth anniversary from the date on which the shares were appropriated to him. If trustees dispose of any of a participant's shares before the release date or (if sooner) the date of his death, the participant is chargeable to income tax under Schedule E for the year of assessment in which the disposal takes place on the *appropriate percentage* of the " locked-in value " of the shares at the time of the disposal. Generally, the locked-in value means the initial market value of the shares, which is generally their market value at the date on which the shares were appropriated to the participant. (Locked-in value has a different meaning where, since the initial appropriation to the participant, there has been a capital receipt in respect of such shares.)

If the event giving rise to the tax charge occurs during the period of retention, the appropriate percentage of the locked-in value which is chargeable to income tax is 100 per cent.; if it occurs after the expiry of the period of retention and before the seventh anniversary of the date on which the shares were appropriated, the appropriate percentage is 50 per cent.; if it is after the seventh anniversary and before the tenth anniversary, the appropriate percentage is 25 per cent. After the tenth anniversary (*i.e.* the release date), there is no Schedule E charge. Any tax charge under Schedule E is collected (so far as possible) under the P.A.Y.E. system.

For the purposes of the capital gains tax, a participant is treated as absolutely entitled to the shares as against the trustees, notwithstanding the conditions which restrict his disposal of them; hence the treatment accorded to settled property (see §§ 16-21 *et seq.*) is excluded. The normal capital gains tax rules apply on a disposal of the appropriated shares.

Dividends on scheme shares belong to the participants, with normal tax consequences (see § 8-20).

Sums expended by the employing company in contributing to an approved profit sharing scheme are deductible in computing trading profits or as management expenses in the case of an investment company.

CHAPTER 4

SCHEDULE D, CASE VI

1. THE SCOPE OF THE CHARGE

4-01 TAX under Schedule D Case VI is charged in respect of:

(1) Certain classes of income specifically directed to be charged under Case VI, such as post-cessation receipts,[1] gains of a capital nature arising from " artificial transactions " in land (§§ 40-16 *et seq.*) and from sales of income derived from personal activities (§§ 40-21 *et seq.*); and

(2) any " annual profits or gains " not falling under any other Case of Schedule D and not charged by virtue of any other Schedule.[2]

Case VI is a residual Case and many different types of income have been brought within (1). These are discussed elsewhere in this book.[3] It might be supposed from (2) that Case VI charges tax on all profits not otherwise chargeable. This, however, is not the case, for the following principles limiting the scope of the charge are firmly established:

First, capital profits are not assessable under Case VI. This is because " annual profits " describes profits of an income nature as distinct from capital profits.[4]

Secondly, under the rule in *Jones* v. *Leeming*,[5] a profit derived from a transaction of purchase and resale is not assessable under Case VI.

> In *Jones* v. *Leeming*,[5] L. and three others obtained options to purchase two rubber estates in the Malay Peninsula, which they later sold at a profit. The Commissioners found that the transaction was not a concern in the nature of trade. *Held*, that the profits were not assessable under Case VI.

" It seems to me," said Lawrence L.J., " that in the case of an isolated transaction of purchase and resale of property there is really no middle course open. It is either an adventure in the nature of trade, or else it is simply a case of sale and resale of property." [6] A sum paid as consideration for the surrender or withdrawal of a legal claim is not assessable under Case VI, for such a transaction would involve the realisation of an asset; nor does Case VI apply where the claimant has only a moral claim or nuisance value.[7]

Thirdly, only profits or gains which are *ejusdem generis* with the profits or gains specified in the preceding five Cases of Schedule D are chargeable

---

[1] *Ante*, §§ 2-88 *et seq.*
[2] I.C.T.A. 1970, s. 109.
[3] Examples are balancing charges (§§ 13-12 *et seq.*); see also Sections 2 and 3 of Chap. 40.
[4] *Scottish Provident Institution* v. *Farmer* (1912) 6 T.C. 34, *per* Lord Inglis at p. 38.
[5] [1930] A.C. 415; 15 T.C. 333 (H.L.).
[6] *Leeming* v. *Jones* [1930] 1 K.B. 279 at p. 301; 15 T.C. 333 at p. 354.
[7] *Scott* v. *Ricketts* (1967) 44 T.C. 303 (C.A.). A sum paid for the surrender of a legal claim might now be chargeable to capital gains tax: see F.A. 1965, s. 22 (3) (c): § 16-08.

under Case VI.[8] For this reason, voluntary gifts,[9] betting winnings [10] and receipts by finding [10] are not chargeable under Case VI.

2. ANNUAL PROFITS ASSESSABLE UNDER CASE VI

4-02 A profit may be assessable under Case VI as an " annual " profit even though it arises from a service rendered on an isolated occasion and outside the normal business of the taxpayer. Thus in *Ryall* v. *Hoare*,[10] a commission paid to directors for guaranteeing an overdraft without security was held to be assessable; and the same principle was applied in *Lyons* v. *Cowcher* [11] where a commission was paid for underwriting shares. In *Brocklesby* v. *Merricks*,[12] a contention that a sum paid to an architect for services rendered by him was in the nature of a voluntary gift was rejected in view of evidence of an enforceable contract for remuneration for those services. In *Hale* v. *Shea* [13] the whole of an annual sum paid to a retiring partner by the continuing partner, as consideration both for the retiring partner's share of profits and his agreement to act as consultant if so requested, and which on the construction of the relevant document it was found impossible to apportion as between the two items of consideration, was held to be assessable under Case VI, and not to be earned income.

The question whether a payment is made for services, or is a gift, or is the price of an asset, is a question of fact.

> In *Hobbs* v. *Hussey*,[14] the appellant (who was not an author by profession) contracted with a newspaper to write his reminiscences in a series of articles for £1,500. The contract involved the sale of the appellant's copyright in the series, which had not been written at the time the contract was made. An assessment was raised on the £1,500.

It was argued that the payment was for the sale of copyright and, therefore, escaped assessment under the rule in *Jones* v. *Leeming* [15]; but the court held that the true nature of the transaction was the performance of services and that any sale of copyright was merely incidental thereto.[16]

The income of furnished lettings may be assessed under Case VI [17]; also the income from leasing chattels otherwise than in the course of a trade.[18] The profits of theatrical backers are now treated as assessable under Case VI, if Cases I and II of Schedule D do not apply.[19]

[8] *Att.-Gen.* v. *Black* (1871) L.R. 6 Ex. 308; 1 T.C. 54.

[9] *Turner* v. *Cuxon* (1888) 22 Q.B.D. 150; 2 T.C. 422.

[10] *Ryall* v. *Hoare* [1923] 2 K.B. 447; 8 T.C. 521. See also *Norman* v. *Evans* (1964) 42 T.C. 188 (sums received under leasing arrangement for racehorses, which included half the prize money, held to be assessable under Case VI).

[11] (1926) 10 T.C. 438.

[12] (1934) 18 T.C. 576 (C.A.). *Cf. Bloom* v. *Kinder* (1958) 38 T.C. 77.

[13] (1964) 42 T.C. 260. See § 8-12 note 20.

[14] [1942] 1 K.B. 491; 24 T.C. 153. See also *Housden* v. *Marshall* (1959) 38 T.C. 233.

[15] *Ante*, § 4-01.

[16] *Cf. Trustees of Earl Haig* v. *I.R.C.* (1939) 22 T.C. 725; *Beare* v. *Carter* [1940] 2 K.B. 187; 23 T.C. 353, where the sums were held to be capital receipts. It would seem that the taxpayers in *Hobbs* v. *Hussey* and *Housden* v. *Marshall* would have escaped tax if there had been an outright sale of copyright in articles written by them; but liability for capital gains tax would now have to be considered in such a case.

[17] *Wylie* v. *Eccott* (1913) 6 T.C. 128; and see *Ryall* v. *Hoare* (1923) 8 T.C. 521, *per* Rowlatt J. at p. 526. See also I.C.T.A. 1970, s. 67: Rule 4 of Schedule A, giving the landlord an option to be assessed under Schedule A: *post*, § 6-11 (27. As to the deductions which are allowed in computing profits of furnished lettings, see Simon's *Taxes*, C 3.206.   [18] See *Norman* v. *Evans*, in note 10.

[19] Hence losses can be set off against other Case VI income: see § 4-05. At one time backers' profits were treated as Case III income and losses as capital losses.

4-03   It will be observed that all the cases which have been referred to of income assessable under Case VI are cases of casual profits for services rendered, where there is no office or employment to bring the profits under Schedule E and no trade, profession or vocation to bring them under Schedule D, Cases I or II. A case in which income of a different character was held to be assessable under Case VI was *Cooper* v. *Stubbs*,[20] where the facts were as follows:

> S. was a member of a firm of cotton brokers and cotton merchants and it was the practice of such firms to deal in " futures," *i.e.* to make contracts to purchase cotton in the future, not with a view to taking delivery but as a hedge against fluctuations in the market. S. had a number of private dealings in futures. The Commissioners found that these were *gambling* transactions and that the profits were not assessable under Case I of Schedule D. *Held*, that Case VI applied.

They were, said Warrington L.J., " dealings and transactions entered into with a view to producing, in the result, income or revenue for the person who entered into them." It would seem from this decision that profits from activities which are *ejusdem generis* with trade but which lack some fundamental characteristic of trade may nevertheless be assessable under Case VI. *Cooper* v. *Stubbs* was followed in *Leader* v. *Counsell*,[21] where subscribers purchased a stallion and sold rights to nominations to the stallion. It was held that the profits were assessable under Case VI, this not being a case (as the taxpayer contended) which was excluded from Case VI as being a transaction of purchase and resale of property (see § 4-01). It is thought that the transactions in *Cooper* v. *Stubbs* (above) would now be held to constitute the carrying on of a trade notwithstanding the element of speculation involved.[22]

It would appear that there is some scope for the extension of Case VI beyond its existing limits.

3. COMPUTATION OF PROFITS UNDER CASE VI

4-04   Tax under Case VI is charged on the full amount of the profits or gains arising (*i.e.* received [23]) in the year of assessment.[24] Although there is no express provision in the Act for deduction of expenses, it seems clear from the use of the phrase " profits or gains " that the charge is limited to the excess of the receipts over such expenses as are necessary to earn them. In this respect Case VI differs from Case III, considered in the next chapter, under which no relief for expenses is available. Case VI income is investment income: see § 8-07 (4).

Losses

4-05   Where a loss is sustained in a transaction falling under Case VI, relief is available under section 176 of the Income and Corporation Taxes Act 1970

---

[20] [1925] 2 K.B. 753; 10 T.C. 29 (C.A.).
[21] [1942] 1 K.B. 364; 24 T.C. 178.
[22] Since the decision in *Edwards* v. *Bairstow and Harrison* (*ante*, § 2-03) the courts have been less reluctant to interfere with the decision of Commissioners on the question whether a transaction can in law constitute " trading."
[23] *Grey* v. *Tiley* (1932) 16 T.C. 414.   [24] I.C.T.A. 1970, s. 125.

by setting off the loss against other Case VI income of the same or a subsequent year. No relief is available against income from any other source, so the taxpayer with a source of Case VI income is less favourably treated in respect of losses than a taxpayer with a source of income falling under Case I or II of Schedule D.

An individual with casual profits from writing, for example, is more favourably treated as regards losses if he can satisfy the Revenue that he is carrying on the vocation of an author (to which Case II of Schedule D applies), for losses may be relieved against other income of the same or any following year.[25]

---

[25] *Ibid.*, s. 171 discussed *post*, §§ 12-02 *et seq.*

CHAPTER 5

THE TAXATION OF PURE PROFIT INCOME: SCHEDULE D

CASE III: SECTIONS 52 AND 53

1. THE CHARGING PROVISION

5-01 TAX under Schedule D Case III is charged [1] on the following:

(1) Any interest of money, whether yearly or otherwise, or any annuity or other annual payment, whether such payment is payable within or out of the United Kingdom, either as a charge on any property of the person paying the same by virtue of any deed or will or otherwise, or as a reservation out of it, or as a personal debt or obligation by virtue of any contract, or whether received and payable half-yearly or at any shorter or more distant periods, but excluding any payment chargeable under Schedule A;

(2) all discounts [2];

(3) income from securities bearing interest payable out of the public revenue, except income charged under Schedule C [3];

(4) certain income specifically directed to be charged under Case III, such as:

    (i) small maintenance payments [4];

    (ii) savings bank interest (if not exempted) [5];

    (iii) loan and share interest paid by industrial and provident societies without deduction of tax. [6]

In this book, only income falling under (1) and (4) (i) is discussed in any detail. Note that dividends and other distributions from the resources of a company are not taxed under Schedule D: see §§ 14-40 *et seq.*

2. INTEREST, ANNUITIES AND OTHER ANNUAL PAYMENTS

Interest, annuities and annual payments

5-02 *Interest* has been judicially defined as " payment by time for the use of money " [7] and as compensation paid by the borrower to the lender for deprivation of use of his money. [8] Where a loan transaction provides for the payment of a premium on redemption, it depends on the nature of the transaction and the surrounding circumstances whether the premium is " interest " or merely a sum paid to recompense the lender for the risk taken in advancing the loan. Generally, where a loan is made at or above a

---

[1] I.C.T.A. 1970, s. 109. The charge is on the persons receiving or entitled to the income: *ibid.* s. 114.
[2] In practice, most discounts are trading receipts and Case III of Sched. D does not apply. See § 5-18.
[3] In practice, Schedule C usually applies (see § 5-17).
[4] I.C.T.A. 1970, s. 65; see § 5-05.   [5] *Ante,* § 1-16.
[6] I.C.T.A. 1970, s. 340.   [7] *Bennett* v. *Ogston* (1930) 15 T.C. 374, *per* Rowlatt J. at p. 379.
[8] *Riches* v. *Westminster Bank Ltd.* (1947) 28 T.C. 159 at p. 189. See also *Re Euro Hotel (Belgravia) Ltd.* [1975] S.T.C. 682.

commercial rate of interest, any sum payable on redemption by way of premium will not be treated as interest.[9] Capital gains tax would be payable on such a sum if the debt was " a debt on a security." [10] Interest awarded by the court under the Law Reform (Miscellaneous Provisions) Act 1934, s. 3, is income chargeable under Case III.[11] In one case where a debenture provided for the payment of " interest " which exceeded the amount of the principal advanced and was payable within a few days after the advance, it was held that this was not interest in law.[12] If a principal debtor defaults in payment of interest and the debt is discharged by a third person pursuant to a contract of indemnity, the payment by the third person has been held itself to be a payment of " interest." [13] Under a contract of *indemnity,* the indemnifier may fall under a primary obligation to perform the debtor's obligations. The position is different in the case of a contract of *guarantee* and the proposition that " if a guarantor of rent pays under the guarantee, he pays rent "[14] must be open to question in view of more recent authority.[15] The difference between " yearly " and " non-yearly " or " short " interest is discussed in § 5-57.

5-03   *Annuity* describes an income which is purchased (usually from an insurance company) with a principal sum which then ceases to exist. It also describes an annual payment which is granted by an instrument. All annuities are " annual payments," [16] but not all annual payments are properly described as annuities.

5-04   *Other annual payments.* The meaning of this phrase was considered by the Court of Appeal in *I.R.C.* v. *Whitworth Park Coal Co. Ltd.*[17] and the following propositions held to be established:

(1) Other annual payments must be construed *ejusdem generis* with interest and annuity. (Thus if X joins a firm of solicitors on terms that he contributes £10,000 on joining plus £2,000 a year for five years, the latter payments are not annual payments.)

(2) The payment must be made under some binding legal obligation, *e.g.* a court order or contract [18] or deed poll, *e.g.* a voluntary deed of covenant. Gifts, however recurrent, are not annual payments. Payments made by trustees in the exercise of a discretion vested in them may be annual payments within Case III, even though the trustees might (consistently with their trust) have made no

[9] *Lomax* v. *Dixon* [1943] K.B. 671; 25 T.C. 353 (C.A.). See especially Lord Greene at pp. 682 and 367 respectively. *Cf. Davies* v. *Premier Investment Co. Ltd.* (1945) 27 T.C. 27.
[10] F.A. 1965, Sched. 7, para. 11 (1); *post*, § 16-14.
[11] *Riches* v. *Westminster Bank Ltd.* [1947] A.C. 390; 28 T.C. 159 (H.L.).
[12] *Ridge Securities Ltd.* v. *I.R.C.* (1964) 44 T.C. 373 at pp. 393F-394.
[13] See *Re Hawkins decd.* [1972] Ch. 714; *cf. Westminster Bank Executor and Trustee Co. (Channel Islands) Ltd.* v. *National Bank of Greece (S.A.)* (1970) 46 T.C. 472 at pp. 485 and 494.
[14] *Holder* v. *I.R.C.* (1932) 16 T.C. 540 (H.L.) at p. 565, *per* Lord Atkin.
[15] *Lep Air Services* v. *Rolloswin* [1973] A.C. 331 at p. 348, *per* Lord Diplock. And see *Holder* v. *I.R.C.* (1932) 16 T.C. 540 (H.L.) at p. 567, *per* Lord Thankerton.
[16] Note that T.M.A. 1970, s. 106 (2), discussed in § 5-48, makes void agreements for the payment of " interest, rent or other annual payment " without allowing for deduction of tax. The section clearly applies to annuities, although they are not expressly mentioned.
[17] [1958] Ch. 792 at pp. 815 *et seq., per* Jenkins L.J.; 38 T.C. 531 at pp. 548 *et seq.*
[18] *Peters' Executors* v. *I.R.C* (1941) 24 T.C. 45 (C.A.) (oral agreement made on separation of spouses).

payment [19]; once the trustees exercise their discretion in favour of a beneficiary, the payment is one to which the beneficiary was entitled by virtue of the gift made by the settlor and has the character of income in his hands. [20] Dividends which are not due unless and until they are declared are not annual payments [21]; nor is a payment which is *ultra vires* the company making it. [22]

(3) The payment must possess the quality of recurrence, which it may do even though the amount may be variable and/or the payments contingent.

Thus in *Moss' Empires Ltd.* v. *I.R.C.* [23] the appellants guaranteed to make up the profits of a company if they fell below a certain amount. It was held that the payments under the guarantees were " annual " even though they were both variable and subject to a contingency.

The fact that payments are to be made weekly or monthly does not prevent the payments being " annual " provided they may continue beyond a year. [24] Periodic payments under separation agreements and under orders made by the court, *e.g.* on divorce, are examples of annual payments.

Not all " annual payments " fall within the scope of Case III of Schedule D: see §§ 5-12 *et seq.*

Small maintenance payments [25]

5-05   Small maintenance payments are payments made under an order made by a court in the United Kingdom (a) by one of the partners to a marriage (including a marriage which has been dissolved or annulled) to or for the benefit of the other party to that marriage for that other party's maintenance, or (b) to any person for the benefit of, or for the maintenance or education of, a person under 21, not being a payment within (a). Payments within (a) must not exceed £21 weekly or £91 monthly. Payments within (b) must not exceed £12 weekly or £52 monthly. Such payments are made without deduction of tax and the recipient is assessable under Case III of Schedule D on payments falling due in the year of assessment.

3. THE BASIS OF ASSESSMENT UNDER CASE III

5-06   Generally tax is charged on the full amount (without any deduction) of the income arising in the year preceding the year of assessment. [26]

---

[19] *Lindus and Hortin* v. *I.R.C.* (1933) 17 T.C. 442; *Cunard's Trustees* v. *I.R.C.* (1946) 27 T.C. 122 (C.A.). These were cases in which trustees were empowered to augment income of a life-tenant out of the *capital* of the trust fund: see *post*, § 9-09.

[20] *Drummond* v. *Collins* [1915] A.C. 1011 at pp. 1019–1021; 6 T.C. 525 (H.L.) at pp. 540–541, *per* Lord Wrenbury.

[21] *Canadian Eagle Oil Co.* v. *R.* [1946] A.C. 119 at p. 135; 27 T.C. 205 at p.245, *per* Viscount Simon.

[22] *Ridge Securities Ltd.* v. *I.R.C.* (1964) 44 T.C. 373 at pp. 395–396 (where the alleged annual payments were unlawful gifts by the company).

[23] [1937] A.C. 785; 21 T.C. 264 (H.L.).   [24] *Taylor* v. *Taylor* [1938] 1 K.B. 320.

[25] I.C.T.A. 1970, s. 65. The weekly and monthly limits stated in the text apply to new orders made after April 30, 1977, to payments under orders varied or reviewed after that date which fall due after the variation or revival, and otherwise to payments falling due after April 5, 1975, under orders in force at April 30, 1977: The Income Tax (Small Maintenance Payments) Order 1977 in (1977) S.T.I. 104.

[26] *Ibid.* s. 119.

Thus if A has a bank deposit account, he is assessed in 1976–77 on the income which arises in 1975–76, *i.e.* on the interest credited to his account in June and December 1975.

Income does not " arise " until it is received by or credited to the taxpayer [27]: thus A (in the example) is not taxed in 1976–77 on the interest which his deposit earns between December 1975 and April 5, 1976; this interest is credited in June 1976 and taxed as income of 1977–78.

5-07   There are special rules which apply where the taxpayer acquires a fresh source of Case III income or where a source ceases. Normally, in the year when the income first arises and in the next year, the assessment is on the income actually arising in those years [28]:

Thus if A opens a bank deposit account on May 15, 1976, he is assessed in 1976–77 on the interest credited in June and December 1976; and he is assessed in 1977–78 on the interest credited in June and December 1977.

In the next year, 1978–79, the normal preceding tax year basis applies and A is assessed on the interest credited in June and December 1977, *i.e.* in the same amounts as for 1977–78; but this is subject to the taxpayer's right to elect that the first assessment on the preceding tax year basis should be adjusted to the actual income arising in that year, *i.e.* to the interest credited in June and December 1978. The taxpayer has six years in which so to elect. [29]

Where a source of Case III income ceases, tax for the year of cessation is assessed on the income arising in that year, and the assessment for the penultimate year (which will have already been made on the preceding tax year basis) will be adjusted to the actual basis, if this gives a greater tax liability. [30] If the taxpayer acquires a new source, or an addition to an existing source, of Case III income the commencement provisions apply thereto:

Thus in *Hart* v. *Sangster* [31] it was held that a deposit of £2 million in an existing deposit account constituted a new source of income to which the commencement provisions of Case III applied.

It is understood not to be the practice of the Revenue to apply this principle strictly.

Small maintenance payments are assessed under Case III on a current year basis: see § 5-05.

Deduction of tax at the source

5-08   Interest, annuities and other annual payments taxable under Case III of Schedule D are generally subject to the system by which income tax at the basic rate is deducted by the payer and collected from him by the Revenue. This system is discussed in detail in Section 4 of this chapter.

If interest on a debt is payable subject to deduction of income tax but

---

[27] *Whitworth Park Coal Co. Ltd.* v. *I.R.C.* [1961] A.C. 31; 38 T.C. 531 (H.L.).
[28] I.C.T.A. 1970, s. 120.
[29] *Ibid.* s. 120 (1) (c).
[30] *Ibid.* s. 120 (1) (c).
[31] (1956) 37 T.C. 231 (C.A.). A transfer of money on deposit with a bank to current account may cause a cessation of the Case III source, namely, the deposit: *Cull* v. *Cowcher* (1934) 18 T.C. 449.

then ceases to be payable subject to deduction, the debt is treated as a new source of income for the purposes of applying the Case III commencement provisions referred to above. Likewise if the debt begins to be payable subject to deduction of income tax, the cessation provisions apply as if the debt were a source of income which the creditor ceased to possess at that time.[32]

" Receivability without receipt "

5-09   Case III income is taxed on an arising basis and it has been held that income " arises " for this purpose when it is received,[33] or enures for the taxpayer's benefit.[34] Thus if interest, an annuity or other annual payment which is due in a year is not paid in that year, whether through default on the part of the debtor or a waiver of rights before the income arises on the part of the creditor, no Case III income arises in that year. " Receivability without receipt is nothing." [35]

5-10   If payment is made in arrears the question arises whether this is Case III income of the year in which payment is made or of the earlier year in which payment was due; and this may be an especially important consideration if the payee's income, or rates of tax, differ in the two years. If the payment is one from which tax is not deducted before receipt, such as interest paid by a bank, the income is income of the year in which payment is made and is taxed on the basis set out in §§ 5-06 *et seq.* If, however, the payment is one from which tax is deducted before receipt, the position differs according to whether deduction is made under section 52, 53 or 54 of the Income and Corporation Taxes Act 1970. In cases where section 52 applies, the income is income of the year in which payment is due; but where section 53 or section 54 applies, it is income of the year when payment was made: § 8-18.

5-11   Tax reliefs available to the person who makes payments which are Case III income of the payee are governed by similar principles: that is, no relief is given until payment is actually made; and relief is given (broadly speaking) in the same year as that in which the payee is taxed.

4. THE SCOPE OF CASE III

The concept of pure profit income

5-12   The Case III charging provisions give no relief for expenses; indeed, it is assumed that no expense will be incurred in earning Case III income. Where expense has to be incurred in earning income, such income disqualifies itself from treatment as Case III income. The phrase " pure income profit " or " pure profit income ". or " pure income " has been used to describe this category of income.

> " The words of Case III . . . make this much plain: that the legislature is there taxing sums which are a profit in the true sense of the word in the hands of the recipient. The full amount is to suffer the tax and there is to be no

[32] I.C.T.A. 1970, ss. 120 (4), 121 (2).   [33] See n. 27 above.
[34] See *Dunmore* v. *McGowan* (1978) S.T.C. 217 (C.A.).
[35] *Leigh* v. *I.R.C.* [1928] 1 K.B. 73; (1928) 11 T.C. 590, 595, *per* Rowlatt J. And see *Lambe* v. *I.R.C.* [1934] 1 K.B. 178; (1934) 18 T.C. 212; *Dewar* v. *I.R.C.* [1935] 2 K.B. 351; (1935) 19 T.C. 561 (C.A.).

deduction from the full amount. When I receive interest from my debtor or an annuity from whomever is obliged to pay me one, I receive a sum which comes to me in its entirety as a profit. I do not have to set some expenses against the interest or the annuity to find out what the profit content is. It is all profit—at least in contemplation of Case III. To distinguish such a receipt from a receipt against which expenses must be set in order to discover the profit, various expressions are used. Interest and annual payments caught by Case III are said to be income *eo nomine* or ' pure income ' or ' profit income.' It does not matter much what label one uses so long as one makes it plain what is being labelled. I will use the term ' profit income ' to denote that kind of annual payment which the legislature has in mind under Case III, namely an annual payment which for tax purposes is all profit in the recipient's hands." [36]

5-13　　The following examples show what is, and is not, Case III income. By a separation agreement a husband agrees or is ordered to pay his wife £x a year. This is an " annual payment " within Case III of Schedule D. It is pure profit income of the wife. By contrast, A agrees to pay his garage (B) £x a year in consideration of B agreeing to maintain A's car at no further cost to A. B is a trader taxed under Case I of Schedule D on the excess of his trading receipts (including the £x received from A) over his trading expenses (including the actual cost of maintaining A's car). The £x in this case is not pure profit income of B. Similarly, if C pays his club £x a year and is entitled to certain benefits or facilities in consideration for his subscription, the £x is not pure profit income of the club. In neither of these cases is the £x an annual payment within Case III of Schedule D. The £x is no more than an element to be taken into account in determining the taxable income of the recipient. To such a payment it would be inappropriate to apply the system by which income tax at the basic rate is deducted by the payer (see §§ 5-30 *et seq.*) which applies only to annual payments, etc. within Case III of Schedule.D.

5-14　　In *Earl Howe* v. *I.R.C.* [37] the question arose whether premiums paid on a policy of assurance were annual payments within the scope of Case III of Schedule D. If they were, Earl Howe (the payer) would have been entitled to deduct them in computing his total income. In a frequently quoted passage Scrutton L.J. said this:

> ". . . if a man agrees to pay a motor garage £500 a year for five years for the hire and upkeep of a car, no one suggests the person paying can deduct income tax from each yearly payment. So, if he contracted with a butcher for an annual sum to supply all his meat for a year, the annual instalment would not be subject to tax as a whole in the hands of the payee, but only that part of it which was profits. . . ."

The premiums were thus held not to be Case III income of the payee (in whose hands they were a trading receipt) and the Earl's claim to a deduction failed. The principle so stated by Scrutton L.J., which takes trading and professional receipts outside the ambit of Case III, is sometimes called " the *Earl Howe* principle."

---

[36] *I.R.C.* v. *Corporation of London (as Conservators of Epping Forest)* (1953) 34 T.C. 293, *per* Donovan J. at p. 303 (whose actual decision was reversed by the House of Lords).

[37] [1919] 2 K.B. 336; 7 T.C. 289. See also *Asher* v. *London Film Productions Ltd.* [1944] 1 K.B. 33. (Where, following the cancellation of his service agreement, A entered into an agreement under which he was to receive 60 per cent. of the takings (if any) in excess of £110,000 from two motion pictures: *held*, to be annual payments from which the payer could properly deduct tax.)

5-15   In the more recent case of *Campbell* v. *I.R.C.* [38] Lord Donovan said that the problem whether an annual payment was Case III income of the recipient

> ". . . must continue to be resolved, in my opinion, on the lines laid down by Scrutton L.J. in *Earl Howe's* case. One must determine, in the light of all the relevant facts, whether the payment is a taxable receipt in the hands of the recipient without any deduction for expenses or the like—whether it is, in other words ' pure income ' or ' pure profit income ' in his hands, as those expressions have been used in the decided cases. If so, it will be an annual payment under Case III. If, on the other hand, it is simply gross revenue in the recipient's hands, out of which a taxable income will emerge only after his outgoings have been deducted, then the payment is not such an annual payment. . . ."

Payments outside the scope of Case III

The following classes of payment fall outside the scope of Case III of Schedule D:

5-16   (1) *Payments chargeable under Schedule A*. Such payments are expressly excluded by section 109 (2) of the Income and Corporation Taxes Act 1970. Thus rentcharges and any other annual payments reserved in respect of, or charged on or issuing out of land in the United Kingdom, are chargeable only under Schedule A: see §§ 6-10 *et seq.*

5-17   (2) *Payments chargeable under Schedule C*. Income from interest-bearing securities payable out of the public revenue which is chargeable under Schedule C is not chargeable under Case III of Schedule D. In practice Schedule C usually applies. Securities chargeable under Case III include 3½ per cent. War Loan and stock held on the National Savings Stock Register or Trustee Savings Bank Register.

5-18   (3) *Payments which are not pure profit income of the recipient*. This concept has been discussed in general terms in §§ 5-12 *et seq.* Payments which are receipts of a trade, profession or vocation carried on by the recipient are not pure profit income of the recipient and so fall outside the scope of Case III. The principle was illustrated in the extract from the speech of Scrutton L.J. in *Earl Howe's* case: see § 5-14; and it explains why, for example, copyright royalties earned by an author carrying on a vocation as such are not chargeable under Case III. [39]

> In *British Commonwealth International Newsfilm Agency Ltd.* v. *Mahany* [40] the appellant company was set up by the Rank Organisation (" Rank ") and the BBC to provide a newsfilm service. Under a deed of covenant Rank and the BBC each agreed to make annual payments to the appellant company equal to half its annual deficit. Pursuant to this covenant Rank paid the appellant company its " share " of the deficit, deducting tax at the standard rate. The appellant company claimed repayment of the tax so deducted, which it could do if the annual payments were Case III income of the appellant company. *Held*, refusing the claim (i) that the payments were trade receipts of the

---

[38] [1970] A.C. 77; 45 T.C. 427 (H.L.).
[39] *Stainer's Executors* v. *Purchase* [1952] A.C. 280; 32 T.C. 367 (H.L.); *Carson* v. *Cheyney's Executors* [1959] A.C. 412; 38 T.C. 240 (H.L.).
[40] (1962) 40 T.C. 550 (H.L.).

appellant company because they were supplements to its trading revenue and were made to preserve its trading stability: they were trade subsidies; and (ii) that the payments were not therefore Case III income of the appellant company.

5-19   Payments which are made to a non-trader but are made in consideration of the provision of benefits or facilities to the payer are also disqualified from treatment as Case III income. Thus club subscriptions are not Case III income, and if they are paid under deduction of tax, the club cannot recover the tax from the Revenue.

> In *I.R.C.* v. *National Book League*,[41] the League (a charity) raised its membership subscription except for members who entered into seven-year covenants to pay their subscriptions at the then existing rates. Club facilities were available to members. A number of members executed covenants expressed as net sums after deduction of tax and the League claimed to recover tax in respect of the sums so paid on the ground that they were annual payments within Case III of Schedule D. *Held*, refusing the claim, that the payments were not annual payments.

The evidence in the *Book League* case

> " clearly established that the so-called annual payment was simply a club subscription in return . . . for the ' annual provision by the League of goods and services,' and so was clearly within the scope of the decision in *Earl Howe's* case." [42]

It should be noted that the principle in the *Earl Howe* case takes trading and professional receipts which are Case I or II income outside the charge under Case III: hence this is not a case in which the Revenue has an option to assess under one case or the other as it chooses.[43]

5-20   It does not follow from the principles stated in §§ 5-18 and 19 that *only* income which is pure bounty in the hands of the recipient falls within Case III of Schedule D. If an individual purchases an annuity from an insurance company, this is Case III income of the individual notwithstanding the absence of any bounty towards him; and property can be sold in exchange for an annuity.[44] It is only where the *Earl Howe* principle takes a payment out of the category of pure profit income that Case III does not apply. It is thought that the *Earl Howe* principle does not apply to annuities: see § 5-23.

5-21   The fact that the payee has expense to incur and the payer makes covenanted payments equal to the expense so incurred does not prevent the payments being pure profit income of the payee.[45]

5-22   *Annual payments to executors and trustees.* Executors or trustees may be rewarded for their services by an annuity or other annual payment. Consistently with the principle in the *Earl Howe* case it appears to be the practice of the Revenue to treat such remuneration as Case III income, except in the case of a professional executor or trustee who brings the payments into the computation of the profits of his profession under Case II of Schedule D.[46]

---

[41] [1957] Ch. 488; 37 T.C. 455 (C.A.).
[42] *Campbell* v. *I.R.C.* (1970) 45 T.C. 427, *per* Lord Donovan at p. 474C.
[43] *Stainer's Executors* v. *Purchase* (1952) 32 T.C. 367, *per* Jenkins L.J. at pp. 402–403.
[44] For other examples, see *Campbell* v. *I.R.C.* (1970) 45 T.C. 427, *per* Lord Donovan at pp. 473–474. See also paras. 5-27 *et seq*.
[45] See the *Epping Forest* case in note 36.
[46] *Jones* v. *Wright* (1927) 13 T.C. 221.

5-23   *Interest and annuities.* It is not clear from the Case III charging provision (see § 5-01) if the principle in the *Earl Howe* case applies to interest and annuities or only to annual payments. If the principle were so applied, interest or annuities which formed a constituent part of the trading receipts of a trader would fall altogether outside the scope of Case III and outside the system by which basic rate income tax is deducted by the payer on making the payment: § 5-56. Also the tax relief for interest payments applies only to Case III and bank interest: §§ 8-57 *et seq.* Interest earned by a trader whose stock-in-trade is money and who earns interest by the use of that money, as by borrowing at one rate and lending at a higher rate, is clearly capable of being a Case I trading receipt. Annuities also are capable of being Case I trading receipts in certain circumstances.[47] If the *Earl Howe* principle applied to interest and annuities, they would be excluded from the Case III charge on the authority of the *British Commonwealth* case discussed in § 5-18. The author is inclined to the view that the *Earl Howe* principle does not apply to interest and annuities. Interest and annuities are in all cases " chargeable " under Case III although, in some cases, they may be charged at the Revenue's option (see § 1-13) under Case I of Schedule D. See also § 8-57. This view appears to accord with Revenue practice. Assume, for example, that interest is paid to a finance company in circumstances where the interest could constitute a trade receipt. Assume that the payer deducts income tax on making the payment, so treating the payment as if Case III applied. Revenue practice is to exclude sums so paid under deduction of tax in computing Case I trading profits but to allow the payer such tax relief as is appropriate to the payment of interest chargeable under Case III: see § 2-49.

5-24   (4) *Payments which are not income of the recipient.* Annual payments which lack the quality of " income " in the hands of the recipient fall outside the scope of Case III of Schedule D, which applies only to income.

> In *Campbell* v. *I.R.C.*[48] a company carrying on business as tutors covenanted for seven years to pay 80 per cent. of its trading profits (less capital allowances) to trustees of a charitable trust, there being an understanding (held on the facts to constitute a legally binding obligation) that the trustees would apply the sums received together with any income tax recoverable in purchasing the company's business. The trustees claimed to recover the tax under what is now section 360 (1) (*c*) of the Income and Corporation Taxes Act 1970 on the grounds that the payments were annual payments within Case III of Schedule D which formed part of the income of the trustees. *Held*, that the payments were not income of the trustees.

This was a case, said Lord Donovan (at p. 473C) " where a person wishing to sell an asset provides the prospective purchaser with the purchase price. That seems to me as clear a case of a gift of capital as one could want." Viscount Dilhorne reached the same conclusion by a different route (at p. 463C):

---

[47] Interest treated as a trading receipt under Case I is taxed in the year of trading: *Bennett* v. *Ogston* (1930) 15 T.C. 374 at p. 379.

[48] (1970) 45 T.C. 427 (H.L.).

". . . in my opinion the condition as to the return of the money to (the company) deprived the payments of the character of income just as much as if, instead of the return of the money, the condition or counter-stipulation had been the provision of goods or services by the (trustees to the company)."

The correctness of this approach to the problem may be questioned since the existence of a condition to provide goods or services (as in the *National Book League* case: see § 5-19) does not deprive the payments of the character of income: it merely disqualifies the income from being treated as Case III income: see §§ 5-18 *et seq.*

5-25   *Campbell* [49] was a case in which the company financed the purchase by trustees of an asset which the company owned, the finance being provided by a seven-year covenant. There were three classes of transaction involved: (i) the provision of finance by the company under the covenant; (ii) the application of the covenanted sums in the purchase of the asset from the company; and (iii) the transfer of the asset to the trustees. *Campbell* was concerned only with the character for tax purposes of the payments made to the trustees under (i). The principles which govern the character for tax purposes of the payments made to the company under (ii), *i.e.* the character of annual payments made as the price of an asset, are considered in a later section of this chapter: see § 5-27.

5-26   (5) *Payments which have a source outside the United Kingdom.* Income which arises from securities or possessions out of the United Kingdom is chargeable under Case IV or V of Schedule D and not under Case III.

Thus in the *Greek Bank* [50] case, the A Bank issued bonds on which interest was payable in London or Athens, at the holder's option. The B Bank guaranteed A's liability under the bonds. The C Bank was universal successor of B. The A and B Banks were incorporated in Greece and neither Bank was resident in or carried on business in the United Kingdom. The C Bank was also incorporated in Greece and not resident in the United Kingdom but carried on business through a branch office in London. The proper law of the bonds and of the guarantee was English law. The C Bank paid interest to the plaintiff and deducted standard rate income tax. The plaintiff sued, claiming that the C Bank had no right to deduct such tax. *Held,* on the facts, that the interest arose from a foreign source and that Case III did not apply. Hence income tax was wrongly deducted.

Annual payments distinguished from instalments of capital
5-27   There is authority for the propositions (1) that if A sells property to B for £10,000 to be paid by instalments of £1,000 without interest, the whole of each instalment is capital; whereas (2) if A sells property to B for ten instalments of £1,000 (*i.e.* with no reference to a lump sum), the whole of each instalment is income. [51] Proposition (1) rests on the principle that paying for property by instalments is like paying off a debt by instalments: the instalments take their character as capital from the antecedent debt or

---

[49] *Ibid.*
[50] *Westminster Bank Executor and Trustee Co. (Channel Islands)* v. *National Bank of Greece (S.A.)* [1971] A.C. 945; 46 T.C. 472 (H.L.).
[51] *I.R.C.* v. *Ramsay* (1935) 20 T.C. 79, *per* Romer L.J. at p. 98; *I.R.C.* v. *Wesleyan and General Assurance Society* (1948) 30 T.C. 11, *per* Lord Greene M.R. at p. 16.

the lump sum expressed in the contract.[52] Proposition (2) rests on the principle that if A purchases an annuity with money or money's worth, the annuity is wholly income.

> In *I.R.C.* v. *Ramsay* [53] R. agreed to purchase a dental practice for £15,000. R. was to pay £5,000 at once and the balance by 10 yearly instalments equal to one-fourth of the net profits of the practice in each of those years. If the annual payments came to more or less than the balance of the purchase price (£10,000), that price was to be treated as correspondingly increased or diminished. *Held*, that the yearly payments were capital and were not deductible in computing R.'s total income for surtax purposes.

These propositions have the attraction of simplicity but they fail to take account of the fact that a commercial bargain which provides for payment by instalments over a period of years will invariably require the purchaser to pay interest. Not surprisingly therefore there have been a number of cases in which the courts have had to consider whether, if property is sold for a lump sum payable by instalments, the instalments can be dissected into capital and income (being the interest element). If an asset has a market value of £10,000 and payment is to be made by instalments, there are two principal ways in which interest can be included in the instalments:

(a) By the purchaser agreeing to purchase the asset for £10,000 and to pay instalments of £1,000 plus interest at an agreed rate. Assume an instalment comes to £1,200. It is clear that the instalment will be treated for tax purposes as made up of capital (£1,000) and income (£200).[54]

(b) By increasing the lump sum to allow for interest so that, *e.g.* the purchaser agrees to pay (say) £30,000 by 10 instalments of £3,000. In the early case of *Foley* v. *Fletcher* [55] (in which the purchaser treated the whole of each instalment as income, apparently on the ground that some part of it must have represented interest but, since the contract did not enable him to quantify that part, he was entitled to treat the whole as income), the court refused to dissect the instalments into capital and income on the ground that there was no warrant for this in the Taxing Acts and held that the whole of each instalment was capital. The significant feature of this case was that there was no *evidence* that the property was worth less than the lump sum provided for in the contract.

In *Vestey* v. *I.R.C.* [56] V. sold shares valued at £2 million for the sum of £5·5 million payable without interest by 125 yearly instalments of £44,000. Although the agreement contained no provision for interest there was evidence

---

[52] *Dott* v. *Brown* [1936] 1 All E.R. 543 (C.A.); *Jones* v. *I.R.C.* [1920] 1 K.B. 711; 7 T.C. 310. In *I.R.C.* v. *Mallaby-Deeley* (1938) 23 T.C. 153 at p. 169 Sir Wilfrid Greene M.R. said: " . . . If there is a real liability to pay a capital sum, either pre-existing or then assumed, that capital sum has a real existence, and, if the method adopted of paying it is a payment by instalments, the character of those instalments is settled by the nature of the capital sum to which they are related. If there is no pre-existing capital sum, but the covenant is to pay a capital sum by instalments, the same result will follow."
[53] (1935) 20 T.C. 79 (C.A.).
[54] *Secretary of State for India* v. *Scoble* [1903] A.C. 299; 4 T.C. 618 (H.L.). In this case the instalments were described as an *annuity* but it was held that this did not determine the character of the payments for tax purposes.
[55] (1853) 3 H. & N. 769; 157 E.R. 678.
[56] *Vestey* v. *I.R.C.* (1961) 40 T.C. 112.

before the Commissioners that the shares were worth £2 million; that if one pays £2 million by annual instalments over 125 years with interest on the unpaid balance at 2 per cent. per annum, the instalments amount to £44,000 per annum; and that the purchasers were so advised by an actuary and acted on this advice. *Held* that the instalments should be dissected into capital and income.

It follows that proposition (1), above, is true only if the lump sum for which the property is agreed to be sold is the value of the property at the time of the contract of sale.

5-28   In *I.R.C.* v. *Church Commissioners,*[57] the Church Commissioners owned properties which were let to Investment Trust Ltd. (" Land Securities ") for rents totalling £40,000 per annum. By an agreement of January 5, 1960, the Church Commissioners agreed to sell the properties to Land Securities for yearly rentcharges issuing out of the properties which were payable for 10 years and totalled £96,000 per annum. On paying the rentcharges, Land Securities deducted income tax at the standard rate. The Church Commissioners, being a charity, claimed repayment of the income tax so deducted.

The Revenue rejected the claim on two grounds. First, the claim was rejected on the broad ground (so expressed in argument) that there is a general principle of tax law that where a capital asset is transferred, or a capital obligation is discharged, or a capital payment is made, in consideration of a series of cash receipts of a *fixed* amount over a *fixed* period, so that the total debt may be immediately calculated, then those cash receipts are, in the hands of the recipient, partly income and partly capital, whether the parties call the series of cash receipts " rent " or " annuity " or " annual sums " or " rentcharges " or " instalments," and whether the payments are secured or unsecured. Secondly, the claim was rejected on the narrower ground, and in reliance on the decision in *Vestey* (§ 5-27, above) that the real bargain between the parties as revealed by certain documents which had been admitted in evidence as showing the negotiations leading up to the agreement of January 5, 1960, was such as to require dissection of the rentcharges into an income and capital element.

5-29   The House of Lords unanimously allowed the Church Commissioners' claim, holding, as regards the first ground, that the propositions stated in the first sentence of § 5-27, above, are now too firmly entrenched in tax law to be displaced otherwise than by legislation. As regards the second ground, it was held that on the true construction of the agreement of January 5, 1960, the payments were of an income character and that the admitted evidence merely confirmed that the bargain had always been conceived in income terms. In this respect the present case was distinguishable on its facts from the *Vestey* case which Lord Wilberforce described as " the high water mark of dissection cases." The large difference between the purchase price of £5½ million and the £2 million which represented the value of the shares at the date of the contract, the fact that payment was spread over 125 years and the absence in the contract in the *Vestey* case of any provision for interest made that case distinguishable from the *Church Commissioners*

---

[57] [1977] A.C. 329; 50 T.C. 516; [1976] S.T.C. 339 (H.L.).

case. Significantly, too, the Church Commissioners merely replaced one form of income (rents) with another (rentcharge income).

5. COLLECTION OF TAX AT THE SOURCE: SECTIONS 52 AND 53

5-30   Interest, annuities and other annual payments are the most important forms of income falling under Case III of Schedule D. Annuities and annual payments (and interest in some cases) are subject to the system by which basic rate income tax is deducted by the payer at the time when he makes the payment and collected from him by the Revenue. This system of collection must now be examined in some detail. The system applies to payments made by the Crown: § 1-17. Interest is separately considered in §§ 5-55 *et seq.* of this chapter.

The Income and Corporation Taxes Act 1970 distinguishes between annuities and other annual payments charged with tax under Case III of Schedule D which are payable out of " profits or gains brought into charge to tax " (s. 52) and those not so payable (s. 53).

> *Example*: X, who carries on a trade, covenants to pay £160 to Y on June 30 each year. In the year ended December 31, 1973, X's trading profits are £1,400; in the year ended December 31, 1974, X's profits are nil. These profits are the income of X for the years 1974–75 and 1975–76 respectively. Section 52 applies to the payment of £160 due in 1974–75; section 53 applies to the payment of £160 due in 1975–76.

Payments out of chargeable profits: section 52

5-31   Under section 52 of the Income and Corporation Taxes Act 1970, where any annuity or other annual payment charged with tax under Case III of Schedule D (not being interest) is payable wholly out of profits or gains brought into charge to income [58] tax, the payer is taxed on the whole of his profits without distinguishing the payment. The payer is entitled, on making the payment, to deduct and retain out of it a sum representing the amount of income tax thereon, *i.e.* income tax at the basic rate in force for the year of assessment in which the amount becomes due. [59]

> Thus, in the example in § 5-30, in the year in which the payment due on June 30, 1974, falls (1974–75), X has sufficient statutory income to support the annual payment. X deducts tax at the basic rate at the time the payment is due (£160 @ (say) 30 per cent. = £48) and pays Y the balance of £112, retaining the amount deducted.

The effect of section 52 can be seen if the position of each of the parties in the example is considered. [60]

5-32   *The payee.* The recipient of an annuity or other annual payment is entitled only to the net amount after deduction of tax at the basic rate for the year in which the payment is due, and is bound (under penalty) to allow

[58] Thus s. 52 does not apply to payments made by companies chargeable to corporation tax: s. 53 applies (I.C.T.A. 1970, s. 240 (4), *post*, § 14-09).

[59] I.C.T.A. 1970, s. 52 (1) (c), read with F.A. 1971, s. 36 (a).

[60] For a judicial analysis of ss. 52 and 53 (then Rules 19 and 21 respectively) see *Allchin* v. *Corporation of South Shields* [1943] A.C. 607; 25 T.C. 445 (H.L.), *per* Viscount Simon L.C. at pp. 618, 460, respectively; *I.R.C.* v. *Frere* [1965] A.C. 402; 42 T.C. 125 (H.L.), *per* Viscount Radcliffe.

the deduction.[61] Payment of the net amount is a full discharge by the payer of his obligation to the payee.[62] The amount deducted is treated as income tax paid by the payee. The gross amount of the payment will enter into the computation of the payee's total income so that (a) if he is not liable to bear tax at the basic rate, he can make a repayment claim; and (b) if he is liable to higher rate income tax or the investment income surcharge, the gross amount forms part of his total income for the year by reference to which basic rate tax was deducted.[63] See §§ 8-16 *et seq.*

5-33   *The payer.* A person who is liable to pay an amount by way of annuity or other annual payment is treated as having alienated part of his income to the payee. In strictness, therefore, if X (having trading income of £5,000) covenants to pay £2,000 annually to Y, Y ought to be assessed on £2,000 (under Case III of Schedule D) and X on £3,000 (under Case I). Section 52 however, directs that X should be assessed on the *whole* of his profits without distinguishing the payment; moreover, the annual payment is not deductible in the computation of X's trading profits, even if it was incurred for the purposes of X's trade.[64] X is relieved from tax on the income he alienates to Y in two ways: (a) when he makes the payment, X is entitled to deduct tax at the basic rate and to retain the amount deducted; (b) X is entitled to deduct the gross amount of the payment (£2,000) in the computation of his total income charged to higher rate and additional rate income tax.

For example see § 8-33.

Payments not made out of chargeable profits: section 53

5-34   Under section 53 of the Income and Corporation Taxes Act 1970, where any annuity or other annual payment charged with tax under Case III of Schedule D (not being interest) is not payable or not wholly payable out of profits or gains brought into charge to income tax, *i.e.* if it is payable wholly or in part out of a source other than profits or gains brought into charge,[65] the person by or through whom the payment is made must, on making the payment, deduct a sum representing the amount of income tax thereon, *i.e.* income tax at the basic rate in force for the year in which the payment is made.[66] Such person must then deliver to the Inspector an account of the payment and an assessment will be duly made to enable the Revenue to collect the tax so deducted.[67] Failure to deliver an account renders the person in default liable to a penalty.

> Thus in the example in § 5-30, in the year in which the payment due on June 30, 1975, fell (1975–76), X had insufficient income to support the annual payment. X deducts tax at the basic rate (under s. 53), but must account to the Revenue for the tax deducted.

---

[61] I.C.T.A. 1970, s. 52 (1) (*d*); T.M.A. 1970, s. 106; F.A. 1971, s. 36 (*a*).
[62] I.C.T.A. 1970, s. 52 (1) (*e*).
[63] I.C.T.A. 1970, s. 528 (3) (*a*).
[64] I.C.T.A. 1970, s. 130 (*l*).
[65] *Ibid.* s. 56.
[66] F.A. 1971, s. 36 (*b*). An annuity payable out of a superannuation fund to a U.K. resident may be taxed under Schedule E and not by deduction under s. 53: see I.C.T.A. 1970, s. 208 (3).
[67] I.C.T.A. 1970, s. 53 (2).

5-35   It should be observed that section 53 provides for the assessment of the person " by or through whom " the payment is made.

> In *Rye and Eyre* v. *I.R.C.*,[68] the appellants were solicitors of an individual who was about to form a company to produce a play written by M. Sacha Guitry whose usual place of abode was outside the United Kingdom. Under an agreement made by the individual with the author's agent, advance copyright royalties became payable to M. Guitry, which the solicitors remitted in full without deducting tax. Section 53 applied to the payment of royalties by virtue of section 25 of the Finance Act 1927, now section 391 of the Income and Corporation Taxes Act 1970. *Held*, that the solicitors were assessable in respect of the tax they ought to have deducted, for they were persons " through whom " the royalties were paid.

Where a person, acting in one capacity, pays interest to himself in another capacity, this is a payment " through " him.

> Thus in *Howells* v. *I.R.C.*,[69] a solicitor lent money to a builder on the security of properties in the course of development and was entitled to interest. The solicitor later acted for the builder in connection with the sale of the properties and he retained, out of the proceeds of sale, the principal due to him and the *net amount* of interest. *Held*, that the solicitor was liable to account to the Revenue under section 53 for income tax on the interest. [Section 53 then applied to interest as well as to annuities and other annual payments.]

The solicitor in *Howells's* case ought to have retained the gross amount of interest due to him out of which to meet his liability to account for basic rate income tax. Since, in practice, the solicitor in such a case will often have no means of knowing whether section 52 or section 53 applies, it is probably safer to effect the transaction by exchange of cheques, the solicitor accounting to his client for the proceeds of sale and the client accounting to his solicitor for the net amount of interest. In this way the solicitor is exonerated from any possible liability to account for tax.

5-36   The duty to account under section 53 arises only if and when " payment " is actually made.

> In *I.R.C.* v. *Oswald*,[70] it was held that the capitalisation of interest on non-payment thereof by a mortgagor was not a " payment " of interest.

The word " payment " in this context has been said to include everything which is in a commercial sense a " payment," including the making of credit entries in books of account.[71]

Which section applies?

5-37   The question whether section 52 or section 53 of the Income and Corporation Taxes Act 1970 applies to a payment is important to the payer because this determines his title to the sum which he deducts when making the payment. If section 52 applies, he may retain it; but if section 53 applies, he must generally account for it to the Revenue.[72] As regards the payee, if

---

[68] [1935] A.C. 274; 19 T.C. 164 (H.L.).
[69] [1939] 2 K.B. 597; 22 T.C. 501.
[70] [1945] A.C. 360; 26 T.C. 435 (H.L.).
[71] *Rhokana Corporation Ltd.* v. *I.R.C.* [1937] 1 K.B. 788 at p. 808; 21 T.C. 552 at p. 573, *per* Lord Wright M.R.
[72] See *ante*, §§ 5-30 *et seq*. See concession A20 in § 5-42.

section 52 applies the payment is included in his total income for the year when the payment is *due*; if section 53 applies the payment is included in his total income for the year when the payment is *made*: see § 8-18.

Section 52 applies to a payment which is " payable wholly out of profits or gains brought into charge to tax." Section 53 applies in any other case, *e.g.* if or to the extent that the profits are insufficient to cover the payment or if the payment can lawfully be made only out of capital.[73] Tax in section 52 means income tax, so section 53 applies to payments made by companies chargeable to corporation tax.[74] A payment which is deductible in computing profits chargeable to income tax is not payable *out of* such profits and section 53 applies.

5-38   " Profits or gains brought into charge to income tax " means income determined in accordance with the rules which apply for computing total income: see § 8-16. These rules require that income should be computed in accordance with the charging provisions applicable to the appropriate Schedule.[75] In the case, for example, of a trader whose accounting year ends on December 31 and whose only income is derived from the trade, his income for the year 1975–76 will be the profits for the year ended December 31, 1974 [76]; and any capital allowances or losses which are brought forward must be deducted from the profits for the purpose of determining whether the payer has sufficient profits or gains brought into charge to support the payment.[77]

5-39   In *Chancery Lane Safe Deposit and Offices Co. Ltd.* v. *I.R.C.*[78] Lord Morris said this:

> " . . . the perplexing words ' payable . . . out of profits or gains brought into charge to tax ' were fully analysed in the *Central London* case. The words ' payable out of ' are words which might often be used to denote an actual payment out of some actual fund. In [sections 52 and 53] the words involve a different conception. There is a statutory figure of ' profits or gains brought into charge to tax.' It is an assessment based at any rate so far as trading profits are concerned upon the actual results of the previous year. It is not, therefore, an actual fund. If the word ' fund ' is used in reference to it it must be classed as a notional fund. An annual payment, on the other hand, is not something notional; it is actual and real. But since, as Lord Macmillan has pointed out, you cannot make an actual payment out of a notional fund the word ' payable ' comes to mean notionally payable. It denotes, therefore, a right which the taxpayer may decide to exercise: he may attribute his payment as being within and under the statutory figure of his profits or gains brought into charge to tax. He can say that in paying tax on his profits or gains brought into charge to tax he has paid tax on the amount of a smaller annual payment which he has to make: he may, therefore, deduct tax in making such annual payment: the recipient must allow that deduction if it is made. It may be, however, that the taxpayer cannot link his annual payment with ' profits or gains brought

---

[73] *Sugden* v. *Leeds Corporation* [1914] A.C. 483; 6 T.C. 211 (H.L.).
[74] I.C.T.A. 1970, s. 240 (4).
[75] *Att.-Gen.* v. *L.C.C.* [1901] A.C. 26; 4 T.C. 265 (H.L.).
[76] *Att.-Gen.* v. *The Metropolitan Water Board* [1928] 1 K.B. 833; 13 T.C. 294 (C.A.).
[77] *Trinidad Petroleum Development Co. Ltd.* v. *I.R.C.* [1937] 1 K.B. 408; 21 T.C. 1 (C.A.); thus when losses are brought forward under I.C.T.A. 1970, s. 171 (*post*, § 12-02), and profits are rendered insufficient to cover annual payments, s. 53 applies.
[78] [1966] A.C. 85; 43 T.C. 83 (H.L.).

into charge to tax ': there may not be any: in that event the annual payment cannot be ' payable out ' of them: there cannot be any attribution to them. In that situation the taxpayer must deduct tax when making his annual payment. He is, so to speak, collecting the tax for the Revenue, to whom he must pay it. The same result will follow if the taxpayer firmly decides not to link and in fact does not link his annual payment with profits or gains. This may be so if he decides to make his annual payment out of capital."

5-40   Where the payer of an annuity or other annual payment has a mixed fund of (i) profits or gains brought into charge to income tax and (ii) profits or gains not so charged (*e.g.* capital) and the payment can lawfully be made in full out of either fund, the payment will normally be treated as made out of (i), with the result that section 52 applies, irrespective of the actual resources out of which the payment is made or is shown by the accounts to have been made.[79] Thus in *Postlethwaite* v. *I.R.C.*[80] in which trustees paid an annuity out of a mixed fund consisting of capital and accumulated income, Wilberforce J. said:

"   . . . I think it is not disputed that, there being in the trustees' accounts a mixed fund consisting partly of capital and partly of taxed income, and the trustees not having made any express declaration as to how the annuity was to be paid, it is open to the taxpayer [in that case the annuitant] to claim that payment has been made out of that portion of the trust fund which yields him the most favourable result for the purposes of taxation. That follows from the analogy of *Sugden* v. *Leeds Corporation*; and following that, it would be open to the taxpayer to say that the payment must be considered as having been made out of the former income element of the fund. I think it is accepted by both sides that the manner in which the trust accounts have been presented is not material in this respect."

5-41   Where, however, the payer of an annuity or other annual payment has secured some fiscal or other advantage by debiting the payment to capital[81] or has made a deliberate decision to charge the payment to capital,[82] section 53 applies even though the payer has sufficient taxed income to support the payment.

Thus in *Chancery Lane Safe Deposit and Offices Co. Ltd.* v. *I.R.C.,*[83] the appellant company borrowed to finance building works. Interest on the borrowings was charged to capital so as not to reduce the fund distributable as dividend. *Held,* the company could not make an inconsistent attribution for tax purposes.

5-42   If in the year when a payment is due and made the payer has insufficient chargeable income to cover the payment, the payer cannot avoid the

---

[79] *Edinburgh Life Assurance Co.* v. *Lord Advocate* [1910] A.C. 143; 5 T.C. 472; *Sugden* v. *Leeds Corporation*, in note 73; *Allchin* v. *Coulthard* [1942] 2 K.B. 228 at pp. 233 *et seq.*; [1943] A.C. 607 at p. 626; 25 T.C. 445 at p. 465.
[80] (1963) 41 T.C. 224.
[81] *Corporation of Birmingham* v. *I.R.C.* [1930] A.C. 307; 15 T.C. 172 (H.L.) (corporation paid interest out of an account drawn to show a deficit recoverable from Exchequer subsidy. Cost of interest shown as gross amount, *i.e.* consistent only with [section 53]. *Held*, corporation could be assessed).
[82] *Central London Ry* v. *I.R.C.* [1937] A.C. 77; 20 T.C. 102 (H.L.); applied in *B. W. Nobes & Co. Ltd.* v. *I.R.C.* (1965) 43 T.C. 133 (H.L.); *Chancery Lane Safe Deposit and Offices Co. Ltd.* v. *I.R.C.* [1966] A.C. 85; 43 T.C. 83 (H.L.); *Fitzleet Estates Ltd.* v. *Cherry* [1977] S.T.C. 95. For payments made by companies liable to corporation tax, see *post*, § 14-10 (1).
[83] [1966] A.C. 85; 43 T.C. 83 (H.L.).

consequences of section 53 by relating the payment back to accumulated profits of earlier years.

> Thus in *Luipaard's Vlei Estate and Gold Mining Co. Ltd.* v. *I.R.C.*[84] a company made no profits for four years. During those years the company paid debenture interest and deducted tax. [Section 53 then applied to interest.] The Revenue sought to recover from the company the tax so deducted (on the basis that section 53 applied to the payments), but the company contended that the debenture interest should be treated as having been paid out of the accumulated profits of past years. It was held that only profits of the year when the interest was paid could be regarded as profits out of which the debenture interest was paid. " You cannot look for the fund brought into charge to tax outside the year in which the interest is paid and the amount deducted . . ."

There is a concession (A20) under which, where annuities, annual payments, etc. (other than interest) are paid in a later year than the due year but in the due year could have been paid wholly or partly out of taxed income, an allowance is made, in fixing the amount to be paid over under section 53, for the tax which the payer would have been entitled (under section 52) to deduct and retain if the payments had been made at the due dates.

5-43   *Foreign cases.* Where the proper law of a deed is English law, the position *as between the parties* is that the payer (whether resident within or outside the United Kingdom) is entitled to deduct tax from an annual payment, whether it is payable within or out of the United Kingdom. There is no such right of deduction in the case of a deed the proper law of which is foreign law.[85]

6. FAILURE TO DEDUCT TAX

5-44   What is the position if a person paying an annuity or other annual payment fails to deduct tax, as he is entitled to do under section 52 of the Income and Corporation Taxes Act 1970 or bound to do under section 53?

(1) *As between payer and payee*

Generally the payer cannot recover the tax by action from the payee, for this is a case of money paid voluntarily under a mistake of law.[86] The payer has a remedy in only three cases:

(a) Where payments are made by instalments, any under-deduction during a tax year can be made good out of any subsequent payments in the same tax year.[87]

(b) Where the basic rate of tax is increased by the Finance Act, so that tax is under-deducted from earlier payments, an adjustment can be made in the next payment after the passing of the Act. If there is no

---

[84] [1930] 1 K.B. 593; 15 T.C. 573 (C.A.).
[85] *Keiner* v. *Keiner* (1952) 34 T.C. 346. (H, by a deed executed in America, agreed to make payments to his divorced wife. H, when resident in the U.K., deducted tax in reliance on what are now ss. 52 and 53. *Held,* that H had no right to deduct tax.)
[86] *Re Hatch* [1919] 1 Ch. 351.
[87] *Taylor* v. *Taylor* [1938] 1 K.B. 320 (C.A.), explained in *Hemsworth* v. *Hemsworth* [1946] K.B. 431. *Cf. Johnson* v. *Johnson* [1946] P. 205 (C.A.).

" next payment," the amount under-deducted may be recovered as if it were a debt.[88]

(c) Where the failure to deduct (or under-deduction) is through a mistake of fact.[89]

(2) *As between the parties and the Revenue*

5-45   Failure to deduct income tax at the basic rate in a case to which section 52 applies does not normally concern the Revenue, for the Revenue recover the tax in the assessment on the profits or gains of the payer, the whole of which are taxed without distinguishing the annuity or other annual payment.[90] Failure to deduct in a case to which section 53 applies does, however, concern the Revenue who may either (i) assess the payee under section 53 in the year in which the payment is made, or (ii) assess the payee [91] under the Schedule and Case appropriate to the nature of the income and in accordance with the rules applicable thereto [92]: thus an annuity or other annual payment may be assessed under Case III of Schedule D on the basis discussed in §§ 5-06 *et seq.* Failure to deduct will not expose the payer to any penalty, notwithstanding that under section 53 the obligation to deduct is mandatory. In no case can relief be claimed under section 33 of the Taxes Management Act 1970,[93] for a failure to deduct is not an error or mistake in a return or statement made by the payer for purposes of assessment.

5-46   In practice, a person who pays an annuity or annual payment gives the payee a certificate stating the gross amount of the payment, the amount of income tax deducted, and the actual amount paid. He is bound to give such a certificate on the request in writing of the recipient, who may enforce the due performance of this duty.[94] Where no such certificate is given, it may be uncertain whether the recipient is to be treated as having received untaxed income (in which case he could be assessed to basic rate tax) or income taxed by deduction at source.

5-47   Where the recipient of an annual payment is assessed the onus lies on him to show either that the payment was made out of profits or gains brought into charge to tax or, alternatively, that the payment was a net amount from which tax had been deducted.[95]

---

[88] I.C.T.A. 1970, s. 521. As to overdeductions in the year 1978–79, when the basic rate was reduced from 34 to 33 per cent., see I.C.T.A. 1970, s. 522 and (1978) S.T.I. 372.

[89] *Turvey* v. *Dentons (1923) Ltd.* [1953] 1 Q.B. 218.

[90] For an example of a case in which the Revenue was unable to recover tax from the payer: see *Hume* v. *Asquith* (1968) 45 T.C. 251 (as regards the B royalties). At that time the payee could not be assessed where [section 53] applied. There is no longer any prohibition against assessment of the payee: I.C.T.A., 1970, s. 52 (1), (*a*), was repealed as from 1973–74 by F.A. 1971, ss. 37 (2), 38 and Sched. 14, Part II.

[91] *Lord Advocate* v. *Edinburgh Corporation* (1905) 7 F. (Ct. of Sess.) 972.

[92] *Grosvenor Place Estates Ltd.* v. *Roberts* [1961] Ch. 148; 39 T.C. 433 (C.A.); where a tenant under a long lease failed to deduct tax as required by the now repealed s. 177 of the Income Tax Act 1952: *held*, the landlord could be assessed under Case VI of Schedule D.

[93] *Post,* § 17-09.

[94] I.C.T.A. 1970, ss. 55 and 232 (4), relating to payments by companies.

[95] See *Hume* v. *Asquith* (1968) 45 T.C. 251 at pp. 271–272 (as regards the C royalties) when the appellant taxpayer failed to discharge this onus.

In *Stokes* v. *Bennett* [96] a husband resident abroad had been ordered by an English divorce court to pay his wife £22 per month free of tax. (It was agreed that an order in that form was to be construed as an order to pay a gross sum of such an amount as after deducting tax would leave £22.) There was no evidence that the husband had any English income which had suffered U.K. income tax; nor was there evidence that he had ever purported to deduct tax. However, the order of the court referred to a net sum and the husband had in fact paid that sum over some years. *Held*, that the husband must be presumed to have paid a net sum after deduction of standard rate tax, so that no assessment to standard rate tax could be raised on the wife under Case III.

7. Tax Free Payments

5-48 A person who agrees to make annual payments may wish to ensure that the payee receives a fixed amount of, say, £x per annum, neither more nor less. Such a wish is commonly expressed in connection with separation agreements. This objective is not easy to achieve; for if A agrees to pay B £x per annum, B is entitled only to £x less tax at the basic rate, which may vary from year to year; and if A agrees to pay B in full without deduction of tax this provision is ineffective. This is because under section 106 (2) of the Taxes Management Act 1970 every agreement for payment of interest, rent or other annual payment in full without allowing any deduction authorised by the Taxes Acts is void. The subsection does not make the agreement void *in toto*, but only the provision for non-deduction of tax [97]; so that, in the result, B is entitled to £x less tax, as before. The prohibition in section 106 (2) applies only to *agreements*, such as a separation agreement, a deed of covenant (even if unilateral) and any settlement which contains an element of bargain. [98] It does not apply, for example, to wills. The effect of section 106 (2) is that only an agreement to pay a taxable sum is permissible, [99] but formulae can be devised which will satisfy this requirement and yet, at the same time, provide the recipient with a sum which will remain constant despite changes in the basic rate of income tax. The conventional formula provides for the payment of

> such a sum as after the deduction of income tax at the basic rate for the time being in force will leave the sum of £x per annum in the payee's hands.

This takes effect as a covenant to pay an amount equal to £x grossed up at the current basic rate [1]: the payee receives a constant annual sum of £x irrespective of changes in the basic rate of tax (hence payment by bankers' order can be easily arranged) and the only variable factor is the gross cost of the agreement to the grantor and the amount which is deductible in computing his total income. [2] Thus if the agreement provides for a net

---

[96] *Stokes* v. *Bennett* [1953] Ch. 566; 34 T.C. 337. *Cf. Hemsworth* v. *Hemsworth* [1946] K.B. 431, where apparently the covenantee was expressed to be entitled to a gross amount and Denning J. held that, in the absence of notification that tax had been deducted, the payment must be taken to have been made without deduction. And see *Butler* v. *Butler* [1961] P. 33 (C.A.).

[97] In *Whiteside* v. *Whiteside* [1950] Ch. 65 (C.A.), the court refused rectification of an instrument which infringed s. 106 (2).

[98] *Brooke* v. *Price* [1917] A.C. 115 (settlement following a divorce). *Cf. Re Goodson's Settlement* [1943] Ch. 101.

[99] *Re Maclennan* [1939] 1 Ch. 750, 755.

[1] *I.R.C.* v. *Cook* [1946] A.C. 1; 26 T.C. 489.

[2] As to total income, see Chap. 8.

annual sum of £500, the gross cost will be £769·23 if the basic rate is 35 per
5-49 cent. and £833·33 if the basic rate is 40 per cent.[3] Two points should be
noted in connection with the conventional formula:

(1) If the payee is liable to higher rate income tax or the investment
income surcharge on the covenanted sum (which must be grossed up
at the basic rate for the purpose of computing the payee's total
income: see § 8-18), the payer is not bound to indemnify the
annuitant in respect of such tax[4];

(2) if the payee is entitled to claim repayment in respect of the tax
notionally deducted by the payer, he is not accountable to the payer
for the tax so reclaimed.[5]

It follows that where the conventional formula is used, the recipient who is
liable to tax in excess of the basic rate will be left with £x less the amount of
tax in excess of the basic rate which is attributable to £x; whereas the
recipient who is not a basic rate taxpayer will be left with £x plus any
repayment due in respect of tax deducted at the basic rate. Practically
speaking this is unavoidable. Forms of words other than those referred to as
" the conventional formula " may be used but care should be taken to
ensure that the consequences referred to in (1) and (2) ensue. An agreement
to pay a specified sum " free of tax " has been held to oblige the payer to
pay such a sum as after deduction of income tax at the basic rate equals the
specified sum.[6]

Wills

5-50   The provisions of section 106 (2) of the Taxes Management Act 1970 do
not apply to wills and there is accordingly no objection to a testator
directing the payment of an annuity of £x per annum tax free. This takes
effect as a direction to pay such a sum as after deduction of tax at the basic
rate will leave £x. In practice, however, tax free annuities in wills should be
avoided for two reasons:

(1) The words " tax free " mean free of all income tax, so that if in any
year the annuitant is liable to tax in excess of the basic rate (including
the investment surcharge), the trustees must indemnify him in
respect of the amount of such tax which is attributable to the gross
amount of the annuity.[7]

(2) The annuitant may be accountable to the deceased's personal
representatives or will trustees for a proportion of any repayment
which he receives.

In *Re Pettit*,[8] an annuity was given by will free of duty and income tax. The
annuitant was not liable to tax at the standard rate and recovered part of the
tax which he had suffered by deduction in respect of the annuity. *Held* that he
was not entitled to retain the whole of the tax so reclaimed, but was

---

[3] To " gross up " £500 when the basic rate is (say) 35 per cent., multiply by 100 and divide the result by
(100–35 = 65).   [4] *Re Bates* [1925] Ch. 157 where the earlier cases were reviewed.
[5] *Re Jones* [1933] Ch. 842.   [6] *Ferguson* v. *I.R.C.* [1970] A.C. 442; 46 T.C. 1 (H.L.).
[7] *Re Reckitt* [1932] 2 Ch. 144 (C.A.); *Re Bates* in note 4, *supra*. For a glimpse of the difficulties which
can arise, see *I.R.C.* v. *Duncanson* (1949) 31 T.C. 257.
[8] [1922] 2 Ch. 765. See also *Re Lyons* [1952] Ch. 129.

accountable to the trustees for a proportion thereof. This is the proportion which the gross amount of the annuity bears to the annuitant's total gross income.[9]

The annuitant in such a case is under a duty to the trustees to make the necessary claim for repayment [9]; and an annuitant who is a married woman can be compelled to apply for separate assessment.[10]

Court orders

5-51   A court order, not being an agreement, may provide for the making of tax free payments.[11] An order to pay £x " tax free " obliges the payer to pay such a sum as after deduction of income tax at the basic rate equals £x.[12] It is common practice in divorce proceedings, however, to order the payment of a sum " less tax." [13] An order to pay £x less tax takes effect as an order to pay £x from which sum the payer will deduct tax at the basic rate under section 52 or section 53 of the Income and Corporation Taxes Act 1970, as appropriate. The rule in *Re Pettit* does not apply to court orders.[14]

Small maintenance payments are subject to special provisions.[15]

Pre-war tax free annuities

5-52   By section 422 of the Income and Corporation Taxes Act 1970, any provision made [16] before September 3, 1939, and not varied on or after that date, for the payment of a stated amount free of income tax, is to take effect in each year of assessment as if the stated amount were reduced in accordance with the following fraction:

The stated amount $\times \dfrac{100 - A}{72 \cdot 5}$ where A is the basic rate of income tax for the year expressed as a percentage.

8. PURCHASED LIFE ANNUITIES

5-53 Until 1956, when a life annuity was purchased, the entire annuity was taxed as income of the annuitant, no account being taken of the capital content in the payments. Through recommendations in the Report of the Committee on the Taxation Treatment of Provisions for Retirement,[17] section 27 of the Finance Act 1956 was passed (now section 230 of the Income and Corporation Taxes Act 1970) providing that the capital element in each periodic payment of a purchased life annuity should be exempt from tax. The capital content is found by dividing the purchase price of the annuity by the normal expectation of life of the annuitant at the date when the annuity

---

[9] *Re Kingcome* [1936] Ch. 566, where the court made a declaration that the annuitant was a trustee of her statutory right to recover the overpaid tax.

[10] *Re Batley* [1952] 1 All E.R. 1036.

[11] *Spilsbury* v. *Spofforth* (1937) 21 T.C. 247; *cf. Blount* v. *Blount* [1916] 1 K.B. 230; *Burroughes* v. *Abbott* [1922] 1 Ch. 86 (agreements made to give effect to court orders).

[12] *Ferguson* v. *I.R.C.* [1970] A.C. 442.

[13] *Wallis* v. *Wallis* [1941] P. 69.

[14] *Jefferson* v. *Jefferson* [1956] P. 136.

[15] *Ante*, § 5-05.

[16] Where an annuity is granted by will, provision is " made " when the testator dies, not when the will is executed: *Berkeley* v. *Berkeley* [1946] A.C. 555. See also *Re Westminster's Deed of Appointment* [1959] Ch. 265 (C.A.).   [17] Cmd. 9063, paras. 496–505.

commences, and this remains constant throughout the life of the annuitant. Tax is then charged each year on the amount by which the annuity payment exceeds this annual capital content, whether or not the annuitant survives the period of normal expectation. The question whether an annuity is subject to these provisions, and the amount of the capital content, is determined by the Inspector, subject to a right of appeal.[18]

Exceptions [19]

5-54   The following annuities are excepted from these provisions:

(1) An annuity which would in any event be treated wholly or partly as capital. An annuity for a *fixed term* is so treated.

(2) Annuities granted in consideration of sums which qualify for relief under the provisions relating to retirement annuities [20] or for life assurance relief.[21] A life annuity which also combines a life policy is within this exception.

(3) Annuities purchased in pursuance of any direction in a will, or to provide for an annuity payable by virtue of a will or settlement out of income of property disposed of by the will or settlement (whether with or without resort to capital).

(4) Annuities purchased under a sponsored superannuation scheme [22] or approved trust scheme,[23] or an annuity purchased in recognition of another's services (or past services) in any office or employment. The full amount of the annuity is taxable but, in the latter case, may be treated as earned income.[24]

9. INTEREST

5-55   Until the Finance Act 1969 the system of deduction of tax at source which now applies to annuities and annual payments applied also to interest, except that for some purposes a distinction was made between " yearly " or " annual " and " non-yearly " or " short " interest. The pre-1969 system is not further discussed in this book.[25] Suffice it to say that sections 52 and 53 of the Income and Corporation Taxes Act 1970 now expressly exclude interest. All interest of money, whether yearly or otherwise, and whether payable within or out of the United Kingdom, is chargeable under Case III of Schedule D,[26] provided the instrument under which the obligation to pay interest arises does not create a foreign source of income outside the scope of the Schedule D charge.[27] Interest is payable in full without deduction of tax, except where section 54 of the Income and Corporation Taxes Act 1970 otherwise provides.

---

[18] See I.C.T.A. 1970, ss. 230–231; Income Tax (Purchased Life Annuities) Regulations 1956 (S.I. 1956 No. 1230).

[19] I.C.T.A. 1970, s. 230 (7).

[20] *Ibid.* s. 227.

[21] *Ibid.* s. 19; *post*, § 8-54.

[22] *Ibid.* s. 226.

[23] *Ibid.* s. 226 (5), (6).

[24] *Post*, § 8-07.

[25] For the pre-1969 law, see the 3rd edition of this book.

[26] I.C.T.A. 1970, s. 109; § 5-01.   [27] See § 5-26.

5-56 Section 54 applies where any yearly interest of money chargeable to tax under Case III is paid:

(*a*) otherwise than in a fiduciary or representative capacity, by a company or local authority, or

(*b*) by or on behalf of a partnership of which a company is a member, or

(*c*) by any person to another person whose usual place of abode is outside the United Kingdom.

In these three cases, the person by or through whom the payment is made is bound, on making the payment, to deduct out of it a sum representing the amount of income tax thereon at the basic rate for the year in which the payment is made [28]; except that this requirement does not apply:

(i) to interest payable in the United Kingdom on an advance from a bank carrying on a bona fide banking business in the United Kingdom, or

(ii) to interest paid by such a bank in the ordinary course of that business.[29]

In these two cases the interest is paid without deduction of tax. Exception (i) applies only where the interest is paid by the person to whom the advance is made; it does not apply to payments made by a guarantor under a guarantee.[30]

Where there is an obligation to deduct tax under section 54, the provisions in section 53 relating to the obligation to render an account to the Inspector apply.[31]

5-57 *Yearly and short interest.* Section 54 of the Income and Corporation Taxes Act 1970 applies only to " yearly interest." Non-yearly or " short " interest is always payable in full without deduction of tax. The main factor which determines whether interest is " yearly " or " short " is the degree of permanence of the loan [32]: if the obligation to pay interest is to continue for less than a year, the interest is " short " interest. Interest paid on unpaid purchase money when completion is delayed has been held to be yearly interest.[33]

5-58 *Bank interest.* Interest paid to a bank carrying on a bona fide banking business in the United Kingdom is payable without deduction, whether the interest is yearly or short.

Tax relief for interest paid is discussed in §§ 8-57 *et seq.*

10. PATENTS AND COPYRIGHTS

Patents

5-59 Sections 52 and 53 of the Income and Corporation Taxes Act 1970, relating to deduction of basic rate income tax, which are discussed *ante,*

---

[28] I.C.T.A. 1970, s. 54 (1), as amended by F.A. 1971, s. 37 and Sched. 6, para. 22. As to payments " through " others, see *ante*, § 15-35. [29] I.C.T.A. 1970, s. 54 (2).

[30] *Holder* v. *I.R.C.* [1932] A.C. 624; 16 T.C. 540 (H.L.). As to whether a payment by a guarantor is itself a payment of " interest," see *Re Hawkins* [1972] Ch. 714.

[31] *Ibid.* s. 54 (3); see *ante*, § 5-34.

[32] *Hay* v. *I.R.C.* (1924) 8 T.C. 636; *I.R.C.* v. *Frere* [1965] A.C. 402; 42 T.C. 125 (H.L.); *Corinthian Securities Ltd.* v. *Cato* [1970] 1 Q.B. 377; 46 T.C. 93 (C.A.).

[33] *Bebb* v. *Bunny* (1854) 1 K. & J. 216; 69 E.R. 436.

§§ 5-30 *et seq.*, apply to " any royalty or other sum paid in respect of the user of a patent." [34] A *royalty* commonly assumes the form of a periodic payment made to an inventor by a manufacturer under an agreement by which the inventor grants to the manufacturer a licence (exclusive or non-exclusive) to exploit the inventor's patent; and the royalty may be an agreed sum for each article manufactured or produced. The words *other sum* include a lump sum awarded to an inventor in respect of the past user of a patent. [35] In one case a non-exclusive licence to use a patent was granted in consideration of the payment of a lump sum plus a royalty and it was held (contrary to the taxpayer's contention) that the lump sum was an income receipt notwithstanding that there was no evidence that the lump sum was arrived at by reference to some anticipated quantum of user. [36] The phrase " royalty or other sum " does not include capital payments, such as a lump sum payment for the grant of an *exclusive* licence [37]; but such a payment may be assessable under section 380 of the Income and Corporation Taxes Act 1970 (see § 5-61) or may be liable to capital gains tax.

5-60   Patent royalties, like annual payments, are payable less income tax at the basic rate. Patent royalties may be " annual payments " within Case III of Schedule D. [38] Where a lump sum royalty or other payment is made in respect of the past user of a patent, there are provisions which allow the payee to spread the payment backwards over a period of years corresponding to the period of past user. [39]

5-61   Where a person resident in the United Kingdom sells any patent rights for a capital sum, he is chargeable under Case VI of Schedule D; but the sum may be " spread forward " over a period of six years. [40] If in a similar case the vendor is not resident in the United Kingdom and the patent is a United Kingdom patent, the vendor is chargeable under Case VI but the purchaser is entitled to deduct tax under section 53 of the Income and Corporation Taxes Act 1970 as if the capital sum was an annual sum payable otherwise than out of profits or gains charged to tax. [41] If the purchaser is also non-resident, his liability to account for the amount he deducts may be difficult to enforce.

Copyrights

5-62   Sections 52 and 53 of the Income and Corporation Taxes Act 1970 do not apply to copyright royalties, which are payable in full without deduction of tax. If the recipient is an author by profession and the royalties are receipts of that profession, they are taxed under Case II of Schedule D or, if the

---

[34] I.C.T.A. 1970, ss. 52 (2) (*a*) and 53 (1) (*b*).
[35] *Constantinesco* v. *Rex* (1927) 11 T.C. 730 (H.L.); *Mills* v. *Jones* (1929) 14 T.C. 769 (H.L.).
[36] *Rustproof Metal Window Co.* v. *I.R.C.* (1947) 29 T.C. 243 (C.A.). See also *Murray* v. *I.C.I. Ltd.* [1967] Ch. 1038; 44 T.C. 175 (C.A.).
[37] *British Salmson Aero Engines Ltd.* v. *I.R.C.* (1938) 22 T.C. 29 (C.A.).
[38] *Rank Xerox Ltd.* v. *Lane* [1978] S.T.C. 449 (C.A.).
[39] I.C.T.A. 1970, s. 384.
[40] I.C.T.A. 1970, s. 380 (1).
[41] I.C.T.A. 1970, s. 380 (2).

profession has ceased, as post-cessation receipts.[42] If the recipient is not an author by profession, the royalties may be taxable under Case VI of Schedule D.[43]

Where an author assigns the copyright in a work, wholly or partially, or grants an interest in the copyright by licence, and he receives a lump sum payment (including a non-returnable advance on account of royalties), the sum is taxable as a receipt of his profession by reference to the year in which it is received, or under Case VI of Schedule D.[44] In the absence of specific relief, the lump sum might therefore be swallowed in tax as income of a single year of assessment. Two alternative forms of relief are available:

5-63   (1) *Relief by spreading the payment backwards* [45]: If the author was engaged on the making of a literary, dramatic, musical or artistic work for a period of more than 12 months, he can claim to spread the lump sum payment backwards over a period of two or three years depending on the period of engagement on the making of the work. If this exceeded 24 months, the lump sum can be treated as if it had been received in three equal annual instalments, the last being received on the date of actual receipt; if it was less than 24 months, the lump sum can be treated as received in two such instalments. A claim for the relief should be made to the Inspector.[46]

5-64   (2) *Relief by spreading the payment forwards* [47]: This relief applies only to the case where the author etc. of the established work sells the residual rights in that work. If not less than 10 years after the first publication of a work the author assigns the copyright therein, wholly or partially, or grants an interest in the copyright by licence in consideration of a lump sum payment (including a non-returnable advance on account of royalties), and the duration of the assignment or grant is not less than two years, he can claim to spread the payment forwards over a period of years depending on the duration of the grant or licence. Except where the duration is less than six years, the payment can be treated as becoming receivable in six equal annual instalments, the first being received on the date of actual receipt; if the duration is less than six years, the payment can be treated as becoming receivable in equal annual instalments corresponding to the number of whole years throughout the duration of the assignment or grant. The relief is available in the case of payments falling to be included in computing profits or gains for the year 1967–68 or any subsequent year of assessment. There are special provisions to meet the cases where, during the period of " spread," the author dies or his profession is otherwise permanently discontinued.

Relief is not available under one of the above heads if relief has already been claimed under the other head.

---

[42] Discussed, *ante*, §§ 2-88 *et seq.*

[43] *Ante*, §§ 4-02 *et seq.*

[44] The Rule in *Sharkey* v. *Wernher* (*ante*, § 2-46) does not apply to an assignment by way of gift or at an undervalue: *Mason* v. *Innes* [1967] Ch. 1079; 44 T.C. 326 (C.A.). The transaction would be a capital gains tax disposal, credit being given in computing the capital gains tax payable for income tax on any sum received by the assignor.

[45] I.C.T.A. 1970, s. 389.

[46] T.M.A. 1970, s. 42 and Sched. 2.   [47] I.C.T.A. 1970, s. 390.

CHAPTER 6

THE TAXATION OF INCOME FROM LAND:
SCHEDULES A AND B

1. INTRODUCTION

6-01 THE feudal structure of English society in the early years of development of the common law made land the subject of special treatment under English law, and it is not surprising that income from land should be differentiated from other sources of income under the Income Tax Acts. The taxation of income from land was put on an entirely new basis by the Finance Act 1963 which became fully effective in and from the year 1964–65, and this chapter is concerned principally with the provisions of that Act, which have now been incorporated in the Income and Corporation Taxes Act 1970. In order that the effect of these provisions may be fully understood, the reader must know something of the law which previously applied and it is the purpose of this Introduction to summarise, in broad outline, the pre-1963 law.

Income from land was taxed under Schedules A and B. Schedule A in its pre-1963 form was a tax on income from the ownership of land capable of actual occupation, except that certain quarries, mines and other concerns were excluded from the charge. For the purpose of taxing income from land, all property in the United Kingdom had a gross annual value representing the value at which it was worth to be let by the year in the open market on the footing that the landlord was responsible for all repairs and that the tenant was liable for rates. From the gross annual value so found by valuation, a statutory repairs allowance was deducted and tax was levied on the resultant net annual value. Schedule A tax was not restricted to the income which landlords derived from letting property: it was also levied on owner-occupiers and, in their case, the net annual value represented a " notional income " from the land. As between landlord and tenant, Schedule A tax was (subject to exceptions) levied on the occupier of the property and the Income Tax Act 1952 contained elaborate provisions to enable the tenant who paid the tax to pass it on to the landlord by deduction from rent. There was an exception in the case of property let on a " long lease " when the rent was treated as an annual payment chargeable under Case VI of Schedule D and paid under deduction of tax. The long lease became an attractive proposition for tenants of luxury flats in the higher income groups because the rent (being an annual payment) was deductible in computing total income for purposes of surtax. The distinction between the short and the long lease has no place in the system introduced by the Act of 1963.

6-02 It was originally intended that a revaluation of property for purposes of Schedule A tax should be made every five years, but the last general valuation was made in 1935–36 (" the preparatory year ") for 1936–37 (" the year of revaluation "). As time passed and rents increased the annual values determined for Schedule A purposes became more and more unrealistic, for the Revenue had no power to revalue property between years of revaluation unless there had been such a change in the character of the property (*e.g.* by structural conversion or development) as to create a new unit of assessment. For this reason the Finance Act 1940 introduced provisions for taxing under Case VI of Schedule D rents received by landlords to the extent that the rents exceeded the annual value for Schedule A. These " excess rent assessments " were made on the landlord; they were not levied on the tenant and the tax passed on to the landlord by deduction.

Maintenance claims

6-03 A statutory repairs allowance was deducted in ascertaining the net annual value of property. This allowance was a fixed fraction of the gross annual value. Where the taxpayer's expenditure on maintenance, repairs, insurance and management of the property, averaged over five years, exceeded the statutory repairs allowance, there were provisions to enable the taxpayer to obtain relief by way of maintenance claim.[1]

Schedule B

6-04 Tax under Schedule B was charged in respect of the occupation of land in the United Kingdom which was chargeable under Schedule A, except that dwelling-houses and land occupied for the purposes of carrying on a trade, profession or vocation were excluded. Farming and market gardening used at one time to fall within Schedule B until these activities were made statutory trades subject to tax under Case I of Schedule D.[2] Schedule B thus applied to amenity lands, lands occupied for non-profit-making purposes (*e.g.* sports grounds), sporting rights and woodlands. The basis of assessment was one-third of the gross annual value and the tax was additional to Schedule A tax. The tax was assessed on the occupier, who had no right of recoupment.

The Finance Acts 1963 and 1969

6-05 The Finance Act 1963 introduced a new code for the taxation of income from land. Schedule A in its original form ceased to have effect in and from the year 1963–64 except that, for the year 1963–64 only, Schedule A tax and the excess rent provisions were preserved for the purpose of taxing landlords on rental income. There was no Schedule A tax (and accordingly no maintenance relief) for owner-occupiers and tenants with a beneficial occupation in 1963–64.[3]

The Finance Act 1963 introduced a new Case VIII of Schedule D to tax income from land. The Finance Act 1969 renamed Case VIII of Schedule D " Schedule A."[4]

---

[1] For details, see the first edition of this book, pp. 19–23.
[2] I.C.T.A. 1970, s. 110. For the history of the relevant provisions, see *Sargent* v. *Eayrs* (1973) 48 T.C. 573; [1973] S.T.C. 50 and see § 2-18A.   [3] F.A. 1963, s. 20.
[4] F.A. 1969, s. 60 and Sched. 20, para. 1 (an amendment which was made for the purposes of the 1970 Consolidation).

Woodlands

6-06   In and from the year 1963–64, Schedule B tax is restricted to the occupation of woodlands in the United Kingdom managed on a commercial basis and with a view to the realisation of profit.[5] Tax under Schedule B is charged on the occupier (which includes every person having the use of lands [6]) on the assessable value of his occupation in the chargeable period, that is on an amount equal to one-third of the woodlands' annual value, or a proportionate part of that amount if the period in respect of which he is chargeable is less than one year.[7] The annual value of land is taken to be the rent which might reasonably be expected to be obtained on a letting from year to year if the tenant undertook to pay all usual tenant's rates and taxes, and if the landlord undertook to bear the costs of the repairs and insurance, and the other expenses, if any, necessary for maintaining the subject of the valuation in a state to command that rent; but the annual value of any woodlands is determined in accordance with this formula as if the land, instead of being woodlands, were let in its natural and unimproved state.[8] Disputes as to annual value are determined by the General Commissioners.[9]

6-07   Under section 111 of the Income and Corporation Taxes Act 1970, any person occupying woodlands managed by him on a commercial basis and with a view to the realisation of profits may elect to be assessed under Schedule D instead of under Schedule B. He is then assessed on the basis of profits (if any) instead of on the basis of annual value. The election must extend to all such woodlands on the same estate; except that woodlands planted or replanted within the previous 10 years can be treated (at the occupier's option) as forming a separate estate. The election has effect for the year of assessment to which it relates and for all future years so long as the woodlands are occupied by the person making the election.

Where profits derived from " commercial woodlands " exceed their assessable value for Schedule B purposes, as would normally be the case where the woodlands have reached maturity, taxation under Schedule B is preferable. Where, however, the woodlands are immature or otherwise unproductive of profits, taxation under Schedule D is preferable because (a) relief for losses may be claimed [10]; and (b) relief for capital expenditure on machinery and plant, forestry buildings, fences, etc., may be available.[11] Once an election has been made under section 111 it applies until there is a change of occupation. A new occupier is at once assessed under Schedule B, unless he elects for assessment under Schedule D.

6-08   Where the occupier elects to be assessed under Schedule D, the profits or gains arising to him from the occupation of the woodlands are to be deemed to be profits or gains of a trade. But this does not mean that the occupier is to be treated as carrying on a trade or that the woodlands are trading stock.

---

[5] I.C.T.A. 1970, s. 91.
[6] *Ibid.* s. 92 (3).
[7] *Ibid.* s. 92 (1), (2).
[8] *Ibid.* s. 92 (2) applying s. 531.
[9] *Ibid.* s. 531 (3).
[10] *Post*, Chap. 12.
[11] *Post*, Chap. 13.

" Merely by deeming the offspring to be something which it is not, the section does not change the nature of the parent. Merely to deem the profits or gains arising from the occupation of the woodlands to be the profits or gains of a trade is not, in my judgment, to say that the occupation of the woodlands is to be deemed to be a trade . . ." [12]

Thus there would be no tax liability under Case I of Schedule D on a sale of the woodlands. [13]

6-09 There is a distinction between occupying woodlands on a commercial basis (when Schedule B applies, subject to the right of election under section 111) and carrying on a trade in relation to the products of the woodlands (when Schedule D, Case I applies as regards the trade itself).

In *Collins* v. *Fraser* [13] the taxpayer manufactured boxes and crates from timber provided from his own woodlands. The mill was some distance from the woodlands. The General Commissioners found that the activities fell within Schedule B to the point when the timber was transported from the woodlands. Megarry J. held the activities ceased to be referable to the Schedule B occupation when something more was done than market the timber.

2. THE TAXATION OF ANNUAL PROFITS OR GAINS FROM RENTS AND OTHER RECEIPTS FROM LAND (OTHER THAN PREMIUMS)

The charging provisions

6-10 By section 67 of the Income and Corporation Taxes Act 1970, tax under Schedule A is charged on " the annual profits or gains arising in respect of any such rents or receipts " as follow, that is to say:

(a) rents under leases [14] of land in the United Kingdom;
(b) rentcharges, ground annuals and feu duties, and any other annual payments reserved in respect of, or charged on or issuing out of, such land; and
(c) other receipts arising to a person from, or by virtue of, his ownership of an estate or interest in or right over such land or any incorporeal hereditament or incorporeal heritable subject in the United Kingdom. Thus payments for easements or other rights to use land are taxed under Schedule A. [15]

It will be convenient to refer to the above-mentioned sources of income as " rents, etc." It should be observed that rents, etc., are not made taxable as such. Schedule A charges tax on the profits or gains arising in respect of rents, etc., and it is therefore necessary to visualise an income and expenditure account in which rents, etc., are credited and certain outgoings are debited. The Act contains a general provision authorising the deductions provided for by sections 72 to 77. [16] Receipts of a capital nature

---

[12] *Coats* v. *Holker Estates Co.* (1961) 40 T.C. 75, *per* Plowman J. at p. 80.
[13] *Collins* v. *Fraser* (1969) 46 T.C. 143.
[14] Lease includes an agreement for a lease and any tenancy; it does not include a mortgage or heritable security: I.C.T.A. 1970, s. 90 (1). As to nature of rent under a lease, see *T. & E. Homes Ltd.* v. *Robinson* [1976] S.T.C. 462.
[15] And see I.C.T.A. 1970, s. 67 (3), for the position where the occupier is taxed under Schedule B. In *Lowe* v. *J. W. Ashmore Ltd.* (1970) 46 T.C. 597 receipts from sales of turf were held to be taxable under (c).
[16] *Ibid.* s. 71 (1). For the allowed deductions, see §§ 6-27 *et seq.*

are not taxed under Schedule A: thus, if A realises a profit on the sale of his dwelling-house, this may be said to be a receipt which arises by virtue of his ownership thereof, but it escapes tax under Schedule A because it is not an annual profit or gain. He might, however, be liable to capital gains or development gains tax.[17] There are special provisions relating to the taxation of premiums which are discussed later.[18]

6-11　　*Exceptions.* The following income from land is not assessed under Schedule A:

(1) Yearly interest and payments charged under section 112 (mines, quarries and other concerns) and section 156 or 157 (mining rents and royalties) of the 1970 Act. These are expressly excluded from Schedule A.[19] Mineral royalties are taxed on a special basis: briefly, half the royalty is taxed as income and half as capital gain.[20]

(2) Furnished lettings. Where rent is paid under a lease entitling the tenant to the use of furniture, and tax in respect of the payment for its use is chargeable under Case VI of Schedule D,[21] tax will be charged on the rent under Case VI unless the landlord, by notice in writing to the Inspector given within two years after the end of the year of assessment, requires that this provision shall not apply.[22] Schedule A would then apply and consequential adjustments would follow. A landlord of a furnished letting would elect for a Schedule A assessment if he was advised that the deductions allowed under the provisions applicable to Schedule A were more favourable to him than those normally permitted in the case of furnished lettings. Where payment for a furnished letting in the United Kingdom is made (whether in the United Kingdom or elsewhere) to a person, whether the landlord or not, whose usual place of abode is outside the United Kingdom, the tenant must deduct tax from the payment and account therefor to the Revenue under section 53 of the Income and Corporation Taxes Act 1970 as if it were an annual payment not payable out of profits or gains brought into charge.[23] It therefore behoves a tenant of a furnished letting to insert in his lease a covenant by the landlord to notify the tenant if the person to whom the rent is payable changes his usual place of abode to a place outside the United Kingdom.

(3) Income from land outside the United Kingdom. This is outside the charging provisions of Schedule A.

Rents receivable but not received

6-12　　Tax under Schedule A is charged by reference to the rents, etc., to which a person *becomes entitled* in the year of assessment.[24] The principle that

---

[17] *Post*, Chap. 16.
[18] *Post*, §§ 6-16 *et seq.* See also § 2-61.
[19] I.C.T.A. 1970, s. 67 (1), para. 3.
[20] F.A. 1970, s. 29 and Sched. 6.
[21] *Ante*, § 4-02.
[22] I.C.T.A. 1970, s. 67 (1), para. 4 and s. 67 (2).
[23] I.C.T.A. 1970, s. 89. See *ante*, § 5-34.
[24] *Ibid.* s. 67 (1), para. 2.

receivability without receipt gives rise to no tax liability has no place in this sphere of income taxation: a person is charged on rents, etc., which he is entitled to receive, whether or not he receives them and whether or not he demands payment. Section 87, however, allows a person to claim relief in respect of rents, etc., which are not received and which would be chargeable under Schedule A in two cases:

(1) If the non-receipt was attributable to the default of the person by whom the rent was payable and the claimant proves that he has taken reasonable steps available to him to enforce payment;

(2) if the claimant waived payment and the waiver was made without consideration and was reasonably made in order to avoid hardship.

Consequential adjustments will then be made. If relief is given and the rent, etc., is subsequentially received, the claimant (or his personal representatives) must notify the Inspector in writing within six months of the receipt. There are penalties for non-compliance.[25] The rent, etc., will then be treated as income of the year to which it relates and will be assessed accordingly; and for this purpose the Inspector has power to make assessments for more than six years back but the assessment must be made within six years from the end of the year when payment was received.[26]

Basis of assessment

6-13   Tax under Schedule A is assessed on a current year basis. Thus tax in 1970–71 is levied on the annual profits or gains from rents, etc., in the year ended April 5, 1971. Since, however, tax for 1970–71 is due on or before January 1, 1971,[27] and assessments have to be made in advance of this date, the assessment has to be provisional, followed by an adjustment (either by way of additional assessment or repayment claim) when the profits of the year are finally agreed.[28] The provisional assessment (for 1970–71 in the above example) is to be made on the basis that all sources of income and all amounts relevant in computing profits or gains are the same as for the last preceding year of assessment (*i.e.* the year ended April 5, 1970).[29] A person who ceases to own property after the beginning of a year of assessment may have this excluded from the provisional assessment for the following year by notifying the Inspector in writing before January 1 in that year. Thus (in the above example) property sold in the year ended April 5, 1970, will be excluded from the computation of the provisional assessment for 1970–71 if notice is given before January 1, 1971. It will not be excluded, however, unless the taxpayer can show that his provisional assessment for 1970–71 will be less than it would have been if he had not ceased to possess the property.

Collection

6-14   (1) *From derivative lessees.*[30] Where any tax under Schedule A is charged to a person who is not the occupier of the land (such as a lessor or licensor)

---

[25] T.M.A. 1970, s. 98.
[27] I.C.T.A. 1970, s. 4 (1).
[28] *Ibid.* s. 69.
[29] *Ibid.* s. 69.

[26] I.C.T.A. 1970, s. 87 (1).
[30] I.C.T.A. 1970, s. 70 (1).

but the tax is not paid by that person (referred to as " the person in default ") the tax may be recovered from any lessee of the land or any part thereof (referred to as " a derivative lessee ") whose interest is derived directly or indirectly from the person in default. The amount demanded from a derivative lessee in any period must not exceed the amount of the rent, etc., arising from the land which is due from him at the end of the period and payable to the person in default or another derivative lessee; and there are provisions which allow the derivative lessee from whom tax has been collected to deduct the tax from any subsequent payment arising from the land and due to the person in default or another derivative lessee. If the subsequent payments are insufficient to cover the tax paid, the difference can be recovered from the Revenue.

(2) *From agents.* [31] Where any person (referred to as " the agent ") is in receipt of rents, etc., on behalf of another person (referred to as " the principal ") and any tax under Schedule A charged on the principal has not been paid, the collector may require the agent to pay in or towards satisfaction of the tax sums received by the agent on behalf of the principal on account of rents, etc. An agent who fails to comply with the requirements of a notice served on him by the Inspector is liable to penalties.

Returns [32]

6-15   For the purpose of obtaining particulars of profits or gains chargeable to tax under Schedule A, the Inspector has power to require information from a number of sources. Thus, lessees and licensees (including former lessees and licensees) may be required to give information as to the terms of the lease or licence; a lessee (or former lessee) may be required to state the consideration given for the grant or assignment to him of the tenancy; and any person who as agent manages land or is in receipt of rents, etc. (which might include a solicitor or accountant), may be required to furnish the particulars relating to payments arising from land. There are penalties for non-compliance.

3. The Taxation of Premiums

6-16   A code of taxation of income from land would not be complete unless premiums on leases were brought into charge. If premiums were not made chargeable to tax as income, landlords seeking to avoid income tax would grant leases at a premium and not at a rent, for a lump sum premium would escape tax under section 67 of the Income and Corporation Taxes Act 1970 (*ante,* § 6-10), because it is not an annual profit or gain. Only capital gains tax would be chargeable. Section 80 (1) accordingly provides as follows:

> Where the payment of any premium is required under a lease, or otherwise under the terms subject to which a lease is granted, and the duration of the lease does not exceed fifty years, the landlord shall be treated for the purposes of the Tax Acts as becoming entitled when the lease is granted to an amount by way of rent (in addition to any actual rent) equal to the amount of the premium reduced by 1/50th of that amount for each complete period of twelve months (other than the first) comprised in the duration of the lease.

---

[31] I.C.T.A. 1970, s. 70 (2).   [32] T.M.A. 1970, s. 19.

The term " premium " is defined to include any like sum, whether payable to the immediate or a superior landlord [33] or to a person connected with either of them within section 533 of the 1970 Act [34]; and any sum (other than rent) paid on or in connection with the granting of a tenancy is presumed to have been paid by way of premium except in so far as other sufficient consideration for the payment is shown to have been given. [35]

6-17   The reader will recall that rents are not taxed as such. The charge under Schedule A is on the annual profits or gains arising in respect of rents, etc., and a premium (or the appropriate part of it) is treated as rent and so falls into charge under section 67. It will be convenient, however, to refer in this chapter to premiums as being " chargeable." The following is an example of the operation of the section:

> A grants a lease for a term of 21 years at a premium of £5,000. The chargeable portion of the premium is £5,000 less 40 per cent. thereof = £3,000. If the term had been 50 years, the chargeable portion would be £5,000 less 98 per cent. thereof = £100. Where the term exceeds 50 years, the premium escapes tax under Schedule A (subject to the qualifications in the next paragraph).

Premiums and sums which are taxed as premiums received by a dealer in land are treated as trading receipts only to the extent that sections 80, 81 or 82 of the 1970 Act do not apply. [36]

The duration of the lease

6-18   It will be appreciated from the example just given that the longer the term of the lease, the lower is the charge to tax. A lease for a term exceeding 50 years escapes the charge under Schedule A; and in the case of leases for 50 years or less, the discount increases as the term increases. In ascertaining the duration of a lease, the following provisions have effect [37]:

(a) where any of the terms of the lease (whether relating to forfeiture or to any other matter) or any other circumstances render it unlikely that the lease will continue beyond a date falling before the expiry of the term of the lease and the premium was not substantially greater than it would have been (on certain assumptions specified in the Act) had the term been one expiring on the date, [38] the lease shall not be treated as having been granted for a term longer than one ending on that date; and

(b) where the terms of the lease include provision for the extension of the lease beyond a given date by notice given by the tenant, account may be taken of any circumstances making it likely that the lease will be so extended; and

(c) where the tenant, or a person connected with him, is or may become entitled to a further lease or the grant of a further lease (whenever commencing) of the same premises or of premises including the

---

[33] I.C.T.A. 1970, s. 90 (1).   [34] F.A. 1972, s. 81 (3).
[35] I.C.T.A. 1970, s. 90 (1), (2). *Quaere* why the word " tenancy " is used in the definition and not " lease."
[36] I.C.T.A. 1970, s. 142.
[37] I.C.T.A. 1970, s. 84.
[38] F.A. 1972, s. 81 (2) amending I.C.T.A. 1970, s. 84 as from August 25, 1971, in order to counteract a number of tax avoidance schemes.

whole or part of the same premises, the term of the lease may be treated as not expiring before the term of the further lease. [39]

Paragraph (a) catches the lease which contains an " escalator clause," *i.e.* a clause reserving a rent which increases to such an extent as to induce the premature determination of the lease by the lessee.

Work carried out by the tenant

6-19   The tax on premiums is not avoided by the landlord requiring the tenant to carry out work on the demised premises, for section 80 (2) of the Income and Corporation Taxes Act 1970 provides as follows:

> Where the terms subject to which a lease is granted impose on the tenant an obligation to carry out any work on the premises, the lease shall be deemed for the purposes of this section to have required the payment of a premium to the landlord (in addition to any other premium) of an amount equal to the amount by which the value of the landlord's estate or interest, immediately after the commencement of the lease, exceeds what its then value would have been if the said terms did not impose that obligation on the tenant.

There is a proviso that this subsection shall not apply in so far as the obligation requires the carrying out of work payment for which would, if the landlord and not the tenant were obliged to carry it out, be deductible from the rent under sections 72 to 76 of the Act. [39]

Thus, if L grants a lease for a term of 21 years to T at a rent and in consideration of a covenant by T to carry out structural alterations, it is necessary to find out to what extent the value of L's reversionary interest immediately following the grant of the lease is increased by virtue of T's covenant. The amount so found is treated as a premium and discounted according to the length of the term. There is an element of double discounting in this case, for the greater length of the term not only increases the amount of the discount but also reduces the value of the works to the hypothetical purchaser. It is thought that no tax would be chargeable in respect of the value of work of a temporary nature.

Delayed premiums

6-20   The charge on premiums is not avoided by arranging for a lump sum to be paid by the tenant on some occasion subsequent to the grant of the lease. The following provisions are relevant in this connection:

(1) By section 80 (3) of the Income and Corporation Taxes Act 1970 where, under the terms subject to which a lease is granted, a sum becomes payable by the tenant in lieu of the whole part of the rent for any period, that sum is treated as a premium payable in the year when it becomes payable by the tenant. The premium is discounted on the basis that the duration of the lease excludes any period other than that in relation to which the sum is payable.

(2) By section 80 (3) where, under the terms subject to which a lease is granted, a sum becomes payable by the tenant as consideration for

---

[39] See *post*, §§ 6-27 *et seq.*

the surrender of the lease, that sum is treated as a premium payable in the year when it becomes payable by the tenant. The premium is discounted on the basis that the duration of the lease extends from its commencement to the date of surrender. It should be noted that this provision does not apply to a surrender which is negotiated after the term has commenced.

(3) By section 80 (4) where, as consideration for the variation or waiver of any of the terms of a lease, a sum becomes payable by the tenant otherwise than by way of rent, this sum is treated as a premium in the year when the contract providing for the variation or waiver is entered into. The premium is discounted on the basis that the duration of the lease is the period during which the variation or waiver is to have effect.

Premiums payable by instalments [40]

6-21   Where a premium (or a sum which is treated as a premium under one of the provisions discussed under the above head " Delayed premiums ") is payable by instalments, the tax chargeable by reference to the premium may, if the recipient satisfies the Board that he would otherwise suffer hardship, be paid at his option by such instalments as the Board may allow over a period not exceeding eight years and ending not later than the time at which the last of the first-mentioned instalments is payable. [41]

Charge on assignment of lease granted at undervalue [42]

6-22   The tax on premiums which has been discussed could be avoided in the following way. Suppose A wished to grant a lease to B at a premium and to avoid tax on the premium. A could grant a lease to a company which he controlled or to a collaborator, which lessee would then assign the lease to B for a consideration equal to the desired premium. Whereas a premium taken on the *grant* of a lease is chargeable under section 80 (1), a lump sum taken on the *assignment* of a lease escapes tax (unless it falls into charge as a trading receipt of a dealer in land or as a taxable capital gain). To prevent this form of avoidance section 81 (1) provides as follows:

> Where the terms subject to which a lease of a duration not exceeding fifty years was granted are such that the grantor, having regard to values prevailing at the time it was granted, and on the assumption that the negotiations for the lease were at arm's length, could have required the payment of an additional sum (hereinafter referred to as " the amount foregone ") by way of premium, or additional premium, for the grant of the lease, then, on any assignment of the lease for a consideration—
> > (a) where the lease has not previously been assigned, exceeding the premium (if any) for which it was granted, or
> > (b) where the lease has been previously assigned, exceeding the consideration for which it was last assigned,
> the amount of the excess, in so far as it is not greater than the amount foregone reduced by the amount of any such excess arising on a previous assignment of

---

[40] I.C.T.A. 1970, s. 80 (6) as substituted by F.A. 1972, s. 81 (1) with effect from April 11, 1972: *ibid.* s. 81 (6).
[41] Where the premium is not payable by instalments, see *post*, § 6-26.
[42] I.C.T.A. 1970, s. 81.

the lease, shall in the same proportion as the amount foregone would under section 80 (1) . . . have fallen to be treated as rent if it had been a premium under the lease, be treated as profits or gains of the assignor chargeable to tax under Case VI of Schedule D.

6-23   Suppose that A grants a lease to B for a term of 21 years and that A demands a premium of £200, but could have demanded £380. On an assignment of the lease by B, B is chargeable on his profit on the assignment up to the amount foregone by A. Thus, if B assigns to C for £350, B is chargeable on his profit (£150) up to the amount foregone (£180), *i.e.* B is treated as receiving a premium of £150, which will be discounted according to the duration of the lease. If C later assigns the lease to D, any profit made by C on the assignment is taxable up to the amount foregone by A (£180) less £150 (the amount charged against B).

The Revenue can therefore recover tax from successive assignors until the lost tax is recovered. Assignors could unwittingly incur tax liability as a result of tax avoidance by the original lessor, whether deliberate or not, and a measure of protection is afforded by section 81 (2) under which if there is submitted to the Inspector, by the grantor or any assignor or assignee of the lease, a statement showing whether or not a charge to tax arises or may arise, and if so the amount on which the charge arises or may arise, then if the Inspector is satisfied as to the accuracy of the statement he shall so certify. The assignee of a lease should, of course, seek indemnities against liability which might arise under the section.

Charge on sale of land with right to reconveyance [43]

6-24   Another method by which the tax on premiums could be avoided is as follows. Suppose A wished to take a premium of (say) £8,000 on the grant of a lease to B for seven years and that A wished to avoid tax on the premium. The transaction could be carried out by A selling the land to B for (say) £15,000 on terms that B would reconvey the land to A at the end of seven years for £7,000. To prevent this form of avoidance, section 82 (1) of the Income and Corporation Taxes Act 1970 provides as follows:

Where the terms subject to which an estate or interest in land is sold provide that it shall be, or may be required to be, reconveyed at a future date to the vendor or a person connected with him, the vendor shall be chargeable to tax under Case VI of Schedule D on any amount by which the price at which the estate or interest is sold exceeds the price at which it is to be reconveyed or, if the earliest date at which, in accordance with those terms, it would fall to be reconveyed is a date two years or more after the sale, on that excess reduced by 1/50th thereof for each complete year (other than the first) in the period between the sale and that date.

Thus, in the example, A will be taxed under Case VI on £8,000 discounted on the footing that there was a lease of a duration of seven years.

Section 82 (1) presupposes that the date of the reconveyance and the reconveyance price are fixed by the terms of the sale. Section 82 (2) deals with the case where the date of the reconveyance is not so fixed, *e.g.* where gravel-bearing land is sold with a provision for reconveyance when extraction is complete.

---

[43] I.C.T.A. 1970, s. 82.

Section 82 (3) deals with the case where land is sold with an arrangement for a lease back to the vendor or a person connected with him. Transactions of this nature are common as methods of financing the development of land and there is an express proviso excluding the operation of the subsection where the lease is granted and begins to run within one month after the sale.

Premiums: capital gains tax

6-25   Schedule A does not charge tax on a premium where the duration of the lease exceeds 50 years; but there may be liability to capital gains tax or development gains tax. Likewise a liability to capital gains tax might arise in respect of the portion of a premium which escapes Schedule A. This is discussed later.[44]

4. PREMIUM TOP-SLICING

6-26   Where a premium (or a sum which is treated as such) is chargeable as income of a single year of assessment, the Act allows an *individual* who is chargeable to avoid having the payment swallowed up in tax by claiming " top-slicing relief." The relief is not available where the person chargeable is not an individual, *e.g.* a company; nor where the premium is payable by instalments. No attempt is made here to summarise the detailed provisions of Schedule 3 to the Income and Corporation Taxes Act 1970 by reference to which relief is given. Broadly speaking the chargeable portion of the premium (called the " chargeable sum ") is spread over the duration of the lease (called " the relevant period ") to give what is termed the " yearly equivalent." If, for example, the chargeable sum is £2,100 and the relevant period is seven years, the yearly equivalent is £300. Outgoings are to be set against rents, etc., as far as possible and only the balance that remains is set against the yearly equivalent. There is then calculated the top rate of tax in the claimant's total income, including what (if anything) remains of the yearly equivalent after deducting outgoings. Tax is then charged at this top rate on the whole of the chargeable sum. If nothing remains of the yearly equivalent after deducting outgoings, tax is charged at the rate applicable to the highest part of the remainder of the claimant's total income for the year of assessment.

5. DEDUCTIONS

What is deductible

6-27   In computing the profits or gains arising to a person in a year of assessment, certain deductions are allowed from the rent or receipts to which he becomes entitled—including premiums which are treated as rent.[45] These are contained in sections 72 to 77 of the Income and Corporation Taxes Act 1970. The person chargeable may, under section 72, deduct payments made by him (but not mere liabilities incurred by him):

(a) in respect of maintenance, repairs, insurance or management;
(b) in respect of services provided under the terms of the lease other than services for which he received separate consideration;

---

[44] *Post*, Chap. 16.
[45] I.C.T.A. 1970, s. 71 (1).

(c) in respect of rates or other charges on the occupier which the person chargeable was obliged to defray;

(d) in respect of any rent, rentcharge, ground annual or other periodical payment reserved in respect of, or charged on or issuing out of, land.

6-28   Maintenance refers to expenditure necessary to maintain the value of property. Repairs has a similar meaning. It is difficult to differentiate these terms and no useful purpose is served by attempting to do so; for the important distinction is that between expenditure on maintenance and repairs (which is deductible) and expenditure on replacements, additions and improvements (which is not deductible).[46] Insurance refers to premiums paid on a policy insuring the building but not its contents. Premiums on a leasehold redemption policy are not allowable.[47] Management includes all the ordinary expenses of managing property, such as the cost of obtaining estimates for repairs, architects' and surveyors' fees,[48] accountants' fees, legal expenses of recovering arrears of rent, the cost of advertising property for letting,[49] etc. Capital allowances may be claimed for certain business or estate management expenditure.[50]

It is the view of the Inland Revenue that there is no material difference in the law relating to expenditure on dilapidations under Schedule A and under Case I of Schedule D as interpreted in *Law Shipping Co. Ltd.* v. *I.R.C.* and *Odeon Associated Theatres Ltd.* v. *Jones.*[51] Thus expenditure on maintenance and repairs will be disallowed as a deduction under Schedule A on the ground that it relates to dilapidations attributable to a period before the currency of the relevant lease if the expenditure would have been disallowed under Case I if the property had been acquired as a fixed asset of a trade at the commencement of the lease; and it will be allowed under Schedule A if it would have been allowed under Case I. It is arguable that the decision in the *Law Shipping* [51] case had no relevance to maintenance claims under Schedule A in the pre-1963 form and now has no relevance to the computation of profits or gains under Schedule A in its present form. Where maintenance and repairs of property are obviated by improvements, additions and alterations, so much of the outlay as is equal to the estimated cost of the maintenance and repairs is (with some qualifications) allowed as a deduction in computing liability in respect of rents under Schedule A.[52]

Principles of deduction

6-29   As a general principle, payments made by the landlord in respect of premises may only be deducted from rent payable in respect of those premises and must relate to expenditure incurred (or, in the case of maintenance and repairs, to dilapidations occurring) during the currency of

---

[46] For the distinction between "repairs" and "improvements," see the discussion, *ante*, § 2-63.
[47] *Pearce* v. *Doulton* (1947) 27 T.C. 405.
[48] *London and Northern Estates Co. Ltd.* v. *Harris* [1939] 1 K.B. 335; 21 T.C. 197.
[49] *Southern* v. *Aldwych Property Trust Ltd.* [1940] 2 K.B. 266; 23 T.C. 707.
[50] I.C.T.A. 1970, s. 78; *post*, § 13-19.
[51] *Ante*, § 2-62.
[52] Concession No. B4.

the lease. No deduction is allowable with respect to dilapidations outstanding at the commencement of the lease or in respect of expenditure incurred by a predecessor in title.[53]

There is an exception to this general principle in the case of a lease at a full rent, when a deduction is allowed for payments made in respect of expenditure incurred prior to the commencement of the lease in a " previous qualifying period " (as defined), *e.g.* when a previous lease at a full rent with the same lessor was subsisting or when no lease was subsisting and the lessor was entitled to possession (called a " void period ").[54] Thus where a lessor grants successive leases at a full rent, the allowable expenditure may be carried forward and deducted from the future rent: the right to carry forward expenditure is lost only by a period of owner-occupation or by a letting which is not at a full rent. A lease is a lease at a full rent if the rent reserved under the lease (including an appropriate sum in respect of any premium under the lease) is sufficient, taking one year with another, to defray the cost to the lessor of fulfilling his obligation under the lease and of meeting any expenses of maintenance, repairs, insurance and management of the premises subject to the lease which fall to be borne by him.[55]

6-30 There are cases in which payments made in respect of demised premises may be deducted from rents from other premises demised by the same lessor. Broadly speaking where rent is payable under a lease at a full rent (including a tenant's repairing lease) and the rent is insufficient to absorb the expenditure, the excess may be set off against rent from another lease at a full rent which is not a tenant's repairing lease.[56] " Tenant's repairing lease " means a lease where the lessee is under an obligation to maintain and repair the whole, or substantially the whole, of the premises comprised in the lease.

6. MANAGEMENT EXPENSES

6-31 A company which owns tenanted property as an investment bears corporation tax on its annual profits or gains arising in respect of rents or receipts from land, computed under the rules applicable to Schedule A; and, in particular, may deduct the cost of managing *the properties*.[57] In addition, tax relief is allowed in respect of the cost of managing *the company*. Before the introduction of corporation tax, the relief was given by way of repayment of income tax [58]; now it is given by way of deduction in computing the profits liable to corporation tax.[59] The same relief for management expenses is available to any company whose business consists mainly in the making of investments and the principal part of whose income is derived therefrom.

---

[53] I.C.T.A. 1970, s. 72 (2).
[54] *Ibid.* s. 72 (3)–(7).
[55] *Ibid.* s. 71 (2).
[56] I.C.T.A. 1970, s. 72 (4).
[57] *Ante,* § 6-27.
[58] I.T.A. 1952, s. 425.
[59] I.C.T.A. 1970, s. 304; see *post,* §§ 14-20 *et seq.*

6-32   A proportion of director's fees may be claimed as management expenses but these will be closely scrutinised.[60] Brokerage and stamp duty paid on a change of investments are not allowable management expenses.[61] A loss arising when rents were misappropriated by a fraudulent agent was held not to be a cost of management for the purposes of a Schedule A maintenance claim [62]; but different principles apply to a management expenses claim.

---

[60] See *Berry Investments Ltd.* v. *Attwooll* (1964) 41 T.C. 547.
[61] *Capital and National Trust* v. *Golder* (1949) 31 T.C. 265; *Sun Life Assurance Society* v. *Davidson* (1957) 37 T.C. 330.
[62] *Pyne* v. *Stallard-Penoyre* (1964) 42 T.C. 183.

CHAPTER 7

THE TAXATION OF FOREIGN INCOME

1. SCHEDULE D

7-01 INCOME which arises from a source within the United Kingdom is generally liable to United Kingdom tax, irrespective of the nationality, domicile, residence or presence of the recipient. There is an exception in the case of interest on certain British Government securities, such as 3½ per cent. War Loan, in the beneficial ownership of a person not ordinarily resident in the United Kingdom.[1] There are also exceptions under double taxation agreements: see §§ 7-25 *et seq.* Foreign income is chargeable to United Kingdom tax only if the recipient is resident in the United Kingdom.[2] All income which originates from a source outside the United Kingdom is " foreign income " including, for example:

(1) Income from a property situated outside the United Kingdom.[3]

(2) Dividends from a company resident outside the United Kingdom.[4]

(3) Income from a trust where the fund is situated outside the United Kingdom.[5]

(4) Income from a trade, profession or vocation carried on *wholly* outside the United Kingdom.[6]

The taxation of foreign income under Schedule C has already been mentioned.[7] Income from employments which have a foreign element is discussed later in this chapter.[8] The taxation of companies and capital gains are discussed in later chapters.[9] Other foreign income is taxed (if at all) under Case IV or Case V of Schedule D.[10]

Case I

7-02 Tax is charged under Case I of Schedule D in respect of any trade carried on in the United Kingdom *or elsewhere* on the annual profits or gains thereof [11]; but it has been held that, notwithstanding the italicised words, Case I does not apply to a trade carried on wholly outside the United Kingdom.[12] The income of such a trade is foreign income; the trade is a " foreign possession "; and United Kingdom tax can be levied only under Case V of Schedule D if and when the income is remitted to a United Kingdom resident.[13]

---

[1] I.C.T.A. 1970, s. 99. Ordinary residence is discussed *post*, § 7-24. The exemption applies only when the securities are owned by the claimant at the time when the interest arises; thus it will not apply when the securities are sold before the coupon date.

[2] *Ibid.* s. 108. Residence is discussed *post*, §§ 7-17 *et seq.*

[3] The general principles as to the situation of property are discussed *post*, § 23-09.

[4] *Bradbury* v. *English Sewing Cotton Co.* [1923] A.C. 744; 8 T.C. 481 (H.L.).

[5] *Baker* v. *Archer-Shee* [1927] A.C. 844; 11 T.C. 749 (H.L.).

[6] *Colquhoun* v. *Brooks* (1889) 14 App.Cas. 493; 2 T.C. 490 (H.L.).

[7] *Ante*, § 1-07.

[8] *Post*, §§ 7-12 *et seq.*

[9] Chaps. 14–16.

[10] *Post*, §§ 7-06 *et seq.*

[11] I.C.T.A. 1970, s. 109 (2), Case I.

[12] *Colquhoun* v. *Brooks* (1889) 14 App.Cas. 493; 2 T.C. 490 (H.L.).

[13] *Post*, § 7-09.

The question therefore arises: when is a trade carried on wholly or partly within the United Kingdom so as to bring Case I of Schedule D into operation? If a company whose trading operations are carried out wholly abroad is controlled from the United Kingdom, so that the company is resident in the United Kingdom,[14] the company is treated as trading partly within the United Kingdom.[15] In one case it was held that a foreign business owned by an individual in the United Kingdom who had the sole right of control of the business was carried on partly within the United Kingdom, even though in fact the individual had at no time exercised control within the United Kingdom: " It is a matter . . . of power and right, and not of the actual exercise of right or power." [16]

7-03   In the case of a trade which is controlled from outside the United Kingdom there is an important distinction between trading *with* and trading *partly within* the United Kingdom. If the activities of the trade consist of selling goods, the place where contracts are concluded may be decisive.

> Thus in *Grainger & Son* v. *Gough* [17] the question arose whether a French wine merchant was trading within the United Kingdom. He had appointed a firm in the City of London agents in Great Britain for the sale of his wines. The agents canvassed for orders and were remunerated on a commission basis; but no orders were accepted in Great Britain. Orders were transmitted to France where the French wine merchant exercised his discretion whether or not to accept them. No offers were accepted on behalf of the French wine merchant in Great Britain. It was held (Lord Morris dissenting) that no part of the trade was carried on in the United Kingdom.

But the place where contracts are made is not only the test and may be inappropriate in the case of a non-mercantile business. In one case, for example, Atkin L.J. propounded the test: where do the operations take place from which the profits in substance arise? [18] Thus if goods are manufactured by X in the United Kingdom and their sale by X is negotiated in the United Kingdom and delivery takes place in the United Kingdom, the clear fact that X is trading within the United Kingdom cannot be altered by executing the contract of sale abroad.

The mere act of purchasing goods from the United Kingdom (*e.g.* for resale abroad) is not trading within the United Kingdom.[19]

Case II

7-04   Tax is charged under Case II of Schedule D in respect of any profession or vocation which is carried on wholly or partly within the United Kingdom; but not in respect of a profession or vocation carried on wholly abroad.[20] Where the activities of a profession or vocation are normally carried on in

---

[14] *Unit Construction Co.* v. *Bullock* [1960] A.C. 351; 38 T.C. 712 (H.L.), *post*, § 7-24.

[15] *San Paulo (Brazilian) Ry. Co.* v. *Carter* [1896] A.C. 31; 3 T.C. 407 (H.L.).

[16] *Ogilvie* v. *Kitton* (1908) 5 T.C. 338 *per* Lord Stormonth-Darling at p. 345. It is difficult to reconcile this decision with the later decision of the House of Lords in *Egyptian Hotels Ltd.* v. *Mitchell* [1915] A.C. 1022; 6 T.C. 542 (H.L.).

[17] [1896] A.C. 325; 3 T.C. 462 (H.L.) and see *Maclaine* v. *Eccott* [1926] A.C. 424; 10 T.C. 481 (H.L.).

[18] *Smidth & Co.* v. *Greenwood* [1922] A.C. 417; 8 T.C. 193 at p. 204 (H.L.). See also *Firestone Tyre & Rubber Co. Ltd.* v. *Lewellin* (1957) 37 T.C. 111 especially the speech of Lord Radcliffe (H.L.).

[19] *Att.-Gen.* v. *Sully* (1860) 2 T.C. 149n. (Exch.Ch.).

[20] I.C.T.A. 1970, s. 109 (2), Case II.

the United Kingdom by a resident of the United Kingdom, it is difficult in practice to show that activities carried on abroad constitute a separate profession.

> Thus in *Davies* v. *Braithwaite,* [21] an actress resident in the United Kingdom was held assessable to tax in respect of earnings from an American contract which she fulfilled during a year in which she also acted in the United Kingdom. It could not be said that the acting in America was a " separate profession " from the acting in the United Kingdom.

The actress in this case entered into a variety of contracts of employment in the course of carrying on a profession within Case II of Schedule D. [22] The fees from the American contract were thus subject to United Kingdom tax, whether or not remitted to the United Kingdom. [23] If the American contract had been a " Schedule E contract " and the duties had been performed wholly outside the United Kingdom, fees paid under that contract but not remitted to the United Kingdom would at that time have escaped United Kingdom tax.

Method of assessment

7-05   The Income Tax Acts contain special provisions to enable the Revenue to assess the profits of non-residents trading in the United Kingdom. They may be assessed and charged in the name (*inter alia*) of any factor, agent, receiver, branch or manager in the United Kingdom, whether or not the factor, etc., has the receipt of the profits or gains. [24] There are provisions for the charge to be based on a percentage of turnover if the profits cannot be otherwise ascertained [25] and for taxation on the basis of merchanting profit. [26]

Cases IV and V

7-06   Case IV of Schedule D charges tax in respect of income arising from *securities* out of the United Kingdom, except income charged under Schedule C. [27] " Securities " in Case IV was held in *Singer* v. *Williams* [28] to denote " a debt or claim the payment of which is in some way secured. The security would generally consist of a right to resort to some fund or property for payment; some form of secured liability is postulated." A debenture or mortgage is a security; stocks and shares are not. [28]

7-07   Case V of Schedule D charges tax in respect of income arising from *possessions* out of the United Kingdom. [29] " Possessions " in Case V is a very wide term which embraces all sources of income other than securities, including income from trades, professions and vocations; income from stocks and shares; income from a foreign trust fund [30]; income from

---

[21] (1931) 18 T.C. 198 at pp. 205 *et seq.* Not reported on this point in [1931] 2 K.B. 628.
[22] *Cf. Fall* v. *Hitchen* (1973) 49 T.C. 433; [1973] S.T.C. 66. See *ante*, § 3-03.
[23] *Post*, § 7-08.
[24] T.M.A. 1970, ss. 78–85.   [25] *Ibid.* s. 80.
[26] *Ibid.* s. 81.   [27] I.C.T.A. 1970, s. 109 (2).
[28] [1921] 1 A.C. 41; 7 T.C. 419.
[29] T.M.A. 1970, s. 80.
[30] *Drummond* v. *Collins* [1915] A.C. 1011; 6 T.C. 525 (where the income was paid at the discretion of the trustees).

unsecured overseas pensions [31]; and alimony. [32] Note that dividends from companies resident outside the United Kingdom are taxed under Case V of Schedule D and not under Schedule F [33]: see § 14-58. Income derived from a partnership controlled outside the United Kingdom may constitute Case V income of partners resident in the United Kingdom. [34] Until 1956, emoluments of foreign employments fell within Case V but these are now assessable (if at all) under Schedule E: see *post*, §§ 7-12 *et seq*.

Foreign income which arises under a trust is not liable to United Kingdom tax if the beneficiary is resident abroad and the income is mandated direct to the beneficiary, even if the trustees are resident in the United Kingdom. [35]

2. THE BASIS OF COMPUTATION UNDER SCHEDULE D

Cases I and II of Schedule D

7-08 The basic rule is that tax is charged under Cases I and II of Schedule D on the whole of the profits from trading, etc., within the United Kingdom, whether or not the profits are remitted to the United Kingdom and whether or not the trader is resident in the United Kingdom. Thus the solicitor who carries on his practice from an office in London is chargeable to tax under Case II on profits arising from work done outside as well as within the United Kingdom. This is because the *source* of his income is a United Kingdom source, being the profession he practises in the United Kingdom; he does not have a separate source of income in each country in which he does business.

This basic rule is qualified in and from the year 1978–79 by provisions contained in section 27 of and Schedule 4 to the Finance Act 1978. Under these provisions an individual resident in the United Kingdom who carries on a trade, profession or vocation in respect of which he is within the charge to income tax under Case I or II of Schedule D can claim a relief from tax if he is absent from the United Kingdom on at least 30 *qualifying days* in a year of assessment. No entitlement to relief arises unless a claim for relief is made within two years after the end of the year of assessment. A *qualifying day* in relation to an individual carrying on a trade is a day of absence from the United Kingdom:

(a) which he devotes substantially to the activities of the trade; or

(b) which is one of at least seven consecutive days on which he is absent from the United Kingdom for the purposes of the trade and which (taken as a whole) he devotes substantially to the activities of the trade; or

(c) on which he is travelling wholly and exclusively for the purposes of the trade.

A day which is devoted to the activities of two or more trades taken together but not to any particular trade is treated as a qualifying day. A day

[31] Some such pensions are exempt from tax: see I.C.T.A. 1970, ss. 213–218.
[32] *I.R.C.* v. *Anderström* (1927) 13 T.C. 482.
[33] *Rae* v. *Lazard Investment Co. Ltd.* (1963) 41 T.C. 1 (H.L.); but *cf. Courtauld's Investments* v. *Fleming* (1969) 46 T.C. 111. See generally Whiteman and Wheatcroft, *Income Tax*, 2nd ed., para. 12-04.
[34] See I.C.T.A. 1970, s. 153; *post*, § 7-24. See *Newstead* v. *Frost* [1978] S.T.C. 239.
[35] *Williams* v. *Singer* [1921] 1 A.C. 65; 7 T.C. 387.

of absence from the United Kingdom which an individual who is a member of a non-resident partnership devotes to its trading operations within the United Kingdom (but not those outside the United Kingdom) may be a qualifying day. An individual is not regarded as absent from the United Kingdom on any day unless he is absent at the end of it. Generally the period of absence begins when the individual boards the vessel or aircraft to leave the United Kingdom and continues until his return to the United Kingdom but a period spent on (for example) a cruise which begins and ends in the United Kingdom is not treated as a period of absence.

The relief is not measured by reference to the actual profits earned outside the United Kingdom but is calculated (under provisions in Sched. 4) by reference to the total profits of the year after taking account of capital allowances and stock relief. The relief is 25 per cent. of the total profits attributable to the number of qualifying days in the year of assessment so that if, for example, the individual spends 35 qualifying days outside the United Kingdom, the amount deductible from his total profits is 25 per cent. of 35/365ths of the total profits. When a day is a qualifying day as being devoted to the activities of (say) two or three trades taken together, it is treated as a fraction of a day—a half or one-third—in calculating the amount which is deductible from the total profits of each trade.

Cases IV and V

7-09   Tax is charged under Cases IV and V of Schedule D on the full amount of the income *arising* in the year preceding the year of assessment, whether the income has been or will be received in the United Kingdom or not.[36] This basis (called " the arising basis ") does not apply as respects income arising up to and including the year 1973–74 in three cases:

(1) To the income of any person who satisfies the Commissioners that he is not domiciled in the United Kingdom or that (being a British subject or a citizen of the Republic of Ireland) he is not ordinarily resident in the United Kingdom.

(2) To any income which is immediately derived by a person from the carrying on by him of any trade, profession or vocation, either solely or in partnership.

(3) To any income which arises from a pension.

In these three cases, tax is charged on the full amount of the sums *received* in the United Kingdom in the year preceding the year of assessment.[37] This is commonly described as the " remittance basis," as contrasted with the normal " arising basis."

> *Example*: Brown, a British subject resident in England, owns a villa in Monte Carlo which he leases during the summer months. The rent is foreign income chargeable to tax under Case V of Schedule D. Brown will be assessed on the full amount of the income, even if it is paid into a bank in France and remains there. If Brown were domiciled in France, he would be assessed only on the income remitted to the United Kingdom.

---

[36] I.C.T.A. 1970, s. 122 (1). There are special rules which apply where a source of income is first acquired or ceases.
[37] I.C.T.A. 1970, s. 122 (3).

For the year 1974–75 and subsequent years of assessment the remittance basis applies only to (1) in § 7-08, the arising basis applying to cases (2) and (3),[38] except that a deduction of one-quarter of the amount of income is allowed in charging it,[39] save in the case of foreign pensions or annuities where the allowable deduction is one-tenth.[40] Since the remittance basis no longer applies in case (2), only a limited saving of United Kingdom income tax (resulting from the 25 per cent. deduction) can be achieved by individuals establishing foreign trading partnerships and accumulating profits outside the United Kingdom, unless case (1) applies.

Where the arising basis applies, income tax paid in the place where the income arises may be deducted, unless this is forbidden by the Income Tax Acts or some other relief is given, *e.g.* under a double taxation agreement. Any annuity or other annual payment payable out of the income to a non-resident may likewise be deducted.[41] Foreign income tax on profits which are not chargeable to tax in the United Kingdom cannot be deducted from income which is so chargeable.[42] The remittance basis does not apply to companies within the charge to corporation tax.[43]

What constitutes a remittance? [44]

7-10   Income is remitted to the United Kingdom if the money or the equivalent of money in normal commercial usage (*e.g.* a cheque or bill of exchange) is received in the United Kingdom, either by the resident taxpayer himself or by another person to whom the taxpayer has directed payment to be made [45] (*e.g.* a creditor), unless the amount remitted has ceased to be the property of the taxpayer before it reaches the United Kingdom.[46] Capital which is remitted to the United Kingdom is not assessable to tax.[47] If income is invested abroad and the investments are later sold and the proceeds of sale remitted to the United Kingdom, this is a remittance of income.[48] Foreign income of a person ordinarily resident in the United Kingdom which is applied abroad in repaying debts in the United Kingdom is deemed to be remitted to the United Kingdom.[49] There are other cases of constructive, or deemed, remittance.[50]

Where a person resident in the United Kingdom is required under the Exchange Control Acts to offer to the Treasury any receipt in a particular foreign currency, any part of the proceeds of that receipt which is remitted abroad immediately is treated for the purposes of assessment to income tax

---

[38] F.A. 1974, ss. 22 (1) and 23 (1).   [39] *Ibid.* s. 23 (3).
[40] *Ibid.* s. 22 (1).
[41] I.C.T.A. 1970, s. 122 (1) (*b*).
[42] *Scottish American Investment Co.* v. *I.R.C.*, 1938 S.C. 234.
[43] I.C.T.A. 1970, s. 243 (1).
[44] See especially *Thomson* v. *Moyse* [1961] A.C. 967; 39 T.C. 291 where the law is reviewed by the House of Lords. It was held that the sale of a cheque in London drawn on a bank abroad was a remittance of the sum realised. See also *Harmel* v. *Wright* (1974) 49 T.C. 149; [1974] S.T.C. 88.
[45] *Timpson's Executors* v. *Yerbury* [1936] 1 K.B. 645; 20 T.C. 155 (C.A.).
[46] *Carter* v. *Sharon* (1936) 20 T.C. 229.
[47] *Kneen* v. *Martin* [1935] 1 K.B. 499 (C.A.); 19 T.C. 33 (remittance of proceeds of sale of investments); *cf. Scottish Provident Institution* v. *Allan* [1903] A.C. 129; 4 T.C. 591 (where interest was intermixed with capital to an extent that made segregation impossible: the onus lies on the taxpayer to show that what is remitted is capital).
[48] *Patuck* v. *Lloyd* (1944) 26 T.C. 284 (C.A.).
[49] See I.C.T.A. 1970, s. 122 (4).   [50] See I.C.T.A. 1970, s. 122 (5)–(7).

on that occasion as though it had not been remitted to the United Kingdom. The term " immediately " is interpreted as covering the period not exceeding three months from the date of crediting of the proceeds, provided that the money in question has not been expended or used during that time in the United Kingdom, and that it has been kept in a specific bank account.[51]

Basic periods

7-11   Cases IV and V of Schedule D charge tax on the income which arises (or is received) in the year preceding the year of assessment. There is, however, a different basis period where a fresh source of foreign income arises.[52] Where the remittance basis applies, tax is charged as if a new source arose when the income was first remitted to the United Kingdom, so if the recipient was not resident in the United Kingdom in that year, the normal preceding year basis will apply if he later becomes resident.[53] Where a non-resident with an existing source of foreign income later acquires a United Kingdom residence, this is not a new " source." [54]

Losses

7- 11A   The methods by which tax relief for losses is given are discussed in Chapter 12. The Finance Act 1974 contains provisions enabling losses to be relieved against foreign income which, in consequence of the changes made by that Act, is now liable to United Kingdom tax.

3. EMPLOYMENTS WITH A FOREIGN ELEMENT

7-12   The Schedule E charging provisions were restructured by the Finance Act 1974, primarily in order to bring into charge to tax emoluments, wherever earned, of persons resident and ordinarily resident in the United Kingdom and to get rid of the provisions under which emoluments earned by such persons outside the United Kingdom previously escaped United Kingdom tax provided they were not remitted to the United Kingdom during any year of assessment in which the office or employment existed.[55] These changes operate for 1974–75 and subsequent years and take effect subject to Double Taxation Agreements. The Finance Act 1977 changes as from 1977–78 provisions in the Act of 1974 giving tax relief on emoluments earned during periods of absence outside the United Kingdom.[56]

The charging provisions

7-12 (1)   Schedule E is now divided into three Cases. The expression " foreign emoluments " which is used in connection with the Cases is defined in § 7-14. The meaning of residence, ordinary residence and domicile is discussed in §§ 7-17 *et seq*.

---

[51] Concession B12.   [52] See I.C.T.A. 1970, s. 123.
[53] *Carter* v. *Sharon* (1936) 20 T.C. 229. See Concession A14 as to the year of commencement or cessation of permanent residence.
[54] *Back* v. *Whitlock* [1932] 1 K.B. 747; 16 T.C. 723.
[55] For the law before 1974–75, see 7th ed. at §§ 7-12 *et seq*.
[56] For the law before 1977–78 and after 1974–75, see 10th ed. at §§ 7-12 *et seq*.

Case I [57] applies where the person holding the office or employment is resident and ordinarily resident in the United Kingdom. The charge is on any emoluments for the chargeable period, [58] *i.e.* the whole of the emoluments are chargeable to tax, subject to the following exceptions [59]:

(1) *Foreign duties performed in periods of long absence from the United Kingdom (365 days or more): 100 per cent. deduction.* [60] Where in any year of assessment the duties of an employment (including an office [61]) are performed wholly or partly outside the United Kingdom [62] and any of those duties are performed during a *qualifying period* which falls wholly or partly in that year of assessment, no tax is chargeable on the emoluments attributable to that qualifying period or such of it as falls in the year of assessment. More precisely, in charging tax under Case I of Schedule E on the amount of the emoluments in question, a deduction equal to the whole of them is allowed. A *qualifying period* means a period of at least 365 consecutive days entirely consisting of days of absence [63] from the United Kingdom; except that where a period of absence from the United Kingdom is preceded by an earlier such period or periods, all the periods of absence can be added together to see if there are 365 days of absence in all, provided (a) there are no more than 62 intervening days between the periods and (b) the number of days in the resulting period which are spent in the United Kingdom does not exceed one-sixth of the total number of days in that period. In reckoning the emoluments attributable to a qualifying period there can be included any emoluments covering a period of leave immediately following the period.

(2) *Foreign duties performed in periods of short absence: 25 per cent. deduction.* [64] Where in any year of assessment the duties of an employment are performed wholly or partly outside the United Kingdom [65] and the number of days in that year which are qualifying days in relation to the employment (together with any which are qualifying days in relation to other employments) amounts to at least 30 days, a deduction of 25 per cent. is allowed from the emoluments chargeable under Case I of Schedule E which are attributable to duties performed outside the United Kingdom in that year. A *qualifying day* in relation to an employment is a day of absence from the United Kingdom [66]:

---

[57] I.C.T.A. 1970, s. 181 (1) substituted by F.A. 1974, s. 21 (1).

[58] Chargeable period means an accounting period of a company or a year of assessment: I.C.T.A. 1970, s. 526 (5).

[59] Exceptions (1), (2) and (3) are contained in F.A. 1977, s. 31 and Sched. 7. Exception (4) is in F.A. 1974, Sched. 2.

[60] F.A. 1977, Sched. 7, para. 1.

[61] *Ibid.* para. 11.

[62] Where an employment is in substance one the duties of which fall in the year of assessment to be performed in the United Kingdom, there shall be treated as so performed any duties performed outside the United Kingdom the performance of which is merely incidental to the performance of the other duties in the United Kingdom: *ibid.* para. 8. For the location of duties performed on ships or aircraft: *ibid.* para. 7.

[63] A person is not regarded as absent from the United Kingdom on any day unless he is so absent at the end of it: *ibid.* para. 6.

[64] F.A. 1977, Sched. 7, para. 2.

[65] *Supra*, n. 61.

[66] F.A. 1977, Sched. 7, para. 2.

(a) which is substantially devoted to the performance outside the United Kingdom of the duties of that employment or of that and other employments; or

(b) which is one of at least seven consecutive days on which the person concerned is absent from the United Kingdom for the purpose of the performance of such duties outside the United Kingdom and which (taken as a whole) are substantially devoted to the performance of such duties as aforesaid; or

(c) on which the person concerned is travelling in or for the purpose of the performance of such duties outside the United Kingdom.

(3) *Foreign employments* [67]: *25 per cent. deduction.* Where in any year of assessment the duties of an employment are performed wholly outside the United Kingdom [68] and the employment is with a person, a body of persons or partnership resident outside, and not resident in, the United Kingdom, a deduction of 25 per cent. is allowed from the amount of the emoluments chargeable under Case I of Schedule E from that employment for that year. Relative periods of absence from, or presence in, the United Kingdom are irrelevant in applying this deduction.

There are elaborate anti-avoidance provisions [69] which prevent a person whose job is performed partly within and partly outside the United Kingdom from obtaining additional tax relief by having two employments, possibly with associated employers, and having the emoluments " loaded " onto the foreign employment.

The same day may be taken into account for the purposes of Exceptions (1) and (2) above, but a deduction is not allowed in respect of the same emoluments under both those exceptions or under either of them as well as under exception (3). [70]

(4) *Foreign emoluments.* When the emoluments are foreign emoluments (see *post*, § 7-14), a deduction of half their amount is allowed, [71] except that if the duties are performed wholly outside the United Kingdom in the chargeable period, Case I does not apply [72] but Case III will apply to emoluments *received* in the United Kingdom. [73]

Thus a person domiciled in the United States of America, employed by an American corporation and posted to the United Kingdom for a tour of duty with its United Kingdom branch will pay United Kingdom tax under Case I on half the emoluments from his United Kingdom job. If he also has a directorship with a foreign company and performs the duties of that office wholly outside the United Kingdom, he will be charged on a remittance basis under Case III in respect of the emoluments of the foreign directorship.

7-12 (2)   *Case II* [74] applies where the person holding the office or employment is not resident or, if resident, is not ordinarily resident in the United Kingdom.

---

[67] *Ibid.* para. 3.   [68] *Supra*, n. 61.
[69] *Ibid.* para. 4.   [70] *Ibid.* para. 10.
[71] I.C.T.A. 1970, s. 181 (1), para. 1 and F.A. 1974, Sched. 2, para. 3. In and after 1976–77, the deduction is one-quarter if the taxpayer is resident in the United Kingdom in the year of assessment and was so resident in the preceding 10 years or in nine of them.
[72] I.C.T.A. 1970, s. 181 (1), para. 1 and F.A. 1974, Sched. 2, para. 4.   [73] *Post*, § 7-12 (3).
[74] I.C.T.A. 1970, s. 181 (1) substituted by F.A. 1974, s. 21 (1).

Thus it applies to a person who normally lives and works abroad (and so is ordinarily resident outside the United Kingdom) but who works in the United Kingdom for periods sufficiently short to become resident but not ordinarily resident there or so short as to become neither resident nor ordinarily resident. The charge is on the whole of the emoluments for the chargeable period [75] in respect of duties performed in the United Kingdom unless the emoluments are foreign emoluments (see *post*, § 7-14) when a deduction of one-half of their amount is allowed. [76] Emoluments for duties performed outside the United Kingdom are not taxable under Case II but are taxable under Case III [77] if the person is resident in the United Kingdom and remits the emoluments to the United Kingdom.

7-12 (3)   *Case III* [77] applies to persons resident in the United Kingdom (whether ordinarily resident there or not) and applies to emoluments *received* in the United Kingdom in circumstances (mentioned above) in which Cases I and II do not apply.

Emoluments are treated as received in the United Kingdom if they are paid, used or enjoyed or in any manner or form transmitted or brought to the United Kingdom. [78]

Where a person who is resident in the United Kingdom receives foreign currency, this has to be surrendered to an authorised dealer under section 2 of the Exchange Control Act 1947. This requirement is satisfied, without there being any remittance for United Kingdom tax purposes, by payment into a bank in the Channel Islands. [79]

Case III does not catch emoluments of years before 1974–75 which, if the new system had been enacted, would have fallen under Cases I or II. [80] Thus persons resident or ordinarily resident in the United Kingdom who performed duties outside the United Kingdom before 1974–75 can now remit their emoluments from those duties without Case III applying.

Non-residents

7-13   Persons who are neither resident nor ordinarily resident in the United Kingdom can be charged to tax in respect of an office or employment only under Case II of Schedule E on the emoluments attributable to the duties performed in the United Kingdom. If the emoluments are foreign emoluments, a deduction of one-half of their amount is allowed.

Foreign emoluments

7-14   The expression " foreign emoluments " means emoluments of a person not domiciled in the United Kingdom from an office or employment under or with any person, body of persons or partnership resident outside, and not resident in, the United Kingdom. [81]

---

[75] Chargeable period means an accounting period of a company or a year of assessment: I.C.T.A. 1970, s. 526 (5).
[76] I.C.T.A. 1970, s. 181 (1), para. 1 and F.A. 1974, Sched. 2, para. 4.
[77] *Supra*, n. 73.
[78] I.C.T.A. 1970, s. 184 (4). See also § 7-10.
[79] Concession B12. See also § 7-10.
[80] F.A. 1974, s. 21 (9).   [81] I.C.T.A. 1970, s. 181 (1), para. 1.

The expression foreign emoluments applies, for example, to an individual whose home is outside the United Kingdom but who works in the United Kingdom for a non-resident company. Note that the word " foreign " does not refer to the place where the duties are performed. Foreign emoluments may be taxable under any one of the three Cases of Schedule E, depending on the residence and ordinary residence status of the taxpayer.

Place of performance of duties

7-15   There are a number of rules which apply for determining the place where duties of an office or employment are to be treated as performed. These are as follows:

(1) Under section 184 (2) of the Income and Corporation Taxes Act 1970 where an office or employment is in substance one the duties of which fall in the year of assessment to be performed outside the United Kingdom, duties of an incidental character performed in the United Kingdom are to be treated as performed outside the United Kingdom. *Semble*, a close examination of all duties performed in and out of the United Kingdom should be made to see to what extent the duties performed in the United Kingdom are incidental to those performed outside the United Kingdom.[82] (Section 184 (2) is ignored in determining when duties are performed or whether a person is absent from the United Kingdom in applying Exceptions (1) and (2) in § 7-12 (1).)[83]

(2) Under section 184 (3) the following duties are to be treated as performed in the United Kingdom:

(a) the duties of any office or employment under the Crown of a public nature[84] of which the emoluments are payable out of public revenue; and

(b) any duties which a person performs on a vessel engaged on a voyage not extending to a port outside the United Kingdom, or which a person resident in the United Kingdom performs on a vessel or aircraft engaged on a voyage or journey beginning or ending in the United Kingdom, or on a part beginning or ending in the United Kingdom of any other voyage or journey.[85]

Expenses in connection with work done abroad

7- 15A   Section 189 (1) of the Income and Corporation Taxes Act 1970 allows as a deduction from Schedule E emoluments expenses in travelling in the performance of the duties of an office or employment and other expenses incurred wholly, exclusively and necessarily in the performance of the duties: § 3-35. Section 32 of the Finance Act 1977, which has effect for 1977–78 and subsequent years of assessment, gives a special relief to employees who are resident and ordinarily resident in the United Kingdom

---

[82] See *Robson* v. *Dixon* (1972) 48 T.C. 527; *post*, § 7-20.

[83] F.A. 1977, Sched. 7, para. 9.

[84] Duties performed by civil servants are of a public nature, whatever the rank or grade of the servant: *Graham* v. *White* (1971) 48 T.C. 163. And see *Wienand* v. *Anderton* [1977] S.T.C. 12.

[85] As to modifications to this provision in applying F.A. 1977, Sched. 7, see *ibid.* para. 7.

and who hold an office or employment (" the overseas employment ") the duties of which are performed wholly outside the United Kingdom. The relief does not apply to foreign emoluments: see § 7-14. The following expenses are treated for the purposes of section 189 (1) as necessarily incurred for the purposes of the overseas employment:

(a) expenses incurred by the employee in travelling from the United Kingdom to take up the overseas employment and in returning to the United Kingdom on its termination;

(b) where the employee holds two or more offices or employments, one outside the United Kingdom, and he travels from one place of duty to the other (either or both of such places being out of the United Kingdom), the expenses of travelling are treated as incurred in performing the duties to be performed at his destination [86];

(c) where a person is absent from the United Kingdom for a continuous period of 60 days or more for the purpose of performing duties outside the United Kingdom, travelling expenses incurred by the employee in visiting (or being visited by) his spouse or child are (within stringent limits) allowed;

(d) where in order to enable him to perform the duties of an overseas employment, board and lodging outside the United Kingdom is provided (or the cost is reimbursed), the cost (or the amount reimbursed, as the case may be) is deductible.

Terminal payments

7-16   The provisions discussed in §§ 3-24 *et seq.* apply to offices and employments in which a foreign element is involved, but subject to the following provisions [87]:

(1) Where the emoluments of the office or employment were foreign emoluments (defined *ante*, § 7-14), only one-half of a lump sum paid on termination of the employment is chargeable to tax;

(2) Where the emoluments of the office or employment were not chargeable to tax, or would not have been charged had there been any earnings, a lump sum paid on termination of the employment is itself not chargeable to tax.

4. THE NATURE OF RESIDENCE AND ORDINARY RESIDENCE

7-17 The Tax Acts contain no definition of the terms " residence " and " ordinary residence," which accordingly have their ordinary dictionary meaning. In the case of an individual, " residence " describes the country where he lives. " Ordinary residence " is broadly equivalent to habitual residence and contrasts with casual or occasional residence. [88] The question whether an individual is ordinarily resident in the United Kingdom in any year of assessment has to be answered by examining his pattern of life over

---

[86] This involves a departure from normal Schedule E principles, which draw a distinction between travelling *on* the job (deductible) and travelling *to* the job (non-deductible).

[87] I.C.T.A. 1970, s. 188 (2) as amended by F.A. 1974, s. 14 (3) and (4).

[88] *I.R.C.* v. *Lysaght* [1925] A.C. 234; 13 T.C. 511 (H.L.).

a period of years: in this respect, the concept of ordinary residence resembles domicile more than residence. A person may be resident but not ordinarily resident in the United Kingdom in a year of assessment; conversely, he may be ordinarily resident but not resident.[89] It will be seen from the cases referred to below that an individual who is physically absent from the United Kingdom for an entire year of assessment is normally not resident there; but it is clear that such a person may be treated as ordinarily resident if, for example, he was ordinarily resident in the previous year and returned to the United Kingdom as a resident in the following year. Thus an individual cannot escape capital gains tax by physically absenting himself from the United Kingdom for one year of assessment during which he disposes of his assets, for he will be treated as ordinarily resident (though not resident) in the United Kingdom in that year.

The concept of " ordinary residence " is important as regards (a) immunity from income tax [90] and capital transfer tax [91] in respect of certain British Government securities; (b) immunity from capital gains tax [92]; (c) the taxation of emoluments [93]; and (d) the application of section 478 of the Income and Corporation Taxes Act 1970.[94]

The six months rule

7-18   Section 51 of the Income and Corporation Taxes Act 1970 provides that a person who is in the United Kingdom for some temporary purpose only and not with a view or intent of establishing his residence there, and who has not actually resided in the United Kingdom at one time or several times for a period equal in the whole to six months in any year of assessment, shall not be chargeable as a United Kingdom resident; but that a person who has so actually resided shall be so chargeable. Thus physical presence in the United Kingdom in a year of assessment for some temporary purpose will not make a person resident in the year unless the physical presence is for a period or periods totalling six months in the year of assessment. Six months is regarded as equivalent to 183 days, whether or not the year is a leap year. Fractions of a day will be taken into account to measure the period spent in the United Kingdom [95] except that, under the present practice of the Revenue, days of arrival and days of departure are normally ignored.[96] An individual physically present in the United Kingdom for more than six months, but not in the same year of assessment, is not thereby made resident.

Presence for less than six months

7-19   It follows from section 51 of the Income and Corporation Taxes Act 1970 (*ante*, § 7-18), that a person who is physically present in the United

---

[89] *Cf.* F.A. 1965, s. 20; *post*, § 16-04.
[90] *Ante*, § 7-01.
[91] *Post*, § 19-26.
[92] *Post*, § 16-04.
[93] *Ante*, §§ 7-12 *et seq.*
[94] *Post*, § 7-26.
[95] *Wilkie* v. *I.R.C.* [1952] Ch. 153; 32 T.C. 395.
[96] See Inland Revenue booklet, " Residents and Non-residents: Liability to Tax in the United Kingdom " I.R. 20, para. 8.

Kingdom for less than six months in a year of assessment may nevertheless be treated as resident there if his presence has a " residential quality." The following numbered paragraphs exemplify this proposition.

(1) *Place of abode in the United Kingdom.* A person who has his home abroad but also has a place of abode available for his occupation in the United Kingdom will be treated as resident in the United Kingdom in any year of assessment in which he visits the United Kingdom, however short his visit. If he visits in four or more consecutive years, or intends to do so from the start, he will be treated as ordinarily resident also.[97]

> Thus in *Lloyd* v. *Sulley,*[98] a merchant who carried on business in Italy (where he ordinarily resided) owned a house in the United Kingdom where he lived with his family for several months in a year. It was held that he was resident in the United Kingdom, for his occupation of the house had the characteristics of a settled residence. The same conclusion was reached in a case where the establishment was leased to,[99] and in another where it was owned by,[1] a company controlled by the taxpayer. By contrast a different conclusion was reached in a case where a merchant living in Madras had a family home in Scotland (where his children lived during the year of assessment) but which the merchant did not visit during the year.[2]

Hence *ownership* of the place of abode is immaterial. Note that physical presence within the United Kingdom is necessary for residence as distinct from ordinary residence. A house owned by a visitor but let on terms which give him no right of occupation is not in practice regarded as available for his use.[3]

7-20   There is an important statutory qualification [4] to the proposition in (1) above which applies where a person works full-time abroad in a trade, profession, vocation, office or employment where all the duties thereof are performed outside the United Kingdom. In this case the question whether he is resident in the United Kingdom must be decided without regard to any place of abode maintained there for his use; and if (in the case of an office or employment) the office or employment is one of which the duties fall in the year of assessment to be performed outside the United Kingdom, merely incidental duties performed within the United Kingdom are treated as performed abroad. Thus a man who works full-time abroad but who keeps his house in the United Kingdom (*e.g.* for use when on leave) is not treated as resident in the United Kingdom merely by virtue of his ownership of the house and his visits when on leave. Further, if his job brings him to the United Kingdom, the duties performed here are disregarded.

> But in *Robson* v. *Dixon* [5] a pilot employed by K.L.M. Airlines and based in Amsterdam occasionally landed in the United Kingdom *en route* to his destination. It was held that the landings in the United Kingdom were not " merely incidental to the performance of the other duties outside the United

---

[97] *Ibid.* para. 21.
[98] (1884) 2 T.C. 37, *per* Lord Shand at p. 44.
[99] *Cooper* v. *Cadwalader* (1904) 5 T.C. 101.
[1] *Loewenstein* v. *De Salis* (1926) 10 T.C. 424.
[2] *Turnbull* v. *Foster* (1904) 6 T.C. 206.
[3] See Inland Revenue booklet in note 96 at para. 28.
[4] I.C.T.A. 1970, s. 50.
[5] (1972) 48 T.C. 527.

Kingdom." The duties performed here had the same quality as those performed elsewhere.

7-21   (2) *Regular visits.* A person who maintains no place of abode in the United Kingdom may nevertheless be held to be resident there if he pays regular visits to the United Kingdom (although for less than 183 days in each year of assessment) if these visits form part of his habit of life. The Revenue's practice in applying this rule is as follows:

> " A visitor who has no accommodation available will be regarded as becoming resident and ordinarily resident after his visits for four consecutive years have averaged three months or more a year. If it is clear when he first comes that he proposes to make such visits, he may be treated as resident and ordinarily resident in the United Kingdom from the start." [6]

Thus a person who comes to the United Kingdom for a period of study or education expected to last more than four years will be regarded by the Revenue as resident and ordinarily resident from the date of his arrival in the United Kingdom.[7] A person who comes to the United Kingdom to work for a period of at least two years is treated as resident for the whole period but not as ordinarily resident until he has been in the United Kingdom for at least three years.[8]

By contrast, a person who visits the United Kingdom over a number of years merely in the course of travel will not be treated as resident there.

Although the purpose of the visitor is relevant in determining whether or not his visits have a residential quality, it is immaterial that the visitor has no freedom of choice, *e.g.* because his presence in the United Kingdom is an exigency of his business.[9]

> In *Levene* v. *I.R.C.*[10] a retired businessman who had been resident and ordinarily resident in the United Kingdom went to live abroad where he lived in hotels, having no fixed abode. For five years thereafter he spent four or five months each year in the United Kingdom obtaining medical advice, visiting relatives, etc.—this being part of his regular system of life. *Held*, he remained resident in the United Kingdom having left the United Kingdom for " occasional " residence abroad (see § 7-22).
>
> In *I.R.C.* v. *Lysaght* [11] a director sold his house in England and went to live with his family in Ireland. He returned to England each month for directors' meetings, remaining for about a week on the company's business and staying in hotels. *Held*, he was resident in the United Kingdom.

7-22   (3) *Former residence.* Section 49 of the Income and Corporation Taxes Act 1970 provides that where a British subject or citizen of the Republic of Ireland, whose ordinary residence has been in the United Kingdom, leaves the United Kingdom for the purpose only of occasional residence abroad, he will be treated during his absence as actually residing in the United Kingdom. In *Levene* v. *I.R.C.*[12] the observation that the appellant

---

[6] See Inland Revenue booklet in n. 96 at para. 21.
[7] *Ibid.* paras. 23–24; *Miesegaes* v. *I.R.C.* (1957) 37 T.C. 493 (C.A.).
[8] *Ibid.* para. 25.
[9] *I.R.C.* v. *Lysaght* [1928] A.C. 234 at p. 248; 13 T.C. 511 at pp. 534–535; *Inchiquin* v. *I.R.C.* (1948) 31 T.C. 125.
[10] [1928] A.C. 217; 13 T.C. 486, *per* Viscount Cave.
[11] *I.R.C.* v. *Lysaght* [1928] A.C. 234 at p. 248; 13 T.C. 511 at pp. 534–535; *Inchiquin* v. *I.R.C.* (1948) 31 T.C. 125.   [12] [1928] A.C. 217; 13 T.C. 486, *per* Viscount Cave.

" changed his sky but not his home " graphically describes the state of mind of an individual with an " occasional " residence abroad. Section 49 creates a presumption that a person ordinarily resident in the United Kingdom retains that ordinary residence; but this presumption may be displaced by proof of abandonment of his United Kingdom residence.

Residence in the year of assessment

7-23   The question whether a person is resident or ordinarily resident in the United Kingdom has to be determined for the year of assessment. Strictly, each tax year has to be looked at as a whole and a person is either resident or not resident for the whole year. He cannot be regarded as resident for part only. There is, however, a published concession [13] which applies when a person leaves the United Kingdom for permanent residence abroad so as to become not ordinarily resident in the United Kingdom or becomes a new permanent resident not previously ordinarily resident in the United Kingdom. In such cases, he is treated as ceasing to be resident (or becoming resident, as the case may be) on the date of departure (or arrival).

Residence of corporations and partnerships

7-24   A corporation is resident in the country (or countries) where the central management and control resides. Central management and control is usually invested by the constitution of the company in its board of directors and therefore lies in the country where the board meets; but if in fact control is exercised elsewhere, the company will be treated as resident elsewhere. [14] A company resident in the United Kingdom may not lawfully cease to be so resident without Treasury consent. [15]

The residence of a partnership is determined on principles similar to those governing corporations. If the control and management of the firm is situate abroad, the trade or business of the firm is deemed to be carried on by persons resident outside the United Kingdom and the firm is deemed to reside outside the United Kingdom, notwithstanding the fact that some of the members are resident in the United Kingdom and some of the trading operations are conducted within the United Kingdom [16]; but the profits of trading operations within the United Kingdom are chargeable to United Kingdom taxation. [17]

5. DOUBLE TAXATION RELIEF

7-25 Income arising in one country to which a person resident in another country is entitled may be subject to tax in both countries. Under English law relief in respect of the foreign tax may take one of the following forms:

---

[13] See Inland Revenue booklet in n. 96 at para. 11.
[14] *Unit Construction* v. *Bullock* [1960] A.C. 351; 38 T.C. 712 (H.L.).
[15] I.C.T.A. 1970, s. 482.
[16] *Ibid.* s. 153 (1).
[17] *Ibid.* s. 153 (2).

(1) *Double taxation conventions* [18]

Many conventions have been entered into between the United Kingdom and foreign governments providing relief from double taxation. Each convention is different but, broadly speaking, the relief may take one of two forms:

(a) Certain classes of income are made taxable only in one of the countries concerned, *e.g.* in the country where the taxpayer resides.

(b) Other income is taxable in both countries but (in the case of United Kingdom residents) the foreign tax is allowed as a credit against United Kingdom taxes.

Where the taxpayer is resident in both countries, the relief in (a) is usually not available.

(2) *Unilateral relief*

Where there is no double taxation convention in force, relief is given in accordance with section 498 of the Income and Corporation Taxes Act 1970.

(3) *Relief by deduction*

Where neither (1) nor (2) applies the foreign tax may be deducted in computing the amount of foreign income which is assessable to United Kingdom income tax.

6. ANTI-AVOIDANCE LEGISLATION

7-26 Income of a person not resident within the United Kingdom which arises outside the United Kingdom escapes United Kingdom income tax. If it were not for the provisions of sections 478–481 of the Income and Corporation Taxes Act 1970, tax could be avoided by an individual resident in the United Kingdom transferring income-producing property to a foreign resident company and enjoying the income abroad. Section 478 comes into operation, however, whenever there is a transfer of assets, whether abroad or not, in consequence of which (whether directly or through " associated operations " [19]) income [20] becomes payable to persons, including companies, resident or domiciled outside the United Kingdom. It is arguable that profits earned by a trading company are not income which " becomes payable " to the company. [21] In the case of an investment company with dividend income, it has been held that it means such income before deduction of management expenses. [22] Broadly speaking, where any individual ordinarily resident in the United Kingdom has power to enjoy income of a person resident or domiciled out of the United Kingdom, [23] such income is treated as his income for all the purposes of the Income Tax

---

[18] I.C.T.A. 1970, s. 497.
[19] Defined *ibid.* s. 478 (4).
[20] This does not include directors' remuneration.
[21] *Cf. Latilla* v. *I.R.C.* [1951] A.C. 421; 32 T.C. 159 (H.L.).
[22] *Chetwode (Lord)* v. *I.R.C.* [1977] S.T.C. 64 (H.L.).
[23] As to which see I.C.T.A. 1970, s. 478 (5) and (6).

Acts. Where assets are transferred to a non-resident company whose shares are then settled on the trusts of a discretionary settlement with a number of beneficiaries ordinarily resident in the United Kingdom it seems that *each* beneficiary could be assessed as a person having power to enjoy the *whole* of any income which the non-resident company does not distribute.[24]

There are provisions [25] which exempt transactions in respect of which the Board are satisfied either (a) that tax avoidance was not the purpose or one of the purposes for which the transfer or associated operations or any of them were effected; or (b) that the transfer and any associated operations were bona fide commercial transactions and were not designed for the purpose of avoiding liability to taxation.[26] The powers of the Revenue to obtain information for the purposes of these sections are unusually wide.[27]

---

[24] Note the wide language of I.C.T.A. 1970, s. 478 (5) (*d*). *Lord Howard de Walden* v. *I.R.C.* (1941) 25 T.C. 121 (C.A.). See also *Vestey* v. *I.R.C.* [1977] S.T.C. 414.

[25] I.C.T.A. 1970, s. 478 (3).

[26] This includes estate duty (*Sassoon* v. *I.R.C.* (1943) 25 T.C. 154), capital transfer tax and capital gains tax.

[27] See I.C.T.A. 1970, s. 481. See the information asked for in *Royal Bank of Canada* v. *I.R.C.* [1972] Ch. 665; 47 T.C. 565; *Clinch* v. *I.R.C.* [1974] Q.B. 76; 49 T.C. 52. *Cf. Wilover Nominees* v. *I.R.C.* (1974) 49 T.C. 559.

CHAPTER 8

TOTAL INCOME: THE COMPUTATION OF THE TAX LIABILITY OF AN INDIVIDUAL UNDER THE UNIFIED SYSTEM

INTRODUCTION

8-01 IN the earlier chapters of this book we have seen what income is chargeable to tax and the detailed provisions of the Schedules and Cases under which income is so chargeable. In this chapter we see how, for each year of assessment ending on April 5, the taxable income of an *individual* is determined and charged to tax. The word " individual " does not include personal representatives or trustees, nor does it include companies.

1. THE METHOD OF CHARGING TAX

8-02 The rates of tax and the " bands " of income taxed at those rates are determined annually by Parliament.[1] The Finance Act 1978, the Budget Resolutions for which were passed on April 11, 1978, fixes the rates and bands for 1978–79.

Lower, basic and higher rate income tax

8-03 Section 32 of the Finance Act 1971 (as amended [2]) prescribes the method of charging income tax. The first band of an individual's *taxable income* is charged at such lower rate or rates as Parliament may determine; and the second band of *taxable income* is charged at the basic rate. Taxable income means the amount of an individual's income after making deductions for personal reliefs, *etc.*, as explained in §§ 8-15 *et seq.* For the year 1978–79 the lower rate is 25 per cent. and the lower rate band ends at £750. The basic rate is 33 per cent. and the basic rate band ends at £8,000.[3]

8-04 Income in excess of £8,000 is not charged at the basic rate but is charged at a higher rate or rates in accordance with a statutory table. Tax at these higher rates may be conveniently referred to as " higher rate tax." The table applicable for 1978–79 is as shown on page 162.[3]

Additional rates on investment income

8-05 Where an individual's taxable income includes investment income (see § 8-07) in excess of a certain amount, income tax is charged at an additional rate or rates, *i.e.* additional to basic rate tax and to higher rate tax. This excess amount is called " income chargeable as investment income." [4] This additional rate tax may be conveniently referred to as the " investment income surcharge."

---

[1] F.A. 1971, s. 32.
[2] F.A. 1978, s. 14 (introducing " lower rate income tax ").
[3] F.A. 1978, s. 13.
[4] F.A. 1971, s. 32 (3).

Higher Rate Table

Part of excess over £8,000	Higher rate %	Tax on full slice £	Cumulative tax at maximum on each slice £
The first £1,000	40	400	, —
The next £1,000	45	450	850
,, ,, £1,000	50	500	1,350
,, ,, £1,500	55	825	2,175
,, ,, £1,500	60	900	3,075
,, ,, £2,000	65	1,300	4,375
,, ,, £2,500	70	1,750	6,125
,, ,, £5,500	75	4,125	10,250
The remainder	83		

For an expanded Table, see § 8-70.

For the year 1978–79, the first £1,700 of an individual's investment income bears no surcharge; the next £550 (£1,701–£2,250) bears surcharge at 10 per cent.; and the excess over £2,250 bears tax at 15 per cent.[5] Thus the top rate of tax on investment income is 83 per cent. + 15 per cent. = 98 per cent.

In the case of a person who or whose spouse is aged 65 or over, the first £2,500 of investment income bears no surcharge; the next £500 (£2,501–£3,000) bears tax at 10 per cent.; and the remainder bears tax at 15 per cent.[6] This may be shown as follows:

Investment Income Surcharge

Under 65		65 and over	
£	%	£	%
1,701–2,250	10	2,501–3,000	10
Over 2,250	15	Over 3,000	15

The first £1,700 (or £2,500) which bears no surcharge is not " income chargeable as investment income." Computation A in § 8-69 is a simple illustration of the operation of these provisions.

8-06   Where an individual's income consists of or includes maintenance payments (as defined) paid to him or for his benefit, those payments are not investment income.[7]

What is investment income?

8-07   Section 32 (3) of the Finance Act 1971 defines investment income as " any income other than earned income," adding one qualification which is referred to in § 8-09 below; and the definition has since been extended to include maintenance payments (see § 8-10) and retirement annuities (see § 8-11). Examples of investment income are given in § 8-13.

---

[5] F.A. 1978, s. 13 (c).
[6] *Ibid.* s. 13.
[7] F.A. 1974, s. 15, as amended by F.A. 1978, s. 21. In 1977–78 only the first £1,500 of maintenance payments was exempt from treatment as investment income. See § 8-10.

Earned income is defined in section 530 of the Income and Corporation Taxes Act 1970 and in other statutory provisions to include (in relation to an individual) the following:

(1) Remuneration from an office or employment, including the annual value of property which the employee is entitled to occupy rent free. [8]

> In *Dale* v. *I.R.C.* [9] it was held that an annuity payable under a will to a trustee for acting as such was income of an office of profit and therefore earned income.

> In *White* v. *Franklin,* [10] F. was the managing director of a family company and held no shares. To induce F. to stay with the company, his mother and brother settled shares in the company on him so long as he should be engaged in the management of the company. *Held* that the settlement income paid to F. was earned income.

(2) Pensions given in respect of past service in an office or employment, whether the pension is paid to the servant or his wife or parent and whether contributory or not.

(3) Payments in connection with the termination of an office or employment which are assessable under section 187 of the Income and Corporation Taxes Act 1970. [11]

(4) Any income charged under Schedule A, Schedule B or Schedule D which is *immediately derived* (see § 8-08) by the individual from the carrying on or exercise by him of his trade, profession or vocation, either as an individual or, in the case of a partnership, as a partner personally acting therein. Thus the income of a sleeping partner and the income of beneficiaries under a trust derived from a business carried on by the trustees is not earned income. [12] Income taxed under Case VI of Schedule D is not earned income. Income from furnished lettings is not earned income unless the activities amount to the carrying on of a trade under Case I of Schedule D.

(5) Post-cessation receipts. [13]

(6) Income from patent rights actually devised by the recipient. [14]

(7) Annuities payable under approved retirement annuity contracts. [15]

Earned income: trades and professions

8-08 The words " immediately derived " in § 8-07 (4) are narrowly construed so as to exclude income which is not exclusively attributable to the carrying on of a trade, *etc.*

> Thus in *Bucks* v. *Bowers* [16] merchant bankers held securities and foreign investments in the course of their business. The share of income of a partner derived from these sources was held not to be earned income on the ground that

---

[8] I.C.T.A. 1970, s. 185; see §§ 3-21 *et seq.*
[9] [1954] A.C. 11; 34 T.C. 468 (H.L.).
[10] (1965) 42 T.C. 283.
[11] I.C.T.A. 1970, s. 187 (4). See §§ 3-27 *et seq.*
[12] *Fry* v. *Sheil's Trustees* (1915) 6 T.C. 583; *M'Dougall* v. *Smith* (1919) 7 T.C. 134.
[13] I.C.T.A. 1970, s. 148. See §§ 2-88 *et seq.*
[14] *Ibid.* s. 383.
[15] *Ibid.* s. 226 (1).
[16] (1970) 46 T.C. 267. In this case Pennycuick J. appears to have attached some importance to the fact that the interest was paid under deduction of tax; but this, it is thought, is not relevant in applying the words " immediately derived." See the case in note 9.

the source of the income was not the trade but the loan obligations and foreign investments.

In *Pegler* v. *Abell* [17] it was held that an annuity received by a retired partner was not earned income because it was derived not from the past carrying on by the partner of his profession but from the contractual liability of the continuing partners to the retired partner.

In *Northend* v. *White & Leonard & Corbin Greener and others* [18] the taxpayer claimed to treat as earned income his share of interest, being interest earned by a firm of solicitors when depositing clients' funds with a bank which the firm was entitled to retain under section 8 (3) of the Solicitors Act 1965. *Held* not to be earned income.

Templeman J. said this (at pp. 324–325):

" . . . if the Solicitors Act 1965 had not been passed, or if the firm had not carried on the exercise of the profession of solicitors, there would have been no deposit account and no interest. But, it does not follow that the interest was ' immediately derived ' from the carrying on of the profession. To produce the interest there must be an intervening event which could not be described as the ' carrying on of the profession of solicitor '; namely, the loan of money by a customer [the firm] to a bank on terms that interest should be paid. The fact that the money lent did not belong to the customer did not prevent the interest deriving from the intervening event; namely, the loan and the contract between the customer and the bank."

He accordingly held that the interest was not " exclusively attributable " to the carrying on of the practice.

Contrast *Peay* v. *Newton* [19] in which the proceeds of the sale of the goodwill of a hairdressers' business (taxable under Case VII of Schedule D as a short-term capital gain) was held to be exclusively attributable to and immediately derived from the carrying on of the business which was sold.

8-09   *Financial concerns.* Section 32 (4) of the Finance Act 1971 provides that where income derived by an individual from a trade, profession or vocation is earned income and (a) the proceeds of sale of any investments; or (b) a debt, if proved to be a bad debt, would be taken into account in computing the profits or gains of that trade, *etc.*, income from those investments or interest on that debt shall not be investment income. The effect of this provision is to prevent the decision in *Bucks* v. *Bowers* (see § 8-08) applying for the purposes of the investment income surcharge: interest and dividends received by a dealer in securities and shares are treated as earned and not as investment income.

8-10   *Maintenance payments.* Section 15 of the Finance Act 1974 (as amended by section 21 of the Finance Act 1978) provides that where an individual's income for any year of assessment consists of or includes amounts paid as maintenance payments to him or for his benefit, those amounts shall not be investment income. " Maintenance payments " means payments made by a party to a marriage by way of provision for the other party or for a child of both or either of the parties, or payments by way of provision for a child which are made by his natural father. " Marriage " includes a marriage

---

[17] (1973) 48 T.C. 564; followed in *Lawrence* v. *Hayman* [1976] S.T.C. 227; and see § 8-11.
[18] (1975) 50 T.C. 121; [1975] S.T.C. 317.
[19] (1970) 46 T.C. 653.

which has been dissolved or annulled; and " child " includes an illegitimate child and an adopted child. The section does not apply only to direct payments made by one party to a marriage to the other party: it applies also to payments which are made under a settlement [20] if the settlement is made by one party to a marriage, and the payments are made during the settlor's life to, or for, the benefit of *the other party* (but not such payments to, or for, the benefit of his or her child).

It should be noted that the section is not limited to payments made on the occasion of divorce or separation. Hence the section may apply where, for example, a father makes annual payments by way of provision for his child aged 18 or over.

8-11　　*Partnership retirement annuities.* In *Pegler* v. *Abell* [21] a retirement annuity paid to a partner was held not to be earned income, on the ground that it was not immediately derived from the carrying on by him of his profession but from the contractual liability imposed under the partnership deed on the continuing partners: see § 8-08. Section 16 of the Finance Act 1974 gives some relief from the effect of this decision. It provides that where a person ceases to be a member of a partnership on retirement, because of age or ill health or on death, and annual payments are made to him or his widow or a dependant of his, such payments are within specified limits to be treated as earned income. The section applies to annual payments which are made under the partnership agreement, or under an agreement replacing it or supplementing it or supplementing an agreement replacing it, or to payments made under an agreement made with an individual who acquires the whole or part of the business. Note that the section does not apply where retirement is due otherwise than to age or ill health. The limit referred to may be roughly expressed as 50 per cent. of the average of the retired or deceased partner's share of profits in the best three of the last seven years of assessment in which he was required to devote substantially the whole of his time to acting as a partner.

Annuities which are treated as earned income cannot be treated as reducing the investment income of the person or persons paying them, *i.e.* they are a charge on income other than investment income. [22]

8-12　　*Consultancy agreements.* Since partnership retirement annuities are, subject to the provisions discussed in § 8-11, investment income, a retiring partner still able to render useful services to his former partners may prefer to continue acting as a consultant on a fee or salary basis, taking a reduced annuity so long as he acts as consultant. [23]

8-13　　*Examples of investment income.* Subject to the qualifications referred to in §§ 8-07 *et seq.*, dividends, interest, annuities, rents, income arising to beneficiaries under a trust and maintenance payments are investment income.

---

[20] " Settlement " includes any disposition, trust, covenant, agreement or arrangement: I.C.T.A. 1970, s. 454 (3), applied by F.A. 1974, s. 15 (2).

[21] See note 17 above.　　　　　　　　　　[22] F.A. 1974, s. 16 (1). See also § 11-13.

[23] *Cf. Hale* v. *Shea* (1964) 42 T.C. 260 in § 4-02, which shows that an indivisible payment which is partly in consideration of the rendering of services and partly in consideration of the transfer of goodwill is not earned income of the recipient.

8-14　*Husband and wife.* In cases where the income of a wife is deemed to be the income of her husband (see § 8-23) the income, if earned income, is treated as earned income of the husband.[24] Where a husband's total income includes earned income of his wife, the wife's earned income is segregated from the total income for the purpose of entitling both spouses (where appropriate) to the benefit of the lower rate band.[25]

Persons other than individuals

8-14A　This chapter is concerned only with the taxation of *individuals.* It should be noted, however, that the levy of income tax at the *basic* rate is not confined to individuals; whereas only individuals are liable to higher rate tax (§ 8-04) and the investment income surcharge (§ 8-05) and are entitled to the benefit of the lower rate (§ 8-03). Trustees may be liable to additional rate tax (§ 9-02).

A company resident outside but not within the United Kingdom may be liable to income tax at the basic rate (§ 14-02). Dividends received by such a company from a United Kingdom resident company are not assessed to income tax at the basic rate but will notionally have suffered such tax under the imputation system (§§ 14-01B *et seq.*).

2. THE COMPUTATION OF TAXABLE INCOME

8-15　In order to compute the amount of an individual's taxable income in a year of assessment, it is first necessary to determine the amount of his total income. Certain deductions are allowed *in computing* total income, *e.g.* for sums paid under deduction of tax such as annuities and other annual payments. These are called " charges on income ": see § 8-31. Other deductions are allowed *from* total income, *e.g.* for personal reliefs.

Since investment income bears tax at the additional rate or rates referred to in § 8-05, the allocation of deductions as between one class of income and another may affect the amount of tax payable. It would be to the advantage of an individual, for example, to deduct interest from investment income (so as to reduce the investment income surcharge) rather than from income other than investment income. In the following sections of this chapter are considered:

(1) The meaning of total income (§§ 8-16 *et seq.*).
(2) Charges on income and other deductions (§§ 8-31 *et seq.*), personal reliefs (§§ 8-36 *et seq.*) and deductions in respect of interest (§§ 8-57 *et seq.*).
(3) The allocation of deductions in quantifying and taxing income (§§ 8-68 *et seq.*).

There then follows in § 8-69 a number of specimen computations showing how the provisions are applied in practice.

---

[24] F.A. 1970, s. 530 (1).
[25] F.A. 1971, s. 32 (1A) and (1B), as inserted by F.A. 1978, s. 14 (2).

3. TOTAL INCOME

8-16 Section 8 (1) of the Taxes Management Act 1970 authorises the Revenue to require a person to deliver a return of his income, computed in accordance with the Income Tax Acts and specifying each separate source of income and the amount of income from each source. Section 528 (1) of the Taxes Act 1970 provides that:

> " ' total income,' in relation to any person, means the total income of that person from all sources estimated in accordance with the provisions of the Income Tax Acts. . . ."

Thus total income means income under Schedules A to F, as set out in section 1 of the Taxes Act 1970. The return will show income of the following categories on which tax will be charged in accordance with the following rules:

8-17 (1) *Income not taxed by deduction before receipt.* The income from each source must be stated, computed by reference to the rules of the appropriate Schedule and Case and making whatever deductions are appropriate to each source. Thus a statement of Schedule A income will show rents received and the amounts deductible from those rents. Income falling under all Schedules, other than Schedule D, is taxed on a current year basis, *e.g.* income of the year ended April 5, 1976, forms part of the total income of the year 1975–76. Income falling under all the cases of Schedule D, other than Case VI, is taxed on a preceding year basis.

> Thus if X carries on a profession and makes up annual accounts to April 30, X's profits for the year ended April 30, 1974, form part of his total income for the year 1975–76: see § 2-79. The total income for the year 1975–76 will include bank interest credited to X in 1974–75: see § 5-06.

A partner's share of partnership income forms part of his total income, as illustrated in § 11-06.

8-18 (2) *Income taxed by deduction before receipt.* A return of income computed in accordance with the Income Tax Acts will include particulars of income from which tax has been deducted before receipt,[26] *e.g.* annuities and other annual payments. Such income must be grossed up at the basic rate for the purpose of computing total income.

> Thus an annuity of £67 net is returned as a receipt of £100, assuming a basic rate of 33 per cent.

Difficulties sometimes arise when a sum which is due in one year is paid in a later year. Is the sum income of the year in which it was due or of the year in which it was paid? It seems from section 528 (3) (*a*) of the Income and Corporation Taxes Act 1970 that it forms part of the total income of the year by reference to which basic rate tax was deducted. If section 52 of the Act applies to the payment (see §§ 5-31 *et seq.*) this is the year when payment was due; whereas, if section 53 (see §§ 5-34 *et seq.*) or section 54 (see § 5-56) of the Act applies, this is the year when payment was made.[27]

---

[26] T.M.A. 1970, s. 8 (8).　　　　　　　　　　　[27] F.A. 1971, s. 36.

Where the sum has to be related back to an earlier year, additional assessments to higher rate income tax and investment income surcharge may have to be made for that earlier year.

Tax credit. The effect of including in total income the grossed up amount of annuities and annual payments is that income tax at the basic rate as well as at the higher and additional rate is charged on the grossed up amount. To avoid a double charge to tax, the taxpayer is entitled to credit against income tax so charged an amount equal to the basic rate tax which was deducted before receipt. For an example, see Computation B in § 8-69.

8-19　　　(3) *Building society interest.* Building society interest is subject to special provisions.[28] The societies pay income tax at a special rate but the investor (who receives his interest " free of tax ") is treated as having had tax at the basic rate deducted before receipt. The interest must be grossed up at the basic rate for the purposes of estimating total income, but a credit is given against total tax payable equal to tax at the basic rate on the grossed up amount; but no refund in tax can be obtained by an investor not liable to basic rate income tax. Building society interest (unlike, for example, bank interest: see § 8-17) is assessed on a current year basis.

> Thus if X receives £67 of Building Society interest, £100 is included in X's total income (assuming basic rate tax of 33 per cent.). But X gets credit against the total tax payable by him of basic rate tax on £100, *i.e.* £33. In the result X is assessed only to higher rate tax and investment income surcharge on this income. If X is not liable to basic rate income tax, he cannot recover any part of the £33 treated as deducted.

This example shows that investment in a Building Society should be avoided by an individual who is not liable to income tax at the basic rate.

8-20　　　(4) *Dividends and other distributions chargeable under Schedule F.* A return of income must separately state the amount or value of the distribution and the amount of the tax credit [29] (see § 14-01B); and the amount to be included in total income in respect of a dividend chargeable under Schedule F is the actual amount or value of the dividend or other distribution plus the tax credit. A dividend is treated as income of the year by reference to which advance corporation tax is calculated.[30] The shareholder deducts the tax credit from the total tax payable by him. See Computation B in § 8-69.

> Thus if in 1978–79 (when the basic rate is 33 per cent.) X receives a dividend of £67 from a U.K. company, this carries a tax credit of 33/67ths of £67, *i.e.* £33. £100 is included in X's total income, *i.e.* the dividend plus the tax credit, but X gets credit against the total tax payable by him equal to £33. In the result X is assessed only to higher rate tax and investment income surcharge on this income. If X is not liable to basic rate income tax, he can make a repayment claim in respect of the whole, or some part of, the £33. See also Computation B in § 8-69.

---

[28] I.C.T.A. 1970, s. 343.
[29] T.M.A. 1970, s. 8 (9).
[30] I.C.T.A. 1970, s. 528 (3) (*b*) and § 14-59.

8-21   (5) *Trust income.* A beneficiary must include in his total income an amount equal to his share of the trust income, grossed up at the basic rate of income tax. The beneficiary is entitled to a tax credit against the total tax payable by him equal to the tax attributable to his share of that income. See Computation A in § 8-69.

8-22   (6) *Salary.*[31] Income tax on salary is deducted before receipt under the P.A.Y.E. system: see § 3-53. The gross amount is included in total income, and the recipient is entitled to a credit for the tax suffered by deduction. Salary is earned income and so not liable to the investment income surcharge.

Aggregation of income: husband and wife [32]

8-23   Subject to the options discussed in §§ 8-26 and 8-29, and except in the first year of marriage (unless the marriage takes place on April 6),[33] the separate incomes of husband and wife must be aggregated for the purpose of determining total income. This is because a woman's income chargeable to income tax, so far as it is income for a year of assessment or any part of a year of assessment (being a part beginning with April 6) during which she is a married woman " living with her husband," is deemed for income tax purposes to be his income and not to be her income.[34] Hence the husband is assessed on the joint income,[35] there being included as income of the woman any sum which (aggregation apart) would have been included in computing her total income.[36] A married woman is treated for tax purposes as " living with her husband " unless either

   (a) they are separated under an order of a court of competent jurisdiction, or by deed of separation; or
   (b) they are in fact separated in such circumstances that the separation is likely to be permanent.[37]

8-24   Where one spouse is resident in the United Kingdom for a year of assessment but the other is not, or both are resident in the United Kingdom but one is absent throughout the year of assessment, they are treated for that year as if they were permanently separated.[38] Hence their separate incomes are not aggregated for that year.

8-25   A husband whose wife's income is substantial would be in difficulties if his wife declined to fund tax on her income for which he is chargeable under

---

[31] *Ibid.* ss. 204–207.

[32] See Inland Revenue publication: " Taxation of Wife's Earnings " (1977) I.R. 13. A government Green Paper on the taxation of the family, including the personal tax allowances and the principle of aggregation, is in course of preparation: [1978] S.T.I. 367.

[33] F.A. 1976, s. 36 (1) and (2). Although the income of husband and wife are not aggregated in the first year of marriage, there are provisions to enable one spouse to transfer specified unutilised reliefs to the other where the transferring spouse has insufficient income: see F.A. 1976, s. 36 (7) and (8).

[34] I.C.T.A. 1970, s. 37 (1), as amended by F.A. 1976, s. 36 (2). In the year of marriage, any income of the wife is apportioned on a time basis and the post-marital income treated as income of the husband. If the wife's income is assessed in a preceding year basis, income apportioned to the husband will include earnings of an earlier year: *Leitch* v. *Emworth* (1929) 14 T.C. 633.

[35] I.C.T.A. 1970, s. 37 (2).

[36] *Ibid.* s. 37 (1), proviso, and (4).

[37] *Ibid.* s. 42 (1).

[38] *Ibid.* s. 42 (2).

the aggregation rule. Section 40 of the Income and Corporation Taxes Act 1970 enables the Revenue to collect tax from the wife in certain circumstances; and section 41 of that Act entitles a husband to disclaim liability for the tax on his deceased wife's income.

Options for separate assessment

8-26　　Either husband or wife may apply to be separately assessed. The application must be made within six months before July 6 in any year of assessment except that, in the case of persons married during the year of assessment, an application has effect for the year for which it is made and for subsequent years, until the application is withdrawn.[39]

8-27　　The effect of an application is that the provisions of the Income Tax Acts governing the assessment, charge, and recovery of income tax apply as if the husband and wife were not married.[40] An application does not have the effect of reducing the total amount of tax payable by husband and wife. Their incomes are aggregated for the purpose of determining the measure of the joint tax liability and reliefs and allowances are apportioned between them.[41] Separate assessment has the effect that each spouse pays his or her respective share of the tax bill. Since the aggregation rule in § 8-23 does not normally apply in the first year of marriage, the option is not needed in that year and is excluded.[42]

8-28　　Although a repayment of tax in respect of the wife's income has to be made to her husband if there has been no application for separate assessment, the wife is beneficially entitled to the amount repaid.[43]

Election for non-aggregation of wife's earned income

8-29　　The provisions discussed in §§ 8-23 *et seq.* requiring that the income of husband and wife should be aggregated for tax purposes are a disincentive to wives who might otherwise go out to work. Accordingly the provisions have been modified as from the year 1972–73. Section 23 of the Finance Act 1971 provides that where a man and his wife living with him jointly so elect, the wife's earnings and their other income shall be chargeable to tax separately, as provided in Schedule 4 to that Act. " Wife's earnings " is defined [44] as earned income of hers, excluding income arising in respect of any pension, superannuation or other allowance, deferred pay or compensation for loss of office given in respect of the husband's past services in any office or employment. These words of exclusion prevent a husband negotiating a " split " pension—part payable to the husband and part payable to his wife—in order to have the two parts taxed separately.

　　Where notice of election is given, the wife's earnings (but not her other income) are charged to income tax as if she were a single woman with no

---

[39] I.C.T.A. 1970, s. 38 (1) (3) (4).　　　　　　　　　　　　　[40] *Ibid.* s. 38 (1).
[41] *Ibid.* ss. 38 (2) and 39.
[42] See note 33, *ante.*
[43] *Re Cameron, decd.* (1965) 42 T.C. 539. But see F.A. 1978, s. 22, which allows tax repayment to wives in some cases.
[44] F.A. 1971, Sched. 4, para. 1.

other income and the husband's other income (including the wife's investment income) is charged as if the wife's income were nil. Any payments made by her which give rise to relief, such as interest in certain circumstances, must be set solely against the wife's earnings: any excess will be unrelieved.[45] Income tax charged on the wife's earnings is taxed on and recovered from her. Section 23 states the procedure for electing. Notice of election must be given by husband and wife jointly not earlier than six months before the beginning of the year of assessment concerned and not later than 12 months after the end of the year. The Board of Inland Revenue may extend the time limit. The election, once given, remains effective until husband and wife give joint notice of withdrawal, which may be given up to 12 months after the end of the year of assessment concerned. Election for non-aggregation does not mean that husband and wife make separate tax returns. This consequence ensues only if they elect for separate assessment: see §§ 8-26 *et seq.* An example of the operation of these provisions is Computation E in § 8-69.

Aggregation of income: parent and child

8-30   For the three years 1969–70 to 1971–72 (both inclusive), an infant's income so far as it was income for a year (or part of a year) of assessment during which he or she was unmarried and not regularly working was treated as income of the infant's parent or parents.[46]

Section 16 (1) of the Finance Act 1971 provided that for the year 1972–73 and subsequent years of assessment the provisions for aggregation should cease to have effect. The income of an infant child is therefore not now taxed as if it were the income of his parent, except in the case of income of the infant under a settlement made by his parent as explained in §§ 10-23 *et seq.* When a child's income exceeds the amount which is specified as the income limit for the year, his parent's claim for child relief is restricted as explained in § 8-47. In his Spring 1974 Budget Speech the Chancellor of the Exchequer announced his intention to reintroduce the aggregation of children's income but this proposal has now been deferred.

4. CHARGES ON INCOME AND OTHER DEDUCTIONS

Charges on income

8-31   A return of income computed in accordance with the Income Tax Acts will include particulars relating to " charges on income," which are defined as " amounts which fall to be deducted in computing total income." [47] These include annuities or other annual payments.[48] The gross amount of any sum payable under deduction of tax by reason of section 52 of the Taxes Act 1970 (see § 5-31), *e.g.* annuities or annual payments, is allowable as a deduction in computing total income; whereas interest paid under

---

[45] F.A. 1971, Sched. 4, para. 4.
[46] I.C.T.A. 1970, ss. 43–48.
[47] T.M.A. 1970, s. 8 (8).

deduction of tax by reason of section 54 of that Act (see § 5-56) is deductible only where statute so allows (see §§ 8-57 *et seq.*).[48]

Difficulties may arise when a sum which is due in one year is paid in a later year. Is the sum deductible in the year in which it falls due for payment, or in the year in which it is actually paid? It seems from section 528 (3) (*b*) of the Income and Corporation Taxes Act 1970, that it is deductible in the year by reference to which basic rate tax is deductible. See and compare § 8-18.

8-32   *Add back of retained tax.* We have seen in § 8-18 that, to avoid a double charge to tax, an individual is entitled to a tax credit where tax at the basic rate has been deducted from income he receives. Where an individual pays an annuity or other annual payment, the gross amount is deductible in computing his total income (see § 8-31) and therefore reduces tax liability at the lower, basic, higher and additional rates. But where section 52 of the Income and Corporation Taxes Act 1970 applies to the payment, the payer is entitled to retain the tax he deducts on making the payment (see § 5-31). To prevent the individual (in effect) obtaining double relief for tax, he is charged to tax on an amount equal to the tax he so deducts.[49]

Example

8-33   X has earned income of £9,000. He pays Y, his ex-wife, maintenance of £2,000 (gross), *i.e.* £1,340 net after deduction of tax at 33 per cent. (£660). X's tax liability is as follows:

	£
Earned income	9,000
less personal relief (§ 8-43)	985
	8,015
less maintenance	2,000
	6,015

Tax		£
750 at 25%		187·50
5,265 at 33%		1,737·45
6,015		1,924·95
Add back retained tax:		
2,000 at 33%		660
		£2,584·95

This example shows that X acts as a tax collector on behalf of the Revenue when he deducts £660 on paying Y and accounts for this amount in his own tax computation. For a further example, see Computation C in § 8-69.

---

[48] T.A. 1970, s. 528 (1) (2) (3) (*b*) and Sched. 13. The absence of any general principle allowing the deduction of interest seems to follow from the speech of Viscount Radcliffe in *Frere* v. *I.R.C.* [1965] A.C. 402; 42 T.C. 125 (H.L.).

[49] T.A. 1970, s. 3 (*a*) read with s. 52 (1) (*b*).

8-34   *Add back of income under the settlement provisions.* There are a number of provisions in the Income Tax Acts relating to settlements which for tax purposes deem income to be the income of the settlor and not income of any other person. These provisions are discussed in Chapter 10. Where they apply, sums are added back in computing the total income of the settlor. See §§ 10-04 *et seq.*

8-34A   Where husband and wife elect for non-aggregation of the wife's earnings (see § 8-29) charges on the wife's income are deductible only from her earnings. Charges on the husband's income are deductible from their joint income excluding the wife's earnings.

Other deductions

8-35   Interest is in some cases deductible in computing total income: see §§ 8-57 *et seq.*

Premiums on retirement annuity contracts are deductible from relevant earnings: see § 39-14.

Deductions are in some cases given in respect of losses and capital allowances: see Chapters 12 and 13.

Deductions in respect of personal reliefs are discussed in §§ 8-36 *et seq.*

Deductions are allowed in respect of small maintenance payments: see § 5-05.

5. PERSONAL RELIEFS

8-36   An individual who makes a claim in that behalf is entitled to personal reliefs.[50] Claims for reliefs are made to the Inspector, subject to a right of appeal to the Commissioners where relief is refused.[51] Claims are normally made by the individual making an entry in his tax return in the section headed " Allowances." These reliefs reduce the amount of the income on which he is liable to tax. Where the taxpayer's income in any year is insufficient to absorb in full the reliefs to which he is entitled, they are to that extent lost: there is no provision for carrying forward unabsorbed personal reliefs.

8-37   Where an individual is entitled to deduct tax at the basic rate on making a payment, *i.e.* where there is a charge on his income equal to the gross amount of the payment (see § 8-31), personal reliefs are restricted to the extent that they reduce the income below an amount equal to the amount of the charge.[52]

> Thus if X, having income of £900, makes a deed of covenant for £100 in favour of Y, X's personal reliefs are limited to reliefs on £800. This ensures that the Revenue collect basic rate income tax on £100.

8-38   Personal reliefs may be claimed only by persons resident in the United Kingdom, except in the case of certain classes of non-resident listed in

---

[50] I.C.T.A. 1970, s. 5.
[51] T.M.A. 1970, s. 42.
[52] I.C.T.A. 1970, s. 25, substituted by F.A. 1971, s. 33 (5).

section 27 of the Income and Corporation Taxes Act 1970, who may claim in respect of their United Kingdom income a proportion of the personal reliefs. [53]

8-39   Before the introduction of the unified system, reliefs were given by deducting from the amount of tax a sum equal to tax at the standard rate on an amount specified as the amount of the relief. Under the unified system, the amount specified as the amount of the relief (shown in the second column of the following Table) is deducted from the individual's total income. [54] Hence income tax at the lower, basic and higher rates is charged on the balance of an individual's income, after deducting personal reliefs and any other allowable deductions. For unified tax the amounts of the personal reliefs have been adjusted to allow for the abolition of earned income relief. Personal reliefs reduce earned before investment income: see § 8-68.

8-40   The following Table shows the reliefs which are available in 1978–79.

Income and Corporation Taxes Act 1970	Amount to be deducted from total income £	Reference to paragraph where discussed
s. 8 (personal relief):		
(1) (a) married	1,535 [55]	8-42
(b) single	985 [55]	8-42
(2) wife's earned income	985 or, if less, amount of wife's earned income.	8-44
s. 10 (children)[56]:		
(1) under 11	300 or 100	
(2) 11 or over but under 16	335 or 135	8-45
(3) 16 or over	365 or 165	
s. 12 (housekeeper)	100	8-48
s. 13 (relative taking charge of younger brother or sister)	100	8-49
s. 14 (additional relief for widows, etc., with children)	550	8-50
s. 16 (dependent relative):		
(1) other than single woman	100 [57]	8-51
(2) single woman	145 [57]	
s. 17 (son or daughter's services)	55	8-52
s. 18 (blind person):		
(1) one spouse blind	180 reduced by tax-free disability payments.	8-53
(2) both spouses blind	360 reduced as above.	

[53] See generally the Revenue booklet (I.R. 20) on " Residents and Non-residents: Liability to Tax in the United Kingdom "—paras. 60 *et seq.*

[54] F.A. 1971, s. 33 (2).

[55] There is an increased personal relief for persons aged 65 or more with a small income, sometimes called " Age Allowance ": see § 8-43.

8-41   *Family allowance deduction (" clawback ").* Family allowances (which were taxable under Schedule E: see *ante*, § 3-02) were increased in 1968–69. There were elaborate provisions in section 24 of the Income and Corporation Taxes Act 1970 which had the effect of depriving basic rate taxpayers of the benefit of the increase. This was achieved by reducing the total deductions to which the individual would otherwise be entitled in respect of personal reliefs by £52 for each child for whom family allowances were due. Family allowances have been replaced by child benefit from April 4, 1977: Child Benefit Act 1975, s. 1 (3). See § 8-45.

The following personal allowances may be claimed in the year 1978–79:

1. *Personal relief* [58]

8-42   A married man is entitled to deduct £1,535 from his total income if he proves:

(1) that for the year of assessment he has his wife living with him (in the sense in which those words are defined in § 8-23); or

(2) that he wholly maintains his wife during the year of assessment and is not entitled in computing his total income for the year to make any deduction in respect of the sums paid for his wife's maintenance (see § 8-31).

Accordingly, if a husband and wife are permanently separated and the wife is wholly maintained under payments made by the husband on a voluntary basis, he is entitled to the married man's deduction of £1,535, but if he maintains her under a court order or deed so that the payments are annual payments which are a charge on his income, he is entitled only to the single person's deduction of £985.

A married man not within (1) and (2) and a single individual, including a widow or widower and including a child, is entitled to the single person's allowance of £985. A man is not entitled to the married man's allowance for a woman to whom he is not married, even though they are living together as man and wife.

The difference between the married man's allowance and the single person's allowance in 1978–79 is £550. In the year when a man marries, the allowance of £1,535 is reduced by one-twelfth of £550, *i.e.* by £45·83, for each complete month in that year prior to the date of marriage. The " month " referred to begins with the sixth day of one month and ends with the fifth day of the next.[59] A man who is entitled to a married man's allowance by virtue of a previous marriage existing in the year will continue to receive the amount of the allowance due by virtue of that previous marriage.

Where husband and wife jointly elect that the wife shall be taxed on her earnings as if she were a single person with no other income (see § 8-29), each of them is entitled only to the single person's deduction of £985. See Computation E in § 8-69.

---

[56] The higher reliefs apply in the cases discussed in § 8-45 B and C.
[57] Reduced by the excess of the dependent relative's income over the basic retirement pension.
[58] I.C.T.A. 1970, s. 8 (1).
[59] *Ibid.* s. 8 (3).

8-43   *Persons aged 65 or more with small incomes: age allowance.*[60] In 1978–79 a person whose total income does not exceed £4,000 and who proves that, at some time in the year of assessment, he or his wife living with him (see § 8-23) is aged 65 or more, is entitled to a personal relief of £2,075 if married and £1,300 if single. If the total income exceeds £4,000, the allowance is reduced by £2 for every £3 of income over £4,000 until it is the same as the ordinary personal allowance in § 8-42.

2. *Relief on wife's earned income* [61]

8-44   Where a husband and wife are living together (§ 8-23) and they have not elected for non-aggregation of the wife's earnings (see § 8-29), their separate incomes are aggregated for tax purposes. Personal reliefs are given to the husband against the total income; no reliefs are given to the wife as such.

If, however, a husband's total income includes any earned income of his wife, the husband is entitled to an additional deduction from total income of £985 or, if less, the amount of his wife's earned income. This allowance is given in addition to the personal relief of £1,535 in § 8-42. See Computation E in § 8-69.

8-45   The following income of the wife (though earned) is excluded for this purpose:

       (a) Pensions and similar payments made to the wife in respect of her husband's past services; and

       (b) benefits under the Social Security Act 1975 (other than the wife's Category A retirement pension).

This additional deduction is not given where husband and wife elect for non-aggregation of the wife's earnings (see § 8-29). Each spouse then gets the single person's allowance only.[62] See Computation E in § 8-69. The additional deduction is not available where, in the first year of marriage, the aggregation rule in § 8-23 does not apply.

3. *Child relief*

(1) *The child benefit reduction in child tax allowances*

8-45A   For many years a relief from tax has been available in respect of a child or children. The effect of the relief is to reduce the amount of tax which would otherwise be payable by the husband, or by husband and wife if each is separately assessed. Alongside, there has existed a system of family allowances taxable under Schedule E. The Child Benefit Act 1975 and Regulations made thereunder have abolished family allowances as from April 4, 1977, and substituted a system of non-taxable child benefits payable usually to the mother and in respect of all children including the first child. In consequence of the introduction of child benefits, the system

---

[60] I.C.T.A. 1970, s. 8 (1A) and (1B).
[61] *Ibid*. s. 8 (2).
[62] F.A. 1971, s. 23 (1) and Sched. 4, para. 3.

of tax allowances for children is to be phased out and sections 23 to 26 of the Finance Act 1977 are intended to implement Government policy in this respect. Child benefit is currently at the rate of £2·30 per week for each child. This will be increased to £4 per week in April 1979, when child tax allowances will cease except in the two special cases discussed in § 8-45 B and C.[63] " Child " means a person who is under 16 or is under 19 and is receiving full-time education by attendance at a recognised educational establishment. There is no child benefit in respect of children aged 19 or over. Since child benefits are tax free and there is no such " clawback " arrangement as applied to family allowances (see § 8-41), the phasing out operation is achieved by reducing the child tax allowances for 1977–78 and again in 1978–79. Subject to two exceptions, the reductions are made whether or not child benefit is actually paid, so higher rate taxpayers cannot keep the unreduced child tax allowances by withholding a claim for child benefit. These exceptions are as follows:

8-45B   (a) *Children living abroad.*[64] Where a child in respect of whom a child tax allowance is claimed is outside the United Kingdom throughout the year of assessment and does not normally live in one of a number of specified countries or territories, and is under 19 at the end of the year, and no child benefit is paid or payable in respect of the child, no reduction is made in the child tax allowance in respect of that child. The object of the legislation is to preserve a taxpayer's right to the unreduced child tax allowance where he is not entitled to child benefit or to a comparable benefit in the country of the child's normal residence.

8-45C   (b) *Students.*[65] No child benefit is payable in respect of a child who is aged 19 or over, even if he is receiving full-time education; but parents will benefit after September 1977 in the adjustments made in the parental contribution scale towards student grants. The right to the unreduced child tax allowance is preserved for a taxpayer whose child was a full-time student on December 31, 1976, and who receives no grant or whose income is below the threshold giving rise to a parental contribution.

(2) *Child tax relief* [66]

8-45D   Child relief is available to certain persons who have a child living at any time during a year of assessment. The amount of the relief varies according to the age of the child at the commencement of the year of assessment (*i.e.* April 6, 1978), and (expressed in terms of a deduction from total income) is as follows. The amounts in column 1 apply to children living abroad (§ 8-45B) and the students referred to in § 8-45C. The amounts in column 2 apply in other cases.

---

[63] For details see [1978] S.T.I. 348. The phasing out of the tax allowance will affect the conditions to which some other allowances are currently subject.

[64] F.A. 1977, s. 25, and F.A. 1978, s. 20 (5).

[65] *Ibid.* s. 26.

[66] I.C.T.A. 1970, ss. 10–11, as amended by F.A. 1978, s. 20 (1) and (2).

Age at commencement of year of assessment	Column 1 £	Column 2 £
(1) under 11	300	100
(2) 11 or over but under 16 . . .	335	135
(3) 16 or over	365	165

A child attains a particular age at the commencement of the relevant anniversary of the date of his birth.[67] The relief in (1) and (2) is granted on proof only of the age of the child. In (3), however, the claimant must also prove that the child

> is receiving full-time instruction at any university, college, school or other educational establishment *or* is undergoing training for any trade, profession or vocation, in such circumstances that the child is required to devote the whole of his time to the training for a period of not less than two years.[68]

If the necessary conditions are satisfied, the claim may be made notwithstanding that the child is over 18 or marries during the year of assessment.

> In *Heaslip* v. *Hasemer*,[69] a child attended the house of a music teacher for regular lessons and the teacher gave her work to do at home. The claim for child relief was rejected (1) because there was no educational establishment; and (2) because the instruction was not full-time. The court would not accept that there was " constructive instruction " while the pupil practised at home under her tutor's directions.

An educational establishment is one whose primary function is education in the sense of training the mind, as distinct from training in manual skills.[70]

8-46 *Avoidance of double claims for relief.* There are two classes of person who are entitled to claim child relief:

(1) The person who has a child, including a stepchild and an illegitimate child whose parents have married each other after the child's birth.

(2) Any other person who has the custody of and maintains a child at his own expense. This includes a person with factual but not legal custody.[71]

If two or more individuals are entitled to relief in respect of the same child, the child relief must be apportioned between them either

(a) as they agree; or

(b) in default of agreement, in proportion to the amount or value of the provision made by them respectively (otherwise than by way of payments deductible in computing their respective total incomes) for the child's maintenance and education for the year of assessment.[72]

---

[67] Family Law Reform Act 1969, s. 9 (1). [68] I.C.T.A. 1970, s. 10 (2) (*b*) and (4).
[69] (1927) 13 T.C. 212.
[70] *Barry* v. *Hughes* (1972) 48 T.C. 586; [1972] S.T.C. 103.
[71] *Robertson* v. *Walton* [1977] S.T.C. 26.
[72] I.C.T.A. 1970, s. 11. As to what payments are deductible, see §§ 8-31 *et seq.* In *Buxton* v. *Buxton* [1978] S.T.C. 122 the High Court refused to disturb an apportionment by the Commissioners on a percentage basis.

Double claims for relief will arise each year if the parents are divorced or separated. Separation agreements often contain a clause providing which of the two spouses shall be entitled to child relief. Where a husband is ordered to maintain his child, the whole of his contribution is a charge on his income (see § 8-31) and so is deductible in computing his total income and is therefore disregarded in making any apportionment. The wife, accordingly, is entitled to the whole of the child relief, unless the husband makes supplementary voluntary payments, in respect of which he will then be entitled to claim part of the child relief. A double claim may also arise if a husband dies during a year of assessment and his widow also makes a claim; or where a woman entitled to relief marries during the year and her husband makes a claim.

8-47 *Child's income limit.* Where a child is entitled in his own right to an income exceeding £500 a year (excluding scholarship, bursary, or other similar educational endowment), the amount of the child relief is reduced by the excess over £500; except that if a child under 18 at the end of the year and unmarried throughout that year has no earned income or has earned income not exceeding £385, the income limit is not £500 but is " investment income not exceeding £115." [73] (The explanation for this exception is that, previously, the income limit was £115; it was increased to £350 in and from 1976–77 to enable children to earn or to top up their income to £350 without reducing the parent's child relief but *not* so as to enable children to receive more than the previous limit of £115 in investment income. The " investment income content " in the child's income limit thus remains at £115.) At the age of 18 or over, or if the child is married, there is a single income limit of £500 for all income, whether earned or investment income. " Income " means income chargeable to tax and therefore does not include any foreign earned income of a child which is not chargeable to United Kingdom income tax. [74] Income to which a child is entitled *in his own right* includes:

(1) Emoluments of an employment, including remuneration under articles. [75] The fact that some part of the wage represents a return of premium paid by the father does not affect its character as income of the child.

(2) Income applied for the child's maintenance, education or benefit under a trust in which the child has a contingent interest, [76] unless the income so applied is deemed to be that of some other person. [77]

(3) Income from a trust in which the child has a vested and absolute interest. This must be contrasted with the case where the child has only a vested life interest, *i.e.* an interest in income only; for in this case, if section 31 of the Trustee Act 1925 applies, the effect of that section is to convert the child's interest in income not actually applied for his maintenance into a contingent interest. [78]

---

[73] *Ibid.* s. 10 (5) as amended by F.A. 1978, s. 20 (3).
[74] *Mapp* v. *Oram* [1970] A.C. 362; 45 T.C. 651 (H.L.).
[75] *Williams* v. *Doulton* (1948) 28 T.C. 522; *Miles* v. *Morrow* (1940) 23 T.C. 465.
[76] *Johnstone* v. *Chamberlain* (1933) 17 T.C. 706.   [77] See Chap. 10.
[78] See *Stanley* v. *I.R.C.* [1944] K.B. 255; 26 T.C. 12 (C.A.). The judgment of Lord Greene M.R. explaining the effect of s. 31 of the Trustee Act 1925 merits careful study.

Income arising under a trust in which the child has a contingent interest and which is accumulated is not income to which the child is entitled in his own right. There are many cases where income, which would appear to be income of the child, is deemed by virtue of some provision of the Income Tax Acts to be income of some other person.[79] In such cases, the child tax relief is not lost.[80]

Where a child marries and her income is deemed to be that of her husband, under the aggregation provisions discussed *ante*, § 8-23, this does not mean the child no longer has an income in her own right in determining whether the child's income limit has been exceeded.[81]

Where in or after 1972–73 husband and wife jointly elect to have the wife's earnings taxed separately, any children of the husband are treated as his children and not hers so that he alone qualifies for the child tax relief.[82] See Computation E in § 8-69.

4. *Housekeeper and similar reliefs*

8-48   (1) *Widower's or widow's housekeeper.*[83] The sum of £100 is deductible from the total income of a widower who has a person resident with him in the capacity of a housekeeper being either a relative of his or of his deceased wife or (there being no such relative able or willing to act in that capacity) some other person who is employed as a housekeeper. The same relief may be claimed by a widow, the relation in this case being a relative of her or her deceased husband. The relief is not allowed where the relative is a man who has claimed and been allowed the higher personal relief applicable to married persons or a married woman living with her husband where the husband has claimed and been allowed the higher personal relief applicable to married persons (§ 8-42); nor where the claimant is entitled to the additional relief in § 8-50.[84] Also the relief is not allowed unless the claimant proves that no other individual is entitled to relief in respect of the relative or, if so entitled, has relinquished his claim thereto.

8-49   (2) *Relative taking charge of unmarried person's young brother or sister.*[85] The sum of £100 is deductible from the total income of an unmarried person who has a relative living with him for the purpose of having the charge and care of any brother or sister of his for whom child relief is allowed, where he maintains the relative at his own expense. The allowance is not available unless the claimant proves that no other individual is entitled to relief in respect of the same person or, if so entitled, has relinquished his claim thereto.

8-50   (3) *Additional relief for widows and others in respect of children.*[86] The sum of £550 is deductible from the total income of a person who proves that

---

[79] See §§ 10-23 and 10-35.
[80] See *e.g. Yates* v. *Starkey* [1951] Ch. 465; 32 T.C. 38 (C.A.). *Cf.* the case in note 81.
[81] *Murphy* v. *Ingram* [1974] Ch. 363; 49 T.C. 410 (C.A.).
[82] F.A. 1971, s. 23 (1) and Sched. 4, para. 3.
[83] I.C.T.A. 1970, s. 12, as amended. See *Barentz* v. *Whiting* (1965) 42 T.C. 267 (C.A.).
[84] F.A. 1971, s. 15 (5).
[85] I.C.T.A. 1970, s. 13, as amended.
[86] *Ibid.* s. 14, as amended.

he is entitled to child relief in respect of a child resident with him (or would be so entitled but for the amount of the child's income: see § 8-47). This additional relief may be claimed by widows, widowers and other persons not entitled for the year to the higher personal relief given to married persons (§ 8-43) and by any married man who is so entitled to the higher personal relief but whose wife was throughout the year totally incapacitated by physical or mental infirmity. There are provisions for apportioning the relief where more than one person is eligible.

The claimant must show that neither he nor any other person is entitled to the relief in § 8-49 or that such entitlement has been relinquished.

The relief is not available in the case of a person who is entitled to the single person's allowance in consequence only of electing for the non-aggregation of wife's earnings (see § 8-29).

5. Dependent relative relief [87]

8-51   The maximum amount of the dependent relative deduction is £100, or £145 when the claimant is a single woman. For the purposes of this allowance, husband and wife are treated as separate persons where they elect for non-aggregation of wife's earnings, so each can claim for his or her own dependent relative. The allowance is deductible from the total income of a person who proves that he maintains at his own expense any person, being a relative of his or of his wife, who is incapacitated by old age or infirmity from maintaining himself, or who maintains his own or his wife's mother (whether incapacitated or not) if she is a widow or divorced or separated from her husband. The amount of the relief is reduced, if the total income of the person maintained exceeds the basic retirement pension (as defined [88]), by the amount of the excess. (The basic retirement pension for a single person is £795·60 for 1977–78.) No relief is given where the dependant's income exceeds the basic retirement pension by more than £100 (or £145 where the claimant is a single woman). If two or more persons jointly maintain a relative, the relief is apportioned in the ratio of their respective contributions.

6. Claimant depending on services of a son or daughter [89]

8-52   The sum of £55 is deductible from the total income of a person who, by reason of old age or infirmity, is compelled to depend upon the services of a son or daughter resident with and maintained by him. A married man is not entitled to the allowance unless his wife is old or infirm. This allowance should not be claimed where the larger housekeeper allowance (see § 8-48) can be claimed. A person cannot claim both.

7. Reliefs for blind persons [90]

8-53   The sum of £180 (reduced by tax-free disability payments receivable) is deductible from the total income of a person who (or whose wife) is a

---

[87] I.C.T.A. 1970, s. 16, as amended.
[88] *Ibid.* s. 16 (2A), inserted by F.A. 1973, s. 12 (2).
[89] I.C.T.A. 1970, s. 17, as amended.
[90] *Ibid.* s. 18, as amended.

registered blind person. Where both husband and wife are registered blind persons, the allowance is £360 reduced by tax-free disability payments receivable. A person entitled to relief under § 8-52 must relinquish that relief as a condition of claiming blind person's relief.

8. *Life insurance relief* [91]

8-54　　Relief is given for premiums paid by the claimant on a policy of insurance made after June 22, 1916, if:

(1) the insurance is on the life of the claimant or on that of his wife; and

(2) the insurance was made by him.

Thus if an employer insures the life of an employee (not being his wife), neither employer nor employee may claim the relief; nor may the assignee of a life policy claim the relief. Again, relief is conditional on the premium being paid by the claimant in the year of assessment, so relief will be refused if the claimant has fallen into arrears. Relief is generally available only on a policy which secures a capital sum payable on death, whether or not in conjunction with any other benefit.

8-55　　The amount of the relief depends on the total amount of premiums qualifying for relief under the section and is as follows:

(1) Premiums totalling not more than £20 in the year of assessment: relief is a deduction equal to income tax at the basic rate on £10 or on the full amount of the premium, whichever is the less.

(2) Premiums totalling more than £20 in the year of assessment: relief is a deduction equal to income tax at half the basic rate on the amount of the premiums, *i.e.* 16½ per cent. when the basic rate is 33 per cent.

The relief is subject to one statutory restriction: the aggregate of the premium on which relief is given must not exceed 1/6th of the claimant's total income. [92] Where husband and wife elect for non-aggregation of the wife's earnings (see § 8-29), they are treated as separate persons for the purposes of this relief; hence each can claim only on premiums which he or she pays to insure his or her own life. See Computation A in § 8-69.

8-56　　*Anti-avoidance legislation.* The Finance Act 1968 introduced elaborate provisions which were designed to prevent tax avoidance by the use of life insurance relief. Previously many companies had offered single-premium policies which assured the payment of a small sum on death (so that the policies qualified for life assurance relief) and a larger sum on the attainment by the insured of a specified age, the life insurance element being small in relation to the endowment element. The " gain " on the maturity of such policies escaped both income tax and capital gains tax but the premiums qualified for tax relief, within the statutory limits in § 8-55.

---

[91] I.C.T.A. 1970, s. 19. For policies made on or before June 22, 1916, relief is given by I.C.T.A. 1970, s. 20. The relief depends on the amount of the claimant's income and is given on the premium, as follows: (a) income not exceeding £1,000 relief half the basic rate; (b) income between £1,000 and £2,000 relief at three-fourths of the basic rate; (c) income exceeding £2,000, relief at the basic rate.

[92] I.C.T.A. 1970, s. 21.

In the case of policies of insurance made after March 19, 1968, premiums do not qualify for life insurance relief unless the policy is a " qualifying policy " within the meaning of Part 1 of Schedule 1 to the Income and Corporation Taxes Act 1970. Briefly, the policy must run for a minimum period of 10 years or until earlier death; there must be a reasonably even spread of premiums; and the capital sum payable on death must be at least 75 per cent. of the total premiums payable under the policy. When a policy is not a qualifying policy, premiums do not qualify for life insurance relief and higher rate income tax is chargeable on the proceeds *less* the premiums paid.[93]

8-56A   *Relief by deduction.*[93a] The method of giving relief on premiums has been altered in and from 1979–80. The payer will be entitled to deduct and retain a percentage of the amount of each premium, such percentage being 17½ per cent. in 1979–80. Hence, tax relief will be given when the premium is paid and not, as before, in assessing the payer to income tax. The £20 limit (see § 8-55) will no longer apply and it will generally be irrelevant whether or not the payer (if a United Kingdom resident) has income chargeable to tax. No claim need be made to the payer.

The new system will apply to insurance and deferred annuity contracts on the life of an individual or his spouse where the contract was made by either of them. The relief applies only to qualifying policies, defined for this purpose to exclude certain short-term policies (such as package holiday insurance) and personal accident policies.

Where husband and wife elect for non-aggregation of wife's earnings, this is to be ignored for the purposes of the 1/6th income limit (§ 8-55). Hence, a husband will be entitled to pay premiums of more than 1/6th of his income provided the total premiums paid by both husband and wife do not exceed 1/6th of their joint income. The life offices will be compensated for their loss of premium income by means of deficiency payments made by the Revenue.

6. RELIEF FOR INTEREST PAID [94]

8-57   By changes made in section 19 of the Finance Act 1974, which apply to interest paid after March 26, 1974, interest is not deductible in computing total income for tax purposes. There are exceptions to this rule which apply where the loan is applied for a qualifying purpose and transitional provisions which give tax relief on interest payable under obligations incurred on or before March 26, 1974. The exceptions and transitional provisions are summarised below. Where the exceptions apply and a claim to relief is made, tax relief is available to a person who pays in any year of assessment—

> (a) annual interest chargeable to tax under Case III of Schedule D (see §§ 5-01 *et seq.*); or

---

[93] *Ibid.* s. 19 (4); ss. 393–402.

[93a] F.A. 1976, s. 34 and Sched. 4, and F.A. 1978, s. 25 and Sched. 3. The Income Tax (Life Assurance Premium Relief) Regulations 1978 (S.I. 1978 No. 1159) in [1978] S.T.I. 432.

[94] For a more detailed treatment of this topic, see the Revenue publication " Tax Treatment of Interest Paid " (1974) I.R. 11 (with 1977 Supplement).

(b) interest payable in the United Kingdom on an advance from a bank carrying on a bona fide banking business in the United Kingdom or from a person bona fide carrying on a business as a member of the Stock Exchange in the United Kingdom or bona fide carrying on the business of a discount house in the United Kingdom.

Relief is given by allowing the interest to be deducted from or set off against the income for the year of assessment, income tax being discharged or repaid accordingly.[95] As regards (a), it is thought that the word " chargeable " does not require that the interest should be actually charged under Case III. All annual interest is chargeable under Case III although in some cases it may be charged under Case I: see § 5-23.

8-58   Interest paid on a bank overdraft or under credit card arrangements is not eligible for relief,[96] except under the transitional provisions summarised in § 8-67.

8-58A   *Anti-avoidance legislation.* Section 38 of the Finance Act 1976 denies tax relief in respect of any payment of interest if a scheme has been effected or arrangements have been made such that the sole or main benefit that might be expected to accrue to the claimant from the transaction under which the interest is paid was the obtaining of a reduction in tax liability by means of such relief.[97]

Relief in respect of interest paid may be available in the following circumstances:

1. *Interest paid as a business expense*

8-59   Interest paid as a business expense, whether short interest or yearly interest, is deductible except in the case of interest paid by companies where yearly interest (other than bank interest) is not deductible as a business expense but is allowed as a charge on income: see *ante*, § 2-75.

2. *Loans for purchase or improvement of land* [98]

8-60   Interest is eligible for relief under section 75 of the Finance Act 1972, if paid by a person owning an estate or interest in land in the United Kingdom on a loan to defray money applied—

(a) in purchasing the estate or interest, or one absorbed into or given up to obtain, the estate or interest; or

(b) in improving or developing the land, or buildings on the land including (i) payments in respect of maintenance or repairs incurred by reason of dilapidation attributable to a period before the estate or interest was acquired (but not otherwise including payments in respect of maintenance or repairs, or any other payments deductible from rent: see §§ 6-27 *et seq.*), and (ii) certain payments in respect of street works, as defined; or

---

[95] F.A. 1972, s. 75 as amended by F.A. 1974, s. 19.
[96] F.A. 1972, s. 75 (1A) as inserted by F.A. 1974, s. 19 (1).
[97] See Inland Revenue Press Release in [1976] S.T.I. 208.
[98] F.A. 1972, s. 75 and Sched. 9, paras. 1–9 as applied by F.A. 1974, s. 19.

(c) in paying off another loan where the claimant could have obtained relief under the section for interest on that other loan if it had not been paid off (and, if free of interest, assuming it carried interest).

The section does not apply to a loan unless made " in connection with the application of the money " *and* either on the occasion of its application or within a reasonable time from the application of the money; and the section does not apply to a loan where the proceeds are applied for some other purpose before being applied as so described. Interest on loans to purchase existing rentcharges, mortgages or charges do not qualify. There are provisions to prevent relief being given more than once and anti-avoidance provisions to prevent claims resulting from transactions between spouses, between a settlor and the trustees of his settlement, and between connected persons.

Interest on a loan to purchase or improve land, buildings or a caravan or house-boat is eligible for relief only if one of two conditions is satisfied [99]:

(1) *Main residence*

8-60A   Loan interest (including mortgage interest) is eligible for relief if, at the time when the interest is paid, the land etc. is used as the only or main residence of the borrower or of a dependent relative or former or separated spouse of his. The relief is available only for loans up to £25,000 [1]: interest on loans in excess of £25,000 does not qualify for relief. If, for example, the loan is £30,000 only 25,000/30,000ths of the interest is eligible. Previous loans have in some cases to be taken into account in determining whether the £25,000 limit has been exceeded. This applies to an earlier loan made after March 26, 1974, in respect of a main residence so that if, for example, A borrows £25,000 to purchase a main residence, interest on a subsequent loan to finance improvements will be ineligible for relief. Earlier loans, whenever made, in respect of a residence have to be taken into account: thus if A spent £15,000 in the purchase before March 1974 of a second residence, interest whereon is allowed under the transitional provisions discussed *post*, § 8-67, a loan of no more than £10,000 will qualify if applied subsequently in the purchase of a main residence. There are special provisions which apply to bridging loans and to cases where interest is payable before the land etc. is used as a residence.

The legislation does not say how the " main " residence is to be determined. This is a question of fact.

(2) *Let property*

8-60B   Where (1) does not apply, loan interest is eligible for relief if, in any period of 52 weeks comprising the time at which the interest is payable, the land etc. is let at a commercial rent for more than 26 weeks and, when not so let, is either available for letting at a commercial rent or used as the main residence of the owner or is prevented from being available for letting by

---

[99] F.A. 1974, s. 19 (2) and Sched. 1, paras. 4–8.
[1] This limit applies for 1978–79 and the four preceding years: F.A. 1976, s. 28; F.A. 1977, s. 21; F.A. 1978, s. 18.

reason of works of construction or repair. Where the borrower owns the land for less than 26 weeks in the year of assessment, it must be let at a commercial rent throughout that period. Interest relief in respect of let property is available only against rental income derived from that or any other let property. [2] There is no £25,000 restriction as in (1).

3. *Loan applied in acquiring interest in close company* [3]

8-61   Interest is eligible for relief under section 75 of the Finance Act 1972 on a loan to an individual to defray money applied—

(a) in acquiring any part of the ordinary share capital of a close company satisfying any of the conditions of paragraph 3A (2) of Schedule 16 to the Finance Act 1972; or

(b) in lending money to such a close company which is used wholly and exclusively for the purposes of the business of the company or of any associated company (being a close company satisfying any of these conditions); or

(c) in paying off another loan where relief could have been obtained under the section for interest on that other loan if it had not been paid off (and, if free of interest, assuming it carried interest).

The conditions in (a) restrict the relief to loans to purchase capital of close companies which are (i) trading companies, (ii) companies which are members of a trading group and (iii) companies of which the whole, or substantially the whole, of the income is estate or trading income, or interest and dividends or other distributions received from a 51 per cent. subsidiary, itself within (i), (ii) or (iii). Relief is given only—

(a) if when the interest is paid the company continues to satisfy any of the conditions (above) and the individual has a material interest (as defined) [4] in the company; and

(b) if, taking the period from the application of the proceeds of the loan until the interest was paid as a whole, the individual has worked for the greater part of his time in the actual management or conduct of the business of the company, or of any associated company of the company; and

(c) if he shows that in that period he has not recovered any capital from the close company: if capital is so recovered and is not used to repay the loan, the individual is treated as having repaid the loan to the extent of the capital recovered and the amount of interest eligible for relief is reduced accordingly. An individual is treated as having recovered an amount of capital if he receives consideration for the sale of ordinary share capital of the company, or by way of repayment of any part of the ordinary share capital; if the company

---

[2] F.A. 1974, Sched. 1, para. 7. It seems unnecessary that the other let property should itself be let at a commercial rent for the period stated in para. 4 (1) (b).

[3] F.A. 1974, s. 19 (2) and Sched. 1, paras. 9–10 and paras. 13–16. And see §§ 15-07 *et seq.*

[4] See I.C.T.A. 1970, s. 285 (6) as applied by F.A. 1974, Sched. 1, para. 16. A person has a material interest who alone, or with associates, controls more than 5 per cent. of the ordinary share capital or would, on a statutory apportionment, have more than 5 per cent. of the distributable income apportioned to him: see §§ 15-28 *et seq.*

repays a loan or advance; or if he receives consideration for the assignment of a debt due from the company. In each case the capital recovered is the amount or value so received or repaid, save that a sale or assignment otherwise than by way of a bargain at arm's length is deemed to be made at market value.

The section does not apply to a loan unless made " in connection with the application of the money " and either on the occasion of its application or within a reasonable time from the application of the money; and the section does not apply to a loan where the proceeds are applied for some purpose before being applied as specified in the section.

4. *Loan applied in acquiring an interest in a partnership* [5]

8-62   This relief is similar to the relief in § 8-61. Under section 75 of the Finance Act 1972 interest is eligible for relief on a loan to an individual to defray money applied—

(a) in purchasing a share in a partnership; or

(b) in contributing money to a partnership by way of capital or premium, or in advancing money to the partnership, where the money contributed or advanced is used wholly for the purposes of the trade, profession or vocation carried on by the partnership; or

(c) in paying off another loan where relief could have been obtained under section 75 for interest on that other loan if it had not been paid off (and, if free of interest, assuming it carried interest).

Relief is given only—

(a) if throughout the period from the application of the proceeds of the loan until the interest was paid, the individual has personally acted in the conduct of the trade, profession or vocation carried on by the partnership; and

(b) if he shows that in that period he has not recovered any amount of capital from the partnership (the provisions in this respect being similar to those summarised in § 8-61).

The section does not apply to a loan unless made " in connection with the application of the money," etc. (see § 8-60).

5. *Loan to purchase machinery or plant used by a partnership or in an office or employment* [6]

8-63   Section 44 of the Capital Allowances Act 1968 provides that in taxing a trade carried on in partnership, the same capital allowances or balancing charges shall be made in respect of machinery or plant used in the trade and belonging to one or more of the partners, but not being partnership property, as would be made in the case of machinery or plant belonging to the partners and being partnership property. For any year of assessment in

---

[5] F.A. 1974, s. 19 (2) and Sched. 1, paras. 11–12 and paras. 13–16.
[6] F.A. 1972, Sched. 9, paras. 10–15 as applied by F.A. 1974, s. 19.

which a partnership is entitled to an allowance or liable to a charge under section 44, the individual to whom the machinery or plant belongs is entitled to relief on interest paid by him in that year on a loan to defray money applied as capital expenditure on the provision of that machinery or plant. Relief will not be given in respect of interest falling due and payable more than three years after the end of the year of assessment in which the debt was incurred.

Thus a partner in a firm of solicitors can claim interest relief (for the three-year period mentioned) on a loan to purchase a car which is used in the practice.

Where the holder of an office or employment is entitled in any year to a capital allowance, or liable to a balancing charge, on machinery or plant purchased for use therein (see § 13-23), and he pays interest in that year on a loan to defray money applied as capital expenditure on the provision thereof, the interest so paid may be deducted from the emoluments of the year in which the interest is paid. The three-year limitation period mentioned in the last paragraph applies.

6. *Loan to pay capital transfer tax* [7]

8-64 Interest on a loan to the personal representatives of a deceased person is eligible for relief if the proceeds are applied—

(a) in paying, before the grant of representation, capital transfer tax in respect of personal property to which the deceased was beneficially entitled immediately before his death; or

(b) in paying off another loan where relief could have been obtained under the section for interest on that other loan if it had not been paid off.

Relief will not be given in respect of interest on so much of any loan as is applied in paying capital transfer tax in respect of property situate in Great Britain which did not vest in the personal representatives or in respect of property which, if it had been situate in Great Britain, would not have vested in them. A certificate of the Board as to the amount of capital transfer tax paid will be sufficient evidence for the purposes of claiming tax relief. Interest paid on a loan within (a), above, in respect of any period ending within one year from the making of the loan will be deducted from or set off against the income of the personal representatives for the year in which the interest is paid.

7. *Loans to purchase life annuity* [8]

8-65 Interest on loans to purchase life annuities for persons aged 65 or more, secured on land in the United Kingdom or in the Republic of Ireland in which the borrower has an interest, are eligible for relief in some cases.

---

[7] F.A. 1974, Sched. 1, paras. 17–22, as amended by F.A. 1975, Sched. 12, para. 19.
[8] F.A. 1974, Sched. 1, para. 24.

8. *Further provisions relating to interest*

8-66 Where credit is given for any money due from the purchaser under any sale, this is to be treated as the making of a loan to defray money applied by the purchaser in making the purchase. Thus if V sells land to P for £10,000 and the purchase money is left unpaid, V is to be treated as having made a loan of £10,000 to P, who may be entitled to relief in respect of interest paid to V.[9] Interest in excess of a reasonable commercial rate is ineligible for relief to the extent of the excess.[10] There are provisions for apportionment in the case of a debt which does not wholly fulfil the conditions required by the relevant sections.[11] Relief will be given under the sections only on the making of a claim [12]; and an appeal on the claim lies to the General Commissioners, or to the Special Commissioners if the appellant so elects.

9. *Transitional provisions* [13]

8-67 Interest payable under an obligation incurred on or before March 26, 1974, is excepted if

(1) the obligation was incurred on an overdraft or credit card (or on similar arrangement) and the interest is payable and paid before April 6, 1975; or

(2) the interest (not on an overdraft or credit card or similar arrangement) is payable on or before April 6, 1980.

Thus interest on mortgages to purchase " second homes " arranged before March 26, 1974, will continue to quality for tax relief for approximately six years from that date.

7. The Allocation of Deductions in Quantifying and Taxing Income

8-68 Since investment income beyond a certain limit is liable to investment income surcharge, it is to the advantage of an individual to apply deductions to which he is entitled in first reducing investment income liable to investment income surcharge (see § 8-05) before reducing income not so chargeable or earned income. The provisions of the relevant Act distinguish between deductions for personal reliefs and other deductions, *e.g.* in respect of interest, annuities and other annual payments (called charges on income: see § 8-31).

The rules are as follows:

(1) Deductions from total income under Chapter II of Part I of the Taxes Act (personal reliefs) must be made *after* any other deductions. Thus deductions in respect of charges on income are made before deductions in respect of personal reliefs. [14]

(2) Deductions in respect of charges on income can be made from income of different descriptions in the order which will result in the greatest

---

[9] F.A. 1972, Sched. 9, para. 14.
[10] F.A. 1972, s. 75 (2).
[11] F.A. 1972, Sched. 9, para. 15.
[12] F.A. 1972, s. 75 (1) as amended by F.A. 1974, s. 19 (1).
[13] F.A. 1974, s. 19 (3)–(7).
[14] F.A. 1971, s. 34 (3).

reduction in liability to income tax.[15] Thus charges can be treated as reducing investment income so as to avoid the investment income surcharge.

(3) Deductions in respect of personal reliefs must in the first instance be disregarded in determining what income is chargeable as investment income and what income is not so chargeable. Such deductions are then treated as reducing income not so chargeable before reducing income so chargeable.[16] The expression " income chargeable as investment income " means income chargeable at the additional rate or rates as enacted in section 32 (1) of the Finance Act 1971 [17]; and the first £1,700 (or £2,500, as appropriate) of investment income is income not so chargeable: see § 8-05.

Thus if in 1978–79 an individual aged under 65 has a salary of £900 and untaxed interest of £2,700 and pays £800 gross in mortgage interest and is entitled to personal reliefs of £1,535, his tax liability is computed as follows:

	£	*Earned income* £	*Investment income* £
Salary	900	900	—
Untaxed interest	2,700	—	2,700
	3,600	900	2,700
less mortgage interest	800	—	800
	£2,800	£900	1,900
less amount not chargeable as investment income (See Note)			1,700
			£200

	£	*Amount not chargeable as investment income* £	*Amount chargeable as investment income* £
	2,800	2,400	200
less personal reliefs	1,535	1,535	—
Taxable income	£1,265	£865	£200

Thus £1,265 is taxed at the lower and basic rates. £200 is also liable to the investment income surcharge.

Note. The personal reliefs (£1,535) cannot be used to reduce investment income from £1,900 to £365 and so avoid surcharge. The deduction of £1,700—see rule (3)—keeps £200 in charge as investment income.

8. COMPUTATIONS

Computation A

8-69   X, who carries on a profession, earned £10,000 (after deduction of expenses and capital allowances) in his accounting period of 12 months ended December 31, 1977. Bank interest credited in June and December 1977 totalled £1,200. Trust income to April 5, 1978, was £900 gross (tax £297). X paid mortgage interest of £200 to a building society in the year ended December 31, 1978, and

---

[15] F.A. 1971, s. 34 (1) and (2).
[16] *Ibid.* s. 34 (4).   [17] *Ibid.* s. 32 (3).

£120 in premiums on qualifying life policies. X's wife and children have no separate incomes. X has two children aged 10 and 14 on April 6, 1978. X's income tax liability for 1978–79 is as follows:

	£	Earned income £	Investment income £
Professional earnings to December 31, 1977	10,000	10,000	
Bank interest (untaxed)	1,200		1,200
Trust income (taxed)	900		900
	12,100	10,000	2,100
less mortgage interest	200	—	200
	£11,900	£10,000	1,900
less amount not chargeable as investment income: see § 8-68			1,700
			£200

	£	£	Amount not chargeable as investment income £	Amount chargeable as investment income £
		11,900	11,700	200
less personal allowance	1,535			
child allowance	100			
	135			
	1,770		1,770	
		£10,130	£9,930	£200

1978–79

Income tax at lower, basic and higher rates (§ 8-04):

£				£
750	@	25%	=	187·50
7,250	@	33%	=	2,392·50
1,000	@	40%	=	400·00
1,000	@	45%	=	450·00
130	@	50%	=	65·00
£10,130				£3,495·00

Income tax at additional rate(s) (§ 8-05):

£				£
200	@	10%	=	20·00
				£3,515·00

less tax credit on trust income (§ 8-21)
£900 @ 33%   297

                                                      £3,218·00

less life assurance relief (§ 8-55):
£120 @ 16½%   19·80

                    Total tax: £3,198·20

Computation B

8-69   X, who carries on a profession, earned £10,000 (after deducting expenses and capital allowances) in his accounting period of 12 months ended December 31, 1977. X received in the year ended April 5, 1979, an annuity of £1,200 gross (tax deducted £396) and dividends of £603 (tax credit £297). X paid mortgage interest of £700 to a building society in the year ended December 31, 1978. X's wife and children have no separate incomes. X has two children aged 10 and 14 on April 6, 1978. X's income tax liability for 1978–79 is as follows:

	£	*Earned income* £	*Investment income* £
Professional earnings to December 31, 1977	10,000	10,000	
Annuity (gross)	1,200		1,200
Dividends £603 plus tax credit £297	900		900
	12,100	10,000	2,100
less mortgage interest	700		700
	£11,400	£10,000	1,400
less amount not chargeable as investment income: see § 8-68			1,700
			nil

	£	£	*Amount not chargeable as investment income* £	*Amount chargeable as investment income* £
		11,400	11,400	nil
less personal allowance	1,535			
child allowances	135			
	100			
		1,770	1,770	
Taxable income		£9,630	£9,630	nil

Income tax at lower, basic and higher rates (§ 8-04):

£		%		£
750	@	25	=	187·50
7,250	@	33	=	2,392·50
1,000	@	40	=	400·00
630	@	45	=	283·50
£9,630				£3,263·50

	£	
less tax credits:		
Annuity £1,200 @ 33%	396	
Dividends	297	693·00
		£2,570·50

No liability to investment income surcharge.

Computation C

8-69   H's salary to April 5, 1979, is £9,000. Bank interest credited in June and December 1977 totalled £600. H, who is divorced and unmarried, paid his ex-wife (W) maintenance of £2,000 gross in the year ended April 5, 1979. (H deducted income tax at the basic rate of 33%, *i.e.* £660, and paid W £1,340: see § 5-31.) H's income tax liability for 1978–79 is as follows:

		Earned income	Investment income
	£	£	£
Salary	9,000	9,000	
Untaxed interest	600		600
	9,600	9,000	600
less maintenance payments	2,000	1,400	600
	7,600	7,600	nil
less personal relief	985	985	
	£6,615	£6,615	nil

Income tax payable:

£		%		£
750	@	25	=	187·50
5,865	@	33	=	1,935·45
				2,122·95

Add back retained tax (§ 8-32)

£2,000	@	33	=	660·00
	Total tax payable:			£2,782·95

Computation D

Facts as in Computation C. W's tax position in 1978–79 is as follows:

	£
Maintenance payments	2,000
less personal relief	985
	£1,015

Tax:

£		%		£	£
750	@	25	=	187·50	
265	@	33	=	87·45	274·95
	less tax deducted by H				660·00
	Tax reclaimable from Revenue				£385·05

Thus W receives: from H	1,340
from the Revenue	385·05
	£1,725·05

As to surcharge on maintenance payments, see § 8-10.

In 1978–79 a husband (H) has earned income of £17,000 and investment income of £200. His wife (W) has earned income of £4,000 and investment income of £500. The children have no income. Column 1 shows the tax position if the option for non-aggregation of wife's earnings (§ 8-29) is *not* exercised; Column 2 shows the tax position if it is exercised.

Computation E

	Column 1	Column 2 Joint income (excluding W's earnings)	W's earnings
	£	£	£
Joint income			
Earned	21,000	17,000	4,000
Unearned	700	700	—
	21,700	17,700	4,000
less	£	£	£
Personal relief	1,535	985	985
Additional personal relief on wife's earnings (§ 8-44)	985	—	—
Child relief	235	235	
	2,755	1,220	985
Taxable income	£18,945	£16,480	£3,015
Tax payable	£8,978·75	£7,291	£934·95

Total tax: £8,225·95

Tax saving: £752·80

Comments on Computations C and D

These Computations show:

(1) That H gets relief from higher rate tax because the gross amount of £2,000 is deductible in computing his total income. (If H had income chargeable as investment income, the maintenance payments would be applied first in reducing such income: see § 8-68.)

(2) That H discharges his obligation to pay £2,000 to W by paying only £2,000, less income tax at the basic rate (£660). This tax is recovered from H under section 3 of the Taxes Act 1970: see § 8-32. H thus acts as a tax collector for the Revenue.

(3) That W receives £1,725·05 from an outlay by H of £1,340, the difference of £385·05 being an amount equal to tax at the basic rate of 33 per cent. on the personal relief of £985 to which W is entitled (£325·05) plus tax at 8 per cent. (being the difference between the basic rate and the lower rate on £750 = £60).

(4) If the £2,000 were not a charge on H's income, H's tax liability would be on £9,600 less H's personal relief. This demonstrates in practical terms the proposition that an income settlement has the effect of removing the top slice of the settlor's income and making it the income of the beneficiary for tax purposes.

1978–79

Tax rates on earned income

8-70

Total taxable income	Top rate band tax at	Total tax	Tax as percentage of total taxable income
£	%	£	%
8,000	33	2,580	32·25
9,000	40	2,980	33·11
10,000	45	3,430	34·30
12,000	55	4,480	37·33
14,000	60	5,655	40·39
15,000	65	6,305	42·03
18,000	70	8,355	46·42
20,000	75	9,830	49·15
22,000	75	11,330	51·50
25,000	83	13,660	54·64
28,000	83	16,150	57·68
30,000	83	17,810	59·37
40,000	83	26,110	65·28
50,000	83	34,410	68·82

" Taxable income " is defined in § 8-03. The amount of tax payable on a *taxable income* of (say) £10,000 is £3,430. To find the amount of tax payable on an income over £8,000 where the amount is not in the left-hand column, take the next lowest income shown in that column and add to the amount of tax shown in the third column a percentage of the excess, taking the per cent. figure in the next line. The tax on £10,500 for example is:

Tax on £10,000	=	£3,430
plus 55% × £500	=	£ 275
		£3,705

Taxable income of £8,000 or less is taxed at the lower and basic rates. Where taxable income includes investment income, additional tax is payable as explained in § 8-05.

CHAPTER 9

TRUST INCOME

1. THE CHARGE ON THE TRUSTEES

A. *Income arising to trustees: basic rate income tax*

9-01   Income received by trustees in the course of administering a trust is assessed to tax at the basic rate, unless the income has already suffered basic rate tax by deduction. There is no provision in the Income Tax Acts specifically charging trustees to basic rate tax on trust income, [1] but they are nevertheless assessable under the Schedule appropriate to the source from which the income arises. [2] Thus trustees who carry on a trade are assessed under Case 1 of Schedule D; trustees in receipt of an income from rents are taxed under Schedule A, and so on. Trustees are chargeable persons in respect of capital gains. [3] Trustees are not entitled to personal reliefs because they are not " individuals " for tax purposes [4] ; but they may claim other reliefs appropriate to the source of the trust income, *e.g.* loss relief in respect of Schedule D income. No deduction is allowable in computing liability to basic rate income tax for expenses incurred by the trustees in managing the trust [5]; nor can trustees make a management expenses claim. [6] Foreign income which arises under a trust is not liable to United Kingdom tax if the beneficiary is resident abroad, even if the trustees are resident in the United Kingdom, if the income is paid direct from the foreign source to the non-resident beneficiary. [7] It appears that a trustee would have a good defence to an assessment to the extent that the income assessed was held on trust for a beneficiary not liable to income tax, such as a company chargeable to corporation tax. [8]

B. *Income arising to trustees: additional rate tax*

9-02   Under the pre-unified system of personal taxation, trustees were not assessable to surtax because they are not " individuals " for tax purposes [4]; and when the unified system was introduced by section 32 (1) of the Finance Act 1971, charging higher rate income tax and additional rates of income tax (the " investment income surcharge ") on the total income of *individuals,* trustees were liable only to basic rate income tax. Had the law remained unchanged, a settlement authorising or directing the accumulation of income with a view to its eventual distribution in capital form would

---

[1] I.C.T.A. 1970, ss. 68 (1) and 114 (1) charge tax under Schedules A and D respectively on " the persons receiving or entitled to the profits or gains " in respect of which tax is directed to be charged. T.M.A. 1970, s. 72, provides for the assessment of trustees of incapacitated persons, including infants (*ibid.* s. 118 (1)).

[2] I.C.T.A. 1970, s. 1. *Williams* v. *Singer* [1921] A.C. 65; 7 T.C. 387; *Reid's Trustees* v. *I.R.C.* (1929) 14 T.C. 512. *Kelly* v. *Rogers* [1935] 2 K.B. 446; 19 T.C. 692 (C.A.).

[3] See *post,* Chap. 16.

[4] This is clear from many statutory provisions. See, *e.g.* the discussion in § 9-02.

[5] *Aiken* v. *MacDonald's Trustees* (1894) 3 T.C. 306.

[6] *Ante,* § 6-31.

[7] *Williams* v. *Singer* [1921] A.C. 65; 7 T.C. 387 (H.L.).

[8] See *Reid's Trustees* v. *I.R.C.* (1929) 14 T.C. 512 at p. 525, *per* Lord Clyde.

have been an attractive vehicle for the accumulation of wealth at a relatively low cost in taxation. Not surprisingly, therefore, section 16 of the Finance Act 1973 altered the law in and from 1973–74 by making certain income which arises to trustees liable to income tax at " the additional rate " (but not higher rate income tax) as well as to basic rate income tax. " The additional rate " in this context means the additional rate mentioned in section 32 (1) of the Finance Act 1971 or, if more than one, the higher or highest of them.[9] This is 15 per cent. in 1977–78 and 1978–79.[10] Thus where the section applies, trust income bears tax at 48 per cent. in 1978–79.[11] The surcharge-free amounts (and the lower rates) which apply to the investment income of individuals (§ 8-05) do not apply to trust income. Hence income being accumulated may, during the period of accumulation, bear a higher rate of income tax than that applicable to the beneficiaries.

9-03   Section 16 of the Finance Act 1973 applies to income arising to trustees in a year of assessment which is subject to a trust for accumulation and also to income which is payable at their discretion, whether or not the trustees have power to accumulate. Thus income tax at the additional rate is charged on the income of a trust for maintenance and accumulation (see § 37-14). Not all the income is chargeable but only the net amount after defraying expenses of the trustees properly chargeable to income (or which would be so chargeable but for any express provisions of the trust).

9-04   The charge does not apply to income which, when it arises, is treated as the income of a beneficiary (see § 9-15); nor to income which is treated as income of the settlor under one of the provisions considered in Chapter 10.

> Thus if trustees of a discretionary trust are required to pay an annuity to X, so much of the trust income as is equal to the gross amount of the annuity does not bear the additional rate income tax.

The charge does not apply to income arising under a trust established for charitable purposes only or to income from investments, deposits or other property held for the purposes of a fund or scheme established for the sole purpose of providing relevant benefits within the meaning of section 26 of the Finance Act 1970 (relating to retirement benefits schemes).

Note that trustees of a charitable trust seeking to secure exemption from additional rate tax are not required to show that the income is " applied to charitable purposes only." [12] Dividends and building society interest received by trustees are treated as income from which income tax from a corresponding gross amount has been deducted.[13]

9-05   Where trustees are participators in a close company and sums are apportioned to them under the provisions discussed in §§ 15-28 et seq., such sums together with the amount of advance corporation tax attributable to them are income chargeable at the additional rate.[14]

---

[9] F.A. 1973, s. 59 (2).
[10] F.A. 1977, s. 17.
[11] F.A. 1973, s. 59 (2) read with F.A. 1978, s. 13.
[12] Cf. ante, § 1-18.
[13] F.A. 1973, s. 16 (5).   [14] Ibid. s. 16 (3) and (4).

Thus if £660 is apportioned to trustees in 1977–78, when the rate of ACT is 34/66ths, the trustees are assessed under section 16 of the Finance Act 1973 to surcharge of 15 per cent. of £1,000 = £150.

9-06 The term " trustees " in the above paragraphs does not include personal representatives, but where personal representatives, on or before the completion of the administration of an estate, pay to trustees any sum representing income which, if personal representatives were trustees within the meaning of section 16 of the Finance Act 1973, would be income to which the section applies, that sum is to be deemed to be paid to the trustees as income and to have borne income tax at the basic rate.[15]

Thus if personal representatives pay £660 of undistributed income to trustees of a discretionary settlement in 1977–78, the trustees are assessed under section 16 of the Finance Act 1973 to additional rate tax of 15 per cent. of £1,000 = £150. (The personal representatives will already have borne income tax at the rate for the year in which the income arose.)

9-07 The Revenue may, by notice given to trustees under section 8 of the Taxes Management Act 1970, require a return of the income arising to them to include particulars of the manner in which the income has been applied, including particulars as to the exercise of any discretion and of the persons in whose favour it has been exercised.[16]

9-08 Tax at the additional rate of 15 per cent. normally becomes due and payable by trustees on July 6 following the end of the year of assessment in which the relevant income arises to the trustees.

C. *Income distributed by trustees: discretionary settlements*

9-09 We have seen that income which arises to trustees of a discretionary settlement in and from 1973–74 is liable to basic rate income tax and tax at the additional rate in the year when the income arises, whether or not the income is distributed in that year or is accumulated.[17] A further charge to tax may arise on the trustees in the year when the income is distributed if the tax rate on trust income (which is 49 per cent. in 1977–78 and 48 per cent. in 1978–79) has increased since the year in which the income arose. Section 17 of the Finance Act 1973 provides that where, in any year of assessment, trustees make a payment to a person in the exercise of a discretion and the sum paid is for all the purposes of the Income Tax Acts *income* of the payee (but would not be his income apart from the payment), the payment shall be treated as a net amount corresponding to a gross amount from which tax has been deducted at a rate equal to the sum of the basic rate and the additional rate in force for the year in which the payment is made.[18]

Thus if trustees make an income-payment of £550 to a beneficiary in a year of assessment when the basic rate is 30 per cent. and the additional rate 15 per

---

[15] F.A. 1973, s. 16 (6).
[16] *Ibid.* s. 16 (8).
[17] *Ante*, §§ 9-02 *et seq.*
[18] F.A. 1973, s. 17 (1), (2). Trustees in this section do not include personal representatives: *ibid.* s. 17 (5).

cent., the payment is treated for tax purposes as a payment of £1,000 from which tax of £450 has been deducted.

The sum treated as deducted (£450) is treated as income tax paid by the payee and, subject to the set-off provisions in § 9-10, as income tax assessable on the trustees.[19]

9-10   Section 17 (3) of the Finance Act 1973 allows the trustees to set off against the amount assessable on them income tax already borne by them on the income as it arose, under the provisions summarised in §§ 9-02 *et seq.*

> Thus if trustees of a discretionary settlement receive income in 1974–75 on which they suffer tax at 48 per cent. and the income is distributed as income in 1975–76 when the tax rate on trust income is 50 per cent., the trustees suffer tax at 2 per cent. on the amount distributed in 1975–76.

There are provisions having the same effect to meet the case where income of a close company which is apportioned to trustees in one year and taxed under section 16 of the Finance Act 1973, is actually distributed to the trustees by way of dividend in a later year, and subsequently distributed by the trustees as income.[20]

9-11   The legislation has to allow for the possibility that income distributed by trustees of a discretionary settlement in or after 1973–74 might have arisen before 1973–74. In such a case it would be right to allow some set-off for tax suffered on the arising of the income and it is accordingly provided that the " amount of tax in respect of income found on a claim made by the trustees to have been available to them for distribution at the end of the year 1972–73 . . . shall be taken to be two-thirds of the net amount of that income." [21] Such income is thus treated as having suffered an average rate of tax of about 40 per cent. It is thought that the words " income . . . available to [the trustees] for distribution " include income which had been accumulated at the end of 1972–73 and thus lost its character as " income " for tax purposes.[22]

9-12   Tax payable by trustees under section 17 of the Finance Act 1973 normally becomes due and payable on July 6 following the end of the year of assessment in which the relevant payment is made. The beneficiaries are entitled to a certificate of tax deducted by the trustees.[23]

2. TOTAL INCOME OF THE BENEFICIARIES

9-13   It will be apparent from Section 1 of this chapter that trust income will have already suffered tax at the basic rate before it reaches the beneficiaries and that, where trust income is to be accumulated or is payable at the discretion of the trustees, it will also have borne additional rate tax. Trustees are under

---

[19] *Ibid.* s. 17 (2) (*b*).
[20] *Ibid.* s. 17 (3) (*b*) and (*c*).
[21] *Ibid.* s. 17 (3) (*d*). Claims are made to the Inspector: T.M.A. 1970, s. 46 (2).
[22] *Cf.* (1973) H.C.Deb., Standing Committee H, Third Sitting, cols. 267–268.
[23] F.A. 1973, s. 17 (4).

no circumstances liable to higher rate income tax.[24] The beneficiary must include in his return of total income the amount of trust income to which he is entitled, grossed up at the rate of tax treated as deducted by the trustees.

> This is tax at the basic rate in the case of a beneficiary with a life interest and tax at the sum of the basic and additional rates in the case of a beneficiary under, *e.g.* a discretionary settlement (see § 9-09).

Where trust income is received direct by the beneficiary under the authority of the trustees, the beneficiary may be assessed instead of the trustees.[25]

9-14   The significance of total income was explained in Chapter 8. In the computation of total income, the following rules apply with respect to trust income:

9-15   (1) Income to which a beneficiary is entitled (whether by virtue of the trust instrument or otherwise, *e.g.* under the Trustee Act 1925) forms part of his total income, whether or not he receives it. This is because

> " Where trustees are in receipt of income which it is their duty to pay over to beneficiaries . . . that income is at its very inception the beneficiary's income." [26]

Consequently, the beneficiary avoids no higher rate income tax or investment income surcharge by refusing to accept payment of the trust income.[27] Note that trustees are not chargeable at the additional rate on income which, before being distributed, is income of a beneficiary.[28]

> Where trustees hold *e.g.* securities upon trust for A for life, the source of A's income for tax purposes is the securities, not the trust instrument.[29]

9-16   (2) Sums which a beneficiary is entitled to have applied for his benefit form part of his total income.

> Thus if a testator directs his trustees to pay the rates and other outgoings on a house occupied by his widow (the tenant for life), the amount so paid by the trustees forms part of his widow's total income.[30]

9-17   (3) A payment to a beneficiary out of trust *capital* is *income* of the beneficiary, if the payment is Schedule D Case III income (*i.e.* an annual payment) in the hands of the beneficiary.[31]

---

[24] See, *ante*, § 8-03.

[25] See T.M.A. 1970, s. 76 (1), which protects trustees who authorise the receipt of " profits arising from trust property " by the persons entitled thereto and who make a return in accordance with s. 13 of that Act.

[26] Sir Wilfrid Greene M.R. in *Corbett* v. *I.R.C.*·[1938] 1 K.B. 567, 577 (C.A.); 21 T.C. 449, 460. *Dreyfus* v. *I.R.C.* (1963) 41 T.C. 441; *cf. Cornwell* v. *Barry* (1955) 36 T.C. 268 where the beneficiary had a vested interest in income which was liable to be divested and the court held that income not specifically appropriated to the beneficiary was not his income for tax purposes.

[27] *Cf.* income under Case III of Schedule D: *ante*, § 5-09.

[28] See, *ante*, § 9-04.

[29] *Archer-Shee* v. *Baker* [1927] A.C. 844; 11 T.C. 749 (H.L.).

[30] *I.R.C.* v. *Miller* [1930] A.C. 222; 15 T.C. 25. The annual value of the house would no longer form part of the widow's total income. As to the effect of the provisions for compensating the beneficiary against higher rate income tax (then surtax): see *Michelham's Trustees* v. *I.R.C.* (1930) 15 T.C. 737 (C.A.).

[31] *Ante*, § 5-04.

In *Brodie's Will Trustees* v. *I.R.C.,*[32] trustees were directed to pay part of the trust income to the testator's widow; and if in any year the widow's share of income did not amount to £4,000, the trustees were directed to raise and pay the deficiency out of capital. *Held*, that the sums so paid out of capital in seven successive years were " annual payments " within Case III of Schedule D and formed part of the beneficiary's total income.[33]

The position is the same where the beneficiary has no right to demand that his income be augmented but has to rely on the trustees' discretion.[34] Care must therefore be taken in drafting any provision in a will or settlement giving trustees power to advance sums out of capital: payments which have the quality of recurrence will be treated as income of the beneficiary, notwithstanding their origin in capital and notwithstanding the parties' own description of the payment.[35] Hence the power should not be expressed as a power to make up deficiencies in income or to maintain the beneficiary in a particular standard of living but should be expressed in general terms and exercised in such a manner as not to give the quality of income (*i.e.* annual payment) to the payments. In the case of a discretionary settlement, the manner in which trustees resolve to exercise their discretion may give payments made by them out of capital the quality of income. Bona fide loans by the trustees are not income of the beneficiary.[36] In one case, the nature of a payment to a beneficiary is determined by the source from which it arises. This is where the beneficiary is absolutely entitled to both income and capital of the fund: the entire income of the fund is income of the beneficiary, and the capital of the fund is capital of the beneficiary.[37] This rule applies whether the beneficiary is paid in a lump sum or by periodic payments.

9-18   (4) **Discretionary payments.** Sums actually paid to a beneficiary in the exercise of a discretion, whether statutory or otherwise, are part of the beneficiary's total income.[38] So, for example, sums paid to an infant beneficiary in exercise of the statutory power of maintenance are income of the infant.

9-19   (5) **Accumulated income.** The question whether income which is accumulated by trustees forms part of the beneficiary's total income depends on whether the beneficiary has a vested or a contingent interest in the income. Whether an interest is vested or contingent must be ascertained by applying general principles of law and

---

[32] (1933) 17 T.C. 432. See also *Cunard's Trustees* v. *I.R.C.* (1946) 27 T.C. 122; *Williamson* v. *Ough* [1936] A.C. 384; 20 T.C. 194; *Milne's Executors* v. *I.R.C.* (1956) 37 T.C. 10; *Lawson* v. *Rolfe* (1969) 46 T.C. 199.
[33] There would be an assessment on the trustees under I.C.T.A. 1970, s. 53 (*ante*, §§ 5-34 *et seq.*) or under F.A. 1973, s. 17 (1) as appropriate: *ante*, §§ 9-09 *et seq.*
[34] *Lindus and Hortin* v. *I.R.C.* (1933) 17 T.C. 442. See also *Peirse-Duncombe Trust (Trustees)* v. *I.R.C.* (1940) 23 T.C. 199, where the deficiency in an annuity was made up out of borrowed moneys and the principle was applied.   [35] *Jackson's Trustees* v. *I.R.C.* (1942) 25 T.C. 13.
[36] *I.R.C.* v. *Sansom* [1921] 2 K.B. 492; 8 T.C. 20 (C.A.).
[37] *Brodie's Will Trustees* v. *I.R.C.* (1933) 17 T.C. 432, *per* Finlay J. at p. 438.
[38] *Drummond* v. *Collins* [1915] A.C. 1011; 6 T.C. 525. See also § 5-04 (2). Higher rate income tax and investment income surcharge due from a beneficiary under a discretionary trust may be recovered from the trustees: I.C.T.A. 1970, s. 36.

especially section 31 of the Trustee Act 1925, as amended by the Family Law Reform Act 1969.[39]

(a) *Vested interest.* If the beneficiary has a vested interest, the income forms part of the beneficiary's total income year by year as it arises, even if it is not received by him.[40] Any claim for personal reliefs by the beneficiary and any assessment on him to higher rate income tax or investment income surcharge must be made within six years after the end of the year.

(b) *Contingent interest.* Income in which a beneficiary has a contingent interest and which is accumulated does not form part of his total income, even retrospectively when the contingency occurs and the accumulations are paid to the beneficiary. The income reaches the beneficiary as capital.[41] Higher rate income tax is thus avoided.[42]

Example: Assume A settles income-producing property on trust for such of his children as shall attain the age of 25 years and that A has two children. The trustees accumulate the whole of the income of each child's share until he attains the age of 18 years when, under section 31 of the Trustee Act 1925, each child's interest in income vests in possession. Each child attains the age of 25 years. The income of each child's share forms part of his total income from the date when he attains 18 years but, before that date, is taxed as income of the trustees at the basic and additional rate.[43] No further income tax is payable on the vesting of each child's share of capital.

Where a foreign element is present, sections 478–481 of the Income and Corporation Taxes Act 1970 may be relevant: see § 7-26.

3. INCOME ARISING DURING THE ADMINISTRATION OF AN ESTATE

9-20 Income which arises from an estate during the course of its administration is treated as income of the personal representatives in their representative capacity and is charged to basic rate income tax (but not to higher rate income tax).

The income of an estate has to be taken into account in computing the total income of the beneficiary entitled thereto, and the method by which this is done is provided in Part XV of the Income and Corporation Taxes Act 1970. These provisions apply only during the " administration period "; that is, from the date of death until the date of completion of the administration of the estate.[44] Although the phrase " the completion of the administration " is used frequently in the Acts, the only definition is that contained in section 433 (*a*) of the Income and Corporation Taxes Act 1970, which is concerned with the application of Part XV to Scotland. From this definition it would appear that the administration is complete when the residue is ascertained. After the completion of the administration, the total income of the beneficiaries is computed in accordance with the rules already discussed (in Section 2) applicable to trust income.

The method of computing total income under Part XV varies with the nature of the interest of the beneficiary in residue:

[39] See *Stanley* v. *I.R.C.* [1944] K.B. 255; 26 T.C. 12 (C.A.).
[40] *Hamilton-Russell's Executors* v. *I.R.C.* (1943) 25 T.C. 200 (C.A.).
[41] *I.R.C.* v. *Blackwell Minor's Trustees* [1924] 2 K.B. 351; 10 T.C. 235.
[42] *Stanley* v. *I.R.C.* [1944] K.B. 255; 26 T.C. 12 (C.A.).
[43] See generally Chaps. 10 and 37.   [44] I.C.T.A. 1970, s. 426 (1).

(1) *Where the beneficiary has a limited interest in residue* [45]

9-21   A beneficiary with a right to income only (such as a life tenant) has a
" limited interest." [46] Such a beneficiary has a right to income from the
date of death but the final determination of the exact amount of the income
to which he is entitled must await the completion of the administration, for
the residue cannot be ascertained until all claims against the estate have
been determined. The general scheme of the Act is as follows:

(1) Any sums which are paid to the beneficiary during the
administration period are treated as part of his total income for the
year when they are paid. Where such sums have already suffered tax
at the basic rate (which is ordinarily the case where the estate is a
United Kingdom estate), [47] they must be grossed up at the basic rate
for the year of payment. Clearly this method of computing the
beneficiary's income can produce only a provisional figure and
adjustments are necessary when the amount of the residue is finally
known.

(2) On completion of the administration, the sums already paid to the
beneficiary are aggregated with any sums then found due to him, and
the aggregate income is deemed to have accrued due and been paid to
the beneficiary from day to day during the administration period.
This reallocation of the income throughout the period of
administration will necessitate fresh computations of total income,
and any additional assessments which are required may be made
at any time within three years from the completion of the
administration. [48]

(2) *Where the beneficiary has an absolute interest in residue* [49]

9-22   A beneficiary has an absolute interest in residue if he has a right to capital
on the residue being ascertained. [50] In this case, the problem is to find what
part of any sum which is paid to the beneficiary during the administration
period represents capital and what part represents income of the capital still
awaiting distribution. The problem is to segregate the income element from
the capital element, for only the former enters into the computation of the
beneficiary's total income. The method by which this process of segregation
is achieved is briefly as follows:

(1) Calculate the " residuary income " of the estate for each year (or
part of a year) of assessment during the administration period. [51]
This, broadly speaking, is the aggregate income of the personal
representatives from all sources, less certain charges on the estate of
an income nature (*e.g.* annuities, interest on legacies) and certain
management expenses. [52]

---

[45] I.C.T.A. 1970, s. 426.   [46] *Ibid.* s. 432 (3).
[47] Defined *ibid*. s. 432 (8). In the case of a " foreign estate " the income is charged to tax at the basic
rate under Case IV of Schedule D: *ibid*. s. 426 (4).
[48] *Ibid*. s. 431 (3).
[49] *Ibid*. s. 427.
[50] *Ibid*. s. 432 (2).
[51] *Ibid*. s. 427 (2), s. 428 (1). Income received under deduction of tax by personal representatives which
covers a period including the date of death is not income of the deceased: *I.R.C.* v. *Henderson's Executors*
(1931) 16 T.C. 282.   [52] *Ibid*. s. 432 (7), s. 428 (1).

(2) Sums which are paid to the beneficiary during the administration period are treated as income up to the amount of the " residuary income." Any excess over this is treated as payment on account of capital.

(3) On completion of the administration, adjustments may be necessary.

4. LEGACIES AND ANNUITIES

General legacies

9-23 Where a general legatee is entitled to interest,[53] the amount of interest actually paid to the legatee forms part of his total income. Such interest is income falling under Case III of Schedule D. Interest which is not paid (*e.g.* because the legatee declines to accept payment [54]) is not " income " of the legatee.

Specific legacies

9-24 Income arising from property which is the subject of a specific disposition by will belongs to the legatee from the date of death, unless the will otherwise provides. It therefore forms part of the legatee's total income year by year as it arises.[55]

Annuities

9-25 An annuity provided by will is payable (unless the will otherwise provides) from the date of death, and therefore forms part of the annuitant's total income from that date. An annuitant is entitled to have a fund set aside which will produce income sufficient to secure the annuity; and where the estate is insufficient to pay the pecuniary legacies in full and also to provide the annuity fund, the annuitant is generally entitled to demand payment of the actuarial value of the annuity (abated with the legacies).[56] In such an event, the annuitant's right is to *capital* only, and all payments to him must be treated as such.[57] A direction in a will to purchase an annuity generally entitles the annuitant to demand the capital value of the annuity, when similar tax consequences ensue.

Purchased life annuities

9-26 These are considered in §§ 5-53 *et seq.*

---

[53] See Snell's *Equity*, 27th ed., p. 356.
[54] *Dewar* v. *I.R.C.* [1935] 2 K.B. 351; 19 T.C. 561 (C.A.). And see § 5-09. For the position where the legacy is abated or payment is delayed and sums are paid on account, see *Re Prince* (1935) 51 T.L.R. 526; *Re Morley's Estate* [1937] Ch. 491.
[55] *I.R.C.* v. *Hawley* [1928] 1 K.B. 578; 13 T.C. 327.
[56] See Snell's *Equity*, 27th ed., pp. 352–355.
[57] *I.R.C.* v. *Castlemaine (Lady)* (1943) 25 T.C. 408.

CHAPTER 10

INCOME AND CAPITAL SETTLEMENTS

1. INTRODUCTION

10-01 THERE are many circumstances in which one person may wish, or be obliged, to provide another person with a source of income. A parent or grandparent may wish to provide a source of income for a child's education or maintenance, or to assist a dependent relative. A person may wish to provide an income for charitable purposes. Divorce and separation are occasions when one spouse may be obliged by law to provide an income for the other or for the children of the marriage.

10-02 A source of income may be provided in one of two ways:

1. Where the provider has income but no capital, in the sense of income-producing property, he may enter into a deed or other instrument transferring part of his income.

> *Example*: X covenants to pay Y during the joint lives of X and Y or for seven years whichever is the shorter period the sum of £2,000 per annum less income tax at the basic rate.

This type of arrangement may be described as an " income settlement " because X merely transfers part of his income to Y.

2. Where the provider has capital, he may enter into a deed or other instrument transferring part of his capital to trustees, directing them to invest the capital and pay or apply the income so produced to or for the benefit of one or more persons.

> *Example*: X transfers £20,000 to trustees upon trust to invest the same, to divide the capital between X's children if and when they attain the age of 25 years and meanwhile to apply the income for the maintenance, education or benefit of such children.

This type of arrangement may be described as a " capital settlement " because X transfers part of his capital to trustees.

10-03 The terms " income settlement " and " capital settlement " are not used in the Tax Acts but the expressions conveniently underline the differences between the two types of arrangement. Because of these differences, income and capital settlements are dealt with separately in the pages that follow. Although many of the statutory provisions which apply to the one type of settlement apply also to the other, their effect is not the same.

The effect of the statutory provisions

10-04 The object of both types of settlement is to transfer a slice of the settlor's income from the settlor to another person or persons. In some cases the settlor is a high rate taxpayer, whereas the beneficiary is taxable at a lower rate or not at all (*e.g.* a charity). The object of the exercise in such a case is to transfer income in such a way that it ceases to be part of the settlor's income taxable at the high rates applicable to him and becomes the beneficiary's income. Whether the settlement is an income settlement or a capital settlement, the income will have suffered basic rate income tax by deduction before it reaches the beneficiary, so that, if the beneficiary is exempt from income tax or not liable to tax at the basic rate on the whole of the income he derives from the settlor, the beneficiary will be able to make a claim for repayment of income tax from the Revenue.

10-05 The statutory provisions which are considered in this chapter operate in one of two ways:

(1) In some cases they deem the income to be that of the settlor for *all* income tax purposes. This renders the settlement wholly ineffective for tax purposes because (a) the settlor gets no relief from tax because the transferred income is added back in computing his tax liability and (b) it denies the beneficiary any right to claim repayment of basic rate income tax.

(2) In other cases, they deem the income to be that of the settlor only for the purposes of " excess liability." Excess liability means the excess of liability to income tax over what it would be if all income tax were charged at the basic rate to the exclusion of any other rate.[1] This means that the transferred income is deemed to be the income of the settlor for the purposes of higher rate income tax and investment income surcharge, with the result that the settlor is denied any relief from tax at these rates; but the beneficiary is not deprived of his right to claim repayment of basic rate income tax in an appropriate case.

10-06 Although voluntary settlements are often used in tax planning where the settlor is a high rate taxpayer and the beneficiary is a low rate taxpayer, it should be kept in mind that the tax position of the parties may become reversed through changed circumstances, in which case the statutory provisions operate to reduce the tax liability of the beneficiary and to increase that of the settlor.

A settlement which is ineffective under the general law, *e.g.* for lack of certainty[2] or for perpetuity[3] is equally ineffective for any tax purpose.

What is a settlement?

10-07 For the purposes of most of the provisions considered in this chapter the word " settlement " is defined as including " any trust, covenant, agreement or arrangement "[4] although, for the purposes of other provisions, it also includes " a transfer of assets."[5]

---

[1] I.C.T.A. 1970, s. 457 (1).
[2] See *Re Baden's Deed Trusts* [1971] A.C. 424 (H.L.).
[3] *Aked* v. *Shaw* (1947) 28 T.C. 286.
[4] I.C.T.A. 1970, s. 454 (3) applying for the purposes of Chapter III (ss. 445–456) and Chapter IV (ss. 457–459). The word " disposition " is so defined in s. 434 (2) for the purposes of Chap. I (ss. 434–436).
[5] I.C.T.A. 1970, s. 444 (2) applying for the purposes of Chapter III (ss. 437–444).

10-08   Although the point has never been fully argued, it seems generally to be accepted that some element of bounty is necessary for an agreement or arrangement lacking the characteristics of a settlement to be treated as a " settlement " for tax purposes.[6] But a transaction which is plainly a settlement, *e.g.* in the conveyancing sense, is a " settlement " for tax purposes even if it is the result of a commercial bargain.

10-09   A court order can constitute a " settlement " and in *Yates* v. *Starkey* [7] (a divorce case) it was held that a consent order directing the husband to make payments *in trust for* each of his children was a settlement of which the husband was settlor. Where the court orders that payments be made *directly* to the child it is Revenue practice not to treat the order as constituting a settlement. Where, however, there is a consent order and the amount ordered is excessive in relation to the legal obligations of the father to maintain his child, the Revenue may contend that there is a settlement.

2. INCOME SETTLEMENTS

10-10   The following is an example of the operative clause in a typical income settlement:

> X covenants to pay Y during the joint lives of X and Y or for seven years, whichever is the shorter period, the sum of £2,400 per annum less income tax at the basic rate, such payments to be made in equal monthly instalments on the first day of each month.

It has been explained in § 5-04 that, provided the agreement between X and Y creates an obligation binding on X (as it will if the agreement is under seal or is otherwise enforceable as a simple contract), the payments made under the agreement are annual payments within Case III of Schedule D. On making the payments X deducts income tax at the basic rate: see § 5-30.

10-11   Let it be assumed that X has an income (all earned) of £9,000 in the year of assessment and that he has covenanted to make Y an annual payment of £2,400. Ignoring the settlement provisions in the Tax Acts, the tax consequences of this arrangement may be summarised as follows:

1. X discharges his obligation to Y by paying to Y each month £200 less income tax at the basic rate. Thus if the basic rate is 33 per cent., X will pay £200 less £66 = £134.
2. Y can reclaim from the Inland Revenue the amount by which the amount deducted by X exceeds Y's tax liability, if any. If Y is a charity or is otherwise exempt from income tax on Case III income, Y can reclaim from the Revenue the whole of the amount deducted by X. If Y is an individual with no other income, and therefore taxable only on his income after deducting the personal reliefs, Y can reclaim tax at the basic rate on an amount equal to his personal reliefs.

---

[6] See *Bulmer* v. *I.R.C.* [1967] Ch. 145; 44 T.C. 1; following *Copeman* v. *Coleman* (1939) 22 T.C. 594 and *I.R.C.* v. *Leiner* (1964) 41 T.C. 589. See also *I.R.C.* v. *Plummer* [1978] 3 W.L.R. 459 (C.A.) and *Berry* v. *Warnett* [1978] S.T.C. 504, *post*, § 16-21.   [7] [1951] Ch. 465; 32 T.C. 38 (C.A.).

3. The gross amount of the annual payment (£2,400) is a charge on the income of X: see § 8-31. Hence X is entitled to deduct the £2,400 in computing his total income. The effect is that X avoids higher rate income tax and investment income surcharge (where appropriate) on the annual payment but has to account for the basic rate tax which he deducts (see § 8-32).

10-12   The practical effect of these consequences is clearly demonstrated by the example in § 8-69 (Computations C and D) and the comments there, to which the reader is referred. Briefly, an income settlement enables an individual to transfer a slice of his income so that it ceases to bear income tax at the rate or rates that would otherwise apply to such income, which becomes taxable at the rate or rates applicable to the transferee. Tax law permits these consequences to ensue only where there is a genuine alienation of income which creates a source of Case III income for the transferee. Not all expenditure has this effect. Thus the example in § 10-10 may be contrasted with the case where X gives £2,400 out of one year's income to Y. Such a gift is not Case III income of Y: it is a mere non-taxable gift of money. The statutory provisions which are discussed in the following paragraphs show the conditions that have to be satisfied for a transfer of income to be effective for tax purposes.

Statutory provisions affecting income settlements

(1) *Higher rate and additional rate relief for settlors*

10-13   We have seen, in § 10-11, that the gross amount of an annual payment made under an income settlement is a charge on the settlor's income and so escapes income tax at the higher rates and, where appropriate, investment income surcharge. As a result of legislation first enacted in 1965 and now in section 457 of the Income and Corporation Taxes Act 1970, the opportunity for an individual to avoid higher rate income tax and surcharge by means of an *income* settlement has been severely restricted. Section 457, which applies to all income settlements made on or after April 7, 1965, other than those which are expressly excepted (see §§ 10-14 *et seq.*) deems the income so settled to be the income of the settlor for the purposes of higher rate tax and the investment income surcharge. Taking the example in § 10-11, the tax consequences of such a settlement, if made after April 7, 1965, are exactly as there stated, except that X will not avoid higher rate income tax and surcharge on the gross amount of the annual payment. But the income arising under the settlement is not deemed to be the income of X for *all* income tax purposes; hence Y's right to recover basic rate income tax is unaffected by section 457. Section 457 restricts reliefs which would otherwise be available to the settlor: it has no impact on the tax position of the beneficiary. Section 457 does not apply to capital settlements, *i.e.* to " income from property of which the settlor has divested himself absolutely by the settlement." [8]

---

[8] I.C.T.A. 1970, s. 457 (1) (*d*).

Settlements excepted from section 457. Annual payments which are made in the following circumstances are excepted from the operation of section 457:

10-14   (a) *Annuities to retired partners and their families.*[9] Annual payments made under a partnership agreement to or for the benefit of a former member (as defined [10]) or to the widow or dependants [11] of a deceased former member of the partnership fall outside section 457, if the payments are made under a liability incurred for full consideration. Continuing partners thus normally get full income tax relief on annuities which they pay to retired partners, their widows or dependants. See also § 8-11.

10-15   (b) *Purchase of a business on an annuity basis.*[12] Annual payments made by an individual in connection with the acquisition by him of the whole or part of a business fall outside section 457 if they are made under a liability incurred for full consideration:

(i) to or for the benefit of the individual from whom it is acquired or (if he is dead) his widow or dependants [13]; or

(ii) if the vendor was a partnership, to or for the benefit of a former member (as defined [14]) or the widow or dependants of a deceased former member of that or any preceding partnership [15] or to or for the benefit of an individual from whom the business or part was acquired by that or any preceding partnership or, if he is dead, to or for the benefit of the widow or dependants of such an individual.

In this context the distinction between annual payments and instalments of capital must be kept in mind (see § 5-27). No income tax relief is given to the purchaser of a business for a capital sum paid by instalments.

10-16   (c) *Payments on divorce, nullity and separation.*[16] Annual payments under a settlement made by one party to a marriage by way of provision for the other after the dissolution or annulment of the marriage, or while they are separated under an order of a court or under a separation agreement or in such circumstances that the separation is likely to be permanent, fall outside section 457 if they are payable to or applicable for the benefit of that other party.

> Thus, if a husband (H) and wife (W) are separated and the separation is likely to be permanent and H agrees to pay £x per annum to W, H is entitled to full tax relief on the gross amount which he pays. If H agrees to pay £y to H's son (S), section 457 applies and H gets no tax relief on the payments to S unless there is a court order directing H to pay S. In that case, section 457 does not apply because there is no " settlement ": see § 10-09.

10-17   *Transactions for full consideration.* There is a feature of the three exceptions in §§ 10-14 to 10-16 which may strike the reader as odd. Section

---

[9] I.C.T.A. 1970, s. 457 (1) (*a*).

[10] " Former member " in relation to a partnership means an individual who has ceased to be a member of that partnership on retirement or death: *ibid.* s. 457 (5) (*a*).

[11] As to the meaning of " dependants," see *Re Baden's Deed Trusts* (*No.* 2) [1972] Ch. 607; [1973] Ch. 9 (C.A.).   [12] I.C.T.A. 1970, s. 457 (2)–(4).

[13] See note 11, *ante.*   [14] See note 10, *ante.*

[15] A partnership becomes a " preceding partnership " of another if it transfers its business or part of its business to another and one or more individuals are members of both, and any preceding partnership of the transferor by reference to any part of the business transferred also becomes a preceding partnership of the transferee: I.C.T.A. 1970, s. 457 (5) (*b*).   [16] I.C.T.A. 1970, s. 457 (1) (*c*).

457 of the Income and Corporation Taxes Act 1970 applies only to " settlements "; and it has been said that bona fide commercial transactions having no element of bounty are not settlements: see § 10-08. Why, therefore, is it necessary to except from the operation of section 457 payments made under a liability incurred for full consideration which would seem to fall outside its scope? The explanation may be as follows. Doubt may arise as to what constitutes a bona fide commercial transaction. Is it necessary, for example, that there should be an enforceable agreement between the payer and the recipient of an annual payment? A partnership deed may provide for the payment of an annuity to a retired partner and/or his widow or dependants. There will normally be a contractual relationship between the continuing partners and the retired partner but none between the continuing partners and the retired partner's widow.[17] The exception in § 10-14 makes it clear that section 457 does not deny full tax relief to the payer of the annuity in such a case.

10-18   *Reverse annuity transactions.* The principle that the settlement provisions in the Tax Acts do not apply to agreements which are bona fide commercial transactions for full consideration in money or money's worth forms the basis of a tax avoidance scheme [17a] whereby, for example, a high rate taxpayer covenants to pay £x per annum out of his income to (say) a charity in consideration of a capital sum. The payer claims the annual payment as a deduction in computing his total income for income tax purposes. The capital sum is non-taxable. This device has now been countered by section 48 of the Finance Act 1977.

The section requires that the annual payment in such a case shall be made without deduction of income tax and shall not be allowed as a deduction in computing income or total income of the payer and shall not be a charge on income for the purposes of the corporation tax. The section does not apply if the capital sum is taxable as income of the payer or if it is received as consideration for any annuity granted in the ordinary course of a business of granting annuities. Nor does the section apply so as to deny full tax relief to the person paying an annuity or other annual payment in any of the cases mentioned in §§ 10-14 to 10-16 above.

Section 48 applies to payments made after March 29, 1977, irrespective of when the liability to make the payments was incurred.

(2) *The period of the settlement*

10-19   To be effective for tax purposes, an alienation of income must be capable of remaining operative for a substantial period of time. Section 434 of the Income and Corporation Taxes Act 1970 provides that where under a disposition [18] income [19] is payable to or applicable for the benefit of a

[17] See *Beswick* v. *Beswick* [1968] A.C. 58 (H.L.).
[17a] See *I.R.C.* v. *Plummer* [1978] 3 W.L.R. 459 (C.A.).
[18] As to what constitutes an effective disposition of income, see *I.R.C.* v. *Lee* (1943) 25 T.C. 485; *I.R.C.* v. *Compton* (1946) 27 T.C. 350. *Cf. Russell* v. *I.R.C.* (1944) 26 T.C. 242.
[19] As to payments of capital, see *I.R.C.* v. *Mallaby-Deeley* (1938) 23 T.C. 153 (C.A.). " Income " means income under the Tax Acts which is chargeable under those Acts. It does not include a non-resident person's income from foreign property: *Becker* v. *Wright* (1965) 42 T.C. 591 (where the taxpayer had foreign income under a deed of covenant made by a covenantor resident outside the U.K. and unsuccessfully relied on s. 434 to escape assessment under Case V of Sched. D).

person for a period which cannot exceed six years, such income shall be deemed for all tax purposes to be that of the disponer, if living. " Disposition " (with one qualification mentioned below) includes any trust, covenant, agreement or arrangement.[20]

This section applies only if the period of payment *cannot* exceed six years. To avoid the section, therefore, the covenantor must choose either:

(a) A definite period which must exceed six years: hence the " seven year covenant "; or

(b) an indefinite period which might exceed six years, such as a covenant for the joint lives of the covenantor and covenantee or for seven years, whichever shall be the shorter period.

If an indefinite period is chosen, it is immaterial that, in the events which happen, the payments cease within six years, whether by mutual agreement between the parties [21] or otherwise.

In *I.R.C.* v. *Black* [22] the respondents covenanted to pay a property-owning company which they controlled an annuity equal to a proportion of the difference between the annual letting value of certain property and the income actually produced. There was to be an overall limit of £100,000. The covenant was made in 1936 and was to expire in 1944. Within two years, however, the limit had been reached. Since the period *might* have exceeded six years, the covenant was not caught by the section.

It should be kept in mind that a covenant which is not limited to the life of the settlor will bind his personal representatives and, if there is a life interest in the covenantor's residuary estate, some part of the covenanted sums will be payable out of capital under the rule of apportionment in *Re Perkins*.[23] The personal representatives will to this extent be liable to account for tax under section 53 of the Income and Corporation Taxes Act, 1970.[24] It is advisable in such a case to exclude the apportionment rule.

10-20   The period of six years referred to in section 434 is the period during which income is payable, and is therefore reckoned from the date when the first payment is due (which cannot be before the date of execution of the settlement) to the date when the last payment is due.[25] Considerable care is required in drafting a deed to ensure that section 434 does not apply.[26]

Section 434 does not apply to a disposition made for " valuable and sufficient consideration "[26a]; so, for example, provision can be made for a retiring partner or his dependants in an appropriate case by covenants made

---

[20] I.C.T.A. 1970, s. 434 (2). As to dispositions by more than one settlor, see *ibid*. s. 436.
[21] If a provision for revocation is contained in the settlement itself, I.C.T.A. 1970, s. 445 (1) will apply: *post*, § 10-26.   [22] (1940) 23 T.C. 715 (C.A.).
[23] [1907] 2 Ch. 596. See Snell's *Principles of Equity* (27th ed.), pp. 332-333.
[24] *Ante*, §§ 5-34 *et seq.*
[25] *I.R.C.* v. *St. Luke's Hostel Trustees* (1930) 15 T.C. 682. Separate from the question of reckoning the six-year period is the question whether sums expressed to be payable in respect of a period prior to the date of execution but paid on or after that date are deductible in computing the covenantor's income. *Semble*, they are not deductible unless they are expressed to be payable on or after the execution of the deed: see *I.R.C.* v. *Nettlefold* (1933) 18 T.C. 235.
[26] See, *e.g. I.R.C.* v. *St. Luke's Hostel Trustees* (1930) 15 T.C. 682; *I.R.C.* v. *Verdon Roe* (1962) 40 T.C. 541 (C.A.); *I.R.C.* v. *Hobhouse* (1956) 36 T.C. 648.
[26a] For a discussion on this phrase see *I.R.C.* v. *Plummer* [1978] 3 W.L.R. 459 (C.A.) especially at pp. 470 *et seq.*

by the continuing partners and expressed to run for a definite period of less than six years. Dispositions made on the occasion of separation or divorce may fall within the words of exception.

10-21   *Covenants for varying amounts.* Where a settlement provides for the payment of fixed sums which vary in amount throughout its duration, only the amount common to the whole period is outside the mischief of section 434. Any excess over this amount in any year is to be treated as income of the settlor for that year. This is because the words of the section require the recurrence in each year of some definable unit of income which is payable for a period which can exceed six years.[27] It seems this requirement is satisfied by a covenant whereby the settlor is to pay a stated fraction of his income (even if it amounts to the whole thereof) or an amount equal to a yearly dividend from a block of ordinary shares.[28]

10-22   *Effect where section 434 applies.* Where a settlement is caught by section 434, the income payable thereunder is deemed for all tax purposes to be the income of the settlor. Such income is deemed to be the highest part of his income and is accordingly liable to tax at the highest rate applicable to him.[29] Under section 435 (1) of the Income and Corporation Taxes Act 1970, there are provisions whereby the amount of the income tax chargeable on and paid by the settlor in consequence of the disposition may be recovered from the trustee or other person to whom the income was payable. The result is that the payee cannot recover any part of the basic rate income tax deducted by the settlor; and the settlor bears the same higher rate income tax and investment income surcharge that would have been payable by him if the settlement had not been made. Having paid such higher rate income tax and surcharge, the settlor is entitled to recover this from the payee.

(3) *Covenants for the covenantor's own children*

10-23   By section 437 of the Income and Corporation Taxes Act 1970, where under a settlement and during the life of the settlor any income is in any year *paid*[30] to or for the benefit of a child[31] of the settlor who at the time of payment is unmarried and below the age of 18, such income is to be treated for all tax purposes as the settlor's income for that year and not that of any other person. There is an exception in the case of sums not exceeding £5.[32] " Settlement " includes any disposition, trust, covenant, agreement, arrangement or transfer of assets.[33] An income settlement by a parent on his infant, unmarried child is thereby rendered ineffective as a means of creating a source of income in respect of which the child can recover basic

---

[27] *I.R.C.* v. *Mallaby-Deeley* (1938) 23 T.C. 153 (C.A.).

[28] *I.R.C.* v. *Black* (1940) 23 T.C. 715 (C.A.); *D'Ambrumenil* v. *I.R.C.* [1940] 1 K.B. 850; 23 T.C. 440; *cf. I.R.C.* v. *Prince-Smith* (1943) 25 T.C. 84.   [29] I.C.T.A. 1970, s. 435 (3).

[30] Income apportioned to a child by virtue of a surtax direction has been held not to have been " paid ": see *Houry* v. *I.R.C.* [1960] A.C. 36 (J.C.). This now applies to statutory apportionments: see §§ 15-28 *et seq.*

[31] Child includes a step-child, an adopted child and an illegitimate child: I.T.A. 1952, s. 403. A step-child includes a child of a former marriage whose parents are alive: *I.R.C.* v. *Russell* (1955) 36 T.C. 83.

[32] I.C.T.A. 1970, s. 437 (3), substituted by F.A. 1971, s. 16 (2) (d).

[33] I.C.T.A. 1970, s. 444 (2). As to arrangements, see *Crossland* v. *Hawkins* [1961] Ch. 537; 39 T.C. 493 (C.A.) and *Mills* v. *I.R.C.* [1975] A.C. 38; 49 T.C. 367 (H.L.).

rate income tax. Settlements for the children of others and on grandchildren of the settlor are outside the scope of section 437, except that reciprocal arrangements between parents to make settlements on each other's children are caught.[34]

The provisions of section 437 cannot be avoided by directing the income to be paid to trustees for the child and directing the trustees to accumulate the income for the child, even if the child's interest in the income so accumulated is contingent. This is because income which *might* become payable to or for the benefit of a child in the future is to be treated as if it were actually paid to him.[35]

10-24   *Effect where section 437 applies.* Where a settlement is caught by section 437, the income payable thereunder is deemed for all tax purposes to be the income of the settlor. Such income is deemed to be the highest part of his income and is accordingly liable to tax at the highest rate applicable to him.[36] Under section 441 (1) of the Income and Corporation Taxes Act 1970, there are provisions whereby the amount of the income tax chargeable on and paid by the settlor in consequence of the disposition may be recovered from the trustee or other person to whom the income was payable. The result is that the payee cannot recover any part of the basic rate income tax deducted by the settlor; and the settlor bears the same higher rate income tax and investment income surcharge that would have been payable by him if the settlement had not been made. Having paid such higher rate income tax and surcharge, the settlor is entitled to recover this from the payee.

10-25   *Covenants for adult or married children.* Section 437 does not apply where the settlor's child is married or has attained the age of 18 at the time of the payment. In such a case, therefore, the income is not deemed to be that of the settlor for all tax purposes so the covenantee may be able to make a claim for repayment of the basic rate income tax suffered by deduction; but the income is deemed to be that of the settlor for the purposes of higher rate income tax and investment income surcharge, as explained in § 10-13 above, so the settlor is denied tax relief on the gross amount of the payments.

(4) *Revocable settlements*

10-26   Section 445 (1) of the Income and Corporation Taxes Act 1970 provides that if the terms of any settlement [37] are such that any person has or may have power either to revoke or otherwise determine the settlement (so that the liability to make the payments thereunder ceases) or to diminish the amount of any payments thereunder, the sum payable under the settlement or a sum equal to the amount of the possible diminution (as the case may be) is to be treated for all tax purposes as the settlor's income. There is a proviso which excepts a power of revocation or of determination or of diminution which is not exercisable for six years from the time when the

---

[34] See the definition of " settlor " in I.C.T.A. 1970, s. 444 (2).
[35] I.C.T.A. 1970, s. 438 (1).   [36] *Ibid.* s. 441 (3).
[37] Defined in I.C.T.A. 1970, s. 454 (3), to include any disposition, trust, covenant, agreement or arrangement.

first annual payment is payable [38]; but this merely suspends the operation of the section, which applies as soon as the power is exercisable after six years. This period during which the section is held in suspense cannot be extended retrospectively. [39]

Section 445 must be kept in mind where the amount payable under a covenant is to be related to the income of the covenantor or to some other variable sum. In a separation deed, for example, the amount payable in each year may be related to the husband's income in that year; or a covenant to guarantee periodical payments may be related to the profits of the covenantee. Two points should be noted in this connection:

10-27   (1) The section applies only to a *power* to revoke, etc. It is thought that the section does not apply if the amount to be paid is defined by reference to a formula, *e.g.* as a defined fraction of the covenantor's income. Thus if, in a separation deed, a husband reserves power to reduce the amount of the payments if his income falls, the section applies; but it will not apply if he covenants to pay one third of his annual income.

    (2) The section applies only to a power contained in the settlement itself.

In *I.R.C.* v. *Wolfson* [40] the settlor controlled a private company. He covenanted to pay periodical sums which were related to the dividends declared by the company, and the Revenue contended that because the settlor could ensure that no dividends were paid, there was therefore a power of revocation. The House of Lords held that the section did not apply because the power was not to be found in the terms of the settlement.

Lest it be thought that the section can always be avoided by the interposition of a company, it should be noted that " settlement " includes an arrangement and that the formation of a company followed by the execution of an income settlement may together constitute a single settlement. [41]

10-28   *Effect where section 445 applies.* Where a settlement is caught by section 445 the income payable thereunder, or the appropriate part thereof, is deemed for all tax purposes to be income of the settlor. Such income is deemed to be the highest part of his income and is accordingly liable to tax at the highest rate applicable to him. [42] Under section 449 (3) there are provisions whereby the tax consequently paid by the settlor may be recovered from the trustee or other person to whom the income was actually paid.

(5) *Undistributed income*

10-29   Income is " undistributed " if it is so dealt with that it does not fall to be treated as the income of the person entitled to it. [43] It is thought that income

---

[38] I.C.T.A. 1970, s. 445 (1), proviso.

[39] *Taylor* v. *I.R.C.* (1945) 27 T.C. 93 (C.A.); *I.R.C.* v. *Nicolson* (1953) 34 T.C. 354.

[40] (1949) 31 T.C. 141 (H.L.).

[41] I.C.T.A. 1970, s. 454 (3); and see *I.R.C.* v. *Payne* (1940) 23 T.C. 610; *Crossland* v. *Hawkins* [1961] Ch. 537; 39 T.C. 493 (C.A.).

[42] I.C.T.A. 1970, s. 449 (5).   [43] See *ibid.* s. 455 for details.

will be treated as distributed if it is applied for the benefit of the beneficiary, *e.g.* by purchase of investments in the beneficiary's name. Income is undistributed if, for example, there is a covenant to pay periodic sums to trustees for an infant beneficiary who is contingently entitled thereto, and the trustees do not distribute the entire income for purposes of maintenance [44]; or if, in a discretionary settlement, the trustees fail to exercise their discretion in respect of the whole of the income. [45]

10-30   (a) *Position where settlor retains interest.* By section 447 (1) of the Income and Corporation Taxes Act 1970, if the settlor has an interest in any income arising under or property comprised in a settlement, undistributed income which arises in any year of assessment during the settlor's life is to be treated for all tax purposes as the settlor's income. A settlor is deemed to have such an interest if any income or property which may at any time arise under or be comprised in the settlement is, or will or may become, payable to or applicable for the benefit of the settlor or the wife [46] or husband of the settlor in any circumstances whatsoever. [47] If, therefore, there is any likelihood that there might be undistributed income it is important to see that there is no possibility, however remote, of a resulting trust to the settlor.

10-31   *Exceptions.* By the proviso to section 447 (2), the settlor is not to be deemed to have an interest within the section if the income or property can only become payable or applicable to him in the events therein stated. [48] In particular, the settlor has no such interest if there is a resulting trust to him (or his spouse) in the event of the death under 25 or some lower age of some person beneficially entitled to the income of property on attaining that age. If the vesting of capital is postponed until the beneficiary attains an age greater than 25, the deeming provision is excluded until the beneficiary attains 25 but not thereafter.

Effect where section 447 applies. The effect is the same as when section 445 applies: see § 10-28.

10-32   (b) *Position where income is left undistributed.* Section 450 of the Income and Corporation Taxes Act 1970 applies if the covenantor pays to the trustees of a settlement any sums which would otherwise be deductible in computing his total income if income remains undistributed in the trustees' hands at the end of the year of assessment. Such income is disallowed as a deduction in computing the settlor's total income, unless it is otherwise disallowed under sections 445, 446, 447 or 448 of the Act. [49]

---

[44] It seems that if a beneficiary has a vested interest and the trustees accumulate income because the infant cannot give a valid receipt, such income is " distributed." See § 9-05.

[45] See *Cornwell* v. *Barry* (1955) 36 T.C. 268: child had vested interest in income liable to be divested—no appropriation of income to child—*held*, not income of child for purpose of enabling child to claim personal reliefs and allowances.

[46] " Wife " does not include " widow ": *Vestey's Executors* v. *I.R.C.* (1949) 31 T.C. 1.

[47] I.C.T.A. 1970, s. 447 (2). In *Glyn* v. *I.R.C.* (1948) 30 T.C. 321, the possibility that the settlor might benefit under a power exercisable jointly with his son was held to be such an interest; but it was said *obiter* that the possibility of a mere voluntary application of income by a beneficiary to a settlor was outside the section notwithstanding the words " in any circumstances whatever."

[48] These events are set out in full in § 10-42.

[49] For s. 445, see § 10-26; for s. 448, see § 10-44.

This prevents income settlements being used to build up funds in the hands of trustees for eventual distribution as capital, the settlor getting relief from higher rate tax and investment income surcharge in the process.

Conclusion on income settlements

10-33   Since 1965 the settlor who makes an income settlement gets relief from higher rate tax and investment income surcharge only in three exceptional cases. These are cases of payments of annuities under partnership agreements (§ 10-14), payments towards the purchase of a business on an annuity basis (§ 10-15) and certain payments made in connection with divorce, nullity or separation (§ 10-16).

Even in these exceptional cases no such relief is given unless further conditions are satisfied. First, the period of the settlement must be capable of exceeding six years (§ 10-19), except where the disposition is for valuable and sufficient consideration (§ 10-20). Secondly, the payments must not be to infant unmarried children of the settlor (§§ 10-23 *et seq.*). Thirdly, the settlement must not be " revocable " in the extended sense in which that word is used (§§ 10-26 *et seq.*). Fourthly, the settlor must retain no interest, subject to certain excepted interests (§§ 10-31 *et seq.*). Fifthly, the income must be distributed and not accumulated at the end of each year of assessment (§ 10-32).

As regards the covenantee, it is not necessary that the settlement should fall within one of the three exceptional cases referred to above in order that the amount covenanted to be paid should be treated as the covenantee's income for tax purposes. But each of the other five conditions referred to above has to be satisfied.

3. CAPITAL SETTLEMENTS

10-34   A capital settlement is one under which a settlor transfers property, usually of an income-producing nature, to trustees and directs the trustees to deal with the income so produced for the benefit of one or more persons. The implications of capital settlements as regards capital transfer tax are considered in Part II of this book. As regards income tax, the objective (in most cases) is that the income shall no longer be treated as part of the income of the settlor for the purposes of income tax but that it shall be treated in accordance with the principles applicable to trust income, which are considered in Chapter 9. It will be recalled that trustees bear tax at the basic rate on trust income and, in some cases, at an additional rate. Where, however, the income is distributed to a beneficiary or he is otherwise entitled to it, the income is treated as the beneficiary's income for tax purposes and bears tax at the rate or rates applicable to him. We now consider the statutory provisions which apply to capital settlements, the effect of which has already been briefly mentioned in §§ 10-04 *et seq.*

(1) *Settlements on children*

10-35   It has been seen in § 10-23 that an income settlement for the settlor's unmarried child below the age of 18 has no tax saving effect. This is because, by section 437 of the Income and Corporation Taxes Act 1970, where under a settlement and during the settlor's life, income is in any year paid to or for the benefit of a child of the settlor who at the time of payment is unmarried and below the age of 18, such income is treated for all tax purposes as the settlor's income for that year and not as the income of any other person. " Settlement " includes any disposition, trust, covenant, agreement, arrangement or transfer of assets.[50] The section thus applies to capital as well as to income settlements.

> In *Thomas* v. *Marshall* [51] a father made payments into a Post Office Savings Bank into accounts opened in the names of his infant unmarried children and purchased Defence Bonds in their names. *Held,* that this was a " settlement " within the section and that the interest on the Savings and Bonds must be treated as the father's income.

Accumulation settlements

10-36   There is an important exception to the statutory provision in section 437, which applies to an irrevocable capital settlement where income is lawfully accumulated under a trust or power to accumulate. The exception is in section 438 of the Income and Corporation Taxes Act 1970. " Irrevocable " is defined in section 439 and has an unusually extended meaning. A settlement is not irrevocable (subject to limited exception [52]) if either:

(1) It can be determined by the act or default of any person; or
(2) if in any circumstances any income or property can be applied for the benefit of the settlor, or the husband or wife [53] of the settlor, during the life of a child-beneficiary; or
(3) if it provides for the payment of any penalty by the settlor in the event of his failing to comply with its provisions.

If and so long as income arising under an irrevocable settlement is *accumulated*, such income is not to be deemed under section 437 to be income of the settlor; but *distributed* income (*e.g.* income applied for the maintenance of an infant and unmarried child under section 31 of the Trustee Act 1925) falls within the deeming provision. The section cannot be avoided by the trustees accumulating income (which thus becomes capital) and making advancements out of capital; for it is expressly provided that distributions of capital shall be treated as distributions of income up to the amount of undistributed income.[54] A settlement of capital (*i.e.* income-producing property) under which the income is accumulated is the only method provided for in the Taxing Acts by which a high-rate tax payer can provide for his own infant unmarried children and avoid higher rate income tax on the income so accumulated. Accumulated income may be liable to the investment income surcharge.[55] The requirement that the settlement should be " irrevocable " makes it essential that the settlor and his spouse

---

[50] I.C.T.A. 1970, s. 444 (2).
[51] [1953] A.C. 543; 34 T.C. 178 (H.L.). For an example of an arrangement, see *Crossland* v. *Hawkins* [1961] Ch. 537; 39 T.C. 493 (C.A.). and the cases cited therein and *Mills* v. *I.R.C.* [1975] A.C. 38; 49 T.C. 367 (H.L.).
[52] I.C.T.A. 1970, s. 439 (1), proviso.
[53] " Wife " does not include " widow ": *Vestey's Executors* v. *I.R.C.* (1949) 31 T.C. 1.
[54] I.C.T.A. 1970, s. 438 (2) (*b*).
[55] See *ante*, § 9-02.

should be excluded from any possible interest under the settlement, other than such interest as is specifically allowed by the proviso to section 439.

Income derived from appropriations of income

10-37   Section 437 of the Income and Corporation Taxes Act 1970 applies where, by virtue or in consequence of the settlement, income is paid to or for the benefit of a child of the settlor. Where income is *appropriated* to a child to be held for the child contingently on his attaining a specified age (pursuant to a power conferred on the trustees) and is invested for the child's benefit, the investment income derived from the appropriations is income which (so it would seem) does not fall to be treated as income of the settlor under section 437. That income is income of which it can be said—using the language of section 438 (1) of the Income and Corporation Taxes Act 1970—that it, or assets representing it, will or may become payable or applicable to or for the benefit of the child in the future; and that subsection is intelligible only on the assumption that such income is *not* income which is " paid to or for the benefit of " a child of the settlor. It would seem, therefore, that income derived from appropriations of income is income of the child, not income of the settlor.

Adjustments between disponer and trustees

10-38   Where income tax is chargeable on and is paid by the settlor in consequence of these statutory provisions, he is entitled to recover the tax so paid from the trustee or other person to whom the income is payable by virtue or in consequence of the settlement.[56]

(2) Revocable settlements

10-39   Section 446 of the Income and Corporation Taxes Act 1970 applies to a settlement if its terms are such that:

   (1) Any person has or may have power to revoke or otherwise determine the settlement or any provision thereof or to diminish the property comprised in it or to diminish the amount of any payments which are or may be payable under the settlement to any person other than the settlor or the wife [57] or husband of the settlor; and
   (2) on the exercise of that power the settlor (or the wife [58] or husband of the settlor) will or may become entitled to the whole or any part of the property then comprised in the settlement or of the income arising from the whole or any part of that property.

Where a settlement is " revocable " as thus defined, the income arising under the settlement is to be treated as that of the settlor (and not as the income of any other person) for all tax purposes, except that if the power of revocation extends only to a part of the property comprised in the settlement, only the income arising from that part is deemed to be income of the settlor.

---

[56] I.C.T.A. 1970, s. 441.
[57] See note 53, *ante.*
[58] *Ibid.*

It will be observed that the mere existence of a power coupled with the possibility of benefit, however remote, to the settlor or the wife of the settlor, will bring the section into operation.[59] The effect of the section is to deny the settlor the tax advantages of a capital settlement where its terms are such that he retains power to regain the capital or income for his or his wife's benefit.

The section contains a proviso excepting a power to revoke which cannot be exercised within a period of six years from the time when property is put into the settlement and suspending the operation of the section during that period.

It should be noted that, where section 446 applies, the settlor retains no *interest* in capital or income: there is a mere opportunity to regain such an interest through the exercise of a power by someone, not necessarily the settlor.

Where section 446 applies, there are provisions for adjustment similiar to those mentioned in § 10-38.[60]

(3) *Undistributed income*

10-40 Income is " undistributed " if it is so dealt with that it does not fall to be treated as the income of the person entitled to it.[61] Income which is accumulated for the benefit of a beneficiary contingently entitled thereto is undistributed.[62]

10-41 (i) *Position where settlor retains interest.* By section 447 (1) of the Income and Corporation Taxes Act 1970 (which has already been referred to in connection with income settlements),[63] if and so long as the settlor has an interest in any income arising under or property comprised in a settlement, any income so arising during the settlor's life in any year of assessment must, to the extent to which it is not distributed, be treated for all tax purposes as the income of the settlor for that year and not as the income of any other person. A settlor is deemed to have an interest for this purpose if any income or property which may at any time arise under or be comprised in the settlement could at any time be payable to or applicable for the benefit of the settlor (or the wife [64] or husband of the settlor) in any circumstances whatever.[65] Defective drafting which produces a resulting trust of income or capital to the settlor will cause section 447 to apply. A mere power reserved to the settlor to direct investment policy is not an " interest " for the purposes of this provision [66]; nor is an investment clause under which the trustees can invest in companies in which the settlor has a financial interest.

---

[59] See *Barr's Trustees* v. *I.R.C.* (1943) 25 T.C. 72; *I.R.C.* v. *Kenmare* [1958] A.C. 267; 37 T.C. 383.
[60] I.C.T.A. 1970, s. 449 (3).
[61] *Ante,* § 9-19.
[62] *Ibid.*
[63] *Ante,* § 10-30.
[64] See note 53, *ante.*
[65] I.C.T.A. 1970, s. 447 (2); *Hannay* v. *I.R.C.* (1956) 37 T.C. 217. For a recent example, see *I.R.C.* v. *Wachtel* [1971] Ch. 573; 46 T.C. 543.
[66] *Vestey's Executors* v. *I.R.C.* (1949) 31 T.C. 1.

10-42   Section 447 will apply if the settlement deed provides for the property comprised in the settlement to revert back to the settlor (or the wife or husband of the settlor) because this will constitute a retained " interest "; but, by a proviso to section 447 (2), the settlor is not deemed to have an interest:

     (a) If and so long as the income or property cannot become payable or applicable as aforesaid except in the event of:

         (i) the bankruptcy of some person who is or may become beneficially entitled to that income or property; or

         (ii) any assignment of or charge on that income or property being made or given by some such person; or

         (iii) in the case of a marriage settlement, the death of both the parties to the marriage and of all or any of the children of the marriage; or

         (iv) the death under the age of 25 or some lower age of some person who would be beneficially entitled to that income or property on attaining that age; or

     (b) if and so long as some person is alive and under the age of 25 during whose life that income or property cannot become payable or applicable as aforesaid except in the event of that person becoming bankrupt or assigning or charging his interest in that income or property.

In most family settlements, the settlor wishes the settled property to revert to himself (or his wife) on failure of the trusts for the children. The proviso to section 447 (2) of the Income and Corporation Taxes Act 1970 enables this wish to be fulfilled. There is generally no objection to the settlor or his spouse being named as the persons entitled on the failure of the trusts, where the settlement provides for the vesting of capital in children at an age not exceeding 25 years.

Where section 447 applies, there are provisions for adjustment similar to those mentioned in § 10-38.[67]

10-43   (ii) *Position where settlor receives a capital sum.* Section 451 of the Income and Corporation Taxes Act 1970 is concerned with capital settlements (including those in which the settlor retains no interest) the trustees of which pay a capital sum (as defined) to the settlor when there is undistributed income in the trustees' hands. Such sum grossed up at the basic rate (and in and after 1973–74 at the additional rate at which investment income surcharge is levied [68]) for the year is treated as income of the settlor for that year up to the amount of the " available income." Any excess is carried forward against " available income " of future years and treated as income of the settlor for that year, and so on.

" Available income " means [69] undistributed income which is not deemed to be income of the settlor under some other provision. " Capital sum " means [70]:

---

[67] I.C.T.A. 1970, s. 441.
[68] Finance Act 1973, s. 16 (7).
[69] I.C.T.A. 1970, s. 451 (2).   [70] *Ibid.* s. 451 (8).

(a) Any sum paid [71] by way of loan or repayment of a loan; and

(b) any sum paid otherwise than as income, being a sum which is not paid for full consideration in money or money's worth,

but it does not include any sum which could not have become payable to the settlor except in one of the events specified in the proviso to section 447 (2) of the Income and Corporation Taxes Act 1970 (see § 10-42).

The reference in the section to sums paid to the settlor includes sums paid to the wife or husband of the settlor [72]; and a capital sum paid by any body corporate connected with the settlement in any year is treated as paid by the trustees in that year. [73] A body corporate is deemed to be connected with a settlement in any year of assessment if it is at any time in the year a close company (or only not a close company because it is not resident in the United Kingdom) and the participants then include the trustees of or a beneficiary under the settlement. [74]

The greatest care must be taken in practice in dealing with any loan transactions between settlor and trustees or between settlor and a company in which the trustees hold shares in a case where there is any possibility that there might be undistributed income in the settlement, for the section is highly penal in its operation and has often proved to be a fiscal death trap for the unwary. Note that the section will apply where a loan made to a company in which the trustees hold shares is repaid to the settlor, even where the loan was made before the settlement was made. There are often ways of preventing section 451 applying.

(4) *The settlor (or his spouse) as the object of a discretion*

10-44   Sections previously considered have dealt with the cases where the settlor retains an interest in the settlement and there is undistributed income (§ 10-41) and where, having no interest, the settlor might regain an interest (§ 10-39). Section 448 of the Income and Corporation Taxes Act 1970 deals with the case of a discretionary settlement where the settlor (or the husband or wife of the settlor) is among the class of beneficiaries for whose benefit the trustees might exercise their discretion to pay income or capital. Section 448 applies whether or not the income is undistributed. The section provides that if the terms of a settlement are such that any person has or may have power to pay to or apply for the benefit of the settlor, or the wife [75] or husband of the settlor, the whole or any part of the income or property which may at any time arise under or be comprised in the settlement, being a power exercisable at his discretion, any income arising under the settlement in any year of assessment shall be treated as income of the settlor for that year for all tax purposes and not as the income of any other person. [76] The section does not apply if the discretionary power is exercisable only in the

---

[71] A transfer of assets may constitute the " payment " of a " sum ": see *McCrone* v. *I.R.C.* (1967) 44 T.C. 142 (Ct. of Sess.).

[72] *Ibid.* s. 451 (8). But a sum paid to a third person on the direction of the settlor may fall outside the section: see *Potts' Executors* v. *I.R.C.* [1951] A.C. 443; 32 T.C. 211 (H.L.).

[73] *Ibid.* s. 451 (4).

[74] *Ibid.* s. 454 (4).

[75] See n. 53, above.

[76] I.C.T.A. 1970, s. 448. See *Blausten* v. *I.R.C.* (1971) 47 T.C. 542.

events specified in the proviso to section 447 (2), which are set out in § 10-42; and there is a provision which suspends the operation of the section where the power cannot be exercised within a period of six years. [77]

The mere existence of the discretionary power brings the section into operation: it is immaterial that in fact the income is paid or applied to or for the benefit of some other person. A provision in the settlement by which the settlor and his spouse for the time being are expressly excluded from any benefit by the exercise of any power or discretion given by the settlement is sufficient to avoid the effects of the section.

Where section 448 applies, there are provisions for adjustment similar to those mentioned in § 10-38.

---

[77] *Ibid.* s. 448 (2).

CHAPTER 11

PARTNERSHIP TAXATION

1. The Existence of a Partnership

11-01 PARTNERSHIP is defined in section 1 of the Partnership Act 1890 as the relation which subsists between persons carrying on business in common with a view to profit; and section 2 of that Act contains a number of rules for determining whether a partnership exists. This is a question of law which must be determined by reference to the facts of the particular case. The execution of a partnership agreement will not of itself constitute a partnership, unless that agreement is put into effect [1]; on the other hand, individuals may be held to be trading in partnership although no formal partnership agreement exists and although they never intended such a relationship to exist. [2] A partnership agreement is not effectual for tax purposes prior to the date on which it was executed, unless a partnership in fact existed before execution, in which case the deed may operate to confirm such a relationship.

> In *Waddington* v. *O'Callaghan* [3] W., who carried on practice as a solicitor, told his son on December 31, 1928, that he intended to take him into partnership as from that date. Instructions for the drafting of a partnership deed were at once given, and on May 11, 1929, a deed was executed expressed to have effect from the previous January 1. Rowlatt J. held that the facts showed clearly that there was to be no partnership unless and until a deed was agreed upon between father and son. " It was a contemplated future partnership the accounts of which were to relate back."

11-02 On the same principles the question whether a partnership has ceased to exist is a question of mixed law and fact. A declaration by the partners that the partnership has terminated or will terminate on a specified date is not necessarily conclusive. Generally speaking, if traders decide to sell off their stock with a view to discontinuing business, they will be treated as trading in partnership until the stock is finally sold off. [4]

2. The Taxation of Partnership Income

11-03 Although a partnership, unlike a company, is not a separate legal entity apart from its individual members, [5] it is to an extent treated as such for tax purposes. Thus under section 152 of the Income and Corporation Taxes Act 1970, where a trade or profession is carried on by two or more persons jointly, the tax in respect of it has to be computed jointly and a joint assessment made in the partnership name. The liability of partners to tax is the *joint* liability of *all* the partners, not the *several* liability of each. [6] A joint

---

[1] *Dickenson* v. *Gross* (1927) 11 T.C. 614 and see *Alexander Bulloch & Co.* v. *I.R.C.* [1976] S.T.C. 514.
[2] *Fenston* v. *Johnstone* (1940) 23 T.C. 29 at p. 36.
[3] (1931) 16 T.C. 187.
[4] *O'Kane & Co.* v. *I.R.C.* (1922) 12 T.C. 303 (H.L.). And see *ante*, § 2-15.
[5] In Scotland a partnership is treated as a separate entity: see the case first cited in note 6.
[6] *Income Tax Commissioners for the City of London* v. *Gibbs* [1942] A.C. 402; 24 T.C. 221 (H.L.); *Harrison* v. *Willis Bros.* [1966] Ch. 619; 43 T.C. 61 (C.A.).

return of the partnership income must be made by the "precedent partner" who is usually the partner resident in the United Kingdom who is first named in the partnership agreement.[7] The income of a partnership is computed by applying the ordinary rules applicable to individuals: so, for example, a trading partnership is assessed under Case I of Schedule D on the normal preceding year basis. There are special provisions which apply where one of the partners is a company chargeable to corporation tax.[8]

Where husband and wife are in partnership, the rules requiring the aggregation of a wife's income with that of her husband (*ante*, § 8-23) are disregarded in applying section 152 (above).[9]

11-04 When the partnership income is determined, it must be allocated to each partner for tax purposes by reference to the share of profits to which he is entitled in the year of assessment of which those profits constitute the statutory income.[10]

> *Example*: The adjusted profits of a firm of solicitors for the year ended December 31, 1975, are £6,000. This is the statutory income of the firm for 1976–77. This amount must be divided between the partners in the shares to which they are entitled under the partnership agreement in the year ending April 5, 1977. It is immaterial that they in fact divided profits in different shares in the basis year 1975.

11-05 Salary paid to a partner is not assessed under Schedule E, for a partner is not an employee.[11] Interest on capital contributed by a partner is not an annual payment and the partner is therefore credited with the full amount of that interest.[12] The following example shows how these items enter into the computation of the assessable income of a partnership.

11-06 *Example*: The adjusted profits of a firm of solicitors for the year ended December 31, 1975, are £10,000. In 1976–77 there are three partners, X, Y and Z, entitled to profits in the following shares: X: 1/5; Y: 2/5; Z: 2/5. The assessment for 1976–77 is computed as follows:

Line		Firm £	X £	Y £	Z £
1	Profits to December 31, 1975 (as adjusted)	10,000			
2	*less* interest on capital and salary .	1,150			
3		8,850	1,770	3,540	3,540
4	*add* interest on capital	450	nil	200	250
5	*add* salary	700	nil	400	300
6		£10,000	£1,770	£4,140	£4,090

---

[7] T.M.A. 1970, s. 9 (1).

[8] I.C.T.A. 1970, s. 155.

[9] I.C.T.A. 1970, s. 37 (2), proviso.

[10] I.C.T.A. 1970, s. 26 (dealing with the allocation of income for the purposes of personal reliefs). And see *Lewis* v. *I.R.C.* (1933) 18 T.C. 174; *I.R.C.* v. *Blott* (1920) 8 T.C. 101 at p. 111.

[11] See *Stekel* v. *Ellice* [1973] 1 W.L.R. 191.

[12] Annual payments are discussed in Chap. 5. A partner has no statutory right to interest on the capital which he contributes: Partnership Act 1890, s. 24 (4). But it is common practice to stipulate that each partner shall be entitled to interest at (say) 5 per cent. per annum on the capital for the time being standing to his credit, such interest to be paid in priority to any division of profits.

Explanatory notes:
Line
1   The £10,000 are the profits of the basis period adjusted for tax purposes, less capital allowances. All debits in the partnership accounts for partners' shares of profits, salaries and interest on capital will have been added back and are thus included in the £10,000. This is because these items are not expenses which are deductible in computing profits under Schedule D, Case II.
2   This is the total of the figures in lines 4 and 5 (see below).
3   Each partner has allocated to him a share of £8,850 corresponding to his share of profits in the year 1976–77.[13]
4   It is usual for a partner to receive interest on any capital contributed by him. Each partner is credited with the full amount due to him in the current year, for this is not an annual payment.[14]
5   The salary credited to each partner is the salary to which he is entitled in the current year, 1976–77.
6   The partnership income allocated to each partner is included in his total income. The profits of each partner (including interest on partnership capital) are treated as earned (not investment) income, unless the partner is a sleeping partner or is not an individual. Interest on capital loaned to the partnership is investment income.
The tax liability of each partner is computed and the total is assessed in the partnership name. The tax is payable by the firm and the amount due from each partner (according to the above computation) is debited to his current account.

Partnership losses

11-07   Where a firm suffers a loss, the loss is apportioned between the partners in the same way that profits are apportioned. Each partner may claim relief in respect of the share of the loss apportioned to him under section 168, 171 or 172 of the Income and Corporation Taxes Act 1970 as he thinks fit.[15] Terminal losses may be the subject of relief under section 174 of that Act.[16] Where there is a change of partners and the partnership business is treated as discontinued (see below), losses can nevertheless be carried forward.[17]

3. CHANGE OF PARTNERS

11-08   Where there is a change in the persons engaged in carrying on a trade, profession or vocation, the amount of the profits or gains of the trade, etc., on which tax is chargeable and the persons on whom it is chargeable have to be determined as if the trade, etc., had been permanently discontinued at the date of the change and a new trade, etc., had been then set up and commenced. This provision in section 154 of the Income and Corporation Taxes Act 1970,[18] comes into operation whenever a partner dies or retires or where a new partner is admitted or where a sole trader takes another person into partnership with him.

---

[13] See *Gaunt* v. *I.R.C.* (1913) 7 T.C. 219 and Simon's *Taxes*, 3rd ed., E.5. 407.
[14] If there is other income of the partnership (*e.g.* fees for appointments held by the partners for which the partners are accountable to the partnership), this also must be brought into account and apportioned between the partners in their profit-ratio.
[15] These reliefs are considered in Chap. 12.
[16] *Post*, § 12-12.
[17] I.C.T.A. 1970, s. 171 (4).
[18] *Ante*, §§ 2-86 *et seq.*

Thus, if A, B and C are trading in partnership and A dies (or retires) on March 14, 1972, the firm of A, B and C will be treated as having discontinued business on that date and a new firm of B and C as having commenced business.

The consequences of this provision have already been explained.[18] Because of it, a change of partners, whether deliberate or otherwise, can have serious tax repercussions; and through recommendations made by the Committee on the Taxation of Trading Profits,[19] a right of election was given on a change in the constitution of a partnership.

The death of a trader and the consequent passing of his business to his successor is an occasion for the application of the discontinuance provisions of the Tax Acts. Where, however, a business passes on death to the trader's husband or wife who has been living with her or him, the discontinuance provisions are not enforced unless claimed. But, in any case, losses and capital allowances for which the deceased had not obtained relief are not permitted to be carried forward.[20]

Election to exclude section 154 (1)

11-09   Under section 154 (2) of the Income and Corporation Taxes Act 1970, where there is a change in the persons engaged in carrying on any trade, profession or vocation, and a person so engaged immediately before the change continues to be so engaged immediately after it, all the persons so engaged immediately before and after the change may by notice elect that section 154 (1) shall not apply. The notice must be signed by all the persons mentioned (including personal representatives of a deceased partner)[21] and must be sent to the Inspector of Taxes within two years[22] after the date of the change. Where the partners elect for a continuation, the assessment on the firm is made as if no change had occurred, *i.e.* on the usual preceding year basis; but there will be an apportionment for the year of change (usually on a time basis) as between the partners. It must not be supposed that it is always advantageous to exercise the right of election under section 154 (2): much depends on the flow of profits of the partnership. Broadly speaking, if profits have been rising in the past and are expected to continue to rise, it is advantageous to exercise the right of election. An election under section 154 (2) is not irrevocable: it is the practice of Inspectors to accept a notice of revocation if given (signed by all interested parties) before the expiry of the two-year limit for making an election.[23]

11-10   If there is in respect of a change of partners an election for continuance under section 154 (2) and, after the change but before the end of the second year of assessment following that in which the change occurred, there is a permanent discontinuance (including a change of partners which is treated as such), the cessation provisions apply giving the Revenue the right to assess the penultimate and pre-penultimate years on an actual basis. Revised assessments on this basis will extend back into the first partnership, but this

[19] Cmd. 8189, para. 72.
[20] Concession No. A8.
[21] I.C.T.A. 1970, s. 154 (6).
[22] Increased from 12 months except where the change occurred before April 6, 1970: F.A. 1971, s. 17.
[23] Inland Revenue Press Notice dated January 17, 1973, in B.T.R. 1973 (No. 1) at p. 811.

is permitted [24] notwithstanding that it may mean additional assessments being raised on the original partners. The election is therefore nullified.

Post-cessation and other receipts

11-11   At one time the rules which bring about a " statutory discontinuance " on a change of partners could be used to avoid tax. Many such forms of avoidance have been countered by the provisions relating to post-cessation receipts which are discussed in §§ 2-88 *et seq.*

4. PARTNERSHIP ANNUITIES

11-12 An annuity payable to a retired partner or to the widow or dependants of a deceased partner is paid under deduction of income tax at the basic rate, as explained in §§ 5-30 *et seq.* The amount of the annuity is deductible in computing the total income of the payer (see § 8-31), provided the annuity is not " caught " by any of the provisions under which income payable under a settlement is treated as income of the settlor (see §§ 10-10 *et seq.* and, in particular, § 10-14). Partnership annuities are frequently paid under commercial arrangements which are not settlements, as explained in §§ 10-08 and 10-17.

11-13   A partnership annuity is investment income of the recipient. [25] Section 16 of the Finance Act 1974 provides an exception to this general rule by treating certain partnership annuities as earned income up to a certain limit, the excess over this limit being treated as investment income. Section 16 applies where a person (" the former partner ") has ceased to be a partner on retirement, because of age or ill-health or on death, and annual payments are made to the former partner or his widow or a dependant, either under the partnership agreement or under an agreement replacing or supplementing it. The limit up to which the annuity is treated as earned income is related to the former partner's share of profits chargeable to income tax [26] and is 50 per cent. of the average of the former partner's share of profits in the best three of the last seven years of assessment in which he was required to devote substantially the whole of his time to acting as a partner. Where the former partner was a member of more than one partnership, his share of profits of all the partnerships of which he was a member have to be aggregated.

---

[24] I.C.T.A. 1970, s. 154 (3) (*b*).
[25] *Pegler* v. *Abell* (1973) 48 T.C. 564; [1973] S.T.C. 23. *Ante*, § 8-11.
[26] Thus unremitted profits of a foreign-controlled partnership to which I.C.T.A. 1970, s. 153 applies (*ante*, § 7-24) are left out of account for relevant years before the year 1974–75: see F.A. 1974, s. 23, *ante*, § 7-09.

CHAPTER 12

LOSSES

12-01 A LOSS arises in a trade where, in a year of assessment, trading expenses exceed trading receipts. There are two principal methods of dealing with a trading loss while a business is a going concern, and these are considered in Sections 1 and 2 of this chapter. Other methods of dealing with losses are considered in Section 3. The methods of dealing with losses of companies liable to corporation tax are considered in Chapter 14.

1. CARRYING LOSSES FORWARD: S. 171

12-02 Under section 171 (1) of the Income and Corporation Taxes Act 1970, where a person has sustained a loss in any trade,[1] profession or vocation carried on by him either solely or in partnership, he may claim to carry forward the loss and set it off against profits of the same trade, etc. assessed to income tax in subsequent years of assessment. The loss can be carried forward indefinitely, but must be set off against the first subsequent assessment and, so far as it remains unrelieved, from the next assessment, and so on.[2] If a loss is partially relieved under some other provision, the unrelieved part may be carried forward. Note that losses may be carried forward against profits of the *same trade*. It is often a difficult question whether one trade is the same as another.[3]

12-03 *Example*: The accounts of a trade are as follows:

		£	Tax Year
Accounting year ended December 31, 1970	Profit	2,000	1971–72
Accounting year ended December 31, 1971	Loss	3,500	1972–73
Accounting year ended December 31, 1972	Profit	3,000	1973–74
Accounting year ended December 31, 1973	Profit	5,000	1974–75

The loss of £3,500 in 1971 will produce a nil assessment for 1972–73. If relief under section 171 is claimed, it must be given in the assessment for 1973–74 (reducing the profit of that year to nil) and 1974–75 (reducing the profit of that year to £4,500).

In a year in which assessable profits are reduced to nil, the trader will lose his personal reliefs, unless he has sufficient income apart from the trade to support them. Section 171 cannot be used to " skim off " the top slice of profits so as to leave sufficient to cover personal reliefs but otherwise avoid tax liability.

12-04 Where the Case I profits of a trade are insufficient to enable relief to be given in respect of a loss brought forward under section 171 (1), interest or dividends taxed at source which would have been taken into account as trading receipts had they not already been taxed will be treated as if they

---

[1] Including woodlands where an election under I.C.T.A. 1970, s. 111 has been made: s. 171 (5); *ante*, § 6-07.

[2] *Ibid.* s. 171 (2). As to the period for making the claim, see, *ibid.* s. 171 (7). Trades etc. carried on outside the United Kingdom, the profits of which would be chargeable to United Kingdom tax, are included, with the qualification (since only 75 per cent. of the profits of such a trade are charged to United Kingdom tax) that only 75 per cent. of the losses are relievable: F.A. 1974, s. 23 (2)–(4), *ante*, § 7-09.

[3] See §§ 2-85 *et seq.* and *Robroyston Brickworks Ltd.* v. *I.R.C.* [1976] S.T.C. 329; *Rolls-Royce Motors Ltd.* v. *Bamford* [1976] S.T.C. 162.

were trading profits.[4] Thus the carried forward losses of a dealer in securities with insufficient profits to absorb the losses would be set off against income taxed at source.

12-05   Where a person has been assessed under section 53 of the Income and Corporation Taxes Act 1970 in respect of a payment made wholly and exclusively for the purpose of a trade, profession or vocation, the amount on which tax has been paid under that assessment must be treated as a loss sustained in the trade, etc., and carried forward under section 171 (above) or under section 172, discussed in § 12-06.[5] Unrelieved interest may in some cases be treated as a loss available for carry-forward.[6]

" Conversion " of business into company

12-06   If a business carried on by an individual, or by individuals in partnership, is transferred to a company in consideration solely or mainly of the allotment of shares of the company, and the individual(s) continue to hold those shares throughout the tax year in question, any unrelieved loss of the former business can be carried forward under section 171 and set off against any income derived by the individual(s) from the company, whether by way of dividends on the shares or otherwise, as if such income were income of the business.[7] The set-off has to be made primarily against income which is directly assessable to tax, such as directors' remuneration or other earned income.[8]

> If an individual or partnership with tax losses is " converted " into a company, care should be taken to arrange the transaction to take advantage of section 172. It is not essential that the vendor(s) should take up all the shares of the company.

This is a method by which carried-forward losses of a business can be set off against income which may derive from a business of an entirely different character.

2. IMMEDIATE RELIEF FOR CURRENT LOSSES: S. 168 (1)

12-07 There are many reasons why a taxpayer may not wish to carry forward a loss under section 171 of the Income and Corporation Taxes Act 1970. In the example in § 12-03, no relief for the loss sustained in 1971 was available until 1973–74, and a trader may not wish to wait so long: he may be uncertain whether the future profits of the trade will be sufficient to support the loss. Again, in periods of falling rates of tax, immediate relief may be preferred.

12-08   Section 168 of the Income and Corporation Taxes Act 1970 enables a trader to obtain relief for a loss in the year in which the loss is sustained. Section 168 (1) provides that where any person sustains a loss in any trade,

---

[4] I.C.T.A. 1970, s. 171 (3).
[5] Ibid. s. 173.
[6] Ibid. s. 175.
[7] I.C.T.A. 1970, s. 172 (1) losses incurred in a foreign business may be relieved under this section where profits of that business would have been subject to United Kingdom tax: see F.A. 1974, s. 23 (2).
[8] Ibid. s. 172 (2).

profession, employment or vocation carried on by him either solely or in partnership, he may, by notice in writing given within two years after the year of assessment, make a claim for relief from income tax on an amount of his income equal to the amount of the loss. Any unrelieved loss may be carried forward under section 171 or 172.[9]

> *Example*: In the example in § 12-03 the trader sustained a loss of £3,500 in 1971. In practice the Revenue allow a loss sustained in an accounting period to be treated as a loss of the tax year in which the accounting period ends [10]; so the loss in 1971 would be treated as a loss in 1971-72. If relief under section 168 (1) were claimed, the tax for 1971-72 (tax on £2,000) would be repaid and the balance of the loss (£1,500) may be carried forward under section 171 to 1973-74.

Generally, relief for a loss under section 168 (1) will be given against income of the corresponding class: thus a loss in a trade would be relieved against earned before unearned income.[11]

12-09   It should be noted that relief under section 168, unlike relief under section 171, is not restricted to profits of the *same trade*. Relief is available against *any* income of the trader in the relevant period. Under section 170, however, a loss is not available for relief under section 168 unless it is shown that, in the year of assessment in which the loss is claimed to have been sustained, the trade was being carried on on a commercial basis and with a view to the realisation of profits in the trade or, where the carrying on of the trade formed part of a larger undertaking, in the undertaking as a whole [12]; and the fact that a trade was being carried on at any time so as to afford a reasonable expectation of profit is conclusive evidence that it was then being carried on with a view to the realisation of profits.[13]

> Thus a " hobby-trader " may be unable to set off a loss in that trade against profits of a trade carried on on a commercial basis.

Generally, a loss incurred in a trade of farming or market gardening cannot be relieved under section 168 if in each of the prior five years (as defined) a loss was incurred in carrying on that trade; and when a loss is so excluded from relief, any related capital allowance (as defined) is also excluded from relief.[14]

Subject to some qualifications, the capital allowances to which a trader is entitled (see Chap. 13) may be used to augment a claim for loss relief under section 168.[15]

---

[9] *Ante*, § 12-02 (s. 171); § 12-06 (s. 172).

[10] Strictly, the loss sustained in a tax year should be computed by apportioning the figures in the trading accounts which overlap the tax year. The Revenue require this method to be adopted in the opening years and in the final year of a trade.

[11] *Ibid.* s. 168 (4). Generally, in the case of husband and wife, relief is given against the joint income, after first exhausting the earned (then unearned) income of the spouse sustaining the loss. Alternatively, the loss can be confined to the spouse who sustains it: *ibid.* s. 168 (3). For the position where, in or after 1972-73, husband and wife jointly elect to have the wife's earnings taxed separately, see F.A. 1971, Sched. 4, para. 4.

[12] I.C.T.A. 1970, s. 170 (1).

[13] *Ibid.* s. 170 (5).

[14] *Ibid.* s. 180.

[15] *Ibid.* s. 169.

3. RELIEF IN THE NEXT YEAR: S. 168 (2)

12-10 Where a trade shows a loss in one year, there will be a nil assessment in the following year. The trader may, however, have another source of income in that following year and, under section 168 (2) of the Income and Corporation Taxes Act 1970 he may set off the loss against the income of that year only, provided the trade, profession or vocation is still then being carried on.

> Thus in the example in § 12-03, the trader sustained a loss in 1971, producing a nil assessment in respect of the trade for 1972–73. Under section 168 (2) the trader can set off the loss against income from another source (*e.g.* investment income) in 1972–73 if the trade was still then being carried on.

4. CARRY-BACK OF NEW BUSINESS LOSSES

12-10A Section 30 of the Finance Act 1978 introduced a new form of relief aimed to encourage individuals to start new businesses. If an individual carrying on a trade (including a profession or vocation) sustains a loss in the trade either in the year of assessment in which it is first carried on by him or in any of the next three years of assessment, he may, by notice in writing given within two years after the year of assessment in which the loss is sustained, make a claim for relief. Briefly, the loss may be carried back against income for the three years of assessment last preceding the year in which the loss is sustained, taking income for an earlier year before income for a later year. Relief is not, however, given in respect of a loss sustained in any period unless it is shown that the trade was carried on throughout that period on a commercial basis and in such a way that profits in the trade (or, where the carrying on of the trade forms part of a larger undertaking, in the undertaking as a whole) could reasonably be expected to be realised in that period or within a reasonable time thereafter. The relief is available whether the individual carries on the trade solely or in partnership. Relief under section 30 is available for losses sustained in and from 1978–79.[16]

Relief is not given in respect of a loss sustained by an individual in a trade if, at the time when it is first carried on by him, he is married to and living with another individual who has previously carried on the trade *and* the loss is sustained in a year of assessment later than the third year of assessment after that in which the trade was first carried on by the other individual.

There are provisions to prevent relief given for the same loss twice over.

5. OTHER METHODS OF DEALING WITH LOSSES

Carry-back of terminal losses [17]

12-11 If a trade, profession or vocation has been permanently discontinued, a loss sustained in the last 12 months of the trade, etc. (called a " terminal loss "), can be set against the profits in the three years preceding the year in

---

[18] *Ante,* § 11-08.
[19] I.C.T.A. 1970, s. 176.

which the discontinuance occurred, unless the loss has been relieved under some other provision. The latest profits are relieved first.

In the case of a partnership, this relief is available (i) on a permanent discontinuance of the partnership; and (ii) on a statutory discontinuance caused by a change of partners,[18] as regards the non-continuing partners.

Case VI losses

12-12   Where a person sustains a loss in a transaction the profits from which (if any) would be assessed under Case VI of Schedule D, the loss may be set off against any other Case VI profits of the same year or carried forward and set off against Case VI profits of future years, without time limit.[19] Case VI losses cannot be set off against income assessable under Cases I or II of Schedule D.

Other losses

Losses under Schedule A and under the legislation taxing capital gains are discussed elsewhere.

---

[16] The set-off rules as between husband and wife are as stated in note 11: see F.A. 1978, s. 30 (7).

[17] I.C.T.A. 1970, s. 174, losses in a foreign trade etc. may be relieved under this section where profits of the trade would have been subject to United Kingdom tax: F.A. 1974, s. 23 (2).

[18] *Ante*, § 11-08.

[19] I.C.T.A. 1970, s. 176.

CHAPTER 13

CAPITAL ALLOWANCES

13-01　THE cost and depreciation of capital assets are not allowable deductions in computing profits under Schedule D,[1] but capital allowances are available in respect of expenditure on:

    (1) Machinery and plant;

    (2) Industrial buildings and structures;

    (3) Agricultural or forestry buildings and works;

    (4) Mines, oil wells, etc.; dredging; and scientific research.

The provisions of the Income Tax Act 1952 and of later statutes granting capital allowances were consolidated in the Capital Allowances Act 1968, which applies as respects allowances and certain charges (called balancing charges) falling to be made for chargeable periods ending after April 5, 1968.[2] " Chargeable period " means a year of assessment or, in relation to a company, an accounting period.[3] The Finance Act 1971 introduced a new system of capital allowances in respect of expenditure on plant and machinery incurred on or after October 27, 1970, which does not, however, supersede the Act of 1968.

13-02　Capital allowances should not be confused with investment grants which, by the Industrial Development Act 1966, the Board of Trade had power to make to any person carrying on a business in Great Britain towards *inter alia* approved capital expenditure incurred in providing new machinery or plant for carrying on a qualifying industrial process (as defined) or for carrying on scientific research relating thereto. Investment grants were not part of the tax system and were abolished in respect of expenditure on or after October 27, 1970, by the Investment and Building Grants Act 1971. Capital allowances are discussed only in outline.

1. ALLOWANCES ON MACHINERY AND PLANT

13-03　The term " plant " was said by Lindley L.J. in *Yarmouth* v. *France* [4] to include

> " whatever apparatus is used by a business man for carrying on his business— not his stock-in-trade . . . but all goods and chattels, fixed or movable, live or dead, which he keeps for permanent employment in his business. . . ."

In one case the House of Lords held (on somewhat unusual facts) that knives and lasts used in conjunction with machinery in shoe manufacture were plant.[5] The Court of Appeal reached the same conclusion on the factual assumption, which the House of Lords found to be wrong, that the

---

[1] *Ante*, § 2-52.

[2] Capital Allowances Act 1968 (C.A.A.), s. 96 (1).

[3] *Ibid.* s. 94 (2). For the meaning of " accounting period," see *post*, § 14-05.

[4] (1887) 19 Q.B.D. 647 at p. 658.

[5] *Hinton* v. *Maden and Ireland Ltd.* (1959) 38 T.C. 391 (H.L.).

knives and lasts were physically integrated with the machines in conjunction with which they were used. In this connection it should be noted that the term " machinery " is defined in the relevant legislation to include a part of machinery.[6] Books purchased by a practising barrister for the purposes of his practice have been held to be plant.[7]

The Court of Appeal has held that movable office partitioning is plant, a distinction being drawn between the premises in which a trade is carried out (which are not plant) and the apparatus with which it is carried on (which may be plant).[8] The function which the object claimed to be plant fulfils in relation to the trade is an important factor. Thus it has been held that a dry dock [9] and a swimming pool [10] were plant but that a pre-fabricated gymnasium,[11] the canopy used in a self-service filling-station [12] and a vessel used as a floating restaurant [12a] were not.

Expenditure incurred in insulating industrial buildings against loss of heat is deemed to be incurred on machinery or plant.[13]

13-04   Certain allowances are available under Part III of the Finance Act 1971 in respect of capital expenditure on machinery or plant where the expenditure is incurred on or after October 27, 1970.[14] The rates of the allowances for expenditure incurred after March 21, 1972, are in section 67 of the Finance Act 1972. The following is a summary of these allowances:

First-year allowances

13-05   An allowance called " a first-year allowance " is available to a person carrying on a trade [15] who incurs capital expenditure on the provision of machinery or plant for the purposes of the trade where, in consequence of his incurring the expenditure, the machinery or plant belongs to him at some time during the chargeable period related to the incurring of the expenditure; and the allowance is given for that period.[16] The condition that the machinery or plant should " belong " to the trader may be satisfied where it is purchased under a hire-purchase or similar agreement.[17] Commitment fees and interest paid to finance the purchase of plant or

[6] C.A.A. 1968, s. 87 (4); F.A. 1971, s. 50 (6).
[7] *Munby* v. *Furlong*, 50 T.C. 491; S.T.C. 232 (C.A.), overruling *Daphne* v. *Shaw* (1926) 11 T.C. 256. See *Rose & Co. (Wallpaper & Paints) Ltd.* v. *Campbell* (1967) 44 T.C. 500 (expenditure on pattern books with minimum useful life of two years not capital expenditure).
[8] *Jarrold* v. *John Good & Sons Ltd.* (1963) 40 T.C. 681.
[9] *I.R.C.* v. *Barclay, Curle & Co.* (1969) 45 T.C. 221 followed in *Schofield* v. *R. & H. Hall Ltd.* [1975] S.T.C. 351 (C.A.(N.I.)).
[10] *Cooke* v. *Beach Station Caravans Ltd.* (1974) 49 T.C. 514.
[11] *St. John's School* v. *Ward* (1974) 49 T.C. 524.
[12] *Dixon* v. *Fitch's Garage Ltd.* (1975) 50 T.C. 509.
[12a] *Benson* v. *Yard Arm Club Ltd.* [1978] S.T.C. 408.   [13] F.A. 1975, s. 14.
[14] F.A. 1971, s. 40 (1). For allowances on expenditure incurred before October 27, 1970, see the 4th edition of this book.
[15] Trade includes professions, employments, vocations and offices and the occupation of woodlands if assessed under Schedule D: *ibid.* s. 47 (1).
[16] *Ibid.* s. 41 (1). The phrase " chargeable period related to " is defined in F.A. 1971, s. 50 (1). Briefly, a company gets the allowance in the accounting period in which the expenditure is incurred. An individual or partnership gets the allowance in the year of assessment appropriate to the basis period in which the expenditure is incurred.
[17] F.A. 1971, s. 45. When a contract provides that a person shall or may become the owner on the performance of the contract, the plant or machinery is treated as belonging to him when he is entitled to the benefit of the contract.

machinery are not " capital expenditure on the provision of " the plant or machinery.[18]

No first-year allowance is available if the chargeable period related to the incurring of the expenditure is also the chargeable period related to the permanent discontinuance of the trade.[19] If machinery or plant ceases to belong to a trader without having been brought into use for the purposes of the trade, no first-year allowance is made or, if made, will be withdrawn; and any necessary assessments or adjustments of assessments can be made.[20]

13-06   The first-year allowance in relation to expenditure incurred after March 21, 1972, is of an amount equal to the whole of the expenditure.[21]

13-07   In some cases a trader will prefer to claim (or, in the case of a company, to disclaim) part of the first-year allowance in order to have higher writing-down allowances in subsequent chargeable periods; and there are provisions under which this can be done.[22] It should be noted that, except in the case of a ship, the tax system does not permit " free depreciation " in the sense that a trader can take his allowances as he pleases. If a trader takes a reduced first-year allowance, the writing-down allowance is calculated on the balance of the expenditure.

13-08   First-year allowances do not apply to capital expenditure on the provision of mechanically propelled road vehicles other than commercial vehicles, vehicles used for public transport and vehicles provided for hire.[23] But writing-down allowances may be claimed.

Writing-down allowances

13-09   Where (a) a person carrying on a trade [24] has incurred capital expenditure on the provision of machinery or plant for the purposes of the trade, and (b) in consequence of his incurring the expenditure, the machinery or plant belongs, or has belonged, to him, and (c) the machinery or plant is or has been in use for the purposes of the trade,[24] he is entitled to writing-down allowances.[25] The condition that the machinery or plant should " belong " to the trader may be satisfied where it is purchased on hire-purchase or similar terms.[26]

13-10   The system of writing-down allowances may be explained by taking a case in which the trader has one machine purchased in year 1 for £10,000, and claims a reduced first-year allowance equal to 80 per cent. of the cost (£8,000) for that year. In year 2 the trader is entitled to a writing-down allowance equal to 25 per cent. of the cost of the machine *less* the allowance

---

[18] *Ben-Odeco Ltd.* v. *Powlson* [1978] S.T.C. 460 (H.L.).
[19] F.A. 1971, s. 41 (1), proviso. But see § 13-13.
[20] *Ibid.* s. 41 (2), (4).   [21] F.A. 1972, s. 67 (2).
[22] C.A.A. 1968, s. 70 (3). F.A. 1971, s. 41 (3): this subsection does not apply to new ships but the first-year allowance may be spread at will under *ibid.* Sched. 8, para. 8.
[23] F.A. 1971, s. 43.   [24] See note 15, *ante.*
[25] F.A. 1971, s. 44 (1). And see F.A. 1976, ss. 39–40.
[26] F.A. 1971, s. 45; and see note 17.

already given, *i.e.* 25 per cent. of £2,000 (£10,000 less £8,000) = £500. In year 3 the writing-down allowance is again 25 per cent. of cost less the allowances already given, that is 25 per cent. of £1,500 (£10,000 less [£8,000 + £500]) = £375, and so on. The formula " cost less allowances already given " produces what the Act describes as the " qualifying expenditure " [27] (commonly described as the written-down value of the machine).

Pooling and balancing adjustments [28]

13-11   Where the trader purchases items of machinery or plant, these are treated for the purposes of the writing-down allowance as falling into a " pool " made up of all the machinery or plant already belonging to him. Thus if at the beginning of year 5 the aggregate qualifying expenditure on all machinery or plant in the pool is £20,000, the writing-down allowance for year 5 is of an amount equal to 25 per cent. of £20,000, leaving qualifying expenditure in the pool of £15,000 at the beginning of year 6.

If during year 6 some items of machinery are disposed of for (say) £7,000, the qualifying expenditure applicable to the machinery or plant in the pool is diminished by the disposal value of the item disposed of. Hence the writing-down allowance in year 6 will equal 25 per cent. of £8,000 (£15,000 less £7,000) = £2,000. This reduction of the qualifying expenditure in the pool by an amount equal to the disposal value of plant leaving the pool is called a " balancing adjustment." [29]

13-12   If the sale proceeds of a machine exceed the amount of qualifying expenditure in the pool, a " balancing charge " is made on the trader on an amount equal to the difference. Thus if, in the example in § 13-10, a trader sold the machinery or plant in year 3 for £2,000 (when the qualifying expenditure was £1,500) there would be a balancing charge of £500.

13-13   It will be seen that if, within a pool of qualifying expenditure of £15,000, there is one item of machinery with a written-down value of £4,000 which is sold for £3,500, the trader is entitled to no " balancing allowance," as under the system of allowances in operation before the 1971 Act. The £3,500 is credited to the pool, so reducing the qualifying expenditure.

No writing-down allowances are given in the chargeable period related to the permanent discontinuance of a trade; but when the trade is permanently discontinued an excess of unrelieved capital expenditure is relieved by way of " balancing allowance." [30]

13-14   If a trade is carried on for part only of a year (not being the year of permanent discontinuance) the amount of the writing-down allowances is proportionately reduced. [31]

A person (other than a company) claiming a writing-down allowance for any period may require that the amount of the allowance be reduced by an

---

[27] F.A. 1971, s. 44 (2), (4).   [28] *Ibid.* s. 44 (2), (3), (4).
[29] Disposal value is elaborately defined in F.A. 1971, s. 44 (6). When machinery is sold it is the net proceeds of sale unless it is sold at an undervalue when market value may be substituted. Insurance moneys must be brought in when machinery is demolished or destroyed.
[30] *Ibid.* s. 44 (2).   [31] *Ibid.* s. 44 (2) (*a*) (ii).

amount specified in the claim. This right would be exercised by an individual whose income would otherwise (after deduction of the full amount of the writing-down allowance) be insufficient to support his personal reliefs.[32]

Cars which cost more than £5,000 and are used in a trade qualify for writing-down allowance but are treated as used in a *separate* trade.[33] Hence they fall into a separate " pool."

Secondhand plant

13-15　　First-year and writing-down allowances are available whether the plant or machinery is purchased new or secondhand. But where an initial allowance has been granted to a person under the pre-1971 law, there are provisions to prevent a connected person getting a first-year allowance in respect of the same machinery or plant.[34]

Machinery and plant on lease

13-16　　Where machinery or plant is purchased and let by a person in the course of a trade, the lessor is entitled to the allowances available to an ordinary trader who does not let the machinery or plant.

13-17　　*Anti-avoidance legislation.* Section 41 of the Finance Act 1976 is aimed at counteracting various schemes under which higher rate taxpayers have joined partnerships formed to purchase plant and machinery in order to secure a share in the 100 per cent. first-year allowance and so avoid tax.

Where machinery or plant so purchased is let by a person otherwise than in the course of a trade, he is treated for the purposes of the 1971 Act as having incurred the expenditure for the purposes of a trade begun to be carried on by him, separately from any other trade which he may carry on.[35] Treating the letting as a separate trade has the effect that " let " machinery or plant falls into a different " pool " of expenditure from other machinery or plant.[36]

No allowances are given in the case of machinery or plant let for use in a dwelling-house.[37] Thus the lessor of a dwelling-house is entitled to no capital allowances in respect of his expenditure on central heating equipment. Dwelling-house is not defined but would presumably not include a block of flats; hence, the landlord of a block of flats would be entitled to allowances in respect of his expenditure on lifts, etc.[38]

The allowances available to a non-trading lessor are made by way of discharge or repayment of tax and are available primarily against income from the letting of the machinery or plant. The amount of the allowance is

---

[32] F.A. 1971, s. 44 (2), proviso.
[33] *Ibid.* Sched. 8, paras. 9–12. The figure of £5,000 was increased from £4,000 in respect of expenditure incurred after April 6, 1976: F.A. 1976, s. 43.
[34] *Ibid.* s. 40 (2). See also F.A. 1972, s. 68.
[35] F.A. 1971, s. 46 (1).
[36] See §§ 13-11 *et seq.*
[37] F.A. 1971, s. 46 (1), proviso.
[38] *Cf. McSaga Investment Co. Ltd.* v. *Lupton* (1967) 44 T.C. 659 (C.A.).

deducted from or set off against his income of that class for the relevant chargeable period and any excess may be carried forward and set off against income of the same class for the next year of assessment and so on. If the amount of the allowance is greater than the amount of the person's income from letting for the first mentioned year, he can elect to have the excess deducted from or set off against his other income for that year.[39]

13-18   Where a lessee incurs capital expenditure on the provision for the purposes of a trade carried on by him of machinery or plant which he is required to provide under the terms of the lease, the machinery or plant is treated as belonging to him for so long as it continues to be used for the purposes of the trade.[40] Thus if a lease of an office block imposes on the lessee an obligation to replace worn-out lifts, the lessee will qualify for capital allowances in respect of his capital expenditure. The lessee is not required on the determination of the lease to bring any disposal value into account in respect of the machinery or plant; hence he will continue to qualify for writing-down allowances until his original expenditure is written off.[40]

13-18A   There are anti-avoidance provisions to prevent first-year allowances being obtained by higher-rate taxpayers by participation in certain types of leasing partnership.[41]

Investment companies, etc.

13-19   Capital allowances may be claimed in respect of machinery or plant used in the maintenance of property or in the management of the business of an investment company.[42]

2. ALLOWANCES IN OTHER CASES

Industrial buildings

13-20   Where a person incurs capital expenditure on the construction of a building or structure which is to be an " industrial building or structure " to be occupied for the purposes of a trade carried on by him or certain lessees, he is entitled to an initial allowance of 50 per cent.[43] and writing-down allowances of 4 per cent.[44] The allowance is in each case based on the initial cost of construction. There are provisions for balancing allowances and charges.[45] An industrial building or structure is defined in section 7 of the Capital Allowances Act 1968 to mean a building or structure in use for one or more of the purposes listed in the section, *e.g.* manufacture, storage,

---

[39] F.A. 1971, s. 48 (2)–(4).
[40] *Ibid.* s. 46 (2).
[41] F.A. 1976, s. 35.
[42] F.A. 1971, s. 47 (2).
[43] C.A.A. 1968, s. 1. The 50 per cent. rate applies to expenditure incurred after November 12, 1974: see F.A. 1975, s. 13.
[44] C.A.A. 1968, s. 2.
[45] *Ibid.* s. 3. F.A. 1972, s. 69 contains provisions to counter certain schemes designed to accelerate industrial buildings allowances.

catching shellfish, etc. Buildings in use as a dwelling-house, retail shop, showroom or office are excluded.

Qualifying hotels are treated as industrial buildings or structures in relation to expenditure incurred after April 11, 1978, and are eligible for initial and writing-down allowances of 20 per cent. and 4 per cent. respectively.[46]

Agricultural land and buildings

13-21   Where the owner or tenant of any agricultural or forestry land incurs any capital expenditure on the construction of farmhouses,[47] farm or forestry buildings, cottages, fences or other work, he is entitled to an initial allowance of 20 per cent. of the expenditure for the chargeable period related to the incurring of the expenditure plus writing-down allowances of 80 per cent. of the expenditure for a period of 8 years beginning with that period.[48] To qualify for the allowances, the expenditure must be incurred for the purposes of husbandry or forestry on the land in question and, in the case of expenditure on the farmhouse, one-third of the expenditure is the maximum which will qualify.[49] There are provisions for transfer of the allowances to a successor in title, or to an incoming tenant (when a tenancy comes to an end) if he pays the outgoing tenant for the asset representing the expenditure in question.[50]

13-22   *Miscellaneous allowances.* Allowances are available in respect of specified capital expenditure in connection with the working of a mine, oil well or other source of mineral deposits of a wasting nature [51]; in respect of expenditure on dredging [52]; in respect of expenditure on scientific research [53]; and in respect of expenditure on sports grounds.[54] Writing-down allowances are available in respect of expenditure after March 19, 1968, on the acquisition of know-how for the purposes of a trade.[55]

13-23   *Employees.* An employee who uses machinery or plant in the performance of his duties is entitled to capital allowances on his expenditure.[56]

---

[46] F.A. 1978, s. 38 and Sched. 6.
[47] As to what constitutes a farmhouse, see *Lindsay* v. *I.R.C.* (1953) 34 T.C. 289.
[48] Capital Allowances Act 1968, ss. 68, 69; s. 87 (1) (*b*), as amended by F.A. 1978, s. 39 as respects expenditure incurred after April 11, 1978.
[49] C.A.A. 1968, s. 68 (3).
[50] *Ibid.* s. 68 (4) (5).
[51] *Ibid.* ss. 51 *et seq.*
[52] *Ibid.* s. 67.
[53] *Ibid.* ss. 91–95.
[54] F.A. 1978, s. 40.
[55] I.C.T.A. 1970, ss. 386–387.
[56] C.A.A. 1968, s. 47.

DIVISION B

THE TAXATION OF COMPANIES

CHAPTER 14

CORPORATION TAX AND
THE TAX TREATMENT OF DISTRIBUTIONS

14-01A THE profits of companies are chargeable neither to income tax [1] nor capital gains tax [2] but only to corporation tax. The Finance Act 1972 introduced the " imputation system " of company taxation and made substantial changes in the system which had been introduced by the Finance Act 1965. Under the earlier system, the profits of companies were charged to corporation tax at the rate then in force (which was 40 per cent. for the year ended March 31, 1972). When a company paid a dividend it deducted income tax at the current standard rate (which was 38·75 per cent. for the year 1972–73) and accounted to the Revenue for the income tax so deducted. Hence the total tax charge on a company which distributed none of its profits was 40 per cent. If it distributed all its profits the total tax charge was 63·25 per cent. If it distributed (say) 60 per cent. of its profits, the total tax charge was 53·95 per cent. Dividends were treated in substantially the same way as annuities or annual payments paid out of profits or gains not brought into charge to income tax and each member included the grossed-up amount of the dividend in his return of total income. Companies could not deduct the income tax paid on dividends or other distributions in computing profits chargeable to corporation tax; hence the profits of companies were, in a sense, taxed twice—once at the corporation tax rate in the hands of the company and again at the income tax rate when they were distributed to members. One criticism often levelled at this system was that it encouraged companies to retain profits in order to avoid income tax on distributions although, in the case of close companies, there were provisions designed to counteract such avoidance of tax when the retention of profits was not justified by the commercial needs of the company. Another criticism was that the system treated a company and its shareholders as separate entities which (it was said) was juristically correct but commercially unrealistic.

The imputation system

14-01B   The essential features of the imputation system (ignoring cases in which there is a foreign element) are as follows:

(1) A company pays corporation tax on its profits, whether distributed or not, at the prescribed rate, which will be assumed in the examples that follow to be 52 per cent. (which is the rate for the year ended March 31, 1978, called " the financial year 1977 ": see § 14-04). There is a lower rate for small companies and for chargeable gains (§ 14-04B).

(2) When making a qualifying distribution (§ 14-41), *e.g.* paying a dividend, the company does not deduct Schedule F income tax as

---

[1] I.C.T.A. 1970, s. 238 (2). Income which arises to a company in a fiduciary or representative capacity is chargeable to income tax: see § 14-03.   [2] *Ibid.* s. 238 (3).

under the pre-imputation system. The company is required to make an advance payment of corporation tax (" ACT ") to the Revenue at a rate which, for the financial year 1978 is 33/67ths of the amount or value of the distribution: § 14-50. This rate applies irrespective of the effective rate of tax suffered by the company on its income.

(3) Advance payments of corporation tax made in respect of dividends or other qualifying distributions paid in an accounting period are available for set-off against corporation tax liability on the profits (excluding chargeable gains) of the period: §§ 14-51 to 14-53.

Thus a company with an income (excluding chargeable gains) in an accounting period of £60,000 is assessed after the end of the period to corporation tax at 52 per cent. = £31,200. If the company pays a dividend of £6,700 it must pay 33/67ths of this amount (£3,300) of ACT to the Revenue. The actual corporation tax payable is therefore £31,200 less £3,300 = £27,900. (*Note* that the company needs a fund of £10,000 in order to pay £6,700 to its members.)

(4) An individual resident in the United Kingdom who receives a qualifying distribution (§ 14-41) is liable to Schedule F income tax on the aggregate of the distribution and the tax credit: § 14-59. The tax credit is set against the tax due: § 14-56. Note that a rate of ACT of 33/67ths of the amount distributed is equivalent to income tax at the basic rate of 33 per cent. on the aggregate of the distribution and the tax credit.

Thus an individual who receives a dividend of £67 is treated as having Schedule F income of £100. If he is liable only to the basic rate of income tax, he has no further tax to pay. An individual with a higher income is liable to higher rate income tax and investment income surcharge, if appropriate. An individual not liable to the basic rate of income tax can claim repayment from the Revenue of an amount equal to the tax credit (§ 14-56).

(5) An individual resident in the United Kingdom who receives a non-qualifying distribution (§ 14-41) incurs no charge to income tax at the basic rate and has no entitlement to a tax credit. Any liability to higher rate income tax or the investment income surcharge is on the amount of the distribution (without the addition of any credit), but any higher rate tax payable is reduced by an amount equal to tax at the basic rate on the amount assessed at higher rates: § 14-60.

(6) A company resident in the United Kingdom which receives a qualifying distribution is chargeable neither to income tax nor corporation tax in respect of it. The company is entitled to a tax credit which can be set off against its liability to ACT on its own qualifying distributions: §§ 14-54 *et seq.*; § 14-63.

14-01C   The new system is described as an " imputation system " because part of the company's liability to corporation tax is imputed to the members and is treated as satisfying their basic rate income tax liability. Effect is given to this imputation by conferring a tax credit on the member in respect of each distribution made to him: see § 8-20. The imputation system removes the bias against distributed profits, for its effect is that a company pays corporation tax at a flat rate on all its profits whether distributed or not.

Non-resident members

14-01D   A member of a company who is not resident in the United Kingdom has
no entitlement to a tax credit. He therefore suffers United Kingdom income
tax at the basic rate and may (if an individual) be assessed under Schedule F
to higher rate income tax and the investment income surcharge, subject to
any relevant double taxation arrangement.

Date of commencement of the imputation system

14-01E   Corporation tax is levied by reference to financial years commencing on
April 1 and ending on March 31 in the following year. The new system
applies to profits attributable to any time after March 31, 1973. When a
company's accounting period straddles March 31, 1973, profits will be
apportioned on a time basis, the imputation system applying only to the
profits attributed to the period falling after March 31, 1973.

The system by which income tax is deducted at the source from dividends
and other distributions applied to dividends etc., paid up to and including
April 5, 1973. Dividends paid after April 5, 1973, are subject to the
imputation system.

In the remainder of this chapter, the taxation of companies is considered
in detail under the following main headings:

A. The Corporation Tax.
B. The Tax Treatment of Distributions.

The special legislation applicable to close companies is considered in
Chapter 15. The pre-imputation system is referred to in this edition only so
far as necessary to explain the imputation system.

A. THE CORPORATION TAX

1. *Introduction*

14-02   All companies resident in the United Kingdom became liable to corporation
tax on trading profits arising after the end of the period which formed the
basis period for the year of assessment 1965–66. Thus a company with a
period of account ending on or after April 6, 1964, became liable to
corporation tax on its trading profits on the day following the end of the
period of account. In respect of most other sources of income, liability to
corporation tax commenced on April 6, 1966.[3] A company which is not
resident in the United Kingdom but which trades in the United Kingdom
through a branch or agency is liable to corporation tax on chargeable
profits from the branch or agency.[4]

14-03   A company resident in the United Kingdom is liable to corporation tax on
all its profits wherever arising.[5] " Company " means any body corporate

---

[3] F.A. 1965, s. 80. Companies resident in the United Kingdom and non-resident companies within the
charge to corporation tax are not liable to income tax after the year 1965–66: *ibid*. s. 46 (2). Profits tax is
not chargeable for accounting periods after the end of 1965–66: *ibid*. s. 46 (3). For transitional provisions,
see ss. 81 and 87 and Sched. 21 (relating to cessations of trades, etc.).

[4] I.C.T.A. 1970, ss. 246 and 527 (1). As to the mode of assessing such companies, see T.M.A. 1970,
s. 85.   [5] *Ibid*. ss. 238 (2) and 243 (1).

or unincorporated association, but does not include a partnership or a local authority.[6] " Profits " means income and chargeable gains.[7] This includes profits accruing for its benefit under any trust or arising under any partnership in any case in which the company would be so chargeable if the profits accrued to it directly; and a company is chargeable to corporation tax on profits arising in the winding-up of the company, but is not otherwise chargeable to corporation tax on profits accruing to it in a fiduciary or representative capacity except as respects its own beneficial interest (if any) in those profits.[8] Thus profits which arise to a company on a sale of assets by its liquidator are chargeable to corporation tax; profits which arise to a company as agent or trustee are chargeable only to income tax.

14-04   Corporation tax (unlike income tax) is levied by reference to financial years ending on March 31.[9] " The financial year 1970 " means the year beginning with April 1970, and so on.[10] The rate of corporation tax for the financial years 1964, 1965 and 1966 was 40 per cent.[11] and for the financial year 1967, 42½ per cent.[12] The rate for the financial years 1968 and 1969 was 45 per cent.[13]; and for 1970, 1971 and 1972 it was 40 per cent.[14] The rate for the financial years 1973, 1974, 1975, 1976 and 1977 is 52 per cent.[15] The rate is fixed in arrears; thus the rate of corporation tax for the financial year 1977 (*i.e.* the year beginning with April 1, 1977) was fixed by the Finance Act 1978, which was enacted on July 31, 1978. When an assessment to corporation tax falls to be made before the rates for the financial year are fixed, the Revenue has power to charge tax at rates fixed for the previous year, subject to adjustment later.[16] There are special provisions relating to the profits of a company in liquidation,[17] where the tax liability has to be finally determined before the rate has been fixed for the year.

Franked and unfranked income

14-04A   Corporation tax is not chargeable on dividends and other distributions received from a company resident in the United Kingdom, nor are such dividends or distributions taken into account in computing income for corporation tax.[18] United Kingdom companies account for advance corporation tax when making a distribution; a United Kingdom company receiving a distribution is entitled to a tax credit. The consequences of this are discussed in §§ 14-54 *et seq.*

The general scheme of the Act is that a company should suffer corporation tax (and not basic rate income tax) on its unfranked investment income, such as interest on debentures and on investments. Such income is assessed to corporation tax under Case III of Schedule D, credit being given for any income tax suffered by deduction.

[6] I.C.T.A. 1970, s. 526 (5).
[7] *Ibid.* s. 238 (4) (*a*).
[8] *Ibid.* s. 243 (2).
[9] *Ibid.* s. 238 (1).
[10] *Ibid.* s. 527 (1).
[11] F.A. 1966, s. 26 (1); F.A. 1967, s. 19 (1).
[12] F.A. 1968, s. 13.
[13] F.A. 1969, s. 9; F.A. 1970, s. 13.
[14] F.A. 1971, s. 14; F.A. 1972, s. 64; F.A. 1973, s. 11.
[15] F.A. 1974, s. 9 and F. (No. 2) A. 1975, s. 26; F.A. 1976, s. 25; F.A. 1977, s. 18; F.A. 1978, s. 15.
[16] I.C.T.A. 1970, s. 243 (5) and F.A. 1974, s. 36.
[17] I.C.T.A. 1970, s. 245. See also F.A. 1974, s. 37.
[18] I.C.T.A. 1970, s. 239.

Special rates for small companies and chargeable gains

14-04B   Under the new system " small companies " pay corporation tax at a lower rate called the " small companies rate." The small companies rate for the financial years 1974, 1975, 1976 and 1977 is 42 per cent.[19] This rate applies to a company with taxable profits (including chargeable gains) in the accounting period not exceeding £50,000 but there are tapering provisions for companies with profits between £50,000 and £85,000.[20] There are provisions for apportionment when an accounting period straddles more than one financial year. There are anti-avoidance provisions designed to prevent the fragmentation of businesses into a number of companies in order to get the benefit of the lower rate.

Under the new system a company's chargeable gains are taxed at a lower rate than the corporation tax rate. This is achieved by excluding a fraction of such gains from the charge to corporation tax and charging corporation tax only on the balance.[21] The effective rate to be charged on gains from April 1, 1973, is 30 per cent.[22]

Accounting periods

14-05   Although the rate of tax is levied by reference to financial years, assessments to corporation tax are made on a company by reference to the company's own accounting period [23] and where the accounting period does not coincide with the financial year, the chargeable amount must be calculated by apportioning the profits of the accounting period (after making all proper deductions) between the financial years in which the period falls.[24] The apportionment is made on a time basis.[25]

> Thus if a company's accounts are made up to December 31, 1975, and the period of account is 12 months, one-quarter of the profits fall in the financial year 1974 and three-quarters in the financial year 1975.

The Act contains elaborate provisions for defining accounting periods. An accounting period cannot, for the purpose of corporation tax, be longer than 12 months; and if accounts are prepared for a longer period, the first 12 months will be treated as the accounting period.[26]

14-06   Generally, corporation tax assessed for an accounting period is payable within nine months from the end of that period or, if the assessment is later, within one month from the making of the assessment.[27]

Administration

14-07   Corporation tax is under the care and management of the Board of Inland Revenue, who may do all such acts as are necessary and expedient for raising, collecting, receiving and accounting for the tax.[28] Detailed provisions relating to the administration of the Corporation Tax Acts are contained in the Taxes Management Act 1970.

---

[19] F. (No. 2) A. 1975, s. 27 (2); F.A. 1976, s. 27 (2); F.A. 1977, s. 20 (1); F.A. 1978, s. 17 (2).
[20] F.A. 1972, s. 95 as amended by F.A. 1978, s. 17 (3). The figures in the text apply for the financial year 1977. The figures in the previous year were £40,000 and £65,000 respectively.
[21] F.A. 1972, s. 93, *post*, § 16-53.   [22] F.A. 1974, s. 10 (1).
[23] I.C.T.A. 1970, s. 243 (3); and see s. 527 (1) for definitions of " accounting date " and " period of account."   [24] *Ibid.* s. 243 (3).
[25] *Ibid.* s. 527 (4).   [26] *Ibid.* s. 247 (2)–(7), as amended by F.A. 1972, s. 107 (1).
[27] *Ibid.* s. 243 (4).   [28] T.M.A. 1970, s. 1.

2. *Charges on Income*

14-08 The general rules governing the computation of the income of a company are discussed in the next section of this chapter; but first it will be convenient to examine the statutory definition of " charges on income " and to see how charges are dealt with under the corporation tax system.

Charges on income *paid* by a company in an accounting period (but not before the year 1966–67), so far as paid out of the company's profits brought in to charge to corporation tax, are allowed as deductions against the total profits for the period as reduced by any other relief from tax, other than group relief.[29] Charges are not a deduction in computing profits; they are deductible after " total profits " have been ascertained and reduced by other reliefs, such as loss relief. It is expressly provided that no payment which is deductible in computing profits shall be treated as a charge on income for the purposes of corporation tax.[30] Dividends or other distributions of a company are not charges on income of the company and, by virtue of the wide definition of " distribution," which is extended in the case of close companies, many payments which fall within the definition of " charges on income " are excluded.[31]

Charges on income defined

14-09 Charges on income are defined [32] as:

> (a) any yearly interest, annuity or other annual payment [33] and any such other payments as are mentioned in section 52 (2) of the 1970 Act, but not including sums which are or, but for any exemption would be, chargeable under Schedule A [34]; and
>
> (b) any other interest payable in the United Kingdom on an advance from a bank carrying on a bona fide banking business [35] in the United Kingdom, or from a person who in the opinion of the Board is bona fide carrying on business as a member of a stock exchange in the United Kingdom or bona fide carrying on the business of a discount house in the United Kingdom [36];

and the interest in (b) is to be treated as paid on its being debited to the company's account in the books of the person to whom it is payable.[32] Subject to this last-mentioned exception, charges on income are not deductible unless and until they are actually paid; but charges which are paid in an accounting period are deductible even though they were due in an earlier period. The difficulties created by the use of the words " paid " and " payable " in sections 52 and 53 of the Income and Corporation Taxes Act 1970,[37] do not therefore exist in the case of companies liable to corporation

---

[29] I.C.T.A. 1970, s. 248 (1). Surplus franked investment income may be treated as an equivalent amount of profits for this purpose: *ibid.* s. 254 (2) (*b*).

[30] *Ibid.* s. 248 (2). See also § 14-17.

[31] *Ibid.* s. 248 (2). As to the meaning of dividends and other distributions, see *post*, §§ 14-40 *et seq.* and §§ 15-21 *et seq.*

[32] *Ibid.* s. 248 (3).   [33] Discussed *ante*, § 5-04.

[34] I.C.T.A. 1970, s. 52 (2), includes patent royalties, mining rents and royalties and payments for easements.

[35] See *United Dominions Trust Ltd.* v. *Kirkwood* [1966] 1 Q.B. 783 as to the meaning of " bona fide banking business."

[36] Non-yearly interest paid to a bank would fall under (b).   [37] *Ante*, §§ 5-37 *et seq.*

tax. Payments of interest within (b), above, may be deductible as a trading expense of a trading company; but generally the payments within (a), above, may not be deducted in computing income and are therefore deductible as charges on income.[38] A company making payments within (a), above, must deduct basic rate income tax from the payments and account to the Revenue for the tax so deducted.[39] Note that the obligation to deduct and account for income tax continues under the imputation system.

Charges in excess of profits

14-09A Where in an accounting period the charges on income paid by a company exceed the amount of profits against which they are deductible, and include payments made wholly and exclusively for the purposes of a trade carried on by the company, then up to the amount of that excess or of those payments (if less) the charges are deductible as if they were a trading expense for the purposes of computing trading losses.[40] The manner in which losses of trading companies are relieved is considered in §§ 14-24 et seq.

There are similar provisions for treating charges on income of an investment company which exceed profits as if they were expenses of management.[41] Charges on income may be surrendered for group relief.[42]

Payments not charges on income

14-10 A payment is not to be treated as a charge on income in the following circumstances:

(1) If the payment is charged to capital [43]: interest on moneys borrowed by property developers to finance a development project may be charged to capital account, thereby increasing the profit available for dividend. Interest so charged is not deductible from profits; but it may be deductible in computing the chargeable gain on a disposal of the property [44];

(2) if the payment is not ultimately borne by the company, e.g. where there is a right of reimbursement against a third party which is effectively exercised [45];

(3) if the payment is not made under a liability incurred for a valuable and sufficient consideration [46]: thus a voluntary annuity is not a charge on income, except that a covenanted donation to charity (defined in § 14-11, below) is deductible [46];

In *Ball* v. *National and Grindlays Bank,*[47] officers employed by the Bank were normally required to spend their whole working lives abroad and had, therefore, to educate their children at boarding schools. The financial burden falling on parents caused much discontent and some resignations or threatened

[38] I.C.T.A. 1970, s. 251 (2) (3).
[39] *Ibid.* ss. 53–54 and s. 240 (4); *ante,* §§ 5-09 *et seq.* and §§ 5-33 *et seq.*
[40] *Ibid.* s. 177 (8).
[41] *Ibid.* s. 304 (2); *post,* § 14-22.
[42] *Ibid.* s. 259 (6); *post,* § 14-41. It is thought that debited bank interest is treated as *paid* for the purposes of *ibid.* s. 259 (6).
[43] *Ibid.* s. 248 (5) (a); *cf. Chancery Lane Safe Deposit Ltd.* v. *I.R.C.* [1966] A.C. 85; 43 T.C. 83 (H.L.).
[44] I.C.T.A. 1970, s. 269.   [45] *Ibid.* s. 248 (5) (a).
[46] *Ibid.* s. 248 (5) (b).   [47] [1973] Ch. 127; 47 T.C. 287 (C.A.).

resignations. The Bank entered into a deed of covenant with trustees to pay monthly sums to be applied in the education of the children and this scheme in fact abated some of the discontent. *Held*, that payments under the deed were not a charge on income, because there was no valuable consideration representing an adequate or fair equivalent for the Bank's expenditure. A business advantage fell short of this requirement.

(4) if, in the case of a non-resident company (which is liable to corporation tax on the profits from trading in the United Kingdom),[48] the payment is not incurred wholly and exclusively for the purposes of a trade carried on by it in the United Kingdom through a branch or agency [49]: thus interest on moneys borrowed for the purposes of its overseas operations is not deductible.

14-11   " Covenanted donation to charity " in paragraph (3) of § 14-10 means a payment under a disposition or covenant made by the company in favour of a body of persons or trusts established for charitable purposes only, whereby the like annual payments (of which the donation is one) become payable for a period which may exceed six years [50] and is not capable of earlier termination under any power exercisable without the consent of the persons for the time being entitled to the payments.[51] Such a payment is not treated as a distribution.[52]

Payments of interest

14-12   A payment of interest is not to be treated as a charge on income unless—

(a) the company exists wholly or mainly for the purpose of carrying on a trade; or

(b) the payment of interest is wholly and exclusively laid out or expended for the purposes of a trade carried on by the company; or

(c) the company is an investment company; or

(d) the payment of interest would, on certain assumptions, be eligible for relief under section 75 of the Finance Act 1972.[53]

Payments by companies to non-residents

14-13   A payment of yearly interest, an annuity or other annual payment and a payment of the kind referred to in section 248 (3) (*a*) of the Income and Corporation Taxes Act 1970 which is made by a company to a non-resident person is not treated as a charge on income [54] unless the paying company is resident in the United Kingdom and either

(a) the company deducts income tax from the payment in accordance with section 53 or 54 and accounts for the tax so deducted [55]; or

(b) the company is carrying on a trade and the payment is a payment of

---

[48] I.C.T.A. 1970, s. 246.   [49] *Ibid.* s. 248 (5) (*b*).
[50] *Ante*, § 10-19.
[51] I.C.T.A. 1970, s. 248 (9).
[52] *Ibid.* s. 248 (8).
[53] I.C.T.A. 1970, s. 248 (6), restored and amended by F.A. 1974, Sched. 1, para. 25; and see *ante*, §§ 8-57 *et seq.*
[54] *Ibid.* s. 248 (4).
[55] *Ante*, §§ 5-30 *et seq.* Where the company would have deducted tax but for the existence of double taxation relief, the company is treated as if tax had been deducted and accounted for: Double Taxation Relief (Taxes on Income) (General) Regulations 1972, No. 488.

interest falling within section 249. Generally, the interest must be payable and paid outside the United Kingdom; and the liability must be on a loan incurred for the purposes of trading activities of the company outside the United Kingdom save where the interest is payable in the currency of a territory outside the scheduled territories; or

(c) the payment is one payable out of income brought into charge to tax under Case IV or V of Schedule D.

The provisions summarised in this paragraph are important in relation to interest on loans from non-resident persons. In such cases condition (a) may not be satisfied by reason of the lender's requirement that interest should be paid without deduction of United Kingdom income tax.

Collection of tax

14-14　　Although the income of companies is charged to corporation tax, a company must account for income tax on payments of interest, annuities and annual payments within sections 53 and 54 of the Taxes Act 1970 and will suffer income tax by deduction on " unfranked " income. Section 104 of and Schedule 20 to the Finance Act 1972 contain provisions for regulating the time and manner in which companies resident in the United Kingdom should account for income tax, and allow income tax suffered by deduction to be offset against income tax for which they are accountable on their own payments.

3. General Rules for Computation of Income

14-15　　Corporation tax is assessed and charged on the profits which arise in the accounting period, subject only to such deductions as the Act allows.[56] Profits means income and chargeable gains.[57] The Act states [58] that, except as otherwise provided,

> " the amount of any income shall for purposes of corporation tax be computed in accordance with income tax principles, all questions as to the amounts which are or are not to be taken into account as income, or in computing income, or charged to tax as a person's income, or as to the time when any such amount is to be treated as arising, being determined in accordance with income tax law and practice as if accounting periods were years of assessment."

The way in which income is determined by reference to accounting periods but tax is levied by reference to financial years has already been mentioned.[59] The expression " income tax law " is defined [60] to mean the law which applies to the charge on individuals of income tax for the year of assessment in which the company's accounting period ends; except that it also includes certain enactments specifically relating to companies and excludes those enactments which apply only to individuals. The incorporation of " income tax law " into corporation tax implies that both statutory exemptions and provisions imposing a charge to income tax also apply.

---

[56] I.C.T.A. 1970, ss. 129 (1), 247 (1). For company partnerships, see s. 155.
[57] *Ibid*. s. 238 (4) (*a*).　　　　　　　　　　　　　　　　　　[58] *Ibid*. s. 250 (1).
[59] *Ante*, § 14-05.　　　　　　　　　　　　　　　　　　[60] I.C.T.A. 1970, s. 250 (2).

14-16   It follows that, for the purposes of corporation tax, income is computed and assessments are made under the like Schedules and Cases as apply for purposes of income tax and in accordance with the rules applicable to those Schedules and Cases.[61]

> Thus if a company carries on a trade, receives rent from land and receives interest, its income in any accounting period must be determined by reference to the rules of Schedule D Case I, Schedule A and Schedule D Case III respectively and assessments to corporation tax will be made under those Cases of Schedule D, except that income of an accounting period is not to be determined by reference to any preceding year or other period.

The amounts which are so computed for the several sources of income, if more than one, together with any amount to be included in respect of chargeable gains must be aggregated to arrive at the *total profits* of the company.[62]

14-17   Dividends or other distributions are not deductible in computing income from any source [63] nor are they charges on income.[64] Yearly interest, annuities, other annual payments and certain payments which are similarly treated are not deductible in computing income [65] but may be a charge on the income of the company, when they are deductible from total profits.[66]

14-18   Where a company begins or ceases to carry on a trade, or to be within the charge to corporation tax in respect of a trade, *e.g.* where a non-resident company carrying on a trade becomes resident and chargeable to corporation tax, the company's income must be computed as if that were the commencement or, as the case may be, discontinuance of the trade, whether or not the trade is in fact commenced or discontinued.[67] Thus stock-in-trade held at the time of the deemed discontinuance must be valued in accordance with section 137 of the Income and Corporation Taxes Act 1970.[68]

Computation of chargeable gains

14-19   Corporation tax (not capital gains tax) is assessed and charged on the chargeable gains which arise in any accounting period of a company, after setting off allowable losses of that and earlier periods, including periods before the company became liable to corporation tax.[69] The chargeable gains of a company are computed in accordance with the principles applying for capital gains tax,[70] subject to some modifications which are discussed elsewhere in this book.[71] Generally, where the provisions of the capital gains tax refer to income tax or the Income Tax Acts, the reference in relation to a company is to be construed as a reference to corporation tax or the Corporation Tax Acts.[72]

---

[61] I.C.T.A. 1970, s. 250 (3).   [62] *Ibid.* s. 250 (3). And see s. 527 (1).
[63] *Ibid.* s. 251 (2).   [64] *Ibid.* s. 248 (2).
[65] *Ibid.* s. 251 (2); but yearly interest paid to a United Kingdom bank may be deductible: *ibid.* s. 251 (3).
[66] *Ante*, §§ 14-08 *et seq.*
[67] I.C.T.A. 1970, s. 251 (1).   [68] *Ante*, §§ 2-34 *et seq.*
[69] I.C.T.A. 1970, s. 265 (1).   [70] *Ibid.* s. 265 (2).
[71] *Post*, §§ 16-53 *et seq.*
[72] I.C.T.A. 1970, s. 265 (3). And see the definitions in s. 526 (1).

Investment companies: management expenses

14-20   A trading company is normally able to deduct expenses of management in computing its income chargeable to corporation tax under Case I of Schedule D. An investment company with income from land, *e.g.* rents, may deduct expenses of managing its *properties* under the Schedule A rules discussed in §§ 6-27 *et seq.*; but expenses of managing the *company* itself, *e.g.* head office administration expenses, may not be allowed under these rules. An investment company with income from stocks and shares would secure no relief for management expenses without the special provisions discussed below.

Section 304 (1) of the Income and Corporation Taxes Act 1970 provides that in computing for the purposes of corporation tax the total profits for any accounting period of an investment company resident in the United Kingdom, there shall be deducted any sums disbursed as expenses of management (including commissions) for that period, except any such expenses as are deductible in computing income for the purposes of Schedule A. It is further provided that there shall be deducted from the amount treated as expenses of management the amount of any income derived from sources not charged to tax, other than franked investment income and group income.[73] The purpose of this not obviously meaningful provision is apparently to enable the Revenue to deduct (for example) bank deposit interest from expenses of management, thus obviating the need for separate Case III or other assessments on the income so deducted. The exception for franked investment income and group income prevents the Revenue from taxing such income indirectly.

14-21   " Investment company " is defined [74] for this purpose as meaning

" any company whose business consists wholly or mainly in the making of investments and the principal part of whose income is derived therefrom, but includes any savings bank or other bank for savings."

It follows that no relief under section 304 is available in the case of a mixed trading and investment company where the principal part of the income is derived from trading and the expenses relate to the management of the investments, for such a company is not an " investment company " as defined. The relief will, however, be available if the two enterprises are segregated into separate companies. An authorised unit trust is treated as if it were an investment company [75]: trustees are not otherwise entitled to relief for management expenses.

The Act contains no definition of the phrase " expenses of management," nor of the term " disbursed," and reference must accordingly be made to cases decided under section 425 of the Income Tax Act 1952 for illumination.[76] Brokerage and stamp duty paid on a change of investments have been held not to be expenses of management of an investment company.[77]

---

[73] I.C.T.A. 1970, s. 304 (1), proviso.
[74] *Ibid.* s. 304 (5).
[75] *Ibid.* s. 354.
[76] See Simon's *Taxes*, 3rd ed., D4.408.
[77] *Capital and National Trust Ltd.* v. *Golder* (1949) 31 T.C. 265 (C.A.).

14-22   Where the deductible management expenses in any accounting period, together with any charges on income paid in the accounting period wholly and exclusively for the purposes of the company's business, exceed the amount of the profits from which they are deductible, the excess can be carried forward to the succeeding accounting period.[78] The amount carried forward is to be treated for this purpose, including any further application of this carry-forward provision, as if it had been disbursed as expenses of management for that accounting period.[79] A claim may be made by a company to set off management expenses against a surplus of franked investment income.[80]

Capital allowances

14-23   Effect is given to allowances and charges for corporation tax purposes by deductions from or additions to profits.[81] In taxing the trade, capital allowances due for an accounting period are treated as a trading expense of the trade (so reducing profits); balancing charges so due are treated as trading receipts (so increasing profits).[82] Allowances and charges of an investment company are similarly treated.[83] Capital allowances can be added to the expenses of management of an investment company for the purposes of relief by carry-forward.[84]

4. *Losses*

14-24   Sections 177 to 179 (inclusive) of the Income and Corporation Taxes Act 1970 contain provisions for the relief of losses of companies liable to corporation tax which are similar to those already discussed in connection with income tax.[85] Losses incurred in a trade are computed in the same way that trading income is computed.[86] In the case of a company carrying on a trade so as to be within the charge to corporation tax in respect of it, losses may be relieved in the following ways:

14-25   (i) *Carry-forward.* The company may claim to set off a trading loss incurred in an accounting period against trading income from the trade in succeeding accounting periods.[87] The trading income must be derived from the same trade as that in respect of which the loss is incurred.[88] " Trading income " means, in relation to any trade, the income which falls or would fall to be included in respect of the trade in the total profits of the company (and thus does not include chargeable gains); but where the trading income is insufficient to support losses carried forward, any interest or dividends on investments which would fall to be treated as trading receipts but for the fact that they have been otherwise taxed are to be treated as if they were trading income.[89] Thus dividends on shares which are trading stock of a share-dealing company may be treated as trading receipts.

---

[78] I.C.T.A. 1970, s. 304 (2). As to capital allowances, see § 14-23. Not all charges on income will satisfy the wholly and exclusively test: covenanted donations to charity may not do so (*ante*, § 14-11).

[79] I.C.T.A. 1970, s. 304 (2).
[81] C.A.A. 1968, s. 73 (1).
[83] I.C.T.A. 1970, s. 306.
[85] *Ante*, Chap. 12.
[87] *Ibid.* s. 177 (1).
[89] I.C.T.A. 1970, s. 177 (7).

[80] *Ibid.* s. 254 (2) (c).
[82] *Ibid.* s. 73 (2).
[84] *Ibid.* s. 304 (3).
[86] I.C.T.A. 1970, s. 177 (6).
[88] *Cf.* § 12-02.

If charges on income paid by a company in an accounting period exceed the profits from which they are deductible, the charges may be treated as a trade expense to the extent that they are payments made wholly and exclusively for the purposes of a trade carried on by the company, thereby creating a loss which is available to be carried forward.[90]

14-26 (ii) *Set-off against the profits (including chargeable gains) of current or past accounting periods.* Where a company incurs a trading loss in an accounting period, it may claim to set the loss off against profits [91] (of whatever description) of that accounting period and, if necessary, against the profits of preceding accounting periods in which the trade was carried on; but this is subject to the limitation that a loss cannot be carried back for a period longer than the duration of the accounting period in which the loss is incurred.[92] Thus if a company suffers a trading loss in an accounting period of 12 months, the company may claim to carry the loss backwards and set it off against the profits of the preceding 12 months, even if this includes more than one accounting period. If the company incurs a trading loss in an accounting period of nine months and the preceding accounting period was of 12 months, the loss may be set off against nine/twelfths of those profits and any excess carried forward under the provisions discussed above. No loss relief is available under this provision unless, in the accounting period in which the loss was incurred, either (i) the trade was being carried on on a commercial basis and with a view to the realisation of gain in the trade or in any larger undertaking of which the trade formed part; or (ii) the trade is one carried on in the exercise of functions conferred by or under any enactment (including an enactment contained in a local or private Act).[93] As regards (i), the fact that a trade was being carried on at any time so as to afford a reasonable expectation of gain is conclusive evidence that it was then being carried on with a view to the realisation of gain; and where in an accounting period there is a change in the manner in which the trade is being carried on, it will for those purposes be treated as having throughout the accounting period been carried on in the way in which it was being carried on by the end of that period.[94] Losses attributable to capital allowances can be carried back three years.[95]

14-27 (iii) *Relief for terminal losses.* The relief which is given to a trading company liable to corporation tax in respect of terminal trade losses is substantially the same as that given by section 174 of the Income and Corporation Taxes Act 1970.[96] Thus a company can claim to set off a loss incurred in the last 12 months of its life against trading income from the trade (not chargeable gains) of the preceding three years.

14-28 *Case VI losses.* If a company suffers a Case VI loss in respect of which it is chargeable to corporation tax, the company may claim to set the loss off

[90] I.C.T.A. 1970, s. 177 (8).
[91] Profits includes chargeable gains: *ibid.* s. 238 (4) (*a*) applied to s. 177 by s. 527 (2).
[92] *Ibid.* s. 177 (2), (3).   [93] *Ibid.* s. 177 (4).
[94] *Ibid.* s. 177 (5).   [95] *Ibid.* s. 177 (3A).
[96] *Ibid.* s. 178. For s. 174, see § 12-12.

against any other Case VI income liable to corporation tax in the same or any subsequent accounting period.[97] This relief does not apply to a loss incurred in a transaction falling within section 80, 81 or 82 of the Act (premiums, leases at undervalue, etc.).[98]

Company reconstructions

14-29   Where a company (called " the predecessor ") ceases to carry on a trade and another company (called " the successor ") begins to carry it on, the trade is treated as continuing in the same ownership if on or at any time within two years after the change the trade or an interest amounting to not less than a three-fourths share in it belongs to the same persons as the trade or such an interest belonged to at some time within a year before the change.[99] A trade carried on by a company may be treated as belonging to the persons owning the ordinary share capital (as defined) in proportion to their shareholdings.[1] Where this provision applies, the position with respect to capital allowances, balancing charges and losses is broadly the same as if no change had occurred: thus the losses of the predecessor may be carried forward and offset against the trading income of the successor as if the predecessor had continued trading.[2] The predecessor is not entitled to terminal loss relief except in certain circumstances where the successor ceases to trade within four years of the succession.[3]

> Thus if A Limited has accumulated tax losses available to be carried forward under section 177 of the Act (see § 14-25), and the trade of A Limited is transferred to B Limited, B Limited will be entitled to carry forward the losses (if the 75 per cent. " common ownership test " is satisfied) and set them off against profits of the transferred trade but not against profits of the original trade of B Limited.

There are provisions to meet the case where only the *activities* of the predecessor's trade (or part of it) are transferred and not the trade itself.[4]

14-30   The provisions just mentioned were widely used for purposes of avoiding tax and elaborate anti-avoidance provisions will be found in section 483 of the Income and Corporation Taxes Act 1970. Briefly, if in any period of three years there is both a change in the ownership of a company and a " major change in the nature or conduct of a trade," past losses will not be available for carry forward. A number of schemes to pass on losses to a purchaser have failed.[5]

Group relief

14-31   The Finance Act 1967 introduced a new form of relief called " group relief " by which a member of a group of companies (called " the surrendering company ") can surrender its claim to relief for capital

---

[97] I.C.T.A. 1970, s. 179 (1).
[98] *Ibid.* s. 179 (2).
[99] *Ibid.* s. 252 (1); and see s. 252 (6) where there are a series of transfers.
[1] *Ibid.* s. 253.   [2] *Ibid.* s. 252 (3).
[3] *Ibid.* s. 252 (3), (5).   [4] *Ibid.* s. 252 (7).
[5] See *e.g. Pritchard* v. *H. M. Builders (Wilmslow) Ltd.* (1969) 45 T.C. 360 and *Ayerst* v. *C. & K. (Construction) Ltd.* [1976] A.C. 167; [1975] S.T.C. 345 (H.L.) where it was held that a company was divested of the beneficial ownership of its assets upon a resolution or order for winding up.

allowances, charges on income and management expenses of an investment company to another company which is a member of the same group (called " the claimant company ").[6] Two companies are deemed to be members of a group if one is a 75 per cent. subsidiary [7] of the other or both are 75 per cent. subsidiaries of a third company. Group relief is also available in certain other cases, *e.g.* where the surrendering company is a trading company which is owned by a consortium and which is not a 75 per cent. subsidiary of any company where the claimant company is a member of the consortium.[8] There are statutory provisions designed to prevent the formation of " artificial " groups in order to secure group relief.[9]

14-32   *Trading losses.* If in an accounting period ending after July 21, 1967, a company incurs a loss in carrying on a trade, the amount of the loss may be surrendered by that company and claimed by another company in the same group, whether a trading company or not. The loss may then be set off against the total profits of the claimant company in the corresponding accounting period (as defined).[10] Profits means income and chargeable gains.[11] Where a claim for group relief is made by a company which is a member of a consortium, only a fraction of the amount of the loss may be set off corresponding to a member's share in the consortium (as defined). There are special provisions where a company joins or leaves a group or consortium.

The right to group relief is not dependent on the claimant company having made any payment to the surrendering company: it is sufficient that the right to loss relief is surrendered by the one company and claimed by the other. In practice, however, a company in a group which makes a loss in an accounting period may have that loss subsidised by a payment (which in earlier legislation was called a " subvention payment ") from a profit-making company in the same group. The legislation relating to subvention payments no longer applies and the phrase " payment for group relief " is now used. This means [12]

> " a payment made by the claimant company to the surrendering company in pursuance of an agreement between them as respects an amount surrendered by way of group relief, being a payment not exceeding that amount."

The agreements referred to must be legally enforceable and must be either under seal or supported by consideration.[13] A payment for group relief is not taken into account in computing profits or losses of either company for corporation tax purposes and is not for any of the purposes of the Corporation Tax Acts regarded as a distribution or a charge on income.

---

[6] See now I.C.T.A. 1970, ss. 258–264.
[7] A body corporate is a 75 per cent. subsidiary of another body corporate if and so long as not less than 75 per cent. of its ordinary share capital is owned directly or indirectly by that other body corporate. Ownership means beneficial ownership and ordinary share capital means all the issued share capital other than capital with a right to a dividend at a fixed rate (or at a rate fluctuating with the standard rate of income tax) and with no other right to share in profits: *ibid.* ss. 258 (5), 526 (5), 532.
[8] See *ibid.* s. 258 (2) and the definitions in s. 258 (8).
[9] See F.A. 1973, ss. 28–29 and [1973] S.T.I. 451 for the Revenue's view of the effect of these provisions.
[10] I.C.T.A. 1970, ss. 259 (1), 261.
[11] *Ibid.* s. 238 (4) (*a*).   [12] I.C.T.A. 1970, s. 258 (4).
[13] *Montague L. Meyer Ltd. and Canusa Ltd.* v. *Naylor* (1961) 39 T.C. 577: *Haddock* v. *Wilmot Breeden Ltd.* (1975) 50 T.C. 132; [1975] S.T.C. 255 (H.L.).   P -9

14-33–   *Other cases.* Group relief is available also in respect of capital allowances,
14-39   management expenses of an investment company and charges on income.[14]

B. THE TAX TREATMENT OF DISTRIBUTIONS

The meaning of distribution

14-40   The term " distribution " is defined in sections 233 to 237 of the Income
and Corporation Taxes Act 1970, as amended by section 106 of and
Schedule 22 to the Finance Act 1972. The definition embraces not only
dividends but also distributions out of assets of a company representing
funds which could have been applied in the payment of dividends.
Distributions in respect of share capital in a winding up are excluded.[15]

14-41   *Qualifying and non-qualifying distributions.*[16] The imputation system,
unlike the earlier system, makes a distinction between qualifying and non-
qualifying distributions. Qualifying distributions are dividends and other
distributions which are similar to dividends. Non-qualifying distributions,
such as issues of bonus debentures or bonus redeemable shares, are
distributions which give the recipient a potential claim on the profits of the
company at a future date. Qualifying distributions require an advance
payment of corporation tax by the company and confer a tax credit on the
recipient.[17] Non-qualifying distributions require no advance payment of
corporation tax and confer no tax credit on the recipient.

Companies are required to make returns of, and provide information
about, non-qualifying distributions.[18] The statutory provisions defining the
term distribution cannot easily be summarised. The following are mere
guide-lines:

14-42   1. Any dividend paid by a company, including a capital dividend, is a
distribution.

14-43   2. The term also includes any other distribution out of assets of a
company (whether in cash or otherwise) in respect of shares in the company,
except so much of the distribution (if any) as represents a repayment of
capital on the shares or is, when it is made, equal in amount or value to any
new consideration received by the company for the distribution.[19] Thus if
sums are returned to shareholders by way of reduction of capital which are
shown to represent no more than the amount subscribed, this is not a
distribution. There is a distribution if sums in excess of the amount
subscribed are returned.[20] Where companies form a 90 per cent. group (as
defined), a distribution by one company in respect of shares in another
company in the group may be caught.[21]

---

[14] The next paragraph is § 14-40.
[15] I.C.T.A. 1970, s. 233 (1). It is not clear what the position is where distributions are made in the course
of the dissolution of a company *without* winding up, pursuant to the Companies Act 1948, s. 208 (1) (*d*).
[16] F.A. 1972, s. 84 (4).   [17] F.A. 1972, s. 86; *post*, § 14-54.
[18] F.A. 1972, ss. 105, 108 (1).
[19] I.C.T.A. 1970, s. 233 (2) (*b*). " New consideration " is defined in s. 237 (1).
[20] Note that in the cases of *Hague* and *Horrocks* (*post*, § 40-02, note 6), the sums returned did not
exceed the amount of the subscribed capital.
[21] F.A. 1972, s. 106 and Sched. 22, para. 10.

14-44   3. *Repayment of share capital with or followed by bonus issue.* If share capital is repaid (after April 6, 1965) and at or after the time of repayment the company issues bonus shares (whether redeemable or not), the amount capitalised in the bonus issue is treated as a distribution in respect of the bonus shares, except in so far as that amount exceeds the share capital repaid.[22]

> Assume a company has a share capital of £50,000 in £1 ordinary shares (all subscribed in cash) and a revenue reserve of £80,000. Assume the company reduces its share capital to £25,000 by repaying 50p on each £1 share. This would not of itself constitute a distribution. But if the company issues 50,000 new bonus shares of 50p each and applies £25,000 out of its revenue reserve to pay for them, the overall effect of the transaction is the same as if the original share capital had remained intact and £25,000 had been distributed by way of dividend. Hence the amount paid up on the bonus shares (£25,000) is treated as distributed. If the amount paid up on the bonus shares exceeded £25,000, only £25,000 would be treated as distributed.

A bonus issue does not give rise to a distribution under this provision if—

    (a) The share capital repaid consists of fully paid preference shares (defined so as to include only normal fixed interest stock)[23]; or

    (b) The bonus issue (on or after April 6, 1973) is of share capital other than redeemable share capital and takes place more than 10 years after the repayment; but this exception does not apply in relation to a company within paragraph D of section 461 of the Income and Corporation Taxes Act 1970.[24] This paragraph embraces closely controlled companies and, in their case, any repayment of non-preference share capital after April 6, 1965, will cause a subsequent bonus issue to be treated as a distribution.[25]

14-45   4. *Bonus issue followed by repayment of share capital.* Where a company (after April 6, 1965) makes a bonus issue which does not rank as a qualifying distribution and subsequently repays the bonus shares, the amount so repaid is treated as a distribution.[26] There is an exception similar to the exception in paragraph 3 (b), above, where the repayment is made more than 10 years after the bonus issue, which, again, does not apply to companies within paragraph D of section 461 of the 1970 Act.[27]

14-46   5. *Bonus shares.* An issue of bonus ordinary shares involves no distribution. But if any bonus redeemable share capital or any security is issued by a company in respect of shares in the company or (after April 5, 1972) in respect of securities of the company, this is treated as a distribution[28] and as a non-qualifying distribution.[29] If a shareholder is

---

[22] I.C.T.A. 1970, s. 234 (1).
[23] *Ibid.* s. 234 (2) (*a*) and (3).
[24] F.A. 1972, Sched. 22, para. 5. For s. 461, see *post*, §§ 40-02 *et seq.*
[25] *Cf. I.R.C.* v. *Horrocks* (1968) 44 T.C. 645.
[26] I.C.T.A. 1970, s. 235.
[27] F.A. 1972, Sched. 22, para. 6. For s. 461, see *post*, §§ 40-02 *et seq. Cf. Hague* v. *I.R.C.* (1968) 44 T.C. 619 (C.A.).
[28] I.C.T.A. 1970, s. 233 (2) (*c*) substituted by F.A. 1972, Sched. 22, para. 2.
[29] *Ante*, § 14-41.

given the option of taking either cash or bonus shares and elects to take the shares he is liable to tax, at the higher rates, on the basis of the equivalent cash dividend grossed up at the basic rate.[30]

14-47   6. *Interest and other distributions in respect of securities.* Interest and other distributions out of assets of a company in respect of the company's securities are treated as distributions where the securities fall into one of a number of specified categories.[31] Interest on bonus redeemable shares or securities within paragraph 5, above, is treated as a distribution. Interest on securities which are convertible directly or indirectly into shares in the company, or securities issued after April 5, 1972, which carry a right to receive shares in or securities of the company, is treated as a distribution, subject to an exception for certain quoted securities. Where the amount of interest is to any extent dependent on the results of the company's business or any part of it, or represents more than a reasonable commercial return for the use of the principal, the interest is treated as a distribution,[32] except that in the latter case only the excess over a reasonable commercial return is so treated. Where companies form a 90 per cent. group (as defined), a distribution by one company in respect of securities in another company in the group may be caught.[33]

14-48   7. *Transfers of assets etc., to or by members.* Where on a transfer of assets or liabilities by a company to its members or to a company by its members the amount or value of the benefit received by the member (taken at its market value) exceeds the amount or value of any new consideration given by him, the company is treated as making the distribution to him of an amount equal to the difference.[34] Thus if a company sells an asset to a member at an undervalue or a member sells an asset to the company at an overvalue, the company is treated as making a distribution. There is an exception to this rule in the case of inter-group company transactions.

14-49   8. *Reciprocal arrangements.* Where two or more companies enter into arrangements to make distributions to each other's members, all parties concerned can be treated as if anything done by either of those companies had been done by the other; and this applies however many companies participate in the arrangements.[35]

Advance corporation tax

14-50   Where a company resident in the United Kingdom makes a qualifying distribution (§ 14-41) after April 5, 1973, it is liable to pay an amount of corporation tax to the Revenue, called " advance corporation tax."[36]

---

[30] F. (No. 2) A. 1975, s. 34 and Sched. 8; this provision also applies where a class of shares gives a *right* to receive bonus shares; and where the shares are not issued by reference to an alternative cash dividend the charge is on the (grossed up) market value of the bonus shares issued.
[31] See I.C.T.A. 1970, s. 233 (2) (*d*).
[32] I.C.T.A. 1970, s. 233 (2) (*d*) (iii) and F.A. 1972, Sched. 22, paras. 3 (2) and (3).
[33] F.A. 1972, s. 106 and Sched. 22, para. 10.
[34] I.C.T.A. 1970, s. 233 (3).
[35] F.A. 1972, Sched. 22, para. 9.
[36] *Ibid.* s. 84 (1).

Virtually all distributions are qualifying distributions other than issues of bonus redeemable shares and bonus debentures.[37] Advance corporation tax is payable on an amount equal to the amount or value of the distribution and is payable at a rate, called " the rate of advance corporation tax," which for the period beginning April 6, 1973, and ending with March 31, 1974, was 3/7ths.[38] Thereafter the rate of advance corporation tax is such fraction as Parliament may from time to time determine.[39] The rate of advance corporation tax for the financial years 1975 and 1976 is 35/65ths.[40] The rate for the financial year 1977 is 34/66ths.[41] The rate for the financial year 1978 is 33/67ths.[42] A distribution attracts the rate of advance corporation tax in force for the financial year in which the distribution is made.[43] The expression " franked payment " is used to describe the sum of the amount or value of the qualifying distribution and the amount of the advance corporation tax attracted to it.[43]

> Thus if a company makes a distribution of £6,700 during the financial year 1978, it is required to make a payment of advance corporation tax to the Revenue of £3,300. The company is said to have made a franked payment of £10,000.

The main due dates for the payment of advance corporation tax are 14 days after the end of the quarterly " return periods " (*i.e.* the quarters ended March 31, June 30, September 30 and December 31).

Set-off of advance corporation tax against corporation tax

14-51   We have seen how the liability of a company to corporation tax is computed by reference to accounting periods.[44] Advance corporation tax paid by a company (and not repaid[45]) in respect of any distribution made by it in an accounting period can be set against its liability to corporation tax " on any income charged to corporation tax for that accounting period."[46] Liability to corporation tax is to that extent discharged.[47] The phrase in quotation marks is defined as meaning the amount of the company's profits for the period on which corporation tax falls finally to be borne exclusive of the part of the profits attributable to chargeable gains.[48] Hence advance corporation tax cannot be credited against that part of the company's profits which is attributable to chargeable gains, the reason being that (under the new system) chargeable gains attract a lower rate of corporation tax than other profits.[49] The amount of the chargeable gains to be excluded is the amount before any deduction for charges on income, expenses of management or other amounts which can be deducted from or set against or treated as reducing profits of more than one description.[50] There is therefore an order of set-off for those reliefs which take effect

---

[37] F.A. 1972, s. 84 (4); *ante*, § 14-41.
[38] *Ibid.* s. 84 (2). This is subject to *ibid.* s. 89: *post*, § 14-65. The period from April 6, 1973, to March 31, 1974, is taken as a " financial year " (*ante*, § 14-04): *ibid.* s. 110 (5).
[39] *Ibid.* s. 84 (2). See also s. 103.
[40] F. (No. 2) A. 1975, s. 28; F.A. 1976, s. 26.
[41] F.A. 1977, s. 19.
[42] F.A. 1978, s. 16.
[43] F.A. 1972, s. 84 (3).
[44] *Ante*, § 14-05.
[45] *Post*, § 14-55.
[46] F.A. 1972, s. 85 (1) and (7).
[47] *Ibid.* s. 85 (1).
[48] *Ibid.* s. 85 (6). And see s. 110 (4).
[49] See *post*, § 16-53.
[50] *Ibid.* s. 85 (6).

against total profits, the rule being that such reliefs must be set off first against income other than chargeable gains. Generally, advance corporation tax paid by a company cannot be set off against its liability to corporation tax on profits attributable to development land tax (see § 16-161) or development gains (F.A. 1974, Sched. 7, paras. 3–4).

14-52   " *Excessive distribution.*" There is an important restriction on the extent to which a payment of advance corporation tax can be set against corporation tax liability. If in an accounting period a company makes distributions which are in excess of or disproportionate to the profits of that period, *e.g.* out of profits of an earlier period or because its commercial profits have been reduced for tax purposes by capital allowances, it would be wrong to allow the whole of the payment of advance corporation tax to be used to eliminate the company's corporation tax liability for that period. Hence it is provided that the amount of advance corporation tax to be set against a company's liability for any accounting period shall not exceed the amount of advance corporation tax that would have been payable in respect of a distribution made at the end of that period of an amount which, together with the advance corporation tax so payable in respect of it, is equal to the company's income charged to corporation tax for that period.[51]

> Assume that a company has profits (not chargeable gains) of £40,000 in an accounting period. Its corporation tax liability for the period is £20,800 (rate 52 per cent.). In the period it pays dividends of £66,000 involving a payment of advance corporation tax of £34,000 (assuming an ACT rate of 34/66ths). This £34,000 cannot be set against the £20,800, reducing the corporation tax liability to nil. The limit of set-off is £13,600 because that would have been the amount of the advance corporation tax on a franked payment equal to the company's income for the period. (A distribution of £26,400 would have attracted advance corporation tax of £13,600 giving a total of £40,000.)

Hence in the example the company's corporation tax liability of £20,800 can be reduced by £13,600. The surplus advance corporation tax paid for the accounting period (£34,000 less £13,600 = £20,400) can be carried back to the two preceding accounting periods (against the company's liability for the more recent accounting period before the remote one) and any surplus still remaining may be carried forward to the next accounting period and so on.[52] Other methods of dealing with surplus advance corporation tax are considered later.[53]

14-53   A company must make a claim to set advance corporation tax against its liability to corporation tax for any accounting period but a claim is treated as made when the company makes a return under section 11 of the Taxes Management Act 1970.[54]

As to the set-off of advance corporation tax by subsidiary companies, see § 14-75.

Tax credits and their utilisation

14-54   The distinction between qualifying and non-qualifying distributions was noted *ante*, § 14-41. Where a company resident in the United Kingdom

---

[51] F.A. 1972, s. 85 (2).   [52] *Ibid.* s. 85 (3) and (4).
[53] *Post*, § 14-68.   [54] *Ibid.* s. 85 (5).

makes a qualifying distribution after April 5, 1973, and the person receiving the distribution is another company resident in the United Kingdom or a person resident in the United Kingdom, not being a company, the recipient of the distribution is entitled to a " tax credit " equal to the advance corporation tax attributable to the distribution.[55] Distributions by non-United Kingdom resident companies attract no tax credit. Distributions to non-United Kingdom resident members attract no tax credit but there is an exception in the case of a qualifying distribution to a non-United Kingdom resident member who claims personal allowances under section 27 of the Income and Corporation Taxes Act 1970.[56] Such a member is brought within the charge to basic rate income tax, and is entitled to a tax credit and is chargeable on the aggregate of the distribution and the tax credit in the same way as a United Kingdom resident member.[56]

14-55   Where a United Kingdom resident company is entitled to a tax credit it may claim to have the amount of the credit paid to it [57] if—

(a) the company is wholly exempt from corporation tax or is only not exempt in respect of trading income (in which case distributions would be exempt); or

(b) the distribution is one in relation to which express exemption is given (other than the exemption from corporation tax for dividends and other distributions).

Hence an incorporated charity can " cash " its tax credit. Where there is no such right to " cash " the tax credit, it can be set against the recipient company's liability to advance corporation tax on its distributions: see § 14-63.

14-56   A person (other than a United Kingdom resident company) who is entitled to a tax credit can claim to set the credit against his tax liability for the year of assessment in which the distribution is received.[58] He can set it either against income tax chargeable at the basic rate on annuities and other annual payments etc., or against tax on his total income for the year of assessment; and where the credit exceeds the tax due, he is entitled to claim payment of the excess.[58] This applies not only to United Kingdom resident individuals but also to non-residents entitled to tax credits. The recipient of a distribution who is not liable to income tax at the basic rate can claim payment of any tax credit, subject to an exception to prevent exempt persons holding 10 per cent. or more of any one class of shares or securities recovering tax on distributions earned before he acquired his holding.[59]

14-57   It was said in § 14-54 that the *recipient* of a distribution may be entitled to a tax credit. But where the distribution falls to be treated as the income of some person other than the recipient, that person is treated as the recipient; and, accordingly, the question whether there is any entitlement to a tax credit is determined by reference to his residence and not the residence of

[55] F.A. 1972, s. 85 (1) (2). See *ante*, § 14-01B.
[56] *Ibid.* s. 98. And see § 8-52.
[57] *Ibid.* s. 86 (3). But see s. 89 (5).
[58] *Ibid.* s. 86 (4).
[59] F.A. 1973, s. 21. See also *ibid.* s. 22.

the actual recipient.[60] Thus if non-United Kingdom resident trustees hold a trust fund upon trust for a United Kingdom resident individual, a distribution which forms part of the income of that resident individual will qualify for a tax credit.[60] Where any qualifying distribution is income of a United Kingdom trust (as defined [61]) the trustees are entitled to a tax credit in respect of it if no other person is entitled.[62]

Income tax on distributions: Schedule F

14-58   The meaning of " distribution " and the distinction between qualifying and non-qualifying distributions has already been discussed in §§ 14-40 *et seq.* For the year 1973–74 and subsequent years of assessment, the recipient of a distribution is chargeable to income tax under the substituted Schedule F.[63] Schedule F charges income tax for a year of assessment in respect of all dividends and other distributions in that year of a company resident in the United Kingdom which are not specially excluded from income tax [64]; and for the purposes of income tax all such distributions are regarded as income however they fall to be dealt with in the hands of the recipient.[65] Hence capital dividends which, as between tenant for life and remainderman, fall to be treated as capital are nevertheless treated as income for Schedule F purposes. Schedule F does not apply to dividends and other distributions of companies not resident in the United Kingdom: these are taxed under Case V of Schedule D. No distribution which is chargeable under Schedule F is chargeable under any other provisions of the Income Tax Acts.[66]

14-59   *Position where distribution carries tax credit.* The charge under Schedule F is on the aggregate of the amount or value of the distribution and any tax credit to which the recipient is entitled, and this aggregate is treated as income of the recipient.[67] Hence an individual who receives a dividend of £6,700 must include in his return of total income for income tax purposes, as his income from the company, the sum of £10,000 being the dividend plus the tax credit of £3,300 attracted to it. (This example assumes a rate of advance corporation tax of 33/67ths.) The recipient of a qualifying distribution is entitled, if he so requests, to a statement in writing showing the amount or value of the distribution and (whether or not he is a person entitled to a tax credit in respect of the distribution) the amount of the tax credit to which a recipient who is such a person is entitled.[68]

14-60   *Position where distribution carries no tax credit.* Where the recipient of a distribution (not being a company resident in the United Kingdom) is not entitled to a tax credit in respect of that distribution, *e.g.* because the distribution is a non-qualifying distribution or because the recipient is not

[60] F.A. 1972, s. 86 (5).   [61] *Ibid.* s. 110 (1).
[62] See note 60, *ante.*
[63] *i.e.* the charging provision in I.C.T.A. 1970, s. 232 (1) substituted by F.A. 1972, s. 87 (2).
[64] *Ibid.* s. 87 (1) (2).
[65] *Ibid.* s. 87 (2).
[66] *Ibid.* s. 87 (3). The " old " Schedule F applied to distributions " not charged under any other Schedule."   [67] *Ibid.* s. 87 (2).
[68] I.C.T.A. 1970, s. 232 (4) substituted by F.A. 1972, Sched. 24, para. 18.

resident in the United Kingdom, no assessment to basic rate income tax can be made on that person in respect of the distribution. Higher rate income tax and the investment income surcharge is levied on the amount or value of the distribution, but any higher rate tax payable is reduced by an amount equal to tax at the basic rate on the amount assessed at higher rates.[69]

> Thus if a company issues bonus redeemable shares this is a non-qualifying distribution. Suppose a shareholder receives such shares having a value [70] of £670. No basic rate income tax is leviable on the £670. Any higher rate income tax is levied on £670 and the amount of tax reduced by an amount equal to tax at the basic rate on £670. Investment income surcharge is levied on £670.

14-61   If in this example the company later repays the bonus shares, this repayment (£670) will be a qualifying distribution (*ante*, § 14-41) in respect of which a payment of advance corporation tax (say, £330) will be made by the company. A tax credit (£330) will then be conferred on the recipient. The recipient is entitled if assessed to higher rate income tax or the investment income surcharge in respect of the repayment of the bonus shares, to take credit for tax levied on the previous non-qualifying distribution.[71]

14-62   The amount or value of a distribution which carries no tax credit is treated for the purposes of sections 52 and 53 of the Income and Corporation Taxes Act 1970 as not brought into charge to income tax.[72] The consequences of this are discussed in §§ 5-34 *et seq.*

Franked investment income

14-63   We have seen that a company resident in the United Kingdom which makes a qualifying distribution is liable to pay advance corporation tax to the Revenue equal (for the financial year 1978) to 33/67ths of the amount or value of the distribution: *ante*, § 14-50. But companies with investments in other companies receive as well as make distributions and this is taken into account in quantifying the company's liability for advance corporation tax. Briefly, a company can take credit for tax imputed to it: hence advance corporation tax is payable only to the extent that the company's qualifying distributions exceed distributions received.

14-64   Income of a company resident in the United Kingdom which consists of a distribution in respect of which the company is entitled to a tax credit is called " franked investment income " of the company.[73]

> Hence if in an accounting period company A receives a dividend from company B of £6,700 (both companies being resident in the United Kingdom), this represents franked investment income of £10,000 (assuming the rate of advance corporation tax to be 33/67ths).
> If during the same period company A made a qualifying distribution to its members of £1,340, it would prima facie have to make a payment of advance corporation tax of £660 (33/67ths of £1,340).

---

[69] F.A. 1972, s. 87 (5).   [70] *Ibid.* Sched. 22, para. 2 (2).
[71] *Ibid.* s. 87 (6).   [72] *Ibid.* s. 87 (5).
[73] *Ibid.* s. 88 (1). And see s. 88 (2). Group income is not franked investment income: § 14-72.

14-65   The Act, however, provides that where in any accounting period a company receives franked investment income, it shall not be liable to pay advance corporation tax in respect of qualifying distributions made by it in that period unless the amount of the franked payments made by it in that period exceeds the amount of its franked investment income.[74] In the example in § 14-64 the franked payment made by company A is £1,340 plus £660 = £2,000. Since this is less than the franked investment income received by the company (£10,000), no advance corporation tax is payable in respect of the distribution of £1,340. If (as in the example) the amount of franked investment income received in an accounting period exceeds the amount of the franked payments made in that period, the excess (£8,000 in the example) must be carried forward to the next accounting period and treated as franked investment income received by the company in the next period, and so on.[75] Such an excess is called a " surplus of franked investment income." [76]

14-66   Where franked payments made by a company exceed franked investment income received in the same accounting period, advance corporation tax is payable on an amount which, when the advance corporation tax payable thereon is added to it, is equal to the excess.[77]

> Assume the franked investment income of a company in an accounting period is £3,500. Assume that the franked payments made by the company in the same period are £10,000. There is an excess of £6,500. The figure which, when advance corporation tax is added to it, equals £6,500 is £4,225. Hence the company must account for advance corporation tax on £4,225 = £2,275. (This is the difference between advance corporation tax on distributions of £6,500 (= £3,500) and £2,275 (= £1,225).)

Certain companies exempt from tax, such as incorporated charities, can claim to be paid the amount of a tax credit.[78] There are provisions to prevent such a company using its franked investment income to frank distributions made by it and thus obtain relief (in effect) twice over.[79]

Anti-avoidance provisions

14-66A   It has been explained that a surplus of advance corporation tax may be carried forward and credited against the corporation tax liability in a subsequent accounting period.[80] Section 101 of the Finance Act 1972 contains provisions designed to frustrate the purchase of companies merely for the purpose of obtaining the benefit of surplus advance corporation tax. The provision is similar to section 483 of the Taxes Act 1970, dealing with tax losses.[81]

Accounting for advance corporation tax

14-67   Schedule 14 to the Finance Act 1972 regulates the time and manner in which advance corporation tax is to be accounted for and paid and the

---

[74] F.A. 1972, s. 89 (1).
[76] *Ibid.* s. 89 (6).
[78] *Ibid.* s. 86 (3); *ante*, § 14-55.
[79] *Ibid.* s. 89 (5).
[80] *Ante*, § 14-52.

[75] *Ibid.* s. 89 (3).
[77] *Ibid.* s. 89 (2).

[81] *Ante*, § 14-30.

manner in which effect is to be given to the provisions allowing franked investment income of a company to be used to frank its distributions.[82] Companies are required to make returns on a quarterly basis. The return must show the franked payments made in the " return period " and the franked investment income received or brought forward from a previous period. Advance corporation tax is payable on the excess of franked payments in the period over the amount of franked investment income.

Set-off of losses, etc., against a surplus of franked investment income

14-68 There is a surplus of franked investment income where the amount of the franked income received by a company in an accounting period exceeds the amount of the franked payments made by it in that period.[83] Such an excess, as explained in § 14-65, may be carried forward to and treated as franked investment income of the next and subsequent accounting periods. Section 254 of the Income and Corporation Taxes Act 1970 [84] provides an alternative form of relief by allowing a company in certain circumstances to claim to treat a surplus of franked investment income in an accounting period as if it were a like amount of profits chargeable to corporation tax in that period and to set against the surplus so treated unrelieved trading losses, charges on income, expenses of management and capital allowances. Such deductions must be made first against profits chargeable to corporation tax before resorting to a surplus of franked investment income treated as if it were profits. For the purposes of a claim under section 254, the surplus of franked investment income for an accounting period must be calculated without regard to the part, if any, carried forward from an earlier period. There are various provisions to prevent more than one relief being obtained in respect of the same franked investment income.[85]

14-69 Where a claim is made under section 254 of the 1970 Act, the claimant company receives payment of the amount of the tax credit comprised in the surplus of franked investment income.

14-70 Section 255 of the Income and Corporation Taxes Act 1970 [86] contains similar provisions under which losses brought forward and terminal losses can be set against a surplus of franked investment income.

Groups of companies

14-71 We have seen that a United Kingdom resident company which makes a qualifying distribution to another such company is required to make a payment of advance corporation tax and that the recipient is entitled to a tax credit.[87] There is an important exception to this principle which applies to dividends (but no other distributions) paid from one member of a group of companies to another member of the same group, where an election is in force under section 256 of the Income and Corporation Taxes Act 1970.[88] In that case no liability to advance corporation tax is incurred and the

---

[82] F.A. 1972, ss. 84 (5), 89 (4).
[84] Substituted by F.A. 1972, s. 90 (1) and Sched. 15.
[85] *Ibid.* s. 90 (2) and (3).
[87] *Ante,* § 14-54.
[83] *Ibid.* s. 89 (6); *ante,* § 14-65.
[86] See note 84, *ante.*
[88] Substituted by F.A. 1972, s. 91 (1) and Sched. 15.

recipient is entitled to no tax credit. Section 256 applies only where both companies are bodies corporate resident in the United Kingdom and where the company paying the dividends is—

(a) a 51 per cent. subsidiary of the other or of a company so resident of which the other is a 51 per cent. subsidiary; or

(b) a trading or holding company owned by a consortium the members of which include the company receiving the dividends.

14-72   Dividends so treated are referred to as " group income " and are not franked investment income of the recipient company.[89]

14-73   The provisions by which dividends may be treated as group income apply also to payments which are corporation tax charges on income of the company making them: thus interest, annuities and other annual payments can be paid by a subsidiary company to its parent company in full, without deduction of basic rate income tax, where the appropriate election is in force.[90]

14-74   Dividends and other payments received by a company on investments cannot be treated as group income if a profit on a sale of those investments would be treated as a trading receipt of the company.[91] Hence dividends on shares forming part of the trading stock of a company dealing in shares cannot be treated as group income. There are provisions for the recovery of tax in respect of dividends and other payments which were wrongly treated as group income.[92] The Board of Inland Revenue has power to make regulations governing the manner in which claims for group treatment are to be made.[93]

Setting off companies' advance corporation tax against subsidiaries' liability

14-75   It has been explained that advance corporation tax paid by a company is deducted from the corporation tax payable on its income.[94] In a group of companies, it might happen that one member of the group has a liability for advance corporation tax but no corporation tax profits, whereas another member of the same group has profits but no liability to advance corporation tax. Section 92 of the Finance Act 1972 (as amended [95]) enables a United Kingdom resident company to surrender advance corporation tax for the benefit of its resident subsidiaries. The subsidiaries must be 51 per cent. subsidiaries (as defined); and the relief only applies to advance corporation tax paid in respect of dividends (not other distributions). Thus if a company makes a bonus issue of ordinary shares which it then repays by way of reduction of capital, this is a qualifying distribution of the amount repaid (see § 14-41 and § 14-43) but the advance corporation tax cannot be surrendered to group subsidiaries under section 92.

---

[89] F.A. 1972, s. 88 (1) and I.C.T.A. 1970, s. 256 (1).
[90] I.C.T.A. 1970, s. 256 (2). For the method of electing, see *ibid*. s. 257.   [91] *Ibid*. s. 256 (2).
[92] F.A. 1972, s. 91 (2).   [93] *Ibid*. s. 91 (3).
[94] *Ibid*. s. 85 (1); *ante*, § 14-51.   [95] F.A. 1973, s. 32 and Sched. 13.

CHAPTER 15

CLOSE COMPANIES

15-01 THE profits of a company, when distributed by way of dividend, form part of the total income of each member. A member liable to income tax at the basic rate will incur no income tax liability on dividend income because, as explained in § 14-01, dividends confer a tax credit equal to tax at the basic rate. The member is treated as having " suffered " income tax at the basic rate by virtue of the company's liability to account for advance corporation tax. Members whose tax liability is not limited to tax at the basic rate will be liable to higher rate income tax on dividend income and, since dividends are not earned income, to the investment income surcharge. Hence it is often in the interests of wealthy shareholders that the company in which they hold shares should not distribute profits but should accumulate them, paying only corporation tax at the general rate or the small companies rate, as appropriate. There is an especially strong inducement to do this where the shareholders are able to extract sufficient for their needs from the company by way of remuneration. For many years statutory provisions have existed to counteract the avoidance of surtax by the retention of profits, where this retention could not be justified by reference to the needs of the company's business; and, under the new unified system, this legislation has been modified to counteract (i) the avoidance of higher rate income tax and the investment income surcharge and (ii) any corporation tax advantage that might otherwise have flowed from failure to pay dividends. The applicable legislation has effect only on companies which are sufficiently closely controlled to enable the shareholders to manipulate the company's affairs to avoid tax in the manner indicated; and such companies are called " close companies." In this chapter the special legislation applicable to such companies is considered.

1. DEFINITIONS

There are a number of general definitions which apply for the purposes of the statutory provisions relating to close companies.

Participator [1]

15-02 A participator is, in relation to any company, a person having a share or interest in the capital or income of the company. Thus in the case of a company with a share capital, it includes every shareholder; and in a company with no share capital, it includes every member. Without prejudice to the generality of these words, " participator " includes:

    (a) any person who possesses, or is entitled to acquire, share capital or voting rights in the company;

    (b) any loan creditor of the company (see § 15-03);

---

[1] I.C.T.A. 1970, s. 303 (1). For the position of debenture holders, see § 15-03A.

(c) any person who possesses, or is entitled to acquire, a right to receive or participate in distributions [2] of the company or any amounts payable by the company (in cash or in kind) to loan creditors by way of premium on redemption; and

(d) any person who is entitled to secure that income or assets (whether present or future) of the company will be applied directly or indirectly for his benefit.

References in (a), (c) and (d) to being entitled to do anything apply where a person is presently entitled to do it at a future date, or will at a future date be entitled to do it. [3] Thus a person who has an option (or right to acquire an option) entitling him to acquire shares at a future date is a " participator " within (a).

There are a number of provisions in the Act which enable a " participator " in one company to be treated as being also a " participator " in another. [3]

Loan creditor

15-03   This definition has to be read in conjunction with paragraph (b) in § 15-02.

Loan creditor, in relation to a company, means a creditor in respect of any debt incurred by the company:

(a) for any money borrowed or capital assets acquired by the company, or

(b) for any right to receive income created in favour of the company, or

(c) for consideration the value of which to the company was (at the time when the debt was incurred) substantially less than the amount of the debt (including any premium thereon),

or in respect of any redeemable loan capital issued by the company. [4]

A person carrying on a business of banking is not deemed to be a loan creditor in respect of any loan capital or debt issued or incurred by the company for money lent by him to the company in the ordinary course of that business. [4]

Note that the term " loan creditor " does not apply only to a person who lends money to a company. It also applies to a person who sells assets or an annuity to a company, leaving the purchase price owing.

A person who is not the creditor in respect of any debt or loan capital to which the provisions summarised in § 15-03 applies, but nevertheless has a beneficial interest therein (*e.g.* under a trust) is, to the extent of that interest, to be treated as a loan creditor in respect of that debt or loan capital. [5]

15-03A   A debenture holder is a participator as being a " loan creditor " unless he is excepted as being a bank lending in the ordinary course of banking

---

[2] " Distributions " is here to be construed without regard to the extended meaning in I.C.T.A. 1970, ss. 284 and 285 (see §§ 15-21 *et seq.*); *ibid.* s. 303 (1) (*c*). For the meaning of " distribution," see §§ 14-40 *et seq.*

[3] *Ibid.* s. 303 (2). See for examples *ibid.* s. 284 (7) in § 15-21; s. 286 (9) and s. 282 (2) in § 15-25.

[4] *Ibid.* s. 303 (7).   [5] *Ibid.* s. 303 (8).

business. Such a bank is not a participator within the definition in paragraph (a) of § 15-02 (unless he is entitled to voting rights *e.g.* because his security is in jeopardy), because a debenture gives an interest in the *assets* of a company, not an interest in its *share capital.* [6] A debenture holder who is entitled to interest which is to any extent dependent on the results of the company's business or represents more than a reasonable commercial return for the use of the principal (*i.e.* who is entitled to participate in " distributions ": see § 14-47) is a participator within the definition in paragraph (c) in § 15-02.

Associate

15-04   This definition is important because, generally, the rights of " associates " of participators can be attributed to the participators [7] (see § 15-09). An " associate " means, [8] in relation to a participator:

(a) any relative (see § 15-05) or partner of the participator;
(b) the trustee or trustees of any settlement in relation to which the participator is, or any relative of his (living or dead) is or was, a settlor (" settlement " and " settlor " having here the same meanings as in section 454 (3) of the Income and Corporation Taxes Act 1970) see §§ 10-07 *et seq.*; and
(c) where the participator is interested (whether beneficially or as trustee [9]) in any shares or obligations of the company which are subject to any trust, or are part of the estate of a deceased person, any other person interested therein. [10]

The term " associate " has a corresponding meaning in relation to a person other than a participator. [11] In *Willingale* v. *Islington Green Investment·Co.,* [12] executors holding shares in a company *qua* executors were held to be associates of a director who held shares in the same company.

Relative and partner

15-05   " Relative " in paragraph (a) of § 15-04 means husband or wife, parent or remoter forebear, child or remoter issue, or brother or sister. [13] Note that this definition does not include " in-laws."

There is no definition of the word " partner " for the purposes of paragraph (a) of § 15-04. General principles of law have to be applied: see § 11-01. Note that although a shareholder's partner can be treated as his associate, and so also a shareholder's relative, a relative of the shareholder's partner cannot be treated as the shareholder's associate.

---

[6] *I.R.C.* v. *R. Woolf & Co. Ltd.* (1961) 39 T.C. 611.
[7] I.C.T.A. 1970, s. 302 (6).
[8] *Ibid.* s. 303 (3).
[9] *Willingale* v. *Islington Green Investment Co.* (1972) 48 T.C. 547 (C.A.).
[10] Beneficiaries under some types of trust are not " associates " under (c). See I.C.T.A. 1970, s. 303 (3) proviso. A legatee in an unadministered estate may not be a person interested within (c): see the case in note 12, *post.* It appears from the proviso to s. 303 (3) that objects of a discretionary trust are persons " interested " within para. (c).
[11] *Ibid.* s. 303 (3). Thus " associate " has the same meaning in relation for example to a director: see s. 303 (5) (c) in § 15-06.
[12] (1972) 48 T.C. 547 (C.A.).
[13] I.C.T.A. 1970, s. 303 (4).

Director

15-06   The word " director " is widely defined [14] so as to include any person occupying the position of director by whatever name called, any person in accordance with whose directions or instructions the directors are accustomed to act, and any person who:

     (a) is a manager of the company or otherwise concerned in the management of the company's trade or business; and

     (b) is, either on his own or with one or more associates (see § 15-04), the beneficial owner of, or able, directly or through the medium of other companies or by any other indirect means, to control 20 per cent. or over of the ordinary share capital of the company.

A person is for this purpose to be treated as owning or, as the case may be, controlling what any associate owns or controls, even if he does not own or control share capital of his own. [15]

> Thus if X has no shares in Y Ltd., but X's relatives or other associates together directly or indirectly control 20 per cent. or more of the ordinary share capital of Y Ltd., X is for the purposes of the close company provisions treated as a director of Y Ltd. if he is concerned in its management although not a member of the Board of Directors.

2. What is a Close Company

15-07   There are two main tests for determining what is a close company. These may be called the " control " test (§§ 15-08 *et seq.*) and the " apportionment " test (§§ 15-12 *et seq.*). There are also a number of cases in which companies which would otherwise be treated as close companies as satisfying one or other of these tests are excepted and so made " non-close " or " open " companies (§§ 15-14 *et seq.*).

1. *The control test*

15-08   Section 282 (1) of the Income and Corporation Taxes Act 1970 provides that a close company is one which is under the control of (i) five or fewer participators or (ii) of participators (however many) who are directors. The terms " participator " is defined in § 15-02 and " director " in § 15-06.

If there is any group of five or fewer participators who together have " control " in any sense in which that term is defined (see § 15-10), the company is a close company. The following examples illustrate the principle:

> *Example 1*: A Ltd. has an issued capital of £90 in £1 shares, all carrying equal voting rights. There are nine members with 10 shares each; no member is an " associate " of any other: see § 15-04. Any group of five members would have 50 shares between them, *i.e.* voting control. A Ltd. is therefore a " close " company.

> *Example 2*: B Ltd. has an issued capital of £90 in £1 shares, all carrying equal voting rights. There are 18 members with five shares each, all disassociated as in Example 1. No group of five members would have more than 25 shares. B Ltd. is therefore an " open " company.

---

[14] I.C.T.A. 1970, s. 303 (5).   [15] *Ibid.* s. 303 (7).

If in Example 2 the shares had unequal voting rights and it was possible to find any group of five or fewer participators who between them had voting control, the company would be a close company.

Attributions

15-09   It is assumed in Example 2 that the 18 members (*i.e.* participators: § 15-02) are " disassociated," *i.e.* that no one is the " associate " of any other in the sense in which the term " associate " is defined in § 15-04. Section 302 (5), however, provides that in applying the control test (see § 15-10) there shall be attributed to any person any rights or powers of a nominee for him, that is to say, any rights or powers which another person possesses on his behalf or may be required to exercise on his direction or behalf. Section 302 (6) provides that in applying the control test there may also be attributed to any person all the rights and powers of any company of which he has, or he and associates of his have, control or any two or more such companies, or of any associate of his or of any two or more associates of his, including those attributed to a company or associate under section 302 (5), but not those attributed to an associate under section 302 (6); and that such attributions shall be made as will result in the company being treated as under the control of five or fewer participators if it can be so treated.

> Thus if, in Example 2, six of the shareholders with five shares each are relatives, they can (in effect) be treated as one participator with 30 shares. Any four others would have 20 shares between them. Hence there would be a group of five or fewer participators with 50 shares between them and, therefore, with voting control. B Ltd. would thus be a close company by virtue of the attributions made under section 302 (6).

These provisions prevent a person with control of a close company making the company " open " by off-loading shares to relatives or (generally) by settling them otherwise than in connection with certain approved superannuation funds and retirement schemes and on certain employee-trusts set out in a proviso to section 303 (3) of the Taxes Act 1970.

The meaning of control

15-10   In the Examples in §§ 15-08 and 15-09, it has been assumed that " control " means voting control; but the statute treats as having control not only a person (or group of persons) who have the lion's share of the votes; it also brings in a person (or group of persons) who together have the lion's share of the income or would, in the event of a liquidation, have the lion's share of the assets available for distribution. More precisely, section 302 (2) provides that a person shall be taken to have control of a company if he (including any rights, etc. attributed to him under the provisions in § 15-09) exercises, or is able to exercise or is entitled to acquire (see § 15-11), control, whether direct or indirect, over the company's affairs, and in particular, but without prejudice to the generality of the preceding words, if he possesses or is entitled to acquire:

(a) the greater part of the share capital or issued share capital of the company or of the voting power in the company; or

(b) such part of the issued share capital of the company as would, if the whole of the income of the company were in fact distributed among the participators (without regard to any rights which he or any other person has as a loan creditor), entitle him to receive the greater part of the amount so distributed; or

(c) such rights as would, in the event of the winding up of the company or in any other circumstances, entitle him to receive the greater part of the assets of the company which would then be available for distribution among the participators.

15-11   Section 302 (3) provides that where two or more persons together satisfy any of the conditions of section 302 (2), they shall be taken to have control of the company. Example 1 in § 15-08 is a case in point. Section 302 (4) provides that a person shall be treated as entitled to acquire something which he is entitled to acquire at a future date, or *will* at a future date be entitled to acquire (but not if he only *may* be so entitled).

> Thus, if C Ltd. has 11 shareholders, all disassociated and with shares carrying equal voting rights, C Ltd. is an open company if no group of five has voting control or any other rights which confer control. But if D (an individual) has an option to acquire sufficient shares to confer " control," the company can be treated as controlled by D.

The definition of " control " is such that more than one person or group of persons can control the same company at the same time; and one person or group may have one type of control whereas another person or group may have a different type of control. Thus if a company has in issue (i) 100 £1 ordinary shares carrying one vote each and (ii) 200 £1 non- voting 10 per cent. preference shares and (iii) 10 £1 participating preference shares carrying one vote each and the right to 60 per cent. of the profits available for distribution by way of dividend in priority to the ordinary shares, the non-voting preference shares in (ii) have control because they possess the greater part of the share capital; the ordinary shares in (i) have control because they have the greater part of the voting power; and the participating preference shares in (iii) have control within paragraph (b) of § 15-10. A company is a close company if there can be found *any* five or fewer participators who, with their associates, have control in *any* sense.

2. *The apportionment test*

15-12   Section 282 (2) of the Income and Corporation Taxes Act 1970 provides an additional test which, if satisfied in relation to a company, makes the company a close company. We shall see in §§ 15-24 *et seq.* that, in certain circumstances where a close company fails to distribute a sufficient part of its income, a statutory apportionment of that income can be made under Schedule 16 to the Finance Act 1972. The persons to whom the income is so apportioned are then taxed (in effect) as if a dividend of the proper amount had been paid. Section 282 (2) of the Income and Corporation Taxes Act 1970 provides that if, on the assumption that it is a close company or on the assumption that it and any other such company or companies are so, more than half of any amount falling to be apportioned under Schedule 16 (including any sum which has been apportioned to it, or could on either of those assumptions be apportioned to it, under that Schedule) could be apportioned among five or fewer participators, or among participators who are directors, the company shall be treated as a close company. This test is especially important in relation to the exemption discussed in § 15-16 and § 15-17, where an example of its operation is given.

15-13 Section 282 (2) provides that in ascertaining under that subsection whether any amount could be apportioned among five or fewer participators or among participators who are directors, account shall, in cases where an original apportionment and any sub-apportionment are involved, be taken only of persons among whom that amount could be finally apportioned as the result of the whole process of original apportionment and sub-apportionment; and those persons shall be treated as participators or directors if they are participators or directors of any company in the case of which either an original apportionment or any sub-apportionment could be made. This is an example of a provision such as is referred to in the last sentence in § 15-02 where a participator in one company can be treated as being also a participator in another company.

Companies which are not Close Companies

(1) Non-resident companies

15-14 The expression " close company " does not include a company which is not resident in the United Kingdom.[16] A company is treated as resident in the country or countries from which it is centrally managed and controlled.[17] Lest it be supposed that a company can easily escape the restrictions imposed on close companies by changing its residence from the United Kingdom to some other country, reference should be made to section 482 of the Income and Corporation Taxes Act 1970, which makes it unlawful for a company resident in the United Kingdom to cease to be so resident or to transfer the whole or part of its trade or business to a non-resident person, without obtaining Treasury consent.[18]

(2) Quoted companies

15-15 A company is not to be treated as being at any time a close company if shares in the company carrying not less than 35 per cent. of the voting power in the company (and not being shares entitled to a fixed rate of dividend, whether with or without a further right to participate in profits) have been allotted unconditionally to, or acquired unconditionally by, *and* are at that time beneficially held by, the public, *and* any such shares have within the preceding 12 months been the subject of dealings on a recognised stock exchange, *and* the shares have within those 12 months been quoted in the official list of a recognised stock exchange.[19] The Finance Act 1965

---

[16] I.C.T.A. 1970, s. 282 (1) (a).   [17] *Ante*, § 7-22.
[18] *Ante*, § 7-22.
[19] I.C.T.A. 1970, s. 283. " Share " includes " stock." " Recognised stock exchange " has the same meaning as in the Prevention of Fraud (Investments) Act 1958, except that it includes the Belfast Stock Exchange and other exchanges outside the United Kingdom designated by order of the Board: I.C.T.A. 1970, s. 535.

contained no definition of the expression " public "; except that it stated the circumstances in which shares would *not* be treated as held by the public. The absence of any definition of " public " in the Act of 1965 gave rise to many difficulties and the Finance Act 1967 defined the circumstances in which shares should be deemed to be held by the public. The relevant provisions (now in s. 283 of the Income and Corporation Taxes Act 1970) are of some complexity and cannot be summarised in an intelligible form. Briefly, shares held by a director or his associate, or by a company controlled by a director or his associate, or by an associated company [20] of the company, or by trustees of a fund held for the benefit of such persons are treated as *not* held by the public; and not more than 85 per cent. of the voting power must be held by " principal members," *i.e.* persons with more than 5 per cent. of the voting power in the company.

(3) *Subsidiaries of non-close companies*

15-16   Section 282 (4) of the Income and Corporation Taxes Act 1970 provides as follows:

> (4) A company is not to be treated as a close company—
>
> > (*a*) if—
> >
> > > (i) it is controlled by a company which is not a close company, or by two or more companies none of which is a close company; and
> > >
> > > (ii) it cannot be treated as a close company except by taking as one of the five or fewer participators requisite for its being so treated a company which is not a close company;
> >
> > (*b*) if it cannot be treated as a close company except by virtue of paragraph (*c*) of section 302 (2) of this Act and it would not be a close company if the reference in that paragraph to participators did not include loan creditors who are companies other than close companies.

If sub-paragraph (i) stood alone, it could be said that a company which is controlled by an open company, or by two or more companies none of which is close, is an open company. Thus if two individuals owned 50 per cent. each of the issued share capital of X Ltd. (which would clearly then be a close company), X Ltd. would cease to be a close company if the individuals granted an option to an open company enabling that company to acquire their shares at a future date. X Ltd. would cease to be close on the granting of the option because the open company would be a participator with control within paragraph (a) in § 15-02. However, sub-paragraph (ii) provides (in effect) that where the participators in a company include an open company or companies and others, the rule is that if you can find five or fewer participators who between them have control *without* including the open company among them, the company is a close company; conversely, if it is necessary to include an open company among the five or fewer participators requisite for close status, the company is not a close company. In the Example, X Ltd. could be treated as controlled by the two individuals *or* as controlled by the open company: therefore, X Ltd. is treated as a close company.

---

[20] I.C.T.A. 1970, s. 302 (1).

15-17 In applying sub-paragraph (ii), the expanded definition of participator in section 282 (2)—see § 15-12 (the apportionment test)—must not be overlooked. Under this test, the participators in one company can be treated as participators in another.

> *Example*: A Limited has 11 shareholders (including X, Y and Z) with nine shares each, all with equal voting and other rights, and no one of which is the associate of any other. Thus A Ltd. is an open company because no group of five members has control. B Ltd. has an issued capital of 100 shares of £1 each. A Ltd. subscribes for 55 shares in B Ltd. The remaining 45 shares in B Ltd. are held as to 15 shares each by X, Y and Z.

At first sight, B Ltd. would appear to be an open company because it is controlled by an open company, A Ltd., which cannot be excluded in applying the control test to B Ltd. But the apportionment test in § 15-12 demands an inquiry as to whom income of B Ltd. would be apportioned if both A Ltd. and B Ltd. were close companies, and on this hypothesis 45 per cent. of the income would be apportioned to X, Y and Z as members of B Ltd. and 3/11ths of 55 per cent. (15 per cent.) would be apportioned to X, Y and Z as members of A Ltd. Hence X, Y and Z can be treated as participators in both A Ltd. and B Ltd. who together are entitled to more than half the distributable income of B Ltd.: see § 15-13. B Ltd. is therefore a close company.

Section 282 (4) (*b*) prevents an otherwise open company becoming a close company merely through taking a substantial loan from a close company giving the lender " loan creditor control ": see § 15-03A.

References in section 282 (4) (see § 15-16) apply to a company which, if resident in the United Kingdom, would be a close company.[21]

15-18 The subsidiary, resident in the United Kingdom, of a foreign company will be an open company if either the subsidiary company or its foreign parent company satisfy the conditions of exemption referred to in § 15-15 (quoted companies). In this connection it should be noted that foreign stock exchanges are not recognised stock exchanges for the purposes of the relevant provisions, unless a double taxation agreement so provides[22]; so the wholly owned United Kingdom resident subsidiaries of foreign quoted companies are not necessarily non-close companies.

(4) *Crown-controlled companies*

15-19 A company controlled by or on behalf of the Crown, and not otherwise a close company, is not a close company.[23] A company is to be treated as controlled by or on behalf of the Crown if, but only if, it is under the control of the Crown or of persons acting on behalf of the Crown, independently of any other person; and where a company is so controlled, it shall not be treated as being otherwise a close company, unless it can be treated as a close company as being under the control of persons acting independently of the Crown.[24]

---

[21] I.C.T.A. 1970, s. 282 (5).
[22] See Double Taxation Relief (Taxes on Income) (France) Order 1968 (S.I. 1968 No. 1869), art. 25 (5).
[23] I.C.T.A. 1970, s. 282 (1) (*c*).
[24] *Ibid*. s. 282 (3).

(5) *Certain societies*

15-20   The expression " close company " does not apply to a registered industrial and provident society (as defined) or to certain building societies.[25]

(6) *Non-resident participators*

15-20A   When a close company, 90 per cent. or more of the ordinary share capital of which is beneficially owned by non-residents, wishes to retain its surplus funds in the United Kingdom, a request that the company should not be liable to apportionment of its income will be favourably considered.[25a]

2. EXTENDED MEANING OF DISTRIBUTION [26]

The term " distribution " has an extended meaning in the case of close companies. The tax consequences of a distribution have already been considered: see § 14-50 (advance corporation tax) and § 14-59 (Schedule F income tax).

Accommodation and other benefits or facilities for participators and associates

15-21   If a close company incurs expense in connection with the provision for any participator (§ 15-02) of living or other accommodation, of entertainment, of domestic or other services, or of other benefits or facilities of whatever nature, the company is treated as making a distribution to him of an amount equal to so much of that expense as is not made good to the company by the participator.[27] The amount of the expense to be taken into account as a distribution is the same as would, under the Finance Act 1976, be the cash equivalent of the resultant benefit to the participator.[28] The tax charge on distributions will be avoided if the expense is " made good " at any time before the relevant assessment becomes final. There are exceptions from the tax charge in the case of benefits taxable under sections 61–68 of the Finance Act 1976 (*i.e.* where the participator is in director's or higher-paid employment: see § 3-40) and in the case of expenses incurred in providing death or retirement benefits for the spouse, children or dependants of a person employed by the company.[29] References to a participator in this paragraph include an associate (§ 15-04) of a participator; and any participator in a company which controls another company is treated as a participator in that other company.[30]

There are anti-avoidance provisions to counter reciprocal arrangements by which two close companies provide benefits or facilities for participators

---

[25] See I.C.T.A. 1970, s. 282 (1) (*b*).

[25a] Inland Revenue Press Release, September 13, 1978 (SP 2/78 (i)); [1978] S.T.I. 456.

[26] The meaning of the term " distribution " is discussed *ante*, §§ 14-40 *et seq*. The provisions there discussed apply to close as well as to non-close companies.

[27] I.C.T.A. 1970, s. 284 (1) (*c*), (2).

[28] I.C.T.A. 1970, s. 284 (3), as substituted by F.A. 1976, Sched. 9, para. 16, in and from 1977–78.

[29] I.C.T.A. 1970, s. 284 (2), proviso, as substituted by F.A. 1976, Sched. 9, para. 15, in and from 1977–78.

[30] I.C.T.A. 1970, s. 284 (7). " Control " is defined in § 15-10.

in the other.[31] There is no " distribution " if the company and the participator are both resident in the United Kingdom and one is the subsidiary of the other or both are subsidiaries of a third company, also so resident, and the benefit to the participator arises on or in connection with a transfer of assets or liabilities of the company to him, or to the company by him.[32]

Interest paid to directors and associates

15-22 Interest paid by a close company to directors or their associates is in some cases treated as a distribution by the company. The relevant section[33] applies where in any accounting period any interest is paid to, or to an associate of, a person

(a) who is a director of the close company, or of any company which controls, or is controlled by, the close company; and

(b) who has a material interest in the close company or, where the close company is controlled by another company, in that other company.

Beneficial ownership, either alone or with associates, of more than 5 per cent. of ordinary share capital or entitlement on a notional statutory apportionment (see §§ 15-28 *et seq.*) to more than 5 per cent. of distributable income constitutes a *material interest*.[34] The expression " interest " includes any other consideration paid or given by a close company for the use of money advanced or credit given, and references to interest " paid " are construed accordingly.[35] Thus the section applies when *e.g.* a director sells an asset to a close company and the company pays interest on the unpaid purchase price.

15-23 The amount of interest to be attributed to a director (or associate) and so treated as a distribution to him is calculated as follows[36]:

(1) Calculate a sum equal to interest at 12 per cent. per annum on whichever is the less of—

(a) the total of the loans, advances and credits to which section 285 applies and on which interest was paid in the accounting period or, if that total was different at different times in the accounting period, the average total over the accounting period; and

(b) the nominal amount of the issued share capital of the company plus the amount of any share premium account (or other comparable account by whatever name called) taking both amounts as at the beginning of the accounting period. The sum so calculated is called " the overall limit."

---

[31] *Ibid.* s. 284 (6).
[32] *Ibid.* s. 284 (4) and (5), defining " subsidiary."
[33] I.C.T.A. 1970, s. 285.
[34] *Ibid.* s. 285 (6).
[35] *Ibid.* s. 285 (5).
[36] *Ibid.* s. 285 (2), (3) and (4). The interest rate can be varied by Treasury order: F.A. 1974, s. 35 (1).

(2) Apportion the " overall limit " between the recipients according to the amount of interest (as defined above) paid to them.

(3) If the total amount paid to the recipient in the accounting period exceeds the amount apportioned to him in (2), the excess is treated as a distribution made by the close company to that person.

Hence interest up to the overall limit, if spread evenly between the recipients according to the amounts of the loans, etc., actually made by them, gives rise to no " distribution."

Disallowed directors' remuneration

15-24 When directors' remuneration is disallowed for corporation tax purposes the disallowance will not rank as a distribution. When such a disallowance has been negotiated with the Inspector of Taxes, the Schedule E liability of the director will be reduced by the amount of that disallowance, provided that the amount disallowed is formally waived and refunded to the company by the director, and a satisfactory settlement of the amount to be apportioned (if any), under Schedule 16 to the Finance Act 1972, for that accounting period is reached.[37]

3. Loans to Participators and their Associates

15-25 Section 286 of the Income and Corporation Taxes Act 1970 provides that where any loan or advance of money is made by a close company to an individual [38] who is a participator [39] in the company or an associate [40] of a participator, there shall be assessed on and recoverable from the company, as if it were an amount of corporation tax for the accounting period in which the loan or advance is made, an amount equal to such proportion of the amount of the loan or advance as corresponds to the rate of advance corporation tax in force for the financial year in which the loan or advance is made.[41]

> Thus if a close company makes a loan of £6,700 to a participator in the financial year 1978, it must pay to the Revenue an amount equal to 33/67ths of £6,700.

The section does not apply to a loan or advance made by a close company in the ordinary course of a business which includes the lending of money [41]; nor does it apply to a loan to a director or employee of a close company (or its associated company [42]) if the amount of the loan including outstanding loans made by such close company (or associated companies [42]) to the borrower (or his husband or wife) does not exceed £15,000, provided the borrower works full-time for the close company or any of its associated

---

[37] Inland Revenue Press Statement [1973] S.T.I. 56; and see §§ 15-28 *et seq.*

[38] References to an individual include a company receiving the loan or advance in a fiduciary or representative capacity, and to a company not resident in the United Kingdom: I.C.T.A. 1970, s. 286 (8). Loans to individuals who are trustees are also included: *ibid.* s. 287 (2), (4).

[39] " Participator " is defined in § 15-02. For the purposes of s. 286, a parent company is treated as a participator in its sub-subsidiary company: see *ibid.* s. 286 (9).

[40] Defined *ante*, § 15-04.

[41] *Ibid.* s. 286 (1).

[42] " Associated company " is defined in I.C.T.A. 1970, s. 302 (1).

companies [42] and does not have a material interest [43] in the close company or in any associated company. [44] Section 286 does not apply where the loan or advance is made by a company which is not a close company, but section 287A (inserted by section 44 of the Finance Act 1976) extends it to certain loans made by companies which are or come under the control of close companies.

15-26   It should be noted that the Act does not expressly provide that the loan or advance shall be treated as a dividend or other distribution made by the company. Hence the tax paid by the company may not be credited against the company's liability for corporation tax. There are provisions to prevent avoidance of the section by the company channelling a loan to a participator through a non-participator. [45] Where the whole or part of the purchase price is left unpaid on a sale to a company, this is not a " loan " or " advance " by the vendor, [46] but when a person incurs a debt to a company, e.g. on a sale of property by the company, this is treated as a loan to the extent of the debt, except where the debt is incurred for the supply of goods or services in the ordinary course of the company's business and the credit does not exceed six months or that normally given to the company's customers. [47] A company is treated as making a loan to a person if, for example, the person borrows from a bank which assigns the debt to the company. [48]

If *after* the company has been assessed to tax under section 286 (above), the loan or advance (or part of it) is repaid to the company, relief is given for the tax by discharge or repayment on a claim being made within six years from the end of the financial year in which the repayment is made. [49]

15-27   The loan or advance is not treated as income of the borrower at the time it is made; but if the company releases or writes off the whole or part of the debt, the borrower is treated for purposes of computing his total income as having then received income equal to the grossed up equivalent of the amount so released or written off. No repayment of income tax will be made in respect of that income and no assessment will be made on him to basic rate income tax on that income. [50] If the loan or advance was made to a person who has since died or to trustees of a trust which has come to an end, the Act applies to the person from whom the debt is due at the time of release or writing off. [51] Loans taxable under section 451 (see *ante*, § 10-43) are excepted from the operation of section 286. [52] By concession, section 286 has been suspended on some loans to executors to pay estate duty. [53]

[43] " Material interest " is defined in I.C.T.A. 1970, s. 285 (6) as applied by s. 286 (9). See § 15-22.
[44] *Ibid.* s. 286 (3).
[45] I.C.T.A. 1970, s. 286 (7).
[46] *Cf. Ramsden* v. *I.R.C.* (1957) 37 T.C. 619.
[47] I.C.T.A. 1970, s. 286 (2).
[48] *Ibid.*
[49] *Ibid.* s. 286 (5).
[50] *Ibid.* s. 287 (1) as substituted by F.A. 1971, s. 37 and Sched. 6, para. 32.
[51] *Ibid.* s. 287 (2).
[52] *Ibid.* s. 287 (3).   [53] Concession No. C2.

4. The Statutory Apportionment of Income

15-28　Where a company resident in the United Kingdom makes a qualifying distribution it must account to the Revenue for advance corporation tax; and the amount distributed plus the tax credit attributable thereto forms part of the total income of the recipient for the purposes of higher rate income tax and the investment income surcharge.[54] If a company withholds income from distribution, its members avoid income tax, and there are accordingly provisions to enable the Revenue to counter such avoidance by directing, in effect, that the members should be taxed as if income had in fact been distributed. These provisions apply only to close companies[55] and, generally speaking, they do not apply where the requirements of the company's business justify the non-distribution of income. The provisions for the statutory apportionment of income of close companies are now to be found in Schedule 16 to the Finance Act 1972 as subsequently amended. A number of terms used in the Schedule, and printed in italics in the following paragraphs, are defined in §§ 15-37 *et seq.* The definitions in §§ 15-02 *et seq.* also apply by virtue of section 94 (3) of the Finance Act 1972.

The power to apportion

15-29　Paragraph 1 (1) of Schedule 16 provides that the income of a close company for any accounting period may be apportioned by the inspector among the *participators.*[56] It is generally thought that the power exists only in the case of a company which is a close company at the end of the accounting period to which the apportionment relates.[57] As a general rule no such apportionment may be made unless the *relevant income* of the company for the accounting period exceeds its *distributions* for the period; and the amount to be apportioned is the amount of the excess.[58] Where the excess is not more than £1,000 no apportionment is made if the company is a *trading company* or *a member of a trading group.*[59] An amount which is apportioned to a close company may be sub-apportioned through that company to its participators.[60]

　　The general rule stated in the preceding paragraph is subject to two exceptions:

15-30　First, in the case of a company which is not a trading company (*e.g.* an investment company), the inspector can if he sees reason for it apportion the whole of the relevant income for an accounting period, whether or not there is an excess of relevant income over distributions for the period (*i.e.* even if the company has distributed the whole of its relevant income) and whether or not the excess is more than £1,000.[61]

15-31　Secondly, if a company has made annual payments which were deducted in arriving at its distributable income (*e.g.* as charges on income) and which,

---

[54] See *ante,* § 14-01.
[55] Defined *ante,* §§ 15-07 *et seq.*
[56] Defined *ante,* § 15-02.
[57] *Cf. C. H. W. (Huddersfield) Ltd.* v. *I.R.C.* (1961) 41 T.C. 92.
[58] F.A. 1972, Sched. 16, para. 1 (2).
[59] *Ibid.* Sched. 16, para. 1 (3).
[60] *Ibid.* Sched. 16, para. 1 (4).
[61] *Ibid.* Sched. 16, para. 2.

in the case of an individual, would not have been deductible or would have been treated as his income in computing his total income, the amount so deducted by the company may be apportioned.[62] It has been explained in § 10-17 that an individual is unable to avoid higher rate income tax by making an income settlement in favour of a charity. This second exception (for example) prevents such an individual who is a participator in a close company from securing tax relief indirectly by getting the company to make the settlement for him. The provision does not apply to annual payments which consist of interest or are made wholly and exclusively for the purposes of the company's trade.[62]

15-32   Paragraph 3A of Schedule 16 allows interest paid by an investment company to be apportioned in certain circumstances. The object of this paragraph is to prevent an individual or individuals avoiding the provisions which restrict interest relief (see §§ 8-57 *et seq.*) by routeing their borrowing through a company.

Manner of apportionment

15-33   An apportionment (or sub-apportionment) is made according to the respective interests in the company in question of the participators.[63] An inspector who proposes to make an apportionment must serve a notice on the company showing the amount to be apportioned and a further notice showing how the amount is apportioned to each participator or, if the inspector thinks fit, to each class of share; and the manner of apportionment may be reviewed on appeal.[64] The inspector may, if it seems proper to him to do so, attribute to each participator an interest corresponding to his interest in the assets of the company available for distribution among the participators in the event of a winding up or in any other circumstances [65]; and in the case of a non-trading company, the inspector may if it seems proper to him to do so treat a *loan creditor* as having an interest to the extent to which the income to be apportioned, or assets representing it, has or have been expended or applied, or is or are available to be expended or applied, in redemption, repayment or discharge of the loan capital or debt (including any premium thereon) in respect of which he is a loan creditor.[66]

Consequences of apportionment: income tax

15-34   The sum apportioned to an individual (whether by original apportionment or by sub-apportionment) is treated as income of the individual received by him at the end of the accounting period to which the apportionment relates and must therefore be included in the computation of his total income. The apportioned amount is deemed to be the highest part of his total income and is therefore liable to bear tax at the highest rate applicable to the individual. The recipient cannot be assessed to basic rate

---

[62] *Ibid.* Sched. 16, para. 3. For charges on income, see §§ 14-08 *et seq.*
[63] F.A. 1972, Sched. 16, para. 4 (1). " Participator " is defined in § 15-02.
[64] *Ibid.* Sched. 16, paras. 15 and 16.
[65] *Ibid.* Sched. 16, para. 4 (2).
[66] *Ibid.* Sched. 16, para. 4 (3).

income tax on the amount apportioned (because liability to this extent is treated as satisfied); but a recipient not liable to tax at the basic rate can make no claim for repayment of tax. The sum apportioned is treated for the purposes of sections 52 and 53 of the Taxes Act as income not brought into charge to income tax.[67] A sum apportioned to trustees may attract the additional rate of tax (15 per cent. in 1977–78 and 1978–79) on trust income.[68]

No individual is to be assessed by virtue of an apportionment [68] unless the sum on which he is assessable amounts at least to £200 or 5 per cent. of the amount apportioned, whichever is the less.[69]

Where income which has been apportioned to an individual and income is actually distributed to him, there are provisions for excluding from charge the amount already taxed.[70]

The Board are normally prepared to regard a non-resident whose dividend income from United Kingdom companies is effectively relieved from higher-rate tax under a Double Taxation Agreement as exempted from the United Kingdom income tax charge on any close company income apportioned to him.[70a]

Payment and collection of income tax

15-35 Income tax chargeable in respect of a sum apportioned to a participator is assessed in the first place on the participator. If the tax so assessed is not paid within 30 days from the date on which the assessment became final and conclusive, or by July 6, in the year next following the year of assessment, whichever is the later, a notice of liability to tax may be served on the company and the tax thereupon is payable by the company on the service of the notice. Where such a notice of liability is served on the company, any interest due on the tax assessed on the participator and not paid by him, and any interest accruing due on that tax after the date of service, is payable by the company. If the company then fails to pay the tax and any interest payable before the expiry of three months from the date of service of the notice, the tax and any interest may, without prejudice to the right to recovery from the company, be recovered from the participator.[71]

Consequences of apportionment: advance corporation tax

15-36 Where a statutory apportionment is made for an accounting period, there are provisions which are designed to put the company into substantially the same position as respects advance corporation tax *as if* a dividend equal to the amount apportioned had been paid at the end of the accounting period. These provisions have to allow for the fact that an apportionment is usually made long after the company's corporation tax liability for the period has been settled, and they are designed, *inter alia*, to avoid unnecessary repayment claims.

---

[67] *Ibid.*Sched.16,para.5(1)(2).
[68] See *ante*, § 9-05.
[69] F.A. 1972, Sched. 16, para. 5 (4).
[70] *Ibid.* Sched. 16, para. 5 (5)–(8).
[70a] Inland Revenue Press Release of September 13, 1978 (SP 2/78 (ii)); [1978] S.T.I. 456.
[71] *Ibid.* Sched. 16, para. 6, as amended by F.A. 1976, s. 45.

It will be recalled that when an *actual* dividend is paid, the company is liable to pay advance corporation tax to the Revenue save to the extent that the company's franked investment income equals or exceeds the sum of the dividend and the advance corporation tax attributable thereto (§§ 14-63 and 14-64). Any advance corporation tax which is payable can be set off against the company's liability to corporation tax (§ 14-51).

One consequence of an apportionment is that the advance corporation tax attributable to the " notional " dividend is set off against what remains of any surplus franked investment income at the time when the apportionment becomes final and conclusive. This cancels the tax advantage which otherwise would arise to the company through withholding income from distribution and thereby " increasing " surplus franked investment income. [72]

Definitions

15-37   It was explained in § 15-29 that no apportionment can be made unless the relevant income of the company for the accounting period exceeds its distributions for the period; and that subject to the provisions summarised in §§ 15-31 to 15-33, the amount apportioned is the amount of that excess. For these purposes and for the purposes of provisions discussed later, the following expressions are used:

15-38   " *Trading company* " [73] means any company which exists wholly or mainly for the purpose of carrying on a trade, and any other company whose income does not consist wholly or mainly of investment income, that is to say, income which, if the company were an individual, would not be earned income (*ante*, § 8-07). An amount which is apportioned to a company is deemed to be income of the company and to be investment income.

15-39   A company is treated as *a member of a trading group* [74]

    (a) If it exists wholly or mainly for the purpose of co-ordinating the administration of a group of two or more companies each of which is under its control and exists wholly or mainly for the purpose of carrying on a trade. The parent company of a group of trading companies may fulfil such a co-ordinating function in which case, although its income may consist substantially if not wholly of dividend income, it will be treated (in effect) as a trading company and not as an investment company; or

    (b) If it exists wholly or mainly for the purpose of a trade or trades carried on by a company resident in the United Kingdom which controls it (and is not itself controlled by a third company). A company which carries on research work which is ancillary to the activities of a group of trading companies may fulfil this function.

15-40   The *distributable income* [75] of a company for an accounting period is the amount of its distributable profits (§ 15-41) for the period exclusive of the part attributable to chargeable gains.

---

[72] *Ibid.* Sched. 16, para. 7. For details of this complex provision, see Bramwell's *Taxation of Companies*, §§ 12-22 *et seq.*
[73] F.A. 1972, Sched. 16, para. 11 (1).
[74] *Ibid.* Sched. 16, para. 11 (2).

15-41 The *distributable profits* [75] of a company for an accounting period is the aggregate of the following amounts:

(i) the amount of any profits on which corporation tax falls finally to be borne (as defined), less the amount of that tax,

(ii) an amount equal to the qualifying distributions comprised in any franked investment income, other than franked investment income against which relief is given under section 254 or 255 of the Taxes Act (*ante*, § 14-68 and § 14-70), and

(iii) an amount equal to any group income (*ante*, § 14-72).

15-42 The *distributable investment income* [76] of a company for an accounting period is the amount of the distributable income, exclusive of the part attributable to estate or trading income (see below), less whichever is the smaller of

(a) 10 per cent. of the estate or trading income and

(b) £1,000 or, if the accounting period is of less than 12 months, a proportionately reduced amount.

15-43 *The estate or trading income* [77] of a company means—

(a) income which is not investment income, and

(b) income which is chargeable to tax under Schedule A or Schedule B, and income (other than yearly or other interest) which is chargeable to tax under Schedule D, and which arises from the ownership or occupation of land (including any interest in or right over land) or from the letting furnished of any building or part of a building. The income derived from investments of certain insurance, banking, money lending and similar trades may be treated as estate or trading income. [78]

Thus the phrase " distributable investment income " means, in relation to a property investment company, its income excluding rental income and chargeable gains.

The estate and trading income is, in the case of a trading company, assumed to be less than its actual amount in some cases: see § 15-51.

15-44 There is an order of set-off of charges on income, expenses of management and other amounts which can be deducted from or set against or treated as reducing profits of more than one description for the purpose of quantifying the amount of each class of a company's income. [79]

The computation of " relevant income "

15-45 (1) *Trading companies and members of trading groups.* Relevant income in the case of a trading company (§ 15-38) or a member of a trading group

---

[75] *Ibid.* Sched. 16, para. 10 (2); and see para. 10 (7).
[76] *Ibid.* Sched. 16, para. 10 (3). The figure of £1,000 in (b) was increased from £500 for accounting periods after October 26, 1977: F.A. 1978, s. 35 (3), (4).
[77] *Ibid.* Sched. 16, para. 10 (4).
[78] F.A. 1972, Sched. 16, para. 10 (5) and (6).
[79] *Ibid.* Sched. 16, para. 10 (8).

(§ 15-39) means so much of the company's distributable income (§ 15-40) for the accounting period as can be distributed without prejudice to the requirements of the company's business; and for the purpose of arriving at the relevant income, regard is to be had not only to the current requirements of the business but also to such other requirements as may be necessary or advisable for the maintenance and development of *that* business.[80]

15-46   The proposition in § 15-45 is subject to the qualification [81] that, in certain circumstances, income has to be treated as available for distribution and not as having been applied, or as being applicable, to the requirements of the company's business, etc. These provisions are especially important as regards debts incurred by a company for the purpose of acquiring the business, undertaking or property which the company was formed to acquire or which was the first business, undertaking or property of a substantial character in fact acquired by the company. Sums applies out of income [82] in discarding such debts (called " first business loans ") will be subject to the apportionment provisions, irrespective of the company's trading requirements.

> Thus if A Limited is formed to acquire A's business in consideration for an issue of redeemable preference shares or loan stock, sums applied out of income in redeeming the shares or repaying the stock will be apportioned irrespective of the trading requirements of A Limited.

15-46A   By amendments made in the Finance Act 1978,[83] regard may be had, for the purpose of arriving at the relevant income of an accounting period, not only to the requirements referred to in § 15-45 but also to any other requirements necessary or advisable for the acquisition of a trade or of a controlling interest (as defined) in a trading company or in a company which is a member of a trading group, including a requirement to repay any debts or meet any other obligations in connection with the acquisition. Hence, if A and B, who carry on a trade in partnership, transfer their trade to a newly formed company in exchange for loan stock, sums applied out of income in discharging the debt to A and B are not now treated as relevant income available for distribution, even if they are " first business loans." [84] This is subject to the qualification that, under the new provisions, regard may not be had to sums expended or applied where the expenditure or application would constitute a distribution by the company, *e.g.* if the acquisition is at an over-value from a participator. Nor may advantage be taken of these relaxed provisions where the purchaser is from, *e.g.* an associated company of the purchaser.

15-47   (2) *Non-trading companies having estate or trading income.* Where a company is not a trading company or a member of a trading group but its

---

[80] *Ibid.* Sched. 16, para. 8 (1) (*a*) and para. 8 (2). For the Revenue's practice in applying these provisions to groups of companies, see Press Statement in [1973] S.T.I. 55. For a recent case on required standard, see *MacTaggart Scott & Co. Ltd.* v. *I.R.C.* (1973) 48 T.C. 708; [1973] S.T.C. 180 (Ct. of Sess.).

[81] *Ibid.* Sched. 16, para. 12.

[82] A sum is not applied out of income if it is an expense to be taken into account in determining income: *Hanstead Investments Ltd.* v. *I.R.C.* [1975] S.T.C. 419 (C.A.).

[83] F.A. 1972, Sched. 16, para. 8 (3)–(5), added by F.A. 1978, s. 36 and Sched. 5.

[84] F.A. 1972, Sched. 16, para. 12, qualifies *ibid.* para. 8 (2) (*a*) but *not* the new para. 8 (3)–(5).

distributable income for an accounting period consists of or includes *estate or trading income* (§ 15-37) (*e.g.* in the case of a land-owning company, its income from rents), the *relevant income* means (i) so much of the estate or trading income as can be distributed without prejudice to the requirements of the company's business so far as concerned with the activities or assets giving rise to estate or trading income, and (ii) its distributable income, if any, other than estate or trading income.[85] There must be treated as available for distribution any sum expended or applied, or available to be expended or applied, out of the income, in or towards the acquisition of an estate or interest in land, or the construction or extension of a building (other than a construction or extension which constitutes an improvement or development of farm land or market garden land).[86]

15-48   (3) *Other companies.* In the case of any other company, *e.g.* a pure investment company, the relevant income for an accounting period is its distributable income for that period.[87] Interest paid by such a company which would not qualify for tax relief if paid by an individual may be apportioned as if it were income.[88]

> Thus no avoidance of income tax is achieved by forming a company to own stocks or shares, for the whole of the distributable income of such a company is apportioned, if it is not distributed.

Maximum amount to be taken as relevant income

15-49   Subject to special provisions applicable to cessations and liquidations (*post*, § 15-53), the relevant income of a company must in no case be taken to exceed the company's distributable investment income (§ 15-42) for the accounting period plus 50 per cent. of the estate or trading income (§ 15-43) for the period.[89]

Special reduction for trading companies [90]

15-50   The " relevant income " of a company will normally not exceed its distributable investment income for the accounting period plus 50 per cent. of the estate or trading income for the period. In the case of a trading company, however, the estate or trading income of an accounting period is assumed to be nil if it is less than £25,000. If it is between £25,000 and £75,000 there are tapering provisions under which the estate or trading income is assumed to be the amount of that income reduced by one half of the amount required to make it up to £75,000 (the latter figure being called " the relevant maximum amount ").

> Thus if the estate or trading income of the accounting period is £45,000, it is assumed for apportionment purposes to be £30,000. The object of these provisions is to remove the need for apportionment in cases where relatively small sums are at stake.

---

[85] F.A. 1972, Sched. 16, para. 8 (1) (*b*) and para. 8 (2).
[86] F.A. 1972, Sched. 16, para. 12 (1) (*d*).
[87] *Ibid*. Sched. 16, para. 8 (1) (*c*).
[88] *Ibid*. Sched. 16, para. 3A, added by Sched. 1, Part V to the F.A. 1974.
[89] F.A. 1972, Sched. 16, para. 9 (1).
[90] F.A. 1972, Sched. 16, para. 9 (2)–(6). Figures increased from £5,000 and £15,000 to £25,000 and £75,000 for any accounting period after October 26, 1977, by F.A. 1978, s. 35 (1), (4).

Where there are a number of associated companies, each is not entitled to the benefit of these reductions. The reductions are applied to the group of companies as a whole.

15-51 It may now be possible to perceive through the maze of definitions how the apportionment procedure operates in relation, for example, to a trading company. First, the distributable income for the accounting period must be quantified. This will be (roughly) the whole of the income from all sources, including dividends but excluding chargeable gains, less charges, losses, etc. (§ 15-40 and § 15-44). Next must be found how much of the distributable income can be distributed without prejudice to the requirements of the company's business or, put in another way, how much of the distributable income needs to be retained by the company for the purposes of its business (§ 15-45). This is principally a matter for the directors but the directors' opinion can be challenged by the inspector. The company wishing to avoid a statutory apportionment should distribute by way of dividend as much as it can afford to distribute without prejudice to its business requirements but need never distribute more than the whole of its investment income plus 50 per cent. of its trading income (§ 15-43). Generally, every trading company may retain 50 per cent. of its trading income without fear of any apportionment and may retain more than 50 per cent. if this can be justified by business requirements. Where the distributions for the accounting period (§ 15-52) fall short of the amount which should have been distributed, an apportionment will be made.

Distributions for an accounting period [91]

15-52 Generally, no apportionment will be made unless the relevant income of the company for the accounting period exceeds its distributions for that period (§ 15-29). The distributions for an accounting period consist of—

(a) any dividends which are declared in respect of the period and are paid during the period or within a reasonable time thereafter, and

(b) all distribution made in the period except dividends declared in respect of an earlier period.

Where dividends are declared in respect of a period which straddles more than one accounting period, they must be apportioned between the accounting periods in proportion to the distributable income of each such period.

Cessations and liquidations [92]

15-53 Where a close company ceases to carry on the trade, or the business of holding investments, in which its activities wholly or mainly consisted, the relevant income of the company for any accounting period in which that event occurs, or which ends in or within the 12 months ending with that event, is calculated on the whole instead of on 50 per cent. of the estate or

---

[91] *Ibid.* Sched. 16, para. 10 (1).
[92] *Ibid.* Sched. 16, para. 13. The operation of this provision may be relaxed in cases of reorganisation carried out for commercial reasons: see [1973] S.T.I. 57.   P-10

trading income (if any) taken into account, and without any deduction in respect of the requirements of the business. The conception underlying this provision is that a company which has ceased to trade has no business requirements to justify the retention of income either in the accounting period with which the cessation occurs [93] or in the previous period. There is an exception where the company shows that distributions of the whole income could not be made without prejudice to the claims of creditors (certain creditors being excluded); in this case, a shortfall in distributions is disregarded to the extent necessary to satisfy the non-excluded creditors. Debts due to participators and their associates will be taken into account only if they are ordinary trading debts or debts for remuneration or rent at a commercial rate.

These provisions also apply where a resolution is passed or an order is made for the winding up of a close company. [94]

Legal restrictions on distributions [95]

15-54 Where a company is subject to any restriction imposed by law as regards the making of distributions, the excess of relevant income over distributions in the period is disregarded to the extent to which the company could not make distributions up to the amount of its relevant income without contravening that restriction. Restrictions contained in a company's articles are not " imposed by law." [96]

Clearances

15-55 There are provisions [97] under which a close company may, at any time after the general meeting at which the accounts for any period are adopted, forward a copy of the accounts to the inspector requesting him to intimate whether or not he proposes to make an apportionment. The inspector has three months from the date of the request in which to make his decision (unless he requires further particulars, when the three months' period runs from the receipt of the particulars). If the inspector does *not* intimate his intention to make an apportionment, he cannot do so unless material information has been withheld or there is a cessation or liquidation within 12 months from the end of the period, when he may reconsider the matter.

---

[93] An accounting period ends with the cessation of trade: I.C.T.A. 1970, s. 247 (3) (c).
[94] See note 92, *ante.* For capital gains tax, see § 16-31 (v).
[95] F.A. 1972, Sched. 16, para. 14, and see F.A. 1974, Sched. 7, para. 6 (relating to development gains).
[96] *Noble* v. *Laygate Investments Ltd.* [1978] S.T.C. 430.
[97] *Ibid.* Sched. 16, para. 18.

DIVISION C

THE TAXATION OF CAPITAL GAINS

CHAPTER 16

THE TAXATION OF CAPITAL GAINS

THIS chapter is divided into three parts. Part I summarises the statutory provisions taxing capital gains, principally contained in the Finance Act 1965. Part II summarises the provisions taxing the development value of land under the Development Land Tax Act 1976. Part III deals with the interaction of Development Land Tax and other taxes.

PART I. CAPITAL GAINS TAX

1. THE SCOPE OF THE CHARGE

16-01   Capital gains tax was introduced by, and is charged under, the Finance Act 1965. It applies in and from the year 1965–66. The tax is levied on the total amount of *chargeable gains* which accrue to a person on the *disposal* of *assets* in a year of assessment (or accounting period, in the case of a company) after deducting *allowable losses*.[1] The expression " chargeable gain " means a gain which accrues after April 6, 1965, such gain being computed in accordance with provisions contained in Schedule 6 to the Finance Act 1965.[2] " Allowable losses " are computed in the same way.[3] The chargeable gain (or allowable loss) on the disposal of an asset is, roughly, the difference between the cost of the asset (plus any expenditure on improvements) and the consideration in money or money's worth for its disposal. Where an asset was acquired before April 1965 it has, in some cases, to be assumed that the asset was sold and re-acquired for its market value on April 6, 1965. The asset is then treated as if it cost this amount.

The main provisions relating to capital gains tax are in the Finance Act 1965, as amended; but there are provisions dealing with companies' capital gains in sections 265–281 of the Income and Corporation Taxes Act 1970: see §§ 14-04B, *ante* and 16-53, *post.*

Rates: individuals

16-02   In the case of an individual, the rate of capital gains tax is 30 per cent.[4] except that, for 1977–78 and subsequent years, there is a nil or lower rate where the individual's *taxable amount* does not exceed £9,500. Section 44 of the Finance Act 1978 provides that an individual shall not be chargeable to capital gains tax for a year of assessment if his *taxable amount* for that year does not exceed £1,000. If his taxable amount exceeds £1,000 but does not exceed £5,000, the amount of tax to which he is chargeable for that year is 15 per cent. of the excess over £1,000. If his taxable amount exceeds £5,000, the amount of tax to which he is chargeable is not to exceed £600 plus one-half of the excess over £5,000. The expression *taxable amount* means the

---

[1] F.A. 1965, ss. 19 (1) (3); 20 (1) (4).
[2] *Ibid.* ss. 45 (1); 22 (10).
[3] *Ibid.* ss. 45 (1); 23 (1).
[4] *Ibid.* s. 20 (3).

total amount of chargeable gains accruing to the individual in the year of assessment after deducting (i) any allowable losses accruing in that year and (ii) any unrelieved losses carried forward from a previous year, except that no deduction is made in such a way as to reduce gains below the tax-free £1,000.[4a]

For 1976–77 and earlier years capital gains tax was levied at a flat rate of 30 per cent.[4] except where less tax would be payable under the " alternative charge." [5] This alternative charge applied if, in the case of an individual, the chargeable gains of the year did not exceed £5,000 and less tax would be payable if he was chargeable to income tax under Case VI of Schedule D on one-half of the chargeable gain. Capital gains tax was then payable of an amount equal to the amount which would be chargeable under Case VI. If the gain exceeded £5,000, the tax liability was £2,500 plus the amount by which the gain exceeded £5,000. This alternative charge ceases to apply in and from the year 1978–79.[6] There is a reduced rate of tax on disposals of shares in authorised unit trusts and investment trusts.[6a]

Rates: personal representatives and trustees

16-02A   For the year of assessment in which an individual dies and for the two following years of assessment, the nil and lower rates applicable to an individual whose gains do not exceed £9,500 apply to disposals by his personal representatives.[6b]

For any year of assessment during the whole or part of which any property is settled property (see § 16-21), the trustees are not chargeable to capital gains tax for a year in which their taxable amount for the year does not exceed £500. If the taxable amount exceeds £500, the tax is not to exceed half the excess over £500. Hence the full rate of 30 per cent. applies to gains which exceed £1,250.[6c] The larger relief applicable to individuals applies to certain trusts for mentally disabled persons and persons in receipt of an attendance allowance [6d]: see § 16-02.

Due date

16-03   Capital gains tax is assessed on a current year basis. The tax is payable at or before the expiration of three months following the year of assessment or at the expiration of 30 days beginning with the date of issue of the notice of assessment, whichever is the later.[7]

Short-term gains

16-03A   The Finance Act 1962 introduced a tax on short-term gains, under Case VII of Schedule D. In its final form it was levied on gains which accrued

---

[4a] F.A. 1978, s. 44 (1)–(5) (9).
[5] F.A. 1965, s. 21. For details see the 11th ed. of this book at § 16-01.
[6] F.A. 1978, s. 36 (10).
[6a] I.C.T.A. 1970, ss. 112–113, and F.A. 1978, s. 44 (8) (9).
[6b] F.A. 1978, s. 44 (6) and Sched. 7, para. 4.
[6c] *Ibid.* s. 44 (6) and Sched. 7, para. 6.
[6d] *Ibid.* s. 44 (6) and Sched. 7, para. 5.
[7] F.A. 1965, s. 20 (6). For companies see I.C.T.A. 1970, s. 243 (4).

where there was an acquisition of an asset and a disposal within 12 months; and whereas capital gains tax was a flat rate tax, gains charged under Case VII of Schedule D were subject to income tax and surtax. After the Finance Act 1965, the gains of companies fell outside the ambit of Case VII and within the ambit of the capital gains tax. Gains which were chargeable as short-term gains were not chargeable to capital gains tax.[8]

Case VII of Schedule D was abolished for the year 1971–72 and subsequent years[9] and is not further considered in this edition.

Chargeable persons

16-04   The capital gains tax applies to all gains accruing to a person in a year of assessment during any part of which he is resident in the United Kingdom, or during which he is ordinarily resident in the United Kingdom.[10] The alternative of " ordinary " residence is introduced to prevent a person normally resident in the United Kingdom avoiding capital gains tax by disposing of assets during a period of " temporary " non-residence. The terms " resident " and " ordinarily resident " have the same meanings as in the Income Tax Acts.[11] An individual who is resident or ordinarily resident but not domiciled in the United Kingdom is taxed on a remittance basis on gains from the disposal of assets situated outside the United Kingdom; losses on the disposal of such assets are not allowable losses.[12] The Act contains provisions for determining the situation of assets.[13] Trustees and personal representatives are not " individuals " so the remittance basis does not apply to disposals by them.[14]

Where any trade or business is carried on by two or more persons in partnership and the control and management of the trade or business is situated abroad, partners resident in the United Kingdom are treated for the purposes of the capital gains tax as resident outside the United Kingdom.[15] This artificial treatment does not extend to *ordinary* residence. Its effect, therefore, is that partners who are ordinarily resident in the United Kingdom are chargeable to capital gains tax on the disposal of partnership assets whereas partners who are not so ordinarily resident are exempt from the charge.

A person who is neither resident nor ordinarily resident in the United Kingdom in a year of assessment is not chargeable to capital gains tax on gains accruing to him in that year unless he is carrying on a trade in the United Kingdom through a branch or agency (as defined[16]), in which case he is chargeable on chargeable gains (and is entitled to relief for allowable losses[17]) which accrue on the disposal—

---

[8] F.A. 1965, Sched. 6, paras. 2 and 3.

[9] F.A. 1971, s. 56 (1). For details of the taxation of short-term gains, see the 4th edition of this book at Chap. 15.

[10] F.A. 1965, s. 20 (1). See Concession No. D2 as to the year of commencement or cessation of permanent residence.

[11] F.A. 1965, s. 43 (1) (2); and §§ 7-17 *et seq.*

[12] *Ibid.* s. 20 (7). As to the amount to be treated as remitted, see s. 45 (6). As to delayed remittances, see § 16-06.

[13] *Ibid.* s. 43 (3).

[14] *Ibid.* Sched. 10, para. 12 (2).

[15] *Ibid.* s. 45 (7) applying I.C.T.A. 1970, s. 153; *ante*, § 7-24.

[16] *Ibid.* s. 45 (1).

[17] *Ibid.* s. 23 (6).

(a) of assets situated in the United Kingdom [18] and used in or for the purposes of the trade at or before the time when the capital gain accrued; or

(b) of assets situated in the United Kingdom [18] and used or held for the purposes of the branch or agency at or before that time, or assets acquired for use by or for the purposes of the branch or agency. [19]

This provision does not apply to a person who is exempt from income tax in respect of the profits or gains of the branch or agency under a double taxation agreement. [20] The position with respect to chargeable gains of non-resident companies is discussed below. [21]

Husband and wife

16-04A Gains and losses of husband and wife are calculated separately for each spouse, losses incurred by one of them being set primarily against that spouse's gains. Chargeable gains accruing to a married woman in any year or part of a year during which she is living with her husband (see § 8-23) are, however, assessed on the husband unless either the husband or wife elect to be separately assessed. [22] Where husband and wife are living together (whether or not an election for separate assessment has been made), unrelievable losses of one spouse in any year can be set against gains accruing to the other spouse for that year or carried forward and set against gains of future years accruing to either spouse. This, however, is subject to either spouse's right to elect to keep his or her own losses for himself or herself. [23]

As between married persons living together, the amounts of £1,000, £5,000 and £600 referred to in § 16-02 are divided between them in proportion to their respective taxable amounts, except that they can agree the apportionment if either has allowable losses to carry forward from previous years. [24] If they live together for part only of the year, the part in which they are separated is treated as a separate year of assessment.

As to transfers between husband and wife, see § 16-17.

Chargeable assets

16-05 The capital gains tax is charged on the disposal of assets [25] and all forms of property are assets for this purpose, [26] whether situated in the United Kingdom or not, including—

(a) options, debts and incorporeal property generally; and

(b) any currency other than sterling; and

(c) any form of property created by the person disposing of it, or otherwise coming to be owned without being acquired, [27] e.g. a

---

[18] The rules for the situation of assets are in F.A. 1965, s. 43 (3).
[19] *Ibid.* s. 20 (2).
[20] *Ibid.* s. 20 (2), proviso.
[21] *Post,* § 16-55.
[22] F.A. 1965, Sched. 10, para. 3.
[23] *Ibid.* s. 20 (5).
[24] F.A. 1978, s. 44 (6) and Sched. 7, paras. 1–3.
[25] *Ibid.* s. 19 (1).
[26] *Ibid.* s. 22 (1).
[27] F.A. 1965, s. 22 (1).

building which the person erects, goods which he manufactures, a pedigree herd bred by him, or the copyright of a book written by him.

Property which is inherently unsaleable, such as the benefit of a contract of personal service, is not " assets." Thus, in one case [28] a sum of £50,000 received by a company for releasing a director from his obligations under a service agreement was held not to be a capital sum derived from assets within section 22 (3) of the Finance Act 1965: see § 16-08.

Relief for delayed remittances

16-06   Capital gains from the disposal of assets outside the United Kingdom are chargeable gains if the disponer is resident or ordinarily resident in the United Kingdom; and tax is levied on an arising basis or, if the disponer is domiciled outside the United Kingdom, on a remittance basis. [29] If the disponer is unable to transfer the gains to the United Kingdom due to the provisions of the foreign law or to some executive action of the foreign government or to the impossibility of obtaining foreign currency, the liability to tax is delayed until remittance becomes possible. [30]

2. DISPOSALS

Disposal

16-07   The charge to capital gains tax arises on the *disposal* of an asset. [31] On each such disposal a computation must be made to determine whether a chargeable gain (or allowable loss) has accrued. The term " disposal " is not defined in the Act so general principles of law have to be applied. Plainly there is a disposal if ownership of an asset is transferred from one person to another, whether by sale, exchange, gift or otherwise. The expression " disposal " includes a part disposal of an asset [32]; and there is a part disposal where an interest or right in or over the asset is created by the disposal, as well as where it subsists before the disposal (*e.g.* where a lease is granted by the freeholder as well as where it is assigned by the leaseholder), and generally there is a part disposal where, on a person making a disposal, any description of property derived from the asset remains undisposed of. [33] Hence a computation has to be made if a person disposes of less than his entire interest in an asset. A person's holding of shares of the same class in a company is treated as a single asset so a disposal of part of a shareholding requires a computation on a part disposal basis (see § 16-31A).

Extended meaning of disposal

16-08   The term " disposal " has an extended meaning for the purposes of capital gains tax. There is a disposal of assets by their owner where a capital

---

[28] *O'Brien* v. *Benson's Hosiery (Holdings) Ltd.* (1978) 122 S.J. 439.
[29] *Ante,* § 16-04.
[30] *Ibid.* s. 40.
[31] *Ibid.* s. 19 (1).
[32] *Ibid.* s. 22 (2) (*a*).
[33] *Ibid.* s. 22 (2) (*b*).

sum is derived from assets notwithstanding that no asset is acquired by the person paying the capital sum; and the relevant provision [34] applies in particular to:

(a) Capital sums received by way of compensation for any kind of damage or injury to assets or for the loss, destruction or dissipation of assets or for any depreciation or risk of depreciation of an asset [35];

(b) capital sums received under a policy of insurance against the risk of any kind of damage or injury to, or the loss or depreciation of, assets [36];

(c) capital sums received in return for forfeiture or surrender of rights, or for refraining from exercising rights, and

(d) capital sums received as consideration for use or exploitation of assets.

The disposal is treated as occurring at the time when the capital sum is received. [37] The expression " capital sum " means any money or money's worth which is not excluded from the consideration taken into account in the computation of chargeable gains, e.g. sums chargeable as income. [38]

In *Davies* v. *Powell* [39] it was held that compensation for disturbance paid to a tenant farmer on surrendering his lease, following a notice to quit from his landlord, was not " derived " from an asset (*i.e.* the lease). It was a sum which had to be paid under section 34 of the Agricultural Holdings Act 1948.

Roll-over relief is available in certain cases where the capital sum is applied in restoring or replacing an asset which is damaged or injured. [40]

16-09   The occasion of the entire loss, destruction, dissipation or extinction of an asset is treated as a disposal of the asset whether or not any capital sum by way of compensation or otherwise is received in respect of the destruction, dissipation or extinction. [41] If the Inspector is satisfied on a claim being made by the owner of an asset that the value of the asset has become negligible, the claimant is to be treated as having sold and immediately re-acquired the asset for a consideration equal to the value specified in the claim, [42] *i.e.* as if he had in fact disposed of it. For the purposes of these provisions, a building can be regarded as an asset separate from the land on which it stands; but if a building is destroyed or its value becomes negligible, the person deemed to dispose of the building is to be

---

[34] F.A. 1965, s. 22 (3).

[35] That part of a " golden handshake " which escapes income tax under Schedule E will be exempt from capital gains tax under F.A. 1965, Sched. 6, para. 2 (1), *post*, § 16-29.

[36] See *ibid.* Sched. 6, para. 13.

[37] *Ibid.* s. 45 (5).

[38] *Ibid.* s. 22 (9). As to what is excluded, see *post*, § 16-29.

[39] [1977] S.T.C. 32. See also *Randall* v. *Plumb* in § 16-31, note 40.

[40] F.A. 1965, Sched. 6, para. 13.

[41] *Ibid.* s. 23 (3).

[42] *Ibid.* s. 23 (4). For some guidance as to the meaning of " negligible," see B.T.R. (1972) " Current Tax Intelligence," at p. 405. It seems that in practice the Revenue treat the deemed sale as occurring in the chargeable period to which the claim relates. The time limit for making the claim is two years from the end of the chargeable period: see [1975] S.T.I. 420.

treated as if he had also sold and immediately re-acquired the site of the building for a consideration equal to its market value at that time,[43] so any gain (or loss) on the site must be brought into the account in the same year of assessment as that in which the loss on the building is brought in. The abandonment of an option is in some cases [44] treated as a disposal of the option.

Roll-over relief is available in certain cases where compensation for the loss of an asset is applied in replacing the asset.[45]

Mortgage and hire-purchase

16-10   The transfer of an asset by way of security and its retransfer on redemption of the security involves no acquisition or disposal.[46] If a mortgagee or chargee (or receiver or manager) enforces the security, his acts are treated as those of the mortgagor or chargor.[47] If a person takes a transfer of property subject to a mortgage or charge, the amount of the liability assumed by him is treated as part of the cost of acquisition.[48] Thus, if P acquires an asset for £5,000 which is charged to secure a debt of £1,000, which P takes over, P's base cost is £6,000.

If an asset is sold on hire-purchase, it is treated as disposed of at the beginning of the hire-purchase period, subject to later adjustment if the customer does not ultimately become the owner of the asset.[49]

Appropriations to and from stock-in-trade

16-11   A trader may acquire an asset otherwise than as trading stock and later appropriate the asset to the trade. If on a sale of the asset at its market value at the time of such appropriation, a chargeable gain or allowable loss would have accrued to him, the appropriation is treated as a disposal of the asset at market value, unless the trader elects to bring the asset into trading stock at its market value reduced by the amount of the chargeable gain or increased by the amount of the allowable loss.[50] By so electing the trader avoids any immediate charge to capital gains tax but any profit (or loss) on the eventual sale of the asset, or the cessation of the trade, will be reflected in the profits (or losses) of the trade. The election applies only if the trader is chargeable to income tax in respect of the profits of the trade under Case I of Schedule D. Conversely, if at any time an asset which is trading stock is appropriated by the trader for some other purpose, or is retained by him on the cessation of the trade, he is treated as having acquired the asset at that time for a consideration equal to the amount brought into the trading accounts in respect of it for tax purposes.[51] Thus the base value of the asset for purposes of capital gains tax is taken as the closing figure for income tax (or

---

[43] *Ibid.* s. 23 (5).
[44] See F.A. 1971, s. 58.
[45] See note 40, *ante.*
[46] F.A. 1965, s. 22 (6).
[47] *Ibid.* s. 22 (7).
[48] *Ibid.* s. 22 (8).
[49] *Ibid.* s. 45 (4).
[50] F.A. 1965, Sched. 7, para. 1 (1), (3). *Cf.* the principle in *Sharkey* v. *Wernher,* discussed *ante*, § 2-46. Where the trade is carried on in partnership, the election must be concurred in by all the partners.
[51] *Ibid.* Sched. 7, para. 1 (2).

corporation tax) purposes. The practical application of these provisions is somewhat restricted in the case of stock-in-trade consisting of tangible movable property by an exemption which is discussed in § 16-44.

Capital distributions by companies

16-12   Where a person receives or becomes entitled to receive in respect of shares in a company any capital distribution from the company (other than a new holding [52]) he is treated as if he had in consideration of that capital distribution disposed of an interest in the shares. [53] " Capital distribution " means any distribution from the company, including a distribution in the course of dissolving or winding up the company, in money or money's worth except a distribution which in the hands of the recipient constitutes income for the purposes of income tax. [54] Thus if a company goes into liquidation each shareholder is treated as disposing of an interest in his shares in consideration of the share of assets to which he becomes entitled in the liquidation. Each distribution in the course of winding up involves a part disposal by each shareholder. If the Inspector is satisfied that the amount of any capital distribution is small, as compared with the value of the shares in respect of which it is made, and he so directs, the occasion of the capital distribution is not treated as a disposal of the asset, but the amount or value of the capital distribution is deducted from any expenditure allowable as a deduction in computing a gain or loss on the disposal of the shares by the person receiving or becoming entitled to receive a distribution of capital. A person who is dissatisfied with the refusal of the Inspector to give a direction may appeal to the Commissioners. [55] The Revenue treat an amount as small in relation to another amount if the first amount does not exceed 5 per cent. of the second amount. [56]

When, on a bonus or rights issue, a company making the issue sells fractional entitlements on the market and distributes the proceeds *pro rata* to the shareholders entitled, the distributions are treated as capital distributions.

Company transactions

16-13   Paragraphs 4–6 of the Seventh Schedule to the Finance Act 1965 contain elaborate provisions which apply to the reorganisation or reduction of share capital, the conversion of securities and to company amalgamations. If, for example, there is a bonus issue or rights issue and shareholders are allotted shares or debentures in proportion to their existing holdings, the new shares or debentures are treated as acquired when the original shares were acquired and the total holding is treated as acquired for a price equal to the cost of the original shares plus any sum paid for the new holding. [57] Similarly, if the rights attached to a class of shares are altered or there is a conversion of

---

[52] *Ibid.* Sched. 7, para. 4 (1).
[53] *Ibid.* Sched. 7, para. 3 (1).
[54] F.A. 1965, Sched. 7, para. 3 (4).
[55] *Ibid.* Sched. 7, para. 3 (2), (3). For the Revenue's practice in charging tax when there is more than one distribution in a liquidation, see B.T.R. (1972) " Current Tax Intelligence," at p. 403.
[56] IR Booklet CGT 8 (1973), para. 117.
[57] F.A. 1965, Sched. 7, para. 4.

when the claim is made. There are similar provisions which apply where a loss is suffered by a guarantor.

Switching of rights [71]

16-16 If a person having control of a company exercises his control so that value passes out of his shares or of those of a person with whom he is connected [71a] into other shares, this is a disposal of the shares out of which value passes, notwithstanding that there is no consideration for the disposal; so also if value passes out of other rights over the company.

> In *Floor* v. *Davis* [72] it was held that the word " person " could, in this context, be read in the plural so as to make the provision apply where two or more persons cause value to pass out of shares. It was further held that deliberate inaction could constitute an " exercise " of control.

An adjustment of the rights and liabilities under a lease following the grant of a lease, such adjustment being favourable to the lessor, is treated as a disposal by the lessee of an interest in the property.

Similarly, the extinction or abrogation of a right or restriction over an asset involves a disposal.

Husband and wife [73]

16-17 If, in any year of assessment, and in the case of a woman who in that year of assessment is a married woman living with her husband,[74] the man disposes of an asset to the wife, or the wife disposes of an asset to the man, both are treated as if the asset was acquired from the one making the disposal for a consideration of such amount as would secure that on the disposal neither a gain nor a loss would accrue to the one making the disposal. The disponee is treated as acquiring the asset for whatever is the base cost of the asset in the hands of the disponer. This general rule does not apply:

(a) if the asset was trading stock of the disponer or is acquired as trading stock of the disponee; or

(b) if the disposal is by way of *donatio mortis causa*.

Partnerships

16-17A For capital gains tax purposes any dealings in partnership assets are dealings by the individual partners.[75] The Board have issued a Statement of Practice [76] concerning the capital gains tax treatment of partnerships and the statements in this paragraph are based thereon. Each partner is regarded as owning a fractional share in the partnership assets (falling to be valued as a proportion of the market value of those assets) rather than as having a particular interest in the " partnership " falling to be valued as such.

---

[71] F.A. 1965, Sched. 7, para. 15.
[71a] See § 16-18A.
[72] [1978] 3 W.L.R. 360 (C.A.). See also §§ 40-28 *et seq.*
[73] *Ibid.* para. 20.
[74] See § 8-23.
[75] *Ibid.* s. 45 (7).
[76] Issued on January 17, 1975: see [1975] S.T.I. 17.

Therefore when any asset is disposed of by the partnership each partner is attributed with his fractional share of the gain accruing, either by reference to the allocation of asset surpluses under the partnership agreement or, in the absence of such allocation, by reference to his profit-sharing ratio. On a distribution of assets among the partners themselves (as, for example, on a dissolution) any partner not receiving a particular asset will be regarded as having disposed of his fractional share therein. Where there is a change in profit-sharing ratios (as on the introduction or retirement of a partner or on a merger), any disposal in underlying goodwill will be treated as made for a consideration equal to the partner's capital gains tax base cost unless actual payment is made (whether made outside the partnership accounts or by adjustment in those accounts). Where partnership assets are revalued and a partner's share therein is subsequently reduced he will be regarded as disposing of the fractional difference in the partnership assets. Likewise the partner whose share increases has his acquisition cost increased. Transactions between partners are not regarded as being made between connected persons [77] unless the partners are connected otherwise than by way of partnership (for example, father and son). Even in the latter case, however, the Revenue will not substitute market value on any transaction if nothing would have been paid had the parties been at arm's length.

Any lump sum paid to a partner on his leaving the partnership represents consideration for the disposal of his share in the underlying assets. Where, however, instead of receiving a capital payment, a retiring partner is to receive an annuity,[78] its capital value will not be treated as consideration for the disposal of his share [79] in the partnership assets if it is no more than can be regarded as a reasonable recognition of his past work and effort.[80] Specific provision is made in the Statement for the pooling of expenditure and consequential elections.

3. DISPOSALS BY WAY OF GIFT OR SETTLEMENT AND ON DEATH

Gifts

16-18   Where a person disposes of an asset by way of gift [80a] or otherwise than by way of a bargain made at arm's length, this is treated as a disposal by the disponer [81] and an acquisition by the disponee for a consideration equal to the market value of the asset at that time.[82] Dispositions to charities and to

---

[77] F.A. 1965, Sched. 7, para. 21 (4). See § 16-18A.

[78] The Statement makes no reference to the possibility of such annuities becoming payable to the widow and dependants of a partner. Furthermore it does not expressly deal with the situation where one form of " rights " in a partnership is given up for another.

[79] Under F.A. 1965, Sched. 6, para. 2 (3).

[80] Provided the partner has been in the partnership for 10 years this requirement is treated as satisfied if the annuity is no more than two thirds of his average share in profits in the best three of the last seven years.

[80a] The word " gift " can include any transfer of property: see *Berry* v. *Warnett* [1978] 1 W.L.R. at p. 963E; and see § 16-21 (2).

[81] *Turner* v. *Follet* (1973) 48 T.C. 614; [1973] S.T.C. 148 (C.A.). Section 22 (4) applies where there is an acquisition otherwise than by way of bargain at arms' length but no concomitant disposal, *e.g.* where there is an acquisition of a new issue of shares or debentures: *Harrison* v. *Nairn Williamson Ltd.* [1978] S.T.C. 67 (C.A.).

[82] *Ibid.* s. 22 (4). In some cases, payment of the tax due can be postponed: see F.A. 1965, Sched. 10, para. 4, substituted by F.A. 1972, s. 117 and amended by F. (No 2) A. 1975, s. 57.

certain bodies, such as the National Gallery, are the subject of a special relief: see § 16-50.

There are elaborate provisions to prevent avoidance of capital gains tax by disposals at an undervalue; in particular, transactions between connected persons are assumed to be otherwise than by way of bargain at arm's length.[83] Where a price is freely negotiated and the market moves in the vendor's favour before contract, the bargain may nevertheless be at arm's length.[84]

Although the donor or the vendor at an undervalue is chargeable with the tax payable under these provisions, the donee or purchaser can be assessed in some cases.[85]

Connected persons

16-18A   Paragraph 21 of Schedule 7 to the Finance Act 1965 (as amended) provides as follows:

(1) For the purposes of, and subject to, the provisions of the Tax Acts which apply this section, any question whether a person is connected with another shall be determined in accordance with the following provisions of this section (any provision that one person is connected with another being taken to mean that they are connected with one another).

(2) A person is connected with an individual if that person is the individual's husband or wife, or is a relative, or the husband or wife of a relative, of the individual or of the individual's husband or wife.

(3) A person, in his capacity as trustee of a settlement, is connected with any individual who in relation to the settlement is a settlor, with any person who is connected with such an individual and with a body corporate which, under section 454 of this Act is deemed to be connected with that settlement (" settlement " and " settlor " having for the purposes of this subsection the meanings assigned to them by subsection (3) of that section).

(4) Except in relation to acquisitions or disposals of partnership assets pursuant to bona fide commercial arrangements, a person is connected with any person with whom he is in partnership, and with the husband or wife or a relative of any individual with whom he is in partnership.

(5) A company is connected with another company—

(a) if the same person has control of both, or a person has control of one and persons connected with him, or he and persons connected with him, have control of the other, or

(b) if a group of two or more persons has control of each company, and the groups either consist of the same persons or could be regarded as consisting of the same persons by treating (in one or more cases) a member of either group as replaced by a person with whom he is connected.

(6) A company is connected with another person, if that person has control of it or if that person and persons connected with him together have control of it.

(7) Any two or more persons acting together to secure or exercise control of a company shall be treated in relation to that company as connected with one another and with any person acting on the directions of any of them to secure or exercise control of the company.

---

[83] F.A. 1965, Sched. 7. para. 17 (2). For " connected persons," see § 16-18A.
[84] *Clark* v. *Follett* (1973) 48 T.C. 677 at 704F.
[85] *Ibid.* Sched. 7, para. 19. *Post*, § 16-25. As to capital transfer tax, see Pt. 2.

(8) In this section—

" company " includes any body corporate or unincorporated association, but does not include a partnership, and this section shall apply in relation to any unit trust scheme (as defined in section 26 (1) of the Prevention of Fraud (Investments) Act 1958 or section 22 of the Prevention of Fraud (Investments) Act (Northern Ireland) 1940) as if the scheme were a company and as if the rights of the unit holders were shares in the company,

" control " shall be construed in accordance with section 302 of this Act,

" relative " means brother, sister, ancestor or lineal descendant.

Free estate: deaths after March 30, 1971

16-19   On the death of an individual after March 30, 1971, the assets of which the deceased was competent to dispose [86] are deemed to be *acquired* on his death by the personal representatives or other person on whom they devolve for a consideration equal to their market value at the date of the death; but the assets are not treated as *disposed* of by the individual on his death. [87] Hence the death of an individual is not an occasion which gives rise to a charge to capital gains tax: assets of which the deceased was competent to dispose are subject only to capital transfer tax [88] on his death and not to capital gains tax. But the death of an individual is an occasion which gives rise to a notional acquisition by the personal representatives at a cost equal to the market value of the assets of the deceased at the time of his death. This exemption from the charge to capital gains tax applies where the assets are not charged to capital transfer tax as being, for example, left to a surviving spouse.

> Thus if A dies owning quoted shares which cost £20,000 and which have a market value at death of £30,000, capital transfer tax is leviable on the shares (unless the assets are exempt, *e.g.* as being left to a surviving spouse) and A's personal representatives are treated as having acquired the shares at a cost of £30,000.

16-20   Is a subsequent disposal by personal representatives in the course of administration an occasion of charge? This depends on whether the disponee acquires as " legatee " or otherwise.

(1) On a person acquiring any asset as legatee, no chargeable gain accrues to the personal representatives: the legatee is treated as if the personal representatives' acquisition of the asset had been his acquisition of it. [89] Hence a legatee's " base cost " is the market value of the asset at the time of the deceased's death. The expression " legatee " is widely defined to include any person taking under a testamentary disposition or on an intestacy or partial intestacy, whether he takes beneficially or as trustee; and

---

[86] Defined F.A. 1965, s. 24 (9), to mean assets of the deceased which he could if of full age and capacity have disposed of by his will, assuming all the assets are situated in England and the deceased was domiciled in England. Assets over which he has a power of appointment are excluded. The deceased's share in assets to which, immediately before his death, he was beneficially entitled as joint tenant is included: F.A. 1971, Sched. 12, para. 2.

[87] F.A. 1965, s. 24 (1), substituted by F.A. 1971, s. 59 and Sched. 12, para. 1. In *Larter* v. *Skone James* [1976] S.T.C. 220 it was held that " on the death " in s. 24 (1) meant the moment immediately after the death.

[88] See *post*, Chap. 18.

[89] F.A. 1965, s. 24 (7).

a person taking under a *donatio mortis causa* [90] is treated as a legatee and as if his acquisition was made at the time of the donor's death. [91] It should be noted that the exemption on acquisitions by legatees is not in express terms limited to disposals made prior to the completion of the administration period. [92]

(2) If personal representatives dispose of assets otherwise than to legatees, *e.g.* if they realise assets in order to pay capital transfer tax, they are chargeable in respect of any gain which accrues on that disposal, subject to their right to relief in respect of allowable losses. [93] There is no provision under which unrelieved losses accruing on disposals by personal representatives can be made available for offset against gains of the deceased accruing before the death or gains of the beneficiaries entitled to the deceased's estate. [94]

Deeds of family arrangement, etc.

16-20A   It sometimes happens that beneficiaries under a will or intestacy agree between themselves, by a deed of family arrangement or similar instrument (*e.g.* formal correspondence) to vary the dispositions made under the will or created by the intestacy. The estate is then administered subject to the agreed variations. Section 68 of the Finance Act 1978 (*post,* § 19-63) deals with the implications of such a variation as respects capital transfer tax. Section 24 (11) of the Finance Act 1965 provides that where within the period of two years after a person's death any of the dispositions (whether effected by will, under the law relating to intestacy or otherwise) of the property of which he was competent to dispose are varied, or the benefit conferred by those dispositions is disclaimed, by an instrument in writing made by the persons or any of the persons who benefit or would benefit under the dispositions, the variation or disclaimer shall not constitute a disposal for the purposes of capital gains tax; and the Act is to apply as if the variation had been effected by the deceased or, as the case may be, the disclaimed benefit had never been conferred.

This provision does not apply to a variation unless the person or persons making the instrument so elect by written notice given to the Board within six months after the date of the instrument or such longer time as the Board may allow. The section does not apply to a variation or disclaimer made for any consideration in money or money's worth other than consideration consisting of the making of the variation or disclaimer in respect of another of the dispositions. The section applies whether or not the administration of the estate is complete or the property has been distributed in accordance with the original dispositions. This provision is expressed to take effect from the date of the passing of the Act and not from April 11, 1978, as does

---

[90] A *donatio mortis causa* is a delivery of property in contemplation of the donor's death on the express or implied condition that the gift shall not be complete until the donor dies.

[91] F.A 1965, s.45 (1), as amended in the case of death after March 30, 1971, by F.A. 1971, s. 59 and Sched. 12, para. 4. Thus if A makes a death-bed gift to B, this is not an occasion of charge under F.A. 1965, s. 22 (4) (a), nor is A's death an occasion of charge. B takes as his base the market value at death.

[92] Completion of the administration is material to the matters discussed in §§ 9-10 *et seq.*

[93] See § 16-37. For the rate chargeable, see § 16-02A.

[94] This follows from the repeal of s. 24 (8), F.A. 1965, when it was replaced by F.A. 1969, s. 24A and from the subsequent repeal of s. 24A by F.A. 1971, Sched. 14, Pt. V.

a corresponding provision relating to capital transfer tax. By concession, however, both provisions will be applied from the earlier date.[95]

Settled property

16-21   (1) *Definition.* Settled property is defined in section 45 (1) of the Finance Act 1965 as meaning, unless the context otherwise requires, " any property held in trust other than property to which section 22 (5) of this Act applies."

Section 22 (5) excludes from the definition of settled property assets held by a person (a) as nominee for another person; or (b) as trustee for another person absolutely entitled as against the trustee (or for two or more persons jointly so entitled); or (c) as trustee for any person who would be absolutely entitled as against the trustee but for being an infant or other person under disability (or for two or more persons who would be jointly so entitled, but for infancy, etc.). A person is so absolutely entitled as against the trustee where he has the exclusive right, subject only to satisfying any outstanding charge, lien or other right of the trustee to resort to the asset for payment of duty, taxes, costs and other outgoings, to direct how the asset shall be dealt with.[96] Assets which are subject to a unit trust scheme are treated separately from settled property[97] and from property to which section 22 (5) applies (which may be described as " nominee property ").

It will be observed that the definition of " settled property " is extremely wide. Property held for persons entitled in undivided shares is not settled property if the interest of each of the beneficiaries is not, *e.g.* contingent or subject to defeasance. Thus if land is held upon trust for X and Y in undivided shares (equal or unequal), the land is not settled property.[98]

> In *Booth* v. *Ellard,*[99] B and 11 other taxpayers transferred their shares in X Limited to trustees to be held on trusts set out in an agreement for 15 years. Each shareholder restricted his right to dispose of the shares and to deal with his beneficial interest therein. *Held* that the shares subject to the agreement were not " settled property ": each of the beneficiaries was " absolutely entitled " because (a) their respective interests were concurrent and not successive; and (b) their interests were quantitatively the same.

(2) *Property put into settlement.* Where property is put into settlement, this is treated as a disposal of the property thereby becoming settled property, whether the settlement is revocable or irrevocable and notwithstanding that the donor is interested as a beneficiary or is a trustee or the sole trustee of the settlement.[1] Thus the act of settling property may give rise to a chargeable gain or an allowable loss.[2] A settlor and the trustees of his settlement are treated as " connected persons " and

---

[95] F.A. 1965, s. 24 (11), as substituted by F.A. 1978, s. 52; and see § 19-63.

[96] F.A. 1969, Sched. 19, para. 9. And see *Tomlinson* v. *Glyns Executor & Trustee Co. and Another* (1969) 45 T.C. 600 (C.A.).

[97] See F.A. 1965, s. 45 (1), defining " settled property " subject to *ibid.* s. 45 (8), which defines " unit trust scheme. " Unit trust schemes are not settled property.

[98] *Kidson* v. *MacDonald* [1974] Ch. 339; 49 T.C. 503; but property held in common subject to the payment of an annuity is settled property: *Stephenson* v. *Barclays Bank Trust Co. Ltd.* (1975) 50 T.C. 374; S.T.C. 151. See also *Crowe* v. *Appleby* [1975] S.T.C. 502. See § 16-23, note 13.

[99] [1978] S.T.C. 487.

[1] F.A. 1965, s. 25 (2).

[2] In some cases, payment of the tax due can be postponed: see F.A. 1965, Sched. 10, para. 4, substituted by F.A. 1972 , s. 117 and amended by F. (No. 2) A. 1975, s. 57.

accordingly a loss which accrues on the making of the settlement is deductible only from a chargeable gain accruing on some other disposal to the trustees, unless the settlement is for charitable or similar purposes.[3] The stamp duty payable on the settlement is an allowable expense in the capital gains computation.[4]

> In *Berry* v. *Warnett* [4a] B owned investments worth £219,880 on which a gain of £150,483 had accrued. B transferred the investments to a Guernsey company as his nominee. A Jersey company paid B £14,500 for a reversionary interest in the investments expectant on B's death; and B then sold his retained life interest to a Bahamian company for £130,753. The transaction involving B, the Guernsey Company and the Jersey company was completed by one tripartite deed. It was common ground that there was a " settlement " after the sale of the reversionary interest to the Jersey company and that the sale of the life interest to the Bahamian company gave rise to no charge to tax (see the exemption in § 16-24). The question arose whether the sale of the reversionary interest was a disposal of all the investments thereby becoming settled property, such disposal being deemed to be at market value (as the Crown contended) or was a mere part disposal for £14,500 (as B contended). *Held* that B's contention was right. Even if the transfer of the reversionary interest was a gift in settlement, there was no basis on which the consideration could be increased beyond the £14,500 actually received by B.

16-22   (3) *Disposals by trustees.* In relation to settled property, the trustees of the settlement are treated as being a single and continuing body of persons distinct from the persons who may from time to time be the trustees.[5] Hence a mere change of trustees gives rise to no disposal. A disposal by trustees of assets comprised in settled property may give rise to a chargeable gain [6] or allowable loss on which the trustees will be assessed or may claim relief. In some cases trustees of settled property are *deemed* to have disposed of assets comprised in settled property. The following is a summary of these cases.

(i) ABSOLUTE ENTITLEMENT AGAINST TRUSTEE. By section 25 (3) of the Finance Act 1965, on the occasion when a person becomes absolutely entitled to any settled property as against the trustee all the assets forming part of the settled property to which he becomes so entitled are deemed to have been disposed of by the trustee, and immediately re-acquired by him in his capacity as a trustee within section 22 (5) of the Act, for a consideration equal to their market value. Market value means the price the assets might reasonably be expected to fetch on a sale in the open market.[7]

> Thus if assets are held upon trust for A contingently on his attaining the age of twenty-five years, the attainment of the specified age is an occasion of charge under section 25 (3). The trustees are treated as having sold the property at its then market value. The point of the reference to section 22 (5) is that the property ceases to be settled property on A becoming absolutely entitled thereto and any subsequent disposal by the trustees is treated as if it were a disposal by A.

---

[3] *Ibid.* Sched. 7, para. 17 (3), as amended.
[4] *Post,* § 16-30.
[4a] [1978] S.T.C. 504.
[5] F.A. 1965, s. 25 (1). When settled property is divided between different trustees, as in the case of settled land, they are treated as together constituting and, so far as they act separately, as acting on behalf of a single body of persons: *ibid.* s. 25 (11).
[6] F.A. 1965, s. 25 (2).   [7] *Ibid.* s. 44 (1).

A person may become *absolutely* entitled although he is not *beneficially* entitled. Thus if trustees exercise a power of advancement so as to cause the advanced assets to be held on new trusts, the new trustees may become absolutely entitled as against the advancing trustees—and certainly will become so entitled if " no one will ever again need to refer to the original settlement except to confirm that it has ceased to exist." [8]

Where, however, a person becomes absolutely entitled to assets forming part of settled property on the termination of a life interest [9] section 25 (3) is modified [10] so as to accord with the general principle that there should be no charge to capital gains tax on a death but only a deemed acquisition at market value and an " uplift " in the capital gains tax " base." On such an occasion no chargeable gain accrues on the disposal. [11]

> Thus if assets are held upon trust for A for life, remainder to B absolutely, there is a notional disposal and re-acquisition by the trustees on A's death under section 25 (3) but no chargeable gain accrues on that disposal. The trustees pay capital transfer tax (if chargeable, subject to an exception mentioned below) on the market value of the assets and start with a new " base cost " for capital gains tax purposes equal to that market value.

There is a special exception to meet the case where there is a " reverter to the disponer." We shall see in § 22-27 that if S transfers property to X for life, with no other dispositions, no capital transfer tax is payable on X's death in respect of the property which then reverts to S. The exception is designed to prevent both capital transfer tax and capital gains tax being avoided by the use of this device. It is provided that if on the life tenant's death the property reverts to the disponer, the disposal and re-acquisition under section 25 (3) of the Finance Act 1965 shall be deemed to be for such consideration as to secure that neither a gain nor a loss accrues to the trustee and shall, if the trustee had first acquired the property at a date earlier than April 6, 1965, be deemed to be at that earlier date. [11]

> Suppose S purchases an asset in 1968 costing £5,000. In 1970 S grants a life interest in the asset (then worth £6,000) to X and the asset thus becomes " settled property." X dies in 1975 when the value of the asset is £7,000. No capital transfer tax is payable on X's death: see *post*, Chapter 18. But for the special exception, section 25 (3) of the Finance Act 1965, would apply on X's death and S would be treated as re-acquiring the asset at its then market value of £7,000. No gain would accrue on the death. By virtue of the exception, S is treated as re-acquiring the asset for £6,000.

A deemed disposal under section 25 (3) of the Finance Act 1965 may produce an allowable loss. If the loss accrues to the trustees in respect of property to which a beneficiary becomes absolutely entitled as against the trustees or in respect of any property represented by that property (*e.g.* if the trustees have realised assets at a loss and invested the proceeds in the

---

[8] *Hoare* v. *Gardner*; *Hart* v. *Briscoe* [1978] S.T.C. 89. See useful notes in [1978] B.T.R. at pp. 1 and 118.

[9] For definition, see § 16-23 and note that F.A. 1965, s. 25 (3) and (4) apply on the termination by death of an annuity which is not a life interest: F.A. 1971, Sched. 12, para. 10.

[10] In the case of deaths occurring after March 30, 1971.

[11] F.A. 1971, Sched. 12, para. 6.

property being transferred to the beneficiary), the loss is treated as if it had accrued to the beneficiary when he becomes absolutely entitled if otherwise the loss would go unrelieved in the hands of the trustees, *i.e.* if no chargeable gains had accrued to the trustees from which the loss could be deducted. This rule applies whether the loss accrues to the trustees in the year of assessment in which the beneficiary becomes absolutely entitled or is carried forward from an earlier year.[12]

Where a deemed disposal gives rise to a chargeable gain, for which the trustees are accountable, there are provisions under which a beneficiary becoming absolutely entitled as against the trustees can be assessed in respect of so much of the gain as is attributable to the property to which he becomes so absolutely entitled: see § 16-25.

16-23   (ii) TERMINATION OF LIFE INTERESTS.   Under section 25 (4) of the Finance Act 1965, as amended by paragraph 7 of Schedule 12 to the Finance Act 1971, on the termination at any time after March 30, 1971, of a life interest in possession in all or any part [13] of settled property, the whole or a corresponding part of each of the assets forming part of the settled property and *not* ceasing at that time to be settled property are to be deemed at that time to be disposed of and immediately reacquired by the trustee for a consideration equal to the whole or a corresponding part of the market value of the asset, but without any chargeable gain accruing.[14] The official view as to the meaning of " interest in possession " is stated in § 22-14.

> Assume that property is settled on A for life, remainder to B for life, remainder to C absolutely. A dies after March 30, 1971. Under section 25 (4), the trustees are deemed to have disposed of and immediately re-acquired the property on A's death for its market value but no chargeable gain accrues on that disposal. Hence there is an " uplift " in the capital gains base without any chargeable gain accruing. The same result would be achieved by the operation of section 25 (3) on the subsequent death of B: see § 16-22 (i).

It should be noted that the above rule applies notwithstanding that the property is exempt from capital transfer tax on the death of the life tenant.

> Thus if property is settled on a husband (H) for life with remainder to his wife (W) either absolutely or for life, no capital transfer tax will be payable on H's death by virtue of the exemption for transfers between spouses discussed in § 19-02, but there will nevertheless be an " uplift " in the capital gains base.

---

[12] F.A. 1965, s. 25 (8).

[13] " Part " includes an undivided fraction of a trust fund: *Pexton* v. *Bell* and *Crowe* v. *Appleby* [1976] S.T.C. 301 (C.A.). In *Crowe* v. *Appleby* T, by his will, directed that his residuary estate (which at all material times consisted of freehold land held on trust for sale) be held in trust for his five children in specified shares which were not all equal. Each child's share was to be held on protective trusts for such child for life, with remainders over. One child (C1) died in 1952 (before capital gains tax), his share devolving on his child (X) absolutely. A second child (C2) died in 1968–69, her share devolving on her children Y and Z absolutely. Each of C1 and C2 was life tenant of a 5/30th part of the trust property. In 1969–70 the entire trust property was sold. *Held,* (i) that on C2's death there was a notional disposal, not of the whole of the trust property (as the Crown contended), but only of C2's 5/30th share; (ii) that the entire trust property remained settled property at the time of the sale in 1969–70 notwithstanding the earlier deaths of C1 and C2, for neither X nor Y and Z had become absolutely entitled as against the trustees to the share which devolved on them. The trust fund was realty and they could not direct the trustees how to deal with the fund nor could they call for the immediate payment of their respective shares thereof. The trustees were accordingly chargeable to capital gains tax in respect of the gain accruing on the disposal of the whole of the fund.

[14] F.A. 1971, Sched. 12, para. 9, and see Revenue Press Release of November 1, 1973, in [1973] S.T.I. at p. 461.

" Life interest "[15] in relation to a settlement—

(a) includes a right under the settlement to the income of, or the use or occupation of, settled property for the life of a person other than the person entitled to the right or for lives:

> Thus if A, a life tenant, assigns his life interest to B, B has an interest during the life of A (an interest *pur autre vie*). B's interest is a " life interest.";

(b) does not include any right which is contingent on the exercise of a discretion of the trustee or of some other person; and

(c) does not include an annuity, notwithstanding that the annuity is payable out of or charged on settled property or the income of settled property.

Where a life interest (as above defined) is terminated by the death of a person who though not entitled thereto at his death was entitled thereto at any time during the period of seven years ending with the death (but prior to March 27, 1974) and capital transfer tax is chargeable on the full value of the property without any reduction, no chargeable gain is to accrue to the trustees. If, however, the value of the property is reduced for capital transfer tax purposes by any percentage, then the benefit of this free uplift is restricted to the amount brought into charge to capital transfer tax. This provision, therefore, only applies to gifts of such interests which are brought into charge to capital transfer tax by the donor failing to survive the seven-year period that secured exemption from estate duty.[16]

Position of the beneficiaries

16-24   No chargeable gain accrues on the disposal of an interest created by or arising under a settlement (including, in particular, an annuity or life interest, and the reversion to an annuity or life interest) by the person for whose benefit the interest was created by the terms of the settlement or by his legatee, except where that person acquired (or derived his title from one who acquired) his interest for a consideration in money or money's worth, other than consideration consisting of another interest under the settlement.[17]

> Thus if property is settled upon trust for A for life, with remainder to B absolutely and B (or B's executor) sells the reversionary interest to P, no chargeable gain accrues to B; but P is chargeable in respect of any gain which accrues to him when (on A's death) P becomes absolutely entitled to the settled property and P is then treated as disposing of his interest.[18] This disposal by P is additional to the notional disposal by the trustees on P becoming absolutely entitled.[18]

If on a partition of settled property A surrenders his life interest in part of the property in consideration of an interest in capital, A is not treated as acquiring an interest by purchase: the consideration obtained by A is

---

[15] *Ibid.* s. 25 (10), as amended by F.A. 1966, Sched. 10, para. 1 (3). A life interest in part of the income of settled property is treated as a life interest in a corresponding part of the settled property: F.A. 1971 Sched. 12, para. 8, and see *Pexton* v. *Bell*, at n. 13, *ante.*

[16] F.A. 1971, Sched. 12, para. 11, as amended by F.A. 1975, Sched. 12, para. 17.

[17] F.A. 1965, Sched. 7, para. 13 (1). The word " settlement " is not defined but it seems to be generally assumed that there is a settlement when there is " settled property " as defined in § 16-21. See, *e.g. Berry* v. *Warnett* in § 16-21.

[18] *Ibid.* Sched. 7, para. 13 (2).

another interest under the settlement. Hence the exemption from capital gains tax for disposals of interests in settled property applies if A disposes of the interest so acquired by him. A life interest in settled property may be a wasting asset: see § 16-33.

Payment of the tax

16-25   Any capital gains tax which arises on a disposal (including a notional disposal) of settled property is assessed on the trustees. If the tax is not paid within six months from the date when it becomes payable by the trustees,[19] and before or after the expiration of that period of six months the asset in respect of which the gain accrued (or any part of the proceeds of sale of the asset) is transferred by the trustees to a person who as against the trustees is absolutely entitled to it, that person may at any time within two years from the time when the tax becomes payable be assessed and charged (in the name of the trustees) to the tax.[20] The beneficiary will generally have been required to indemnify the trustees in respect of their liability to capital gains tax.

There are provisions to enable tax assessed on the donor of assets and not paid by him to be recovered from the donee.[21]

Non-resident trusts

16-26   Section 42 of the Finance Act 1965 applies as respects chargeable gains accruing to trustees of a settlement[22] if the trustees are not resident and not ordinarily resident in the United Kingdom and if the settlor (or one of the settlors) is domiciled and either resident or ordinarily resident in the United Kingdom, or was so domiciled, etc., when he made the settlement.[23] The trustees of a settlement are treated as a single and continuing body of persons (distinct from the persons who may from time to time be the trustees) and are treated as being resident and ordinarily resident in the United Kingdom unless (i) the general administration of the trusts is ordinarily carried on outside the United Kingdom *and* (ii) the trustees or a majority of them for the time being are not resident or not ordinarily resident in the United Kingdom. When the trustees or a majority of them are or are treated as not resident in the United Kingdom, the general administration of the trust is treated as carried on outside the United Kingdom.[24] As regards (ii), a person carrying on a business which consists of or includes the management of trusts, and acting as trustees of a trust in the course of that business, must be treated in relation to that trust as not resident in the United Kingdom if the whole of the settled property consists of or derives from property provided by a person not at the time domiciled, resident or ordinarily resident in the United Kingdom.[25]

Where section 42 applies, every chargeable gain which accrues to the

---

[19] See § 16-03.
[20] F.A. 1965, s. 25 (9).
[21] *Ibid.* Sched. 7, para. 19.
[22] Settlement is defined in I.C.T.A. 1970, s. 454 (3); F.A. 1965, s. 42 (7).
[23] F.A. 1965, s. 42 (1).
[24] F.A. 1969, Sched. 19, para. 8 (3).
[25] F.A. 1965, s. 25 (1).

trustees must be apportioned to a beneficiary who is domiciled and either resident or ordinarily resident in the United Kingdom at the time when the chargeable gain accrues. The gain must be apportioned as is just and reasonable between persons having interests in the settled property (including beneficiaries under a discretionary trust) so that the gain is divided according to the respective values of the interests in capital and income.[26] There are special provisions relating to the apportionment of gains to beneficiaries under a discretionary settlement.[27] The section does not allow apportionment of a loss accruing to the trustees.[28]

4. COMPUTATION OF GAINS OR LOSSES

16-27   The main rules which govern the computation of chargeable gains are to be found in Schedule 6 to the Finance Act 1965. The basic principles are stated in the following paragraphs.

General rules for assets acquired on or after April 5, 1965

16-28   The amount of the gain (or loss) which accrues on the disposal of an asset is computed in accordance with Schedule 6 to the Finance Act 1965.[29] The main rules may be summarised as follows:

16-29   1. There should be excluded from the consideration for a disposal of assets any money or money's worth which is charged to income tax (or corporation tax) as income of the disponer or which is taken into account as a receipt in computing income or profits or gains or losses of the disponer.[30] Thus, there is excluded that part of the premium on the grant of a lease which is chargeable as income under Schedule A: see § 6-16. The special provisions which apply to certain sale and lease-back transactions are discussed in § 2-61.

Where the consideration consists of a rentcharge or similar right to income, the capitalised value of the rentcharge or other income is taken into account.[31] The treatment of annuities payable to retiring partners as consideration for the disposal of their interest is referred to in § 16-17A.

16-30   2. In calculating the gain accruing to a person on the disposal of an asset there may be deducted from the consideration[32]—

(a) the cost of acquisition of the asset (including any incidental costs) or, if the asset was not acquired, the expenditure incurred in producing it;

(b) expenditure for the purpose of enhancing the value of the asset which is reflected in the state or nature of the asset at the time of

---

[26] F.A. 1965, s. 42 (2).
[27] *Ibid*. s. 42 (3).
[28] *Ibid*. s. 42 (6).
[29] *Ibid*. Sched. 6, para. 1.
[30] *Ibid*. Sched. 6, para. 2 (1), and see para. 21 (2). As to corporation tax, see § 16-53.
[31] *Ibid*. Sched. 6, para. 2 (3); but see *post*, § 16-35, as to the spreading of tax liability.
[32] *Ibid*. Sched. 6, para. 4 (1).

disposal, and expenditure in establishing, preserving or defending the taxpayer's title to or right over the asset [33];

(c) the incidental costs of making the disposal.

Incidental costs means expenditure wholly and exclusively incurred for the purposes of the acquisition, [34] including fees, commission, or remuneration paid for the professional services of any surveyor or valuer, or accountant, or agent or legal adviser and costs of transfer or conveyance (including stamp duty), together with the costs of advertising to find a seller (in the case of acquisition) and costs of advertising to find a buyer and of valuation (in the case of disposal). [35] This rule is subject to the overriding qualifications that no deduction is allowed for expenditure which is otherwise allowed as a deduction in calculating liability to income tax or corporation tax or if, in the case of losses, it is covered by capital allowances (other than investment allowances); and that no deduction is allowed for any sum which would have been deducted if the asset to which the expenditure related had at all times been a fixed asset in use for the purposes of a trade. [36] This last qualification excludes normal maintenance expenditure, *e.g.* the cost of painting a house which is not a principal residence. No deduction is allowable more than once from any sum or from more than one sum. [37] No adjustment to take account of inflation is made in a computation of chargeable gains. [38]

16-31   There are a number of special provisions:

(i) Insurance premiums on a policy to cover the risk of damage or injury to, or loss or depreciation of, the asset are not deductible. [39]

(ii) Certain contingent liabilities are not allowed as a deduction unless they are enforced, when an appropriate adjustment in the tax liability is made. The restriction applies to the contingent liabilities of the assignor of a lease in respect of default by the assignee; to the liabilities of the vendor or lessor of land in respect of the covenants for quiet enjoyment; and to warranties given on the sale or lease of property other than land. [40]

---

[33] *Ibid.* Sched. 6, para. 4 (1).

[34] See *I.R.C.* v. *Richard's Executors* (1971) 46 T.C. 626 (H.L.Sc.): executors' costs of producing inventory to obtain confirmation of shares held to be expenditure wholly and exclusively incurred in establishing title thereto. See also *I.R.C.* v. *Chubb's Trustee* (1971) 47 T.C. 353 (Ct. of Sess.); *Cleveleys Investment Trust Co.* v. *I.R.C.* [1975] S.T.C. 457; *Allison* v. *Murray* [1975] S.T.C. 524; *Emmerson* v. *Computer Time International Ltd.* [1977] S.T.C. 170 (C.A.).

[35] F.A. 1965, Sched. 6, para. (4) (2).

[36] *Ibid.* Sched. 6, para. 5.

[37] *Ibid.* Sched. 6, para. 21 (1).

[38] *Secretan* v. *Hart* (1969) 45 T.C. 701.

[39] F.A. 1965, Sched. 6, para. 12.

[40] *Ibid.* Sched. 6, para. 15, and see *Randall* v. *Plumb* [1975] S.T.C. 191; (1974) 50 T.C. 392, where V owned farmland. In consideration of the deposit with V of £25,000, V granted an option to enable a company to purchase V's land at an agreed price. The deposit was returnable in certain circumstances, *e.g.* if the company failed to obtain planning consent for the extraction of sand and gravel etc. If the company exercised the option, the £25,000 was to be treated as part payment of the purchase price. It was conceded that V had received a capital sum derived from assets, with the consequence that there was a deemed disposal within s. 22 (3) and (9) of the Finance Act 1965 (see § 16-08). The issue was whether the consideration for the disposal was £25,000 or some lesser sum. *Held,* that the possibility of V having to return the £25,000 could not be disregarded and a valuation should be made to take account of this possibility. Walton J. rejected the Crown's submission that only the contingencies referred to in paragraphs 14 (5) and 15 of Sched. 6 could be taken into account.

(iii) Expenditure incurred by a person absolutely entitled as legatee or as against trustees of settled property in relation to the transfer of the asset to him (including similar expenditure of the personal representatives or trustees) is allowable on a disposal by the beneficiary.[41]

(iv) No deduction is allowed for expenditure which is borne by the Crown or any public or local authority in the United Kingdom or elsewhere.[42]

(v) Income tax paid by the disponer of shares as a result of a statutory apportionment is deductible in computing the gain on the disposal of the shares, unless there has been an actual distribution of the amount apportioned.[43]

(vi) Overseas tax charged on the disposal of an asset is deductible so far as this fails to qualify for double taxation relief under section 39 of the Finance Act 1965.[44]

(vii) Interest is not deductible, except as provided by section 269 of the Income and Corporation Taxes Act 1970.[45]

If capital allowances have been given in respect of expenditure on the asset, any such allowances (including renewals allowances) must be taken into account in computing the amount of any loss.[46]

16-31A   On the part disposal of an asset there are provisions for apportionment of expenditure between the part retained and the part disposed of.[47] The portion of the cost attributable to the part disposal is that arrived at by applying the fraction $\dfrac{A}{A + B}$ to the original total cost, where A equals the consideration for the part disposal and B equals the market value of the property retained.

> Suppose A owns an asset with a base cost of £10,000 and that he disposes of a part for £7,000 at a time when the market value of the remainder is £13,000. The cost attributable to the part disposed of is $£10,000 \times \dfrac{£7,000}{£7,000 + £13,000} = £3,500$. Consequently the amount of the gain is £3,500. The cost attributable to the part retained is £10,000 less £3,500 = £6,500.

Special rules of identification exist in the case of shares and securities.[48] There are special provisions which apply to small part disposals of land.[48a]

16-32   3. *Wasting assets.*   In the case of wasting assets not exempt from capital gains tax (see § 16-44), the original expenditure must be written down over

---

[41] *Ibid.* Sched. 6, para. 16.
[42] *Ibid.* Sched. 6, para. 17.
[43] *Ibid.* Sched. 6, para. 18. See the Statement of Practice in (1977) S.T.I. 12.
[44] F.A. 1965, Sched. 6, para. 20.
[45] *Ibid.* Sched. 6, para. 4 (3).
[46] *Ibid.* Sched. 6, para. 6.
[47] *Ibid.* Sched. 6, para. 7.
[48] See *Ibid.* Sched. 6, para. 22, Sched. 7, para. 2 and F. (No. 2) A., 1975, s. 58 (being enacted to counteract " bed and breakfast " transactions by companies) and s. 59 (losses on disposals of gilt-edged securities replaced within a prescribed period).
[48a] F.A. 1969, Sched. 19, para. 10, as amended by F.A. 1978, s. 51.

the period between acquisition and disposal. The principle is that if a person has the enjoyment of a wasting asset over a period of years, he should not be able to claim loss relief based on the difference between buying and selling price; the buying price must be reduced to take account of the use and enjoyment of the asset.

16-33   Wasting asset is defined to mean an asset with a predictable life not exceeding 50 years, excluding freehold land.[49] " Life " in relation to tangible movable property means useful life, having regard to the purpose for which the asset was acquired or provided by the disponer.[50] Plant and machinery is in every case regarded as having a predictable life of less than 50 years, and in estimating its life it must be assumed that its life will end when it is finally put out of use as being unfit for further use, and that it is going to be used in the normal manner and to the normal extent and is going to be so used throughout its life as so estimated.[50] A life interest in settled property is not a wasting asset until the predictable expectation of the life tenant is 50 years or less.[51]

The expenditure incurred on the acquisition of a wasting asset, reduced by the residual or scrap value of the asset,[52] is to be treated as written off to nil at a uniform rate day by day over the life of the asset from the time of acquisition; and expenditure on the improvement of a wasting asset is to be treated as written off in the same manner from the time when it is first reflected in the state or nature of the asset.[53] There are provisions dealing with the case where the expenditure has qualified for capital allowances.[54]

16-34   In the case of leasehold interests,[55] whether of land or other property, the line of wastage is curved and the rate of wastage accelerates as the end of the term approaches. A lease of land is treated as a wasting asset only when its duration is not more than 50 years but there are rules for determining the duration of a lease for this purpose. There is a table in the Act which sets out the rate at which the expenditure on a lease for 50 years is to be deemed to waste away and there is a formula for determining the amount of the original expenditure which is to be attributable to the consideration received on an assignment of the lease. Reference should be made to Schedule 8 to the Finance Act 1965, as amended, for the detailed provisions.

16-35   4. *For consideration payable by instalments.* Where an asset is sold for payments to be made by instalments, such as a rentcharge or other series of income payments, the consideration for the disposal is the capitalised value of the payments,[56] no discount being allowed in making the valuation for

---

[49] F.A. 1965, Sched. 6, para. 9 (1) (*a*).
[50] *Ibid.* Sched. 6, para. 9 (1) (*c*) (*d*).
[51] *Ibid.* Sched. 6, para. 9 (1) (*e*). This will be ascertained from actuarial tables approved by the Board.
[52] Defined F.A. 1965, Sched. 6, para. 9 (2) (3), as the predictable value at the end of the predictable life of the asset.
[53] *Ibid.* Sched. 6, para. 10.
[54] *Ibid.* Sched. 6, para. 11.
[55] *Ibid.* see Sched. 8.
[56] *Ibid.* Sched. 6, para. 2 (3).

the postponement or for the risk that the payments might not be recovered. If any part of the consideration proves to be irrecoverable, such adjustment must be made (whether by way of discharge or repayment of tax or otherwise) as is required in consequence. It is provided that if the consideration or part of the consideration is payable by future instalments over a period exceeding 18 months, then, if the person making the disposal satisfies the Board that he would otherwise suffer undue hardship, the tax on the chargeable gain may, at his option, be paid by such instalments as the Board may allow over a period not exceeding eight years and ending not later than the time at which the last of the future instalments is payable.[57]

> In *Coren* v. *Keighley* [58] V sold land to P for £3,750. The sale agreement provided that V should advance £2,250 on mortgage to P, repayable over 10 years at interest. The conveyance acknowledged the receipt by V of £3,750 and a legal charge, executed on the same day, acknowledged the advance to P. *Held,* V was assessable to capital gains tax on the footing that he had received £3,750: this was not a sale by instalments.

> In *Marren* v. *Ingles* [58a] V sold shares to P for a fixed price per share plus an amount to be determined later by reference to profits. The Crown contended that there were two disposals by V: the first when the shares were sold, and the second when the amount was determined. *Held* there was no such second disposal.

General rules for assets held on April 6, 1965

16-36   The Act charges capital gains tax only on gains which accrue after April 6, 1965. In the case of quoted shares or securities, the general rule is that the gain (or loss) is calculated by reference to their quoted market value on April 6, 1965, except that the calculation must be by reference to the original cost price if this would show a smaller gain (or loss).[59] Where shares acquired on different dates are disposed of, the general rule is first in, first out. The rule for the valuation of land in the United Kingdom which has a development value is similar.[60]

In the case of other assets, the gain (or loss) is assumed to accrue at a uniform rate over the period of ownership; so that if, for example, the asset was acquired on April 6, 1962, and disposed of on April 6, 1966, one-quarter of the total gain is chargeable because, out of the period of ownership of four years, one year fell after April 6, 1965[61]; but the disposer can elect to have his gain (or loss) computed by reference to the market value of the asset on April 6, 1965.[62] He cannot, however, get relief for a larger loss than the loss actually realised.[63] There are provisions for

---

[57] *Ibid.* Sched. 6, para. 14 (1), as amended by F.A. 1972, s. 116. For the mode of testing hardship, see B.T.R. (1972) " Current Tax Intelligence," at pp. 404 and 441.
[58] (1972) 48 T.C. 370.
[58a] Decided July 10, 1978, by Slade J.
[59] F.A. 1965, Sched. 6, para. 22. But see also F.A. 1968, s. 32. The rule by which the market value of quoted securities is determined by reference to the official quotation does not apply " where in consequence of special circumstances prices so quoted are by themselves not a proper measure of market value ": F.A. 1965, s. 44 (3). See *Hinchcliffe* v. *Crabtree* [1972] A.C. 707 (H.L.); 47 T.C. 419.
[60] *Ibid.* Sched. 6, para. 23, as amended by F.A. 1974, s. 48, and see *Watkins* v. *Kidson* [1978] S.T.C. 367 (C.A.).
[61] *Ibid.* Sched. 6, para. 24.
[62] *Ibid.* Sched. 6, para. 25 (1), as amended by F.A. 1968, Sched. 12, para. 5.
[63] *Ibid.* Sched. 6, para. 25 (2).

identifying unquoted shares which are disposed of with earlier acquisitions.[64]

The market value of assets means the price those assets might reasonably be expected to fetch on a sale in the open market.[65] The rules which determine the market value are substantially the same as those which apply for the purposes of capital transfer tax.[66]

5. LOSSES

16-37— Generally, losses are computed in the same way as gains are computed [67];
16-38 and the provisions of the Act which distinguish gains which are chargeable gains from those which are not, or which make part of a gain a chargeable gain and part not, apply also to distinguish losses which are allowable losses from those which are not, and to make part of a loss an allowable loss and part not. References to the term " allowable loss " have to be construed accordingly.[68]

Capital gains tax is charged on the total amount of chargeable gains accruing to a person in a year of assessment, after deducting any allowable losses.[69] Allowable losses accruing in a year of assessment are deducted primarily from chargeable gains of that year and any surplus of unrelieved losses is carried forward to future years without time limit. Losses may not be carried back and relieved against gains of earlier years, except that allowable losses sustained by an individual in the year in which he dies may, so far as they cannot be deducted from chargeable gains accruing in that year, be deducted from chargeable gains accruing to the deceased in the three years preceding the year in which the death occurs, taking chargeable gains accruing in a later year before those accruing in an earlier year.[70] Losses brought forward will, in and from 1977–78, be used only so far as necessary to reduce gains to £1,000.[70a] Losses incurred on a disposal to a connected person are only allowable against gains made on subsequent disposals to the same connected person.[71] Short-term losses to which Case VII of Schedule D applied were not " allowable losses " and could not be offset against long-term gains to which the capital gains tax applied [72]; but Case VII having been abolished for the year 1971–72 and subsequent years of assessment, it has been provided that Case VII losses not relieved against Case VII income in 1970–71 and earlier years shall be treated as allowable losses for the purposes of the capital gains tax, subject to a restriction in the amount allowable where the loss arose on a transaction between connected persons.[73] Individuals resident or ordinarily resident within (but domiciled

---

[64] *Ibid.* See generally *ibid.* Sched. 6, paras. 26–27.
[65] F.A. 1965, s. 44 and F.A. 1973, s. 51 and Sched. 20 (valuation of shares not quoted on a stock exchange).
[66] See F.A. 1965, s. 26 as substituted by F.A. 1975, Sched. 12, para. 13.
[67] F.A. 1965, s. 23 (1).
[68] *Ibid.* s. 23 (2).
[69] *Ibid.* s. 20 (4).
[70] *Ibid.* s. 24 (5).
[70a] See § 16-02.
[71] F.A. 1965, Sched. 7, para. 17 (3).
[72] *Ibid.* s. 23 (2).
[73] F.A. 1971, s. 56 and Sched. 10, para. 2.

outside) the United Kingdom are taxed in respect of chargeable gains accruing from the disposal of assets situated outside the United Kingdom only on the amount received in the United Kingdom; and accordingly losses accruing on the disposal of assets situated outside the United Kingdom to any such individual are not allowable losses.[74] The treatment of losses in connection with settled property has already been mentioned.[75] Where in the case of a woman who in a year of assessment is a married woman living with her husband there is an allowable loss (whether of that year or carried forward from an earlier year) which would be deductible but for an insufficiency of chargeable gains, the loss is deductible from chargeable gains of the husband, unless either party makes application to the inspector before July 6, in the next following year of assessment.[76]

6. EXEMPTIONS AND RELIEFS

The following is a summary of the principal exemptions and reliefs:

1. *Miscellaneous exemptions*

16-39   Private motor-cars are not chargeable assets [77] ; thus no chargeable gain or allowable loss accrues on their disposal.[78] Saving certificates and non-marketable securities (as defined [79]) are not chargeable assets.[80] Gains on the disposal of currency acquired for personal expenditure abroad are not chargeable gains.[81] Betting winnings and winnings from prizes are not chargeable assets.[82] Sums obtained by way of compensation or damages for any wrong or injury suffered by an individual in his person or in his profession or vocation are not chargeable gains.[83] Gains on disposals of certain gilt-edged securities which are retained for 12 months after acquisition are exempt from capital gains tax.[84]

2. *Life assurance and deferred annuities*

16-40   Where a person effects a policy of life assurance, whether on his own life or on that of some other person in whose life he has an insurable interest, the occasion of the payment of the sum assured or the occasion of the surrender of the policy are treated as a disposal by the policy holder of his rights under the policy in consideration of the amount then payable. Likewise, the occasion of the payment of the first instalment of a deferred annuity is treated as a disposal of the rights thereunder in consideration of the market value at that time of the right to that and further instalments of the annuity.[85] Similar provisions apply where the policy provides not

---

[74] *Ibid.* s. 20 (7).
[75] *Ante*, § 16-22 (3).
[76] *Ibid.* s. 20 (5), as amended by F.A. 1967, Sched. 13, para. 1 for the years therein mentioned.
[77] F.A.1965, s. 27 (1).
[78] *Ibid.* s. 27 (10).
[79] *Ibid.* s. 27 (9).
[80] *Ibid.* s. 27 (4) (10).
[81] *Ibid.* s. 27 (5).
[82] *Ibid.* s. 27 (7) (10).
[83] *Ibid.* s. 27 (8).
[84] F.A. 1969, s. 41 and Sched. 18; F.A. 1971, Sched. 10, para. 4.
[85] F.A. 1965, s. 28 (3).

for the payment of money but for the transfer of investments or other assets; the consideration for the disposal being in such case the market value of the assets at the time of the disposal.[86]

It is provided that no chargeable gain shall accrue on a disposal in the circumstances mentioned in the preceding paragraph, except where the person making the disposal is not the original beneficial owner and acquired the rights or interests for a consideration in money or money's worth.[87] Thus if A takes out a policy of life assurance, no liability to capital gains tax arises on payment of the policy moneys to A on a surrender of the policy, or on their payment to A's personal representatives on A's death, or on their payment to the trustees of a voluntary settlement to whom A transferred the policy. If A assigns the policy for money or money's worth, the exemption does not apply on payment of the policy moneys to the assignee. Furthermore A will be chargeable on the consideration received on, *e.g.* the disposal of his rights under a fire insurance policy which has matured, in so far as the property insured was a chargeable asset.[88]

3. *Private residences*

16-41   A gain which accrues on the disposal by an individual of a dwelling-house or part of a dwelling-house is not a chargeable gain if the house was the individual's only or main residence throughout his period of ownership (as defined [89]), or throughout the period of ownership except for all or any part of the last 12 months of that period.[90] If this condition is not satisfied throughout the period, a fraction of the gain is exempted corresponding to the period of occupation as a residence [91]; except that a period of absence not exceeding three years (or periods which do not together exceed three years) during which the dwelling-house was not the individual's only or main residence and throughout which he had no residence or main residence eligible for relief under the section are disregarded in certain circumstances.[92] This (and other provisions [92]) protect the person who is compelled to leave his normal residence, *e.g.* because of a temporary posting. If the gain accrues from the disposal of a dwelling-house part of which is used exclusively for the purposes of a trade or business or of a profession or vocation, the gain is apportioned and the exemption applies to that part of the gain apportioned to the non-business portion.[93] There are provisions for apportionment where a residence is reconstructed or converted.[94]

---

[86] I.C.T.A. 1970, s. 321.

[87] F.A. 1965, s. 28 (1) (2).

[88] F. (No. 2) A. 1975, s. 61, reversing the decision in *I.R.C.* v. *Montgomery* (1975) 49 T.C. 679; [1975] S.T.C. 182.

[89] *Ibid.* s. 29 (13).

[90] *Ibid.* s. 29 (2). The section applies to an individual's dwelling-house or part of a dwelling-house which is, or has at any time in his period of ownership been, his only or main residence; together with its garden or grounds up to a specified limit: see *ibid* s. 29 (1). By concession the period of the last 12 months may be extended where, *e.g.* the owner has been unable to find a purchaser. See (1977) S.T.I. 12.

[91] *Ibid.* s. 29 (3).

[92] *Ibid.* s. 29 (4) and (4A) added by F.A. 1978, s. 50 (temporary occupation of job-related living accommodation).

[93] *Ibid.* s. 29 (5) and as to apportionment, see s. 29 (12). See [1975] S.T.I. 507 as to the effect of letting accommodation, *e.g.* to students.

[94] *Ibid.* s. 29 (6).

The exemption applies only to the individual's only or main residence and, in the case of a man and his wife living with him,[95] there can only be one residence or main residence.[96] A person with two or more residences may nominate one of them for exemption; and if he does not do so, the inspector may determine the matter subject to the individual's right of appeal to the General or Special Commissioners.[97] The exemption applies to a disposal by a trustee of settled property of an asset which is the only or main residence of a person entitled to occupy it under the terms of the settlement.[98] By concession the exemption is given in respect of a residence occupied by permission of the trustees by an individual who is entitled under the settlement to the whole income from the residence or from its proceeds on sale.[99]

There is no exemption if the dwelling-house was acquired wholly or partly for the purpose of realising a gain from the disposal; nor is there any exemption in relation to a gain which is attributable to expenditure incurred during the period of ownership for the purpose of realising a gain from the disposal.[1]

If as a result of the breakdown of a marriage one spouse ceases to occupy his or her matrimonial home and subsequently as part of a financial settlement disposes of the home, or an interest in it, to the other spouse (or, if the transfer is after a divorce, ex-spouse) the home may be regarded for the purposes of section 29 of the Finance Act 1965 as continuing to be a residence of the transferring spouse from the date his (or her) occupation ceases until the date of transfer, provided that it has throughout this period been the other spouse's only or main residence. Thus if a married couple separate and the husband leaves the matrimonial home while still owning it, the exemption is given on a subsequent transfer to the wife, provided she has continued to live in the house and the husband has not elected that some other house should be treated for capital gains tax purposes as his main residence for this period.[2]

4. Chattels sold for £2,000 or less

16-42   A gain accruing on a disposal of an asset which is tangible movable property is not a chargeable gain if the amount or value of the consideration for the disposal does not exceed £2,000.[3] If the consideration exceeds £2,000, five-thirds of the difference between the consideration and £2,000 is excluded from any chargeable gain.[4]

---

[95] See n. 5, *ante*, § 16-01.
[96] *Ibid.* s. 29 (8). Gains on the disposal of a residence provided for a dependent relative are in some cases exempt: see *ibid.* s. 29 (10).
[97] *Ibid.* s. 29 (7). For the position where there are development gains, see F.A. 1974, Sched. 3, para. 21.
[98] *Ibid.* s. 29 (9). In *Sansom* v. *Peay* [1976] S.T.C. 494 the exemption was held to apply where the occupation was that of beneficiaries under a discretionary settlement. " . . . looking at the matter *at the date of the disposal*, the beneficiaries were persons who, in the events which happened, were entitled to occupy the house and did occupy it under the terms of the settlement ": Brightman J. at p. 499.
[99] Concession No. D3.
[1] F.A. 1968, Sched. 12, para. 2.
[2] Concession D9.
[3] F.A. 1965, s. 30 (1). Amount increased from £1,000 for 1978–79 and subsequent years: F.A. 1978, s. 45 (1), (6). The section does not exempt certain gains on the disposal of commodities dealt in on a terminal market or of currency: F.A. 1965, s. 30 (6).
[4] F.A. 1965, s. 30 (2), as substituted by F.A. 1978, s. 45 (2).

There is a corresponding restriction on relief for losses. If a chattel acquired for more than £2,000 is disposed of for less than £2,000, the allowable loss is calculated as if the asset had been disposed of for £2,000.[5]

If two or more assets forming part of a set of articles (such as a set of chairs) are disposed of by the same seller to the same buyer,[6] whether on the same or different occasions, the two or more transactions are treated as a single transaction disposing of a single asset.[7] Their value is therefore aggregated for the purpose of applying the exemption limit. For the purpose of calculating the value of the set, chattels disposed of after November 11, 1964, and before April 7, 1965, must be included,[7] but not so as to tax gains accruing before April 7, 1965.

5. *Works of art, etc.*

16-43　　Gains which accrue on the disposal of works of art, etc., given or bequeathed to a body not established or conducted for profit are not chargeable gains if the asset would qualify for relief from capital transfer tax under paragraph 13 (2) (*f*) of Schedule 6 to the Finance Act 1975.[8] The Treasury may require an undertaking to be given and that undertaking must remain in force until the asset is disposed of.[9]

The exemptions referred to in this paragraph are withdrawn if the asset is later sold or if the undertaking referred to is not carried out.[10]

Any capital gains tax payable on a subsequent sale or a breach of the undertaking is allowed as a deduction from the amount chargeable to capital transfer tax.[11]

An exemption also exists for assets given in connection with preservation of land for the public benefit.[12]

6. *Exemption for tangible movables which are wasting assets* [13]

16-44　　No chargeable gain is to accrue on the disposal after March 19, 1968, of, or of an interest in, an asset which is tangible movable property and which is a wasting asset, *i.e.* even if the consideration exceeds the amount in § 16-42. An asset is a wasting asset if it has a predictable life of less than 50 years: see § 16-33. The exemption does not apply to a disposal of commodities of any description by a person dealing on a terminal market or dealing with or through a person ordinarily engaged in dealing on a terminal market. The exemption does not apply to chattels used for the purposes of a trade in respect of which capital allowances are or could be claimed.

7. *Replacement of business assets*

16-45　　A relief may be claimed where business assets are sold and replaced by others. There is no exemption from the tax: relief is given by allowing the

---

[5] F.A. 1965, s. 30 (3). Amount increased from £1,000 for 1978–79 and subsequent years.
[6] Or to different buyers who are acting in concert or are connected persons: see *ibid.* s. 30 (4) and § 16-18A.
[7] *Ibid.* s. 30 (4), as amended by F.A. 1978, s. 45 (3).
[8] *Ibid.* s. 31 as amended by F.A. 1975, Sched. 12, para. 14; and see *post*, § 19-33.
[9] F.A. 1965, s. 31 (7).　　　　　　　　　　　　[10] *Ibid.* s. 31 (5).
[11] *Ibid.* s. 31 (8).　　　　　　[12] *Ibid.* s. 32, as amended by F.A. 1975, Sched. 12, para. 15.
[13] F.A. 1968, Sched. 12, para. 1.

trader to deduct the gain from the cost of acquisition of the replacement and thus defer payment of tax until the assets are disposed of and not replaced. The relief is thus a " roll-over " relief.

Section 33 (1) of the Finance Act 1965, as amended, [14] provides that if the whole of the consideration which a trader [15] obtains for the disposal of assets [16] (called " the old assets ") used only for the purposes of the trade throughout the period of ownership is applied by him in acquiring other assets (called " the new assets ") which on the acquisition are taken into use and used only for the purposes of the trade *and* the old assets and the new assets fall within the classes listed in the section, [17] then the trader may claim to have the consideration so applied treated:

(a) as if the consideration for the disposal of the old assets were such as to produce neither gain nor loss;

(b) as if the cost of the new assets were reduced by the amount of the chargeable gain.

Section 33 (2) gives a limited relief where less than the whole consideration obtained for the old assets is applied in purchasing new assets provided the amount not so applied does not exceed the gain on the disposal of the old assets (whether chargeable gain or not).

The relief is available only if the acquisition of the new assets takes place, or an unconditional contract for the acquisition is entered into, within 12 months before or not later than three years [18] after the disposal of the old assets; and in the case where there is an unconditional contract, the relief is given provisionally. [19]

16-46   The classes of assets listed in the section are as follows [20]

(1) Any building or structure in the nature of a building occupied and used only for the purposes of the trade and any land so occupied and used; fixed plant and machinery

(2) Ships

(3) Aircraft

(4) Goodwill

(5) Hovercraft.

The relief is withheld if the new assets are bought wholly or partly for the purposes of realising a gain on their disposal. [21]

There are provisions for apportionment if a building is used partly for the purposes of a trade [22] or if the old assets were not so used throughout the

---

[14] The amendment in F.A. 1967, Sched. 13, para. 2, relates to the case where not all the gain on the disposal of the old assets is chargeable gain. Then only the amount of the chargeable gain is deducted from the cost of replacement.

[15] This includes a person who carries on a profession or vocation and the occupier of woodlands on a commercial basis: F.A. 1965, s. 33 (10). Roll-over relief is also available to certain non-profit-making bodies formed to protect or promote the interests of traders and professional people: F.A. 1972, s. 118. See also F.A. 1974. s. 31.

[16] This includes an interest in assets: F.A. 1965, s. 33 (1).

[17] F.A. 1971, s. 60. Where the new asset is a depreciating asset, see F.A. 1969, Sched. 19, para. 16.

[18] F.A. 1965, s. 33 (3), as amended by F.A. 1973, s. 37.

[19] F.A. 1965, s. 33 (3). The Board may allow an extension of the period referred to.

[20] *Ibid.* s. 33 (6). See also F.A. 1968, Sched. 12, para. 3.

[21] F.A. 1965, s. 33 (5).   [22] *Ibid.* s. 33 (7).

period of ownership [23] or if assets within the section are mingled with those outside it. [24] A partner will not qualify for the relief unless he is interested in both the old assets and the new assets. [25]

There are special provisions which apply when the old assets include land with development value: see § 16-165.

8. *Transfer of business on retirement*

16-47   Section 34 of the Finance Act 1965 (as originally enacted) provided a relief from capital gains tax which applied where an individual who had attained the age of 60 disposed by way of sale or gift of a business owned by him or of shares in a company which owned a business. The relief has been recast by section 48 of the Finance Act 1978 in its application to any disposal which takes place after April 11, 1978.

Section 34 (1) in its amended form now affords relief from capital gains tax where an individual who has attained the age of 60 years:

(a) disposes by way of sale or gift of the whole or part of a business [26]; or

(b) disposes by way of sale or gift of shares or securities of a company.

These may be referred to as Situations (a) and (b). The relief is given only if *the relevant conditions* have been fulfilled throughout a period of at least one year ending with the disposal; but the amount of the relief depends *inter alia* on the period of years (up to 10 years) during which the relevant conditions have been satisfied: see §16-48. This relief applies to the deemed disposal of shares on the liquidation of a company. [27]

Situation (a)

The relevant conditions are fulfilled at any time in Situation (a) if at that time:

" the business in question is owned either by the individual or by a company with respect to which the following conditions are at that time fulfilled, namely:
(i) it is a trading company;
(ii) it is the individual's family company; and
(iii) he is a full-time working director of it. " [28]

Hence, the relief applies where a business at first owned indirectly through shares in a family company has come into the direct ownership or part-ownership of the disponer at the time of the disposal *e.g.* as a result of the liquidation of the company.

---

[23] *Ibid.* s. 33 (8).

[24] *Ibid.* s. 33 (12). For the position where there is more than one trade, see *ibid.* s. 33 (9), as substituted by F.A. 1978, s. 47 (1). For the position where a trade is transferred to a family company, see F.A. 1965, s. 33 (9A), added by F.A. 1978, s. 47 (2) (3).

[25] F.A. 1965, s. 33 (4). This does not apply in the case of an acquisition of assets on or after April 20, 1971: F.A. 1971, s. 60. As to replacements in a group of companies, see I.C.T.A. 1970, s. 276, and [1978] S.T.I. 25.

[26] There is a difference between the disposal of part of a business and the disposal of an asset comprised in a business: *McGregor* v. *Adcock* [1977] S.T.C. 206.

[27] F.A. 1966, Sched. 10, para. 2.

[28] F.A. 1965, s. 48 (1A), added by F.A. 1978, s. 48 (1).

" *Trading company* " has the meaning in §15-38. [29]

" *Family company* " means, in relation to an individual, a company the voting rights in which are (a) as to not less than 25 per cent. exercisable by the individual or (b) as to not less than 51 per cent. exercisable by the individual or a member of his family, and, as to not less than 5 per cent. exercisable by the individual himself. [30]

" *Family* " means, in relation to an individual, the husband or wife of the individual, and a relative of the individual or the individual's husband or wife, and *relative* means brother, sister, ancestor or lineal descendant. [31]

" *Full-time working director* " means a director who is required to devote substantially the whole of his time to the service of the company in a managerial or technical capacity. [31] There is a concession which relates to directors of groups of companies. [32]

Situation (b)

The relevant conditions are fulfilled at any time in Situation (b) if at that time:

> " either conditions in paragraphs (i) to (iii) . . . above are fulfilled with respect to the company in question or the individual owns the business which, at the time of the disposal, is owned by the company." [33]

Hence the relief applies where a business which is at first in the direct ownership of the disponer has come to be owned by a family company at the time of the disposal.

Amount of the relief

16-48 The term " *qualifying period* " describes the period, up to a maximum of ten years, ending with the particular disposal during which the " *relevant conditions* " (see above) are fulfilled. The expression " *relevant percentage* " means a percentage determined according to the length of the qualifying period on a scale rising arithmetically from 10 per cent. where that period is precisely one year to 100 per cent. where it is 10 years. [34]

In the case of an individual who has attained the age of 65 years, the relief is the relevant percentage of £50,000. Thus if the relevant conditions have been satisfied for 10 years, the amount of the relief is £50,000; if for nine years, the relief is 90 per cent. of £50,000, and so on. In the case of an individual who has not attained the age of 65 years, the amount of the relief is the relevant percentage of the aggregate of £10,000 for every year by which his age exceeds 60 and a corresponding part of £10,000 for any odd part of the year. [35]

The relief is given only on the " *chargeable business assets* " defined to include assets (including goodwill) used for the purposes of the trade, etc.,

---

[29] F.A. 1965, s. 34 (6).
[30] F.A. 1965, s. 34 (6), as amended by F.A. 1978, s. 48 (4).
[31] See n. 29, above.
[32] Concession D4.
[33] See n. 28, above.
[34] F.A. 1965, s. 34 (1B), added by F.A. 1978, s. 48 (1).
[35] F.A. 1965, s. 34 (2)–(5).

but to exclude assets held as investments and assets on the disposal of which no chargeable gain accrues, *e.g.* trading stock.[36]

So far as the amount available for relief is applied on a disposal, it is not available as any other disposal; and the relief is applied in the order in which disposals take place.[37]

There are a number of concessions which relate to retirement relief.[38]

9. *Relief for gifts of business assets*

16-49   Section 46 of and Schedule 8 to the Finance Act 1978 introduced a new form of relief which applies where an individual (called " the transferor ") makes a disposal after April 11, 1978, otherwise than under a bargain at arm's length, to a person resident or ordinarily resident in the United Kingdom (" the transferee ") of (a) an asset which is, or is an interest in, an asset used for the purposes of a trade, profession or vocation (as defined [39]) carried on by the transferor or by a company which is his family company (as defined [39a]) or (b) shares or securities of a trading company (as defined [39a]) which is the transferor's family company.

The relief enables business assets to be given away during the donor's lifetime without any charge to capital gains tax arising until the donee sells those assets. The relief has to be claimed by the transferor and the transferee. Its effect is that the chargeable gains that would have accrued to the transferor but for section 46 (called the " held-over gain ") is deducted from the transferor's chargeable gain and from the transferee's base cost.[39b]

> Thus if A (aged 50) gives business assets to B and A's chargeable gain, applying section 22 (4) (*a*) of the Finance Act 1965 (see §16-18), would be £20,000 (cost £10,000: Market value £30,000), A's gain is reduced to nil and B's " base cost " is £10,000 (*i.e.* £30,000 less the held over gain of £20,000).

If in the example A had sold the asset to B at an undervalue (say for £18,000), A would pay tax on his chargeable gain of £8,000 and may claim relief on the rest of the gain (£12,000). B's base cost would be £30,000 less £12,000 = £8,000.

Any retirement relief due to the transferor under the provisions in §16-47 is given first, only the non-exempt excess being " rolled over " under section 46.[39c]

The relief applies to gifts of agricultural property which is not used for the purposes of a trade carried on as in (a), above, but only if a chargeable transfer of the property would qualify for relief from capital transfer tax under the provisions discussed in §§ 19-40 *et seq.*

---

[36] F.A. 1965, s. 34 (4).

[37] Concession D4.

[38] See Inland Revenue Press Release of January 4, 1973, published [1973] S.T.I. 2 and the revised Concession in [1976] S.T.I. 334. See also [1978] S.T.I. 140.

[39] Trade, profession and vocation have the same meaning as in the Income Tax Acts (see § 2-01) and " trade " includes the occupation of woodlands on a commercial basis and with a view to the realisation of profits: F.A. 1978, s. 46 (7) (8).

[39a] Definition in F.A. 1965, s. 34, applied by F.A. 1978, s. 46 (7). See § 16-47.

[39b] F.A. 1978, s. 46 (3)-(6).

[39c] *Ibid.* s. 46 (2).

The relief may also apply to an asset used in a trade, etc., carried on by a trustee, or to shares or securities in a trading company, where the trustee has not less than 25 per cent. of the voting rights, when there is a deemed disposal by the trustee under section 25 (3) or (4) of the Finance Act 1965 (see §§ 16-22 and 16-23).

10. *Charities*

16-50 A gain which accrues to a charity and is applicable and applied for charitable purposes is not a chargeable gain.[40] The tax exemptions which apply to High Commissioners, etc., apply also to capital gains tax.[41]

A disposal to a charity, if made after March 21, 1972, is exempt from capital gains tax.[42] This applies to disposals by way of gift (including gifts in settlement) and sales for a consideration not exceeding the expenditure allowable for capital gains tax purposes. The disposal and acquisition are treated as made for such a consideration as will secure that neither a gain nor a loss accrues on the disposal; and a gain accruing to the charity on a later disposal by it will be exempt from capital gains tax only if it is applicable and applied for charitable purposes. If not so exempt, the acquisition of the asset by the disponer will be treated as the charity's acquisition. The exemption on disposals to a charity applies also to deemed disposals, *e.g.* on the termination of a life interest.[43]

The exemption applies also to disposals to the bodies referred to in Schedule 6 to the Finance Act 1975: *post*, § 19-21.

11. *Historic houses, etc.*

16-50A A disposal by way of gift or under section 25 (3) or (4) of the Finance Act 1965, to which section 34 of the Finance Act 1975 (historic houses, etc.), applies or might apply is treated as being for a consideration securing neither gain nor loss to the person making the disposal.[44] See, *post*, § 19-38. The same treatment is applied where assets are disposed of to trustees after May 2, 1976, and the disposal is exempt from capital transfer tax under section 84 of the Finance Act 1976 (maintenance funds for historic buildings)[45]: see *post*, § 19-37.

12. *Superannuation funds*

16-51 A gain is not a chargeable gain if it accrues to a person from his disposal of investments held as part of a superannuation fund approved under section 208 of the Income and Corporation Taxes Act 1970.[46] If part only of the fund is approved, there is a partial exemption.[46] A similar exemption applies to approved retirement annuity schemes.[47]

---

[40] F.A. 1965, s. 35 (1). But see s. 35 (2).
[41] *Ibid.* s. 35 (2).
[42] F.A. 1972, s. 119.
[43] See F.A. 1972, s. 116 (4).
[44] F. (No. 2) A. 1975, s. 56.
[45] F.A. 1976, s. 55.
[46] I.C.T.A. 1970, s. 208 (2).
[47] *Ibid.* s. 226 (6).

13. *Employee trusts*

16-51A Section 90 of the Finance Act 1976 (*post*, § 19-70) exempts from capital transfer tax dispositions made by close companies and individuals into trusts for the benefit of employees which satisfy certain stringent conditions. Section 55 of the Finance Act 1976, enables such transfers to be made without liability to capital gains tax.

14. *Double taxation relief*

16-52 Double taxation relief is granted against United Kingdom capital gains tax for any capital gains tax imposed on the same gains by another country. The relief is similar to that given for income tax.

7. Chargeable Gains of Companies

16-53 The chargeable gains of companies are liable to corporation tax and not to capital gains tax.[49] The amount to be included in respect of chargeable gains in a company's total profits for any accounting period is the total gains accruing to the company in the period, after deducting allowable losses, including unrelieved losses brought forward from an earlier period.[50] The principles which determine whether a company has gains or losses and the amount thereof are the same as those which apply to persons other than companies.[51] The alternative method of assessing capital gains by reference to Case VI does not apply to companies.[52]

As from April 1, 1973, only a part of the chargeable gains of a company is included in the total profits for an accounting period, for section 93 (1) of the Finance Act 1972 directs that the chargeable gains to be so included shall be reduced by such fraction as Parliament may from time to time determine. The fraction as from April 1, 1973, for companies other than authorised unit trusts and investment trusts is eleven twenty-sixths,[53] giving an effective tax rate of 30 per cent. The nil and lower rates referred to in § 16-02 and § 16-02A do not apply to companies. There are special provisions applicable to unit trusts and investment trusts.[53a]

Groups of companies

16-54 There are special provisions relating to capital gains of companies which are members of a group of companies (as defined). Broadly speaking, the disposal of an asset from one member-company of the group to another such company gives rise to no chargeable gain or allowable loss. A gain (or loss) arises only when the asset is disposed of outside the group or a company ceases to be a member of a group.[54]

Gains of non-resident companies

16-55 The circumstances in which a non-resident company is liable to capital gains tax are discussed elsewhere.[55] Section 41 of the Finance Act 1965

---

[49] *Ibid.* s. 238 (3).
[51] *Ibid.* s. 265 (2) (3); for an exception, see F. (No. 2) A. 1975, s. 58.
[52] *Ibid.* s. 265 (3). See § 16-01, para. (2).
[53a] I.C.T.A. 1970, ss. 354–359.
[55] *Ante*, § 16-04.

[50] I.C.T.A. 1970, s. 265 (1).
[53] F.A. 1974, s. 10 (1).
[54] I.C.T.A. 1970, ss. 272–279.

applies to a non-resident company which would be a close company if it were resident in the United Kingdom.

Every person who, at the time when the chargeable gain accrues to the company, is resident or ordinarily resident in the United Kingdom and holds shares in the company is treated as if a part of the chargeable gain had accrued to him.[56] That part is the proportion of the assets of the company to which that person would be entitled on a liquidation of the company at the time when the chargeable gain accrues to the company.[57] A part of the gain attributable to a person which is less than one-twentieth is disregarded.[58] Any amount which is distributed to the shareholder within two years from the time when the gain accrued is excepted from the charge, if that amount is subject to tax in the shareholder's hands.[59] Gains on the disposal of certain trading assets are excluded.[60]

[The next paragraph is 16-100]

---

[56] F.A. 1965, s. 41 (1) (2).

[57] *Ibid.* s. 41 (3).

[58] *Ibid.* s. 41 (4).

[59] *Ibid.* s. 41 (4) (*a*). Adjustments will be necessary if an assessment has been made: *ibid.* s. 41 (6). The tax is deducted on an actual disposal of the shares: *ibid.* s. 41 (7).

[60] *Ibid.* s. 41 (5) (*b*).

PART II. DEVELOPMENT LAND TAX

1. INTRODUCTION

16-100 Attempts have been made at different times to levy relatively high rates of tax on gains realised from the development value of land. The betterment levy, discussed in the third edition of this book, and Development Gains Tax (DGT), discussed in the ninth edition of this book, are two examples. The philosophy which underlies this form of taxation is that profits which stem from the grant of planning consent, which gives land a value in excess of its " current use value," belong to the community and should be taken from the land owner in taxation. New machinery has now been introduced so as to achieve this object. Under the Community Land Act 1975 local authorities, etc., will, ultimately, be directed to acquire all land which is to be developed at its existing " current use value." In the meantime the realisation of development values will fall to be taxed under the Development Land Tax Act 1976 which, subject to transitional provisions, replaces DGT. References to statutory provisions in this Part and in Part III of this chapter are, except where otherwise stated, references to the Development Land Tax Act 1976.

16-101 Development Land Tax (DLT), unlike DGT, is an entirely separate tax from Capital Gains Tax (CGT). It therefore applies whether the land is held as an investment or as stock in trade. The appointed day for the commencement of the tax was August 1, 1976.[1] This part of this chapter is concerned with the structure of the tax whilst Part III is concerned with its interaction with other taxes and the transitional provisions relating to the phasing out of DGT.

The charge to tax applies to the realised development value accruing to any person, whether resident or not, from the disposal of an interest in land in the United Kingdom after the appointed day.[2] A disposal on which such development value may accrue may be either actual or deemed. The word " disposal " is not specially defined and has its ordinary meaning. It therefore includes a sale, exchange, grant of a lease, etc. A deemed disposal occurs on the commencement of a project of material development.[3] Except on the commencement of a project of material development DLT, unlike CGT, does not charge tax on anything other than the actual consideration received. In the case of a gift, for example, special provisions apply but there is no charge on the market value of the land at the date of gift.[4]

16-102 DLT is a tax on the *realised development value* or *betterment* that accrues as a consequence of the grant of planning permission and, in this connection, the following definitions are important:

---

[1] s. 46 (1) and see [1976] S.T.I. 293.
[2] s. 1.
[3] s. 2, *post*, §§ 16-107 *et seq.*
[4] s. 10, *post*, § 16-131.

16-103   " *Market value* " is defined by section 7 (1) as the consideration which an interest in land might reasonably be expected to fetch on a sale in the open market (free of any mortgage), with no reduction for the fact that the whole of the land is to be placed on the market at one and the same time.

16-104   " *Current use value* " is defined by section 7 (2) as the market value of an interest in land on the assumption that planning permission would be granted for any development within a class specified in Schedule 8 to the Town and Country Planning Act 1971 (*i.e.* development not constituting new development) but would not be granted for any *material development* other than that comprised in a project of material development already begun.[5]

16-105   *Material development* is defined in section 7 (7) of and Schedule 4, Part II to the Act. It means any development other than that for which planning permission is granted by a General Development Order but excluding [6]:

    (a) works for the maintenance, improvement, enlargement, alteration or complete rebuilding of any building provided that the cubic content of the *original building* is not exceeded by more than one-tenth. The development of two buildings within the same curtilage may be regarded as one and where two buildings result from the development of one they may be regarded as one.[7] The original building, by reference to which the 10 per cent. tolerance is determined, is the first such building existing on the site on or after September 12, 1974, and not any building which has constituted a rebuilding after that date [8];

    (b) the carrying out on any land used for agriculture or forestry of any building or other operations required for the purposes of that use;

    (c) operations concerning the display of an advertisement or car parking (provided that such use does not exceed six years);

    (d) the use of land for any other purpose falling within the same class as that for which it was used at the relevant time or at the last such time prior to being unoccupied;

    (e) where part only of the building is used for a particular use the use of an additional part not exceeding one-tenth of the cubic content of the original part;

    (f) the resumption of an original use after temporary user or lack of occupation.

The various classes of use are defined in paragraph 7 of Schedule 4.

16-106   " *Interest in land* " is defined by section 46 as any estate or interest in land (including the interest of a beneficiary under a bare trust), any right in

---

[5] If a project of material development had already begun a charge to tax would have been triggered under s. 2, *post*, §§ 16-107 *et seq.* with the consequences that the value of that development forms part of current use value, see *post*, § 16-112.

[6] See Sched. 4, para. 5 (1).

[7] *Ibid.* para. 5 (3). " Curtilage " means a small court or yard ancillary to some main building: *Heron Service Stations Ltd.* v. *Coupe* [1973] 1 W.L.R. 502; and see *Re St. George's, Oakdale* [1976] Fam. 210 and *Sinclair-Lockhart's Trustees* v. *Central Land Board* [1950] 1 P. & C.R. 195.

[8] *Ibid.* para. 6 (3).

or over the land or affecting the use or disposition of land such as a restrictive covenant, and any right to obtain such an interest or right which
is conditional on another's ability to grant the same. It does not include the
interest of a mortgagee, and any conveyance or transfer by way of security
is not to be treated as constituting a disposal or acquisition.

2. DEEMED DISPOSAL

16-107 Section 2 provides that there is a deemed disposal on the commencement of
a project of material development of every major interest in the land which
is comprised within that project. Three questions thus arise: (i) what is a
major interest; (ii) what is a project of material development and what land
is comprised in it; and (iii) when does the project commence.

Major interest

16-108 An interest in land is a major interest [9] unless

> (i) it is in reversion to one or more long leases (being leases of 35
> years' duration [10] or more including such leases determinable at
> any time after the death of any person) and the rent thereunder
> does not and cannot be made to reflect the value of the
> development; or
> (ii) the market value of the interest on the date on which the project
> is begun is less than £5,000 and the interest does not confer,
> either absolutely or conditionally, and whether on that date or at
> any later time, a right to possession as defined in section 205 (1)
> of the Law of Property Act 1925. Thus the benefit of an
> easement or restrictive covenant may fall within this provision
> but a rentcharge (or chief rent) [11] will not.

A project of material development

16-109 A project of material development is taken to be begun at the earliest time
at which any specified operation (as defined) [12] comprised therein is begun.
Examples of specified operations are the digging of a trench, laying of any
underground pipe, any work of construction in the course of erection of a
building, laying out of a road or change in the use of any land. There is
provision for a developer to serve notices on the Board specifying the date
of commencement of the project, its extent, and any subsequent variation
or addition. [13] Subject to certain reservations [14] such notices determine the

---

[9] s. 2 (3).
[10] In determining the duration of a lease the same principles apply as under I.C.T.A. 1970, s. 84:
Sched. 1, Pt. III and see *ante*, § 6-18.
[11] A rentcharge would not normally, however, reflect development value.
[12] See Sched. 1, para. 2 (2).
[13] See Sched. 1, para. 2 (3) and Sched. 8, paras. 36 and 37.
[14] For example on a variation or addition the DLT liability may have to be recomputed: see Sched. 1,
paras. 2 (3), 4 (2) and (3), and 6 as if the variation or addition were comprised within the original project.
Where the addition extends to land not comprised in the original project it will always constitute a separate
project: Sched. 1, para. 6 (4). Where notice of a new project, as opposed to an addition, is given under
Sched. 8, para. 36 within three years from the commencement of an earlier project the Board has power to
treat the new project, having regard to its nature and scope, as being comprised in the original: Sched. 1,
para. 6 (7). In such circumstances it is considered that works on land not comprised in the original project
must, again, be treated as a separate project.

scope, etc., of any particular project for the purposes of the Act. These provisions are of some significance in determining DLT liability since if further material development falls to be treated as additional development (and does not appear to the Board to constitute a separate project) [15] it is taken into account for the purposes of the charge on the commencement of the original project so that if, for example, that project was commenced before the Appointed Day DLT would not be leviable.

16-110   A project of material development comprises all the development carried out in pursuance of the project including the clearing of the land. [16] Where a project was begun but not completed before the Appointed Day no material development is regarded as comprised within 'it unless it was, on the Appointed Day, authorised by planning permission then in force. To the extent that it was not, it falls to be regarded as a separate project. [17] Outline planning permission is not sufficient for these purposes so that the only development deemed to be comprised within the project will be that which was authorised, without reservation, or approved in the manner applicable on or before the Appointed Day. Any garage, outbuildings, etc., constructed with and for the purposes of a building is deemed to be comprised within the same project as the building. [18] Where the only material development in the project is the change of use of any hereditament (or any part thereof) then the land comprised therein is that hereditament, *i.e.* that which forms the subject of a single entry in the valuation list. [19] Thus if several private houses are converted to use as offices each original house will be deemed to constitute a separate project.

Disposal at market value

16-111   Immediately before the commencement of the project every major interest in the land comprised therein is deemed to be disposed of and re-acquired at market value. In determining market value at this time it is to be assumed that it is lawful for everything comprised in the project to be carried out (and to this extent incumbrances are disregarded) and that all existing development has been carried out. [20] Account is taken of any conditions imposed by planning permission authorising the project (such as those often imposed under section 52 of the Town and Country Planning Act 1971). If incumbrances such as restrictive covenants and easements exist they are treated as contingent liabilities assumed by the chargeable person on the assumed disposal and if he subsequently incurs expenditure in removing those incumbrances that expenditure is taken to reduce the market value of his interest on the date of the deemed disposal and the DLT liability recalculated accordingly. [21]

16-112   If a project extends to only a part of the land in which an interest is held the whole of that interest is deemed to be disposed of immediately prior to the commencement of the project but at the market value of that interest in

---

[15] See Sched. 1, para. 6.   [16] *Ibid.* para. 4.
[17] *Ibid.* para. 5 and this new separate project is commenced by a specified operation referable *only* to development outside the original project: *ibid.* para. 5 (3).
[18] *Ibid.* para. 4 (4).   [19] *Ibid.* para. 4 (5) and (6).
[20] s. 2 (1) and Sched. 1, para. 8.   [21] Sched. 1, para. 9.

the project land alone.[22] Correspondingly the base value is deemed to be the appropriate proportion of the actual base value attributable to the project land.[23] On the deemed re-acquisition of the interest the remaining proportion of the original base value is brought in together with the market value of the project land. For the purpose of determining the current use value of the land on the deemed re-acquisition it is assumed that that re-acquisition occurred immediately after the beginning of the project so that the value thereof is reflected in the current use value.[24]

> *Example.* A person acquires 50 acres of land for £100,000, obtains planning permission and commences an initial project on only five acres, the market value of which (on the above assumptions) immediately before the project is commenced is £50,000. Therefore the interest in the whole 50 acres is deemed to be disposed of for £50,000 with a base value attributable to only the five acres of, say £10,000. The deemed re-acquisition will then take place at £140,000 (*i.e.* £50,000 + £90,000) and the current use value increased by the value of the development.

3. COMPUTATION OF REALISED DEVELOPMENT VALUE

16-113 Section 4 provides that the realised development value accruing to a chargeable person on a disposal shall be the amount (if any) by which the net proceeds of the disposal exceed the relevant base value of his interest. There are three alternative base values, Base A, Base B and Base C and the highest of them is the relevant base value.

Disposal proceeds

16-114 The net proceeds of a disposal are the consideration therefor less the incidental costs of making the disposal.[25] Schedule 2, Part V contains detailed rules for determining what constitutes the consideration for a disposal and an acquisition.

The consideration is brought into account without any discount for postponement of the right to receive it and, in the first instance, without any regard to any contingent liability or the risk of its being irrecoverable.[26] If it subsequently proves to be irrecoverable the original liability is recomputed. Foreign tax may be deducted.[27] If an interest is disposed of subject to a mortgage the principal outstanding thereon is added to the consideration.[28] On the grant of a lease the consideration is deemed to be the aggregate of the right to receive the rents reserved and any other payment (such as a premium) given for the grant.[29] On a disposal to an authority possessing compulsory powers the disturbance element is excluded.[30] On a distribution from a company in respect of shares the disposal consideration is deemed to be equal to market value.[31]

---

[22] *Ibid.* para. 11.
[23] Sched. 2, para. 18 and s. 4 (5).
[24] Sched. 1, para. 12.
[25] s. 4 (3).
[26] Sched. 2, paras. 21 and 22.
[27] *Ibid.* para. 23.
[28] *Ibid.* para. 24.
[29] *Ibid.* paras. 26 and 27. In determining the consideration no account can be taken of obligations assumed by the lessor so as to achieve the rents reserved; such obligations may, however, be treated as improvement expenditure: see *post*, § 16-118 and § 16-128.
[30] *Ibid.* para. 29.
[31] *Ibid.* para. 31.

The incidental costs are those incurred wholly and exclusively for the purposes of the disposal or acquisition on fees, etc., to a lawyer, surveyor, valuer, auctioneer, accountant or agent and any other costs of conveyance or transfer (including stamp duty) together with the costs of advertising to find a buyer or seller and costs incurred for the purposes of determining the DLT liability. [32] Such costs would not normally extend to the salary costs of employees undertaking such work.

If a vendor undertakes to bear all or part of the costs of erecting a building on the land disposed of the consideration payable must be apportioned and that attributable to the value of the obligation to carry out the works, etc., excluded from the DLT disposal consideration. [33]

Base A [34]

16-115   This is the aggregate of the following:

16-116   (i) *The cost of acquisition.* This is the amount or value of the consideration given by the chargeable person or on his behalf wholly and exclusively for the acquisition of the interest together with the incidental costs thereof excluding any part provided by the Crown or local authorities etc. [35]

16-117   (ii) *Any expenditure on relevant improvements.* Relevant improvements means that part of the expenditure on improvements which remains after deducting therefrom a sum equal to the amount by which the current use value of the interest has increased as a result of the expenditure. [36] Thus only those improvements which increase development value *e.g.* the cost of obtaining planning permission, as opposed to current use value are deductible. Expenditure on most building works, etc., will, therefore, not constitute expenditure on relevant improvements since they will take place after the commencement of a project of material development which will bring the value of the buildings into current use value.

16-118   Expenditure on improvements (in general) extends to any expenditure incurred in enhancing the value of the interest being expenditure reflected in the state of the land or the market value of the land at disposal or in establishing, preserving or defending title thereto or the enjoyment of the land. [37] Thus expenditure anticipated or contracted for at the date of disposal will not qualify: the expenditure must actually have been incurred by the date of disposal. There is one exception to this rule where, on a lease (or agreement for a lease) being granted, the lessor undertakes to carry out works of improvement. Since these works will be reflected in the rents reserved under the lease (and therefore the disposal consideration [38]) the lessor is entitled to treat the amount of such expenditure as having been actually incurred. [39] This exception only applies on the grant of a lease and not to a sale where the burden of such an obligation will normally reduce

---

[32] Sched. 2, para. 32.
[33] s. 4 (5); the payment attributable to the obligation to carry out the works will constitute expenditure on improvements as far as the acquirer is concerned.   [34] s. 5 (1) (*a*).
[35] s. 5 (2) and (4).   [36] Sched. 3, para. 2.
[37] *Ibid.* para. 1 (1).   [38] See *ante*, § 16-114.
[39] Sched. 2, para. 13A, as inserted by F.A. 1977, s. 55; see *post*, § 16-128.

the disposal consideration. Work of maintenance repair or decoration is, however, excluded.[40] Where the acquisition is a deemed re-acquisition under section 2 no expenditure on improvements incurred prior to that time qualifies to be treated as such on any subsequent disposal unless that expenditure was *not* reflected in the deemed re-acquisition value.[41] Interest charges, it is considered, would not qualify since they represent the cost of providing the expenditure and not the expenditure itself.

Also included as expenditure on improvements on the relevant land is any loss in current use value on other land which has been caused by the imposition of a condition regulating its development or use as a term of granting planning permission over the relevant land [42] (or as part of an arrangement relating thereto).[43] In virtually all cases the whole of this loss of current use value on the affected land would constitute relevant improvements. Correspondingly the base value of the affected land is reduced by the smaller of the addition to improvements on the relevant land or the amount (if any) by which current use value at acquisition or April 6, 1965, exceeds current use value at the time of its disposal.[44] If an authority possessing compulsory purchase powers acquires an interest in land and the compensation is reduced because of " betterment " of an interest in other land then the excess, if any, of 110 per cent. of current use value of the interest acquired over the compensation is regarded as expenditure on improvements to the bettered interest.[45] Again any expenditure provided or met by the Crown or local authorities, etc., is excluded.

16-119   (iii) *The increase in current use value (to the date of disposal) from the date of acquisition or April 6, 1965, if later.* Current use value has been defined above: *ante*, § 16-104. Where parts of the relevant interest have been acquired at different times the current use value at the dates of acquisition (or April 6, 1965, if later) of the various parts are aggregated.[46]

16-120   (iv) *The Special Addition.* Section 6 provides that where an interest in land is acquired before May 1, 1977, a special addition is included in the calculation of Base A which is equal to $D \times E$ per cent. of actual acquisition cost, where D equals the number of years of ownership (subject to a maximum of four) and E is 15 if the acquisition was prior to September 13, 1974, and 10 in any other case. Special Addition is not given *after* a deemed disposal and re-acquisition under section 2 unless on that occasion Base A exceeded the deemed disposal proceeds.[47] In the latter case the Special Addition attributable to a proportion of the original actual acquisition cost (equal to the proportion that the excess on the deemed disposal bears to Base A on that disposal) can be carried forward to a subsequent disposal although D above is reduced by the number of years between actual acquisition and the deemed disposal.

> *Example.* A developer acquired land on April 1, 1972, for £100,000. He commences his development on April 1, 1977, and at that time the market value of the land is £120,000. The Special Addition applicable on that deemed

---

[40] *Ibid.* para. 1 (2).   [41] Sched. 2, para. 1 (4).
[42] *Ibid.* para. 3.   [43] *Ibid.* para. 6.
[44] *Ibid.* para. 4.   [45] *Ibid.* para. 7.
[46] *Ibid.* para. 5.   [47] s. 6 (4)–(9).

disposal is £60,000 (4 × 15 per cent.). Therefore the proportion of the original acquisition cost which can be carried forward for the purposes of Special Addition is £25,000 (*i.e.*

$$\frac{£160,000 \;-\; £120,000}{£160,000} \times £100,000).$$

If the land is subsequently disposed of on say April 1, 1979, then a Special Addition of £7,500 (*i.e.* 30 per cent. of £25,000) will be added to the base cost of £120,000.

Where the relevant interest was acquired in parts at different times Special Addition is applied separately to each part.[48]

In the case of groups of companies, and amalgamations and reconstructions, Special Addition is preserved until the occurrence of a deemed disposal under section 2 or an actual disposal outside the group.[49]

16-121   (v) *The Further Addition.* If in determining Base A an amount is to be included in respect of both relevant improvements and Special Addition a further addition is given which is equal to the formula $RI \times \dfrac{A}{C}$ where RI is expenditure on relevant improvements, A is the Special Addition and C is the cost of acquisition.[50]

16-122   *Connected transfers.*[51] Neither the Special Addition nor the Further Addition is available where the chargeable person acquired the interest (or a part as regards that part) within the 12 months preceding its disposal from a person who was connected with him. This does not apply to personal representatives in the course of administration or a disposal treated as made on death by the deceased.

Base B [52]

16-123   This is the aggregate of 110 per cent. of current use value at the time of disposal and of any expenditure on relevant improvements.

Base C [53]

16-124   This is 110 per cent. of the aggregate of the cost of acquisition and of any expenditure on improvements (*i.e.* it is not restricted to only those improvements which increase development value). Where the interest was acquired by a connected transfer satisfying the conditions set out at *ante*, § 16-122, only the actual cost of acquisition and not 110 per cent. thereof is allowable but the allowance for 110 per cent. of improvements remains the same.

Part disposals

16-125   A part disposal occurs where an owner grants a lease or other interest out of or by virtue of his ownership (*i.e.* a true part disposal) or merely disposes

---

[48] Sched. 2, para. 5.
[49] ss. 20 (3) and 22 (7) and see §§ 16-144 and 16-145.
[50] Sched. 3, para. 8.
[51] s. 5 (6) and (7).
[52] s. 5 (1) (*b*).
[53] s. 5 (1) (*c*) and (6).

of a part of the land in which his interest subsists.[54] There is also a part disposal where he derives any sum from his ownership which is neither rent nor part of the acquisition cost of the person paying the sum, in particular [55]:

    (a) sums received as compensation for damage to land or its depreciation or risk of depreciation [56];

    (b) sums received for forfeiture or surrender of or refraining from exercising rights;

    (c) sums received for the use or exploitation of the land and assets (other than minerals) in, on or under the land.

Such part disposals take place at the time when the sums are received unless, the right to receive payment having accrued, the interest is disposed of.

16-126   On a part disposal the various items which go to make up the base value of the totality are reduced for the purposes of the part disposal computation by applying to each of them the fraction $\dfrac{PD}{PD + MR}$ where PD equals the net proceeds of the part disposal and MR is the market value of the interest retained immediately after the disposal.[57] Where the proceeds of the part disposal are less than market value that value is substituted for the purposes of the fraction. The remainder of the items which go to make up the base value of the totality then constitute the various bases for the retained interest. Special provisions [58] apply where the asset which is the subject of the part disposal was itself acquired in various parts at different times or where the part disposal is a disposal of part and, for example, certain improvement expenditure is only referable to a particular part.

16-127   In determining the applicable base values on a part disposal the amount which would have been the current use value of the totality at disposal is reduced by the current use value of the retained interest immediately after that time and, for the purposes of Base A, in determining current use value at acquisition (or April 6, 1965, if later) that value for the totality is reduced by applying to it the fraction $\dfrac{CW - CR}{CW}$ where CW equals the current use value of the whole at disposal and CR equals that value for the retained interest immediately after that time.[59] The remainder then constitutes the relevant base for the retained interest. Again there are provisions which override these rules where the current use value of the particular part is identifiable.

Leases and reversions

16-128   Schedule 2, Part III contains particular rules applying to the disposal of leases and reversions. As we have seen [60] the consideration for the disposal

---

[54] s. 3 (1).

[55] s. 3 (2), a sum includes money or money's worth.

[56] If the policy of insurance extended only to the risk of damage to a building the consideration received is reduced to the current use value of the building so as to come outside the charge to DLT: Sched. 2, para. 30.

[57] Sched. 2, para. 10.

[58] See *ibid.* paras. 10 and 11.

[59] *Ibid.* para. 12.

[60] *Ante*, § 16-114, Sched. 2, paras. 26 and 27.

on a grant of a lease is deemed to be the aggregate of the right to receive the rent reserved thereunder and any other consideration (such as a premium) given for the grant. This takes no account of any obligation undertaken by the lessor such as to erect a building where that building is pre-let. To overcome this problem and to ensure that the lessor is not charged to tax on his building expenditure paragraph 13A of Schedule 2 to the Act [61] provides that the amount of such expenditure to be undertaken (which the lessor is obliged to incur under the terms on which the lease or agreement for lease is made) qualifies as expenditure on improvements, or relevant improvements as the case may be. Also to ensure that no development profit (as opposed to a profit attributable to the obtaining of planning permission) is charged to tax the realised development value accruing on such a disposal is restricted to the amount that would have accrued had the land been disposed of at its market value on the date that the lease was granted. [62] Consequential amendments are made for the purpose of determining the further addition.

When a lease is granted any element of development value in the rent will be charged to DLT by taking into account the capital value of the rent. Consequently on a subsequent assignment of a lease the new capital value of the rents is taken into account for the purposes of the DLT computation. The ordinary rules are adjusted so as to ensure that, on the disposal of a reversion, the DLT charge is confined to any development value attributable to the right to re-occupy.

Options [63]

16-129   The grant of an option (or the forfeiture of a deposit on an abortive sale) is treated as the disposal of a newly created interest in land and not a part disposal of the grantor's interest. If the option is exercised the two transactions are regarded as one disposal and acquisition taking place at the time of the exercise for a consideration equal to the price of the option and the consideration payable thereunder.

Time of disposal and acquisition [64]

16-130   If an interest in land is disposed of under a contract then, if the contract is conditional (and, in particular, if it is conditional on the exercise of an option) the time of disposal and acquisition is the time when the condition is satisfied and in any other case the time of disposal and acquisition is the time when the contract is made. [65] Where an interest in land is acquired compulsorily by an authority possessing compulsory powers the time of disposal and acquisition is the time at which the compensation is agreed or otherwise determined (variations on appeal being disregarded for this purpose) or, if earlier, the time when the authority entered on the land in pursuance of its powers. [66] If the disposal of an interest in land under a

---

[61] As inserted by F.A. 1977, s. 55.   [62] Sched. 2, para. 13A (3).
[63] s. 8.
[64] s. 45.
[65] s. 45 (2). As to what constitutes a conditional contract see *Eastham* v. *Leigh London and Provincial Properties Ltd.* [1971] Ch. 871; 46 T.C. 687.
[66] s. 45 (4).

conditional contract entered into before September 13, 1974, is made for a consideration not depending wholly or mainly on the value of the interest at the time the condition is satisfied the contract is treated as if it had never been conditional with the consequence that no charge to DLT can accrue.[67] If an owner had entered into an arrangement, evidenced in writing, before September 13, 1974, to dispose of his interest in land and he in fact disposes of that interest within the period of twelve months beginning on the Appointed Day, in terms not materially different from the arrangement or not more beneficial to the owner, the disposal is treated as occurring before the Appointed Day.[68] The same result is prescribed if land is disposed of on or after the Appointed Day to an authority possessing compulsory powers if the notice to treat was served before September 13, 1974.[69]

Devolution on death, gifts, etc.

16-131   Other than on the deemed disposal prescribed by section 2, DLT, unlike CGT, does not impose a charge on the market value of an interest on disposals by way of gift, etc. It is concerned with the actual consideration received. Therefore special rules apply to devolution on death and disposals for no consideration.

Section 9 provides that there is no disposal on death. Personal representatives are deemed to have acquired an interest in land on its acquisition by the deceased and to have incurred the expenditure which he incurred.

Where no consideration (disregarding incidental costs of disposal) is given for the chargeable person's acquisition of an asset then, in determining his base value, the cost of acquisition is deemed to be equal to the donor's cost, and any expenditure on improvements (or relevant improvements) incurred by the donor are deemed to have been incurred by the chargeable person who also acquires the current use value on the donor's acquisition.[70] The donee is entitled to no Special Addition of his own but, instead, is entitled to take that Special Addition that would have been available to the donor on the disposal to the donee.

> *Example.* A acquires land for £100,000 in 1970, dies in 1973, his personal representatives transfer the land to B, his residuary legatee, in 1976 and B sells the land for £200,000 in 1977. No disposal occurs on A's death but a disposal and acquisition for no consideration occurs in 1976. In computing the DLT charge on B's disposal his cost of acquisition is £100,000 and he may include the cost of any improvements incurred by A or the personal representatives and may take the Special Addition that was available to the personal representatives on their disposal to him in 1976 (*i.e.* £60,000).

An acquisition at an undervalue by a charity or body specified in Finance Act 1975, Sched. 6, para. 12 (*i.e.* transactions constituting exempt transfers for capital transfer tax) is also treated as an acquisition for no value if to do so would give the acquirer a higher base value.[71]

---

[67] s. 45 (6).
[68] s. 45 (7).   None of these provisions affect the acquisition: s. 45 (9).
[69] s. 45 (8).
[70] s. 10; an assignment of a lease can never be treated as being for no consideration since the value of the landlord's rights is deemed to constitute consideration: s. 10 (7).
[71] s. 10 (5) and see *post*, § 19-21.

4. RATE OF TAX

16-132 The first £10,000 of realised development value accruing to any person in a financial year is exempt from the charge.[72] The exemption is applied in the order in which the disposals are made. This exemption is excluded where the disposal occurs within 12 months from an acquisition from a connected person or where the disposal is made otherwise than by an individual and the land was acquired from a connected person for less than its market value after September 12, 1974, and within the six years prior to the disposal.[73] If a part of the interest disposed of was so acquired the exemption is excluded as regards the development value accruing on that part only.[74] Where DLT is deferred on any disposal the circumstances are still determined by reference to the date of the disposal. For these purposes a partnership is treated as a single person, not being an individual, in respect of disposals of partnership assets. Thus, in the case of partnerships, it is plainly preferable that the individuals should own the freehold whilst the partnership, as such, only have an occupational lease.

16-133 In respect of disposals occurring on or before March 31, 1980, a reduced rate applies so that the first £150,000 of development value accruing in any one year is charged at 66⅔ per cent.[75] This reduced rate is excluded in the same circumstances as apply to exclude the first £10,000 of development value save that for this purpose a partnership is regarded as an individual.

16-134 Subject to the above, the rate of DLT is 80 per cent.[76]

5. EXEMPTIONS, DEFERMENTS AND OTHER RELIEFS

Exempt bodies

16-135 Certain bodies (*e.g.* local authorities, police and fire authorities) are exempted completely from DLT.

Private residences [77]

16-136 Section 14 provides that any realised development value accruing on the disposal of a private residence is exempt from DLT unless the residence was acquired wholly or partly for the purpose of realising its development value. A private residence is a dwelling-house which is the individual's only or main residence together with its garden or grounds up to an area of one acre (or such larger area as the Commissioners may determine, having regard to the size and character of the dwelling-house, as being required for the reasonable enjoyment of the house).[78] Where an apportionment is required that which is most suitable for occupation with the dwelling-house is taken to be within the exemption. A husband and wife may each have their own

---

[72] s. 12.
[73] ss. 12 (5) and 5 (6); see *ante*, § 16-122. It is considered that these provisions cannot apply to transactions between members of the same group of companies to which s. 20 applies: see *post*, § 16-144.
[74] s. 12 (6) and (7).
[75] s. 13 as amended by F.A. 1978, s. 76.
[76] s. 1 (3).
[77] Compare the similar exemption from CGT at *ante*, § 16-41.   [78] s. 14 (2).

separate main residences for the purposes of this exemption provided that they can establish, as a matter of fact, that the particular house is their main residence.

The ownership must have been for not less than six months and the house must have been the individual's only or main residence during at least one year out of the last two years ending with the disposal (or half the total period if less than two years).[79] An apportionment is prescribed where part of the premises are used for the purposes of a trade, profession or vocation.[80]

16-137   The exemption extends to a dwelling-house and land owned by trustees which is occupied as his only or main residence by an individual entitled to do so under the terms of the settlement or entitled to the whole of the income therefrom or from the proceeds of sale thereof.[81] It is also extended to disposals by personal representatives within two years of the death of a person who would have satisfied the primary conditions of exemption on the date of his death (excluding the requirement of a minimum of six months' occupation).[82] The exemption also applies to a house provided rent-free for a dependent relative.[83]

Houses built for owner-occupation

16-138   Section 15 provides an exemption from the charge on a deemed disposal under section 2 for a person building a single dwelling-house for occupation by himself or an adult member of his family if he owned the land on September 12, 1974. The exemption may extend to two such buildings provided one is built on land within the curtilage of a dwelling-house owned and occupied by him on September 12, 1974.[84]

Stock-in-trade

16-139   Section 16 provides that a trader is exempt in respect of any development value realised on the disposal of stock-in-trade held by him as such on September 12, 1974, to the extent that the development was authorised by planning permission in force on that date. Land is *deemed* to have planning permission on that date if [85]:

(a) the Secretary of State makes a determination after that date and before the relevant disposal on an application made to him before that date under the calling-in procedure or on an appeal against a decision of a planning authority given before that date; or

(b) by virtue of the default provision the appeals provision applies (although the applicant makes or pursues no appeal) as if permission had been refused before September 12, 1974, and the applicant is subsequently granted permission on a further application which does not significantly differ from the first.

---

[79] s. 14 (3).
[80] s. 14 (4).
[81] s. 14 (6).
[82] s. 14 (7).
[83] s. 14 (9).
[84] s. 15 (2).
[85] See Sched. 5, para. 1.

Outline planning permission in force on September 12, 1974, will suffice for the purposes of the section but, in such a case, the exemption will only extend to the value of development which was actually authorised on September 12, 1974, subsequently approved in the manner applicable to the permission in force on that date or was such as might on that date reasonably have been expected to be granted in that manner.[86]

16-140 Where a person acquires an interest in land for no consideration (for example as donee or member of the same group of companies) or as personal representative of a person who, as regards that land, fulfilled the conditions set out above, then the exemption is extended to apply to a disposal made by the recipient.[87] The exemption also applies where the person's only interest in the land was under a conditional contract entered into on or before September 12, 1974.[88]

Minerals

16-141 Section 17 provides that on a deemed disposal any development value which consists of the winning or working of minerals [89] and is authorised by planning permission in force at that time, is excluded from the project of material development. On an actual disposal of land with planning permission for the winning or working of minerals the amount of realised development value is reduced to the aggregate of:

(a) the market value, immediately after the disposal, of the interest on the assumption that it was at that time and would continue to be unlawful to carry out material development consisting of the winning or working of minerals; and

(b) one half of the difference between that market value and the gross realised development value.[90]

From the above it will be seen that it is plainly preferable to commence a project of winning or working minerals prior to an actual disposal since, in that event, a complete exemption will apply on the deemed disposal and the full value of the project will be taken into current use value for the purposes of the subsequent actual disposal.

Projects begun within three years of acquisition

16-142 Section 18 provides an exemption on the deemed disposal under section 2 (§§ 16-107 *et seq.*) where the Board are satisfied that the relevant interest had been acquired within the period of three years ending on the date of the deemed disposal and that if the project had been commenced immediately

---

[86] Sched. 5, para. 2.   [87] s. 16 (3) and (4).
[88] s. 16 (8).
[89] Defined in s. 17 (7) so as to include the grading, washing, grinding etc. of minerals and the carrying out of ancillary operations. " Minerals " are defined in s. 47.
[90] s. 17 (3) and (4). In a case of a disposal which consists of the grant of a mineral lease or agreement within the meaning of s. 29 of the Finance Act 1970, no realised development value whatsoever shall be taken to accrue unless a part of the gross consideration received does not constitute " mineral royalties " within the meaning of that section. Thus, where development value is entirely attributable to the value of minerals, the existing basis of taxation (50 per cent. as capital gain and 50 per cent. as income) is left undisturbed (s. 17 (6) and see *ante*, § 6-11).

after that original acquisition no significant amount of realised development value would have accrued. There are provisions whereby when he proposes to commence a project, a developer can obtain a decision from the Board as to whether or not it is satisfied that the conditions apply.[91]

Development for industrial use

16-143   Section 19 provides that where realised development value accrues to a trader on a deemed disposal under section 2 relating to a building or other land to be used, in whole or part, for the industrial purposes of his trade (or that of another member of the same group of companies [92]) then liability to DLT (or that proportion relating to the part to be used for industrial purposes) is deferred until the first subsequent disposal thereof which is not a deemed disposal, a disposal to another member of the same group, a disposal as a consequence of reorganisation or amalgamation or a sale and lease-back transaction. A building is used for the industrial purposes of a trade if it is used for or incidental to manufacturing, altering and repairing processes, etc., or, otherwise than as a dwelling-house, for the welfare of workers employed in such a trade.[93] Buildings within the same curtilage used for ancillary services or facilities are deemed to constitute such property.[94] The Board are prepared to allow the exemption where the building is constructed prior to the commencement of the trade.[95]

If the land, without being disposed of, ceases to be used for a qualifying purpose by the trader (or another member of the same group) it is deemed to be disposed of so as to bring into charge the deferred tax.[96]

Groups of companies

16-144   For DLT purposes a group of companies is defined in the same way as that applicable to companies' chargeable gains save that it extends to non-resident companies.[97] Section 20 provides that a disposal by one member of a group to another is treated as a disposal (and acquisition) for which no consideration is given (unless the disposal is by a resident to a non-resident member of the group or is to a body exempt from DLT within section 11). Thus the procedure laid down in section 10 applies (see § 16-131) but the company acquiring the asset is treated as having acquired it for all purposes at the date of acquisition of the original group member (*i.e.* so as not to lose Special Addition or the availability of the 10 per cent. tolerance of current use value under section 5 (6)).[98]

Where a company ceases to be a member of a group (other than being wound up, dissolved, or another member being wound up or dissolved) owning land, which it had acquired after September 12, 1974, and within the six-year period ending at the time of severance from another member of the group, it is treated as having disposed of and immediately re-acquired at market value the land at the date of severance.[99] There are provisions

---

[91] s. 18 (3).
[92] s. 20 (5).
[93] s. 19 (2).
[94] s. 19 (3).
[95] See the Revenue booklet DLT 2, para. 198.
[96] s. 19 (5).
[97] s. 47 (2).
[98] s. 20 (3).
[99] s. 21.

providing exemption from this charge where, in certain circumstances, the two companies leave the group at the same time. Any exemption available to the original group member, for example that relating to stock in trade, will apply on the disposal outside the group by any other member of the group.

Amalgamations and reconstructions etc.

16-145   Section 22 provides that disposals of land in the course of an amalgamation or reconstruction are to be treated as disposals (and acquisitions) for which no consideration is given. Thus section 10 applies but so that the Special Addition and the availability of the 10 per cent. tolerance to current use value are preserved. Likewise relief under section 18 is preserved.

Statutory undertakers

16-146   Section 23 provides that DLT is deferred on the deemed disposal of land owned by a statutory undertaker which is to be used for the purposes of its undertaking in a similar manner to that provided by section 19.

Charities

16-147   Section 24 provides a complete exemption from DLT in respect of development value accruing to a charity on the disposal of land held by it (or another charity) on September 12, 1974 (or subsequently acquired by it under a conditional contract entered into prior to that date [1]). An interest in land is deemed to be held by a charity on September 12, 1974, if the charity would on that date have been absolutely entitled to the interest if the administration of a deceased's estate had been completed. [2] There are provisions dealing with the merger of leases and options held by charities on September 12, 1974. [3] If a body subsequently ceases to be a charity a charge accrues at that time by reference to the amounts previously exempt under this section though not so as to exceed the assets then ceasing to be held on charitable trusts. [4] If a charity acquires an interest in land after September 12, 1974, the complete exemption does not apply but section 25 provides that tax on a deemed disposal is deferred (until sale) to the extent that the project of material development relates to a building or other land to be used for the purposes of the charity.

The Housing Corporation and certain housing associations

16-148   Section 26 provides exemption from the charge on a deemed disposal accruing to approved co-operative housing associations and self-build societies. There is a more limited deferment from tax granted on deemed disposals or disposals to other such bodies, accruing to the Housing Corporation and other registered housing associations.

[1] s. 24 (8).
[2] s. 24 (1).
[3] s. 24 (3) and (4).
[4] s. 24 (6) and (7).

6. TRUSTS, SETTLED PROPERTY, PARTNERSHIPS, MORTGAGEES AND LIQUIDATORS

Bare trusts and settled property

16-149   Where an interest in land is held on trust for a person absolutely entitled as against the trustees or for a person who would be so entitled but for being a minor or under a disability (a " bare trust ") the acts of the trustees are regarded as the acts of the person so entitled.[5] An interest in land held on trust other than a bare trust is settled property, the trustees of which are treated as being a single and continuing body of persons distinct from the persons who may from time to time be the trustees.[6] Consequently the trustees (and not the beneficiaries) of settled property are the chargeable persons for DLT purposes. Where a person becomes absolutely entitled to an interest in land which was settled property the trustees are deemed to dispose of the land and re-acquire it for no consideration so that section 10 applies,[7] *ante*, § 16-131. A person is absolutely entitled when he has the exclusive right subject only to satisfying any outstanding charge or lien, etc., to direct how the interest should be dealt with.[8] Two or more persons may be jointly so absolutely entitled as joint tenants, tenants in common or co-parceners.[9]

A disposal of his interest by a beneficiary under a bare trust is treated as a disposal of the whole or part of the land as the case may be.[10] Where there is only a disposal of part of the land the original base value of the whole is apportioned by reference to the ratio of the market values on disposal unless the chargeable person had acquired his interest or a part thereof from another beneficiary.

Partnerships

16-150   Any partnership dealings are treated as dealings by the individual partners and not the firm as such,[11] although, as we have seen, *ante*, §§ 16-132 to 16-133, for the purposes of applying the £10,000 exemption and the reduced rate of tax they are treated as a single body in respect of disposals of partnership assets.

Mortgagees and creditors

16-151   Where a person entitled to a security in any land (or a receiver and manager on his behalf) deals with that land for the purpose of enforcing that security he is regarded as a bare trustee for the person entitled to the land subject to the security.[12] Where by foreclosure an interest in land becomes vested beneficially in a creditor the interest is deemed to be disposed of by the borrower and acquired by the creditor for a consideration equal to the amount of principal, interest and costs outstanding.[13]

---

[5] s. 28 (1) and compare the less precise definition for CGT purposes considered at *ante*, § 16-21.
[6] s. 30.
[7] s. 28 (2).
[8] s. 28 (3).
[9] s. 28 (4).
[10] s. 29.
[11] s. 31.
[12] s. 32 (1).
[13] s. 32 (3).

Liquidators and trustees in bankruptcy

16-152   Where any interest in land is vested in a liquidator or trustee in bankruptcy his acts are deemed to be the acts of the company, bankrupt or debtor in whom the land, for DLT purposes, is regarded as vested.[14] On the death of a bankrupt his trustee in bankruptcy is treated as acquiring the land as a personal representative[15] so that section 9 applies, see *ante*, § 16-131. DLT has the same priority in a bankruptcy or liquidation as income tax.[16]

7. DEDUCTION, ADMINISTRATION AND COLLECTION

16-153   Where an interest in land is disposed of to a local authority, etc., a Minister of the Crown or an exempt body within section 11, that body or person is required to make a deduction from the consideration on account of DLT and the chargeable person is deemed to have paid an amount of DLT equal to the deduction.[17] This deduction falls to be made even so as to prejudice the rights of a mortgagee in the land unless his mortgage was created prior to May 11, 1976.[18] Detailed provisions are set out in Schedule 7. All persons purchasing land from a non-resident are required to make a deduction of 50 per cent. of the purchase price and to account for the same to the Board[19] if planning permission exists in respect of the land and no project of material development comprising that within the permission has been commenced prior to the date of disposal. A clearance procedure exists whereby a non-resident vendor can obtain a certificate from the Board whereby no deduction or a lower deduction can be made.[20] Such a clearance would be applicable where, for example, the non-resident vendor has a high base value.

16-154   DLT is placed under the care and management of the Board of Inland Revenue and the detailed rules governing its administration are set out in Schedule 8. Appeals are to be made to the Special Commissioners except where the only question relates to the exemption for private residences and houses built for owner-occupation.[21] Error or mistake claims can be made within six years and the normal time-limit (subject to fraud, wilful default and neglect) for making assessments is six years from the year of disposal.[22] There are provisions whereby a chargeable person realising chargeable development value is required to notify the Board within one year of the disposal and within 60 days prior to or 30 days after the commencement of a project of material development.[23]

Payment

16-155   DLT is payable either three months after the date of disposal or, if later, 30 days after the date of issue of the assessment.[24] Interest commences to

---

[14] s. 33 (1).
[15] s. 33 (3).
[16] s. 42.
[17] s. 39 and Sched. 7.
[18] See Sched. 7, para. 8.
[19] s. 40 and DLT (Disposals by Non-Residents) Regulations 1976 (see [1976] S.T.I. 306).
[20] DLT (Disposal by Non-Residents) Regulations 1976, reg. 6.
[21] Sched. 8, para. 3.
[22] *Ibid.* paras. 5, 6 and 7.
[23] *Ibid.* paras. 35 and 36.
[24] *Ibid.* para. 43.

run from the due date of payment, *i.e.* three months after the disposal.[25] However on a deemed disposal, grant of a lease for a rent not exceeding the commercial rent, or the triggering, otherwise than by disposal, of a deferred liability, a person liable to DLT may elect to pay the tax by yearly or half yearly instalments.[26] The instalments are normally eight yearly or 16 half yearly instalments with the first payable 12 months after disposal.[27] In such cases interest only runs from the various dates for the payment of instalments.[28] A similar instalment provision exists where the consideration for a disposal consists of payment by instalments and the chargeable person satisfies the Board that he would otherwise suffer undue hardship.[29] In this case, however, interest runs on the total consideration from the normal date, *i.e.* three months after the disposal.[30] There is also provision for postponing payment of tax where the disposal arises as part of the transfer of a business to a company in exchange for shares.[31]

[The next paragraph is 16-156]

---

[25] *Ibid.* para. 21 inserting a new s. 86A in T.M.A. 1970. The rate of interest is 6%: see [1978] S.T.I. 452.
[26] *Ibid.* para. 44.
[27] *Ibid.* para. 45.
[28] See n. 21, above.
[29] Sched. 8, para. 50.
[30] See n. 25, above.
[31] *Ibid.* para. 52.

PART III. THE INTERACTION OF DEVELOPMENT LAND TAX WITH OTHER TAXES

1. TRANSITIONAL PROVISIONS

16-156 The Appointed Day for the introduction of DLT was August 1, 1976. However, since the charge to tax under DLT operates in a different way to that under DGT certain transitional provisions apply.

(1) *Section 38 of the Finance Act 1974*

16-157 Section 35 provides that, subject to certain exceptions, no part of a chargeable gain accruing after the Appointed Day shall be chargeable to DGT under Chapter I of Part III of the Finance Act 1974 (*i.e.* ordinary disposals other than the first letting charge under section 45 of the Finance Act 1974).[1] For this purpose in determining when such a gain accrues, the provisions applicable to DGT apply rather than those under DLT[2] (*ante*, § 16-130). Thus, for example, where DLT is excluded on the basis that a conditional contract existed before September 13, 1974,[3] the charge to DGT will continue to apply on the date, after the Appointed Day, when the condition is satisfied. The other exceptions are as follows:

16-158 (a) *Material development commenced after December 17, 1973, but before the Appointed Day.*[4] If there has been no disposal of such land in the period from the commencement of the development up to the Appointed Day, then the DGT charge continues and will apply to the first disposal after the Appointed Day which is not a no gain/no loss disposal. Provision exists to prevent the value of fresh development (charged to DLT) from being brought within the charge to DGT.[5]

16-159 (b) *Interests acquired before the Appointed Day on a no gain/no loss basis.*[6] The charge to DLT is computed by reference to actual acquisition and disposal consideration whereas for DGT and CGT purposes in certain circumstances assets are deemed to be disposed of and acquired at a consideration giving rise to no gain or loss.[7] Where an interest was so acquired before the Appointed Day (otherwise than within a group of companies) the DGT charge is preserved so as to apply to the first disposal after the Appointed Day not being itself a no gain/no loss disposal.[8] Special provisions apply similarly to reversions on leases.

(2) *Section 45 of the Finance Act 1974*

16-160 The first letting charge is abolished on and after the Appointed Day unless the relevant development relating to the chargeable building was

---

[1] See the 9th ed. of this Book at §§ 16-100 *et seq.*
[2] s. 35 (2).
[3] s. 45 (6) and see *ante*, § 16-130.
[4] s. 36.
[5] s. 36 (5).
[6] s. 37.
[7] *e.g.* disposals between spouses (see *ante*, § 16-17) and within groups of companies (see *ante*, § 16-54).
[8] s. 37 (1).

begun before May 18, 1976.[9] Thus if a project of material development (which also constitutes relevent development of a chargeable building within the Finance Act 1974, s. 46 and Sched. 3, para. 9) was commenced after May 18, 1976, and before August 1, 1976, the subsequent grant of a lease at a full rack rent escaped both DGT and DLT.

2. DLT DISPOSAL PRECEDES OR IS CONTEMPORANEOUS WITH CGT DISPOSAL OR TRADING DISPOSAL

16-161 DLT is an entirely separate tax against which one cannot set off any losses or reliefs. As it is an entirely separate tax, in the absence of relieving provisions persons would be chargeable to DLT as well as CGT, income tax, corporation tax or capital transfer tax (CTT) in respect of the same gain or profit. The DLT itself is not allowable as a deduction in computing chargeable gains or trading profits.[10] However Schedule 6 provides complex rules which, in most cases, prevent the double taxation which would otherwise arise. In this part of this Chapter a DLT disposal means a disposal of an interest in land other than one for which no consideration is given.[11]

Contemporaneous CGT disposal

16-162 Where a DLT disposal is also a CGT disposal the amount of the chargeable realised development value charged to DLT is available as a deduction for the purposes of tax on chargeable gains.[12] Where the DLT is reduced as a consequence of the provisions considered at *post*, § 16-168, the amount of the deduction is restricted by reference to that reduction. The deduction is not allowed to create an allowable loss.[13]

DLT disposal precedes CGT disposal

16-163 The chargeable realised development value accruing on a deemed disposal under section 2 may be deducted on a subsequent CGT disposal [14] except where that disposal occurs on death when any growth in value is not charged to CGT.[15]

Part disposals

16-164 The above provisions also apply where the DLT disposal is a part disposal consisting of the grant of a lease or the subsequent CGT disposal is a part disposal.[16] Where the part disposal is the grant of a lease for no premium it is deemed to be a CGT disposal by assuming a notional premium of £1.[17] The consideration for DLT purposes on the grant of a lease is higher than

---

[9] s. 38.
[10] s. 34 (2).
[11] *i.e.* so that s. 10 applies, see *ante*, § 16-131.
[12] Sched. 6, para. 1.
[13] *Ibid.* para. 1 (6).
[14] *Ibid.* para. 2.
[15] *Ibid.* para. 2 (2) and see *ante*, § 16-19 *et seq.*
[16] *Ibid.* para. 3.
[17] *Ibid.* para. 3 (2).

that for CGT purposes since the former includes the value of rents.[18] Consequently the deduction on the CGT disposal is reduced by applying the fraction $\dfrac{\text{CGT consideration}}{\text{DLT consideration}}$.[19] Similarly where the contemporaneous DLT disposal follows a deemed disposal under section 2 the DLT consideration in the above fraction is taken as the aggregate of the consideration for the earlier deemed DLT disposal and any subsequent improvement expenditure (*e.g.* construction costs, etc.). On subsequent disposals of the retained interest the further CGT consideration is added to the earlier in the above fraction so as to bring in a further slice of the relief (or the remainder if the whole of the retained interest is disposed of).[20] Even though part of the premium on the grant of a lease is charged to income tax it is still brought in as part of the CGT consideration and the relief is given primarily against it.[21]

CGT roll-over relief

16-165　　Where relief under section 33 of the Finance Act 1965 applies on the CGT disposal[22] the amount of the DLT deduction is calculated as if the roll-over relief did not apply and the deduction may be carried forward to be set off against any chargeable gain arising on the disposal of the new assets until it is exhausted.[23]

Contemporaneous trading disposal

16-166　　Where a DLT disposal is also a trading disposal then the amount of chargeable realised development value is allowable (in the form of a trading expense) as a deduction in computing the profits or gains of the trade.[24] If the disposal occurs before April 1, 1980 (*i.e.* in a period when the reduced rate applies),[25] and the trader would have paid more in income tax on the realised development value than he pays under DLT he is assessed under Case VI of Schedule D on an amount such that income tax thereon at the basic rate is equal to the excess.[26] Again this provision is modified where the DLT disposal is a deemed disposal[27] (see *ante*, § 16-163) or there is a part disposal[28] (see *ante*, § 16-164).

Apportionment of income of close companies

16-167　　Schedule 6, paragraph 9, applies where the person making the DLT disposal is a company which owns land as trading stock or is liable to corporation tax on the receipt of a premium for the grant of a lease as if it were income. In such cases if the reduced rate of DLT applies[29] and a

---

[18] See *ante*, § 16-114 and § 16-128.
[19] Sched. 6, para. 3 (3) and (4).
[20] *Ibid.* para. 3 (6), (7) and (8).
[21] *Ibid.* para. 4.
[22] See §§ 16-45 *et seq.*
[23] Sched. 6, para. 5.
[24] *Ibid.* para. 6.
[25] See *ante*, § 16-133.
[26] Sched. 6, para. 6 (3)–(9). In these provisions the excess is referred to as a " deficiency of tax." *Quaere* the application of the higher rates of tax to the Case VI charge so as to create a greater liability than was intended.
[27] *Ibid.* para. 7.
[28] *Ibid.* para. 8.
[29] See *ante*, § 16-133.

deduction is given under the provisions considered above against the company's other tax liability, then 30 per cent. of the difference between that part of the deduction (represented by the part charged at the lower rate) and the amount of the DLT charged thereon is treated as increasing the maximum amount of relevant income for apportionment purposes within the Finance Act 1972, Sched. 16, para. 9.[30]

3. CGT DISPOSAL OR TRADING DISPOSAL PRECEDES DLT DISPOSAL

16-168   A CGT or trading disposal may occur on an occasion which is not also a DLT disposal, for example, an appropriation to or from stock-in-trade or the making of a gift. In such cases the amount of tax on the CGT disposal (including DGT) [31] or the trading disposal, to the extent that it represents tax on the then development value of the land, may be set off against the subsequent DLT liability.[32] For the relief to apply, the DLT disposal must occur within 12 years from the primary CGT or trading disposal. There are provisions allowing the carry forward of the relief to disposals of the retained interest where the first DLT disposal is a part disposal, provided the subsequent disposals still occur within the 12-year period.[33] These rules are modified where the subject matter of the CGT disposal has become part of an assembly.[34]

4. LIABILITY FOR CTT OR ESTATE DUTY PRECEDES CHARGE TO DLT

Set off of CTT against chargeable realised development value

16-169   Where CTT is payable on the acquisition of an interest in land (which does not constitute a DLT disposal) the part of that tax which is referable to the then development value of the land may be deducted from the chargeable realised development value accruing on a subsequent DLT disposal occurring within the next 12 years.[35] The amount of the deduction is determined by the formula $\dfrac{A \times C}{B}$ where A is the chargeable realised development value that would have accrued on the CTT disposal if it had been a DLT disposal; B is the market value of the land at the time of the CTT disposal and C is the amount of CTT paid in respect of the land.[36] For these purposes the amount of CTT is determined as if the donee had borne the tax (*i.e.* there is no grossing up).[37] Where the interest in land was acquired for a price less than market value and the transaction constituted a DLT disposal as well as a CTT transfer the transferee may claim a CTT deduction restricted to the amount of that tax borne by him.[38]

16-170   There are provisions allowing the carry forward of the relief to disposals of the retained interest where the first DLT disposal is a part disposal,

[30] See *ante*, §§ 15-46 *et seq.*
[32] Sched. 6, paras. 10–12.
[34] *Ibid.* paras. 14 and 15.
[35] *Ibid.* paras. 18–20.
[36] *Ibid.* para. 20 (2).
[37] *Ibid.* para. 19 (3) and (4) and see *post*, § 20-10.
[31] *Ibid.* para. 16.
[33] *Ibid.* para. 13.
[38] *Ibid.* para. 18 (3) and para. 19 (5).

provided the subsequent disposals still occur within the 12-year period.[39] The provisions are modified where the subject matter of the CTT disposal has become part of an assembly.[40] Where the rate of CTT is subsequently increased because of the transferor's death within the three-year period [41] the amount of the deduction is redetermined by reference to the new rate of tax.[42]

Set off of estate duty against chargeable realised development value

16-171   Where an interest in land was subject to estate duty on a person's death the part of that duty which is referable to the development value of the land at the date of death or disposition on which it was acquired may be deducted from the chargeable realised development value accruing on a subsequent DLT disposal [43] again in accordance with the formula $\dfrac{A \times C}{B}$.

This deduction is restricted to DLT disposals occuring within six years from the date of death or disposition on the occasion of which the interest was acquired.[44] Where the DLT disposal is a part disposal any excess of the deduction can be carried forward subject, of course, to the six-year time-limit.[45] Again the general provisions are modified in the case of assemblies.[46]

---

[39] Sched. 6, para. 21.
[40] *Ibid.* paras. 22 and 23.
[41] See *post*, § 20-03.
[42] *Ibid.* para. 24.
[43] *Ibid.* paras. 25–27 and see *ante*, § 16-169.
[44] *Ibid.* para. 25 (1).
[45] *Ibid.* para. 28.
[46] *Ibid.* paras. 29 and 30.

ADMINISTRATION, ASSESSMENTS AND
BACK DUTY—CORPORATE AND
NON-CORPORATE BODIES

CHAPTER 17

ADMINISTRATION, ASSESSMENTS AND BACK DUTY

1. ADMINISTRATION

17-01 INCOME tax, corporation tax and capital gains tax are under the care and management of the Commissioners of Inland Revenue who constitute the Board of Inland Revenue (hereinafter called " the Board "). Their principal office is at Somerset House, London. The day-to-day administration is carried out by inspectors and collectors of taxes who are full-time civil servants appointed by the Board who act under the direction of the Board.[1] Collectors, as their name implies, are responsible for the collection of the tax which is assessed by the inspector.

The general administration of the tax system underwent a major reform when the Income Tax Management Act 1964 came fully into force on April 6, 1965. That Act and later amending Acts were consolidated in the Taxes Management Act 1970.

2. RETURNS AND ASSESSMENTS

17-02 Any person may be required by a notice given to him by an inspector or other officer of the Board to deliver to the officer within the time limited by the notice a return of his income, computed in accordance with the Income Tax Acts and specifying each separate source of income and the amount from each source.[2] The return in every case must include a declaration by the person making the return that it is to the best of his knowledge correct and complete.[3] Liability to a penalty arises where a return of income is not made or is incorrect.[4] There is an obligation to provide information about chargeable gains,[5] including particulars of assets acquired, of the person from whom they are acquired and the consideration for the acquisition. A person chargeable to tax who has not delivered a return is required to give notice that he is chargeable not later than one year after the end of the year of assessment to which the return relates.[6]

Persons who receive income in a representative capacity (such as personal representatives and trustees) are under a similar obligation to make returns when required by notice to do so.[7]

17-03 Employers are under a duty when required to do so to disclose the names and particulars of payments to employees.[8] The inspector has power to

---

[1] Taxes Management Act (T.M.A.) 1970, s. 1. Inspectors were called " surveyors " in earlier Acts.

[2] T.M.A. 1970, s. 8 (1). As to what may be required in a return, see *ibid*. s. 8 (3) (4) (8) and (9).

[3] *Ibid*. s. 8 (7).

[4] T.M.A. 1970, ss. 93–107. Generally as to penalties and interest, see the Board's practice in [1977] S.T.I. 110.

[5] *Ibid*. s. 12. See also ss. 25–28. But see F.A. 1978, s. 44 (5) and s. 45 (5).

[6] T.M.A. 1970, s. 7 and (for companies) s. 10.

[7] *Ibid*. s. 8 (2).

[8] *Ibid*. s. 15.

require every person carrying on a trade or business and every body of persons carrying on any other activity to make a return of payments for services rendered otherwise than by employees, including periodical or lump sum payments in respect of copyright. Payments not exceeding £15 and certain other payments are excluded.[9] There are extensive provisions which require the disclosure of payments of interest and rent.[10]

Companies

17-04   A company may be required to deliver to an inspector or other officer of the Board a return of its profits computed in accordance with the Corporation Tax Acts specifying the income taken into account in computing those profits, with the amount from each source, giving particulars of all disposals giving rise to chargeable gains or allowable losses, and giving particulars of all charges on income.[11] For partnership returns, see § 11-03.

Claims

17-05   Section 42 of the Taxes Management Act 1970, and Schedule 2 set out the procedures for claiming reliefs and allowances and the rights of appeal from decisions on such claims.

Production of documents

17-06   Sections 20, 20A, 20B, 20C and 20D of the Taxes Management Act 1970 (inserted by s. 57 of and Sched. 6 to the Finance Act 1976), empower an inspector by notice in writing to require a person to deliver to him such documents as are in the person's possession or power and as (in the inspector's reasonable opinion) contain, or may contain, information relevant to any tax liability to which the person is or may be subject, or to the amount of any such liability. The documents must be specified or described in the notice. Such a notice may also be directed to (for example) the taxpayer's spouse and any son or daughter of his and, where the taxpayer carries on or carried on a business, any other person concerned in the same business. Notices cannot be issued by an inspector save with the prior authority of the Board and with the consent of a General or Special Commissioner (who must be satisfied that the inspector is justified in using the powers conferred by the section). The Board also has powers to require the delivery of documents to one of its officers.

In practice, the Board can enforce production of relevant books, etc., by using its power to make an estimated assessment on the taxpayer.[12] The taxpayer must then either appeal or accept the assessment; and if he appeals, the appellate Commissioners have power to confirm the estimated assessment, unless it is shown by the appellant taxpayer to be excessive.[13] If the taxpayer appeals, the appellate Commissioners have power to issue a

---

[9] *Ibid.* s. 16.
[10] *Ibid.* ss. 17–18 (nterest); s. 19 (rent) and see § 6-15.
[11] T.M.A. 1970, s. 11.
[12] See *ibid.* s. 29 (1) (2) (3); and see below.
[13] *Ibid.* s. 50 (6). See *e.g. Hellier* v. *O'Hare* (1964) 42 T.C. 155.

precept ordering *the appellant* to deliver *inter alia* all such books, accounts or documents in his possession or power which in the Commissioners' opinion contain or may contain information relating to the subject-matter of the appeal. [14]

Assessments

17-07   Assessments are made either by an inspector or the Board. Assessments are made by an inspector unless the Act otherwise provides. [15] If an inspector is satisfied that a return affords correct and complete information concerning the income of the taxpayer, he will make the assessment accordingly; but if the inspector is dissatisfied with any return, he may make an assessment to the best of his judgment. [16] This may be called an " estimated assessment."

17-08   If an inspector (or the Board) *discover*

    (a) that any profits which ought to have been assessed to tax have not been assessed, or

    (b) that an assessment to tax is or has become insufficient, or

    (c) that any relief which has been given is or has become excessive,

the inspector (or the Board) may make an assessment in the amount, or the further amount, which ought in his (or their) opinion to be charged. [17] It will be observed that such an assessment cannot be made unless there is first a *discovery* by the inspector (or the Board). [18] " An Inspector of Taxes ' discovers ' (that income has not been assessed when it ought to have been), not only when he finds out new facts which were not known to him or his predecessor, but also when he finds out that he or his predecessor drew a wrong inference from the facts which were then known to him: and, further, when he finds out that he or his predecessor got the law wrong and did not assess the income when it ought to have been." [19]

The time limits for making assessments are discussed later. [20] Leave of the General Commissioners or Special Commissioners is in some cases necessary before an assessment is made. [21]

An assessment is not void merely by reason of a formal defect or mistake. [22]

Relief for error or mistake

17-09   If a person who has paid tax charged under an assessment alleges that the assessment was excessive by reason of some error or mistake in a return he

---

[14] *Ibid.* s. 51. *Cf.* the powers discussed in the previous paragraph, which are not restricted to *the appellant.*

[15] *Ibid.* s. 29 (1). Before 1964, assessments were made by the Commissioners. The change in the law makes it unnecessary for an appellate court to send a case back to the Commissioners to amend the assessment: see *McMann* v. *Shaw* (1972) 48 T.C. 330.

[16] T.M.A. 1970, s. 29 (1).

[17] *Ibid.* s. 29 (3).

[18] *Cf.* I.T.A. 1952, s. 41 (now repealed), and the cases thereon. See *Commercial Structures Ltd.* v. *Briggs* (1948) 30 T.C. 477 (C.A.); *Cenlon Finance Co. Ltd.* v. *Ellwood* [1962] A.C. 782; 40 T.C. 176; *Jones* v. *Mason Investments (Luton) Ltd.* (1966) 43 T.C. 570.

[19] *Parkin* v. *Cattell* [1971] T.R. 177.   [20] *Post,* §§ 17-19 *et seq.*

[21] T.M.A. 1970, s. 41.   [22] *Ibid.* s. 114.

may, not later than six years after the end of the year of assessment within which the assessment was made (or of the accounting period in the case of a company), make a claim to the Board for relief.[23] The Board must consider the claim and may give such relief by way of repayment as is reasonable and just.[24] The Board must have regard to all the relevant circumstances of the case, and in particular whether the granting of relief would result in the exclusion from charge to tax of any part of the profits (as defined) of the claimant and assessments made on him in respect of chargeable periods other than that to which the claim relates.[25] There is a right of appeal to the Special Commissioners.[26] No relief is available under this provision in respect of the error or mistake as to the basis on which the liability of the claimant ought to have been computed where the return was in fact made on the basis or in accordance with the practice generally prevailing at the time when it was made.[27]

3. APPEALS

Appellate Commissioners

17-10   Tax appeals are heard by the General and Special Commissioners from whose decisions there is a further right of appeal to the High Court by way of case stated on a point of law only.

The General Commissioners are appointed locally for divisions.[28] In England and Wales they are appointed by and hold office during the pleasure of the Lord Chancellor. They receive no remuneration and the great majority of them have no special qualifications in law or accountancy or in tax matters generally. Thus they resemble the lay magistrates and appeals which raise difficult questions of law are usually not brought before them. The General Commissioners for every division appoint a Clerk (and in some cases an assistant Clerk in addition) to assist them.[29]

The Special Commissioners are appointed by the Treasury. They are full-time civil servants and are selected from persons with some practical experience of tax matters obtained in government service or in private practice. Appeals which raise questions of law or which may be prolonged are usually brought before them. Questions as to the value of land are determined by the Lands Tribunal and as to the value of unquoted shares or securities by the Special Commissioners.[30]

Appeals are commonly heard by two Commissioners but in certain circumstances appeals before the Special Commissioners may be heard by a single Commissioner.[31]

General and Special Commissioners take an oath not to disclose any information received in the execution of their duties except for the purpose of those duties.[32]

---

[23] *Ibid.* s. 33 (1).
[24] *Ibid.* s. 33 (2) (3).
[25] *Ibid.* s. 33 (3) and (5).
[26] *Ibid.* s. 33 (4).
[27] *Ibid.* s. 33 (2), proviso.
[28] T.M.A. 1970, s. 2.
[29] *Ibid.* s. 3.
[31] *Ibid.* s. 45.
[30] *Ibid.* s. 47.
[32] *Ibid.* s. 6 and Sched. 1.

Appeals to the Commissioners

17-11   A notice of assessment to tax must be served on the person assessed and must state the date on which it is issued and the time within which any appeal against the assessment may be made.[33] There is a right of appeal against every assessment and the appeal is commenced by giving notice in writing to the person issuing the assessment,[34] such notice to be given within 30 days after the date on which the notice of assessment was issued.[35] Some appeals lie only to the Special Commissioners,[36] but otherwise the appeal will be heard by the appropriate body of General Commissioners,[37] unless the appellant elects to bring the case before the Special Commissioners instead of the General Commissioners.[38] This right of election should be exercised by a notice combined (in the case of an appeal) with the notice of appeal, by a separate notice in writing to the Inspector or other officer of the Board within the time limited for bringing the proceedings.[39] If no such notice of election is given the appeal will be brought before the General Commissioners. There is, however, a procedure for transferring proceedings brought before the General Commissioners to the Special Commissioners and vice versa.[40]

The notice of appeal against any assessment must specify the grounds of appeal but, on the hearing of the appeal, the Commissioners may allow the appellant to put forward any ground not specified in the notice and take it into consideration if satisfied that the omission was not wilful or unreasonable.[41]

If an assessment is not appealed against within the time limit, it becomes final and conclusive and the amount assessed becomes payable on the due date.[42]

Once an assessment has been served on the person assessed, it cannot be lawfully altered except in accordance with the express provisions of the Taxes Act.[43] If, therefore, a person seeks to have an assessment altered, he must give notice of appeal and allow the appeal to be determined by the Commissioners or, under section 54 of the Taxes Management Act 1970, by agreement with the Inspector (see § 17-14).

Once the appeal machinery has been set in motion, the appellant cannot withdraw the notice of appeal [44] and the Commissioners are bound to hear the appeal unless an agreement is reached under section 54.

The amount of tax covered by an assessment is deemed not to be finally determined until that assessment can no longer be varied, whether by any Commissioners on appeal or by the order of any court.[45]

---

[33] *Ibid.* s. 29 (5). For service, see *ibid.* s. 115.
[34] *Ibid.* s. 31 (2).
[35] *Ibid.* s. 31 (1) read with F.(No. 2)A. 1975, s. 67 (1). For appeals to the Commissioners brought out of time, see T.M.A. 1970, s. 49 (1).
[36] See *ibid.* ss. 31 (3) and 47 (3).
[37] *Ibid.* s. 44.
[38] *Ibid.* s. 31 (4).
[39] *Ibid.* s. 46 (1).
[40] *Ibid.* s. 44 (3).
[41] *Ibid.* s. 31 (5).
[42] But see *ibid.* s. 49.
[43] *Ibid.* s. 29 (6).
[44] *Ex p. Elmhirst* [1936] 1 K.B. 487; 20 T.C. 381.   [45] T.M.A. 1970, s. 118 (4).

Postponement of tax

17-12   The Tax Acts prescribe dates on which tax of different descriptions is due and payable.[46] Where there is an appeal against an assessment, the due date for payment was at one time deferred until the appeal was determined: hence it was often to the advantage of the taxpayer to appeal against the assessment for the sake of the interest earned on unpaid tax during the period of deferment. Section 55 and section 86 (§ 17-13) of the Taxes Management Act 1970 [47] contain provisions to remove this advantage. The provisions of section 55 may be summarised as follows:

(1) An appellant who has grounds for believing that he is overcharged by an assessment and who wishes to appeal against the assessment may apply to the Commissioners to determine the amount of tax, payment of which should be postponed pending the determination of his appeal. The application for postponement is made by written notice to the Inspector within 30 days of the issue of the notice of assessment and must state the amount of the alleged overcharge and the grounds on which the appellant believes he is overcharged. The application for postponement is separate from the notice of appeal.

(2) If no application to postpone payment is made, the tax payable by the assessment is payable as if there were no appeal.

(3) If an application to postpone is made, it is heard and determined in the same way as an appeal; but this does not preclude the Commissioners from hearing the appeal itself. If the application is successful, the Commissioners will postpone payment of the tax which is prima facie overcharged until the determination of the appeal; but the remainder of the tax in respect of which payment is not postponed becomes due and payable as if it were tax charged by an assessment notice of which was issued on the date of the Commissioners' determination and in respect of which no appeal was pending. If the Inspector and the taxpayer reach agreement as to the amount of tax payment of which should be postponed, this has the same effect as if the matter has been determined by the Commissioners.

(4) On the determination of the appeal itself,
     (a) any tax payable becomes due and payable as if it were tax charged by an assessment notice of which was issued on the date on which the Inspector issues to the appellant a notice of the total amount payable in accordance with the determination and in respect of which no appeal was pending; and
     (b) any tax overpaid must be repaid.

When, on an appeal against an assessment, the Commissioners increase or reduce the amount assessed, the tax charged by the assessment is taken to be increased or reduced accordingly.[48]

---

[46] See T.A. 1970, s. 4 (income tax); F.A. 1972, s. 84 (5) (advance corporation tax); F.A. 1965, s. 20 (6) (capital gains tax).
[47] These sections were substituted for earlier provisions of T.M.A. 1970 by F. (No. 2) A. 1975, ss. 45 and 46.
[48] T.M.A. 1970, s. 50 (8).

Interest on overdue tax

17-13   Section 86 of the Taxes Management Act 1970 provides that tax charged by an assessment to which the section applies shall carry interest at the prescribed rate (currently 9 per cent. per annum [49]) from " the reckonable date." This date is the date on which the tax becomes due and payable except that, where an application to postpone payment of tax has been made under section 55 (see § 17-12) the reckonable date is either

(a) the date on which tax would have been due and payable if there had been no appeal; or

(b) the date mentioned in a Table in section 86 (4), whichever is the later.

Example (i): X, a solicitor, is assessed under Case II of Schedule D for the year 1975–76 in the sum of £10,000. He disputes the assessment, considering himself overcharged by £3,000. The normal dates for payment of Schedule D tax are January 1, 1976, and July 1, 1976, in equal instalments: T.A. 1970, s. 4 (2). No application to postpone is made in respect of the tax on £7,000, which is accordingly due and payable on January 1, 1976, and July 1, 1976, and interest on that tax runs from these dates. An application to postpone is made as regards tax on £3,000 and, at the hearing of the application to postpone which is determined on October 6, 1976, X makes out a prima facie case of overcharge in respect of £2,000 but not in respect of the remaining £1,000. Tax on the £1,000 is due and payable as if an unappealed notice of assessment were issued on October 6, 1976, *i.e.* within 30 days thereof. Interest in respect of tax on this £1,000 runs from July 1, 1976. Assume X pays the tax on £1,000 before the due date.

X's appeal is finally determined on June 1, 1977. If the appeal is unsuccessful, tax on the £2,000 falls due within 30 days of the determination. Interest runs from July 1, 1976. If the appeal is successful, X is entitled to have the tax on the £3,000 repaid with interest calculated from April 5, 1977 (see § 17-14).

Example (ii): On March 1, 1978, T is assessed to income tax under Schedule D in respect of profits of the year 1971–72. The tax is due 30 days later, on March 31, 1978. There is no Table date applicable to this case, so interest on unpaid tax runs from March 31, 1978.

Repayment supplement

17-14   Where in the case of an individual, a partnership or United Kingdom trust or estate, the tax paid for a year of assessment is repaid after the end of the 12 months following that year of assessment and the amount repaid is not less than £25, the repayment is increased by an amount (called a " repayment supplement ") equal to interest on the amount repaid at the rate of 9 per cent. per annum for the period (if any) between " the relevant time " and the end of the tax month in which the order for the repayment is issued.[50] Briefly, if the repayment is of tax that was paid after the end of the 12 months following the year of assessment for which it was payable, the relevant time is the end of the year of assessment in which the tax was paid; otherwise the relevant time is the end of the 12 months following the year of assessment to which the tax relates. " Tax month " means the

---

[49] Income Tax (Interest on Unpaid Tax) Order 1974.
[50] F. (No. 2) A. 1975, s. 47 (1), (11) and (12).

period beginning with the sixth day of a calendar month and ending with the fifth day of the following calendar month.[51]

> Assume T is assessed to capital gains tax for the year 1976–77 and the tax is due on (say) August 1, 1977. T appeals against the assessment and his appeal, which is determined more than one year after the end of the year 1976–77 (say on July 1, 1979) succeeds. T is entitled to a repayment supplement equal to interest at 9 per cent. per annum from April 6, 1978, until July 5, 1979.

There are similar provisions which apply to companies.[52]

Settling appeals by agreement [53]

17-15   Where a person gives notice of appeal and, before the appeal is determined by the Commissioners, the Inspector or other proper officer of the Crown and the appellant come to an agreement, whether in writing or otherwise, that the assessment or decision under appeal should be treated as upheld without variation, or as varied in a particular manner or as discharged or cancelled, the like consequences are to ensue for all purposes as would have ensued if, at the time when the agreement was come to, the Commissioners had determined the appeal and had upheld the assessment or decision without variation, had varied it in that manner or had discharged or cancelled it, as the case may be. Any such agreement is ignored if, within 30 days from the date when the agreement was come to, the appellant gives notice in writing that he desires to repudiate or resile from it. Where an agreement is not in writing the section does not apply unless the fact that an agreement was come to, and the terms agreed, are confirmed by notice in writing given by the Inspector or other proper officer of the Crown to the appellant or by the appellant to the Inspector or other proper officer. It is a question of fact whether, in any particular case, an " agreement " can be spelled out of negotiations between the Inspector and the appellant (or the person acting on his behalf in relation to the appeal).[54] An agreement under the section precludes any further assessment in relation to the matter in dispute.[55]

Conduct of appeals

17-16   At the hearing of an appeal before the Commissioners the appellant may appear by counsel or by a solicitor or accountant.[56] The Crown is usually represented by the inspector. The proceedings are conducted in accordance with normal court procedure and the rules of evidence apply.[57] There are, however, no formal pleadings before the Commissioners. The Commissioners have power to summon any person (other than the appellant) to appear before them and to examine a witness on oath.[58] The Commissioners decide by a majority and where there are two Commissioners sitting who cannot agree, the normal practice is to discharge

---

[51] *Ibid.* s. 47 (4) and (12).
[52] *Ibid.* s. 48.
[53] T.M.A. 1970, s. 54.
[54] See *Cansick* v. *Hochstrasser* (1961) 40 T.C. 151; *Delbourgo* v. *Field* [1978] S.T.C. 234 (C.A.).
[55] *Cenlon Finance Co. Ltd.* v. *Ellwood* [1962] A.C. 782; 40 T.C. 176 (H.L.).
[56] T.M.A. 1970, s. 50 (5).
[57] *Cooksey and Bibbey* v. *Rednall* (1949) 30 T.C. 514.
[58] T.M.A. 1970, s. 52 (2). As to production of documents, see *Soul* v. *I.R.C.* (1963) 41 T.C. 517.

the assessment. The Commissioners have no power to make any order as to costs, so each party bears his own costs. As to the power to obtain information, see § 17-06.

Onus

17-17   Initially the onus lies on the taxpayer to adduce evidence showing that he has been overcharged by the assessment [59]; so where the taxpayer adduces no evidence on the basis of which the Commissioners can reduce this amount of the assessment, they must confirm it in the amount assessed. [60] Hence, when the quantum of the assessment is the only point in issue (as is common in a back-duty case) the onus may be said to lie solely on the taxpayer. [61] Where fraud, wilful default or neglect is alleged by the Crown, however, the onus lies on the Crown to prove such fraud, etc. [62]

Although the initial *evidential* onus lies on the taxpayer, this does not exonerate the Appeal Commissioners from satisfying themselves that the taxpayer is properly chargeable to tax nor the Crown from satisfying the Commissioners on this point. [63] For example, where the issue is whether activities of the taxpayer do, or do not, constitute the carrying on of a trade, and the taxpayer adduces facts consistent with either alternative, it is for the Crown to satisfy the Commissioners that the activities constitute the carrying on of a trade. [64]

Appeals from the Commissioners

17-18   Either the taxpayer or the inspector (who usually represents the Crown before the Commissioners) may appeal from the Commissioners to the High Court. [65] If there is no appeal within the due time, the decision of the Commissioners is final. [66] The appeal is by way of case stated and lies only on a point of law. The limits on the power of the High Court to disturb the findings of the Commissioners have already been discussed. [67] No appeal to the High Court may be brought unless the appellant expresses dissatisfaction with the decision of the Commissioners immediately after the determination of the appeal. [68] If the decision is notified to the parties by letter, dissatisfaction should be expressed by way of immediate reply.

The appeal is commenced by notice in writing to the clerk to the Commissioners given within 30 days after the determination of the appeal requiring the Commissioners to state a case for the opinion of the High Court. [69] The case sets out the facts found by the Commissioners and their

---

[59] T.M.A. 1970, s. 50 (6).

[60] *Eke* v. *Knight* [1976] S.T.C. 1 and [1977] S.T.C. 198 (C.A.); *Nicholson* v. *Morris* [1976] S.T.C. 269 at p. 280.

[61] *Haythornthwaite* v. *Kelly* (1927) 11 T.C. 657.

[62] *Eagles* v. *Rose* (1945) 26 T.C. 427; *Barney* v. *Pybus* (1957) 37 T.C. 106. See also *Amis* v. *Colls* (1960) 39 T.C. 148 and *Hudson* v. *Humbles* (1965) 42 T.C. 380.

[63] *Partington* v. *Att.-Gen.* (1869) L.R. 4 H.L. 100 at p. 122 (quoted in § 36-02); *Russell* v. *Scott* [1948] A.C. 422 at p. 433; 30 T.C. 394 at p. 424 *per* Lord Simonds; *D'Avigdor-Goldsmid* v. *I.R.C.* [1953] A.C. 347 at p. 361 *per* Viscount Simon; *Re Ralli's Settlement* [1965] Ch. 286 at p. 327 *per* Russell L.J.; *Hochstrasser* v. *Mayes* [1960] A.C. 376 at p. 389; *I.R.C.* v. *Reinhold* (1953) 34 T.C. 389 at pp. 393 and 396.

[64] See *I.R.C.* v. *Reinhold* (1953) 34 T.C. 389.   [65] *Ibid.* s. 56 (2).

[66] *Ibid.* s. 46 (2).   [67] *Ante*, § 2-03.

[68] T.M.A. 1970, s. 56 (1) (2). As to the meaning of " immediately " in this section, see *R.* v. *General Commissioners of Income Tax, ex p. Clarke* (1971) 47 T.C. 691.

[69] *Ibid.* s. 56 (2). The cost is £1; *ibid.* s. 56 (3). A *Written* notice is obligatory: *R.* v. *Edmonton Income Tax Commissioners, ex p. Thomson* (1928) 14 T.C. 313.

decision.[70] The case is prepared by the Commissioners and settled by the parties. If the case, when stated and signed, is defective, mandamus is the appropriate remedy.[71] The appellant must transmit the case to the High Court within 30 days [72] after receiving it but there is no time-limit within which it must be set down.

The High Court may reverse, affirm or amend the determination of the Commissioners or may remit the case to them or make such other order as the court thinks fit.[73] The High Court will make an order as to costs but no such order can be made by the Commissioners: thus each party bears his own costs in any event. The High Court has no power to make a consent order for the withdrawal of an appeal on terms giving effect to an agreement between the appellant and the respondent.[74]

From the High Court there is a further right of appeal to the Court of Appeal and thence, with leave, to the House of Lords.[75]

17-19   Notwithstanding that a case has been required to be stated or is pending before the High Court, tax must be paid in accordance with the determination of the Commissioners. If the High Court decides that too much tax has been paid, the amount overpaid will be refunded with interest; and if the High Court decides that too little tax has been charged, the amount undercharged is due and payable at the expiration of 30 days beginning with the date on which the Inspector issues to the other party a notice of the total amount payable in accordance with the judgment of the court.[76]

4. BACK DUTY

17-20   A " back duty case " arises when a taxpayer is found not to have disclosed his true income or has claimed reliefs or allowances to which he is not entitled or has otherwise evaded tax. There are three courses open to the Revenue in such a case:

(1) To commence criminal proceedings.
(2) To make assessments in respect of the tax lost to the Revenue, with interest.
(3) To claim penalties.

Each will be separately considered.

---

[70] *Ibid.* s. 56 (4).
[71] In *Kirby* v. *Steele* (1946) 27 T.C. 370, Wrottesley J. (at p. 373) allowed the appellant to read affidavits supplementing a case; see also *Calvert* v. *Wainwright* (1947) 27 T.C. 475 at p. 477. In *Cannon Industries Ltd.* v. *Edwards* (1966) 42 T.C. 625, Pennycuick J. declined to allow affidavit evidence to be filed supplementing or contradicting the case stated. The High Court can send a case back to the Commissioners for amendment: T.M.A. 1970, s. 56 (7).
[72] *Ibid.* s. 56 (4) (5).
[73] *Ibid.* s. 56 (6).
[74] *Slaney* v. *Kean* (1969) 45 T.C. 415 (K. succeeded in appeal before General Commissioners; when case was stated, K. agreed Crown's appeal should be allowed. *Held*, court could not make consent order for withdrawal of appeal). In such a case the Crown has therefore to satisfy the court that the appeal ought to succeed on its merits: see *e.g. Knight* v. *Parry* (1973) 48 T.C. 580; [1973] S.T.C. 56.
[75] *Ibid.* s. 56 (8). In some cases the appellant can " leapfrog " the Court of Appeal: see the Administration of Justice Act 1969.
[76] *Ibid.* s. 56 (9).

A. Criminal Proceedings

17-21 There are relatively few cases in which the Board take criminal proceedings. Section 5 of the Perjury Act 1911 makes it an offence knowingly and falsely to make any statement false in a material particular in any of the documents referred to in the section. The making of false statements or accounts knowing them to be false (including certificates of full disclosure such as are required by the Revenue in back duty cases) is a common law offence.[77]

B. Assessments for Past Years

17-22 Under section 34 of the Taxes Management Act 1970, an assessment can be made at any time not later than six years after the end of the chargeable period to which the assessment relates. In cases of fraud or wilful default,[78] there is generally no time limit (except in the case of assessments made against personal representatives[79]), but an assessment can be made only with leave of a General or Special Commissioner.[80]

The Revenue can make assessments for years before the six years referred to in section 34 (above) (called " normal years "), where the taxpayer was guilty of " neglect "; but leave of a General or Special Commissioner must first be obtained.[81] Neglect means—

> " negligence or a failure to give any notice, make any return or to produce or furnish any document or other information required by or under the Taxes Acts."[82]

Negligence, broadly speaking, means doing what a reasonable man would not do or failing to do what a reasonable man would do. The powers of the Revenue in cases of neglect are not as extensive as those which exist under section 34 (above) in cases of fraud or wilful default. The position in cases of neglect is as follows:

(1) Assessments for " earlier years "

17-23 Where an assessment has already been made for a normal year for the purpose of making good to the Crown a loss of tax caused through fraud, wilful default or neglect, the Revenue can make assessments for any of the six years preceding the normal year (called " earlier years ") provided the assessment is made not later than one year from the end of the year when the assessment for the normal year is finally determined, *i.e.* when no appeal is possible or outstanding.[83] No assessment may be made for the earlier year except to make good a loss of tax attributable to the taxpayer's neglect.[84]

---

[77] *R.* v. *Hudson* (1956) 36 T.C. 561.

[78] See *Clixby* v. *Pountney* (1967) 44 T.C. 515.

[79] See *post*, § 17-25.

[80] T.M.A. 1970, ss. 36, 41. The Commissioner exercises an administrative function in deciding whether or not to grant leave under T.M.A. 1970, s. 41, so natural justice does not require that the taxpayer should be heard: *Pearlberg* v. *Varty* (1972) 48 T.C. 14 (H.L.); *Nicholson* v. *Morris* [1977] S.T.C. 162 (C.A.).

[81] *Ibid.* ss. 37, 41.

[82] *Ibid.* s. 118 (1).

[83] T.M.A. 1970, s. 37 (1) (3) (4). It is not necessary that the normal year assessment should state that its " purpose " was to recover tax attributable to fraud, etc., or that the Inspector should do so when the assessment is made. It is sufficient if there was tax lost as described in section 37 (1) and that the normal year assessment recovered it: see *Thurgood* v. *Slarke* (1971) 47 T.C. 130.

[84] *Ibid.* s. 37 (2).

On November 5, 1962, assessments are made for 1956–57 (a normal year) when tax was lost through fraud, wilful default or neglect. Under section 37, the Revenue can make assessments for any one of the preceding six years, *i.e.* 1950–51 onwards, in which loss through neglect is proved if they do so before April 5, 1964.

It should be observed that no assessments can be made for an earlier year under section 37 unless tax is shown to have been lost through fraud, wilful default or neglect, in one of the normal years.

(2) *Assessments for years before " earlier years "*

17-24   If an assessment has been made for a year outside the normal six-year period, *i.e.* where there was fraud or wilful default, or neglect in an " earlier year," the Revenue can make an assessment for any of the previous six years in order to recover tax lost through the taxpayer's neglect; but such an assessment can be made only by leave of the General or Special Commissioners on proof of reasonable grounds for believing such neglect to have occurred.[85]

17-25   *Assessments on personal representatives.* Under section 40 (1) of the Taxes Management Act 1970 an assessment on personal representatives must be made not later than three years from the end of the tax year in which the death occurs.[86]

Under section 40 (2), assessments can be made (within the three years referred to) for any years of assessment ending not earlier than six years before the death, provided the assessment is to make good a loss of tax through fraud, wilful default or neglect. Leave of the General or Special Commissioners must first be obtained.[87]

Death occurs November 5, 1962. The Revenue can make assessments for the years 1956–57 to 1962–63, provided they do so before April 5, 1966.

These rules apply even if tax was lost through fraud or wilful default.

17-26   *Interest on tax recovered by assessment.* Section 88 of the Taxes Management Act 1970 gives the Revenue power to charge interest at 9 per cent. on tax not paid at the due date by reason of the fraud, wilful default or neglect of the taxpayer. The Commissioners may at their discretion mitigate the interest chargeable.[88]

C. Penalties [89]

17-27   Reference should be made to Part X of the Taxes Management Act 1970 for details of the penalties chargeable for failure to make returns, making incorrect returns or accounts, and so on.

A common type of back duty case is one in which a trader has submitted incorrect accounts to the inspector, for which the penalty in respect of each

---

[85] T.M.A. 1970, s. 37 (5) (6) (7) and s. 41.
[86] See *Harrison* v. *Willis Bros.* (1966) 43 T.C. 61 (C.A.), where A. and B. were partners trading as " A. and B. Bros." and, more than three years after B.'s death, an assessment was made on " A. and B. Bros. (A and executors of B. deceased)." *Held*, the assessment was bad as against B. and his executors.
[87] T.M.A. 1970, s. 41.
[88] T.M.A. 1970, s. 88 (4); 9 per cent. is the prescribed rate under the Income Tax (Interest on Unpaid Tax) Order 1974.
[89] For the law before 1960, see *I.R.C.* v. *Hinchy* [1960] A.C. 748; 38 T.C. 625.

year in which such accounts were rendered is (a) a sum not exceeding £50, plus (b) the amount of tax lost to the Revenue. Where there is fraud, the amount in (b) is doubled.[90]

The time limit for proceedings

17-28   Under section 103 of the Taxes Management Act 1970 the normal time limit for recovering penalties (even in proceedings against personal representatives) is six years from the date of the offence, with an extension in cases of fraud or wilful default to three years from the date of the final determination of the tax.

---

[90] T.M.A. 1970, s. 95.

CHAPTER 14

Part 2

CAPITAL TRANSFER TAX

CHAPTER 18

THE MAIN CHARGING PROVISIONS

1. INTRODUCTION

18-01 CAPITAL transfer tax is a tax on all lifetime transfers of property other than certain exempt transfers. It is also a tax on property comprised in a person's estate at the time of his death. It thus fulfils the role of a gifts tax and of estate duty, which ceased to be leviable on deaths occurring after March 13, 1975.[1]

2. LIFETIME TRANSFERS

Chargeable transfers

18-02   Capital transfer tax is charged on the value transferred by a *chargeable transfer*.[2] A chargeable transfer is any *transfer of value* made by an *individual* after March 26, 1974, other than an exempt transfer.[3] A transfer of value is defined [4] as

> any disposition (including a disposition effected by associated operations [5]) made by a person (" the transferor ") as a result of which the value of his estate immediately after the disposition is less than it would be but for the disposition; and the amount by which it is less is the value transferred by the transfer.

Note that not every transfer of value (as defined) is a chargeable transfer: a transfer of value made otherwise than by an individual (*e.g.* by a company or by trustees) is not a chargeable transfer although, as will be seen later, certain dispositions made by trustees of settled property give rise to charges to tax *as if* they were chargeable transfers.[6] A transfer made by a company is not a chargeable transfer but may be a transfer of value and, as such, may give rise to tax liability under provisions discussed in §§ 21-01 *et seq.*

18-03   It is important to grasp at the outset that capital transfer tax is levied by reference to the diminution in value of the transferor's estate, not by reference to the increase in value of the transferee's estate. The difference may be illustrated by a simple example:

> A has a library of rare books including a number of volumes which form a set. A gives one volume out of the set to B. The diminution in the value of the set, on which tax is levied, may greatly exceed the value of the single volume which B acquires.

Where the transferor pays the capital transfer tax, the diminution in his estate will include the amount of the tax. This is because payment of the tax forms part of the cost to the transferor of making the transfer. Tax is consequently charged on the amount or value of the property transferred plus the tax thereon paid by the transferor; and the amount of the tax is

---

[1] F.A. 1975, s. 49 (1); and see § 26-01. The Revenue has published a booklet (CTT 1) which provides a general guide to capital transfer tax: see S.T.I. (1978) 42.   [2] *Ibid.* s. 19 (1).
[3] *Ibid.* s. 20 (1) and (5). Exempt transfers are discussed in §§ 19-01 *et seq.*
[4] *Ibid.* s. 20 (2).
[5] *Ibid.* s. 51 (1); and see § 18-05.   [6] *Post*, Chap. 22.

found by a grossing-up process. The reader might find it helpful to read now §§ 20-02 to 20-05 to see how the tax is charged.

18-04   The definition of transfer of value requires that there should be a *disposition*.[7] But it is provided that where the value of a person's estate is diminished and that of another person's estate or of settled property in which no interest in possession subsists is increased by the first-mentioned person's omission to exercise a right, he shall be treated as having made a disposition at the time, or the latest time, when he could have exercised the right, unless it is shown that the omission was not deliberate.[8] Thus A's failure to pursue a just claim for damages against B or to pursue a claim for indemnity may constitute a chargeable transfer by A. A deliberate omission to exercise an option or to vote at a company meeting may constitute a disposition. An omission to exercise a right would not be " deliberate " if *e.g.* the person in question was able to prove that he was genuinely mistaken in thinking that he did not have the right.

The word " disposition " is not expressly defined. A loan of money involves a disposition and if, for example, A lends B £30,000 interest-free for a fixed term of three years, this will diminish A's estate since £30,000 is of greater value than the right to receive £30,000 in three years' time. Loans, etc., are considered in §§ 21-09 *et seq.*

Waiver of remuneration and dividends

18-04A   A waiver or repayment of remuneration which, apart from the waiver or repayment, would be assessable to income tax under Schedule E (*i.e.* because the remuneration has already been earned and the employee is entitled to it: see § 3-06), but which, because of the waiver or repayment is not taxed under Schedule E, is not a transfer of value. But where the payer would have been entitled to a tax deduction had the remuneration been actually paid, the exemption from capital transfer tax applies only if the payer gets no deduction or the amount is otherwise brought into charge to tax.[9]

A waiver of a dividend on shares is not a transfer of value provided the waiver is *within* 12 months before any right to the dividend has accrued.[10]

Associated operations

18-05   A series of " operations " which bring about a diminution in value in a person's estate will constitute a " disposition " where they are " associated operations " as defined in section 44 (1) of the Finance Act 1975: " disposition " includes a disposition effected by associated operations.[11]

---

[7] F.A. 1975, s. 20 (2) and § 18-02. " Disposition " is a word with a wide meaning and some guidance may be found in the stamp duty cases in which the word " conveyance " has been considered: see §§ 28-03 *et seq.*

[8] *Ibid.* s. 20 (7), as amended by the insertion of the words relating to settled property by F.A. 1978, s. 74. See §§ 22-14 *et seq.* The amendment deals with the situation where *e.g.* a shareholder with 51 per cent. of the shares in X Limited declines to take up a rights issue with the result that trustees of a discretionary settlement holding 49 per cent. of the shares acquire control. Trustees have no " estate ": see § 18-09.

[9] F.A. 1976, s. 91 (applying retrospectively to waivers after March 26, 1974). And see S.T.I. (1975) 394. And see § 3-06 as to the position under Schedule E.

[10] F.A. 1976, s. 92 (applying retrospectively to waivers after March 26, 1974).

[11] F.A. 1975, s. 51 (1).

Associated operations means any two or more operations of any kind, being:

(a) operations which affect the same property, or one of which affects some property and the other or others of which affect property which represents, whether directly or indirectly, that property, or income arising from that property, or any property representing accumulations of any such income; or

(b) any two operations of which one is effected with reference to the other, or with a view to enabling the other to be effected or facilitating its being effected, and any further operation having a like relation to any of those two, and so on;

whether those operations are effected by the same person or different persons, and whether or not they are simultaneous. " Operation " includes an omission. [12]

> Thus if a husband (H) makes an exempt transfer of property to his wife (W) on condition that W shall transfer the property to X, the transfer to X may be treated as if H were the transferor, *e.g.* for the purposes of considering the possible application of the exemptions and reliefs discussed in Chapter 19. [13]

18-06   By way of qualification to this broad definition, the granting of a lease for full consideration in money or money's worth is not to be taken to be associated with any operation effected more than three years after the grant; and no operation effected on or after March 27, 1974, is to be taken to be associated with an operation effected before that date. [14]

> Assume L leases land to T for full consideration. After three years, when the rent being paid is no longer a full market rent, L sells his reversion to P for full consideration. L's sale cannot be " associated " with the lease so as to enable the Revenue to treat L as having made a transfer of value to P; *i.e.* on the basis that L could have obtained more from P if he had been able to increase the rent. If L sells the reversion to P within three years from the grant, the lease and subsequent sale can be treated as a single disposition, with the consequence that L will be treated as if he had sold the land unincumbered by the lease.

This example shows that the provisions relating to associated operations prevent a reduction in liability to capital transfer tax by an operation or omission which reduces the value of the property disposed of.

18-07   Where a transfer of value is made by associated operations carried out at different times, it is treated as made at the time of the last of them; but where any one or more of the earlier operations also constitute a transfer of value made by the same transferor, the value transferred by the earlier operations is to be treated as reducing the value transferred by all the operations taken together, except to the extent that the transfer constituted by the earlier operations but not that made by all the operations taken together is exempt under the relief for transfers between spouses (see §§ 19-02 *et seq.*). [15]

---

[12] F.A. 1975, s. 44 (1).
[13] Inland Revenue Press Notice of April 8, 1975, in S.T.I. (1975), 191 commenting on s. 44.
[14] F.A. 1975, s. 44 (2).
[15] *Ibid.* s. 44 (3).

Assume a husband (H) owns 90 per cent. of the shares of a company. H wishes his son (S) to have an 80 per cent. holding. H gives his wife (W) a 40 per cent. holding. W and H then each give S a 40 per cent. holding. This is a gift by H to S of an 80 per cent. holding effected by associated operations.

Meaning of estate

18-08   A chargeable transfer is one which diminishes the value of the transferor's " estate." [16] The expression estate is defined [17] as follows:

> . . . a person's estate is the aggregate of all the property to which he is beneficially entitled, except that the estate of a person immediately before his death does not include excluded property.

18-09   The word property includes rights and interests of any description. [18] Property to which a person is not beneficially entitled, such as property held by him as trustee, is not part of his " estate." But it is not necessary that a person should own property in order to be treated as beneficially entitled to it. Thus a person is treated as beneficially entitled to property (not being settled property) over which he has a general power of appointment. Section 23 (2) of the Finance Act 1975 provides that:

> A person who has a general power which enables him, or would if he were *sui juris* enable him, to dispose of any property other than settled property, or to charge money on any property other than settled property, shall be treated as beneficially entitled to the property or money; and for this purpose " general power " means a power or authority enabling the person by whom it is exercisable to appoint or dispose of the property as he thinks fit.

The last four words in the subsection exclude the power or authority of a person having a power of attorney or a mortgagee. The exclusion of powers over settled property means that if, for example, property is held upon trust for X for life and thereafter to such person or persons as X shall appoint, an appointment by X falls to be dealt with under the rules relating to settled property (§§ 22-14 *et seq.*). A person is not beneficially entitled to property to which he is entitled as a corporation sole. [19]

Dispositions without donative intent

18-10   Dispositions at market value are outside the ambit of the tax because they produce no diminution in the value of the transferor's estate. But if A sells property to B for £10,000 and there is evidence that A could have obtained (say) £14,000, this transaction may be explained either (i) on the basis that A intended to confer a benefit on B or (ii) on the basis that A made a bad bargain, having no intention of conferring any benefit on B. Tax is payable in the first but not the second of these cases.

18-11   This result is achieved by a provision in section 20 (4) of the Finance Act 1975 which provides that a disposition is not a transfer of value if it is shown that it was not intended, and was not made in a transaction intended, to confer any gratuitous benefit on *any* person *and* either:

---

[16] F.A. 1975, s. 20 (1), (2).
[17] *Ibid.* s. 23 (1).
[18] *Ibid.* s. 51 (1).
[19] *Ibid.* s. 51 (5).

(a) that it was made in a transaction at arm's length between persons not connected with each other,[20] or

(b) that it was such as might be expected to be made in a transaction at arm's length between persons not connected with each other.

Note that two conditions have to be satisfied for there not to be a transfer of value. As well as the transferor's (subjective) intention not to confer a benefit, the objective criteria in (a) or (b) have also to be satisfied.[21] The onus lies on the transferor to prove that the conditions have been satisfied. If, in the example in § 18-10, A had sold the property to B for (say) £4,000, A would probably find it almost impossible to prove lack of donative intent. When a disposition is effected by associated operations (see § 18-05), the conditions have to be applied to the operations considered as a whole.

Transfers of money or property pursuant to an order of the court in consequence of a decree of divorce or nullity of marriage will often be exempt from capital transfer tax as falling within section 20 (4) of the Finance Act 1975.

18-12   The subsection in § 18-11 does not apply [22]:

(i) to certain acquisitions of reversionary interests, as to which see *post*, § 22-75; and

(ii) to a sale of shares or debentures not quoted on a recognised stock exchange, unless a third condition is satisfied, *i.e.* that it is shown that the sale was at a price freely negotiated at the time of the sale *or* at a price such as might be expected to have been freely negotiated at the time of the sale. Thus a sale at a price predetermined by the articles of a company may give rise to a charge to capital transfer tax.

Exempt property and excluded property

18-13   A chargeable transfer is defined as a transfer of value made by an individual other than an exempt transfer.[23] The cases in which transfers are " exempt transfers " are discussed in §§ 19-01 *et seq.*

The Act provides that no account is to be taken of the value of excluded property which ceases to form part of a person's estate as a result of a disposal.[24] Excluded property is discussed in §§ 23-01 *et seq.* Property situated outside the United Kingdom in the beneficial ownership of an individual who is domiciled outside the United Kingdom is excluded property; so also are British Government securities in the beneficial ownership of persons neither domiciled nor ordinarily resident in the United Kingdom: see § 19-26.

Certain lifetime transfers for the maintenance etc. of the transferor's family are expressed not to be transfers of value: see §§ 19-55 *et seq.*

---

[20] See F.A. 1975, s. 51 (4) which applies the definition of " connected persons " in F.A. 1975, Sched. 7, para. 21, with some modifications: see § 16-18A.

[21] The application of section 20 (4) of the F.A. 1975, to payments by employers to their employees or their dependants under certain accident insurance schemes has been the subject of an Inland Revenue Press Release of January 6, 1976: see S.T.I. (1976) 4.

[22] F.A. 1975, s. 20 (4).

[23] *Ibid.* s. 20 (5).   [24] *Ibid.* s. 20 (3).

3. TRANSFERS ON DEATH

18-14 On the death of any person after March 12, 1975 (the Act initiating the capital transfer tax became effective on March 13, 1975), tax is charged as if, immediately before his death, he had made a transfer of value and the value transferred by it had been equal to the value of his estate immediately before his death.[25] The value of the estate is the price it would fetch if sold in the open market at that time (§ 20-17) less liabilities (§ 20-12), subject to special provisions which apply where the death itself affects the valuation " immediately before " the death (see §§ 20-25 *et seq.*). The estate of a person immediately before his death does not include excluded property but otherwise it includes all the property to which he was beneficially entitled [26]: see §18-08. Thus it includes the following:

(a) Property (other than settled property) over which the deceased had a general power of appointment or a special power if he was competent to appoint in his own favour. If the deceased was entitled to a lump sum payment under a superannuation scheme which the deceased could have appointed to a third person but did not, this is taxable as part of his estate;

(b) policies of insurance, whether on the life of the deceased or of a third person, if the deceased was entitled to the sums payable thereunder;

(c) purchased annuities continuing after the deceased's death, but not those ceasing on his death (§ 20-25) or those arising on his death in which the deceased had no beneficial interest. There is a special rule which applies to annuities continuing on death and payable under approved retirement annuity schemes (see § 19-25);

(d) an undivided share and the severable share of a joint tenant;

(e) the share of a deceased partner in partnership property;

(f) an interest in possession in settled property (see § 22-17).

Tax chargeable on death is attributed to the respective values of the items of property comprised in the deceased's estate in the proportions which they bear to the aggregate, subject to any provision reducing the amount of tax attributable to the value of any particular property and subject to any specific provisions of the deceased's will.[27] Deeds of family arrangement, disclaimers and other matters which may affect the devolution of property on death are considered in §§ 19-63 *et seq.*

18-15 *Commorientes.* When it cannot be known which of two or more persons who have died survived the other or others, they are assumed to have died at the same instant.[28] Where this provision does not apply, because the order of deaths is known, quick succession relief may be available: see § 19-31.

4. RATES OF TAX

18-16 The rates of capital transfer tax and the method of computing the charge to tax are discussed in Chapter 20. Transfers made on, or at any time within

---

[25] F.A. 1975, s. 22 (1); and see § 20-25.   [26] *Ibid*. s. 23 (1).
[27] *Ibid*. s. 43 (1); and see § 24-16.   [28] *Ibid*. s. 22 (9).

three years of, the transferor's death are taxed at lower rates than transfers on death: see § 20-03. Briefly capital transfer tax is charged whenever an individual makes a transfer of value after March 26, 1974, and it is charged at a rate determined by reference to the cumulative total of all chargeable transfers made since that date, except that the first £25,000 of value transferred is tax-free and exempt transfers are excluded in reckoning the total. For an example of the working of the tax, see § 20-04.

5. SETTLED PROPERTY

18-17 The rules which apply to transfers of settled property and interests in settled property are discussed in Chapter 22. Briefly, and at the risk of considerable inaccuracy, the legislation draws a distinction between settlements in which no person has an interest in possession, such as a common form discretionary settlement, and other types of settlement in which a beneficiary has a vested interest, such as a life interest. In the case of discretionary settlements, a distinction is drawn between those made before and after the advent of capital transfer tax. In the case of discretionary settlements made before the advent of capital transfer tax, the trustees are (in effect) treated as if they were the chargeable persons: thus the first £25,000 of value transferred by them in capital distributions from the fund is exempt and thereafter tax is payable at the lifetime scale on further distributions. In the case of settlements made after the advent of capital transfer tax, the settlor is treated as the chargeable person. The transfer by him into settlement attracts tax at the rate appropriate to the settlor; a special non-cumulative rate of tax is payable when the trustees distribute the fund which has so borne tax, *i.e.* up to the amount or value settled; but beyond this limit tax is payable by the trustees on a cumulative basis, *i.e.* as if further dispositions were made by the settlor beyond the amount initially settled. In the case of settlements in which a beneficiary has a vested interest, such as a life interest, he is treated as the owner of so much of the settled property as corresponds to the value of his interest. Thus a life tenant entitled to the income of the fund is treated as entitled to the fund itself. A life tenant entitled to one-third of the income of a fund is treated as entitled to one-third of the fund, and so on.

CHAPTER 19

RELIEFS AND RELATED PROVISIONS

1. EXEMPT TRANSFERS

19-01 SECTION 20 (5) of the Finance Act 1975 defines a chargeable transfer as any transfer of value made by an individual after March 26, 1974, other than an exempt transfer; and Schedule 6 to the Act provides for "exempt transfers." The provisions of Schedule 6 are summarised in the following paragraphs. The exemptions numbered 2 to 5 do not apply to deemed transfers on death. The application of the exemptions to settled property is referred to *post*, § 22-22.

A transfer of value which is exempt only to a limited extent is treated as an exempt transfer up to the limit of exemption and as a chargeable transfer beyond that limit. [1]

Details of certain exempt transfers are not required in returns made for the purposes of capital transfer tax. [2]

1. *Transfers between spouses*

19-02 *Unlimited exemption.* A transfer of value is an exempt transfer to the extent that the value transferred is attributable to property which becomes comprised in the estate of the transferor's spouse or, so far as the value transferred is not so attributable, to the extent that that estate is increased. [3] The exemption applies to lifetime transfers and transfers on death and it applies whether or not the spouses are living together at the time of the transfer. Thus transfers between spouses which are made as part of the arrangements leading up to a decree absolute of divorce or nullity fall within the exemption whereas transfers made thereafter do not. [4] A transfer of value made by one spouse to a company of which the other spouse is sole shareholder is exempt because the latter's estate is thereby increased in value.

19-03 The exemption does not apply if the disposition takes effect on the termination after the transfer of value of any interest or period or if it depends on a condition which is not satisfied within 12 months of the transfer, except that the exemption is not excluded by reason only that the gift is conditional on one spouse surviving the other for a specified period. [5] Property is for this purpose treated as given to a spouse if it is given to or held on trust for him. [6]

---

[1] F.A. 1975, s. 20 (6).
[2] (1976) S.T.I. 101.
[3] F.A. 1975, Sched. 6, para. 1 (1) as amended by F.A. 1976, s. 94, in relation to transfers after April 6, 1976. Previously a transfer was exempt " to the extent that the value of the estate of the transferor's spouse is increased." Before the amendment, if H had a set of valuable books and broke the set by giving one book to W, his wife, the exemption applied only to the value of the one book: now it applies to the diminution in the value of H's estate.
[4] But see § 18-11.
[5] F.A. 1975, Sched. 6, para. 15 (1) (2).
[6] *Ibid.* Sched. 6, para. 15 (5).

Thus if a husband (H) gives property to A for life with remainder to his wife (W) absolutely, or to W after 60 days, the exemption does not apply; but if H gives property to W if she shall survive him by 60 days, which she does, the exemption applies.

19-04 *Limited exemption.* The unlimited exemption on inter-spouse transfers in § 19-02 does not apply if, immediately before the transfer, the transferor but not the transferee is domiciled in the United Kingdom. Then the value in respect of which the transfer is exempt (calculated as a value on which no tax is payable) is limited to £25,000 less any amount previously taken into account for the purposes of this limited exemption.[7] Thus if a series of transfers are made to a non-United Kingdom domiciled spouse, the exemption stops when £25,000 in value has been transferred. Gifts made to a non-domiciled spouse which would have been liable to estate duty under the old law as gifts made within the seven years before the transferor spouse's death are (to the extent of the amount which would have been liable to estate duty) to be brought into account for the purposes of the £25,000 limit.[8]

It follows that if one spouse wishes to transfer property to the other who is about to acquire a domicile of choice outside the United Kingdom, the transfer should be made before the domicile is acquired so as to obtain the benefit of the unlimited exemption. It is unlikely in practice that spouses will have separate domiciles while they are living together, but this may occur after they have separated as a result of section 1 of the Domicile and Matrimonial Proceedings Act 1973.

19-05 *Settled gifts.* A person who is beneficially entitled to an interest in possession in settled property is treated for capital transfer tax purposes as beneficially entitled to the property in which the interest subsists: see § 22-17. It follows from this that if a person settles property, whether *inter vivos* or by will, on his spouse for life, the transfer into settlement is exempt from capital transfer tax because the property becomes comprised in the estate of the transferor's spouse.

19-06 *Estate duty.* The exemption for transfers between spouses is applied for estate duty in relation to deaths after November 12, 1974, and before March 13, 1975.[9]

2. *Values not exceeding £2,000*

19-07 Transfers of value made by a transferor in any one year are exempt to the extent that the values transferred by them (calculated as values on which no tax is payable)[10] do not exceed £2,000.[11] " Year " means a period of 12 months ending with April 5.[12] A transferor who does not " use " the relief

---

[7] F.A. 1975, Sched. 6, para. 1 (2), as amended by F.A. 1976, s. 94 in relation to transfers after April 6, 1976. Limit of £25,000 increased from £15,000 in the case of transfers of value made after October 26, 1977, by F.A. 1978, s. 63.

[8] *Ibid.* Sched. 6, para. 1 (3) (4).   [9] *Ibid.* Sched. 11, para. 2.

[10] *i.e.* ignoring capital transfer tax in calculating the £2,000.

[11] *Ibid.* Sched. 6, para. 2 (1), increased from £1,000 by F.A. 1976, s. 93, but not so as to affect the operation of para. 2 in relation to transfers made before April 6, 1976, and not so as to affect the amount which can be carried forward to the year beginning on that date.

[12] F.A. 1975, Sched. 6, para. 2 (3), which also includes transitional provisions.

in a year may carry forward the unused part and add it to the exempt £2,000 in the next following year but not in a later year.[13]

> Thus if A makes transfers of £1,400 in the year ending April 5, 1977 (£600 of the exemption being unused), he can make exempt transfers of up to £2,600 in the year ending April 5, 1978. But the unused £600 cannot be used thereafter.

A transfer of any form of property may qualify for this exemption, which applies to gifts in settlement as well as to direct gifts but not to transfers on death.[14] Husband and wife are separate chargeable individuals for the purposes of capital transfer tax, so each of them is entitled to the annual £2,000 exemption.

19-08   Where the values transferred in a year exceed £2,000, it becomes necessary to determine which transfers are exempt and which not exempt, because the transferee may be liable for capital transfer tax on the non-exempt transfer. The Act provides that the excess over £2,000

  (a) shall, as between transfers made on different days, be attributed, so far as possible, to a later rather than an earlier transfer, *i.e.* so as to exempt the earlier transfers; and

  (b) shall, as between transfers made on the same day, be attributed to them in proportion to the values transferred by them.[13]

> Thus, if on the same day A gives £800 in value to B and £2,400 in value to C, the excess of £1,200 is apportioned as to £300 to B and £900 to C.

19-09   *Transitional provisions.* Capital transfer tax applies to transfers of value after March 26, 1974, but the Finance Act 1975 was not enacted until March 13, 1975. There are transitional provisions to enable exempt transfers of up to £2,000 to be made before April 5, 1975, for the period ended April 5, 1974, and the year ended April 5, 1975. Where " small gifts " (£500 to each donee) in excess of £2,000 were made in the period to April 5, 1975, which, under the old estate duty law, would have been exempt, the higher estate duty exemption applies instead of the lower capital transfer tax exemption.[15]

3. *Small gifts to same person*

19-10   Transfers of value made by a transferor in any one year by outright gifts to any one person are exempt to the extent that the values transferred by them (calculated as values on which no tax is chargeable[10]) do not exceed £100. A year means the period of 12 months ending with April 5.[16]

Note that the exemption applies only to " outright gifts to any one person." It is thought that a gift to trustees to hold on the trusts of a settlement falls outside this exemption, although such a gift will fall within the £2,000 exemption referred to in § 19-07. Transfers of value in the form of a free loan or free use of property (see §§ 21-09 *et seq.*) are treated as outright gifts.[17] The small gifts exemption and the £2,000 exemption are

---

[13] F.A. 1975, Sched. 6, para. 2 (2). But see n. 11, above.
[14] *Ibid.* Sched. 6, para. 8.
[15] *Ibid.* Sched. 6, paras. 3 and 2 (3).
[16] *Ibid.* Sched. 6, para. 4.   [17] F.A. 1976, s. 117 (3).

cumulative. Thus in any one year an individual can make any number of transfers of up to £100 per person in addition to transfers up to £2,000.

4. *Normal expenditure out of income*

19-11   A transfer of value is an exempt transfer if, or to the extent that, it is shown:

(a) that it was made as part of the normal expenditure of the transferor; and

(b) that (taking one year with another) it was made out of his income; and

(c) that, after allowing for all transfers of value forming part of his normal expenditure, the transferor was left with sufficient income to maintain his usual standard of living. [18]

Expenditure is " normal " if it is habitual. Premiums of reasonable amount which are regularly paid by an individual on a policy of his life for the benefit of a donee may fall within this exemption. Dispositions for the maintenance or education of the disponer's family (including dispositions under " income settlements ": see §§ 10-10 *et seq.*) will frequently fall within this exemption but those which do not may be exempt under section 46 of the Finance Act 1975 (*post,* § 19-56). Thus a parent who pays for the education of his children out of income may secure relief from tax under the normal expenditure exemption; whereas, if he has to resort to capital, relief under section 46 may be available. The exemption applies to gifts in settlement as well as to other gifts.

19-12   *Back to back policies.* A common method of estate duty avoidance involved the purchase by A for a capital sum of an annuity and the simultaneous purchase of a policy on A's life, expressed to be for the benefit of B. By this means A substituted dutiable capital for an annuity which ceased and so would not be dutiable on his death and also created an asset for B (the policy proceeds) by the payment of premiums constituting part of A's normal expenditure out of income. In this way dutiable capital of A was replaced by the benefit to B of a non-dutiable policy. Paragraph 5 (2) of Schedule 6 to the Finance Act 1975 now excludes the normal expenditure exemption by the following provision:

> A payment of a premium on a policy of insurance on the transferor's life, or a gift of money or money's worth applied, directly or indirectly, in payment of such a premium, shall not for the purposes of this paragraph be regarded as part of his normal expenditure if, when the insurance was made, or at any earlier or later time, an annuity was purchased on his life, unless it is shown that the purchase of the annuity and the making of any variation of the insurance or of any prior insurance for which the first mentioned insurance was directly or indirectly substituted, were not associated operations.

There is a special charge to capital transfer tax on back to back arrangements: see § 21-12.

---

[18] F.A. 1975, Sched. 6, para. 5 (1).

19-13   It has been the practice of the Revenue not to regard the purchase of an annuity and the effecting of a policy of assurance as " associated operations " if it is shown that the policy was issued after evidence of health had been obtained and the terms on which it was issued would have been the same even if the annuity had not been bought. Hence the normal expenditure exemption has been treated as not applying only if the purchase of the annuity enabled life cover to be obtained which would not otherwise have been available.

19-14   *Purchased life annuity.* The capital element in a purchased life annuity is not now to be regarded as income for the purposes of the normal expenditure exemption. This applies after April 5, 1975, but only in regard to life annuities purchased after November 12, 1974. [19]

5. *Gifts in consideration of marriage*

19-15   There are three requisites for a gift in consideration of marriage: (i) it must be made on the occasion of a marriage; (ii) it must be made conditional on the marriage taking place; and (iii) it must be made by a person for the purpose of or with a view to encouraging or facilitating the marriage. [20] It is a question of fact whether these requisites are present.

19-16   Transfers of value made by gifts in consideration of marriage are exempt to the extent that the values transferred by such transfers made by any one transferor in respect of any one marriage (calculated as values on which no tax is payable) do not exceed

   (a) in the case of gifts satisfying the conditions in § 19-17 by a parent of a party to the marriage, £5,000;

   (b) in the case of other gifts satisfying those conditions, £2,500; and

   (c) in any other case, £1,000.

Any excess is attributed to the transfers in proportion to the values transferred. [21]

19-17   A gift may qualify for the £5,000 or £2,500 exemption if

   (a) it is an outright gift to a child or remoter descendant of the transferor, or

   (b) the transferor is a parent or remoter ancestor of either party to the marriage, and either the gift is an outright gift to the other party to the marriage or the property comprised in the gift is settled by the gift, or

   (c) the transferor is a party to the marriage, and either the gift is an outright gift to the other party to the marriage or the property comprised in the gift is settled by the gift. [22]

---

[19] F.A. 1975, Sched. 6, para. 5 (3).
[20] See the estate duty case of *Re Park, decd. (No. 2)* [1972] Ch. 385 (C.A.).
[21] F.A. 1975, Sched. 6, para. 6 (1).
[22] *Ibid.* para. 6 (2). " Child " in para. 6 includes an illegitimate child, an adopted child and a step-child and " parent," " descendant " and " ancestor " are construed accordingly.

19-18   The estate duty exemption for gifts in consideration of marriage was
shown by the decision of the House of Lords in *Rennell* v. *I.R.C.*[23] to be
much wider than had hitherto been supposed, for it was held to apply to a
discretionary settlement for the benefit of a class which included issue of the
settlor, who was the bride's father. This decision was nullified by section 53
(1) of the Finance Act 1963, by provisions which are carried forward into
capital transfer tax and which provide [24] that a disposition shall not be
treated as a gift made in consideration of marriage:

(a) in the case of an outright gift, if or in so far as it is a gift to a person
other than a party to the marriage;

(b) in the case of any other disposition (*e.g.* a settled gift), if the persons
who are or may become entitled to any benefit under the disposition
include any person other than the following:

(i) the parties to the marriage, issue [25] of the marriage, or a wife
or husband of any such issue [25];

(ii) persons becoming entitled on the failure of trusts for any
such issue [25] under which trust property would (subject only to
any power of appointment to a person falling within sub-para. (i)
or (iii) of this para.) vest indefeasibly on the attainment of a
specified age or either on the attainment of such an age or on some
earlier event, or persons becoming entitled (subject as aforesaid)
on the failure of any limitation in tail;

(iii) a subsequent wife or husband of a party to the marriage, or
any issue,[25] or the wife or husband of any issue,[25] of a subsequent
marriage of either party;

(iv) persons becoming entitled under such trust, subsisting under
the law of England or of Northern Ireland, as are specified in
section 33 (1) of the Trustee Act 1925 (protective trusts), the
principal beneficiary being a person falling within sub-paragraph
(i) or (iii) of this subsection, or under such trusts modified by the
enlargement, as respects any period during which there is no such
issue [25] as aforesaid in existence, of the class of potential
beneficiaries specified in paragraph (ii) of the said section 33 (1);

(v) persons becoming entitled under trusts subsisting under the
law of Scotland and corresponding with such trusts as are
mentioned in sub-paragraph (iv);

(vi) as respects a reasonable amount by way of remuneration,
the trustees of the settlement.

[The next paragraph is 19-20.]

6. *Gifts to charities and political parties*

19-20   Transfers of value to charities (as defined [26]) and political parties (as
defined [27]) are exempt transfers, with limits of £100,000 in the case of gifts

---

[23] [1964] A.C. 173.   [24] F.A. 1975, Sched. 6, para. 6 (3).
[25] References in the section to issue apply as if any person legitimated by a marriage, or adopted by the
husband and wife jointly, were included among the issue of that marriage: *ibid.* para. 6 (4).
[26] *Ibid.* s. 51 (1) applying I.C.T.A. 1970, s. 360.   [27] *Ibid.* Sched. 6, para. 11 (2).

made on or within a year of the transferor's death.[28] Where the value transferred (*i.e.* the loss to the transferor's estate) exceeds the value of the gift in the hands of the donee, the exemption extends to the whole of the value transferred.[29] A gift of property out of a settlement in which there is no interest in possession to a charity is not a distribution payment for the purposes of Schedule 5 to the Finance Act 1975 (*post*, § 22-43).[30] As to free loans, etc., see § 21-11.

7. *Gifts for national purposes etc.*

19-21   A transfer of value is an exempt transfer to the extent that the value transferred by it is attributable to property which becomes the property of certain galleries, museums, national collections, university libraries, the National Trust, local authorities, Government departments and universities and university colleges in the United Kingdom.[31] There is no £100,000 limit as in § 19-20. There is a list of bodies qualifying for this exemption in the Revenue booklet CTT 1, Appendix III at p. 125.

8. *Gifts for public benefit*

19-22   Transfers of value to a body not established or conducted for profit are exempt transfers, if the Treasury so direct, if the property transferred falls into one of a number of categories which include [32] —

   (a) land which in the opinion of the Treasury is of outstanding scenic or historic or scientific interest;
   (b) a building (including the grounds used with it) for the preservation of which special steps should in the opinion of the Treasury be taken by reason of its outstanding historic or architectural or aesthetic interest and the cost of preserving it;
   (c) an object which at the time of the transfer is ordinarily kept in, and is given with, the building within (b);
   (d) property given as a source of income for the upkeep of any of the above; and
   (e) a picture, print, book, manuscript, work of art or scientific collection which in the opinion of the Treasury is of national, scientific, historic or artistic interest.

The Treasury have wide powers to give directions and require undertakings to be entered into for the purpose generally of securing the preservation of the property or its character and reasonable access to it for the public.

9. *Estate duty exemptions applied to capital transfer tax*

19-23   Any transfer of value made before December 10, 1974, which would have been exempt from estate duty if the transferor had died immediately after

---

[28] F.A. 1975, Sched. 6, paras. 10 and 11. There are provisions which deny the exemption where the transfer takes effect later or is conditional and where property is given for a limited period or may be used for other purposes: see *ibid.* Sched. 6, para. 15 as amended by F.A. 1976, s. 95.

[29] (1976) S.T.I. 145. Press Release of April 15, 1976.

[30] F.A. 1975, Sched. 6, para. 10 (2) as substituted by F.A. 1976, s. 111. The same rule applies to gifts to political bodies and to bodies specified in paras. 12 and 13 of Sched. 6 to the Finance Act 1975.

[31] *Ibid.* Sched. 6, para. 12. See also n. 29 and the text thereto, which applies also to this exemption.

[32] *Ibid.* Sched. 6, para. 13 as amended by F.A. 1976, s. 85. See also n. 28 and the text thereto, which applies also to this exemption. For the corresponding capital gains tax exemption, see § 16-50A.

that date is exempt from capital transfer tax.[33] The date is that on which the Bill introducing capital transfer tax was first published. Examples of such transfers include gifts of foreign property by persons who, under the general law (but not the Act: see § 23-10) would be treated as domiciled outside the United Kingdom.

Supplementary provisions

19-23A   Where a transfer of value falls into one or more of the exemptions numbered 1, 7, 8 or 9, above, but is not wholly exempt, paragraphs 16–23 of Schedule 6 to the Finance Act 1975 apply for the purpose of determining the extent of the exemption. Where the transfer is exempt up to a limit but not exempt as to the rest, these provisions (which are of considerable complexity) show how the non-exempt part is to be attributed to the gifts and how the exemption is to be allocated as between the gifts.

2. Miscellaneous Exemptions and Reliefs

Section 29 of and Schedule 7 to the Finance Act 1975 confer the miscellaneous exemptions and reliefs which are summarised in the following paragraphs.

1. *Death on active service, etc.*[34]

19-24   There is an exemption from the capital transfer tax otherwise leviable on death where the deceased is certified by the appropriate authority as having died from a wound inflicted, accident occurring or disease contracted while he was a member of the armed forces, provided he was (i) on active service against an enemy or (ii) on other service of a warlike nature or which, in the opinion of the Treasury, involved the same risks as service of a warlike nature. The exemption also applies where the deceased died from a disease contracted at some previous time, the death being due to or hastened by the aggravation of the disease during a period when the deceased was on service as mentioned in (i) or (ii). The exemption also applies to members of certain women's services.

2. *Cash options under approved annuity schemes*[35]

19-25   Where under a contract or trust scheme approved by the Board under section 226 or 226A of the Taxes Act or (before the commencement of that Act) under section 22 of the Finance Act 1956 (retirement annuities), an annuity becomes payable on a person's death to a widow, widower or dependant of that person, and under the terms of the contract or scheme a sum of money might at his option have become payable instead to his personal representatives, he is not, by virtue of section 23 (2) of the Finance Act 1975 (*ante*, § 18-09), to be treated as having been beneficially entitled to that sum. The sum of money is thus not chargeable to capital transfer tax on death as property forming part of the deceased's estate.

---

[33] *Ibid*. Sched. 6, para. 14.
[34] F.A. 1975, Sched. 7, para. 1.   [35] *Ibid*. Sched. 7, para. 2.

3. *Government securities free of tax while in foreign ownership* [36]

19-26   Certain United Kingdom securities are issued by the Treasury subject to a condition for exemption from taxation so long as the securities are in the beneficial ownership of persons neither domiciled nor ordinarily resident in the United Kingdom. Such securities are " excluded property " if, not being settled property, they are in the beneficial ownership of such a person or, being settled property, such a person is beneficially entitled to an interest in possession in them.

> Thus if " exempt Government securities " are held by trustees upon trust for A for life with remainder to B absolutely and A is neither domiciled nor ordinarily resident in the United Kingdom, no capital transfer tax is payable on the termination of A's interest in possession.

If the securities are settled property and no interest in possession subsists in them, as where Government securities are held on discretionary trusts, the property is excluded property only if it is shown that all known persons for whose benefit the settled property or income from it has been or might be applied or who might become beneficially entitled to an interest in possession in it are persons neither domiciled nor ordinarily resident in the United Kingdom. Where property is held on discretionary trusts for a class of persons which includes such non-domiciled etc. persons and others, capital transfer tax cannot be avoided by the trustees advancing or appointing part of the property into a second settlement for the exclusive benefit of the non-domiciled etc. persons and investing such property in Government securities. This is because the conditions as to beneficial entitlement have to be satisfied as respects the head settlement and the sub-settlement.[37] Further, where a close company is a beneficiary, the principle stated in § 22-39 applies.[38]

The extended definition of " domicile " in section 45 of the Finance Act 1975 (*post*, § 23-10) does not apply for the purposes of this provision.

4. *Overseas pensions* [39]

19-27   The estate duty arrangements in relation to pensions formerly due from India, Pakistan and various ex-colonial governments are continued for capital transfer tax.

5. *Savings by persons domiciled in the Channel Islands or Isle of Man* [40]

19-28   The Act treats as excluded property national savings certificates, premium savings bonds and certain other savings where the person beneficially entitled is domiciled in the Channel Islands or the Isle of Man.

The extended definition of domicile in section 45 of the Finance Act 1975 (*post*, § 23-10) does not apply for the purposes of this exemption.

---

[36] *Ibid.* Sched. 7, para. 3.
[37] See F.A. 1975, Sched. 7, para. 2A, added by F.A. 1978, s. 72 (1), as respects advances, etc. after April 20, 1978: *ibid.* s. 72 (2). See generally [1978] B.T.R. pp. 172–173.
[38] F.A. 1975, Sched. 7, para. 2B, added by F.A. 1978, s. 72 (1), and applying after April 20, 1978: *ibid.* s. 72 (2).
[39] F.A. 1975, Sched. 7, para. 4.
[40] *Ibid.* Sched. 7, para. 5.

6. *Visiting forces and staff of allied headquarters* [41]

19-29   The Act continues certain reliefs for members of overseas forces visiting this country and for the staff of allied headquarters. Certain property belonging to them is excluded property and the period of a visit to the United Kingdom is not treated as a period of residence in the United Kingdom or as creating a change in residence or domicile.

7. *Double taxation relief* [42]

19-30   This provides for double taxation agreements and double taxation relief in respect of capital transfer tax.

3. " QUICK SUCCESSION RELIEF " ON DEATH

19-31   This relief applies on a death where the death which gives rise to the charge to capital transfer tax, under section 22 of the Finance Act 1975, is preceded by a chargeable transfer to the deceased made not more than four years before (called " the previous transfer ") which increased the value of the deceased's estate. The relief takes the form of a reduction in the tax chargeable on death under section 22, the reduction being a " percentage of the tax charged on so much of the value transferred by the previous transfer as is attributable to the increase." [43]

The percentage reduction varies with the period between the previous transfer and the death and is

> 80 per cent. if the period is one year or less;
> 60 per cent. if the period is two years or less;
> 40 per cent. if the period is three years or less;
> 20 per cent. if the period is four years or less.

Suppose A gives B £50,000. B pays capital transfer tax of £x. B dies after 3½ years, leaving £100,000. The capital transfer tax on £100,000 will be reduced by 20 per cent. of £x.

Quick succession relief is not available where the relief in paragraph 5 of Schedule 5 to the Finance Act 1965 (successive charges on settled property) applies [44] : see *post*, § 22-40.

19-32   *Estate duty.* Section 30 (3) of the Finance Act 1975, as substituted by section 97 (1) of the Finance Act 1976, extends the relief to cases where the value of a person's estate was increased (a) on a death on which estate duty was payable; or (b) in consequence of a gift *inter vivos* or a disposition or determination of a beneficial interest in possession in any property comprised in a settlement where, by reason of the gift or interest, estate duty or capital transfer tax under section 22 (5) of the Finance Act 1975 was payable on a subsequent death.

---

[41] *Ibid.* Sched. 7, para. 6.
[42] *Ibid.* Sched. 7, para. 7.
[43] F.A. 1975, s. 30 (1).
[44] *Ibid.* s. 30 (2).

4. RELIEF FOR WORKS OF ART, HISTORIC BUILDINGS ETC.

19-33 The Finance Act 1975 provided an exemption for transfers of value of works of art, etc., which applied only to transfers on death. This exemption was discussed in § 19-33 of the ninth edition of this book. The Finance Act 1976 has replaced the earlier exemption in relation to transfers of value made after April 6, 1976, by new provisions which apply to transfers on death, lifetime transfers and transfers made by trustees of discretionary settlements.[45] The purpose of the relief is to preserve, for enjoyment by all, pictures, collections and buildings etc. which form part of the national heritage.

Section 76 (1) of the Finance Act 1976 makes a transfer of value after April 6, 1976, an exempt transfer to the extent that the value transferred by it is attributable to property (a) which, on a claim made for the purpose, is designated by the Treasury under section 77 (below); and (b) with respect to which the requisite undertaking is given by such persons as the Treasury think appropriate in the circumstances of the case. Such a transfer is called a " conditionally exempt transfer." [46]

Section 77 (1) allows the Treasury to designate the following:

(*a*) any pictures, prints, books, manuscripts, works of art, scientific collections or other things not yielding income which appear to the Treasury to be of national, scientific, historic or artistic interest;

(*b*) any land which in the opinion of the Treasury is of outstanding scenic or historic or scientific interest;

(*c*) any building for the preservation of which special steps should in the opinion of the Treasury be taken by reason of its outstanding historic or architectural interest;

(*d*) any land which adjoins such a building as is mentioned in paragraph (*c*) above and which in the opinion of the Treasury is essential for the protection of the character and amenities of the building;

(*e*) any object which in the opinion of the Treasury is historically associated with such a building as is mentioned in paragraph (*c*) above.

In the case of property within (*a*), the requisite undertaking is to keep the property in the United Kingdom and to take reasonable steps for its preservation and (save in the case of confidential documents) to secure reasonable access to the public. In the case of property within (*b*), the requisite undertaking is to maintain the land and to preserve its character and to secure reasonable access to the public.[47]

No exemption can be claimed for a lifetime transfer unless the transferor or his spouse (or both spouses between them) have been beneficially entitled to the property throughout the six years ending with the transfer or, alternatively, the transferor acquired the property on a death which was

---

[45] As from April 7, 1976, the 1975 Act provisions have effect subject to amendments: see F.A. 1976, s. 76 (5) and Sched. 11. And see *ibid*. s. 83.

[46] F.A. 1976, s. 76 (2).

[47] *Ibid*. s. 77 (2)–(5).

itself a conditionally exempt transfer (or the property was left out of account under previous statutory provisions).[48]

The exemption being here discussed does not apply to a transfer of value which is exempt under provisions relating to transfers between spouses (§ 19-02) or transfers to charities (§ 19-20).[49]

Chargeable events

19-34   Where the exemption under section 76 (1) of the Finance Act 1976 applies, the transfer is conditionally exempt (§ 19-33). Tax becomes chargeable under section 78 on the first occurrence thereafter of a *chargeable event* with respect to the property.[50] The following are chargeable events:

(1) *Non-observance of the undertaking.* Tax becomes chargeable if the Treasury are satisfied that the undertaking (see § 19-33) has not been observed in a material respect. The person liable for the tax in that event is the person who, if the object were sold at the time the tax becomes chargeable, would be entitled to receive (whether for his own benefit or not) the proceeds of sale or any income arising from them.[51]

(2) *Death, or disposal of the property.* Tax becomes chargeable if the person beneficially entitled to the property dies or the property is disposed of, whether by sale or gift or otherwise. The person liable for the tax in the case of death is the person who, if the property were sold immediately after the death, would be entitled to receive (whether for his own benefit or not) the proceeds of sale or any income arising from them. The person liable for the tax on a disposal is the person by whom or for whose benefit the property is disposed of.[52] There are two exceptions to this general rule:

(a) a death or disposal otherwise than by sale is not a chargeable event if it is itself a conditionally exempt transfer, which requires that the undertaking previously given with respect to the property is replaced by a corresponding undertaking given by such person as the Treasury think appropriate in the circumstances of the case.[53]

Thus if property which is accorded conditional exemption from CTT on A's death passes to B and B dies, CTT is payable unless B's personal representatives claim and obtain relief under section 76. Similarly, if C gives property to D and C's gift is accorded conditional exemption from CTT, and D gives the property to E, CTT is payable on D's gift unless D makes a successful claim for relief under section 76. The claimants in each case (B's personal representatives and D) would have to procure fresh undertakings from the appropriate persons.

(b) a death or disposal is not a chargeable event with respect to any property if the deceased's personal representatives within three years of the death (or, in the case of settled property, the trustees or the

---

[48] *Ibid.* s. 76 (3). This qualification makes it difficult for wealthy individuals to invest in assets forming part of the national heritage mainly for the purpose of avoiding CTT.

[49] *Ibid.* s. 76 (4).

[50] *Ibid.* s. 78 (1).

[51] F.A. 1976, s. 78 (2).

[52] *Ibid.* s. 78 (3) as amended by F.A. 1977, s. 53. As to associated properties, see F.A. 1975, s. 78 (6)–(7).

[53] F.A. 1975, s. 78 (4).

person next entitled) sell the property by private treaty (or give it) to
one of the bodies mentioned in paragraph 12 of Schedule 6 to the
Finance Act 1975 (museums, etc., see § 19-21) or apply it in
satisfaction of the Board's claim for capital transfer tax.[54]

Amount of the tax charge

19-35   Where tax becomes chargeable under section 78 of the Finance Act 1976
(see § 19-34), it is charged on an amount equal to the value of the property
at the time of the chargeable event (or the proceeds of sale in the case of an
arm's length sale). If the relevant transferor (see below) is alive, tax is
charged at the rates applicable to lifetime transfers (§ 20-02) as if the
transferor had made a transfer of value of that amount at the time of the
chargeable event; if he is dead, tax is charged at the rates applicable to
transfers on death and as if the amount had been added to the value
transferred on his death and had formed the highest part thereof.[55]

The relevant transferor in relation to the tax chargeable on the occasion
of a chargeable event in respect of any property is [56]:

(*a*) if there has been only one conditionally exempt transfer of the
property before the event, the person who made that transfer;

(*b*) if there have been two or more such transfers and the last was before,
or only one of them was within, the period of 30 years ending with
the event, the person who made the last of those transfers;

(*c*) if there have been two or more such transfers within that period, the
person who made whichever of those transfers the Board may select.

The purpose of (*c*) appears to be to enable the Revenue to counter schemes
for avoiding capital transfer tax by, *e.g.* a person with a large estate
(including conditionally exempt property) channelling transfers through a
person with a small or nil estate.

The scheme of the legislation is to treat a conditionally exempt transfer
followed by a chargeable event as if the transferor (or the relevant
transferor) had made a non-exempt gift of property (valued, not at the date
of the gift, but at the date of the chargeable event). Consistently with this
concept, there are provisions in section 80 of the Act for reinstatement of
the transferor's cumulative total by reference to the no-longer-exempt
transfer.

Assume A makes a conditionally exempt transfer of a Rembrandt to B. A later
makes a non-exempt transfer to C of £40,000 and pays CTT at the rate
appropriate to that transfer. Later B sells the Rembrandt, *i.e.* there is a
chargeable event and B is liable for the tax occasioned thereby. The proceeds of
sale are £450,000.

Under section 80 of the Finance Act 1976 the rate or rates of tax
applicable to A's transfer to B fall to be determined as if the amount on
which tax was chargeable was £490,000. If A is dead at the time of the sale

[54] *Ibid.* s. 78 (5).
[55] *Ibid.* s. 79 (1)–(4). For the position where the death (or the ceasing of a settlement to exist) and the
chargeable event straddle October 26, 1978, see F.A. 1978, s. 62 (6).
[56] F.A. 1975 s. 79 (5).

by B, the amount transferred on A's death is increased by £450,000. If the property is comprised in a settlement at the time of the sale, there are provisions for adding the taxable amount to the settler's cumulative total of gifts in certain circumstances.[57]

Where after a conditionally exempt transfer of any property there is a chargeable transfer the value transferred by which is wholly or partly attributable to that property, any tax charged on that value so far as attributable to that property shall be allowed as a credit—

(a) if the chargeable transfer is a chargeable event with respect to the property, against the tax chargeable in accordance with this section by reference to that event;

(b) if the chargeable transfer is not such a chargeable event, against the tax chargeable in accordance with this section by reference to the next chargeable event with respect to the property.[58]

Settled property

19-36   Sections 81 and 82 of the Finance Act 1976 provide an exemption from capital transfer tax which would otherwise arise under provisions discussed later in this book (see §§ 22-41 *et seq.*) on distributions by trustees of a discretionary settlement of property designated by the Treasury under section 77 of the Act (§ 19-33).

Maintenance funds for historic buildings

19-37   Section 84 of the Finance Act 1976 enables property to be settled on trusts to secure the maintenance, repair or preservation of historic buildings, etc. without liability to capital transfer tax.

5. MUTUAL AND VOIDABLE TRANSFERS

Mutual transfers

Assume that A makes a gift to B and the capital transfer tax is duly paid. Later the parties wish to unscramble the transaction, *i.e.* by B making a gift back to A. But for the provisions about to be considered A could recover no tax on his original transfer; and B's gift back would itself attract liability to capital transfer tax. In certain situations, relief is available to both A and B in such a case.

19-38   (1) *Donee's relief.* Section 86 of the Finance Act 1976 provides a relief from capital transfer tax where a person (" the donor ") makes a chargeable transfer (" the donor's transfer ") which increases the estate of another person (" the donee ") and the donee subsequently makes a transfer of value (" the donee's transfer ") which either—

(i) is made in the donor's life-time and increases the value of the estate of the donor or his spouse; or

---

[57] F.A. 1975, s. 80 (3).
[58] *Ibid.* s. 79 (7).

(ii) is made within two years after the donor's death and increases the value of the estate of the donor's widow or widower.[59]

Section 86 exempts the donee's transfer (or transfers) from capital transfer tax to the extent that it (or they) merely restore to the donor the amount by which his (the donee's) estate was increased in value by the donor's transfer.[60] There is no requirement that the donee's transfer should be of the same property as he received from the donor. The section applies to a transfer back to the donor's spouse, widow or widower only if at the relevant time both the donor and that person were, or neither of them was, domiciled in the United Kingdom (see § 19-04); and for this purpose the relevant time is, in the case of a spouse, the time of the donor's transfer, and in the case of a widow or widower, the time of the donor's death.[61]

(2) *Donor's relief.* Section 87 provides relief in respect of the donor's gift and enables it to be treated as cancelled to a stated extent. By section 87 (1) the donor may, within six years after the donee's transfer, claim that the donor's transfer shall be treated as cancelled by the donee's transfer to the extent specified in section 87 (3); and thereupon, so the section provides,

(a) tax on the cancelled value paid or payable (whether or not by the claimant) shall be repaid to him by the Board or, as the case may be, shall not be payable; and

(b) the rate or rates of tax applicable to any chargeable transfer made by the donor after the claim shall be determined as if the values previously transferred by chargeable transfers made by the donor were reduced by the cancelled value.

Section 87 (3) has the effect that if the donee's transfer is within 12 months of the donor's transfer, the whole of the donor's transfer can be treated as cancelled. If the donee's transfer is more than 12 months after the donor's transfer, the amount to be treated as cancelled is the amount restored reduced by 4 per cent. for every 12 months thereafter. Thus the donor has no right of cancellation if the donee's transfer is made more than 25 years after the donor's transfer.

If the donor dies within three years of his gift there is no liability to additional tax under section 37 of the Finance Act 1975 (see § 20-05) to the extent that the gift has been cancelled by a gift back from the donee made before the death.[62]

Voidable transfers

19-38A　　Where on a claim made for the purpose it is shown that the whole or any part of a chargeable transfer (" the relevant transfer ") has by virtue of any enactment or rule of law been set aside as voidable or otherwise defeasible—*e.g.* on a bankruptcy of the transferor—

---

[59] F.A. 1976, s. 86 (1). Where the donor died before April 1, 1975, the two year period in (ii) is reckoned from that date: *ibid.* s. 86 (5). See *ibid.* s. 86 (3) as to the meaning of " transfer."

[60] *Ibid.* s. 86 (2).

[61] *Ibid.* s. 86 (4).

[62] For the position where the donor's and donee's transfers straddle October 26, 1978, see F.A. 1978, s. 62 (7).

(a) tax paid or payable by the claimant, both in respect of the relevant transfer or any other chargeable transfer made before the claim, that would not have been payable if the relevant transfer had been void *ab initio*, is repayable by the Board or, as the case may be, is not payable; and

(b) the rate or rates of tax (including interest on tax) applicable to any chargeable transfer made after the claim by the person who made the relevant transfer is to be determined as if that transfer or part of it had been void.

Tax repayable carries interest (which is not income for any tax purposes) from the date on which the claim is made. The section applies in relation to transfers before as well as after the passing of the Finance Act 1976.[63]

> Thus if A makes a voidable transfer in 1977 and a valid transfer in 1978, and the 1977 transfer is set aside, and a claim is made as respects the 1977 transfer in 1979, any tax paid on the 1977 transfer is repayable with tax-free interest from the date of the claim; and the tax paid on the 1978 transfer has to be recomputed as if the 1977 transfer had not been made, any overpaid tax being repayable with tax-free interest from the date of the claim.

6. RELIEF FOR BUSINESS PROPERTY

19-39   Section 73 of and Schedule 10 to the Finance Act 1976 provide that where the whole or part of the value transferred by a transfer of value made after April 6, 1976, is attributable to the value of any *relevant business property*, such whole or part of the value (calculated as a value on which no tax is chargeable) shall be reduced by " the appropriate percentage." [64]

The relief applies to all transfers of value, including lifetime transfers, transfers on death and the charges on settled property [65] which are considered in Chapter 22.

Relevant business property

19-39A   Relevant business property means, in relation to any transfer of value [66] —

(a) property consisting of a business or an interest in a business, *e.g.* a partner's interest in a partnership business (including a business carried on in the exercise of a profession or vocation but excluding a business carried on otherwise than for gain);

(b) shares or securities of a company which, by themselves or with other shares or securities owned by the transferor, gave him control [67] of the company immediately before the transfer; and

(bb) shares in a company outside (b) and are not quoted on a recognised stock exchange (*i.e.* a minority holding of unquoted shares); and

---

[63] F.A. 1976, s. 88. The section operates retrospectively to March 27, 1974.
[64] F.A. 1976, Sched. 10, para. 2. The expression " appropriate percentage " is substituted for " 30 per cent." in the case of a transfer of value made after October 26, 1977: F.A. 1978, s. 64 (1), (2) and (7). For the meaning of " value," see *ibid*. para. 6.
[65] F.A. 1976 Sched. 10, para. 1, as amended by F.A. 1978, s. 64 (6) and (7).
[66] *Ibid*. Sched. 10, para. 3 (1). Para. (bb) was inserted by F.A. 1978, s. 64 (3).
[67] Defined in Sched. 10, para. 13 (2), and F.A. 1978, s. 66.

(c) any land or building, machinery or plant which, immediately before the transfer, was used wholly or mainly for the purposes of a business carried on by a company of which the transferor then had control [67] or by a partnership in which he then was a partner. (In this case the relief applies only if the transferor's interest in the business or company immediately before the transfer was relevant business property.) [68]

The relief does not apply where the business (or the business carried on by the company) consists wholly or mainly of dealing in securities, stocks or shares, land or buildings or making or holding investments; except that the relief applies where the business is that of a jobber or discount house in the United Kingdom and to shares or securities in a holding company for one or more companies whose business is not within the exception. [69]

There are special provisions which apply where property which would be relevant business property is subject to a binding contract of sale at the time of the transfer and where a company is in liquidation at the time when its shares are transferred. [70]

There are also provisions for excluding from the value of the property qualifying for relief assets which are not used wholly and exclusively for the purpose of the business or required for future use therein. [71]

Amount of relief

19-39B   The amount of the relief depends on which of the paragraphs (a) to (c) in § 19-39A applies. The relief in the case of transfers of value made after October 26, 1977, is " the appropriate percentage " of the value transferred, which is 50 per cent. where paragraphs (a) or (b) apply, 20 per cent. where paragraph (bb) applies and 30 per cent. where paragraph (c) applies. [72]

In the case of a transfer of shares or securities, paragraph (b), and consequently the 50 per cent. relief, applies only to a transfer of shares or securities which, immediately before the transfer, were sufficient to give the transferor control [67] without other property. [73]

> Thus if X, with 70 out of 100 issued shares in Y Ltd., makes a transfer of value of 51 shares, the 50 per cent. relief applies; whereas if he makes such a transfer of 49 shares, the 30 per cent. rate applicable to shares in paragraph (bb) applies.

The 50 per cent. relief does not apply where the relief in paragraph 9A of Schedule 10 to the Finance Act 1975 applies (§ 20-19) on a sale within three years of a death where a related property valuation made on the death is reduced on the sale. [73]

Minimum period of ownership

19-39C   To qualify for the relief the transferor must have owned the relevant business property throughout the two years immediately preceding the

---

[68] F.A. 1976, Sched. 10, para. 3 (6).   [69] *Ibid.* Sched. 10, para. 3 (2), (3).
[70] *Ibid.* Sched. 10, para. 3 (4), (5).   [71] *Ibid.* Sched. 10, para. 8.
[72] *Ibid.* Sched. 10, para. 2 (1A), added by F.A. 1978, s. 64 (2).
[73] *Ibid.* Sched. 10, para. 3 (1A), added by F.A. 1978, s. 64 (4).

transfer. Alternatively, it must have replaced other relevant business property and it, and the property it replaced, must have been owned for at least two years falling within the five years immediately preceding the transfer of value. Where the transferor became entitled to the property on the death of his spouse, the deceased's period of ownership can be reckoned in the transferor's period of ownership.[74]

7. RELIEF FOR AGRICULTURAL PROPERTY

19-40 Section 35 of and Schedule 8 to the Finance Act 1975 give relief where the value transferred by a chargeable transfer is determined by reference to the value of agricultural property. The relief applies to lifetime transfers and transfers on death; and it applies to transfers into settlement as well as to " outright " transfers. The method of calculating the relief by reference to a multiple of rental value was replaced by section 74 of the Finance Act 1976, which substituted the 50 per cent. reduction in agricultural value referred to in § 19-41.

Definitions

The following definitions apply for the purposes of this relief:

Farming has the same meaning as in the Tax Acts but with the inclusion of market garden land. The question whether a person carries on farming as a trade is to be determined as for the purposes of income tax or, as the case may be, corporation tax.[75]

Agricultural property means agricultural land or pasture and includes woodland if occupied with agricultural land or pasture and the occupation is ancillary to that of the agricultural land or pasture. It also includes such cottages, farm buildings and farm-houses, together with the land occupied with them, as are of a character appropriate to the property.[76]

Agricultural value in relation to agricultural property means the value of that property on the assumption that it is subject to a perpetual covenant prohibiting its use otherwise than as agricultural property.[77] Thus development value which is inherent in agricultural property is excluded from the definition of agricultural value.

The unreduced value in relation to a chargeable transfer means the value transferred, calculated before the reduction (*i.e.* the agricultural relief) and as if no tax were chargeable on it.[78]

Nature of relief

19-41 The relief for agricultural property applies to land in the United Kingdom which, for this purpose, is extended to include land in the Channel Islands and the Isle of Man.[79] The person liable to pay the whole or part of the tax

---

[74] F.A. 1976, Sched. 10, para. 4.
[75] F.A. 1975, Sched. 8, para. 6.
[76] *Ibid.* Sched. 8, para. 7.
[77] *Ibid.* Sched. 8, para. 8.
[78] *Ibid.* Sched. 8, para. 1 (3).
[79] *Ibid.* Sched. 8, para. 1 (1) and (10).

on the value transferred must make a claim for agricultural relief to the Board within two years of the transfer or such longer time as the Board may allow.[80]

In the absence of relief, capital transfer tax would be levied on the value of agricultural property which was transferred, including any value attributable, for example, to the prospect of development. The relief excludes from capital transfer tax (up to a specified limit) one half of the agricultural value of the agricultural property (called " the part eligible for relief ").[81]

Conditions for relief

19-42   Two conditions have to be satisfied before the relief is available—one confining the relief to a transferor who has been an established farmer principally engaged in farming; the other confining the relief to property actually occupied for farming. Each of these conditions must be considered separately.

19-43   (1) *The transferor.* It is a condition that the transferor was, in not less than five out of the seven years ending with April 5 immediately preceding the transfer, wholly or mainly engaged in the United Kingdom in farming as a trader (alone or in partnership), employee or director of a farming company or as a full-time student.[82] The wholly or mainly condition is taken to be satisfied where, *inter alia*, not less than 75 per cent. of the transferor's relevant income (as defined [83]) was immediately derived from agriculture.[84] If the condition is satisfied by the transferor's spouse, who dies having transferred the property to the transferor, this condition is treated as satisfied as regards the transferor.[85] Thus a widow who inherits property on the death of her husband is herself treated as satisfying this condition and will therefore be able to transfer the farm with benefit of agricultural relief even before two years (see § 19-45), her occupation being treated as beginning on the death.[86]

19-44   (2) *The property.* It is a condition that the property was occupied by the transferor (or by a company controlled by him [87]) for the purposes of agriculture at the time of the transfer and throughout the immediately preceding two years. If one farm has replaced another and the replacement farm has not been occupied for two years immediately preceding the transfer, it is sufficient if there was occupation of both farms during two out of the five years immediately preceding the transfer.[88] Occupation acquired on the death of another person is treated as beginning at the time of such death.[89]

---

[80] F.A. 1975, Sched. 8, para. 1 (1) (*b*).
[81] *Ibid.* Sched. 8, para. 2 as amended by F.A. 1976, s. 74 (4) in relation to chargeable transfers after April 6, 1976.
[82] *Ibid.* Sched. 8, para. 3 (1) (*a*) and (2).
[83] The definition excludes pensions, compensation for loss of office and wife's income taxed as the husband's income under I.C.T.A. 1970, s. 37.
[84] F.A. 1975, Sched. 8, para. 3 (3).
[85] *Ibid.* Sched. 8, para. 3 (6) (*b*).
[86] *Ibid.* Sched. 8, para. 3 (6) (*a*); *post*, § 19-45.   [87] *Ibid.* Sched. 8, para. 3 (7) and (8).
[88] *Ibid.* Sched. 8, para. 3 (1) (*b*).   [89] See n. 86, *ante*.

19-45   In one case the requirement of two years' occupation does not apply. This is where one person transfers agricultural property to another in circumstances where the relief applies and the transferee makes a transfer of value of the same property within two years which satisfies condition (1) because he is, or is treated as, a qualifying farmer, but not condition (2). In this case condition (2) is treated as satisfied.[90]

> Thus a widow who inherits agricultural property on the death of her husband and is treated as satisfying condition (1) can transfer the property with benefit of agricultural relief without herself having to remain in occupation for two years.

19-46   Where both conditions (1) and (2) are satisfied except that the transfer is immediately preceded by a period during which the property is occupied for purposes of agriculture by a member of the transferor's family (as defined [91]), the relief is available.[92]

> Thus if the farmer retires from farming and allows a member of his family to occupy and farm the property, agricultural relief is available on the farmer's death if such occupation continues until that time.

Shares and debentures in farming companies

19-47   Transfers of shares or debentures in a company owning agricultural property will qualify for agricultural relief [93] if

    (a) the agricultural property forms part of the company's assets and part of the value of the shares or debentures can be attributed to the agricultural value of the agricultural property; and

    (b) the shares or debentures gave the transferor control [94] of the company immediately before the transfer; and

    (c) the main activity of the company is, and has been throughout the two years immediately preceding the transfer farming in the United Kingdom; and

    (d) the agricultural property was at the time of the transfer occupied by the company for the purposes of farming and either was so occupied by it throughout the two years immediately preceding the transfer or replaced other agricultural property and was so occupied by it for a period which, when added to any period during which it so occupied the replaced property comprised at least two years in the five years immediately preceding the transfer.

Condition (b) replaces condition (2) referred to in § 19-44 but the person transferring the shares or debentures must satisfy condition (1) in § 19-43.

Limitation of relief

19-48   Agricultural relief is limited in the case of each transferor, the limit being measured by reference to value and acreage and taking account of all previous transfers by the same transferor. First the part eligible for relief,

---

[90] F.A. 1975, Sched. 8, para. 1 (2).   [91] *Ibid.* Sched. 8, para. 3 (9).
[92] *Ibid.* Sched. 8, para. 3 (4).
[93] *Ibid.* Sched. 8, para. 4.
[94] Defined *ibid.* Sched. 4, para. 13, as amended by F.A. 1978, s. 66.

when added to the part eligible for relief under any previous chargeable transfer made by the same transferor, must not exceed £250,000 (apparently calculated on the basis that the relief applies). Secondly, the area of the agricultural property by reference to which the relief is given, together with that of any agricultural property by reference to which relief was given under previous chargeable transfers made by the same transferor, must not exceed 1,000 acres (the area of rough grazing land being counted as one-sixth of its actual area). The relief is limited to whichever is the more beneficial of these two alternatives.[95]

Relationship with business relief

19-48A On the transfer of a farming business or of shares or debentures in a farming company, agricultural relief may be claimed in respect of the agricultural value of agricultural property, and business relief (§ 19-39) as respects other relevant business property.

8. WOODLANDS

19-49 Section 35 of and Schedule 9 to the Finance Act 1975 give relief where the value transferred by a chargeable transfer made on death is determined by reference to the value of woodlands.

Nature of relief

19-50 The relief is available where any part of a deceased person's estate includes land in the United Kingdom on which trees or underwood are growing but which is not agricultural property as defined in § 19-40. Where the relief is given the value of the trees or underwood are left out of account in determining the value transferred on death.[96]

Condition of relief

19-51 The relief is not available unless the deceased was beneficially entitled to the land throughout the five years immediately preceding his death or became beneficially entitled otherwise than for a consideration in money or money's worth.[97]

The person liable for the tax on the death must claim the relief by giving written notice to the Board within two years of the death or such longer time as the Board may allow.[98]

Tax chargeable

19-52 If the value of trees or underwood is left out of account on a death and all or part of the trees or underwood are subsequently disposed of (otherwise than to the disponer's spouse), whether together with or apart from the land on which they were growing, tax is chargeable if the disposal occurs before

---

[95] F.A. 1975, Sched. 8, para. 5 as amended by F.A. 1976, s. 74 (6).
[96] *Ibid.* Sched. 9, para. 1 (1).
[97] *Ibid.* Sched. 9, para. 5 (1) as amended by F.A. 1977, s. 52.
[98] *Ibid.* Sched. 9, para. 1 (2).

any part of the value transferred on the death of any other person is attributable to the value of that land, *i.e.* if the disposal occurs before a death in connection with which relief is not given for the whole of the woodlands. The disponer is liable for the tax.[99] The relief in respect of woodlands thus takes the form of a deferred charge to tax.

19-53   Tax is charged on the net proceeds of sale if the disposal is a sale for full consideration in money or money's worth; and in any other case tax is charged on the net value of the trees or underwood at the time of the disposal. Tax is charged at the rate or rates at which it would have been chargeable on the death if the amount so chargeable (including any amount on which tax was previously chargeable in relation to the death) had been included in the value transferred on death and the amount on which the tax is chargeable had formed the highest part of that value.[1] This is subject to the qualification that if business relief (see §§ 19-39 *et seq.*) would have been available on the death if " woodlands relief " under § 19-49 had not been claimed, the amount of tax chargeable is reduced by 50 per cent.; and for this purpose it is to be assumed that Schedule 10 to the Finance Act 1976 (§ 19-39) was in force at the time of the death.[2]

19-54   When the disposal on which tax is chargeable is a chargeable transfer, the value transferred is calculated as if the value of the trees or underwood had been reduced by the tax chargeable.[3] Where tax is charged on a disposal, it is not again charged in relation to the same death on a further disposal of the same trees or underwood.[4]

9. LIFETIME DISPOSITIONS FOR MAINTENANCE OF FAMILY

19-55   The exemptions referred to in this section are those which enable one party to a marriage to make provision for the other (by way of settlement or otherwise) or for a child of either on the occasion, for example, of a decree of divorce or nullity; and those which enable provision to be made for the maintenance of a child not wholly in the care of the transferor, for an illegitimate child of his, and for the care of a dependent relative. The exemptions discussed below do not apply to deemed transfers on death.

19-56   A disposition is not a transfer of value if it is made by one party to a marriage in favour of the other party or of a child (including a step-child or adopted child [5]) of either party and is—

(a) for the maintenance of the other party, or

(b) for the maintenance, education or training of the child for a period ending not later than the year in which he attains the age of 18 or, after attaining that age, ceases to undergo full-time education or training.[6] (" Year " means any period of 12 months ending with April 5.[7])

---

[99] F.A. 1975, Sched. 9, para. 2 (1)–(3). The first of the new Tables (§ 20-02) is applied where the death occurred on or before October 26, 1977: F.A. 1978, s. 62 (5).   [1] *Ibid.* Sched. 9, para. 3.
[2] F.A. 1978, s. 65, applying to disposals after October 26, 1977.   [3] F.A. 1975, Sched. 9, para. 4.
[4] *Ibid.* Sched. 9, para. 2 (4).   [5] *Ibid.* s. 46 (6).
[6] *Ibid.* s. 46 (1).   [7] *Ibid.* s. 46 (6).

19-57   The term " maintenance " is not defined nor is there any qualification as to the amount which may be provided. Contrast in this respect the exemption for a disposition in favour of a dependent relative (*post*, § 19-60), which refers to " reasonable provision " for care and maintenance. It is thought, however, that a disposition in excess of the amount the court would order on an application for maintenance etc. would fall outside the exemption and would be a transfer of value as regards the excess. Annual payments out of capital to pay for a child's education (which will fall outside the normal expenditure exemption in § 19-11) will be exempt under this provision.

19-58   Section 46 (6) provides that

> Marriage, in relation to a disposition made on the occasion of the dissolution or annulment of a marriage, and in relation to a disposition varying a disposition so made, includes a former marriage.

The exemption discussed in § 19-56 is not needed as regards maintenance of a party to the marriage where the parties are married at the time of the disposition because the exemption for transfers between spouses will apply. It is no condition of that exemption that the parties should be living together at the time of the disposition: hence transfers of value in separation and maintenance agreements made during marriage are exempt as transfers between spouses. Spouses cease to be husband and wife on the granting of the decree absolute.[8] Relief under section 46 (1) of the Finance Act 1975, is needed if the disposition takes effect after a decree of divorce or of nullity: then the Act requires that the disposition (to be exempt) must be made either on the occasion of the decree or by way of variation of a disposition so made. Thus if the first disposition by way of maintenance is delayed too long after the decree, the exemption from capital transfer tax under section 46 (1) may be lost. In such a case it might be possible to escape tax on the footing that the disposition was no more than was needed to settle a delayed claim of the transferee.

19-59   A disposition in favour of a child (including a step-child or adopted child[9]) who is not in the care of a parent of his is not a transfer of value provided the child has been in the care of the person making the disposition for substantial periods before the child attains the age of 18. The disposition must be made for the purpose and for the period mentioned in (b) in § 19-56.[10]

19-60   A disposition is not a transfer of value if it is made in favour of a dependent relative (as defined[11]) of the disponer and is a reasonable provision for his care or maintenance.[12]

19-61   A disposition in favour of an illegitimate child of the person making the disposition is not a transfer of value if it is for the purpose and period mentioned in (b) in § 19-56.[13]

---

[8] See *Fender* v. *St. John Mildmay* [1938] A.C. 1 (H.L.).   [9] See n. 97, *ante*.
[10] F.A. 1975, s. 46 (2).   [11] *Ibid*. s. 46 (6).
[12] *Ibid*. s. 46 (3).   [13] *Ibid*. s. 46 (4).

19-62   Where a disposition satisfies the conditions of the above exemptions to a limited extent only, so much of it as satisfies them and so much of it as does not satisfy them are treated as separate dispositions [14]; and where an exempt disposition is of an interest in possession in settled property, there is an exemption from the charge which would otherwise arise under paragraph 4 (1) of Schedule 5 to the Act [14]: *post*, § 22-24.

10. DEEDS OF FAMILY ARRANGEMENT ETC.

19-63   It sometimes happens that beneficiaries under a will or intestacy agree between themselves, by a deed of family arrangement or similar instrument (*e.g.* formal correspondence), to vary the dispositions made under the will or created by the intestacy. The estate is then administered subject to the agreed variations. Section 47 (1) of the Finance Act 1975 (which has been repealed as respects any variation or disclaimer made on or after April 11, 1978 [15]) provided that such a variation should not be a transfer of value if it was made not more than two years after the death and that the Act should apply as if the variations had been effected by the deceased. The Revenue view was that section 47 did not apply to a redistribution of assets which introduced an object who was not an original beneficiary and who was not a member of the family of the deceased; or to an arrangement whereby a beneficiary redirected a gift from which he had already accepted some advantage for himself. There is a similar provision which applies for capital gains tax: *ante*, § 16-20. [16]

Section 68 of the Finance Act 1978, which applies to any variation or disclaimer made on or after April 11, 1978, contains a new provision which supersedes section 47 (above) and no longer requires " a deed of family arrangement or similar instrument." Thus, any written instrument will now suffice and benefits can be directed to anyone even if the redirector has accepted some advantage for himself. The variation or disclaimer must be made within two years after the death and written notice electing that section 68 shall apply must be given to the Board within six months after the date of the instrument or such longer time as the Board may allow. The notice must be given by the person or persons making the instrument *and* by the personal representatives if the variation results in additional tax being payable, except that personal representatives cannot decline to join in an election if they hold sufficient assets to discharge the additional tax.

Section 68 applies whether or not the administration of the estate is complete or the property concerned has been distributed in accordance with the original disposition.

Section 68 applies only to property which was comprised in the deceased's estate immediately before his death (see § 18-08), save that " excluded property " (§ 23-02) is included. Settled property to which the deceased was treated as beneficially entitled under paragraph 3 (1) of Schedule 5 to the

---

[14] F.A. 1975, s. 46 (5).
[15] F.A. 1978, s. 68 (7) and Sched. 13, Pt. V.
[16] Note that the capital gains tax provision in F.A. 1978, s. 52, (*ante*, § 16-20) takes effect from the date of the Royal Assent and not from April 11, 1978, as does s. 68. By " concession " both provisions will be applied from the earlier date: *Hansard*, July 6, 1978, col. 610.

Finance Act 1975 (see § 22-17) is not included, so if property is held for A during the life of X and A predeceases X giving his interest *pur autre vie* to B, section 68 does not apply if B redirects his interest to C.

Section 68 does not apply to a variation or disclaimer made for any consideration in money or money's worth, other than consideration consisting of the making, in respect of another of the dispositions, of a variation or disclaimer to which section 68 applies.

19-64   Three forms of arrangement which were outside the terms of section 47 are made exempt from capital transfer tax by sections 1A and 1B of the Finance Act 1975, as inserted by section 121 of the Finance Act 1976 and by section 68 (4) of the Finance Act 1978. These are:

(1) where property is left on discretionary trusts and, within two years after the death, the trustees distribute it by exercising their discretion: section (1A) prevents a further charge to tax arising on the distribution, *i.e.* in addition to the charge on death; and it treats the distribution as not being a capital distribution [17-18] and as having been made by the deceased's will. This enables a testator to settle property on discretionary trusts, leaving it to his trustees to decide on the disposition of the property. Provided the trustees make the distribution within two years of the death and before any interest in possession subsists in the property, there will be no adverse tax consequences. If the trustees (having power to do so) appoint the property to the settler's spouse, the exemption in § 19-05 will apply and any tax paid on the death will be repayable.

(2) where assets are left to a legatee subject to a request (not legally binding) that the legatee should distribute them in accordance with the testator's wishes: section (1B) prevents a tax charge arising if the legatee carries out the testator's request within two years after the death. The transfer by the legatee is not a transfer of value and the provisions relating to capital transfer tax apply as if the property transferred had been bequeathed by the testator's will.

(3) where a variation results in property being held in trust for a person for a period which ends not more than two years after the death: the disposition at the end of the period is treated as taking effect from its beginning (but not so as to affect the application of the Act to any distribution or application of property during the period).

19-65   On an intestacy, the surviving spouse may, under section 47A of the Administration of Estates Act 1925, elect to redeem his or her life interest for a capital sum. Section 47 (3) of the Finance Act 1975 provides that such an election is not a transfer of value: the surviving spouse is treated as having at all times been entitled to the capital sum.

19-66   Where a person becomes entitled to an interest in settled property but disclaims the interest, then, if the disclaimer is not made for a consideration

---

[17-18] But it is a distribution payment. See § 22-43.

in money or money's worth, the capital transfer tax provisions apply as if he had not become entitled to the interest.[19]

19-67   The Inheritance (Provision for Family and Dependants) Act 1975 empowers the court to make a provision for the family and dependants of a deceased person out of the " net " estate and, in effect, to rewrite the deceased's will, by changing the destination of property. Section 122 of the Finance Act 1976 ensures that when such an order is made there will be the same charges to and exemptions from capital transfer tax as if the will had been made in the terms of the order.

11. DISPOSITIONS ALLOWABLE FOR INCOME TAX OR CONFERRING RETIREMENT BENEFITS

19-68   By section 89 (1) of the Finance Act 1976 a disposition made by a person is not a transfer of value if it is allowable in computing that person's profits or gains for the purposes of income tax or corporation tax or would be so allowable if those profits were sufficient and fell to be so computed. Thus gifts to employees or former employees or their dependants which are deductible as a trade expense (see § 2-51 *et seq.*) are not transfers of value. Section 89 does not apply to gifts which are *not* deductible as a trade expense. Section 89 (1) applies to dispositions after March 26, 1974, and replaces paragraph 9 of Schedule 6 to the Finance Act 1975, which ceases to have effect.

19-69   By section 89 (2), contributions to approved retirement benefits schemes for employees and dispositions to provide benefits on or after retirement for an employee not connected with the disponer or, after death, for the employee's widow or dependants are exempt, provided, in the latter case, the benefits are no greater than could be provided under an approved scheme. The right to occupy a dwelling rent-free or at a rent less than might be expected to be obtained in a transaction at arm's length between persons not connected with each other is treated as a pension of an amount equal to the difference between the rent paid and the rent that might be obtained. Where a disposition satisfies the conditions to a limited extent only, so much of it as satisfies them and so much of it as does not satisfy them are treated as separate dispositions.

12. DISPOSITIONS ON TRUST FOR BENEFIT OF EMPLOYEES

19-70   Dispositions of property to trustees to be held on employee trusts of the description specified in paragraph 17 (1) of Schedule 5 to the Finance Act 1975 are not transfers of value if strict conditions are satisfied.[20] In the case of dispositions by a close company, the trust must permit the property to be

---

[19] F.A. 1975, s. 47 (4).
[20] F.A. 1976, s. 90, as amended by F.A. 1978, s. 67 and Sched. 11.

applied for all or most of the persons employed by or holding office with the company or any one or more of its subsidiaries. In the case of dispositions by an individual, (a) the trustees must at the time of (or within one year after) the transfer hold more than half of the ordinary shares in the company and have powers of voting on all questions affecting the company as a whole which if exercised would yield a majority of the votes capable of being exercised thereon; and (b) there must be no provisions whereby condition (a) can cease to be satisfied without the consent of the trustees.

The exemptions do not apply if the trusts permit any of the property to be applied at any time for the benefit of—

  (a) a person who is a participator in the company making the disposition or, as the case may be, the company whose shares are disposed of; or

  (b) any other person who is a participator in any close company that has made a disposition whereby property became comprised in the same settlement, being a disposition which but for section 90 would have been a transfer of value; or

  (c) any other person who has been a participator in any such company as is mentioned in paragraph (a) or (b) at any time after, or during the 10 years before, the disposition made by that company or, as the case may be, the disposition of its shares; or

  (d) any person who is connected with any person within paragraph (a), (b) or (c).

The participators referred to do not include any participator who on a winding up of the company would not be entitled to 5 per cent. or more of its assets.

It is thought that the conditions of exemption are so strict as to make the exemption of limited use.

CHAPTER 20

THE COMPUTATION OF THE CHARGE

1. GENERAL

20-01 CAPITAL transfer tax is charged on the value transferred by a transfer of value, being any disposition which lessens the value of the transferor's estate; and the amount by which it is less is the measure of the value transferred. A comparison has therefore to be made between the value of the transferor's estate immediately before and immediately after the disposition. The following factors enter into the computation:

(1) The amount or value of the property which forms the subject of the disposition.

(2) Tax and any other costs or expenses incurred by the transferor as a consequence of the disposition. (If it costs the transferor £2,000 in tax and other expenses to transfer assets worth £30,000, the loss to the transferor's estate by reason of the disposition is £32,000. This is the amount on which capital transfer tax is payable.)

Section 2 of this chapter gives the rates of capital transfer tax and explains the cumulative basis on which it operates. Section 3 of this chapter explains how tax and other expenses of the transfer are dealt with. Section 4 summarises the rules of valuation. These are similar to the rules which apply for capital gains tax but there are special provisions (called " related property " rules) to prevent avoidance of capital transfer tax by splitting up valuable assets into a number of less valuable parts as, for example, by splitting a controlling shareholding in a company into a number of minority holdings.

2. RATES OF TAX

The statutory tables

20-02   Capital transfer tax is charged at a rate or rates which are set out in two tables in section 37 (3) of the Finance Act 1975. These tables, which apply to any chargeable transfer made after October 26, 1977,[1] are as follows (the tables applying to any chargeable transfer made on or before that date being in the Appendix in § 26-08):

---

[1] See F.A. 1978, s. 62 (1) and (2) and Sched. 10.

First (Higher Rate) Table

Portion of value		Rate of tax
Lower limit	Upper limit	Per cent.
£	£	
0	25,000	Nil
25,000	30,000	10
30,000	35,000	15
35,000	40,000	20
40,000	50,000	25
50,000	60,000	30
60,000	70,000	35
70,000	90,000	40
90,000	110,000	45
110,000	130,000	50
130,000	160,000	55
160,000	510,000	60
510,000	1,010,000	65
1,010,000	2,010,000	70
2,010,000	—	75

Second (Lower Rate) Table

Portion of value		Rate of tax
Lower limit	Upper limit	Per cent.
£	£	
0	25,000	Nil
25,000	30,000	5
30,000	35,000	7½
35,000	40,000	10
40,000	50,000	12½
50,000	60,000	15
60,000	70,000	17½
70,000	90,000	20
90,000	110,000	22½
110,000	130,000	27½
130,000	160,000	35
160,000	210,000	42½
210,000	260,000	50
260,000	310,000	55
310,000	510,000	60
510,000	1,010,000	65
1,010,000	2,010,000	70
2,010,000	—	75

20-03 The first table applies to transfers made on, or at any time within three years of, the death of the transferor. The second table (with lower rates) applies to any other transfer. It will be noted that each slice of value transferred is charged to tax at rates which progress from nil per cent. for the first £25,000 of value transferred to 75 per cent. where the value transferred exceeds £2,010,000. Note that the rates of tax levied under the first table are double those levied under the second table where the upper limit does not exceed £90,000. Lifetime transfers are thus less costly than transfers on or within three years of death.

The cumulative nature of the tax

20-04 Capital transfer tax applies on a cumulative basis to all chargeable transfers made by an individual from his cradle to his grave. The following example illustrates this. (Exempt transfers are not chargeable transfers (see § 18-02) so exemptions and reliefs are ignored in the example.)

In year 1 A makes a first chargeable transfer of £40,000. The tax payable is as follows (applying the second table):

On the first £25,000	nil	nil
On the next £ 5,000	5 %	£ 250
On the next £ 5,000	7½%	£ 375
On the next £ 5,000	10 %	£ 500
£40,000		£1,125

If in year 2 A makes a second chargeable transfer of £20,000, the amount which was previously transferred (£40,000) is taken into account and is the starting point in the table when computing tax on the £20,000, which is:

On the first £10,000	12½%	£1,250
On the next £10,000	15 %	£1,500
£20,000		£2,750

If in year 6 A dies with a net estate of £45,000, the total amount previously transferred (£60,000) is taken into account and is the starting point in applying the *first* table to the computation of the tax on £45,000, which is:

On the first £10,000	35%	£ 3,500
On the next £20,000	40%	£ 8,000
On the next £15,000	45%	£ 6,750
£45,000		£18,250

The example shows that a cumulative record of all non-exempt gifts made by A since March 26, 1974, is needed to determine the tax payable on any later disposition.

20-05 Where a chargeable transfer (taxed at the lower rates under the second table) is followed by the transferor's death within three years thereafter, extra tax becomes payable in respect of that transfer since, by reason of the transferor's failure to survive the three-year period, the higher rates under the first table apply.[2] The incidence of liability in such a case is discussed in § 24-02. Section 99 of and Schedule 12 to the Finance Act 1976 (applying to tax chargeable on deaths after April 6, 1976) reduce the additional tax payable on transfers made within three years of death where the gift has fallen in value between the time of the gift and the date of the death. The additional tax payable on death is not to exceed the difference between the tax already paid and the tax at the appropriate death rate on the value of the gift at the time of death or, if the property has been sold before the transferor's death, the tax at the appropriate death rate on the sale proceeds. There are special provisions which apply to wasting assets.

---

[2] Where the chargeable transfer is made on or before October 26, 1977, and the transferor dies after that date and within 3 years of the transfer, extra tax is payable only if it would have been chargeable if the first of the new tables had applied to the transfer: F.A. 1978, s. 62 (3). Transfers in fact made after October 26, 1977, but treated as made later by reason of being reported late (§ 25-30A) are to count as made on the earlier date for the purposes of the " 3-year rule ": *ibid*. s. 62 (8).

Transfers of more than one property

20-05A   Section 43 (1) of the Finance Act 1975 provides that where the value transferred by a chargeable transfer is determined by reference to the values of more than one property, the tax chargeable on the value transferred shall be attributable to the respective values in the proportion which they bear to their aggregate, but subject to any provision reducing the amount of tax attributable to the value of any particular property. (An example is a provision which gives relief for foreign tax payable on the same transfer.)

Transfers on the same day

20-05B   Section 43 (2) of the Finance Act 1975 provides that where the value transferred by more than one chargeable transfer made by the same person on the same day depends on the order in which the transfers are made, they shall be treated as made in the order which results in the lowest value chargeable. Subject to this, the rate at which tax is charged on two or more such transfers is the effective rate at which tax would have been charged if those transfers had been a single chargeable transfer of the same total value.[3]

Transfers reported late

20-05C   There are special provisions which apply where, for example, a transfer of value is made in 1978, and the appropriate amount of tax is paid thereon, and the Revenue then discover that an undisclosed transfer was made in (say) 1976. See § 25-30A.

3. LIABILITIES

20-06   Capital transfer tax is charged on the value transferred by a disposition which lessens the value of the transferor's estate. The value transferred is the amount by which the estate is less.

A. *Liabilities resulting from the chargeable transfer*

20-07   A chargeable transfer may give rise to capital transfer tax, capital gains tax, development gains tax, development land tax or stamp duty; and other incidental expenses may be incurred, such as conveyancing costs. All of these, if paid by the transferor, will lessen the value of his estate and, but for some express provision to the contrary, would enter into the computation of the value transferred on which capital transfer tax is leviable. Paragraph 1 (2) of Schedule 10 to the Finance Act 1975 requires that in determining the value of the transferor's estate immediately after the transfer, his liability (and in one case his spouse's liability) to capital transfer tax on the value transferred shall be taken into account but not his liability (if any) for any other tax or duty resulting from the transfer (*e.g.* capital gains tax or stamp duty). Paragraph 6 (*a*) of Schedule 10 likewise requires that incidental expenses incurred by the transferor in making the transfer shall be left out of account. Where tax is taken into account no allowance is made for the fact that it is not due immediately.[4]

---

[3] F.A. 1975, s. 43 (3) added by F.A. 1976, s. 113 in relation to chargeable transfers made after April 15, 1976.   [4] F.A. 1975, Sched. 10, para. 1 (2) (*a*).

20-08   It should be appreciated that the effect of taking a liability into account *immediately after* the transfer is to *increase* the diminution in value of the transferor's estate and so *increase* the value transferred which is chargeable to capital transfer tax. Conversely, the effect of leaving a liability out of account is to reduce the value transferred. The effect of paragraph 1 (2) of Schedule 10 is to require *capital transfer tax* paid or payable by the transferor to be included in reckoning the amount on which such tax is payable: " grossing up " is required: see § 20-10. Where the transferee agrees to pay (or pays) the capital transfer tax, no grossing up is needed: see § 20-15.

20-09   Capital gains tax borne by the donee in respect of chargeable gains of the transferor is treated as reducing the value transferred by the chargeable transfer [5]; so also are the transferor's incidental expenses in making the transfer which are borne by the person benefiting from the transfer. [6]

Grossing up for capital transfer tax

20-10   In the case of many lifetime transfers, the capital transfer tax on the disposition of property is paid by the transferor and has therefore to be taken into account in computing the value transferred, in accordance with the basic principle stated in § 18-03. If A wishes to give a house to B who has no resources out of which to pay the tax or, if B has such resources, A nevertheless pays the tax (having no right of indemnity against B: see § 20-15), the value transferred (on which tax is levied) is the value of the house plus the amount of the tax.

> Thus if A makes a lifetime transfer of an asset worth £40,000, this is treated as a transfer of value of such an amount as, after deduction of capital transfer tax calculated on that amount, leaves £40,000. If this is the first chargeable transfer made by A, the " grossed up " amount in the case of a lifetime transfer made after October 26, 1977, is £41,285·71. The tax on this grossed up amount is £1,285·71.

There is no grossing-up in the case of a lifetime transfer if the transferee pays, or agrees to pay, the tax: see § 20-15. There are many advantages where the transferee pays the tax: there is no grossing-up, so less tax is payable, and there are many cases in which the tax can be paid by instalments and (within limits) free of interest: see §§ 25-26 *et seq.*

> Thus if in the previous example A pays the tax, the tax is on £40,000. The tax is therefore £1,125 and not £1,285·71.

If the asset had been worth £150,000, the tax payable (on the lifetime scale) by A would be £45,000 because A would be treated as making a transfer of value of £195,000. If B paid the tax (on £150,000 only), the tax would be £26,625.

Table A and Table B apply to transfers made otherwise than on or within three years before the death. [7] Table A shows the amount of tax which is

---

[5] *Ibid.* para. 4 (1). See F.A. 1965, Sched. 7, para. 19 in § 16-18.
[6] F.A. 1975, Sched. 10, para. 6. " Incidental expenses " are not defined but *cf.* F.A. 1965, Sched. 7, para. 4 in § 16-30.
[7] Capital transfer tax tables are available from law bookshops.

payable where the transferee bears the tax on a transfer having a value in the range in the left-hand column, *i.e.* where there is no " grossing up." Table B applies where grossing up is necessary because the transfer is a " net " transfer.

Table C gives the scale of rates applicable to transfers on death or within three years before death.

20-11

Table A

Lifetime transfers—transferee bearing the tax

Gross cumulative total		Rate of tax on value within range	Capital transfer tax payable				
£	£	%	£	£			£
25,000—	30,000	5	Nil +	1/20	of each £ over		25,000
30,000—	35,000	7·5	250 +	3/40	,, ,, ,, ,,		30,000
35,000—	40,000	10	625 +	1/10	,, ,, ,, ,,		35,000
40,000—	50,000	12·5	1,125 +	1/8	,, ,, ,, ,,		40,000
50,000—	60,000	15	2,375 +	3/20	,, ,, ,, ,,		50,000
60,000—	70,000	17·5	3,875 +	7/40	,, ,, ,, ,,		60,000
70,000—	90,000	20	5,625 +	1/5	,, ,, ,, ,,		70,000
90,000—	110,000	22·5	9,625 +	9/40	,, ,, ,, ,,		90,000
110,000—	130,000	27·5	14,125 +	11/40	,, ,, ,, ,,		110,000
130,000—	160,000	35	19,625 +	7/20	,, ,, ,, ,,		130,000
160,000—	210,000	42·5	30,125 +	17/40	,, ,, ,, ,,		160,000
210,000—	260,000	50	51,375 +	1/2	,, ,, ,, ,,		210,000
260,000—	310,000	55	76,375 +	11/20	,, ,, ,, ,,		260,000
310,000—	510,000	60	103,875 +	3/5	,, ,, ,, ,,		310,000
510,000—1,010,000		65	223,875 +	13/20	,, ,, ,, ,,		510,000
1,010,000—2,010,000		70	548,875 +	7/10	,, ,, ,, ,,		1,010,000
over 2,010,000		75	1,248,875 +	3/4	,, ,, ,, ,,		2,010,000

Table B

Lifetime transfers—transferor bearing the tax
Grossing up table

Net cumulative total		Capital transfer tax payable				
£	£	£	£			£
25,000—	29,750	Nil +	1/19	of each £ over		25,000
29,750—	34,375	250 +	3/37	,, ,, ,, ,,		29,750
34,375—	38,875	625 +	1/9	,, ,, ,, ,,		34,375
38,875—	47,625	1,125 +	1/7	,, ,, ,, ,,		38,875
47,625—	56,125	2,375 +	3/17	,, ,, ,, ,,		47,625
56,125—	64,375	3,875 +	7/33	,, ,, ,, ,,		56,125
64,375—	80,375	5,625 +	1/4	,, ,, ,, ,,		64,375
80,375—	95,875	9,625 +	9/31	,, ,, ,, ,,		80,375
95,875—110,375		14,125 +	11/29	,, ,, ,, ,,		95,875
110,375—129,875		19,625 +	7/13	,, ,, ,, ,,		110,375
129,875—158,625		30,125 +	17/23	,, ,, ,, ,,		129,875
158,625—183,625		51,375 +	1	,, ,, ,, ,,		158,625
183,625—206,125		76,375 +	11/9	,, ,, ,, ,,		183,625
206,125—286,125		103,875 +	3/2	,, ,, ,, ,,		206,125
286,125—461,125		223,875 +	13/7	,, ,, ,, ,,		286,125
461,125—761,125		548,875 +	7/3	,, ,, ,, ,,		461,125
over 761,125		1,248,875 +	3	,, ,, ,, ,,		761,125

Table C

Scale of Rates of Tax for transfers on death or within 3 years before death

Gross cumulative total		Rate of tax on value within range	Capital transfer tax payable						
£	£	%	£	£					£
Exceeds 25,000 but not	30,000	10	Nil +	1/10	of each £	over	25,000
,, 30,000 ,, ,,	35,000	15	500 +	3/20	,,	,,	,,	,,	30,000
,, 35,000 ,, ,,	40,000	20	1,250 +	1/5	,,	,,	,,	,,	35,000
,, 40,000 ,, ,,	50,000	25	2,250 +	1/4	,,	,,	,,	,,	40,000
,, 50,000 ,, ,,	60,000	30	4,750 +	3/10	,,	,,	,,	,,	50,000
,, 60,000 ,, ,,	70,000	35	7,750 +	7/20	,,	,,	,,	,,	60,000
,, 70,000 ,, ,,	90,000	40	11,250 +	2/5	,,	,,	,,	,,	70,000
,, 90,000 ,, ,,	110,000	45	19,250 +	9/20	,,	,,	,,	,,	90,000
,, 110,000 ,, ,,	130,000	50	28,250 +	1/2	,,	,,	,,	,,	110,000
,, 130,000 ,, ,,	160,000	55	38,250 +	11/20	,,	,,	,,	,,	130,000
,, 160,000 ,, ,,	510,000	60	54,750 +	3/5	,,	,,	,,	,,	160,000
,, 510,000 ,, ,,	1,010,000	65	264,750 +	13/20	,,	,,	,,	,,	510,000
,, 1,010,000 ,, ,,	2,010,000	70	589,750 +	7/10	,,	,,	,,	,,	1,010,000
,, 2,010,000		75	1,289,750 +	3/4	,,	,,	,,	,,	2,010,000

20-12   The provisions discussed in § 20-07 relate to the taking into account of liabilities immediately after the transfer. Subject to those provisions and to the qualifications that follow, the general rule is that in determining the value of the transferor's estate at *any* time, his liabilities at that time shall be taken into account.[8] Thus in the case of a person's death, capital transfer tax is payable on the value of the estate less liabilities.

B. *Other liabilities*

20-13   Except in the case of a liability imposed by law, only liabilities incurred by the transferor for a consideration in money or money's worth are taken into account.[9] Thus if A voluntarily charges his estate with the payment of £3,000 per annum to B for seven years, this liability is ignored in applying the capital transfer tax rules to each payment which is made to B and in valuing A's estate on A's death.

20-14   A liability which falls to be discharged after the time at which it is to be taken into account is to be valued when it is to be taken into account.[10] Thus if at the time of A's death A owes £x to B, payable five years hence, the amount of £x has to be discounted to allow for the time before payment is due (unless the debt is for capital transfer tax).

20-15   A liability in respect of which there is a right to reimbursement may be taken into account only to the extent (if any) that reimbursement cannot reasonably be expected to be obtained.[11] Thus if A owes B £x but A has the right to recover this amount from C, A's debt is left out of account if A can reasonably be expected to recover the debt from C. If A makes a transfer of value to B, A is primarily liable to pay the capital transfer tax: § 24-01; but

---

[8] F.A. 1975, Sched. 10, para. 1 (1).
[10] *Ibid.* para. 1 (4).
[11] F.A. 1975, para. 1 (5).
[9] *Ibid.* para. 1 (3).

if B agrees to bear the capital transfer tax attributable thereto, A's right to reimbursement equals his liability to the Revenue for tax and so no grossing up is required.

20-16   Where a liability, such as a mortgage, is an incumbrance on any property, it must so far as possible be taken to reduce the value of *that* property. Where a liability is not an incumbrance on property in the United Kingdom and is a liability to a person resident outside and falling to be discharged outside the United Kingdom, it must so far as possible be taken to reduce the value of property outside the United Kingdom although not an incumbrance on such property.[12] These rules may be important as affecting the incidence of liability as between different transferees.

4. VALUATION

Open market value

20-17   Section 38 (1) of the Finance Act 1975 states that, except as otherwise provided, the value at any time of any property shall for the purposes of capital transfer tax be the price which the property might reasonably be expected to fetch if sold in the open market at that time. No reduction is to be allowed on the ground that the whole property is hypothetically to be placed on the market at one and the same time.

This is the rule as to valuation which applies for capital gains tax purposes and which applied for estate duty purposes. Market value as ascertained for the purposes of capital transfer tax is to be taken to be the market value for the purposes of capital gains tax.[13] There are, however, a number of special provisions which apply for capital transfer tax and which are considered in the following paragraphs.

Where the provisions relating to capital transfer tax have to be applied on the *death* of an individual, the property to be valued is the whole of the property comprised in the deceased's estate: see § 18-14. Where the provisions have to be applied to a *lifetime transfer* by an individual, the inquiry is directed to finding the diminution in the value of the transferor's " estate " in consequence of that transfer, so the property to be valued is the actual property transferred or, if the property transferred diminishes the value of other property of which it previously formed part, that other property. Then in the example in § 18-03, the set of books before and after the transfer has to be valued.

Restriction on freedom to dispose

20-18   Paragraph 5 of Schedule 10 deals with the case where a contract, such as the grant of an option, excludes or restricts the right to dispose of property (thereby diminishing its value) and the property is later disposed of. The exclusion or restriction is taken into account on the later disposal only to the extent (if any) that consideration in money or money's worth was given for

---

[12] *Ibid.* paras. 2 and 3.
[13] F.A. 1965, s. 26, as substituted by F.A. 1975, Sched. 12, para. 13.

it; but if the contract itself was a chargeable transfer on which tax was charged (or was part of associated operations which together were a chargeable transfer), a deduction is allowed for the value transferred thereby (calculated as if no tax had been chargeable on it) or by so much of it as was attributable to the exclusion or restriction.

Examples

(i) A grants B an option to purchase property at any time within three years for £20,000, its then market value. B exercises the option when the property is worth £39,000. No consideration was paid by B on the grant of the option. The option is ignored when it is exercised, so A makes a transfer of value of £19,000.

(ii) A grants B an option to purchase property at any time within three years for £20,000. The property is then worth £35,000. (This is a chargeable transfer by A and tax is payable on the value transferred thereby, say, £15,000.) After two years B exercises the option, paying £20,000 when the property is then worth £39,000. This is a further chargeable transfer by A. The value transferred by the contract (£15,000) is deductible from the value of the property. Thus the value transferred on the exercise of the option (assuming B pays the tax) is (£39,000 — £15,000) less £20,000 = £4,000.

Where the contract was made before March 27, 1974, these provisions apply only if the first chargeable transfer is on death.[14] Thus if after March 26, 1974, an option is exercised which was granted before that date, any diminution in the value of the grantor's estate resulting from the grant of the option is taken into account and the value transferred reckoned accordingly.

Valuation of related property

20-19 Property is related to the property comprised in a person's estate if either (a) it is comprised in the estate of his spouse; or (b) it is, or is part of, the property comprised in a settlement made by him or his spouse before March 27, 1974, where no interest in possession subsists in that property or part. (See Chap. 22.)

Paragraph 7 of Schedule 10 to the Finance Act 1975 is designed to prevent the owner of an asset avoiding capital transfer tax by dividing up the asset into a number of less valuable parts by a transfer of part to the owner's spouse and/or trustees of a discretionary settlement made by him or his spouse. But for paragraph 7 an owner of (say) 90 per cent. of the shares in XYZ Limited could make an exempt transfer of half of his holding to his wife, with the consequence that each would have a 45 per cent. holding with an aggregate value less than the value of the owner's original 90 per cent. shareholding. Other property which may be reduced in value in this way includes, for example, an area of land which becomes less valuable when divided into a number of smaller units.

The Act provides that where the value of any property comprised in a person's estate would be less than the appropriate proportion of the value of the aggregate of that and any related property, the value shall be the appropriate proportion of the value of that aggregate. Thus in the example

---

[14] F.A. 1975, Sched. 10, para. 5 (2).

mentioned above the owner's 45 per cent. holding (if transferred) is treated as having a value equal to one-half of the value of a 90 per cent. holding.

Section 103 of the Finance Act 1976 extends the related property provisions to property exempted on a transfer to a charity or other privileged body specified in paragraphs 11–13 of Schedule 6 to the 1975 Act (§§ 19-20 to 19-22). The section applies to transfers after March 26, 1974.

Paragraph 9A in Schedule 10 to the Finance Act 1975 provides a relief where property valued on death on a related property basis is sold within three years of the death at less than the value at the time of death.

Value of lessor's interest

20-20 A lease of property not granted for full consideration in money or money's worth is treated as a settlement in certain circumstances: *post*, § 22-09. Where this applies, paragraph 8 of Schedule 10 to the Finance Act 1975 provides that the value of the lessor's interest in the property shall be taken to be a proportion of the value of the property, the proportion being that which the value of the consideration at the time the lease was granted bore to what would then have been the value of full consideration in money or money's worth.

Thus if L grants a lease to T for no consideration, the value of L's interest is taken to be nil if L subsequently transfers that interest. If L grants a lease to B at what was then 80 per cent. of full consideration, L's interest is treated as worth 80 per cent. of the value of the property. The balance represents the value of T's interest: see § 22-21. L's interest in the case of a lease which is treated as a settlement is not excluded property (see § 23-03) so a charge to capital transfer tax may arise on any transfer of value by L.

Value of amounts due

20-21 In determining the value of a right to receive a sum due under any obligation, paragraph 10 of Schedule 10 to the Finance Act 1975 requires it to be assumed that the obligation will be duly discharged, except if or to the extent that recovery of the sum is impossible or not reasonably practicable and has not become so by any act or omission of the person to whom the sum is due. If, for example, X is entitled to a sum of money which a foreign exchange control authority will not allow to be remitted to the United Kingdom for five years, due account of this has to be taken in valuing the right.

Value of life policies, etc.

20-22 Paragraph 11 of Schedule 10 to the Finance Act 1975 provides for the value of certain life assurance policies and deferred annuities which are transferred otherwise than on the death of the life assured. Briefly, their value is not to be less than their total cost allowing for adjustment where there has been, *e.g.* a partial surrender. There are exceptions which apply to term policies and unit linked policies.

Farm cottages

20-23 Where agricultural property is valued and the property includes cottages occupied by persons employed solely for agricultural purposes in connection with the property (*i.e.* tied cottages), paragraph 12 of Schedule 10 to the Finance Act 1975 requires that no account is to be taken of the fact that the cottages are suitable for residential occupation by persons other than agricultural workers.

Open market price of unquoted shares and securities

20-24 In determining the price which unquoted shares or securities (*i.e.* those not quoted on a recognised stock exchange) might reasonably be expected to fetch if sold in the open market, paragraph 13 of Schedule 10 to the Finance Act 1975 requires it to be assumed that in that market there is available to any prospective purchaser all the information which a prudent prospective purchaser might reasonably require if he were proposing to purchase them from a willing vendor by private treaty and at arm's length.

Value transferred on death

20-25 Capital transfer tax is charged on the death of a person as if, immediately before his death, he had made a transfer of value equal to the value of his estate at that time. A valuation " immediately before " the death will take no account of changes in value which occur, or liabilities which arise, because of the death. It will take no account, for example, of an annuity purchased by the deceased which ceases on his death or the proceeds of an insurance policy taken out by a third person and which is payable on the deceased's death: the former should be excluded and the latter included in computing liability to capital transfer tax.

Paragraph 9 of Schedule 10 to the Finance Act 1975 meets this situation by providing that where, *by reason of* a person's death, the property comprised in his estate is added to or there is an increase or decrease in its value, any change having this effect is treated as having occurred *before* the death. The termination on death of any interest or the passing of any interest by survivorship does not fall within this rule: hence the terminated interest, such as a life interest or an interest passing by survivorship, is treated as terminating immediately after the death and is kept in charge to capital transfer tax. It follows that an annuity ceasing on death which is payable out of settled property will give rise to tax because the deceased had an *interest* in that property; whereas an annuity ceasing on death which exists only in contract will give rise to no liability. Decreases in the value of unquoted shares by alterations in rights to take effect on the deceased's death also fall outside the rule so the full value of the shares (ignoring the alterations) is kept in charge to tax.

Where on the death there is an undischarged liability to capital transfer tax, it is deductible from the value of the estate only if the tax is actually paid out of the estate, *i.e.* and not by another liable person, *e.g.* the donee in the case of a lifetime transfer.[15]

---

[15] F.A. 1976, s. 100 (applying to deaths after April 5, 1976).

20-26   An allowance is made for reasonable funeral expenses including (by concession) a reasonable amount for mourning.[16]

20-26A   A liability to make payments or transfer assets under a disposition within section 40 of the Finance Act 1975 (*post*, § 21-07) is to be computed as if the amount or value of the payments or assets were reduced by the chargeable portion thereof.

20-27   Where property is situated outside the United Kingdom, extra expense may be incurred in administering or realising the property and, where the expense is shown to be attributable to the situation of the property, an allowance is made against the value of the property of up to 5 per cent. of its value.

20-28   There are special provisions which apply with respect to the valuation of qualifying investments (including unquoted securities) which are sold at a loss within 12 months immediately following the date of the death.[17] The provisions, which are of considerable complexity, are to be found in Part II of Schedule 10 to the Finance Act 1975. Section 101 of and Schedule 13 to the Finance Act 1976 (applicable to deaths after April 6, 1976) contain relieving provisions where land is sold within three years of the death for less than its market value at the time of death. In both cases, a claim for reduction in the value of the deceased's estate as at the date of his death may be made.

20-29   Paragraph 9A in Schedule 10 to the Finance Act 1975 provides a relief where property valued on death on a related property basis (see § 20-19) is sold within three years of the death at less than the value at the time of death.

Open market price of quoted shares and securities

20-30   The market price of quoted shares and securities is found by applying the " quarter-up " rule, *i.e.* if the quotation is 104–106, the market price is found by adding to 104 one-quarter of the difference between 104 and 106, *i.e.* 104½.

A special relief is available if shares or securities are sold within 12 months of a death for less than the market price at the time of death.[18]

---

[16] Concession E1.
[17] And see F.A. 1976, s. 104, which applies when a quotation is temporarily suspended.
[18] F.A. 1975, Sched. 10, Pt. II.

CHAPTER 21

OTHER CHARGES

1. CLOSE COMPANIES

21-01 CAPITAL transfer tax is charged on the value transferred by a chargeable transfer, which is defined as a transfer of value made by an individual: *ante*, § 18-02. Hence a company is not chargeable to capital transfer tax: but a company may make a disposition which is a transfer of value, the company's property being for this purpose treated as its " estate." Transfers of value by United Kingdom companies will be rare but may occur if, for example, assets are sold at an undervalue or purchased at an overvalue. Section 39 of the Finance Act 1975 enables the Revenue, in effect, to treat a transfer of value made by a close company as if it had been made by its participators. For this purpose " close company " means a company within the meaning of the Corporation Tax Acts which is, or would, if resident in the United Kingdom, be a close company for the purposes of those Acts (§§ 15-07 *et seq.*) [1]; and " participator " has the meaning in § 15-02 except that a person who qualifies as a participator by reason only of being a loan creditor is excluded. [1]

21-02 Section 39 (1) of the Finance Act 1975 provides that where a close company makes a transfer of value, tax shall be charged as if each individual to whom an amount is apportioned under the section had made a transfer of value of such amount as after deduction of tax (if any) would be equal to the amount so apportioned, less the amount (if any) by which the value of his estate is more than it would be but for the company's transfer. For this purpose his estate is treated as not including any rights or interests in the company: thus the measure of the liability is the value transferred by the company, not the amount by which the value of the participator's shares or other interest in the company is diminished in consequence of the transfer. The participator's estate will increase in value where the company's transfer is to the participator himself (or to another company in which the participator has an interest [2]): the exclusion of this increase is necessary to avoid a double charge to capital transfer tax. It follows that where a company makes a transfer of value to one of several participators, an apportionment can be made to all of them; but the participator to whom the transfer was made gets credit to the extent to which his estate was enriched by the transfer. A surrender for group relief of surplus advance corporation tax is not a transfer of value. [3]

21-03 Where an apportionment is made under section 39, the value transferred by the company's transfer is apportioned among the participators according

---

[1] F.A. 1975, s. 39 (6).
[2] See F.A. 1975, s. 39 (8D) inserted by F.A. 1976, s. 118.
[3] F.A. 1975, s. 39 (6A) inserted by F.A. 1976, s. 118.

419

to their respective rights and interests in the company immediately before the transfer, including rights and interests in the assets of the company available for distribution among the participators in the event of a winding up or in any other circumstances. Apportionments will not be made to preference shares where this has only a small effect on their value.[4] An amount which is apportioned to a close company can be further sub-apportioned among its participators, and so on.[5] There are special provisions which apply when the participators are trustees of settled property (see *post*, § 22-38) and where there are inter-group transfers.[6]

21-04   In two cases no apportionment is made [7]:

(a) where the value transferred by the company is attributable to any payment or transfer of assets to any person which falls to be taken into account in computing that person's profits or gains or losses for the purposes of income tax or corporation tax: thus if a company purchases an asset at an overvalue from a trader, no apportionment to any participators can be made in respect of that transfer of value;

(b) where the amount, if apportioned, would be apportioned to an individual domiciled outside the United Kingdom and the amount is attributable to the value of any property outside the United Kingdom.

" Golden handshakes," in the sense of payments made by a company for no consideration, may fall within the exemption in (a).

Liability for tax

21-05   The persons liable for the tax chargeable under section 39 are [8] the company and, so far as the tax remains unpaid after it ought to have been paid, the persons to whom any amounts have been apportioned and any individual (whether such a person or not) the value of whose estate is increased by the company's transfer; but

(a) a person to whom not more than 5 per cent. of the value transferred is apportioned is not as such liable for any of the tax and the deemed transfer by him is left out of account where, on a subsequent transfer by that person, it becomes necessary to decide what previous transfers have been made [9];

(b) each of the other persons to whom any part of the value has been apportioned is liable only for such part of the tax as corresponds to that part of that value; and

(c) a person is not, as a person the value of whose estate is increased, liable for a greater amount than the amount of the increase.[8]

---

[4] F.A. 1975, s. 39 (8A) inserted by F.A. 1976, s. 118.
[5] *Ibid.* s. 39 (2) and (8).
[6] *Ibid.* s. 39 (8B) inserted by F.A. 1976, s. 118.
[7] *Ibid.* s. 39 (2).
[8] *Ibid.* s. 39 (3).
[9] *Ibid.* s. 39 (4).

Alterations in capital as deemed dispositions

21-06   Section 39 (5) of the Finance Act 1975 provides that where there is at any time an alteration (including an extinguishment [10]) in a close company's share or loan capital not quoted on a recognised stock exchange or any alteration in any rights attaching to such shares or debentures, the alteration shall be treated as having been made by a disposition made at that time by the participators and shall not be taken to have affected the value immediately before that time of the shares or debentures not so quoted. [11] Hence an alteration or extinguishment of share or loan capital by which value passes out of the shares may give rise to a charge to capital transfer tax. (Compare the capital gains tax provision, *ante*, § 16-36.)

2. DELAYED TRANSFERS OF VALUE

21-07   Section 40 of the Finance Act 1975 deals with the situation where a disposition made for a consideration in money or money's worth is a transfer of value (as in the case of a sale by the transferor at an undervalue or a purchase by the transferor at an overvalue) and any payments made or assets transferred by the transferor in pursuance of the disposition are made or transferred more than one year after the disposition is made. Supposing, for example, P agrees to buy an asset worth £20,000 from V for £35,000, payment to be made by five equal instalments of £7,000 payable over a five-year period. In such a case value is transferred by P in stages and section 40 imposes a tax charge in stages. It achieves this by providing that tax (if any) shall be charged as if (i) any payment made or asset transferred in pursuance of the disposition were a separate disposition made, without consideration, at the payment or transfer date; and (ii) as if the amount of the payment made or the value of the asset transferred on each of those separate dispositions were the chargeable portion of the payment or asset. [12]

21-08   The chargeable portion of any payment made or asset transferred at any time is such portion of its value at that time as if found by applying to it the fraction of which—

(a) the numerator is the value actually transferred by the disposition in (i) above, calculated as if no tax were payable on it; and

(b) the denominator is the value, at the time of that disposition, of the aggregate of the payments made or to be made and assets transferred or to be transferred by the transferor in pursuance of it. [13]

Thus (in the example) P is treated as making five separate transfers

$$\text{of } £7,000 \times \frac{£15,000}{35,000} = £3,000.$$

---

[10] F.A. 1975, s. 39 (6).
[11] See generally F.A. 1976, s. 118.
[12] *Ibid*. s. 40 (1). And see § 20-26A.
[13] *Ibid*. s. 40 (2).

3. Free Loans etc.

21-09 Where an *individual* (" the lender ") allows another person (" the borrower ") the use of money or other property in any year, the lender is treated as making a disposition as a result of which the value of his estate is reduced by the amount (if any) by which any consideration for the use falls short of the cost to him of allowing it. The disposition is treated as made at the end of the year or, if earlier, at the time when the use comes to an end. " Year " means the period of 12 months beginning with April 6. An individual who makes a revocable gift of property is treated as allowing its use, so long as the gift continues revocable. [14]

This provision in section 115 (1) of the Finance Act 1976 does not apply in the following cases [15]:

(1) where the use of the property is allowed for a period specified in advance, or where in any other case the lender has no right to terminate the use immediately after it begins: section 115 (1) does not apply in relation to use before the expiration of the specified period or, as the case may be, before the earliest time when the lender could terminate the use if he exercised his right to do so at the earliest opportunity.

The explanation for (1) is that if L lends money at no interest (or a low rate of interest) for a fixed or minimum period (L having no right of recall until the expiration of that period), this is a transfer of value under general CTT principles (see § 18-04) and the diminution in L's estate is measured as the difference between the amount lent and the value of L's rights under the agreement. Section 115 (1) applies in and from the year in which the period expires.

(2) In relation to any use of property allowed to the borrower at a time when it is mainly used by the lender or the lender's spouse.

This lets out, *e.g.* the " loan " of a house normally used by the lender.

(3) In relation to the use of property for a period which is less than 12 months unless that period falls within a period of 24 months during which the lender allows the borrower the use of that property or similar property for periods which amount in aggregate to 12 months or more. In calculating the aggregate period, (i) periods which are within exceptions (1) and (2) and (ii) periods during which a commercial rate of interest or a commercial rent was charged, are left out of account.

(4) Where the borrower is a company if (a) it is not a close company [16]; or (b) the lender or his spouse is beneficially entitled to not less than 90 per cent. in nominal value of its issued ordinary shares; or (c) it is not an investment company and either (i) the lender or his spouse is a participator in the company or its holding company or has been such a participator at any time during the year or either of the two

---

[14] F.A. 1976, s. 115 (9).
[15] *Ibid.* s. 115 (2)–(8). Definitions are in s. 115 (10).
[16] See § 21-01.

preceding years; or (ii) the lender's spouse died during the year or either of the two preceding years and was at any time during the three years ending with the year in which he died a participator in the company or its holding company.

(5) Where the borrower is a firm if (a) the lender or his spouse is a partner or has been a partner at any time during the year or either of the two preceding years; or (b) the lender's spouse died during the year or either of the two preceding years and was a partner at any time during the three years ending with the year in which he died. There is no requirement that the lender (or his spouse) should actively participate in the partnership business: it is sufficient that the lender (or his spouse) is, or was during the period referred to, a partner.

(6) To a loan on which a person is chargeable to income tax under Schedule E by virtue of section 66 (1) of the Finance Act 1976 (see § 3-49). Note that section 115 of the Finance Act 1976 applies only to free loans, etc., by *individuals*; it does not apply to free loans, etc., by *companies*.

The exemptions discussed in Chapter 20 have to be considered in relation to free loans, etc. Thus, for example, transfers between spouses (§ 19-02), transfers within the annual £2,000 limit (§ 19-07), transfers within the normal expenditure out of income exemption (§ 19-11) and loans to charities are exempt.

Measure of liability

21-10   The measure of liability where section 115 (1) of the Finance Act 1976 applies is the cost to the lender of allowing the use of the money or other property. In the case of money or land, the cost is taken to be equal to the consideration which might be expected in a transaction on the same terms as those on which the use is allowed (apart from terms as to consideration) made at arm's length between disconnected persons.[17] In the case of other property, such as chattels (including wasting assets) it is the annual value of the use of the property plus any expense incurred by the lender (*e.g.* on maintenance). If the property is hired to the lender and the annual value of the hire charges is greater than the annual value of the use of the property, the former is substituted.[18]

21-11   Capital transfer tax is charged by reference to the diminution in the estate of the transferor (§ 18-03). If the lender of money or land in fact received interest or rent, this would be taxable as income: hence the diminution in the estate consequent on not charging interest or rent is the net loss after income tax. Consistently with this principle, section 116 (3) of the Finance Act 1976 requires that if the property is money or land the amount arrived at under section 115 (1) shall be reduced by the income tax which would be chargeable in respect of that amount (after taking account in the case of land of any deductions which might be made for the purposes of Schedule A

---

[17] F.A. 1976, s. 115 (1).
[18] *Ibid.* s. 115 (2).

(§§ 6-27 *et seq.*)) if it were the highest part of the lender's total income. In calculating that income, any sums mentioned in section 529 of the Taxes Act 1970 (top-slicing relief) are to be disregarded.

Section 117 of the Finance Act 1976 makes a number of modifications to the exemptions from capital transfer tax in Schedule 6 to the 1975 Act (see §§ 19-01 *et seq.*) to take account of these provisions which supersede, as from April 6, 1976, the provisions in section 41 of the Finance Act 1975.[19] For example, the £100,000 limit in § 19-20 does not apply to loans, etc., to charities and political parties.

4. Annuity Purchased in Conjunction with Life Policy

21-12 The nature of back to back insurance arrangements was mentioned briefly in § 19-12. Section 42 of the Finance Act 1975 imposes a special charge in respect of back to back life policies where such policies are taken out with an annuity on the same life as part of an associated operation. In certain circumstances the person taking out the policy is treated as making a transfer of value.

---

[19] F.A. 1976, s. 115 (11).

CHAPTER 22

SETTLED PROPERTY

1. INTRODUCTION

22-01 THIS chapter begins by first considering the definition for capital transfer tax purposes of the term " settlement " and related expressions. The settlement provisions in the legislation differentiate between

    (1) settled property in which some person is beneficially entitled to an interest in possession, such as a life interest or an annuity; and

    (2) settled property in which there is no interest in possession, *e.g.* property held on discretionary trusts; and

    (3) special classes of trust such as superannuation schemes, trusts for employees, protective trusts and trusts for the benefit of mentally disabled persons etc.

22-02 It is important to observe that the charges to tax are imposed by reference to settled property and property comprised in a settlement and not by reference to settlements as such. This is because a single settlement may require that some property should be held on one class of trusts and other property on a different class of trusts; or the trusts on which property is held may change from time to time.

22-03 In the case of settled property falling within (1), it is inevitable that the interest in possession will at some time come to an end, either on death or by effluxion of time, if the holder of the interest has not previously disposed of it. The legislation makes the coming to an end of the interest (*e.g.* the death of a life tenant) the occasion of charge to capital transfer tax and, where the interest is disposed of otherwise than for full consideration in money or money's worth (*e.g.* where the life tenant surrenders his interest to the remainderman), this is treated as if it were the coming to an end of the interest.

    In the case of settled property falling within (2) there is by definition no interest which will come to an end. In this case capital transfer tax is charged on all capital distributions made or treated as made; and property which remains undistributed is subject to a periodic charge as if it had been distributed.

Property put into settlement

22-04 The disposition by which property becomes comprised in a settlement will be a chargeable transfer unless either the transfer is exempt or is not a transfer of value or the property is excluded property or falls to be left out of account under one of the reliefs etc., discussed in Chapter 19. Tax on the making of a settlement is primarily payable by the settlor in the case of a lifetime transfer or by the settlor's personal representatives in the case of a will trust: see § 24-01 and § 24-05. This chapter is, however, concerned with

425

charges to capital transfer tax which may arise *after* the property has become settled property.

2. DEFINITION OF " SETTLEMENT " AND RELATED EXPRESSIONS

Settlement

22-05　The word " settlement " is defined [1] for purposes of capital transfer tax as meaning any disposition or dispositions of property, whether effected by instrument, by parol or by operation of law (*e.g.* under the statutory provisions which apply on an intestacy), or partly in one way and partly in another, whereby the property is for the time being

(a) held in trust for persons in succession (*e.g.* to A for life with remainder to B absolutely) or for any person subject to a contingency (*e.g.* to A if he shall attain the age of 25 years); or

(b) held by trustees on trust to accumulate the whole or part of any income of the property or with power to make payments out of that income at the discretion of the trustees or some other person, with or without power to accumulate surplus income (*e.g.* the common type of discretionary settlement); or

(c) charged or burdened (otherwise than for full consideration in money or money's worth paid for his own use or benefit to the person making the disposition), with the payment of any annuity or other periodical payment payable for a life or any other limited or terminable period.

22-06　The definition includes property which would be so held or charged or burdened if the disposition or dispositions were regulated by the law of any part of the United Kingdom; or whereby, under the law of any other country, the administration of the property is for the time being governed by provisions equivalent in effect to those which would apply if the property were so held, charged or burdened. [2]

22-07　Note that the definition of settlement in § 22-05 requires a disposition or dispositions of property. The word " disposition " is not defined but it seems from the use of the term " whereby " and the sub-paragraphs (a)–(c) that follow that any instrument or court order, etc., which causes property to be held in trust or charged or burdened in one of the ways enumerated in the sub-paragraphs is a " disposition " whether or not any actual transfer of property is made. An instrument whereby A declares himself trustee of property for B for life is as much a settlement as is a disposition by A to trustees to hold upon trust for B for life. Thus if A voluntarily charges his property with the payment of an annuity to B during B's life, it is thought that this creates a settlement under sub-paragraph (c) and that a charge to capital transfer tax will arise on the cesser of the annuity. Note that there is

---

[1] F.A. 1975, Sched. 5, para. 1 (1) and (2). In Scotland an entail and a deed charging an annuity on rents or other property is a settlement: *ibid.* para. 1 (4) and (5). For the capital gains tax definition of " settled property," see *ante*, § 16-21.

[2] F.A. 1975, Sched. 5, para. 1 (2).

no settlement where property is charged with the payment of a perpetual annuity; nor where the annuity is granted for full consideration paid to the grantor.

> Thus if A sells Blackacre to B in consideration of an annual rentcharge secured on Blackacre and payable to A for life or for any other limited or terminal period, Blackacre is not settled property.

22-08 *Annuities to retired partners.* Where annuities payable to retiring partners are secured only by the personal covenants of continuing partners, there is no " settled property." The position is otherwise where such annuities are *charged* on property: then a charge to capital transfer tax will arise on the coming to an end of the annuity, unless it can be shown that the persons paying the annuity obtained full consideration in money or money's worth. It is thought that this condition will normally be satisfied in the case of annuities of a reasonable amount provided under commercial partnership agreements for the benefit of partners and their widows.

22-09 *Leases for lives.* A lease of property which is for a life or lives, or for a period ascertainable only by reference to a death, or which is terminable on, or at a date ascertainable only by reference to, a death is treated as a settlement and the property as settled property unless the lease was granted for full consideration in money or money's worth.[3] Hence the rules relating to settled property cannot be avoided by the disponer granting a lease for life and not a life interest. Leases for a life or lives, etc., take effect as determinable leases for 90 years, as provided in section 149 (6) of the Law of Property Act 1925. As to the valuation of the lessor's interest: see *ante*, § 20-20. As to the valuation of the lessee's interest: see *post*, § 22-21.

22-10 *Undivided shares.* Property held for beneficiaries absolutely entitled in undivided shares is not settled property for the purposes of capital transfer tax.

Settlor

22-11 The expression " settlor " in relation to a settlement includes any person by whom the settlement was made directly or indirectly, and in particular (but without prejudice to the generality of these words) includes any person who has provided funds directly or indirectly for the purpose of or in connection with the settlement or has made with any other person a reciprocal arrangement for that other person to make a settlement.[4] Settlor is thus defined as in section 454 (3) of the Taxes Act 1970.

Where more than one person is a settlor in relation to a settlement and the circumstances so require, the Act applies in relation to it as if the settled property were comprised in separate settlements.[5]

---

[3] F.A. 1975, para. 1 (3).
[4] *Ibid.* para. 1 (6). See §§ 10-07 *et seq.*
[5] *Ibid.* para. 1 (8).

Trustee

22-12   The expression " trustee " in relation to a settlement of which there is no trustee in the ordinary meaning of the word means any person in whom the settled property or its management is for the time being vested.[6]

Excluded property [7]

22-13   We have seen that the value of " excluded property " is left out of account on a transfer of value by an individual, including the deemed transfer on death, so that excluded property falls outside the tax charge: see § 18-13. Section 24 (2) of the Finance Act 1975 provides that property situated outside the United Kingdom is excluded property; and by section 24 (3), reversionary interests not acquired by purchase are excluded property unless they are expectant on the determination of a lease for lives treated as a settlement under the provisions discussed in § 22-09.

In relation to settled property, paragraph 2 of Schedule 5 to the Finance Act 1975 provides that where property comprised in a settlement is situated outside the United Kingdom the property (but not a reversionary interest in the property) is excluded property unless the settlor was domiciled in the United Kingdom at the time the settlement was made. Section 24 (2), above, applies to a reversionary interest in the property but does not otherwise apply.

Note that the key factors in relation to settled property are the domicile of the settlor at the time of the settlement and the situation of the property at the time when the tax charge would otherwise arise. The domicile of the beneficiary is not a material factor except where the property disposed of is a reversionary interest, when the reversionary interest is excluded property under section 24 (2), above, of the Act if the disponer is an individual domiciled outside the United Kingdom.

> Thus if S (being domiciled outside the United Kingdom) settles property on A for life with remainder to B absolutely, no charge to capital transfer tax arises on A's death on property comprised in the settlement which is then situated outside the United Kingdom. The domiciles of S and A at the time of A's death are immaterial. If B gives his reversionary interest to C, this is a chargeable transfer by B, unless B is an individual domiciled outside the United Kingdom and the settled property is situated outside the United Kingdom.

This example shows that a person domiciled outside the United Kingdom who intends to acquire a domicile of choice in the United Kingdom should make any settlements he intends to make before he acquires the domicile of choice.

3. SETTLED PROPERTY IN WHICH THERE IS A BENEFICIAL INTEREST IN POSSESSION

The meaning of interest in possession

22-14   The phrase " beneficially entitled to an interest in possession " is not defined in the capital transfer tax legislation [8] and general principles of

---

[6] F.A. 1975, para. 1 (7).
[7] See generally, Chap. 23.
[8] See *ibid*. para. 1 (9) as to the position in Scotland.

property law have to be applied. An interest in possession must be distinguished from a contingent interest and an interest in remainder. If property is held by trustees upon trust for A for life with remainder to B absolutely, A has an interest in possession. B's interest does not vest in possession until A dies. If property is transferred to trustees upon trust for A if he attains the age of 25 years, A's interest in *capital* is contingent until he attains that age; but his interest in *income* vests in possession when he attains the age of 18 if by statute or otherwise he becomes entitled to the income on attaining that age.[9] Possession of the right to income or to the use or enjoyment of property is the test of an interest in possession for the purposes of capital transfer tax, since this is treated (see §§ 22-17 *et seq.*) as equivalent to ownership of the property from which the income, use or enjoyment is derived.[10] In the case of property which produces no income (*e.g.* a settled life policy which has not yet matured), the person has an interest in possession who would be entitled to the income if there were any (*e.g.* if the insurance company was in liquidation and the trustees had invested the proceeds of the liquidation [11]).

The Board of Inland Revenue has stated the official view as to the nature of an interest in possession in the following terms.[12] "An interest in possession exists where the person having the interest has the immediate entitlement (subject to any prior claim by the trustees for expenses or other outgoings properly payable out of income) to any income produced by that property as the income arises; but that a discretion or power, in whatever form, which can be exercised after income arises so as to withhold it from that person negatives the existence of an interest in possession. For this purpose a power to accumulate income is regarded as a power to withhold it, unless any accumulations must be held solely for the person having the interest or his personal representatives. On the other hand the existence of a mere power of revocation or appointment, the exercise of which would determine the interest wholly or in part (but which, so long as it remains unexercised, does not affect the beneficiary's immediate entitlement to income) does not in the Board's view prevent the interest from being an interest in possession." This official view applies also for the purposes of section 25 (4) of the Finance Act 1965 (see § 16-23).

Where trustees exercise their powers so as to cause an interest in possession to cease to be such an interest, a tax charge may arise under the provisions discussed in § 22-23.

22-15   Paragraph 11 (10) of Schedule 5 to the Finance Act 1975 provides that " interest in possession " means (for the purposes of paras. 6 to 10

---

[9] See Trustee Act 1925, s. 31, as amended.
[10] See *Re Jones' Will Trusts* [1947] Ch. 48 and *cf. Att.-Gen.* v. *Power* [1906] 2 I.R. 272. See also S.T.I. (1975) p. 469.   [11] See *Re Midwood's Settlement* [1968] Ch. 238.
[12] S.T.I. (1976) 75. Press Release of February 12, 1976. The text is also in CTT 1 at p. 126. But see the digest of *Pearson* v. *I.R.C.* in [1978] S.T.I. 457 when Fox J. held that the interest of a person who is immediately entitled to the income of property subject only to a power in the trustees to accumulate is an interest in possession. Property was settled by S on trust for such one or more of S's children and their issue as the trustees should appoint. Pending appointment the trustees had a power to accumulate all or any of the income. Subject thereto the trustees were to hold capital and income for S's children who attained 21 or married under that age, in equal shares. In February 1974 all 3 children of S had attained 21. An appointment was made in 1976. *Held*, (contrary to the contention of the Revenue) that S's children had interests in possession since 1974.

inclusive of the Schedule) an interest in possession to which an individual is beneficially entitled or, if certain conditions are satisfied, an interest in possession to which a company is beneficially entitled. The significance of this provision is discussed in § 22-41.

22-16   Where a person would have been entitled to an interest in possession in the whole or part of the residue of the estate of a deceased person if the administration of that estate had been completed, he is treated as if he had become entitled to an interest in possession in the unadministered estate (as defined) and in the property (if any) representing ascertained residue (as defined), or in a corresponding part of it, on the date as from which the whole or part of the income of the residue would have been attributable to his interest had the residue been ascertained immediately after the death of the deceased person.[13]

Quantifying the interest in possession

22-17   A person beneficially entitled to an interest in possession in settled property is treated as beneficially entitled to the property in which the interest subsists,[14] apparently for all the purposes of the capital transfer tax.[15]

> Thus if Blackacre is held upon trust for A for life with remainder to B absolutely, A is treated as beneficially entitled to Blackacre and not merely to a life interest in it.

22-18   Where the person entitled to the interest is entitled to part only of the income (if any) of the property, the interest is taken to subsist in such part only of the property as bears to the whole of it the same proportion as the part of the income to which he is entitled bears to the whole of the income.[16]

> Thus if property is held upon trust to pay one-third of the income thereof to A for life, A is treated as having a beneficial interest in one-third of the property.

22-19   Where the beneficiary is entitled to an annuity of a fixed amount, or to the whole of the income of the property less a specified amount, he is treated as beneficially entitled to such part of the property as will produce that amount.[17] This is calculated by reference to the income yield of the property. The Treasury has power [18] to prescribe higher and lower rates which operate as limits beyond which variations in the actual income yield of the property are disregarded. The higher rate applies when the interest in the annuity comes to an end; the lower rate applies when the interest in the remainder of the property comes to an end. By the Capital Transfer Tax (Settled Property Income Yield) Order 1975 (S.I. 1975 No. 610) [19] which applies to interests in possession coming to an end after May 7, 1975, the rates are prescribed by reference to the Financial Times Actuaries Share Indices. The higher rate is the current yield from 2½ per cent. Consols; the lower rate is the current gross dividend yield from the Financial Times

[13] F.A. 1975, para. 22.
[15] *Ibid.* s. 21.
[16] *Ibid.* Sched. 5, para. 3 (2).
[18] *Ibid.* para. 3 (4) and (7).

[14] *Ibid.* para. 3 (1).
[17] *Ibid.* para. 3 (3).
[19] S.T.I. (1975) at p. 260.

Actuaries All Share Index. If no yield has been calculated for the date on which the property falls to be valued, the relevant Indices for the latest earlier date are used. Details of these yields can be obtained on any working day from the Estate Duty Office.

22-20   Where the person entitled to the interest is not entitled to any income of the property but is entitled, jointly or in common with one or more other persons, to the use and enjoyment of the property, his interest is taken to subsist in such part of the property as corresponds to the proportion which the annual value of his interest bears to the aggregate of the annual values of his interest and that or those of the other or others.[20] Thus if a settlement provides that Blackacre and Whiteacre shall be occupied by B and W respectively during their lives, B is treated as beneficially entitled to a proportion of the property corresponding to the proportion which the annual value of Blackacre bears to the aggregate annual values of Blackacre and Whiteacre.

22-21   Where a lease of property is treated as a settlement (see § 22-09), the lessee's interest in the property is taken to subsist in the whole of the property less such part of it as corresponds to the proportion which the value of the lessor's interest (*ante*, § 20-20) bears to the value of the property.[21]

The basis of the charge to tax

22-22   Paragraphs 4 and 5 of Schedule 5 to the Finance Act 1975 contain the principal provisions which apply for charging capital transfer tax in the case of settled property in which some person is entitled to a beneficial interest in possession.

The event on the happening of which tax is chargeable under these provisions is the coming to an end of an interest in possession in the settled property or the happening of certain other events which are treated as such and, by section 51 (2) of the Finance Act 1975, such events give rise to assumed transfers of value by the person beneficially entitled to the interest, who is accordingly treated as the " transferor." Thus if property is settled on trust for A for life with remainder to B absolutely and A dies, in which case there is an assumed transfer by A of the property comprised in the settlement at the time of A's death (see § 22-23), the capital transfer tax provisions apply as if A had then made a transfer of his own property. The questions whether any exemptions or reliefs are available, or at what rate or rates tax is chargeable, or which table of rates applies, or whether the settled property is excluded property, have all to be answered by reference to the personal circumstances of A. The only respect in which the general rules do not apply is that the measure of the tax charge is related exclusively to the property comprised in the settlement: questions as to the value by which A's " estate " is diminished in value do not arise.

---

[20] F.A. 1975, Sched. 5, para. 3 (5).
[21] *Ibid.* para. 3 (6).

The charging provisions

There are two basic rules of charge which are subject to a number of qualifications and exceptions which are referred to in § 22-25, below. The rules are as follows:

22-23   (1) Where at any time during the life of a person beneficially entitled to an interest in possession in any property comprised in a settlement his interest comes to an end, tax is chargeable as if at that time he had made a transfer of value and the value transferred had been equal to the value of the property in which his interest subsisted.[22] Where part only of an interest in settled property comes to an end, the value treated as transferred is the corresponding proportion of the property.[23]

22-24   (2) Where a person beneficially entitled to an interest in possession in any property comprised in a settlement disposes of his interest, the disposal is not a transfer of value but is treated as the coming to an end of his interest.[24]

> Thus if property is settled on A for life with remainder to B absolutely and A assigns his interest by way of gift, this is not a transfer of value of A's life interest but is a transfer of value of the settled property itself.

Examples of the way in which these rules operate are given in §§ 22-32 *et seq.*

Exceptions

The basic charging rules stated in § 22-22 to § 22-24 take effect subject to the following exceptions:

(1) *Beneficial entitlement*

22-25   If the person whose interest in possession in the property comes to an end becomes, on the same occasion, beneficially entitled to the property or to another interest in possession in the property, tax is not chargeable unless the value of the property (or part) to which or to an interest in which he so becomes entitled is less than the value of the property in which his interest terminated. Tax is then chargeable on the difference.[25]

(2) *Sales for full consideration*

22-26   If the interest in possession comes to an end by being disposed of by the person beneficially entitled thereto, and the disposal is for a consideration in money or money's worth of equal value to the property in which the interest subsisted, no tax is chargeable; but if its value is less, tax is chargeable as if the value of the property in which the interest subsisted were reduced by the amount of the consideration. For the purposes of this provision the value of a reversionary interest in the property or of any interest in other property comprised in the same settlement is left out of account.[26]

---

[22] F.A. 1975, para. 4 (2) and s. 51 (2). See § 22-22.
[23] *Ibid.* para. 4 (10) (*a*).
[24] *Ibid.* para. 4 (1). But disposals by way of disclaimer may be exempt: see *ante*, § 19-66. See also § 19-62.
[25] *Ibid.* para. 4 (3) and (10) (*b*).   [26] *Ibid.* para. 4 (4).

(3) *Reverter to settlor*

22-27   If an interest in possession comes to an end during the settlor's life and on the same occasion the property in which the interest subsisted reverts to the settlor, no tax is chargeable unless the settlor or his spouse had acquired a reversionary interest in the property for a consideration in money or money's worth.[27]

> Thus if S transfers property to A for life, no tax is payable in respect of the property which on A's death reverts to S. Tax is chargeable on A's death if S has predeceased him.
>
> If S settles property on A for life with remainder to B absolutely and S purchases B's reversionary interest, the exemption does not apply when on A's death the property reverts to S.
>
> If as part of the financial arrangements on divorce H transfers the matrimonial home to his wife (W) until the children attain a certain age, the exemption applies to the reverter of the property to H.

(4) *Reverter to spouse of settlor*

22-28   If on the termination of an interest in possession, whether on death or otherwise, the settlor's spouse becomes beneficially entitled to an interest in possession, no tax charge arises if the settlor's spouse is then domiciled in the United Kingdom.[28] " Spouse " includes the settlor's widow or widower, but only where the settlor died less than two years before the interest comes to an end or the interest comes to an end before April 1, 1977.[29]

> (i) Thus if H (husband) transfers property to trustees to hold upon trust for A for life with remainder to W (H's wife) absolutely, the transfer by H is not exempt because of A's intermediate life interest: see *ante*, § 19-03; but no capital transfer tax is payable on the coming to an end of A's life interest if the conditions as to domicile and residence in the United Kingdom are then satisfied.
>
> (ii) Assume H (husband) transfers property to trustees to hold upon trust for X for life, with remainder to W (H's wife). H dies after April 1, 1977. No capital transfer tax is payable if X surrenders his life interest, provided he does so within two years from the date of X's death.

The effect is that there is only one occasion of charge to capital transfer tax where an interest in possession is interposed in a transfer between spouses.

22-29   The exemption in § 22-28 does not apply where either the settlor or his spouse had acquired a reversionary interest in the property for a consideration in money or money's worth.[30]

> Thus if H (husband) settles property on A for life with remainder to B absolutely and H's wife (W) acquires B's reversionary interest by purchase, a tax charge arises on the termination of A's interest.

(5) *Surviving spouse exemption*

22-30   Where one party to a marriage dies before November 13, 1974 (so that estate duty would have been leviable on his estate), and the other dies after

---

[27] F.A. 1975, s. 22 (2) and Sched. 5, para. 4 (5), as amended by F.A. 1978, s. 69 (1). For a brief explanation for the reason for the amendment, see B.T.R. (1978), p. 170.
[28] F.A. 1975, s. 22 (3) and Sched. 5, para. 4 (6) as amended by F.A. 1976, Sched. 14, para. 13 (*a*).
[29] F.A. 1976, s. 110 (1), (2).   [30] F.A. 1975, Sched. 5, para. 4 (6). And see n. 33.

the passing of the Finance Act 1975 on March 13, 1975 (when estate duty law no longer applies), but the surviving spouse exemption would have applied on the second death if estate duty were chargeable, the exemption applies for capital transfer tax.[31] The exemption applies howsoever the surviving spouse's interest in possession comes to an end. The " surviving spouse exemption " was an exemption from estate duty which applied on the second-to-die of spouses where estate duty was paid on property passing on the death of the first-to-die and the survivor had only a limited interest, *e.g.* a life interest, in that property.[32]

(6) *Trustee's remuneration*

22-30A Where a trustee is remunerated for his services by being given an interest in possession in settled property, and the interest does not represent more than a reasonable amount of remuneration, this is left out of account in valuing the estate of the trustee immediately before his death and also when the interest comes to an end.[33]

(7) *Transitional relief*

22-31 There is a provision limiting the tax charge where, in the case of a settlement made before March 27, 1974, the interest in possession came to an end before December 10, 1974. Tax is chargeable on the basis that the only previous chargeable transfers by the person beneficially entitled were those in respect of any post-March 26, 1974, terminations of an interest in the property.[34] There are special provisions with respect to approved superannuation schemes, trusts for the benefit of employees and newspaper trusts: see Finance Act 1975, Sched. 5, paras. 16, 17 and 17A (as amended or inserted by the Finance Act 1976, ss. 107–108).

The application of the charging provisions to concrete situations

(1) *Advancement*

22-32 If settled property is held upon trust for A for life with remainder to B absolutely and the trustees, in exercise of powers contained in the trust instrument, make an advance of capital to A, A's interest to this extent comes to an end: see § 22-23; but since A becomes beneficially entitled to the property advanced, no tax charge arises: see § 22-25. If the trustees advance capital to B, A's interest in the capital advanced comes to an end (see § 22-23) and a tax charge arises unless B is A's spouse (§ 22-28).

(2) *Partition*

22-33 Assume that settled property is held upon trust for A for life with remainder to B absolutely. A and B agree to divide the fund between

---

[31] F.A. 1975, s. 22 (4) and Sched. 5, para. 4 (7).
[32] For details, see the 8th edition of this book at § 23-54.
[33] F.A. 1975, Sched. 5, para. 19A, inserted by F.A. 1976, s. 109.
[34] F.A. 1975, Sched. 5, para. 4 (8).

themselves in proportion to the respective values of their interests. Assume that A and B accordingly agree that the fund shall be divided as to one-third to A and two-thirds to B. A's interest in possession in two-thirds of the fund comes to an end (§ 22-23); and a tax charge arises (§ 22-25).

Similarly if A assigns the whole of his interest to B for its full value, A's interest is treated as coming to an end (§ 22-24); but no tax charge arises (§ 22-26). A tax charge would arise if A assigned his interest to B for less than the full value of the property in which the interest subsists (§ 22-26).

(3) *Enlargement and reduction of interests*

22-34   If settled property is held upon trust for the children of X in equal shares and X has three children, the birth to X of a fourth child will reduce the share of each existing child from one-third to one-fourth. To this extent the beneficial interest of each of the three children comes to an end and a tax charge arises under § 22-23. See also § 22-48.

(4) *Interests pur autre vie*

22-35   The tax charge arises under § 22-23 where at any time *during the life of* the person beneficially entitled to an interest in possession, his interest comes to an end. If settled property is held upon trust for A during the life of X, a tax charge will arise on the termination of A's interest whether by the death of A, or X before A. If A dies before X and A's interest passes under his will or intestacy to B, a further charge to tax will arise on the termination of B's interest (subject to possible relief under § 22-40).

(5) *Failure of interest*

22-36   The tax charge arises when an interest in possession comes to an end: there is no tax charge when an interest fails before it vests in possession. Thus if property is held upon trust for A for life with remainder to B for life with remainder to C absolutely, and B predeceases A, no tax charge arises on B's death. But note that if property is held on trust for A if he shall attain the age of 25 years, and A dies aged 17, no tax charge then arises; but if A dies after attaining the age of 18 years, when his interest vests in possession (see § 22-14), a tax charge arises on A's subsequent death even before attaining the age of 25 years.

Depreciatory transactions

22-37   Since the tax charge under consideration is levied by reference to the value of the settled property at the time of the termination (or deemed termination) of the interest, any transaction which depreciates the value of the property before that time will result in a saving of tax. Paragraph 4 (9) of Schedule 5 to the Finance Act 1975 accordingly provides that where a transaction is made between the trustees of the settlement and a person who is, or is connected with:

(a) the person beneficially entitled to an interest in the property; or
(b) a person beneficially entitled to any other interest in that property or to any interest in any other property comprised in the settlement; or

> (c) a person for whose benefit any of the settled property may be applied,

and, as a result of the transaction, the value of the first-mentioned property is less than it would be but for the transaction, a corresponding part of the interest shall be deemed to come to an end unless the transaction is such that, were the trustee beneficially entitled to the settled property, it would not be a transfer of value. A loan by trustees to a beneficiary may give rise to a tax charge under this provision. To take extreme examples, an unsecured interest-free loan which was not repayable on demand would depreciate the value of the settled property and so give rise to a charge under paragraph 4 (9). A secured loan on commercial terms would not do so. A lease of trust property to a beneficiary on uncommercial terms is an example of a depreciatory transaction.

Close companies

(1) *Transfers of value by close companies*

22-38   Section 39 of the Finance Act 1975 enables value transferred by a close company to be apportioned between the participators in certain circumstances: *ante*, §§ 21-01 *et seq.* Where the participators are trustees of settled property in which there is an interest in possession, paragraph 24 of Schedule 5 to the Finance Act 1975 enables the value transferred by the company to be apportioned through to the interest-holder. This is achieved by deeming there to be a termination of his interest.

(2) *Interests in possession vested in close company*

22-39   Where a close company is entitled to an interest in possession in settled property, the persons who are participators in relation to the company are treated as being the persons beneficially entitled to that interest according to their respective rights and interests in the company. Thus if the company's interest in possession comes to an end, or is treated as coming to an end, the participators can be treated as making transfers of value in proportion to their rights or interests in the company.[35]

Relief for successive charges on interest in possession

22-40   Paragraph 5 (1) of Schedule 5 to the Finance Act 1975 provides relief for successive charges on interests in possession. The relief applies if an interest in possession comes to an end within four years of a previous chargeable transfer of the settled property. The value chargeable is reduced by a percentage depending on the period since the last chargeable transfer. The reduction is:

> 80 per cent. if the period is one year or less;
>
> 60 per cent. if the period is more than one year but not more than two years;
>
> 40 per cent. if the period is more than two years but not more than three years;
>
> 20 per cent. if the period is more than three years.

---

[35] F.A. 1975, Sched. 5, para. 24 (5). See also § 22-41.

There is a transitional provision which applies if the transferor became entitled to his interest in possession on the death of a person where estate duty was payable on that death. The four-year period is then calculated from the death.[36]

Quick succession relief under section 30 of the Finance Act 1975 (*ante*, § 19-31) is excluded where relief under paragraph 5 (above) is given.[37]

4. SETTLED PROPERTY IN WHICH THERE IS NO BENEFICIAL INTEREST IN POSSESSION [38]

The meaning of interest in possession

22-41   The expression " interest in possession " is defined,[39] for the purposes of the provisions relating to settled property in which there is no beneficial interest in possession, as an interest in possession to which an individual is beneficially entitled or, if the following conditions are satisfied, an interest in possession to which a company is beneficially entitled. These conditions are (a) that the business of the company consists wholly or mainly in the acquisition of interests in settled property; and (b) that the company acquired the interest for full consideration in money or money's worth from an individual who was beneficially entitled to the interest. Thus if an individual with a life interest in settled property sells his interest to such a company, the rules which apply to settled property in which there is a beneficial interest in possession (§§ 22-14 *et seq.*) continue to apply.

Where, however, a close company which is not a company of this description has what, apart from this definition, would be an " interest in possession," the effect of the provision is to treat the close company itself as *not* having an interest in possession; but there is a separate provision which treats the participators in the company as beneficially entitled to the company's interest according to their respective rights and interests in the company.[40] Hence the rules which apply to settled property in which there is a beneficial interest in possession apply: see in particular § 22-39.

When a charge arises

22-42   The main events on the happening of which a tax charge may arise in the case of settled property in which there is no interest in possession are as follows:

A. the making of a capital distribution [41];
B. the coming into existence of an interest in possession in the whole or part of the settled property;
C. the expiry of a period of years from the " relevant anniversary " (the periodic charge);
D. the coming into existence of an " accumulation and maintenance settlement."

---

[36] *Ibid.* para. 5 (2) as substituted by F.A. 1976, s. 97 (2).   [37] *Ibid.* s. 30 (2).
[38] The provisions in this section of the book do not apply to charitable trusts, and certain compensation funds or approved superannuation schemes and there are special provisions applying to trusts for employees and trusts for mentally disabled persons: see F.A. 1975, paras. 16–21.
[39] F.A. 1975, Sched. 5, para. 11 (10).
[40] *Ibid.* Sched. 5, para. 24 (5). See § 22-39.   [41] *Ibid.* Sched. 5, para. 6 (4), and § 22-45.

Each of these is discussed in sections A–D below. Where the events in B, C or D occur, a capital distribution as in A is treated as having been made.[42] There are also provisions to prevent avoidance of tax by depreciatory transactions similar to those referred to in § 22-37.[43] There are also provisions for the apportionment to trustee-participators of value transferred by a close company similar to those in § 22-38.[44] The manner in which tax is charged where there is a capital distribution is considered in § 22-45 and §§ 22-55 *et seq.* A number of detailed amendments have been made to the charging provisions in sections 69 and 70 of the Finance Act 1975, which are " aimed " at various tax avoidance schemes.[45]

Definitions

The following definitions are used in connection with the charging provisions.

22-43   " *Distribution payment* " means any payment (including the transfer of assets other than money) which (a) is not income of any person for any of the purposes of income tax and would not for any of those purposes be income of a person not resident in the United Kingdom if he were so resident; and (b) is not a payment in respect of costs or expenses.[46] (The circumstances in which payments made by trustees are treated as income of the beneficiary are discussed *ante*, §§ 9-13 *et seq.*) Thus payments made by trustees which are income in the hands of the beneficiary (or would be income if he were resident in the United Kingdom) and payments to meet expenses or in the purchase of investments give rise to no liability to capital transfer tax. A loan is thought not to be a distribution payment, but it may be treated as such if it is a depreciatory transaction.

22-44   " *Capital distribution* " means a distribution payment made out of property comprised in a settlement at a time when no interest in possession subsists in the property or in the part of it out of which the payment is made,[47] except that a distribution payment which is made to the settlor or the settlor's spouse is not a capital distribution if the settlor or, as the case may be, the settlor's spouse is domiciled in the United Kingdom at the time the payment is made.[48] " Spouse " does not include a widow or widower of the settlor, subject to a statutory exception in the case of a distribution payment made less than two years after the settlor's death or made before April 1, 1977.[49] Payments to charities and political parties made after April 5, 1976, are not capital distributions.[50]

22-44A   Note the events enumerated in § 22-42 when a capital distribution is *treated as having been made.* The expression " capital distribution "

---

[42] See *ibid.* Sched. 5, para. 6 (2) for Event B (§ 22-46); *ibid.* Sched. 5, para. 12 (1) for Event C (§ 22-50); *ibid.* Sched. 5, para. 15 (3) for Event D (§ 22-54).
[43] See *ibid.* para. 6 (3).
[44] See F.A. 1975, para. 24 (2).
[45] The reader who wishes to know what they were may see B.T.R. (1978), pp. 170 *et seq.*
[46] F.A. 1975, Sched. 5, para. 11 (7).
[47] *Ibid.* para. 6 (1).
[48] *Ibid.* para. 6 (6), as amended by F.A. 1976, s. 112 and Sched. 14, para. 13 (c).
[49] F.A. 1976, s. 110 (3).
[50] F.A. 1975, Sched. 6, paras. 10 (2) and 11 (1A).

throughout the capital transfer tax legislation includes capital distributions treated as so made,[51] even though those events involve no " distribution payment." However, it is provided that the amount of any capital distribution *treated* as made in events B and D (but not event C) shall also be *deemed* to be a distribution payment.[52]

> Thus not all distribution payments are capital distributions and not all capital distributions are distribution payments. No tax charge arises unless there is a capital distribution or an event treated as such. A distribution payment which is not a capital distribution gives rise to no tax charge but is taken into the reckoning of the total of transfers and so may affect the rate of tax on later transfers.

The charging provisions

A. *The making of a capital distribution*

22-45 Where a capital distribution is made after March 12, 1975, tax is charged as it is on the value transferred by a chargeable transfer where the value so transferred less the tax payable on it is equal to the amount of the capital distribution, *i.e.* the amount or value of the property distributed.[53] The value treated as transferred is thus the amount of the capital distribution plus the tax payable on it (*i.e.* the distribution is " grossed up ") except, that if the tax is payable by the recipient of the distribution, the value treated as transferred is the amount of the capital distribution without the tax payable on it (*i.e.* the distribution is not grossed up).[54]

> Thus if trustees of a settlement made before March 27, 1974, make a first capital distribution of £40,000, the value transferred is
>
> (i) if the beneficiary pays the tax, £40,000—tax £1,125;
> (ii) if the trustees pay the tax, such a sum as after deduction of capital transfer tax will leave £40,000, *i.e.* £41,285·71—tax £1,285·71.[55]

The second (lower-rate) table (see § 20-02) is applied for the purpose of determining the rates of tax. As to the method of computing the charge, see §§ 22-55 *et seq.*

B. *The coming into existence of an interest in possession*

22-46 Where a person becomes entitled to an interest in possession in the whole or any part of the property comprised in a settlement at a time when no such interest subsists in the property or that part, a capital distribution is treated as being made out of the property or that part of the property; and the amount of the distribution is taken to be equal to the value at that time of the property or, if the interest is in part only of that property, of that part.[56]

> Thus if Blackacre and Whiteacre are held on discretionary trusts and the trustees appoint that Blackacre shall be held upon trust for A for life with remainders over, the trustees are treated as making a capital distribution equal to the value of Blackacre at the time of the appointment.

The distribution is not " grossed up " as in § 22-45.[57] There is no tax charge where the person who becomes entitled to an interest in possession is

---

[51] *Ibid.* s. 51 (1) defining " capital distribution."   [52] *Ibid.* Sched. 5, para. 11 (8).
[53] F.A. 1975, Sched. 5, para. 6 (1) and (4).   [54] *Ibid.* paras. 6 (4) (5) and 11 (5) (8).
[55] The transitional relief in § 22-62 has been ignored in this example.
[56] *Ibid.* paras. 6 (2) (4) and 11 (5) (8).
[57] *Ibid.* para. 6 (5) as amended by F.A. 1976, Sched. 14, para. 11.

the settlor or the settlor's spouse and is then domiciled in the United Kingdom.[58]

Exceptions. There are two exceptions to the provision which deems there to be a capital distribution when an interest in possession is created:

22-47   (1) *Temporary abeyance of interest in possession: survivorship clauses*: where under the terms of a will or otherwise property is held for any person on condition that he survives another for a specified period of not more than six months, the settlement provisions apply as if the disposition taking effect at the end of the period or, if he does not survive until then, on his death (including any such disposition which has effect by operation of law or is a separate disposition of the income from the property) had had effect from the beginning of the period.[59]

> Suppose property is settled by H's will on W for life provided W shall survive H by 30 days with a gift over to X if W shall not so survive. On H's death no person will then have an interest in possession and, but for the exception, a tax charge would arise on W (or Z) becoming entitled in possession at the expiry of 30 days. The exception excludes this tax charge.

22-48   (2) *Enlargement of the interest of a class member*: where a person entitled to an interest in possession in part of the property comprised in a settlement became so entitled as member of a class, there is no deemed capital distribution on his becoming entitled, as such a member, to an interest in possession in another part of that property, if he becomes so entitled on the death under full age of another member of that class.[60]

> Suppose property is held upon trust for the children of X who shall attain the age of 25 years. There are two children, A and B, who have attained the age of 18 years (and so have interests in possession: see *ante,* § 22-14) and a third child, C, who dies before attaining the age of 18 years. On C's death there is no interest in possession in C's one-third share. The exception prevents a tax charge arising when C's one-third share accrues to A and B.

C. *The periodic charge*

22-49   But for the provisions about to be considered, the charge to capital transfer tax could be avoided so long as, in a settlement (such as a discretionary settlement) in which no beneficiary has an interest in possession, the trustees make no distribution payments and accumulate surplus income as it arises. The Act accordingly imposes a periodic charge to tax at 10-yearly intervals in the case of a United Kingdom resident trust and annually in the case of a non-resident trust.

United Kingdom settlements

22-50   Paragraph 12 (1) of Schedule 5 to the Finance Act 1975 provides that where, at a relevant anniversary, no interest in possession subsists in the property comprised in a settlement or in a part of that property, a capital distribution of an amount equal to the value immediately before that anniversary of that property or part shall be treated as made out of that

[58] *Ibid.* Sched. 5, para. 6 (6) and (6A); but see para. 6 (6B) inserted by F.A. 1978, s. 69 (2).
[59] F.A. 1975, Sched. 5, para. 22A inserted by F.A. 1976, s. 105.   [60] *Ibid.* para. 6 (8).

property or part. There is no " grossing up " of the amount notionally distributed, as there is in the case of an actual capital distribution: see § 22-45.

Tax is charged on the capital distribution so treated as made at 30 per cent. of the rate at which it would be chargeable on a capital distribution of the same amount made at the same date (with an adjustment where additions to the settled property have been made).[61]

22-51   The " relevant anniversary " means the end of the 10 years beginning with the date of the transfer of value which is the relevant transfer (as defined) in relation to the settlement and the end of every subsequent 10 years; except that no date falling before April 1, 1980, is a relevant anniversary.[62]

> Thus if a settlement is made in July 1970, the first periodic charge to tax will arise in July 1980; whereas if the settlement is made in March 1970, the first periodic charge will arise in March 1990.

22-52   Where there is a periodic charge to tax and, on or not later than 20 years thereafter, an actual capital distribution is made by the trustees out of the same property, credit is given for tax payable in consequence of the periodic charge.[63] The effective rate at which tax is charged under the 10-year periodic charge reduces the rate at which tax would otherwise be chargeable on the capital distribution, except that the amount of the reduction is not to exceed the amount of the tax charged under the 10-year charge.

Overseas settlements

22-53   Where the trustees of a settlement are not resident in the United Kingdom a capital distribution of the amount in § 22-50 is treated as made, not only at the end of each period of 10 years, but also at the end of each of the intervening years. There is no tax charge for any year ending before January 1, 1976. Tax is charged at 3 per cent. of the rate at which it would be chargeable on a capital distribution of the same amount made at the same date.[64] There is no " grossing up " of the amount notionally distributed, as there is in the case of an actual capital distribution: see § 22-45.

Any tax so charged is allowed as a credit against the tax chargeable on the next capital distribution made out of the property or treated as made under the 10-yearly periodic charge.[65]

For the purposes of this provision, the trustees of a settlement are regarded as not resident in the United Kingdom unless the general administration of the settlement is ordinarily carried on in the United Kingdom and the trustees or a majority of them (and, where there is more than one class of trustees, a majority of each class) are for the time being resident in the United Kingdom.[66]

---

[61] F.A. 1975, para. 12 (1) and (4).
[62] *Ibid.* paras. 12 (6) and 11 (2). And see F.A. 1976, s. 112 and Sched. 14, paras. 15–16.
[63] *Ibid.* para. 13.
[64] *Ibid.* para. 12 (2).
[65] *Ibid.* para. 12 (3) as amended by F.A. 1976, s. 112 and Sched. 14, para. 8.
[66] *Ibid.* para. 12 (5).

D. *The coming into existence of an accumulation and maintenance settlement*

22-54   An accumulation and maintenance settlement means a settlement which satisfies certain conditions stated in § 22-68. An example of such a settlement is a trust for the children of A upon attaining the age of 25 years: each child has a contingent interest in capital but attains a vested interest in income on attaining the age of 18 years, prior to which date the income can be either applied for maintenance or accumulated under section 31 of the Trustee Act 1925. A special feature of such a settlement is that no charge to capital transfer tax arises when the beneficiary becomes entitled to an interest in possession.

Paragraph 15 (3) of Schedule 5 to the Finance Act 1975 makes the occasion of transforming settled property in which there is no interest in possession into property held on the trusts of an accumulation and maintenance settlement an occasion of charge to capital transfer tax. A capital distribution is treated as made out of the settled property and the amount of the distribution is taken to be equal to the value of the property with respect to which the conditions become satisfied. There is no " grossing up " of the distribution as in § 22-45. Tax planning aspects of accumulation settlements are discussed in § 37-14.

The rate of charge

22-55   Paragraphs 7–9 of Schedule 5 to the Finance Act 1975 provide the basis for calculating the rate of tax chargeable on a capital distribution including the happening of an event which is treated as a capital distribution. There are two main provisions:

(1) *Capital distributions following chargeable transfers*

22-56   Paragraph 7 applies where there is a capital distribution out of a settlement or after the making of which there has been a transfer of value which satisfies certain conditions. The principal conditions are that the property out of which the capital distribution is made was taken into account in determining the value transferred on that earlier transfer of value and that that earlier transfer was a chargeable transfer (or would have been had certain exemptions not applied).[67]

22-57   If the amount of the capital distribution (grossed up where necessary: see § 22-45) plus the amount of all previous distribution payments made out of the property does not exceed the initial value, the rate charged on the capital distribution is that which the settlor would have paid at the time of the settlement on a chargeable transfer equal to the value of the property in settlement.[68] " Initial value " means the value, immediately after the relevant transfer, of the property then comprised in the settlement.[69]

---

[67] See F.A. 1975, Sched. 5, paras. 7 (1) and 11 (2).
[68] *Ibid.* para. 7 (2).
[69] *Ibid.* para. 11 (9).

Assume S makes a settlement of £80,000 on August 1, 1978. Assume this is the first transfer of value made by S and the tax (paid by S out of the £80,000) is £9,531. The " relevant transfer " is the transfer of £80,000 to the trustees and the " initial value " is £70,469 (£80,000—£9,531). The rate of tax on this transfer is $\frac{9,531}{70,469}$ = 13·52%. (See Table B in § 20-11.)

If the trustees make a first capital distribution of £30,000 (the beneficiary paying the tax) the tax charge is

$$£30,000 @ 13·52\% = £4,056$$

and subsequent capital distributions up to £70,469 are taxed at the same rate.

If the trustees make a first capital distribution of £30,000 (the trustees paying the tax out of other resources), grossing up is necessary (*ante*, § 22-45) and the tax charge is

$$£30,270·27 @ 13·52\% = £4,092·54.$$

22-58   If more than one settlement was made on the same occasion the values of the properties in all the settlements (called " related settlements ") have to be aggregated for the purpose of determining the rate of tax.[70]

Assume S makes a settlement of £80,000 and another of £20,000 on August 1, 1978. Assume these are the first transfers of value made by S and the tax (paid in each case out of the property transferred) totals £11,875. The rate of tax on these transfers, taking the two together, is

$$\frac{£11,875}{£88,125} = 13·47\%$$

This is the tax rate on distributions out of either settlement up to the initial value.

22-59   Once the initial value is exceeded the rate charged on successive capital distributions is the rate the settlor would have paid on successive chargeable transfers of the same amount after having made the settlement or settlements.[71]

22-59A   Where the rate of tax on a capital distribution made after October 26, 1977, falls to be determined by reference to a relevant transfer made before that date, the amount of tax is calculated as if the second of the new Tables (§ 20-02) had applied to the transfer.[72]

(2) *Other capital distributions*

22-60   Paragraph 8 applies where paragraph 7 (§ 22-56) does not apply, *e.g.* to capital distributions out of property settled before March 27, 1974. Tax chargeable on a capital distribution is that which would have been due from an individual on a chargeable transfer equal to the capital distribution if he had made chargeable transfers equal to the total of previous distribution payments.

Assume S makes a settlement of £80,000 before March 27, 1974. No tax is payable on that transfer because capital transfer tax did not then exist. If the trustees make a first distribution of £12,000, the same tax is payable as would have been payable on a first transfer of value by an individual, *i.e.* nil. If the

---

[70] F.A. 1975, paras. 7 (2) (*a*) and 11 (6).
[71] *Ibid.* para. 7 (3).
[72] F.A. 1978, s. 62 (4).

trustees make a second capital distribution of £28,000 the previous distribution payment of £12,000 is brought into account and tax charged as when an individual's cumulative transfers total £40,000, *i.e.* £1,125 if the beneficiary pays the tax or £1,285·71 if the trustees pay it.

Property added to the settlement

22-61 Property which is added to a settlement by the settlor after March 26, 1974, is treated for the purpose of determining the rate of charge on a subsequent distribution as property comprised in a separate settlement. Paragraph 9 of Schedule 5 contains provisions for determining whether a distribution is to be treated as coming out of the property originally settled or the property added later.

Transitional relief

22-62 Paragraph 14 of Schedule 5 to the Finance Act 1975 applies exclusively to settled property in which there is no interest in possession (principally discretionary settlements and accumulation settlements which do not satisfy the conditions referred to in § 22-68), and it enables such settlements to be wholly or partially terminated by capital distributions made before April 1, 1980, at reduced rates of charge. The relief applies only to settlements made before March 27, 1974, except that it does not apply to such settlements in respect of funds added after March 26, 1974.

The rate at which tax is chargeable on any capital distribution made before April 1, 1980, is a percentage of the rate at which it would be chargeable without the relief and is as follows:

Date of capital distribution	Relief	
Before April 1, 1976	10	per cent.
After March 31, 1976, and before April 1, 1977	12½	per cent.
After March 31, 1977, and before April 1, 1978	15	per cent.
After March 31, 1978, and before April 1, 1979	17½	per cent.
After March 31, 1979, and before April 1, 1980	20	per cent.
On or after April 1, 1980	Nil	

22-63 Where a capital distribution made after March 31, 1976, but before April 1, 1977, could not have been made except as the result of some proceedings before a court, the distribution is treated as if it had been made before April 1, 1976.[73]

22-64 As regards the periodic charge to tax, the above relief is not needed in the case of United Kingdom settlements because the periodic charge does not commence until April 1, 1980.[74] The relief is expressly excluded in relation to the periodic charge on overseas settlements.[75] The relief, where applicable, does not apply unless the recipient of the capital distribution is an individual domiciled in the United Kingdom at the time the capital distribution is made.[76] Where the occasion of charge is the conversion of a

---

[73] F.A. 1975, Sched. 5, para. 14 (3).   [74] *Ibid.* para. 12 (6).
[75] *Ibid.* para. 14 (4).
[76] *Ibid.* para. 14 (5) as amended by F.A. 1976, s. 112 and Sched. 14, para. 13 (*d*). See also F.A. 1978, s. 69 (3), which prevents the relief being obtained by the trustees making a contingent appointment to a U.K. domiciled beneficiary who sells his interest to a foreign domiciled beneficiary who then gets the appointed property on the occurrence of the contingency.

discretionary settlement into an accumulation and maintenance settlement (see § 22-54), this condition is regarded as satisfied if all the *existing* " beneficiaries " under the trust as modified are so domiciled and resident; and for this purpose possible unborn beneficiaries will be disregarded.[77]

Sequence of capital distributions

22-64A   Capital transfer tax is levied on a cumulative basis and one capital distribution may attract a higher tax rate than an earlier distribution. In some cases tax may be saved or not according to the order in which distributions are made. Suppose, for example, discretionary trustees wish to appoint funds to A, who is domiciled and resident outside the United Kingdom and to B who is domiciled and resident within the United Kingdom. The appointment to B, but not the appointment to A, qualifies for transitional relief under the provisions in § 22-62. The appointment to A should be made first to take advantage of the £25,000 exemption and lower rates in § 20-02. Section 43 (2) of the Finance Act 1975 provides that where the value transferred by more than one chargeable transfer made by the same person *on the same day* depends on the order in which the transfers are made, they shall be treated as made in the order which results in the lowest value chargeable; but section 43 (3) of that Act now provides that the *rate* chargeable on such transfers shall be the effective rate that would have been chargeable if the transfers had been a single transfer of the same total amount.[78]

Where a capital distribution is made on the same day and out of property comprised in the same settlement as a distribution payment that is not a capital distribution (see §§ 22-43 *et seq.*), the capital distribution is treated as made first.[79]

Where a capital distribution is made on the same day as a distribution payment which is not a capital distribution, the capital distribution is to be treated as made before the distribution payment.[79]

Capital distributions after termination of interest of settlor or settlor's spouse

22-65   Paragraph 10 of Schedule 5 to the Finance Act 1975 deals with the case where, for example, *part* (called " the chargeable part ") of settled property is settled by a husband (H) after March 26, 1974, on his wife (W) for life or for some other terminable period, with remainder on trusts under which there is no interest in possession. W's interest comes to an end (so capital transfer tax is chargeable under paragraph 4 (2) of Schedule 5: see § 22-23). A capital distribution is then made to a remainderman giving rise to a tax charge under paragraph 6 (2) of Schedule 5: see § 22-45.

22-66   The initial transfer by H into settlement is exempt from capital transfer tax as regards the part settled by H on W (see § 19-02) but the remaining

[77] See Inland Revenue Press Release in [1975] S.T.I. 469.
[78] Added by F.A. 1976, s. 98 and applicable to chargeable transfers after April 15, 1976, other than transfers on death.
[79] F.A. 1975, Sched. 5, para. 10 A, added by F.A. 1976, Sched. 14, para. 14 in relation to distribution payments made after April 15, 1976.

part is a chargeable transfer: hence the initial transfer into settlement by H is a " relevant transfer " under paragraph 11 (2) of Schedule 5 by reason of the non-exempt part [80]; the initial value is the value of the settled property immediately after the settlement; and the numerator in the fraction for determining the effective rate of tax on capital distributions (see § 22-57) will be low by reason of the exemption from tax on the part settled on W. In this way the exemption from tax on transfers between spouses operates to reduce the tax that would otherwise be levied on capital distributions after the death of W.

22-67   To prevent tax being avoided in this way paragraph 10 of Schedule 5 requires that the chargeable part should be treated as comprised in a separate settlement made by W when her interest comes to an end; that the termination of her interest should be treated as the relevant transfer; and that the subsequent termination of any interest of W in any other part of the settled property should be treated as an addition made by her to the property comprised in that separate settlement. In this way the effective rate of tax on capital distributions is measured without taking account of the exemption for transfers between spouses.

5. OTHER SETTLEMENTS

(1) *Accumulation and maintenance settlements*

22-68   Paragraph 15 of Schedule 5 to the Finance Act 1975 [81] applies to any settlement where

    (a) one or more persons (referred to as beneficiaries) will, on or before attaining a specified age not exceeding twenty-five, become entitled to, or to an interest in possession in, the settled property or part of it; and

    (b) no interest in possession subsists in the settled property or part and the income from it is to be accumulated so far as not applied for the maintenance, education or benefit of a beneficiary; and

    (c) either

        (i) not more than twenty-five years have elapsed since the day on which the settlement was made or, if it was later, since the time (or latest time) when the conditions stated in paragraphs (a) and (b) above became satisfied with respect to the property or part; or

        (ii) all the persons who are or have been beneficiaries are or were either grandchildren of a common grandparent or children, widows or widowers of such grandchildren who were themselves beneficiaries but died before the time when, had they survived, they would have become entitled as mentioned in paragraph (a) above.

The effect of (c) is to limit the period for which tax relief is available in the case of such settlements.

22-69   It is not necessary that the age for vesting of capital should be 25 years or less, for condition (a) is satisfied, whatever the age for vesting of capital, provided the beneficiaries will, on or before attaining a specified age not

---

[80] Where the *whole* of the property is settled on W for life, the initial transfer is not a relevant transfer and para. 10 of Sched. 5 is not needed.
[81] As amended by F.A. 1976, s. 106. There are transitional provisions for settlements in existence on April 15, 1976.

exceeding 25, become entitled to an interest in possession in the settled property, including a vested interest in income: see § 22-14. In settlements to which section 31 of the Trustee Act 1925 applies, beneficiaries will acquire a vested interest in income at the age of 21 years (or at the age of 18 years if section 31 applies as amended by the Family Law Reform Act 1969). Condition (a) is not, however, satisfied unless it can be predicated that the condition referred to *will* be satisfied. Hence the existence of an overriding power of revocation or of appointment may prevent condition (a) being satisfied; and the removal of such a power may give rise to a tax charge under the provisions discussed in § 22-54. By concession,[82] the Board will treat condition (a) as satisfied even if no age is specified in the trust instrument, provided it is clear that a beneficiary will in fact become entitled to the settled property (or to an interest in possession in it) by the age of 25. The concession would apply if, *e.g.* the trust instrument provided for vesting in beneficiaries at the expiry of 21 years from the date of the settlement and in fact the eldest beneficiary was aged three years when the settlement was made.

The Board of Inland Revenue has stated the official view on some points of detail which have been raised on the application of paragraph 15 of Schedule 5 to the Finance Act 1975 to certain situations. The statement was made in a Press Release of January 19, 1976, of which the following is the main part:

1. *Powers of Appointment and Revocation limited to the Class of Beneficiaries*

Where there is a trust for accumulation and maintenance of a class of persons who become entitled to the property (or to an interest in possession in it) at a specified age not exceeding 25 it would not be disqualified under paragraph 15 (1) (*a*) by the existence of a power to vary or determine the respective shares of members of the class (even to the extent of excluding some members altogether) provided the power is exercisable only in favour of a person under 25 who is a member of the class.

2. *Transitional Relief under paragraph* 14 *of Schedule* 5

The transitional relief provided by paragraph 14 of Schedule 5 applies to any capital distribution treated as made under paragraph 15 (3), provided that the conditions in paragraph 14 (5) are met.

3. The examples set out below are based on a settlement for the children of X contingently on attaining 25, the trustees being required to accumulate the income so far as it is not applied for the maintenance of X's children.

A. The settlement was made on X's marriage and he has as yet no children.	Paragraph 15 of Schedule 5 will not apply until a child is born and that event will give rise to a charge for tax under sub-paragraph (3), subject, if it occurs before April 1, 1980, to relief under paragraph 14 of that Schedule.

[82] Inland Revenue Press Release of September 2, 1977: [1977] S.T.I. 262.

B. The trustees have power to apply income for the benefit of X's unmarried sister.

Paragraph 15 does not apply because the condition of sub-paragraph (1) (*b*) is not met.

C. The trustees have power to apply capital for the benefit of X's unmarried sister.

Paragraph 15 does not apply because the condition of sub-paragraph (1) (*a*) is not met.

D. X has power to appoint the capital not only among his children but also among his remoter issue.

Paragraph 15 does not apply (unless the power can be exercised only in favour of persons who would thereby acquire interests in possession on or before attaining 25). A release of the disqualifying power would give rise to a charge for tax under paragraph 15 (3). Its exercise would give rise to a charge under paragraph 6 (2). Either charge is subject to relief under paragraph 14.

E. The trustees have an over-riding power of appointment in favour of other persons.

F. The settled property has been revocably appointed to one of the children contingently on his attaining 25 and the appointment is now made irrevocable.

If the power to revoke prevents paragraph 15 from applying (as it would, for example, if the property thereby became subject to a power of appointment as at D or E), tax will be chargeable under sub-paragraph (3) when the appointment is made irrevocable. This is subject to relief under paragraph 14.

G. The trust to accumulate income expressed to be during the life of the settlor.

As the settlor may live beyond the 25th birthday of any of his children, the trust does not satisfy the condition in sub-paragraph (1) (*a*) and the paragraph does not apply.

Tax advantages

22-70   Where the conditions in § 22-68 are satisfied, paragraph 15 (2) of Schedule 5 to the Finance Act 1975 provides:

(1) that a payment made to a beneficiary out of the settled property (or the part in respect of which the conditions are satisfied) is not a capital distribution and the capital distribution is not treated as made on a beneficiary's becoming entitled to an interest in the property or part; and

(2) that no capital distribution is treated as made under the provisions relating to periodic charges at any time during the period for which the income is to be accumulated as mentioned in condition (b) above.

22-71   Where conditions (a) and (b) are satisfied at any time when there is only one beneficiary, they are not treated as ceasing to be satisfied on his death or on his attaining the specified age, if they would again be satisfied on the birth of another person. [83]

22-72   Thus if property is settled upon trust for the children of X who shall attain the age of 25 years and X has one child, A, who either dies or attains the age of 25 years, the conditions will be treated as continuing to be satisfied so long as X may have further children.

22-73   The occasion of transforming settled property in which there is no interest in possession into property held on accumulation and maintenance trusts is an occasion of charge to capital transfer tax: see § 22-54.

(2) Protective trusts

22-74   Paragraph 18 of Schedule 5 (as amended [84]) gives relief for settled property held on protective trusts, such as those specified in section 33 of the Trustee Act 1925. Tax is not charged when the principal beneficiary's interest comes to an end during the trust period; and a distribution payment to him is not a capital distribution. The periodic charges are deferred until a capital distribution is made or the trust period comes to an end.

6. THE PURCHASE OF A REVERSIONARY INTEREST

22-75   The estate of a person is the aggregate of all the property to which he is beneficially entitled other than excluded property. A reversionary interest acquired by purchase is not excluded property: § 23-03. Nevertheless, section 23 (3) of the Finance Act 1975 provides that where a person entitled to an interest (whether in possession or not) in any settled property acquires a reversionary interest expectant (whether immediately or not) on that interest, the reversionary interest is not part of his estate. This is complementary to the provision by which section 20 (4)—see *ante*, § 18-12—is made not to apply to a disposition by which a reversionary interest is acquired on arm's length terms. The explanation for these somewhat obscure provisions is as follows.

22-76   Suppose property is settled on A for life with remainder to B absolutely. A has £50,000 of free estate and the settled property is worth £100,000. B's reversionary interest has a market value of £40,000. The aggregate value of A's estate for capital transfer tax purposes is £150,000. If A purchases B's interest for £40,000, the value of A's estate would appear to be reduced to £110,000, *i.e.* £10,000 of free estate plus £100,000 of former settled property. The above provisions prevent tax being avoided in this way. First, section 20 (4) causes A's payment of £40,000 to be treated as a chargeable transfer, even though for full value: see § 18-12. Secondly, section 23 (3) treats the reversionary interest as not part of A's estate. Thus A is treated as having an estate worth £100,000 plus £10,000 and as having made a chargeable transfer of £40,000.

---

[83] F.A. 1975, Sched. 5, para. 15 (4).
[84] By F.A. 1976, s. 112 and Sched. 14, para. 19. There are amendments in F.A. 1978, s. 71, designed to counter various avoidance devices: see B.T.R. (1978), p. 172.

CHAPTER 23

EXCLUDED PROPERTY

23-01 WE have seen that a transfer of value is defined as any disposition which diminishes the value of a person's estate but that no account is to be taken of the value of excluded property which ceases to form part of the estate: *ante,* § 18-13. And although on the death of a person capital transfer tax is charged as if, immediately before his death, he had made a transfer of value equal to the value of his estate immediately before his death, it is expressly provided that the estate of a person immediately before his death does not include excluded property: *ante,* § 18-08. Thus the value of excluded property is left out of account on all transfers of value, whether lifetime transfers or transfers on death.

1. MEANING OF EXCLUDED PROPERTY

23-02 (1) Subject to § 23-06, property situated outside the United Kingdom is excluded property if the person beneficially entitled to it is an individual domiciled outside the United Kingdom.[1] Thus an individual domiciled outside the United Kingdom will avoid capital transfer tax by investing in assets situated outside the United Kingdom.

23-03 (2) Subject to § 23-06, a reversionary interest (as defined) is excluded property unless (a) it has at any time been acquired (whether by the person entitled to it or by a person previously entitled to it) for a consideration in money or money's worth; or (b) it is one to which either the settlor or his spouse is beneficially entitled[2]; or (c) it is an interest expectant on the determination of a lease treated as a settlement by virtue of the provisions discussed in § 22-09.[3]

> Thus if property is settled on A for life with remainder to B absolutely, no capital transfer tax is payable on a disposition by B of his reversionary interest before it falls into possession, unless B acquired his interest by purchase or by way of succession from a purchaser or is A's spouse.

23-04 The rationale of excluding the reversionary interest is that capital transfer tax will eventually be payable when the life interest comes to an end so the (then) reversioner will suffer the tax indirectly. The rationale of *not* excluding the reversionary interest acquired by purchase is that, without this exclusion, an individual could avoid capital transfer tax by purchasing a reversionary interest for its market value (thereby reducing the value of his estate by the purchase price) and making a gift or settlement of the interest so purchased. The special provisions applicable to the purchase of reversionary interests by life tenants etc. are considered in § 22-75.

---

[1] F.A. 1975, s. 24 (1) and (2).
[2] F.A. 1975, s. 24 (3) (*aa*) inserted by F.A. 1976, s. 120, but not so as to apply to a reversionary interest under a settlement made before that date.
[3] *Ibid.* s. 24 (1) and (3). And see Sched. 5, para. 2 (2). The exception in (c) keeps in charge to tax any transfer of value on the disposal of a reversionary interest: see § 20-20.

23-05   A " reversionary interest " means a future interest under a settlement, whether it is vested or contingent (including an interest expectant on the termination of an interest in possession which, by virtue of paragraph 3 of Schedule 5 to the Finance Act 1975 is treated as subsisting in part of any property).[4] It thus includes a future interest in remainder as well as a future interest in reversion. It also includes an interest which is expectant on the determination of a lease for life or lives treated as a settlement: see § 22-09.

23-06   (3) Paragraph 2 of Schedule 5 to the Finance Act 1975 provides that where property comprised in a settlement is situated outside the United Kingdom, the property (but not a reversionary interest in the property) is excluded property unless the settlor was domiciled in the United Kingdom at the time when the settlement was made. Thus if the settlor was domiciled outside the United Kingdom when the settlement was made, the property may be excluded property irrespective of the domicile of the beneficiary. The rule in § 23-02 is thus ousted except in the case of a reversionary interest, which is excluded property only if the beneficiary is an individual domiciled outside the United Kingdom.[5]

23-07   (4) Government securities in the beneficial ownership of persons neither domiciled nor resident in the United Kingdom are excluded property: see § 19-26.

23-08   (5) Certain savings by persons domiciled in the Channel Islands or the Isle of Man are excluded property: see § 19-28.

2. THE SITUATION OF PROPERTY

23-09   Under English law all property, whether corporeal or incorporeal, has to be treated as situated somewhere. The following table shows briefly the main rules of English law for determining the situation of the assets mentioned; but where a Double Taxation Convention applies, reference must be made to the text of the Convention to see if there are different rules.

Nature of property	*Where situate*
Land (including land subject to a mortgage) and other tangible assets.	Where the land or other asset is physically situated.
Debts:	
Simple contract debts.	Where the debtor resides.[6]
Specialty debts.	Where the specialty is situated.
Judgment debts.	Where the judgment is recorded.
Mortgages of land:	
If there is a personal obligation to repay the mortgage debt.	Same as for other debts (above).
If there is no such obligation but only a charge on the land.	Where the land is situate.

---

[4] F.A. 1975, s. 51 (1).   [5] *Ibid.* Sched. 5, para. 2 (1) (*b*).
[6] See *New York Life Insurance Co.* v. *Public Trustee* [1924] 2 Ch. 101, especially the judgment of Atkin L.J.; *English, Scottish and Australian Bank* v. *I.R.C.* [1932] A.C. 238 (H.L.).

Nature of property	Where situate
Securities:	
Bearer securities.	Where the document of title is situate.
Registered or inscribed securities.	Where the register is required to be kept.[7]
Bank balances.	Where the branch at which the debt is payable is situated.
Business assets, including a share in a partnership business and goodwill attached to a business.	Where the business is carried on.
Yacht situated in Great Britain but registered in Jersey.	Great Britain.[8]

3. EXTENDED MEANING OF DOMICILE

23-10 The general meaning of the word " domicile " in English law is discussed in textbooks on private international law, to which reference should be made. For capital transfer tax purposes, however, a person who would not otherwise be regarded as domiciled in the United Kingdom at any time (called " the relevant time ") is to be treated [9] as domiciled in the United Kingdom at the relevant time if

(a) he was domiciled in the United Kingdom on or after December 10, 1974, and within the three years immediately preceding the relevant time, *i.e.* three years' domicile outside the United Kingdom is needed to acquire a foreign domicile; or

(b) he was resident in the United Kingdom on or after December 10, 1974, and in not less than 17 of the 20 years of assessment ending with the year of assessment in which the relevant time falls; or

(c) he has, since December 10, 1974, become and has remained domiciled in the Islands (*i.e.* Channel Islands and the Isle of Man) and, immediately before becoming domiciled there, he was domiciled in the United Kingdom. This does not apply in the case of a person with a domicile of origin in the Islands or in the case of a person who, when he became so domiciled in the Islands was incapable of having an independent domicile.[10]

Hence a person of full age who was domiciled in the United Kingdom on or after December 10, 1974, and did not have a domicile of origin in the Islands cannot acquire a non-United Kingdom domicile by becoming domiciled there.

23-11 For the purposes of (b), the question whether a person was resident in the United Kingdom in any year of assessment is to be determined as for the purposes of income tax (*ante*, §§ 7-17 *et seq.*), but without regard to any dwelling house available in the United Kingdom for his use (see § 7-19).[11]

---

[7] See *Standard Chartered Bank Ltd.* v. *I.R.C.* (1978) S.T.C. 272 (a case on duplicate registers: test is where in the ordinary course of affairs the owner would have dealt with the shares).

[8] *Trustees Executors and Agency Co. Ltd.* v. *I.R.C.* [1973] Ch. 254; (1973) S.T.C. 96.

[9] F.A. 1975, s. 45 (1).

[10] F.A. 1977, s. 41 (1).

[11] F.A. 1975, s. 45 (2).

23-12   The property of a person who is treated as domiciled in the United Kingdom only by virtue of (c) in § 23-10 is nevertheless treated as " excluded property " if it represents (i) emoluments from an office or employment in the Islands at a time when he was domiciled there (using the term " domiciled " in its non-extended sense) or (ii) profits from the carrying on of a business there at such a time, either by him or by a company under his control. (i) does not apply to an office or employment with a connected person. (ii) applies to any business, which includes a profession or vocation but not a business of dealing in securities, stocks or shares or in land or buildings situated outside the Islands or making or holding investments being, in the case of investments consisting of land or buildings, land or buildings situated outside the Islands. [12]

23-13   The word " domicile " is normally construed in the legislation in this extended sense. [13]

4. UNILATERAL RELIEF

23-14 When the same transfer of value attracts capital transfer tax in the United Kingdom and a similar tax in a foreign country, relief may be available under treaties between the two countries but, where it is not, unilateral relief may be available. Where the relief is given, a credit is allowed for the foreign tax against the capital transfer tax. [14]

---

[12] F.A. 1977, s. 49. Settled property which represents (i) or (ii) may, if situated outside the United Kingdom, be " excluded property ": see *ibid*. s. 49 (4).

[13] F.A. 1975, s. 51 (3).

[14] See F.A. 1975, Sched. 7, para. 8 for details.

CHAPTER 24

LIABILITY AND INCIDENCE

WHERE a transfer of value is made, there is a duty to deliver an account to the Board. The obligations with respect to the delivery of an account are discussed in §§ 25-02 *et seq.* The first section of this chapter shows who is liable to *account* to the Board for the tax found to be due and it will be seen that the person or persons so liable may not be the same person or persons as are liable to *deliver* an account. Thus in the case of a lifetime transfer, the transferor is the person required to deliver an account whereas the Board can recover the tax either from the transferor or the transferee or, in the case of a transfer into settlement, from the settlor or the trustees or a beneficiary in respect of capital or income. When the tax has been paid to the Revenue the question next arises who has to bear the tax: in the case of a chargeable transfer on death, for example, does the tax attributable to an item of property comprised in the deceased person's estate fall on the residuary fund or on a specific legatee or devisee of that property? This is discussed in the second section of this chapter.

1. LIABILITY

The persons liable to account to the Board for capital transfer tax on the value transferred by a chargeable transfer are as follows; and where two or more persons are liable for the same tax, each is liable for the whole of it.[1] The basic rules in §§ 24-01 to 24-07 have to be read subject to qualifications in the paragraphs that follow.

(1) *Lifetime transfers*

24-01   Where the chargeable transfer is made by a disposition (including an omission treated as a disposition: see § 18-04) of the transferor, the persons liable are:

(a) the transferor and the transferee, *i.e.* the person the value of whose estate is increased by the transfer [2]; and

(b) so far as the tax is attributable to the value of any property, any person in whom the property is vested [3] (whether beneficially or otherwise) at any time after the transfer or who at any time is beneficially entitled to an interest in possession in the property; and

(c) where by the chargeable transfer any property becomes comprised in a settlement, any person for whose benefit any of the property or income from it is applied.[4]

---

[1] F.A. 1975, s. 25 (1).
[2] *Ibid.* s. 25 (9). The transferor is primarily liable: see § 24-14.
[3] This includes any person who takes possession of or intermeddles with, or otherwise acts in relation to, property so as to become liable as executor or trustee and any person to whom the management of property is contracted on behalf of a person not of full legal capacity: *ibid.* s. 25 (6).
[4] *Ibid.* s. 25 (2).

Note that the transferor is liable to account to the Board under (a) even if, as between himself and the transferee, the latter has agreed to bear the tax: and see § 20-15. Note that, in the case of a transfer into settlement, the trustees are liable under (b).

24-02 Where the chargeable transfer is made within three years of the transferor's death and extra tax becomes payable by reason of his failure to survive the three-year period (see § 20-05), the transferee (not the transferor's estate) is liable for the extra tax.[5]

(2) *Transfers of settled property*

24-03 Where the chargeable transfer is one made under Schedule 5 to the Act (see Chap. 22) the persons liable are:

(a) the trustees of the settlement; and
(b) any person entitled (whether beneficially or not) to an interest in possession in the settled property; and
(c) any person for whose benefit any of the settled property or income from it is applied at or after the time of the transfer; and
(d) where the chargeable transfer is made during the life of the settlor and the trustees are not for the time being resident in the United Kingdom, the settlor.[6]

24-04 Where the chargeable transfer is made within three years of the transferor's death and extra tax becomes payable by reason of his failure to survive the three-year period, the settlor is not liable for the extra tax.[7] The persons listed in paragraphs (a)–(c) in § 24-03 are liable.

Thus if S settles property on A for life with remainder to B absolutely and A assigns his interest to B and dies within three years thereafter, S is not liable for the extra tax. (In the example A is the assumed transferor by virtue of section 51 (2) of the Finance Act 1975: see § 22-22.) The trustees are primarily liable.

(3) *Transfers on death*

24-05 Where the chargeable transfer is made on the death of any person, under section 22 of the Act (*ante,* § 18-14), the persons liable are:

(a) the deceased's personal representatives (as defined)[8] as respects unsettled property and as respects settled United Kingdom land devolving on them as personal representatives[9];
(b) as respects settled property, the trustees of the settlement;
(c) so far as the tax is attributable to the value of any property, any

---

[5] F.A. 1975, s. 25 (4). In such a case the estate of the transferor may suffer both capital gains tax (on the original transfer) and capital transfer tax at the higher rates.

[6] *Ibid.* s. 25 (3). The trustees are primarily liable: see § 24-14. For residence of trustees, see *ibid.* s. 25 (10). Para. (*d*) does not apply in relation to a settlement made before December 11, 1974, if the trustees were resident in the United Kingdom when the settlement was made and, in the case of a chargeable transfer made after December 10, 1974, the trustees have not been resident in the United Kingdom at any time during the period between that date and the time of the transfer: F.A. 1976, s. 112 and Sched. 14, para. 20.

[7] F.A. 1975, s. 25 (4).

[8] *Ibid.* s. 51 (1).

[9] Settled land may now devolve on personal representatives: see n. 19 below.

person in whom the property is vested [10] (whether beneficially or otherwise) at any time after the death or who at any such time is beneficially entitled to an interest in possession in the property;

(d) so far as the tax is attributable to the value of any property which, immediately before the death, was settled property, any person for whose benefit any of the property or income from it is applied after the death. [11]

For the purposes of these provisions, a person entitled to part only of the income of any property is deemed to be entitled to an interest in the whole of the property. [12]

(4) *Inter-spouse transfers*

24-06   Where a transferor is liable for any tax and, by another transfer of value made by him on or after March 27, 1974, any property became the property of a person who at the time of both transfers was his spouse, that person is liable for so much of the tax as does not exceed the value of property at the time of the other transfer. [13] This prevents a person escaping liability to pay capital transfer tax on a chargeable transfer to one person by thereafter making an exempt transfer of the funds out of which tax on the first transfer would be payable to his (the transferor's) spouse.

> Thus if H gives property to his son (S) who is domiciled outside the United Kingdom and the rest of his property to his (H's) wife (W), and the tax cannot be recovered from H or S, the Revenue can seek recovery from W.

" *Property* "

24-07   References in the above paragraphs to " property " include references to any property directly or indirectly representing it. [14] Hence the tax charge is not avoided by selling the original property and reinvesting the proceeds of sale in other property.

Exception from liability for purchasers

24-08   A purchaser of property, and a person deriving title from or under such a purchaser, is not liable for tax attributable to the value of the property purchased, unless the property is subject to an Inland Revenue charge. [15] " Purchaser " in this context means a purchaser in good faith for consideration in money or money's worth other than a nominal consideration and includes a lessee, mortgagee or other person who for such consideration acquires an interest in the property in question. [16]

> Thus if A makes a lifetime transfer of property to B who sells the property to a purchaser P, only A and B are liable for the tax on A's transfer notwithstanding (b) in § 24-01. Inland Revenue charges are referred to in § 25-31.

---

[10] See n. 3, above.   [11] F.A. 1975, s. 25 (5). But see *ibid.* s. 25 (7).
[12] F.A. 1975, s. 25 (5) and see § 22-18.
[13] *Ibid.* s. 25 (8). As to the " value " for this purpose, see F.A. 1976, s. 119.
[14] *Ibid.* s. 25 (10).
[15] *Ibid.* s. 26 (1). *Post*, § 25-31.
[16] *Ibid.* s. 51 (1).

Special exemptions from liability in relation to objects and buildings forming part of the national heritage, woodlands, charities and political parties have been referred to elsewhere.[17]

Limitation of liability

24-09 The above paragraphs refer to various classes of person who may be liable for capital transfer tax; but section 27 of the Finance Act 1975 imposes some limit to their liability, as follows:

(1) *Personal representatives*

24-10 Generally a personal representative of a deceased person is not liable for tax attributable to the value of any property except to the extent of the assets he has received as personal representative or might have so received but for his own neglect or default. There is an exception as regards tax attributable to settled property consisting of land in the United Kingdom which devolves on or becomes vested in the personal representative: his liability is then limited to so much of that property as is at any time available in his hands for the payment of the tax or might have been so available but for his own neglect or default.[18] Settled land (within the meaning of the Settled Land Act 1925) may now devolve on personal representatives.[19]

(2) *Trustees*

24-11 A person is not liable for tax as trustee in relation to any property, except to the extent of:

(a) so much of the property as he has actually received or disposed of, or as he has become liable to account for, to the persons beneficially entitled thereto; and

(b) so much of any other property as is for the time being available in his hands as trustee for the payment of the tax or might have been so available but for his own neglect or default.[20]

(3) *Vested or beneficial interest in property*

24-12 A person not liable for tax as personal representative or trustee but liable for tax as a person in whom property is vested, or as a person entitled to a beneficial interest in possession in any property, is not liable for tax except to the extent of that property.[21]

Where the transferor dies within three years after the transfer and extra tax becomes payable, a person is not liable for this extra tax as a person in whom property is vested otherwise than beneficially except to the extent of so much of the property as is vested in him at the time of the death; and a

---

[17] *Ante*, Chap. 19.
[18] F.A. 1975, s. 27 (1).
[19] This is the consequence of the repeal of s. 53 (3) of the Administration of Estates Act 1925 by Sched. 13 to the F.A. 1975.
[20] F.A. 1975, s. 27 (2).
[21] *Ibid*. s. 27 (3).

person is not liable for the extra tax as a trustee in relation to any property except to the extent of

  (a) so much of the property as is vested in him at the time of the death; and

  (b) so much of the property as, after the death, he has actually received or disposed of or as, after the death, he has become liable to account for to the persons beneficially entitled thereto.[22]

> Thus if S transfers property to trustees for a number of beneficiaries and, when S dies within three years of the transfer, the trustees have already distributed the trust property (or part of it) to the beneficiaries, the trustees are not liable for the extra tax save to the extent that it is attributable to the undistributed funds. The beneficiaries are so liable.

(4) Beneficiaries

24-13   A person liable for capital transfer tax as a person for whose benefit any settled property, or income from any settled property, is applied is not liable for the tax except to the extent of the amount of the property or income (reduced in the case of income by the amount of any income tax borne by him in respect of it).[23]

Primary and secondary liability

24-14   The person primarily liable for the tax in the case of a lifetime transfer is the transferor and, in the case of a chargeable transfer made under Schedule 5 to the Act, the trustees of the settlement. The other persons referred to above are liable only if the tax remains unpaid after it ought to have been paid.[24] Their liability is thus of a secondary nature. Where any part of the value transferred is attributable to the tax on it (*i.e.* where tax is taken into account in determining the diminution in the transferor's estate in consequence of the transfer), the person secondarily liable is liable to no greater extent than he would have been had the value transferred been reduced by the tax remaining unpaid.[25]

> Assume A makes a lifetime transfer of £40,000 to B and that the tax for which A is primarily accountable is £5,000, *i.e.* the value transferred by A is £40,000 plus £5,000 equals £45,000. If A pays none of the tax, B's liability is calculated on the basis that the value transferred is £40,000. If A pays (say) £3,000 of the tax, leaving £2,000 unpaid, B's liability is calculated on the basis that the value transferred is £45,000 *less* £2,000 equals £43,000.

A is in both cases liable for the tax for which B is not liable. A is exclusively liable for the excess tax payable in the event of A dying within three years of the transfer.[26]

2. INCIDENCE

(1) Lifetime transfers

24-15   The question who, as between donor and donee (or settlor and trustees), should bear the tax on a lifetime transfer is a matter they must decide

---

[22] *Ibid.* s. 27 (4).   [23] F.A. 1975, s. 27 (5).
[24] *Ibid.* s. 27 (6). As to when tax ought to be paid, see §§ 25-24 *et seq.*
[25] *Ibid.* s. 27 (6).   [26] *Ibid.* s. 27 (7).

between themselves and this decision will determine the amount by which the estate of the donor (or settlor) is diminished and, accordingly, the amount of tax payable. If A gives £100,000 to B and A agrees to or in fact pays the tax, having no right of reimbursement against B, the £100,000 has to be grossed up as explained in § 20-10. There is no such grossing up if B pays the tax.

(2) Death

24-16   Personal representatives have to deliver an account to the Board specifying to the best of their knowledge and belief all the property which formed part of the deceased's estate immediately before his death and the value of that property (see §§ 25-02 et seq.) and, on delivery of their account, must pay all the tax for which they are liable and may also pay tax for which they are not liable at the request of the persons who are liable (see § 25-24). Where, as is commonly the case, the deceased's estate comprises a number of different assets, the amount of tax attributable to each item is found by dividing the total tax payable between the various assets according to their respective values, but subject to any provision reducing the amount of tax attributable to the value of any particular property.[27]

The capital transfer tax legislation has followed the estate duty principle of providing that certain property should be the subject of an Inland Revenue charge and so carry its own burden of tax, whereas tax on other property should be treated as a testamentary expense payable in accordance with provisions contained in the Administration of Estates Act 1925 (normally out of the testator's residuary estate). The property which is the subject of an Inland Revenue charge and so bears its own tax is realty (wherever situated) and property (whether real or personal) situated outside the United Kingdom.[28] Tax attributable to personal or movable property situated in the United Kingdom which was in the beneficial ownership of the deceased immediately before his death and which vests in the deceased's personal representatives is generally payable out of residue; and, for this purpose, leasehold property and undivided shares in land held on trust for sale are treated as personal property: see § 25-32.

Varying the incidence of tax

24-17   The incidence of capital transfer tax can be varied by the testator by appropriate provisions in his will. The following example illustrates the effect of the normal rules:

> The property chargeable to capital transfer tax on T's death is as follows: freehold property in England; leasehold property in England; foreign personalty; a joint interest in English freehold land; and shares in English companies. By his will T gives the freehold to A; the leasehold to B; the foreign personalty to C; and the residue of his estate to D. The total amount of tax payable is £50,000 which is apportioned rateably between the assets comprised in the estate.

---

[27] F.A. 1975, s. 43.
[28] Ibid. Sched. 4, para. 20.

Under the normal rules, the freehold and the foreign personalty carry their own burden of tax payable by A and C respectively. There is an Inland Revenue charge on that property and section 28 (1) of the Finance Act 1975 enables T's personal representatives, having paid the tax, to have it repaid to them.[29] Tax on the leasehold property is a testamentary expense and would be payable out of the residue given to D. Duty on the joint property (which passes to the surviving joint tenant and does not vest in T's personal representatives) is payable by the surviving joint tenant. Duty on the shares, which comprise the residuary estate, is payable out of residue. Much of the residuary estate given to D will therefore go in capital transfer tax. (It is assumed in the example that none of the beneficiaries was T's wife: the problems that arise in the case of partially exempt transfers are discussed in § 24-20).

The testator may, if he wishes, vary the incidence of tax by appropriate provisions in his will. Thus, in the example, if T wished A and B to be in the same position as regards liability for tax, he could devise the freehold " free of capital transfer tax," when the burden of tax would be thrown on to residue; or alternatively, he could provide that B should bear a rateable part of the tax, thereby freeing the residue from this liability.

24-18 Under estate duty law it was held that when a testator wishes to throw the burden of duty on to residue, a clause directing that " testamentary expenses " should be paid out of residue was insufficient to transfer estate duty which was a specific charge on property.[30] More specific provision was usually necessary, such as a direction to pay estate duty out of residue.[31] It is thought that a similar principle may apply as respects capital transfer tax. Section 49 (5) of the Finance Act 1965 provides that any provision in a document which refers to estate duty or death duties is to be taken as referring to capital transfer tax (see § 26-07); hence a provision in a will devising a freehold property " free of death duties " or " free of estate duty " suffices to free a property from liability to capital transfer tax.

Apportionment

24-19 Where there is a direction in a will that legacies should be paid out of a mixed fund comprising both realty and personalty, it was held (under the old estate duty law) that the legacy was presumed to have been paid out of realty according to the proportion of realty to personalty in the fund. The legatee had to bear that part of the estate duty which was apportioned to the realty.[32] It is thought that a similar principle applies to capital transfer tax.

---

[29] *Ibid.* s. 28 (1) provides that where the personal representatives have paid tax on property on which there is an Inland Revenue charge, the tax " shall, where occasion requires, be repaid to them by the person in whom the property is vested." Occasion would so require unless the testator had directed the tax to be paid out of residue. The personal representatives can raise the tax by sale or mortgage of the property: see *ibid.* s. 28 (3).

[30] *Re Owers* [1941] Ch. 17.

[31] *Re Pimm* [1904] 2 Ch. 345; *cf. Re King* [1942] Ch. 413; *Re Phuler's Will Trusts* [1965] 1 W.L.R. 68; *Re Neeld, decd. (No. 2) (Note)* [1965] 1 W.L.R. 73n. (C.A.); *Re Walley* [1972] 1 W.L.R. 257; *Re Rosenthal* [1972] 1 W.L.R. 1273; *Re Williams* [1974] S.T.C. 123.

[32] *Re Spencer Cooper* [1908] 1 Ch. 130. See generally the eighth edition of this book, §§ 29-10 *et seq.*

Partially exempt transfers

24-20   Part III of Schedule 6 to the Finance Act 1975 contains provisions to meet
the case where a transfer of value is partially exempt, as in a case where a
person dies having by will given legacies and residue in a combination of
taxable and exempt transfers. Under the law as it existed before the
enactment of section 96 of the Finance Act 1976, a procedure was adopted
which can be exemplified as follows [33]:

> T dies with an estate of £100,000 giving a legacy of £40,000 to his son and the
> residue to T's wife, who survives T. Assume that T has made no previous
> chargeable transfers. Tax on the legacy of £40,000 is a testamentary expense
> and is payable out of residue. The amount of the exempt residue is computed as
> follows. Tax on a total estate of £100,000, if it was all taxable, would be
> £28,250 giving an " estate rate " of 28·25 per cent. Grossing up the legacy of
> £40,000 at this rate would produce a figure of £55,759. Tax notionally
> attributable to the legacy would be £12,459. Hence T's son received £40,000.
> The exempt residue to which T's wife was entitled was £60,000 less £12,459.

This example shows that the legacy had to be grossed up at a rate which
assumed the *whole* estate to be liable to tax. The amount of the exempt
residue would be increased by T giving a larger legacy and making it bear its
own tax.

24-21   Section 96 of the Finance Act 1976, which applies to transfers of value
after April 6, 1976, has made substantial alterations to the law. The stages
under the new procedure are as follows:

(1) Gifts are grossed up at the rate of tax that would be appropriate if
they alone comprised the transfers of value;

(2) by reference to the gross figure so obtained, the exempt and
chargeable parts of the transfer are calculated;

(3) the gifts (at their original net value) are grossed up again by reference
to the rate of tax appropriate to the chargeable part of the transfer
ascertained at (2);

(4) the exempt and chargeable parts of the transfer are finally
recalculated by reference to the gross figure ascertained at (3).

If the only taxable gifts are gifts not bearing their own tax, only stages (1)
and (2) of the calculation need be made.

> Taking the simple example in § 24-20, the legacy of £40,000 is now grossed up
> at the rate appropriate to a transfer of £40,000, not £100,000 as before. This
> produces a figure of £42,250. Thus T's son receives £40,000, as before. The tax
> is £2,250. The widow receives the balance of £57,750.

If in this example T had made lifetime transfers of (say) £50,000, the
legacy of £40,000 would be grossed up at the rate applicable taking the
lifetime transfers into account, and the residue would be determined
accordingly.

24-22   The calculations become much more complicated where some of the
residue is exempt and some is not. To take a simple example:

---

[33] The example is based on the Tables in operation before 1977.

T's estate is £200,000. Assume there have been no previous chargeable transfers. T gives a legacy of £40,000 to his son. Tax on the legacy is a testamentary expense payable out of residue. T gives the residue of his estate to his widow (W) and daughter (D) equally. (The gift of residue to T's widow (W) is exempt: see § 19-02.)

In this case the problem is to ensure that the widow's exempt share of residue does not bear the tax attributable to the daughter's taxable share of residue. The computations proceed as follows:

(1) The legacy is £40,000. The grossed up amount appropriate to this sum is £42,250 on which the tax is £2,250.

(2) On the basis of (1) the residue is £200,000 less £42,250 equals £157,750. Half of this (£78,875) is exempt. The chargeable part of the estate is £200,000 less £78,875 equals £121,125.

(3) The tax on £121,125 is £33,812 (a rate of 27·92 per cent.). At this rate £40,000 grosses up to £55,494.

(4) On this basis the residue is £200,000 less £55,494 equals £144,506. Half of this (£72,253) is exempt. The chargeable part is £200,000 less £72,253 equals £127,747. The tax on this is £37,123.

The estate is thus disposed of as follows:

	£
S	40,000
W	72,253
D	35,130
Tax — attributable to S's legacy	15,494
— attributable to D's share of residue	37,123
	£200,000

CHAPTER 25

ADMINISTRATION AND COLLECTION

25-01 CAPITAL transfer tax is under the care and management of the Board.[1] Section 19 of and Schedule 4 to the Finance Act 1975 provide for its administration and collection.

1. DELIVERY OF AN ACCOUNT

The duty to account

25-02 The personal representatives of a deceased person and every person who:

(a) is liable as transferor for tax on the value transferred by a chargeable transfer, or would be so liable if tax were chargeable on that value; or

(b) is liable as trustee of a settlement for tax on the value transferred by a transfer of value made after March 26, 1974, or would be so liable if tax were chargeable on that value; or

(c) is liable as trustee of a settlement for tax on a capital distribution, or would be so liable if tax were chargeable on it [2];

is required to deliver to the Board an account specifying to the best of his knowledge and belief all " relevant property " and the value of that property.[3]

25-03 Where the account is to be delivered by personal representatives the relevant property is all property which formed part of the deceased's estate immediately before his death; but if the personal representatives, after making the fullest inquiries that are reasonably practicable in the circumstances, are unable to ascertain the exact value of any particular property, their account is in the first instance sufficient as regards that property if it contains a statement to that effect, a provisional estimate of the value of the property and an undertaking to deliver a further account of it as soon as its value is ascertained. The Board may from time to time give such general or special directions as they think fit for restricting the property to be specified by personal representatives.[4]

25-04 In other cases the relevant property is any property to the value of which the tax is or would be attributable.[5]

---

[1] F.A. 1975, Sched. 4, para. 1. The Board means the Commissioners of Inland Revenue: F.A. 1975, s. 51 (1).

[2] Para. (c) added by F.A. 1976, s. 112 and Sched. 14, para. 4.

[3] F.A. 1975, Sched. 4, para. 2 (1).

[4] *Ibid.* para. 2 (2). A person who is executor only in respect of settled land in England and Wales is excluded and " relevant property " has the meaning in § 25-04.

[5] *Ibid.* para. 2 (3).

463

25-05 Except in the case of an account to be delivered by personal representatives, a person is not required to deliver an account under paragraph 2 of Schedule 4 (§ 25-03) with respect to any property if a full and proper account of that property, specifying its value, has already been delivered to the Board by some other person who is or would be liable for the tax attributable to the value of the property, unless that other person is or would be liable with him jointly as trustee.[6]

Time for delivering account

25-06 An account must be delivered:

(a) in the case of an account to be delivered by *personal representatives*, before the expiration of the period of 12 months from the end of the month in which the death occurs, or, if it expires later, the period of three months beginning with the date on which the personal representatives first act as such; and

(b) in the case of an account to be delivered by *any other person*, before the expiration of the period of 12 months from the end of the month in which the transfer is made or, if it expires later, the period of three months beginning with the date on which he first becomes liable for tax.[7]

25-07 A person liable for tax under section 32 (§ 19-34) or section 34 (§ 19-39) or paragraph 2 of Schedule 9 to the Finance Act 1975 (§ 19-52) must deliver an account before the expiration of the period of six months from the end of the month in which the event by reason of which the tax is chargeable occurs.[8]

Corrective and supplementary accounts

25-08 If a person who has delivered an account under the above provisions discovers at any time that the account is defective in a material respect by reason of anything contained in or omitted from it he must, within six months of that time, deliver to the Board a further account containing such information as may be necessary to remedy the defect.[9]

2. RETURNS BY CERTAIN PERSONS ACTING FOR SETTLORS

25-09 Where any person, in a course of a trade or profession carried on by him, other than the profession of a barrister, has been concerned with the making after March 26, 1974, of a settlement and knows or has reason to believe

(a) that the settlor was domiciled in the United Kingdom, and

(b) that the trustees of the settlement are not or will not be resident in the United Kingdom;

---

[6] F.A. 1975, para. 2 (4).
[7] *Ibid*. para. 2 (5). For transfers of value made more than six months before March 13, 1975, substitute for " 12 months " in (b) " six months from March 13, 1975 ": *ibid*. para. 2 (6).
[8] *Ibid*. para. 2 (7).
[9] *Ibid*. para. 3.

he must, within three months of the making of the settlement or, if it was made before March 13, 1975 (when the Act was passed), within three months of the passing of the Act, make a return to the Board stating the names and addresses of the settlor and of the trustees of the settlement.[10]

25-10   This requirement does not apply to:

(a) any settlement made by will, or

(b) any other settlement, if such a return in relation to that settlement has already been made by another person or if an account has been delivered in relation to it under paragraph 2 of Schedule 4: §§ 25-02 *et seq*.[11]

3. POWER TO REQUIRE INFORMATION AND INSPECT PROPERTY

25-11   The Board may by notice in writing require any person to furnish them within such time, not being less than 30 days, as may be specified in the notice with such information as the Board may require for the purposes of the capital transfer tax provisions.[12] The notice may be combined with a notice relating to income tax.[13]

25-12   A barrister or solicitor is not obliged in pursuance of a notice under this provision to disclose, without his client's consent, any information with respect to which a claim to professional privilege could be maintained; except that

(a) a solicitor may be so obliged to disclose the name and address of his client; and

(b) if his client is resident outside the United Kingdom and carries on outside the United Kingdom a business which includes the provision for persons in the United Kingdom of services or facilities relating to the formation of companies outside the United Kingdom, the making of settlements outside the United Kingdom, or the securing of control over, or the management or administration of, such companies or settlements, a solicitor may also be so obliged to disclose the names and addresses of persons in the United Kingdom for whom such services or the facilities have been provided in the course of that business.[14]

25-13   If the Board authorise any person to inspect any property for the purpose of ascertaining its value for the purposes of capital transfer tax, the person having the custody or possession of the property must permit him to inspect it at such reasonable times as the Board may consider necessary. If any person wilfully delays or obstructs a person acting in pursuance of this provision he is liable on summary conviction to a fine not exceeding £20.[15]

---

[10] F.A. 1975, para. 4 (1).
[11] *Ibid*. para. 4 (2).
[12] *Ibid*. para. 5 (1).
[13] *Ibid*. para. 5 (2).
[14] *Ibid*. para. 5 (3).
[15] *Ibid*. para. 11.

4. Assessment and Appeals

25-14 Income tax, corporation tax and capital gains tax are generally charged by notices of assessment and appeals against assessments may be brought before the General or Special Commissioners. In the case of capital transfer tax, however, the Board give notice of determination of certain matters and an appeal lies against the Board's determination.

25-15 Where it appears to the Board that a transfer of value has been made, or where a claim has been made to the Board in connection with a transfer of value, the Board may give notice in writing to any person who appears to the Board to be the transferor or the claimant or to be liable for any of the tax chargeable on the value transferred, stating that they have determined the matters specified in the notice.[16] Reference here to transfers of value or to the values transferred by them include capital distributions or the amounts on which tax is chargeable in respect of them.[17]

25-16 The matters that may be specified in a notice in relation to any transfer of value are all or any of the following:
  (a) the date of the transfer;
  (b) the value transferred and the value of any property to which the value transferred is wholly or partly attributable;
  (c) the transferor;
  (d) the tax chargeable (if any) and the persons who are liable for the whole or part of it;
  (e) the amount of any payment made in excess of the tax for which a person is liable and the date on which and the rate at which tax or any repayment of tax overpaid carries interest; and
  (f) any other matter that appears to the Board to be relevant for the purposes of the capital transfer tax part of the Act.[18]

25-17 A determination of any fact relating to a transfer of value will, if that fact has been stated in an account or return and the Board are satisfied that the account or return is correct, be made by the Board in accordance with that account or return; but may, in any other case, be made by the Board to the best of their judgment.[19] Thus the Board can make estimated determinations of value transferred in the same way that estimated assessments can be made for income tax purposes.

25-18 A notice of determination must state the time within which and the manner in which an appeal against any determination in it may be made.[20]

Conclusiveness of a notice

25-19 Subject to any variation by agreement in writing or on appeal, a determination in a notice is conclusive against the person on whom the

---

[16] F.A. 1975, para. 6 (1).
[17] *Ibid.* para. 6 (6), added by F.A. 1976, s. 112 and Sched. 14, para. 5.
[18] *Ibid.* para. 6 (2).
[19] *Ibid.* para. 6 (3).
[20] *Ibid.* para. 6 (4).

notice is served; and if the notice is served on the transferor and specifies a determination of the value transferred by the transfer of value or previous transfers of value, the determination, so far as relevant to the tax chargeable in respect of later transfers of value (whether or not made by the transferor) is conclusive also against any other person, subject, however, to any adjustment under the provisions which may apply where too much or too little tax has been paid.[21]

Appeals

25-20   A person on whom a notice has been served may, within 30 days of the service, appeal against any determination specified in it by notice in writing given to the Board and specifying the grounds of appeal.[22] The appeal is to the Special Commissioners except in two cases:

(a) where it is agreed between the appellant and the Board (or, in default of agreement, if the High Court is satisfied on an application made by the appellant and gives leave) that the matters to be decided on the appeal are likely to be substantially confined to questions of law, the appeal may be to the High Court;

(b) any question as to the value of land in the United Kingdom must be determined by the Lands Tribunal.[23]

Many questions on capital transfer tax are questions of construction, and proceedings in the High Court (commenced by originating summons) are appropriate.

Appeals out of time

25-21   An appeal may be brought out of time with the consent of the Board or the Special Commissioners. The Board

(a) must give that consent if satisfied, on an application for the purpose, that there was a reasonable excuse for not bringing the appeal within the time limited and that the application was made thereafter without unreasonable delay; and

(b) must, if not so satisfied, refer the application for determination by the Special Commissioners.[24]

Procedure before Special Commissioners

25-22   This is similar to the procedure where other taxes are involved. The Board may be represented by any of its officers; and any party to the appeal may be represented by a barrister, solicitor or any accountant who has been admitted a member of an incorporated society of accountants or, with the leave of the Special Commissioners, by any other person.[25] The Special Commissioners have wide powers to require the delivery of particulars and information, and to summon witnesses.[26]

The Special Commissioners may allow the appellant to put forward any ground of appeal not specified in the notice of appeal and may take it

---

[21] F.A. 1975, para. 6 (5) and paras. 23 and 24.   [22] *Ibid.* para. 7 (1).
[23] *Ibid.* para. 7 (2), (3), (4).   [24] *Ibid.* para. 8.
[25] *Ibid.* para. 9 (1).   [26] *Ibid.* para. 9 (2)–(3).

into consideration if satisfied that the omission was not wilful or unreasonable.[27] The Commissioners are required to confirm the determination appealed against unless they are satisfied that the determination ought to be varied or quashed.[28]

Statement of case

25-23   Within 30 days of the determination by the Special Commissioners of an appeal, any party to the appeal may question the determination on a point of law by a written request to the Special Commissioners to state and sign a case for the opinion of the High Court. The procedure and the powers and duties of the High Court with respect to such an appeal are similar to those in cases involving other taxes.[29]

5. PAYMENT OF TAX

25-24   Generally capital transfer tax is due six months after the end of the month in which the chargeable transfer is made or, in the case of a transfer made after April 5 and before October 1 in any year otherwise than on death, at the end of April in the next year.[30]

Personal representatives must, on delivery of their account, pay all the tax for which they are liable and may also pay any part of the tax chargeable on the death for which they are not liable, if the persons liable therefor request them to make the payment.[31]

Extra tax payable by virtue of the transferor dying within three years of the transfer (or one year in the case of a transfer to a charity or political party) is due six months after the end of the month in which the death occurs.[32]

Tax chargeable under section 32 or section 34 or paragraph 2 of Schedule 9 is due six months after the end of the month in which the event by reason of which it is chargeable occurs.[33]

25-25   The Board have power in the first instance, and without prejudice to the recovery of the remainder of the tax, to accept or demand payment of an amount by reference to the value stated in an account or supplementary or corrective amount delivered to the Board.[34]

None of the above provisions authorise the recovery from, or require the payment by, any person to tax in excess of his liability as limited by section 27 of the Finance Act 1975 (§§ 24-09 *et seq.*).[35]

Payment of tax by instalments

25-26   Paragraph 13 of Schedule 4 to the Finance Act 1975 contains elaborate provisions, which cannot be conveniently summarised, for tax to be paid by

---

[27] F.A. 1975, para. 9 (4).
[28] *Ibid.* para. 9 (5).
[29] *Ibid.* para. 10; and see §§ 17-11 *et seq.*
[30] *Ibid.* para. 12 (1).
[31] *Ibid.* para. 12 (2).
[32] *Ibid.* para. 12 (3).
[33] *Ibid.* para. 12 (4) and see §§ 19-34, 39 and 52.
[34] *Ibid.* para. 12 (5).
[35] *Ibid.* para. 12 (6).

instalments where the value transferred is attributable to the value of land of any description, wherever situated, shares or securities giving control (as defined)[36] of a company and other shares or securities not quoted on a recognised stock exchange in respect of which certain conditions are satisfied. The provisions apply to transfers on death; and they apply to transfers otherwise than on death if either (a) the tax is borne by the person benefiting from the transfer or (b) the property is settled and remains in settlement after the transfer. If the property is sold before all instalments have been paid the balance of the tax becomes immediately payable.

25-27   Payment by instalments is (at the option of the taxpayer) by eight yearly or 16 half-yearly instalments and, generally, interest is chargeable on the whole of the unpaid tax at each instalment date. The rates of interest are 6 per cent. if the transfer was made on death and 9 per cent. in any other case.

25-28   Paragraphs 14 and 15 of Schedule 4 provide for payment by instalments where the property transferred is a business or an interest in a business, and where there is a lifetime disposal of timber.

25-29   Paragraph 16 of Schedule 4 provides that the instalments are to be free of interest where the value transferred represents a business or shares or securities other than in a company whose business is wholly or mainly dealing in shares or land or the making or holding of investments. Land or buildings may qualify for this relief as business assets. There is an overriding limit of £250,000 on the value on which instalments may be interest-free.

Acceptance of property in satisfaction of tax

25-30   Paragraph 17 of Schedule 4 (as amended) [37] gives the Board power to accept certain types of property, such as a work of art which the Treasury are satisfied is pre-eminent for aesthetic merit or historical value, in satisfaction of a claim for capital transfer tax.

Transfers reported late

25-30A   Section 114 of the Finance Act 1976 provides that where an earlier transfer is not notified to the Board until after payment has been accepted in full satisfaction of tax on a later transfer, the earlier transfer is to be treated as made on the date on which it was discovered or, if the later transfer was on death, immediately before that transfer. But where either transfer was a transfer into a discretionary trust, the section does not affect the tax chargeable on a distribution out of the trust.

Inland Revenue charge for unpaid tax

25-31   Where any tax charged on the value transferred by a chargeable transfer, or any interest on it, is for the time being unpaid, a charge for the amount

---

[36] And see now F.A. 1978, s. 66.
[37] See F.A. 1976, s. 124.

unpaid (called an Inland Revenue charge) is imposed in favour of the Board
on

(a) any property to the value of which the value transferred is wholly or
partly attributable; and

(b) where the chargeable transfer is made by the making of a settlement
or is made under Schedule 5 to the Act, any property comprised in
the settlement.[38]

Property includes any property directly or indirectly representing it.[39]

25-32   Where the chargeable transfer is made on death, personal or movable
property situated in the United Kingdom which was beneficially owned by
the deceased immediately before his death and vests in his personal
representatives is not subject to the Inland Revenue charge; and for this
purpose " personal property " includes leaseholds and undivided shares in
land held on trust for sale, whether statutory or not, and the question
whether any property was beneficially owned by the deceased is for this
purpose determined without regard to paragraph 3 (1) of Schedule 5
(§ 22-17).[40]

25-33   The Inland Revenue charge imposed on any property takes effect subject
to any incumbrance thereon which is allowable as a deduction in valuing
that property for the purposes of the tax.[41]

25-34   A disposition of property subject to an Inland Revenue charge takes
effect subject to that charge [42] unless the disposition is to a purchaser and,
at the time of the disposition (as defined) certain conditions are satisfied,
when the purchaser takes the property free from the charge; but the
property for the time being representing it is subject to the charge.[43] Thus if
in the case of land in England or Wales the charge is not registered as a land
charge or, in the case of personal property situated in the United Kingdom,
the purchaser had no notice of the facts giving rise to the charge, the
purchaser takes free from the Inland Revenue charge but the proceeds of
sale in the hands of the vendor become subject to it. Where property subject
to an Inland Revenue charge, or an interest in such property, is disposed of
to a purchaser in circumstances where it does not then cease to be subject to
the charge, it ceases to be subject to it on the expiration of the period of six
years beginning with the later of the following dates:

(a) the date on which the tax became due; and

(b) the date on which a full and proper account of the property was first
delivered to the Board in connection with the chargeable transfer
concerned.[44]

---

[38] F.A. 1975, para. 20 (1).
[39] *Ibid.* para. 20 (2).
[40] *Ibid.* para. 20 (3), and see (4).
[41] *Ibid.* para. 20 (5).
[42] *Ibid.* para. 20 (6).
[43] *Ibid.* para. 21 (1) and (3).
[44] *Ibid.* para. 21 (2).

CHAPTER 26

CAPITAL TRANSFER TAX AND ESTATE DUTY

1. ABOLITION OF ESTATE DUTY

26-01 ESTATE duty is not leviable on deaths occurring after March 12, 1975 [1]; capital transfer tax is leviable. [2]

It follows that if A makes an outright gift or settlement before March 27, 1974 (*i.e.* before capital transfer tax applied to lifetime transfers) and dies within seven years of his gift, but after March 12, 1975, no estate duty is leviable on A's death in respect of the gift or settlement. In order to prevent loss of tax in these circumstances, there is a " clawback " provision in section 22 (5) of the Finance Act 1975. [3] This subsection provides that where a person who dies after March 12, 1975,

  (a) had, before March 27, 1974, but not more than seven years before his death, made a gift *inter vivos* of any property; or

  (b) had, before March 27, 1974, but not at any time thereafter, a beneficial interest in possession in any property comprised in a settlement

and, by reason thereof, any property would have been included in the property passing on his death had estate duty not been abolished, then in determining for the purposes of capital transfer tax the value of his estate immediately before his death, there shall be included the value which for the purposes of estate duty would have been the principal value of the property so included. If the tapering rules for deaths after four or more years would have applied for estate duty, they will be applied for capital transfer tax; so also the reduced rates in respect of agricultural property or business property.

Note that this clawback provision does not apply to gifts made more than seven years before the transferor's death which would have been subject to estate duty by reason of a reservation of a benefit. In such a case only capital transfer tax is payable on the value of the reserved benefit forming part of the deceased's estate. Note also that there is no clawback for capital transfer tax in respect of dispositions made by trustees of discretionary or accumulation trusts which would have brought about a claim to estate duty under head (iii) or (iv) of section 2 (1) (*b*) of the Finance Act 1894.

2. DEATHS IN THE INTERIM PERIOD

26-02 The White Paper on capital transfer tax [4] gave notice that the Government would amend the estate duty law in certain respects in its application to

---

[1] F.A. 1975, s. 49 (1).
[2] *Ibid.* s. 22 (1).
[3] And see F.A. 1976, s. 98.
[4] Cmnd. 5705.

deaths after Budget Day (November 12, 1974) and before the passing of the Act (March 13, 1975). This period may be called " the interim period." As respects deaths on and before Budget Day, the normal estate duty rules continue to apply. [5]

26-03   Schedule 11 to the Finance Act 1975 contains provisions for altering the enactments relating to estate duty in relation to deaths occurring in the interim period. [6] The principal alterations are, briefly, as follows:

(1) Estate duty is charged at the rates of tax which would apply if the aggregate principal value of the property passing on death were the value transferred by a chargeable transfer made on death where the transferor had made no previous chargeable transfers. [7]

(2) Property passing to a spouse on death is generally exempt from estate duty, and not exempt only up to the £15,000 limit provided under the estate duty law. If both husband and wife die in the interim period, property which is exempt on the first death under this provision is not also exempt on the second death under the surviving spouse exemption. [8]

(3) The reduced rates of duty on agricultural property and on certain business assets do not apply except in relation to property which, by reason of an interest which came to an end or a gift which was made before November 13, 1974, passes on a death by virtue of section 2 (1) (b) (i) or section 2 (1) (c) of the Finance Act 1894. [9]

26-04   The relief from capital transfer tax for agricultural property has been discussed in §§ 19-40 *et seq.* Similar provisions are made to apply for estate duty for deaths occurring in the interim period. [10]

26-05   There are special provisions relating to interest on repayment of estate duty and on instalments of duty. [11]

3. OTHER PROVISIONS

26-06   Section 49 (3) of the Finance Act 1975 provides that where, under the estate duty law, any property was treated as passing on a death occurring before the passing of the Act (March 13, 1975) by virtue of any disposition made or interest subsisting after March 26, 1974, that disposition or the coming to an end of that interest shall not be a chargeable transfer. This ensures that the same event does not give rise to charges both to estate duty and capital transfer tax. Thus if A makes a gift to B after March 26, 1974, and A dies before March 13, 1975, estate duty is leviable on the gift but not capital transfer tax.

---

[5] See the 8th edition of this book, Chaps. 18 *et seq.*
[6] F.A. 1975, s. 49 (1).
[7] *Ibid.* Sched. 11, para. 1.
[8] *Ibid.* Sched. 11, para. 2.
[9] *Ibid.* Sched. 11, para. 3.
[10] *Ibid.* s. 49 (2) and Sched. 8, Pt. II.
[11] See *ibid.* s. 48.

26-07   Section 49 (5) provides that so far as any provision in any document, whether executed before or after the passing of the Finance Act 1975, refers (in whatever terms) to estate duty or death duties it shall have effect, as far as may be, as if the reference included a reference to capital transfer tax chargeable under section 22 (*ante*, § 18-14). [12]

26-08   APPENDIX

Tables applicable to chargeable transfers on or before October 26, 1977

First (Higher Rate) Table

Portion of value		Rate of tax
Lower limit	Upper limit	Per cent.
£	£	
0	15,000	Nil
15,000	20,000	10
20,000	25,000	15
25,000	30,000	20
30,000	40,000	25
40,000	50,000	30
50,000	60,000	35
60,000	80,000	40
80,000	100,000	45
100,000	120,000	50
120,000	150,000	55
150,000	500,000	60
500,000	1,000,000	65
1,000,000	2,000,000	70
2,000,000	—	75

Second (Lower Rate) Table

Portion of value		Rate of tax
Lower limit	Upper limit	Per cent.
£	£	
0	15,000	Nil
15,000	20,000	5
20,000	25,000	7½
25,000	30,000	10
30,000	40,000	12½
40,000	50,000	15
50,000	60,000	17½
60,000	80,000	20
80,000	100,000	22½
100,000	120,000	27½
120,000	150,000	35
150,000	200,000	42½
200,000	250,000	50
250,000	300,000	55
300,000	500,000	60
500,000	1,000,000	65
1,000,000	2,000,000	70
2,000,000	—	75

[12] And see § 24-17.

Part 3

STAMP DUTIES

CHAPTER 27

INTRODUCTION

1. SOURCES AND ADMINISTRATION

27-01 THE imposition of stamp duties is now governed by the Stamp Act 1891,[1] as amended and supplemented by Revenue Acts and by annual Finance Acts. Many administrative provisions are contained in the Stamp Duties Management Act 1891, and some exemptions from duty are to be found in other Acts. The rules which govern the construction of revenue statutes will be discussed in a later chapter.[2]

27-02 The Stamp Act 1891 is in three parts.[3] Part I begins with a section (s. 1) which charges duty on the instruments set forth in the First Schedule, where there is a list of instruments, in alphabetical order, with the duty which each instrument attracts. The remaining sections of Part I (ss. 2-17) contain detailed provision as to the manner in which instruments should be stamped and the effect of failure to stamp. Part II (ss. 18-111) amplifies some of the heads of charge in the First Schedule, dealing with them in the order in which they appear in the Schedule. Part III (ss. 112-125) contains miscellaneous provisions. At the end of the First Schedule there is a list of instruments exempt from all duties. In addition to the statute law, there is a mass of case law, much of which dates from before 1891, but which is nevertheless useful because it aids in the interpretation of sections of older statutes which were repeated in the Act of 1891. In assessing the value of the older cases, it should be kept in mind that, until 1850, all questions of stamp duty were decided in open court upon an instrument being tendered in evidence, and that the Commissioners had no opportunity of being heard. Disputes as to the proper stamping of an instrument may still arise in this way[4] but there has, since 1850, been a procedure in existence by which the opinion of the Commissioners can be obtained as to the proper stamping of an executed instrument presented to them for " adjudication."[5] This opinion may then be challenged in the higher courts in proceedings in which the Commissioners are parties.

There are a number of extra-statutory concessions affecting stamp duties which are published in annual reports of the Commissioners.

The administration of stamp duties is under the care and management of the Commissioners of Inland Revenue,[6] who delegate the day-to-day administration to the Controller of Stamps.

---

[1] In this book, " stamp duties " means those duties which are imposed by the Stamp Act 1891, as amended. Other taxes which may be levied by means of stamps are disregarded.

[2] *Post*, Chap. 36.

[3] For a judicial analysis of the S.A. 1891, see the judgment of Fletcher Moulton L.J. in *Maple & Co. (Paris) Ltd.* v. *I.R.C.* [1906] 2 K.B. 834.

[4] See, *e.g. Re Waterhouse's Policy* [1937] 2 All E.R. 91.

[5] The adjudication procedure is discussed *post*, §§ 27-41 *et seq.*

[6] Stamp Duties Management Act 1891, s. 1.

The process of stamping in outline

27-03   The stamp duties imposed by the Acts are of two kinds:

(1) *Fixed duties*, such as the duty of 50p on a deed. The amount of the duty does not depend on the consideration or other amount expressed in the instrument.

(2) *Ad valorem duties*, such as the duty of £2 per cent. of the amount or value of the consideration on a transfer of shares.

Payment of the duty is indicated by a stamp which is impressed upon the instrument itself. The instrument must be presented to the Stamp Office [7] so that the stamp may be impressed thereon by the use of dies in the exclusive possession of the stamping authorities. The use of adhesive stamps is no longer permitted except in the case of contract notes. [8] Where an impressed stamp is required, the normal practice (for example, in the case of a conveyance on sale) is that the purchaser's solicitor takes the instrument to the local stamp office where it is scrutinised by a clerk who marks in pencil the amount of the duty. The appropriate stamp is then impressed. It is the practice of solicitors not to erase the pencilled marking.

2. BASIC PRINCIPLES

27-04   The subject of stamp duties is one of some complexity; but there are a number of principles or rules which are of general application in stamp duty law and practice. These are as follows:

27-05   (1) *Stamp duty is charged on instruments, not on transactions*

This principle is fundamental: if there is no instrument, there can be no duty. See also § 27-10, *post.*

27-06   (2) *The head of charge under which an instrument falls and, therefore, the amount of the duty, is determined by the nature of the transaction effected by the instrument*

In determining the nature of the transaction which is effected, the court will look to the substance of the instrument, not merely to its form:

" In order to determine whether any, and if any what, stamp duty is chargeable upon an instrument, the legal rule is that the real and true meaning of the instrument is to be ascertained; that the description of it given in the instrument itself by the parties is immaterial, even although they may have believed that its effect and operation was to create a security mentioned in the Stamp Act, and they so declare." [9]

So, for example, an instrument described as a deed of dissolution of partnership may operate as a conveyance on sale [10]; and a covenant not to

[7] For details as to the location of the Stamp Offices, see Sergeant, p. 461.
[8] *Post*, §§ 27-35 *et seq.*
[9] *Limmer Asphalte Paving Co.* v. *I.R.C.* (1872) L.R. 7 Ex. 211 at pp. 214-215, *per* Martin B. See also *I.R.C.* v. *Duke of Westminster* [1936] A.C. 1 and *I.R.C.* v. *Europa Oil (N.Z.) Ltd.* [1971] A.C. 760; *post,* § 36-03. See also § 28-48, *post.*
[10] *Garnett* v. *I.R.C.* (1899) 81 L.T. 633; *post,* § 28-12.

compete given by the vendor of a business to the purchaser may operate as an agreement to assign goodwill.[11]

27-07 (3) *If a transaction can be effected in more than one way, duty must be charged which is appropriate to the instrument actually used*

Thus if A transfers a mortgage for £35,000 to B by way of gift, the instrument must be stamped as a voluntary disposition [12] (at £2 per cent. = £700). But if A gives B £35,000 to enable B to purchase the mortgage from him, the instrument transferring the mortgage will bear no stamp duty whatsoever.[13]

27-08 (4) *The liability of an instrument to stamp duty depends on the circumstances which exist at the time when the instrument is executed*

Thus if property is transferred at a time when there is no subsisting agreement for the sale of that property to the transferee, the transfer is not dutiable as a conveyance or transfer on sale, even if the transfer is made in contemplation of a possible future sale. The application of this principle is demonstrated in the decision of the House of Lords in *Wm. Cory & Son Ltd.* v. *I.R.C.*,[14] which was nullified as regards instruments executed on or after August 1, 1965, by the Finance Act 1965.[15] The principle above stated is not, however, in any way abrogated by the provisions of the statute. Although the time of execution is the material time for determining the effect of an instrument for stamp duty purposes, the court will have regard to what is said and done thereafter in order to discover the true position when the instrument was executed.[16]

27-09 (5) *If an instrument is ineffective for the intended purpose, it is not liable to duty*

Thus, if an appointment of trustees is made by the wrong person, the instrument is not liable to duty; and if a stamp has already been impressed, the duty may be recoverable.[17]

27-10 (6) *A transaction effected orally normally attracts no duty* [18]

This follows from the principle already stated that stamp duty is a duty on instruments, not on transactions. Thus if a contract is concluded orally, or the title to property is transferred by delivery, duty is avoided. In some cases, to avoid duty, property which is not transferable by delivery can be converted into a deliverable state; for example, by severing fixtures before transfer. A common method of avoiding the duty on a transfer of shares is

---

[11] *Eastern National Omnibus Co.* v. *I.R.C.* [1939] 1 K.B. 161, *post*, § 29-08.

[12] *Anderson* v. *I.R.C.* [1939] 1 K.B. 341 and F.A. 1971, s. 64 (2); *post*, §§ 29-53 and 30-10.

[13] Mortgage duty was abolished as from August 1, 1971, by F.A. 1971, ss. 64 (1) (c) and 64 (2); *post*, § 27-53.

[14] [1965] A.C. 1088 (H.L.). Discussed *post*, § 28-22. There are a number of other cases (cited in the *Cory* case) illustrating this principle. The principle was relied on by the Revenue in *Western United Investment Co. Ltd.* v. *I.R.C.* [1958] Ch. 392 at p. 398.   [15] See *post*, § 28-23.

[16] [1965] A.C. 1088 (H.L.), *per* Lord Reid at p. 1105.   [17] See *post*, § 27-51.

[18] Some transactions cannot be effected without the use of a written instrument. Thus (i) a deed is necessary to convey a legal estate in land (Law of Property Act 1925, s. 52 (1)); (ii) transfer of shares must be in writing (Companies Act 1948, s. 75); (iii) a disposition of an equitable interest must be in writing (Law of Property Act 1925, s. 53): see *Grey* v. *I.R.C.* [1960] A.C. 1, *post*, § 28-08.

for a company to issue shares on renounceable letters of allotment thereby enabling the person to whom the letter is issued to transfer his right to the shares by renouncing his right to allotment.[19]

27-11   *Records of oral transactions.* If a transaction is effected without the use of a written instrument and subsequently a written record of that transaction is made, the written record is generally not liable to duty. This is because the transaction is not *effected* by the written instrument; the instrument merely records a transaction which has already been effected. There is an exception to this rule:

Under the principle established in *Cohen and Moore* v. *I.R.C.,*[20] the court will in certain circumstances treat an oral transaction and a subsequent written record thereof as one single transaction effected by the instrument. The facts of the case were as follows:

> Settlors orally declared that they would hold certain securities on trust until other trustees were appointed in their place. The securities were set forth in schedules to a draft deed and the trusts were set forth in the deed. Some five weeks after the verbal declaration of trust, the draft deed was executed reciting the verbal declaration and appointing trustees. *Held*, that the verbal declaration and the later deed formed one transaction and that the deed was liable to settlement duty.

" I think," said Finlay J., " that the transaction was really all one transaction and that, being one transaction, the whole was recorded in the document—the only document which has been drawn up—which is the settlement." [21] It should be noted that the deed was in draft at the time of the verbal declaration.[22]

27-12   (7) *The leading and principal objects rule*

" There is no better established rule as regards stamp duty than that all that is required is that the instrument should be stamped for its leading and principal object, and that this stamp covers everything accessory to this object." [23]

> *Examples:* (i) The stamp on a lease covers an option to purchase the reversion,[24] and a guarantee of the rent.[25]
> (ii) The stamp on the creation of a settlement covers the appointment of the first trustees.
> (iii) The stamp on a conveyance or assent under seal covers any acknowledgment for production, undertaking for safe custody or any restrictive covenants.

If by virtue of the leading object the document is exempt from duty, an accessory provision is also exempt.

> *Example:* The exemption from duty on an assent not under seal covers any warranties as to title or acknowledgment for production.

---

[19] See [1961] B.T.R. 83 (J. G. Monroe).   [20] [1933] 2 K.B. 126; and see *post*, § 28-18.
[21] *Ibid.* at pp. 137-138.   [22] Contrast *Grey* v. *I.R.C.* [1958] Ch. 375 at pp. 379-380 (on this point).
[23] *Limmer Asphalte Paving Co.* v. *I.R.C.* (1872) L.R. 7 Ex. 211 at p. 217, *per* Martin B.
[24] *Worthington* v. *Warrington* (1848) 5 C.B. 635. *Cf.* an option to purchase *other* property, which attracts a separate duty: see *post*, § 27-15, Example (iii).
[25] *Price* v. *Thomas* (1831) 2 B. & Ad. 218. *Cf.* a guarantee for payment of penalties in the event of default by the lessee: *Wharton* v. *Walton* (1845) 7 Q.B. 474.

27-13 (8) *Transactions effected by operation of law attract no duty*

> *Example:* (i) On an appointment of a new trustee by deed (which attracts duty of 50p under the head " Appointment "), no duty is chargeable by virtue of the implied vesting declaration under section 40 of the Trustee Act 1925.
>
> (ii) No duty is attracted by the constructive trust for the purchaser which arises under a contract of sale.[26] *Cf.* the position where there is an express trust in the agreement.[27]

27-14 (9) *Documents containing separate instruments*

Sections 3 and 4 of the Stamp Act 1891 are intended to prevent evasion of duty by the use of one document to effect more than one transaction. Section 3 (2) provides that

> " If more than one instrument be written upon the same piece of material, every one of the instruments is to be separately and distinctly stamped with the duty with which it is chargeable."

By section 122 (1), " instrument " includes every written document, and " material " includes every sort of material upon which words or figures can be expressed. In *Prudential Assurance Co. Ltd.* v. *I.R.C.*,[28] a memorandum indorsed on a life policy increasing the sum assured by the policy, following disclosure that the assured's age had been incorrectly stated, was held to be a separate instrument separately chargeable with duty by virtue of section 3 (2). An alteration of an instrument after execution may in some cases constitute a new instrument requiring a fresh stamp.[29]

27-15 (10) *Instruments to be separately charged with duty*

By section 4 of the Stamp Act 1891, except where express provision to the contrary is made by that or any other Act [30]:

> " (*a*) An instrument containing or relating to several distinct matters is to be separately and distinctly charged, as if it were a separate instrument, with duty in respect of each of the matters;
>
> (*b*) An instrument made for any consideration in respect whereof it is chargeable with *ad valorem* duty, and also for any further or other valuable consideration or considerations, is to be separately and distinctly charged, as if it were a separate instrument, with duty in respect of each of the considerations."

The word " matters " in section 4 (*a*) is not defined in the Act and some doubt has been expressed as to its proper interpretation. It is generally supposed, however, that it refers to the matters in respect of which duty is chargeable,[31] so that more than one duty is charged if the instrument either (i) falls under more than one head of charge, or (ii) effects more than one

---

[26] *I.R.C.* v. *Angus & Co.* (1889) 23 Q.B.D. 579 (C.A.). See *post*, § 28-20.
[27] *Chesterfield Brewery Co.* v. *I.R.C.* [1899] 2 Q.B. 7. See *post*, § 28-19.
[28] [1935] 1 K.B. 101.
[29] See Alpe, *Law of Stamp Duties*, pp. 15-16.
[30] The contrary provisions are listed in Alpe, *op. cit.*, p. 16. There is a useful list of the cases in which assessments under s. 4 are commonly made in Alpe, *op. cit.* , pp. 21-22.
[31] This view is supported by *Reversionary Interest Society Ltd.* v. *I.R.C.* (1906) 22 T.L.R. 740. *Cf.* Rowlatt J. in *Ansell* v. *I.R.C.* [1929] 1 K.B. 608 at p. 617.

transaction.[32] Examples of the application of section 4 which commonly arise in practice are as follows:

(i) A separation deed containing a settlement of property attracts a deed stamp (50p) and *ad valorem* voluntary disposition duty.

(ii) A lease containing an option to buy land other than the demised land attracts lease duty and a 50p stamp in respect of the option (or *ad valorem* conveyance or transfer duty if there is separate consideration for it [33]).

(iii) In *Freeman* v. *I.R.C.*,[34] executors used one document to transfer to four residuary legatees shares in nine companies forming part of the testator's residuary estate. *Held*, that four transfer stamps were required.

27-16   (11) *If one transaction is effected by more than one instrument only one ad valorem duty can be charged if the ad valorem duty exceeds 50p*

This is important in connection with settlements of land and other property which are commonly effected by two instruments. The relevant provisions are discussed later.[35] Where there are several instruments of conveyance for completing the purchaser's title to property sold, only the principal instrument of conveyance is chargeable with *ad valorem* duty; the other instruments are chargeable with such other duty as they may be liable to, such duty not to exceed the *ad valorem* duty payable on the principal instrument.[36]

27-17   (12) *Choice of head of charge*

If an instrument falls under more than one head of charge in the Act, the Crown is entitled to claim duty under only one head, at its choice; but it may choose whichever head yields the most duty.

Examples: (i) In *Speyer Bros.* v. *I.R.C.*,[37] certain notes issued by the United States of Mexico were both promissory notes and marketable securities for the purposes of the Stamp Act. *Held*, that they were liable to the higher duty imposed on marketable securities.

(ii) In *Anderson* v. *I.R.C.*,[38] a voluntary transfer of a mortgage was held liable to the higher duty as a voluntary disposition.[39]

The principle in this paragraph must not be confused with the principle mentioned in § 27-15. *Speyer's* case,[37] for example, was not a case of an instrument effecting more than one transaction; the instrument effected only one transaction but, looked at in different ways, it fell under more than one head of charge.

27-18   (13) *The contingency principle*

If the sum payable under an instrument is uncertain at the time of its execution, any *ad valorem* duty is assessed on the maximum which might become payable and which can be calculated in advance at the date of the instrument.

---

[32] *Lovelock* v. *Franklyn* (1847) 8 Q.B. 371; *cf. ante*, § 27-12, Example (i).
[33] See *post*, § 28-20.
[34] (1871) L.R. 6 Ex. 101.
[35] *Post*, §§ 30-16 *et seq.*
[36] S.A. 1891, s. 58 (3).
[37] [1908] A.C. 92.
[38] [1939] 1 K.B. 341; and see *post*, § 30-10.
[39] This is still the case, even after the abolition of mortgage duty: see F.A. 1971, s. 64 (2); *post*, § 27-53.

Example: A beer house is conveyed for £x, with an undertaking by the purchaser to pay £y if a spirit licence is obtained. *Ad valorem* conveyance or transfer duty is assessed on £x + £y.[40]

There are two leading cases on this principle.

In *Underground Electric Railways Co. etc.* v. *I.R.C.*,[41] A Ltd. agreed that *if* a sufficient number of stockholders in B Ltd. would exchange their ordinary stock for guaranteed stock, A Ltd. would guarantee 4 per cent. interest on such stock *if* the profits of B Ltd. were insufficient to pay interest at 4 per cent. It was known at the date of the deed that if the first condition was satisfied, and if B Ltd. made no profits, A Ltd. would have to make periodic payments of a maximum sum of £120,000. *Held*, that the deed was a primary security for the maximum which *might* be payable, namely £120,000, and was liable to bond covenant duty [42] thereon.

The instrument, said Warrington L.J. " is a security for the payment of a sum of money notwithstanding that events may happen which enable one or other of the parties to put an end to the obligation of which the security is a part and notwithstanding that in the event the obligation may not result in the recovery from the obligor of any particular sum of money." [43] The principle applies also to lease duty.[44]

27-19   *Minimum only calculable in advance.* If only a minimum sum payable can be calculated in advance, *ad valorem* duty is assessed on this minimum.[45]

Example: In assessing the *ad valorem* duty on a life policy, no account is taken of bonuses; but if a minimum bonus is provided, duty is assessed on this minimum.[46]

27-20   *Neither maximum nor minimum calculable in advance.* If neither a maximum nor a minimum can be calculated, no *ad valorem* duty can be charged, except where a sum can be ascertained which *might* be payable.

Example: In *Independent Television Authority and Associated-Rediffusion Ltd.* v. *I.R.C.*,[47] "A.R." agreed to provide TV programmes for a fixed period of approximately nine years and to pay to the Authority a fee of £495,600 a year for 2½ years and £536,900 thereafter. The agreement provided for an increase or decrease of such payments depending on variations in a certain index figure. *Held*, that *ad valorem* bond covenant duty [48] was payable on the total sum which *might* become payable under the agreement, namely over £4 million.

" I take it, therefore, to be a well-settled principle," said Lord Radcliffe, at p. 443, " that the money payable is ascertained for the purposes of charge without regard to the fact that the agreement in question may itself contain provisions which will in certain circumstances prevent it being payable at all. If that is so, there is at least no better reason for adopting a different principle where there are found clauses which merely vary the amount to be paid according to specified contingencies."

---

[40] Alpe, *op. cit.*, p. 180.
[41] [1914] 3 K.B. 210; affirmed [1916] 1 K.B. 306 (C.A.).
[42] Bond covenant duty was abolished as from August 1, 1971, by F.A. 1971, s. 64 (1) (*c*); *post*, § 27-53.
[43] [1916] 1 K.B. 306 at pp. 318-320.
[44] *Coventry City Council* v. *I.R.C.* [1978] S.T.C. 151 (duty assessed on the maximum rent which could become payable).   [45] See *Underground Electric Railways Co.* v. *I.R.C.* [1906] A.C. 21.
[46] See *post*, § 34-03.   [47] [1961] A.C. 427.
[48] Bond covenant duty was abolished as from August 1, 1971, by F.A. 1971, s. 64 (1) (*c*); *post*, § 27-53.

3. THE CONSEQUENCES OF FAILING TO STAMP INSTRUMENTS

27-21 The act of failing to stamp a document, or of failing to stamp a document correctly, does not generally render any person liable to any action against him by the Revenue; nor does the want of the stamp invalidate the document.[49] In the ordinary case, the stamp authorities have no means of knowing when instruments are executed which are not duly stamped. The Stamp Act deals with the problem primarily in two ways:

(1) By rendering unstamped (including insufficiently or improperly stamped) instruments inadmissible in evidence and generally useless, whilst they remain unstamped; and

(2) By levying penalties when instruments are presented for stamping outside the time limits prescribed by the Act.

Each of these matters will be considered.

A. *Admissibility, etc. of Unstamped Instruments*

27-22 Section 14 (4) of the Stamp Act 1891 provides that an instrument

" shall not, except in criminal proceedings, be given in evidence or be available for any purpose whatsoever, unless it is duly stamped in accordance with the law in force at the time when it was first executed."

An instrument delivered as an *escrow* is only *executed,* for this purpose, when it becomes unconditional.[50] An instrument is not " duly stamped " if, though stamped, it bears the wrong kind of stamp. Thus, in *Ashling* v. *Boon,*[51] an instrument bearing an adhesive postage stamp appropriate to a receipt but which should have been stamped with an appropriated " bill or note " stamp as a promissory note was not allowed in evidence to prove payment of the money for which it was given. When an original document is inadmissible, secondary evidence of it is likewise inadmissible.

The rule against admissibility has no application to criminal proceedings (including proceedings before justices for recovery of a penalty) and it is arguable that it does not apply in proceedings before the General and Special Commissioners.[52] Further, an unstamped instrument has been admitted in evidence to prove an act of bankruptcy [53]; to prove fraud [54]; and it may be put to a witness to refresh his memory.[55]

Collateral purpose

27-23 It was at one time thought that an unstamped instrument was admissible in evidence for a collateral purpose: thus, in *Fengl* v. *Fengl,*[56] and in reliance on cases decided before 1891, it was argued that an unstamped

---

[49] In *Re Indo-China Steam Navigation Co.* [1917] 2 Ch. 100 at p. 106, Eve J. suggested *obiter* that the legal title to shares would not pass if the transfer was not properly stamped. This is generally thought to be wrong: Alpe, *op. cit.*, p. 79; Sergeant, *Stamp Duties,* p. 76.

[50] See *Terrapin International Ltd.* v. *I.R.C.* [1976] 1 W.L.R. 665.

[51] [1891] 1 Ch. 568.

[52] See Monroe's *Stamp Duties,* 5th ed., para. 22. The point was left open in *Sinclair* v. *I.R.C.* (1942) 24 T.C. 432 at pp. 442, 444.

[53] *Re Gunsbourg* (1919) 88 L.J.K.B. 562.

[54] *Re Shaw* (1920) 90 L.J.K.B. 204.

[55] *Birchall* v. *Bullough* [1896] 1 Q.B. 325 (D.C.).

[56] [1914] P. 274 (D.C.).

separation deed (which clearly would not have been admissible in proceedings to enforce its provisions) was admissible in proceedings before justices on the issue of the voluntary nature of the separation. Sir Samuel Evans P., however, held that the old cases had been overruled by the very wide terms of section 14 (4) of the Stamp Act 1891, making a document inadmissible in civil proceedings " for any purpose whatsoever." This view is supported by the decision of the Privy Council in *Ram Rattan* v. *Parma Nand*,[57] decided on comparable words in the Indian Stamp Act; so it now seems to be established [58] that an unstamped instrument is inadmissible even to prove some matter collateral to it.

The Revenue will not give effect to unstamped deeds of covenant [59] or other settlements, which are thus ineffective as a means of tax saving until and unless the instrument is stamped on payment of the appropriate penalty: see § 27-27.

Taking stamp objections

27-24   By section 14 (1) of the Stamp Act 1891, if an instrument is produced in evidence in a civil court, the judge, arbitrator, or referee [60] is required to take notice of the omission or insufficiency of any stamp. He is thus under a statutory obligation to protect the Revenue, and it is not open to the parties to waive a stamp objection. The section further provides that if the instrument is one which may be legally stamped after execution,[61] it may be received in evidence on payment of the amount of the duty, of the penalty for stamping out of time, and of a further sum of £1. The usual practice is to allow an unstamped instrument to be put in evidence on a personal undertaking given by the solicitor of the party producing it to have it stamped and to pay the statutory penalty.[62]

Stamp objections by counsel

27-25   The General Council of the Bar has ruled that " save in revenue cases, it is unprofessional that a counsel should object to the admissibility of any document upon the ground that it is not, or is not sufficiently, stamped, unless such defect goes to the validity of the document; and counsel should not take part in any discussion that may arise in support of an objection on such a ground unless invited to do so by the court." [63]

If a dispute arises in the course of proceedings as to the proper stamp for an instrument tendered in evidence, the dispute must be settled in open court. It seems, however, that section 14 (1) of the Stamp Act 1891 does not oblige the judge to try doubtful questions of stamp duty law, but merely requires that he should intervene in a clear case of omission or insufficiency of the stamp.[64] The modern practice in cases of doubt is to require an undertaking to have the instrument adjudicated.

[57] (1945) L.R. 73 Ind.App. 28.
[58] But not, perhaps, in Scotland. See *Watson* v. *Watson*, 1934 S.C. 374, 379.
[59] As from August 1, 1971, a deed of covenant attracts no stamp whatsoever; *post*, § 27-53.
[60] But not a Rent Tribunal: *R.* v. *Fulham, etc., Rent Tribunal* [1951] 2 K.B. 1 (D.C.).
[61] *Post*, § 27-28.
[62] *Re Coolgardie Goldfields Ltd.* [1900] 1 Ch. 475 at p. 477; *Parkfield Trust* v. *Dent* [1931] 2 K.B. 579.
[63] Boulton, *Conduct and Etiquette at the Bar*, 6th ed., p. 70.
[64] See *Don Francesco* v. *De Meo*, 1908 S.C. 7.

27-26 *Appeals.* No appeal lies against the ruling of a judge [65] that an instrument is sufficiently stamped or requires no stamp [66]; but appeal lies from a ruling rejecting an instrument as insufficiently stamped. [67]

B. *Penalties for Stamping Out of Time*

27-27 The word " penalty " is commonly used to describe a punishment, in the form of a fine or other money payment, imposed by a court of criminal jurisdiction. The word is not used in this sense in the Stamp Act, for no criminal proceedings may be instituted for failure to stamp an instrument; nor is a penalty recoverable by civil action. A penalty is the price exacted by the Revenue for stamping an instrument out of time; the amount of the penalty increasing with the delay in the stamping of the instrument.

27-28 Section 15 (1) of the Stamp Act 1891 provides that an unstamped or insufficiently stamped instrument may be stamped after execution [68] only on payment of:

(1) the unpaid duty;

(2) a penalty of £10; and

(3) a further penalty, if the unpaid duty exceeds £10, of interest on such duty at 5 per cent. per annum from the date of first execution [68] of the instrument to the time when the interest equals the additional duty.

27-29 Section 15 (2), however, contains different penalty provisions affecting the instruments listed in a Table in the section. This Table as amended is as follows:

Title of instrument as described in the First Schedule to the Act	Person liable to penalty
Bond, covenant, or instrument of any kind whatsoever. [69]	The obligee, covenantee or other person taking the security.
Conveyance on sale.	The vendee or transferee.
Lease or tack.	The lessee.
Unit trust instrument.	The trustees. [70]
Voluntary disposition. [71]	The grantor or transferor.

It will be noted that not all the principal instruments liable to *ad valorem* duty are included in the Table. An instrument of the class referred to in the Table (as amended) (if not written on stamped material) must be stamped within 30 days after its first execution, [72] unless:

(a) it was first executed out of the United Kingdom, when it must be stamped within 30 days of its arrival in the United Kingdom [73]; or

---

[65] But *semble* that a ruling of the Special Commissioners could be the subject of a case stated.

[66] R.S.C., Ord. 59, r. 11 (5).

[67] *The Belfort* (1884) 9 P.D. 215.

[68] " Execution," in the case of instruments not under seal, refers to the act of signing: S.A. 1891, s. 122 (1). Often an instrument has to be executed by a number of parties and there is no means of telling when it was " first " executed. In practice, the stamp authorities accept the date which is inserted on the instrument as the date from which time starts to run. See a useful article by J. G. Monroe on " The Dating of a Document " in [1960] B.T.R. 180.

[69] This head of charge was abolished as from August 1, 1971, by F.A. 1971, s. 64 (1) (*c*); *post*, § 27-53.

[70] Added to the Table by the F.A. 1962, s. 30 (1).

[71] Added to the Table by the F. (1909-10) A. 1910, s. 74 (3).

[72] See note 68, *ante*.

[73] S.A. 1891, s. 15 (2) (*a*).

(b) it was lodged for adjudication, when it must be stamped within 14 days after notice of the assessment.[74]

The instruments in the Table can be stamped out of time only on payment of the unpaid duty, the penalties in (2) and (3) in § 27-28 and a further penalty equal to the stamp duty on the instrument. In addition, the person in the right-hand column of the Table is liable to a fine of £10 (even if the instrument is not presented for stamping).

Theory and practice

27-30   It seems clear from section 15 that the Stamp Act 1891 contemplates that all instruments executed in the United Kingdom will be stamped *before* execution, except for those instruments listed in section 15 (2) which must be stamped (generally) within 30 days *after* execution. In practice, however, most impressed stamping is done after execution and the Commissioners (who have statutory power to mitigate or remit penalties) [75] will stamp most instruments presented within 30 days after execution without demanding the penalty prescribed by the Act.

C. Other Sanctions for the Payment of Duty

(a) Recovery of stamp duty by action

27-31   Duty cannot normally be recovered by action. Exceptionally, however, in the case of the following duties, proceedings in the High Court may be taken for the recovery of the duty as a debt due to the Crown:

(a) loan capital duty [76];

(b) the capital duty in respect of chargeable transactions of capital companies [77];

(c) the duty payable on the assignment of a policy of life assurance where the policy moneys have been paid to the assignee without stamping the assignment [78];

(d) the amount of the duty remitted under section 55 of the Finance Act 1927, where the remission has been improperly obtained or certain conditions are broken.[79]

(b) Fines

27-32   Many sections of the Stamp Act impose fines,[80] which are recoverable as civil debts. Two of these sections merit special mention:

Section 5 of the Stamp Act 1891 provides that

" All the facts and circumstances affecting the liability of any instrument to duty, or the amount of the duty with which any instrument is chargeable, are to be fully and truly set forth in the instrument; and every person who, with intent to defraud Her Majesty,

---

[74] S.A. 1891, s. 15 (2) (b).
[75] *Ibid.* s. 15 (3) (b), amended by F.A. 1895, s. 15.
[76] F.A. 1899, s. 8; *post,* § 32-01. This duty was abolished with effect from January 1, 1973: F.A. 1973, s. 49 (2).
[77] F.A. 1973, s. 47 (7); *post,* § 32-02.
[78] S.A. 1891, s. 118 (2).
[79] F.A. 1927, s. 55 (6); *post,* § 33-07.
[80] For a list of these sections, see Sergeant,˙ 3rd ed., pp. 7-8.

(a) executes any instrument in which all the said facts and circumstances are not fully and truly set forth; or

(b) being employed or concerned in or about the preparation of any instrument, neglects or omits fully and truly to set forth therein all the said facts and circumstances;

shall incur a fine of £10."

It is not always practicable or desirable to set forth in an instrument *all* the facts and circumstances affecting liability for duty; but no offence is committed unless an intent to defraud is present, so it is sufficient in practice to disclose material facts separately when presenting an instrument to the Commissioners for adjudication.

Section 17 of the Stamp Act 1891 provides that

" If any person whose office it is to enrol, register, or enter in or upon any rolls, books, or records any instrument chargeable with duty, enrols, registers, or enters any such instrument not being duly stamped, he shall incur a fine of £10."

Thus the secretary of a company incurs a fine if he registers an improperly stamped transfer of shares.[81] If the secretary refuses registration on the ground of the insufficiency of the stamp but the transferee questions his refusal, he should present the transfer for adjudication and, after adjudication, re-present it for registration. Mandamus is not the proper procedure.[82] The secretary or other officer concerned is entitled, when considering whether a transfer is duly stamped, to go behind the consideration stated in the transfer.

Thus in *Maynard* v. *Consolidated Kent Colliers Corp.*,[83] the stamp on a transfer of shares was in accordance with the consideration stated on the face of the document, but it was found that the consideration actually given exceeded this amount. *Held*, the directors were entitled to refuse registration of the transfer.

There is a two year time limit for the recovery of fines, such two years being reckoned from the time when the fine is incurred.[84]

(c) *Conveyancing practice*

27-33 A purchaser is entitled to insist that every deed which forms a link in the vendor's title is duly stamped. This is because, by virtue of section 14 (4) of the Stamp Act 1891, a purchaser cannot use an unstamped, or insufficiently stamped, deed for any purpose whatsoever, whether to defend his title or to attack a wrongdoer.

Thus in *Whiting* v. *Loomes*[85] a mortgage deed was stamped with a 10s. deed stamp. *Held*, that a purchaser from the mortgagors was entitled to have the deed stamped before completion to the full *ad valorem* duty at the vendor's expense, notwithstanding that the mortgagee had consented to join in the conveyance.

---

[81] A master has been held vicariously liable for a fine imposed on his servant acting in the course of his duties: *Att.-Gen.* v. *Carlton Bank Ltd.* [1899] 2 Q.B. 158.

[82] *R.* v. *Registrar of Joint Stock Companies* (1888) 21 Q.B.D. 131. As to the duties and liability of the registering officer, see the circular issued by the Revenue in Sergeant, pp. 63 *et seq.*

[83] [1903] 2 K.B. 121 (C.A.).

[84] Inland Revenue Regulation Act 1890, s. 22 (2).

[85] (1881) 17 Ch.D. 10 (C.A.); followed in *Maynard's* case in note 83.

" The court," said Lush J., " is not entitled to speculate whether the purchaser may or may not have occasion to use the deed. A purchaser is entitled to have every deed forming a step in his title in such shape that he can, if he need it, give it in evidence."

A purchaser is entitled to rescind the contract if the vendor refuses to stamp an unstamped instrument; and section 117 of the Stamp Act (which applies to instruments executed after May 16, 1888) invalidates any condition of sale framed with the view of precluding objection or requisition upon the ground of absence or insufficiency of stamp, or providing for the purchaser to undertake liability for the duty.

27-34   *Omnia rite esse acta.* There is a presumption that a document is duly stamped: *omnia praesumuntur rite et solemniter esse acta.* If, therefore, the consideration expressed in a deed which forms a link in the title appears to be inadequate, but the deed is stamped in accordance with the consideration therein expressed, the purchaser is not entitled to raise objection to the sufficiency of the stamp.[86]

A lost document is presumed to have been duly stamped[87] and the Commissioners will stamp a replica free of charge, or repay the duty if a replica has already been stamped.[88]

4. METHOD OF STAMPING

(1) *Impressed and adhesive stamps*

27-35   Payment of stamp duty must now be denoted by means of impressed stamps in all cases except contract notes where appropriated adhesive stamps may be used.[89] Stamp duty under the following headings, prior to their abolition, could be denoted by means of adhesive postage stamps—

(a) agreements under hand only[90];

(b) bills of exchange and promissory notes[91];

(c) receipts.[92]

Postage stamps are no longer valid for stamp duty purposes.

27-36   *Cancellation of adhesive stamps.* Where an adhesive stamp was used, the instrument was not duly stamped unless either—

(a) the stamp was cancelled by the appropriate person writing across it his name or initials together with the true date; or

(b) it was otherwise proved that the stamp was affixed at the proper time.[93]

---

[86] *Re Weir and Pitt's Contract* (1911) 55 S.J. 536; and see Law Society's *Digest,* Vol. 1 (1954), p. 80, Opinion 268.
[87] *Marine Investment Co.* v. *Haviside* (1872) L.R. 5 H.L. 624; and see Monroe's *Stamp Duties,* 5th ed., para. 57.
[88] See Concessions Nos. F1 and F2.
[89] S.A. 1891, s. 2; *post,* § 27-37.
[90] *Ibid.* s. 22; abolished as from August 1, 1970, F.A. 1970, Sched. 7.
[91] F.A. 1961, s. 33 (2); abolished as from February 1, 1971, F.A. 1970, Sched. 7.
[92] S.A. 1891, s. 101 (2); abolished as from February 1, 1971, F.A. 1970, Sched. 7.
[93] *Ibid.* s. 8.

(2) *Appropriated stamps*

27-37 An appropriated stamp is one which bears words on its face which limits its use to a particular description of instrument. The only instrument which, before August 1, 1970, required an appropriated stamp was a contract note [94]; and such an instrument was not duly stamped unless it bore the appropriated stamp [95] or duty was paid out of sums deposited with the Commissioners pursuant to an agreement made under section 46 of the Finance Act 1966. In the case of instruments executed on or after August 1, 1970, a contract note may bear an impressed stamp.

(3) *Denoting stamps*

27-38 Where the duty with which an instrument is chargeable depends in any manner on the duty paid on another instrument, the payment of the last-mentioned duty will, on application to the Commissioners and production of both instruments, be denoted on the first-mentioned instrument. [96] The following denoting stamps are in use:

27-39 (a) *The duplicate denoting stamp.* The duplicate or counterpart of an instrument is not duly stamped unless either
  (i) it is stamped as an original; or
  (ii) it appears by some stamp impressed thereon that the full and proper duty has been paid on the original, *i.e.* unless the instrument is denoted.

The counterpart of a lease does not require denoting unless it is executed by the lessor. [97] In addition to the denoting stamp, a duplicate must bear a fixed stamp under the head " Duplicate or Counterpart of any instrument chargeable with duty." This stamp is 50p (or the same as the original, if the stamp on the original is less than 50p).

27-40 (b) *The duty paid denoting stamp.* This is used on the following instruments:
  (i) On a conveyance, where *ad valorem* duty has already been paid on the agreement for sale under section 59 of the Stamp Act [98];
  (ii) On a lease, where *ad valorem* duty has already been paid on the agreement for the lease under section 75 (1) of the Stamp Act [99];

The stamp in these cases bears the inscription: " Duty paid *ad valorem* £x."

---

[94] This is a note issued by a broker to his principal on a sale or purchase of shares or debentures. It attracts *ad valorem* duty.
[95] S.A. 1891, s. 10; *Ashling* v. *Boon* [1891] 1 Ch. 568 (a case of a promissory note); but see now F.A. 1961, s. 33.
[96] *Ibid.* s. 11.
[97] *Ibid.* s. 72.
[98] *Ibid.* s. 59 (3); *post*, § 29-02.
[99] *Post*, § 31-08.

The denoting stamp is obtained by leaving the instruments at the stamp office. The denoting stamp is, however, no guarantee that the original or principal instrument was duly stamped: a formal adjudication is necessary for this purpose.

(4) *Adjudication stamps*

27-41   Under section 12 of the Stamp Act 1891, any person may require the Commissioners to express their opinion with reference to any *executed* instrument on the questions (a) whether the instrument is chargeable with any duty; and (b) with what amount it is chargeable.[1] If the Commissioners are of opinion that the instrument is not chargeable with duty, it will be stamped accordingly (" Adjudged not chargeable with any duty ")[2]; otherwise, they will assess the duty and, when the instrument has been stamped in accordance with the assessment, they will add the adjudication stamp (" Adjudged duly stamped ").[3]

27-42   *Appeals.* Any person who is dissatisfied with the assessment of the Commissioners may, within 21 days after the date of the assessment and *on payment of the duty* in conformity therewith, appeal to the High Court.[4] The appeal is by way of case stated and the Commissioners may be required to state and sign a case setting forth the question on which their opinion was required and the assessment made by them. In practice, the stated case is settled in draft by the Commissioners and then agreed with the appellant. The case is heard by the Chancery judge taking the revenue list. It is the duty of the judge to determine the question submitted to him and to assess the duty, if any.[5] It may be necessary to call evidence, for example, as to the value of property.[6] If the court decides that the assessment of the Commissioners was wrong, the court will order that the duty (or the excess duty) be repaid, together with any fine or penalty paid in consequence of the erroneous assessment.[7] The court has power to award such interest as it may determine on the sum repaid.[8]

A further appeal from the order of the judge lies to the Court of Appeal and thence, with leave, to the House of Lords.

27-43   *Procedure for obtaining adjudication.* Briefly, the instrument on which adjudication is required must be presented or sent to the stamp office.[9] According to the strict terms of section 5 of the Stamp Act 1891,[10] the

---

[1] S.A. 1891, s. 12 (1).

[2] *Ibid.* s. 12 (3).

[3] *Ibid.* s. 12 (4).

[4] *Ibid.* s. 13. For a criticism of the adjudication procedure, see *E.C. (Holdings) Ltd.* v. *I.R.C.* (1959) 38 A.T.C. 73 at p. 74, *per* Roxburgh J.

[5] *Ibid.* s. 13 (3).

[6] See, *e.g. Speyer Bros.* v. *I.R.C.* [1906] 1 K.B. 318 (where evidence was heard on the question whether " gold coupon treasury notes " issued by the Mexican Government were capable of being dealt in according to the ordinary practice of the Stock Exchange).

[7] S.A. 1891, s. 13 (4).

[8] F.A. 1965, s. 91, nullifying the decision in *Western United Investment Co. Ltd.* v. *I.R.C.* [1958] Ch. 392.

[9] Details of the procedure are published in a circular issued by the Commissioners in March 1959. See Alpe, pp. 38 *et seq.*

[10] *Ante,* § 27-32.

instrument should itself set forth all the facts and circumstances affecting liability to duty; but this is not always practicable and indeed the Commissioners have power to obtain any information they require.[11]

27-44 *Effect of adjudication.* Any executed instrument can be presented for adjudication. In six cases, adjudication is obligatory inasmuch that the instrument is not duly stamped without adjudication. These cases are:

(a) voluntary dispositions [12];

(b) conveyances and leases to charities stamped at the reduced rate of duty [13];

(c) transactions exempt from capital duty within Part III of Schedule 19 to the Finance Act 1973 [14];

(d) conveyances and transfers relieved from duty in connection with schemes of reconstruction and amalgamation of companies [15];

(e) conveyances and transfers relieved from duty as between associated companies [16];

(f) conveyances or transfers of property in contemplation of a sale thereof. [17]

In practice the court requires an undertaking that any orders made under the Variation of Trusts Act 1958 be adjudicated.[18] In other cases, however, adjudication is advantageous because it is generally conclusive as to the sufficiency of the stamp: the instrument is " admissible in evidence, and available for all purposes notwithstanding any objection relating to duty." [19] It is conclusive, therefore, as against a purchaser. But there are some exceptions to this rule of conclusiveness:

(a) an instrument which by law cannot be stamped after execution is not duly stamped, even if it bears an adjudication stamp impressed after execution [20];

(b) the court could probably go behind an adjudication stamp which was proved to have been obtained by fraud or misrepresentation [21];

(c) an adjudication stamp is not retrospective.

Thus in *Prudential Assurance Investment and Loan Association* v. *Curzon*,[22] a document was insufficiently stamped at the trial and objected to on this ground. After the trial and before the appeal, the instrument was adjudicated. *Held*, that this did not remove the objection to the sufficiency of the first stamp.

The procedure by adjudication and subsequent appeal is the normal procedure for obtaining an authoritative decision on some point of stamp

---

[11] S.A. 1891, s. 12 (2).

[12] F. (1909-10) A. 1910, s. 74 (2); *post*, § 30-12.

[13] F.A. 1974, s. 49 (2).

[14] F.A. 1973, s. 47 (6); *post*, §§ 32-09 *et seq.*

[15] F.A. 1927, s. 55 (1), proviso (*a*); *post*, § 33-05.

[16] F.A. 1930, s. 42 (1), proviso; *post*, § 33-10.

[17] F.A. 1965, s. 90 (3); see *post*, § 28-23.

[18] For the practice, see Practice Note in [1966] 1 W.L.R. 345.

[19] S.A. 1891, s. 12 (5). But a " produced stamp " may be required. See § 27-45.

[20] *Ibid.* s. 12 (6) (*b*); *Vallance* v. *Forbes* (1879) 6 R. (Ct. of Sess.) 1099.

[21] Monroe's *Stamp Duties*, 5th ed., para. 65.

[22] (1852) 8 Ex. 97. This was a case under the Stamp Duties Act 1850, s. 14, where the " denoting " stamp therein referred to corresponds with the modern " adjudication " stamp. This decision has been applied in a case involving the validity of proxies presented at a meeting of shareholders: *Marx* v. *Estates and General Investments Ltd.* [1976] 1 W.L.R. 380; [1975] S.T.C. 671, *post*, § 34-06.

duty law. Further, it has been used as a means of obtaining a determination of the court as to whether a body is a legal charity. [23]

(5) *Produced stamps*

27-45　The following instruments are not duly stamped, even if adjudicated, unless they are produced to the Commissioners and stamped with the " produced " (or " P.D.") stamp [24]:

(a) any conveyance on sale of the fee simple in land (including a conveyance where the consideration is under £15,000 [25]);

(b) any lease or agreement for a lease of land for a term of seven years or more;

(c) any transfer on sale of such a lease (even if there are less than seven years to run);

(d) an instrument dutiable on issue as a bearer instrument. [26]

The object of the " produced " stamp is to give the authorities information about land values. A voluntary conveyance does not require a produced stamp; nor does a counterpart lease executed by the grantee or lessee only.

5. FOREIGN ELEMENT

(1) *The territorial limits of the Stamp Act*

27-46　Section 14 (4) of the Stamp Act [27] (which states the consequences which follow where an instrument is not duly stamped in accordance with the law) applies to:

(a) instruments executed in any part of the United Kingdom; and

(b) instruments, wheresoever executed, relating to any property situate, or to any matter or thing done or to be done, in any part of the United Kingdom.

The subsection thus defines the territorial limits within which the Stamp Act operates. [28] A court order has been held to be " an instrument executed." [29]

With regard to (a), it will be noted that an instrument executed in the United Kingdom must be stamped, even though it operates abroad. Thus a conveyance of foreign land which is executed in England is inadmissible in evidence in the British courts unless it bears the *ad valorem* conveyance or transfer duty. [30]

The words in (b) were considered by the House of Lords in *I.R.C.* v. *Maple & Co. (Paris) Ltd.* [31] The facts were as follows:

Property in France was transferred from one English company to another English company by an instrument (an *acte d'apport*) executed in France. The

[23] *I.R.C.* v. *Baddeley* [1955] A.C. 572.
[24] F.A. 1931, s. 28.
[25] *Post,* § 28-24.
[26] F.A. 1963, s. 60 (3); *post,* § 32-11.
[27] *Ante,* § 27-22.
[28] There are other sections which deal specifically with certain instruments executed abroad.
[29] *Sun Alliance Ltd.* v. *I.R.C.* [1972] Ch. 133.
[30] *Re Wright* (1855) 11 Ex. 458.
[31] [1908] A.C. 22.

consideration for the transfer consisted of shares in the latter company which were to be issued and delivered to the former company in England. *Held*, that the instrument was liable to *ad valorem* duty as a conveyance on sale.

" The instrument," said Lord Macnaghten, " relates to the capital of the new company, out of which it was agreed that a specified number of shares should be appropriated and allotted to the old company. The share capital of the new company, if it was situate anywhere, was situate in England. In my opinion this instrument does relate to property situate in England. Be that as it may, it certainly relates to something to be done in England. It relates to the registration in the name of the old company of shares which were to be allotted in an English company as the consideration for the purchase of the French property." [32]

> In *Faber* v. *I.R.C.*,[33] an engineer executed a deed of covenant in Canada whereby he covenanted to pay to a Canadian company a proportion of the income from his profession (which he carried on in England), so long as he practised that profession. *Held*, that the deed related to something done or to be done in the United Kingdom (namely, the practice of the profession) and was liable to *ad valorem* duty.

If an instrument is executed abroad and relates wholly to property or matters abroad, the Stamp Act has no application.

If an instrument executed abroad conveys both foreign and English property, it is arguable (from s. 4 (*a*) of the Stamp Act) that it attracts duty only in respect of the English property.[34]

27-47   *Time for stamping.* It should be kept in mind that, although an instrument executed abroad may be liable to stamp duty, no penalty is payable until 30 days after it has been first received in the United Kingdom.[35] To avoid stamp duty, therefore, an instrument may be left outside the United Kingdom until such time as it is required within the United Kingdom.[36]

(2) *Conflict of laws*

27-48   The courts do not take notice of the revenue laws of a foreign state, except where they render an instrument void and not merely inadmissible.[37]

(3) *Double taxation relief*

27-49   No relief from stamp duty is given by the Stamp Act on instruments which are also dutiable in other countries.

27-50   There is an exception to this rule in the case of Northern Ireland and the Republic of Ireland [38]: If an instrument is dutiable in Great Britain and in

---

[32] [1908] A.C. 22 at p. 26.   [33] [1936] 1 All E.R. 617.
[34] Alpe, *Law of Stamp Duties*, 25th ed., p. 57. See *ante*, § 27-15.   [35] *Ante*, § 27-29.
[36] Furthermore it would appear to be possible to give secondary evidence of a document executed and retained abroad or, at least, of the effect of such a document: see *English, Scottish and Australian Chartered Bank* [1893] 3 Ch. 385 (C.A.).
[37] *Bristow* v. *Sequeville* (1850) 5 Ex. 275; *Government of India* v. *Taylor* [1955] A.C. 491; *Brokaw* v. *Seatrain U.K. Ltd.* [1971] 2 Q.B. 476.
[38] Government of Ireland Act 1920, s. 29 (1), as amended by the Irish Free State (Consequential Provisions) Act 1922 (Session 2), s. 1. For text, see Alpe, *op. cit.*, p. 400. As to bearer instruments, see F.A. 1963, s. 61 (9). The position is now governed by the Northern Ireland Constitution Act 1973 and the Northern Ireland Act 1974 under which, for the time being, stamp duties are levied by the United Kingdom government.

Northern Ireland and is properly stamped in one of those countries, it is deemed to be properly stamped in the other; except that if the duty in such other country is higher, the instrument is not deemed to be duly stamped in that country unless the instrument is stamped for the excess. If an instrument is exempt from stamp duty in one country by virtue of a composition operating there, it is deemed to be stamped with the amount which would have been payable but for the composition.

There are similar provisions relating to the Republic of Ireland.[39]

6. STAMPS SPOILED OR WASTED

27-51　Section 9 of the Stamp Duties Management Act 1891 authorised the Commissioners to make an allowance where, in any of the cases listed in the section, a stamp is " spoiled." The following are examples of cases in which relief may be granted:

> *Examples*: (i) A stamped instrument is found after execution to have been void *ab initio*. (But no relief is available under section 9 where a contract is voidable and is avoided; or where an instrument fails through non-fulfilment of a condition precedent.)
>
> (ii) A stamped instrument is found after execution to be unfit, through error or mistake therein, for the purpose originally intended, *e.g.* where an appointment of trustees was made by the wrong person.
>
> (iii) A stamped instrument becomes insufficient for the purpose for which it was intended through failure of some necessary party to sign it or to complete the transaction. But relief is available in this case only if the instrument has not been made use of for any purpose whatsoever.
>
> (iv) Stamped material is, before execution, inadvertently spoiled or rendered unfit for the purpose intended.

Relief under section 9 is available only if the following conditions are satisfied [40]:

(a) The application for relief must be made within two years after the stamp has been spoiled or becomes useless or, in the case of an executed instrument, after the date of the instrument or, if not dated, after its execution.[41]

(b) In the case of an executed instrument, no legal proceeding must have been commenced in which the instrument could or would have been given or offered in evidence.[42]

(c) In the case of an executed instrument, the instrument must be surrendered for cancellation.[42]

Relief, if granted, may take the form of a repayment in cash or the giving of stamps.[43]

The provisions in section 9 (above) should be contrasted with those in

---

[39] Relief in respect of Double Taxation (Irish Free State Declaration) 1923 (S.R. & O. 1923 No. 406), Schedule, Part III. The Stamp Act 1891 applies in the Republic but the rates of duty are different from those in the United Kingdom, *e.g.* the duty on a conveyance on sale in the Republic is at the rate of £3 per cent. where the consideration exceeds £2,500.

[40] Regulations have been made by the Commissioners as to the procedure for claiming relief. See Sergeant, pp. 29-30.

[41] Stamp Duties Management Act 1891, s. 9 (7), proviso (*a*).

[42] *Ibid.* s. 9 (7), proviso (*b*).

[43] *Ibid.* s. 11. See also Concession No. F2.

section 59 of the Stamp Act 1891,[44] which requires that agreements for the sale of certain classes of property should be stamped as conveyances on sale but which directs the Commissioners to return the duty if the agreement is rescinded or annulled or for any other reason is not substantially performed or carried into effect. There are no conditions restricting the relief, such as those in (a), (b) and (c), above.

7. GENERAL EXEMPTIONS FROM ALL STAMP DUTIES

27-52 The following are the principal instruments which are exempt from all duties:

(1) *Under the Stamp Act 1891*

    (a) Transfers of shares in the Government or parliamentary stocks or funds.

    (b) Instruments for the sale, transfer, or other disposition, either absolutely or otherwise, of any ship or vessel, or any part interest, share, or property of or in any ship or vessel.[45]

    (c) Instruments of apprenticeship, etc.

    (d) Testaments, testamentary instruments, and dispositions *mortis causa* in Scotland.

    (e) Instruments made by, to, or with the Commissioners of Works for any of the purposes of the Commissioners of Works Act 1852.

(2) *Under the Finance Act 1948, s. 74*

Transfers of the stock of certain undertakings carried on under national ownership or control, when the Treasury so directs.

(3) *Under the Finance Act 1949, Schedule 8*

    (a) Articles of clerkship to a solicitor.

    (b) Bonds given pursuant to the directions of any Act, or of the Commissioners or the Commissioners of Customs, or any of their officers, for or in respect of any duties of excise or customs, or for preventing frauds or evasions thereof, or for any other matter or thing relating thereto.

    (c) Bonds on obtaining letters of administration in England or Ireland, or a confirmation of testament in Scotland.

    (d) Charterparties.

(4) *Under the Finance Act 1953, s. 31*

Certain receipts given in connection with National Savings.

(5) *Under the Finance Act 1959, s. 30*

    (a) Cover notes, slips, and other instruments usually made in anticipation of the issue of a formal policy, not being instruments relating to life insurance.

---

[44] *Post,* § 29-03.
[45] See *Deddington Steamship Co. Ltd.* v. *I.R.C.* [1911] 2 K.B. 1001 (C.A.).

   (b) Instruments embodying alterations of the terms or conditions of any policy of insurance other than life insurance.

   (c) Policies of insurance on baggage or personal and household effects only, if made or executed out of Great Britain.

(6) *Under the Finance Act 1960, s. 74*

Certain documents connected with the housing, training and health and efficiency of visiting forces.

(7) *Under the Finance Act 1963, s. 65 (3)*

Certain legal aid agreements and documents.

(8) *Under the Finance Act 1964, s. 23*

Contracts of employment and memoranda thereof.

27-53 **(9)** *Under the Finance Act 1971, s. 64 (1) and (2)*

Section 64 (1) abolished stamp duties under the following headings—

   (a) " Bond, Covenant, or Instrument of any kind whatsoever ";

   (b) " Bond of any kind whatsoever not specifically charged with any duty "; and

   (c) " Mortgage, Bond, Debenture, Covenant."

Section 64 (2) provides that, subject to instruments relating to several distinct matters [46] and the charge on voluntary dispositions, any instrument falling within any of the above headings is not to be chargeable with duty under any other heading in the First Schedule to the Stamp Act. Such an instrument, if executed under seal, will not even attract the 50p duty as a Deed. Examples are a seven year Deed of Covenant and a transfer of mortgage (other than a voluntary disposition [47]). Thus a very material distinction may arise between a transfer of mortgage (which operates to transfer the debt) and a sale of an unsecured debt. [48]

---

[46] *Ante*, § 27-15.
[47] *Ante*, § 27-07.
[48] See Law of Property Act 1925, s. 114, and *Wale* v. *I.R.C.* (1879) 4 Ex.D. 270.

CHAPTER 28

CONVEYANCE OR TRANSFER DUTY

HEAD OF CHARGE [1]

28-01 THE Act imposes duty under two heads:

Head (1)

Conveyance or transfer on sale of any property.

Duty: Ad valorem on the amount or value of the consideration for the sale of £1 per £50 (or fraction of £50). [2]

Head (2)

Conveyance or transfer of any kind not hereinbefore described.

Duty: Fixed duty of 50p.

Conveyance or transfer duty is also charged on certain agreements (s. 59; Chap. 29); on voluntary dispositions (Finance (1909-10) Act 1910, s. 74; Chap. 30); and on certain conveyances or transfers made in contemplation of a sale. [3]

INTRODUCTION

28-02 These heads of charge are of great practical importance. Head (1), which has been described as " the most productive and the most complicated of all heads of charge," [4] charges *ad valorem* duty on a conveyance on sale of any property. The basic rate of duty is £1 per £50 of the amount or value of the consideration, but there are reduced rates where the consideration does not exceed £30,000 and the instrument contains a certificate of value. [5] These reduced rates do not apply on a transfer of stock or marketable securities, [6] other than Commonwealth government stock. [7] However the rate is only 50p per £50 where the conveyance, transfer or lease is to a charity and where the transfer is of stock or marketable securities transferred to a non-resident person. Generally, payment of conveyance or transfer duty is denoted by means of an impressed stamp on the instrument of conveyance. Transfers of shares are the most important class of instruments to attract this duty. Under the Stock Transfer Act 1963 the duty

---

[1] S.A. 1891, Sched. 1. A third head was repealed by F.A. 1963, s. 62 (1), as from August 1, 1963.
[2] For reduced rates, see *post*, § 28-24.
[3] *Post*, § 28-23.
[4] Alpe, *Law of Stamp Duties*, 25th ed., p. 156.
[5] *Post*, § 28-24.
[6] The expression " stock " includes (*inter alia*) any share in the stocks or funds of any foreign or colonial state or government, or in the capital stock or funded debt of any county council, corporation, company or society in the United Kingdom, or of any foreign or colonial corporation, company or society. It also includes a unit under a unit trust scheme (F.A. 1946, s. 54 (1)). The expression " marketable security " means a security of such a description as to be capable of being sold in any stock market in the United Kingdom (S.A. 1891, s. 122), *e.g.* debentures in a public company.
[7] § 28-24.

should be impressed on the Stock Transfer Form where that form alone is used and on the Brokers Transfer Forms if these forms are used.

1. WHAT IS A CONVEYANCE ON SALE?

28-03 Under section 54 of the Stamp Act 1891 the expression " conveyance on sale " includes every instrument, and every decree or order of any court or of any commissioners, whereby any property, or any estate or interest in any property, upon the sale thereof is transferred to or vested in a purchaser, or any other person on his behalf or by his direction. The expression " instrument " includes every written document.[8] If no instrument is used, as where the title to goods is transferred by delivery, no duty can be levied.[9]

An instrument is not a conveyance on sale under section 54 unless (a) it transfers property (b) upon a sale thereof.

What is a Sale?

28-04 A transaction is not a " sale " unless there is:

(1) Mutual assent as to the sale and purchase of property.[10] If this contractual element is absent, the transaction is not one of sale. It is for this reason that some assents escape liability to *ad valorem* duty.[11] Likewise, orders for the transfer of property made under section 24 of the Matrimonial Causes Act 1973 attract *ad valorem* duty only " in unusual circumstances," for their purpose is to compensate the spouse and not to confer bounty.[12] However the general application of this principle must be doubted in view of the decisions in *Ridge Nominees Ltd.* v. *I.R.C.*[13] and *Sun Alliance Ltd.* v. *I.R.C.*[14] In the *Ridge* case an instrument executed on behalf of a dissentient shareholder which brought about a transfer of his shares under section 209 of the Companies Act 1948 was held to be a conveyance on sale; and in the *Sun Alliance* case the same conclusion was reached in regard to a court order under section 206 of the Companies Act 1948.

(2) A price in money paid or promised.[15] It is this requirement which differentiates a sale from an exchange. An exchange is " a transaction in which property belonging to one person is transferred to another person in consideration of that other person's property being transferred to the first." [16] There is no " price " in the legal sense. Instruments which effect an exchange of real or heritable property are dutiable under a separate head of charge in the Stamp Act 1891.[17]

---

[8] S.A. 1891, s. 122.
[9] But the F.A. 1963, s. 67, prohibits the circulation of blank transfers pursuant to a sale or voluntary disposition of stock.
[10] *Att.-Gen.* v. *Felixstowe Gaslight Co.* [1907] 2 K.B. 984.
[11] See *post*, §§ 28-13 *et seq.*   [12] See Sergeant, p. 50.
[13] [1962] Ch. 376 (C.A.).   [14] [1972] Ch. 133.
[15] *Benjamin on Sale*, 8th ed., p. 2, quoted in *Littlewoods Mail Order Stores Ltd.* v. *I.R.C.* [1961] Ch. 597 at p. 631; [1963] A.C. 135 at p. 152 (H.L.).
[16] *Viscount Portman* v. *I.R.C.* (1956) 35 A.T.C. 349; *post*, § 28-48.   [17] *Post*, §§ 28-47 *et seq.*

For the purposes of stamp duty, however, the following instruments are conveyances on sale:

(a) A transfer of property in consideration of the transfer of any stock [6] or security, whether marketable or non-marketable. [18]

(b) A transfer of property in consideration of a debt due to the transferee. [19]

(c) An exchange of stock [6] or securities. [20]

A conveyance in consideration of marriage or of services is not a conveyance on sale.

The instrument must transfer property or an interest in property

28-05 An instrument cannot effectively transfer property unless the transferor has the interest which he purports to transfer. *Nemo dat quod non habet.*

Thus in *Limmer Asphalte Paving Co.* v. *I.R.C.* [21] the grant for value of an exclusive licence to carry on the business of asphalte paving in two counties, where the grantor had no right to make such a grant, was held not to be a conveyance of property.

" Property " has been defined as " that which belongs to a person exclusive of others and which can be the subject of bargain and sale to another." [22]

In *Thames Conservators* v. *I.R.C.* [23] it was held that a grant of a permissive licence, revocable at will, to erect a jetty on the River Thames was not a conveyance of " property."

28-06 It is the instrument which operates in law to transfer property which attracts conveyance or transfer duty. [24]

In *Oughtred* v. *I.R.C.* [25] trustees held shares on trust for A for life, with remainder to B absolutely.

On June 18, 1956, it was orally agreed that B would on June 26 exchange his reversionary interest for certain shares (the " free " shares) owned by A beneficially, to the intent that A should become absolute owner of the settled shares.

On June 26, 1956, three deeds were executed:

(i) A deed of release, reciting the earlier oral agreement and that the settled shares were " accordingly now held by the trustees " for A absolutely.

(ii) A transfer by A of the free shares to B's nominee for a nominal consideration of 10s. (This instrument was stamped 10s.)

(iii) A transfer by the trustees to A of the legal title to the settled shares, also for a nominal consideration of 10s. (This instrument was stamped 10s. under Head (2) on the footing that it was not a conveyance *on sale* but a conveyance in which no beneficial interest passed. [26])

---

[18] s. 55, *post*, § 28-33.
[19] s. 57, *post*, § 28-39.
[20] *Post*, § 28-49.
[21] (1872) L.R. 7 Ex. 211.
[22] *Potter* v. *I.R.C.* (1854) 10 Exch. 147 at p. 156.
[23] (1886) 18 Q.B.D. 279. But this was a case under the Stamp Act 1870, s. 70, wherein the words " or any estate or interest in any property " do not appear in the definition of conveyance. Contrast S.A. 1891, s. 54, *ante*, § 28-03.
[24] Lord Esher in *I.R.C.* v. *Angus* (1889) 23 Q.B.D. 579 at p. 589.
[25] [1960] A.C. 206. And see *Henty and Constable (Brewers) Ltd.* v. *I.R.C.* [1961] 1 W.L.R. 1504 (C.A.); *Fitch Lovell Ltd.* v. *I.R.C.* [1962] 1 W.L.R. 1325.
[26] *Post*, § 28-44.

The issue was whether the transfer in (iii) was correctly stamped. It was held by a majority of the House of Lords that the transfer was liable to *ad valorem* duty as a conveyance on sale. If the legal title had remained vested in the trustees *ad valorem* duty would have been avoided.

28-07   It will be observed that the terms of the bargain and sale were that A should transfer the free shares to B in return for B's reversionary interest or, more precisely, for the legal title to the shares in which B's interest subsisted. The transfer by the trustees of the bare legal title to A was an implementation of B's part of the bargain and was therefore a conveyance " on sale."

> " The parties to a transaction of sale and purchase may no doubt choose to let the matter rest in contract.[27] But if the subject-matter of a sale is such that full title to it can only be transferred by an instrument, then any instrument they execute by way of transfer of the property sold ranks for stamp duty purposes as a conveyance on sale notwithstanding the constructive trust in favour of the purchaser which arose on the conclusion of the contract." [28]

On the point (which was taken by the appellant) that the disputed transfer was made by the trustees and not by B, Lord Jenkins said (at p. 243):

> " Where property sold is outstanding in some person other than the vendor, being a trustee for or nominee of the vendor so as to be bound to transfer the property according to the vendor's directions, then in my view a transfer by such person at the direction of the vendor is for the present purposes equivalent to a transfer by the vendor himself."

28-08   It was immaterial that no " beneficial interest " passed under the conveyance, this having already passed under the prior oral agreement.

> In *Grey* v. *I.R.C.*[29] H transferred the bare legal title in 18,000 shares to trustees as his nominees. [This transfer was correctly stamped 10s. under head (2), since no beneficial interest passed to the trustees.[30]] He then had a subsisting equitable interest and later *orally* directed the trustees to hold 3,000 of the shares on trusts set forth in other settlements previously made on his grandchildren. [No stamp because no instrument.] Five weeks later, the trustees executed declarations (which H signed) reciting their title to the shares and H's oral directions, and acknowledging that they held the shares on the trusts of the other settlement. [Stamped 10s. as a declaration of trust.]

The question in *Grey's* case was whether the declaration executed by the trustees and stamped 10s. was correctly so stamped. It was held that the oral directions given by H regarding the 3,000 shares were ineffective to dispose of his equitable interest (because writing is required by section 53 (1) (c) of the Law of Property Act 1925); therefore the later declaration transferred H's equitable interest to the beneficiaries and was accordingly a conveyance.[31]

28-09   If a written instrument operates to transfer property, that instrument is liable to conveyance or transfer duty irrespective of the manner in which the instrument is described or of its form. This principle can be illustrated by considering particular transactions in which a conveyance or transfer of property is effected.

---

[27] For an explanation of this phrase, see *post*, § 28-19.
[28] [1960] A.C. 206, *per* Lord Jenkins at p. 241.
[29] [1960] A.C. 1 (H.L.). See also *Vandervell* v. *I.R.C.* (1966) 43 T.C. 519 (H.L.) (*held* that s. 53 (1) (c) of the Law of Property Act 1925 did not apply where V caused the legal interest in shares to be transferred with the intention of simultaneously transferring the beneficial interest).   [30] *Post*, § 28-44.
[31] Not a conveyance *on sale* but a conveyance by way of voluntary disposition: see § 30-01.

(a) *Partnership transactions*

28-10   Any instrument under which payment is made for a share of partnership assets is a conveyance on sale, whether payment is made by an incoming partner or to an outgoing partner.

> Thus in *Christie* v. *I.R.C.*[32] a retiring partner transferred his interest in the partnership property to the continuing partner at a price equal to the sum due to the retiring partner in respect of capital. *Held,* that this was a conveyance on sale.

But where the incoming partner merely brings in cash capital, this is not a sale unless there is a simultaneous withdrawal of capital by another partner, when it is the practice to charge *ad valorem* duty.[33]

28-11   *Saving of duty on a dissolution.* Care must be taken in dissolving a partnership to avoid the use of an instrument which operates as a conveyance on sale.

> In *Garnett* v. *I.R.C.*[34] a deed of dissolution of partnership recited (a) that the retiring partner's credit was £41,752; (b) that the partnership realty had been conveyed to the continuing partner; (c) that the partnership chattels were in the possession of the continuing partner; and (d) that the continuing partner had given the retiring partner a promissory note for £41,752. The deed witnessed that the partnership was dissolved and that the retiring partner accepted the promissory note in satisfaction of his interest in the partnership.

It was held that the deed, notwithstanding that it purported to recite a conveyance of property which had already taken place, actually brought about a transfer of the interest therein referred to and was accordingly liable to duty as a conveyance on sale.

28-12   A mere withdrawal of capital by an outgoing partner does not operate as a conveyance on sale, if the capital is withdrawn under the terms of an instrument providing for the distribution of assets *in specie* on a dissolution. Such an instrument operates as a partition and is liable to a fixed duty of 50p.[35]

The following passage from *Lindley on Partnership*[36] was approved in *Garnett* v. *I.R.C.*[34] (at p. 637):

> " If the retiring partner, instead of assigning his interest, takes the amount due to him from the firm, gives a receipt for the money, and acknowledges that he has no more claims on his co-partners, they will practically obtain all they want; but such a transaction, even if carried out by deed, could hardly be held to amount to a sale; and no *ad valorem* stamp, it is apprehended, would be payable."

This suggests another method of avoiding duty on a dissolution.

(b) *Assents*

28-13   An assent under hand is normally exempt from duty; and an assent under seal is liable to a 50p stamp.[37] Where, however, a contractual element is

---

[32] (1866) L.R. 2 Ex. 46; 4 H. & C. 664 (a better report). See also *Phillips* v. *I.R.C.* (1867) L.R. 2 Ex. 399.
[33] Alpe, *op. cit.*, p. 171.   [34] (1899) 81 L.T. 633.
[35] *Macleod* v. *I.R.C.* (1885) 12 R. (Ct. of Sess.) 105. In *Henniker* v. *Henniker* (1852) 1 E. & B. 54 it was held that a partition was not a sale. See also *Cormack's Trustees* v. *I.R.C.*, 1924 S.C. 819. See *ante*, § 27-47.
[36] 11th ed., p. 549; 12th ed., p. 478.
[37] *Kemp* v. *I.R.C.* [1905] 1 K.B. 581; Administration of Estates Act 1925, s. 36 (11).

present, the instrument operates as a conveyance on sale and is liable to the *ad valorem* duty. The following assents must be stamped as conveyances:

(1) An assent by a personal representative to give effect to a contract of sale entered into by the deceased.[38]

(2) An assent appropriating specific assets to a pecuniary legatee in satisfaction, or in part satisfaction, of a legacy (including the statutory legacy due to a surviving spouse on intestacy), where the legatee's consent is required. This applies whether the appropriation is under the statutory power of appropriation[39] or under an express power contained in the will.[40]

28-14   No *ad valorem* duty is payable on an assent in the following cases:

(i) Where the will authorises the personal representatives to appropriate without the legatee's consent. It is common practice, therefore, in order to save stamp duty on a subsequent appropriation, to include in a will a clause directing that the statutory power of appropriation should be exercisable without any consents required by the Act.

(ii) Where the legatee is sole personal representative. The Revenue, it seems, take the view that a person cannot " sell " property to himself.

(iii) Where the assent is to a residuary beneficiary in satisfaction, or in part satisfaction, of his share of residue.[41]

(iv) Where, on an intestacy, the surviving spouse insists on an appropriation of the matrimonial home.[42]

(v) Where, on an intestacy, the net estate is less than the statutory legacy and is vested in the surviving spouse.[43]

If an assent is made in favour of a residuary beneficiary and the value of the assented property exceeds the value of the beneficiary's entitlement, so that he pays a sum to make up the difference, duty is payable on the excess,[44] unless the residuary beneficiary is sole personal representative.

28-15   *Family arrangements.* If the deceased's estate is divided up under a scheme of family arrangement, this is merely a partition[45] and no *ad valorem* duty is chargeable on any deed or assent used to give effect to the arrangement; but if any person gets more than his share, the instrument operates *pro tanto* as a gift (or as a sale if he pays a sum to make up the difference) and *ad valorem* duty will be charged. Where the arrangement is effected by a separate deed of family arrangement, it may be desirable to stamp this deed *ad valorem* and to have a duty paid denoting stamp on the assent.

---

[38] *G.H.R. Co.* v. *I.R.C.* [1943] K.B. 303.
[39] Administration of Estates Act 1925, s. 41; *Dawson* v. *I.R.C.* [1905] 2 Ir.R. 69; followed in *Jopling* v. *I.R.C.* [1940] 2 K.B. 282.
[40] *Re Beverly* [1901] 1 Ch. 681.
[41] There are dicta to the contrary in *Re Beverly, supra.*
[42] See Intestates' Estates Act 1952, s. 6 and Sched. 1.
[43] Alpe, *op. cit.*, p. 168.
[44] (1951) *Law Notes,* pp. 51-52.
[45] *Post,* § 28-47.

(c) *Receipts and acknowledgments*

28-16   A document, though described by the parties as a receipt, or acknowledgment, or memorandum, may nevertheless take effect as a conveyance.

> In *Horsfall* v. *Hey* [46] a document signed by both parties to the transaction recorded that " A has sold B all the goods, stock-in-trade, and fixtures in a certain shop for £50." *Held,* that notwithstanding the use of the past tense, the document meant: " A hereby sells to B " and was a conveyance on sale.

In *Garnett* v. *I.R.C.,* [47] as we have seen, a deed which in terms amounted to little more than a receipt and acknowledgment was held to be a conveyance on sale. Both *Horsfall* v. *Hey* [46] and *Garnett's* case [47] were relied on by Finlay J. in *Cohen and Moore* v. *I.R.C.* [48]

28-17   The authority of these cases may be questioned since the decision of the Court of Appeal in *Fleetwood-Hesketh* v. *I.R.C.* [49] The facts were as follows:

> Property was settled on a father for life, with remainder to his son in tail. The son disentailed with the consent of his father. Thereafter, an oral agreement was concluded by which the son purported to sell to the father for £160,000 and the father agreed to buy the son's reversionary interest. The only written instrument relating to this transaction was an acknowledgment signed by the son stating that he had received from the father £160,000 and stating what the payment was for.

The Crown claimed that the instrument was liable to *ad valorem* conveyance or transfer duty either (a) as a conveyance on sale, or (b) as an agreement for sale under section 59 of the Stamp Act 1891. [50] Finlay J. (at first instance) held that the instrument was chargeable as a conveyance on the ground that it was a contemporaneous record of the transaction of sale. In the Court of Appeal, however, it was held that the instrument was chargeable under section 59; and only two of the three judges expressed opinions on the alternative claim, Romer L.J. holding that there was no conveyance on sale, and Maugham L.J. holding that there was.

28-18   It would seem, therefore, that a receipt or acknowledgment is chargeable with duty as a conveyance only if:

    (1) It can be shown to have been the intention of the parties that the property should pass at the time of the execution of the document, and it did so pass; or

    (2) the document, and the antecedent oral transaction under which the property passed, can be shown to have been one single transaction under the principle established in *Cohen and Moore* v. *I.R.C.* [48]

---

[46] (1848) 2 Ex. 778.
[47] (1899) 81 L.T. 633; *ante,* §§ 28-11 *et seq.*
[48] [1933] 2 K.B. 126; *ante,* § 27-11.
[49] [1936] 1 K.B. 351 (C.A.). And see *Oughtred* v. *I.R.C.* [1960] A.C. 206 at p. 260.
[50] *Post,* § 29-02.

(d) *Dispositions of equitable interests*

28-19   An instrument by which A transfers an equitable interest to a purchaser is dutiable as a conveyance on sale, [51] even if it is in the form of a declaration of trust.

If, however, A agrees to sell a legal estate in land to B, the agreement itself operates to transfer an equitable interest to B, and A holds as bare trustee for B; but this is not a conveyance on sale: the very fact that the instrument is one of which equity will decree specific performance fixes it at once as an " agreement " and not as a " conveyance." [52]

This principle is frequently used to avoid stamp duty.

> Suppose, for example, that X wishes to convey land to XYZ Ltd., a company controlled by X. X agrees to sell the land to the company for a sum to be paid on the execution of the agreement; and the contract provides for completion to take place within (say) seven weeks. The contract is not liable to stamp duty and completion is postponed indefinitely. (If the contract provided for completion to take place (say) seven days after a notice given by the company to X, the Revenue might contend that the parties intended that the agreement should be the only instrument of title and that the agreement should be stamped as a conveyance.)

The parties thus " let the matter rest in contract." [53] But although X is a constructive trustee for the company by virtue of the contract, a subsequent conveyance by X to the company of the legal estate is a conveyance on sale: it is not liable to the fixed duty of 50p as a conveyance passing no beneficial interest. [54]

(e) *Options*

28-20   It was held in *George Wimpey & Co. Ltd.* v. *I.R.C.* [55] that the grant of an option over land was an instrument which vested an interest in property, on the sale thereof, in a purchaser within section 54 of the Stamp Act 1891. Consequently *ad valorem* duty was chargeable on the consideration paid for the grant of the option. The grant of an option is, however, merely an offer to sell which, by operation of law, gives rise to an interest in the property. This decision can only be reconciled with the principle that a contract of sale is not chargeable under section 54 [53] on the basis that the grant of an option is not capable of completion by conveyance or transfer. An option may, alternatively, be chargeable within section 60 of the Stamp Act 1891. [56]

(f) *Miscellaneous cases*

28-21   A foreclosure order is a conveyance on sale by virtue of the Finance Act 1898, s. 6. A family arrangement may be a conveyance [57]; and an

---

[51] *Chesterfield Brewery Co.* v. *I.R.C.* [1899] 2 Q.B. 7. Wills J. held also that there was an agreement for the sale of an equitable interest dutiable under S.A., 1891, s. 59, *post*, § 29-02.

[52] *I.R.C.* v. *Angus & Co.* (1889) 23 Q.B.D. 579 (C.A.), *per* Lord Esher M.R. at p. 591. And see § 27-13.

[53] See the first passage from *Oughtred* v. *I.R.C.* [1960] A.C. 206 quoted *ante*, § 28-07.

[54] *Oughtred* v. *I.R.C.* [1960] A.C. 206 (H.L.), *ante*, § 28-06. But the purchaser may acquire a title under the Limitation Act 1939.

[55] [1975] 1 W.L.R. 995; [1975] S.T.C. 248 (C.A.).

[56] See *post*, § 28-38.

[57] *Bristol (Marquess)* v. *I.R.C.* [1901] 2 K.B. 336; *cf. Cormack's Trustees* v. *I.R.C.*, 1924 S.C. 819.

amalgamation of companies usually involves a conveyance, whether it is effected by agreement [58] or otherwise, *e.g.* by Act of Parliament.

28-22   The liability of an instrument to stamp duty has to be determined at the moment when it is executed. [59] An instrument which transfers an interest in property at a time when there is no subsisting agreement for the sale of that property but which is executed in contemplation of a possible sale which may never take place is not a conveyance " on sale."

> Thus in *Wm. Cory & Son Ltd.* v. *I.R.C.* [60] the appellant company agreed in principle to purchase certain shares and a draft sale agreement was prepared fixing the completion date as November 1, 1957. On October 24, 1957, the appellant company demanded that the share-vendors grant the company an immediate option to purchase the shares and the option was duly granted. The option agreement dated November 1, 1957, provided that, in order to protect the rights of the appellant company, the share-vendors would forthwith transfer their shares to the appellant company, such shares to be held in trust for its registered holders but without passing any beneficial interest to them; and there were provisions for the re-transfer of the shares if the option lapsed. The shares were transferred in accordance with the option agreement and the option was exercised orally on November 8, 1957. It was held (i) that the transfers of the shares were not conveyances or transfers on sale; and (ii) that the option agreement itself was merely an offer to sell: it was not an agreement for sale which attracted *ad valorem* duty under section 59 of the Stamp Act 1891.

28-23 The *Cory* decision revealed a device by which *ad valorem* duty on conveyances on sale could be avoided; and the Finance Act 1965 now provides that any instrument whereby property is conveyed or transferred to any person in contemplation of a sale of that property shall be treated for the purposes of the Stamp Act 1891 as a conveyance or transfer on sale of that property for a consideration equal to the value of that property. [61] The instrument must be presented for adjudication [62] and the value of the property will be determined by the Commissioners in accordance with the principles which apply to voluntary dispositions [63]; in particular, the provisions of section 90 (5) of the Finance Act 1965 [64] (which are designed to prevent avoidance of duty on voluntary dispositions by devices to reduce the value of the property transferred) apply also to conveyances or transfers made in contemplation of a sale. The provisions of the Act of 1965 came into force on August 1, 1965, [65] and apply to instruments executed on or after that date.

If when a conveyance or transfer of property in contemplation of a sale thereof is stamped in accordance with the section and the sale does not take place and the property is re-conveyed or re-transferred to the vendor or transferor (or to a person to whom his rights have been transmitted on

---

[58] *Brotex Cellulose Fibres* v. *I.R.C.* [1933] 1 K.B. 158.
[59] See *ante*, § 27-08.
[60] [1965] A.C. 1088 (H.L.).
[61] F.A. 1965, s. 90 (1) (4).
[62] *Ibid.* s. 90 (3); and see *ante*, § 27-41.
[63] *Post*, § 30-06.
[64] Discussed *post*, § 30-08.
[65] F.A. 1965, s. 90 (7).

death or bankruptcy), or the sale takes place for a consideration which is less than the value in respect of which duty is payable under the section, the Commissioners will repay the duty (or excess duty) on a claim being made to them not later than two years after the making or execution of the dutiable instrument.[66]

It should be noted that section 90 of the Finance Act 1965 does not impose *ad valorem* duty on a mere option agreement: it applies only where property is conveyed or transferred under the agreement. Further, it does not apply unless the property is conveyed or transferred in contemplation of a *sale*: it does not apply, for instance, where property is transferred as security for a loan if there is a subsequent sale to the transferee which was not in contemplation at the time of the transfer.

2. RATES OF DUTY AND CERTIFICATES OF VALUE

28-24 The current full rate of *ad valorem* conveyance or transfer duty is £1 for every £50 (or part of £50) of the amount or value of the consideration. The rate of duty is only 50p for every £50 where:

(1) the conveyance, transfer or letting is made to a charity and the instrument is adjudicated [67]; and

(2) stock or marketable securities are transferred to a non-resident for full consideration in money or money's worth and the instrument is certified as such by an authorised depositary.[68]

There are reduced rates applicable to instruments transferring property other than stock and marketable securities [69] executed on or after May 1, 1974,[70] which are as follows:

	Instrument certified at:	Rate per £50 or part thereof
Consideration £15,000 or under	£15,000	Nil
,, £20,000 ,,	£20,000	25p
,, £25,000 ,,	£25,000	50p
,, £30,000 ,,	£30,000	75p

There is a sliding scale of duty where the consideration is less than £300.[71] There are special rates on transfers of Commonwealth government stock [72]; but not on other transfers of stock or marketable security.

The reduced rates referred to above are conditional on the instrument containing a certificate to the effect " That the transaction effected by the instrument does not form part of a larger transaction or series of

---

[66] F.A. 1965, s. 90 (2); but see the proviso.

[67] F.A. 1974, s. 49 (2).

[68] *Ibid.* Sched. 11, Pt. III; a non-resident is a person who resides outside the Scheduled territories for exchange control purposes. See also the complete exemption for transfers of *loan capital* in F.A. 1976, s. 126 referred to *post*, § 28-45.

[69] See the general exemption from duty in the case of loan capital referred to in § 28-45, *post*. It would now appear that most transfers of stock and marketable securities will be within the exemption.

[70] F.A. 1974, s. 49 and Sched. 11.

[71] See F.A. 1974, Sched. 11, para. 3.

[72] Defined in F.A. 1963, s. 62 (6). The rate is normally 50p for every £100: *ibid.* s. 62 (2), as amended by F.A. 1974, Sched. 10, para. 5.

transactions in respect of which the amount or value, or aggregate amount or value, of the consideration exceeds [£15,000, £20,000, £25,000 or £30,000 as the case may be]." [73]

> Thus if A conveys Blackacre to B for £16,000, the conveyance must be certified at £20,000 and the duty (to be paid by B) is @ 25p per £50 = £80.

The object of the certificate of value is to prevent the avoidance of stamp duty by the artificial splitting up of transactions.

The words of the statutory certificate give rise to two problems:

(1) When does a transaction form part of a larger transaction or series of transactions?

(2) How is the amount or value of the consideration to be determined?

Is there a larger transaction or series? [74]

28-25 The type of problem which often arises in practice is as follows:

> A agrees to purchase two properties from B, each for £9,000. Each property is separately conveyed. If there was one transaction for £18,000, of which each conveyance formed a part, the duty on each conveyance @ 25p per £50 would be £90; but if there were two separate transactions, each conveyance would be certified at £15,000 and the duty would be nil.

Not very much guidance on this question is to be had from the cases, and none from the Act. It seems, however, that where there are simultaneous transfers of property by one transferor to one transferee, these must be taken to form one transaction if there is any degree of interdependence or linkage between the transactions. Thus, in the example above, if B could not (or would not) have purchased the one property without also purchasing the other, such interdependence would, it seems, be present.

Auction sales may be taken as an exception to this general rule, for in *Att.-Gen.* v. *Cohen* [75] it was held that if a purchaser buys separate lots of property by auction from one vendor, and there are separate contracts and conveyances, there is no series even if the contracts are for convenience evidenced by one memorandum. There would, however, be a series if the lots were included in one conveyance, or if several unsold lots were purchased in one block *after* an auction sale. [76]

What is the amount or value of the consideration?

28-26 All property which passes under the transaction or series must be taken into account in deciding if a certificate of value can be included, even property which is not included in any document; except that, under the Finance Act 1958, s. 34 (4), any goods, wares or merchandise may be disregarded, provided they are excluded from the conveyance. A sum paid for fixtures may not be disregarded.

---

[73] F.A. 1958, s. 34 (1).
[74] See also *post*, § 28-28 (building plots); § 28-34 (periodical payments); § 28-42 (sub-sales).
[75] [1937] 1 K.B. 478 (C.A.).
[76] (1954) L.S.G., p. 369.

Example: A agrees to sell his business as a going concern for £21,500. The consideration is apportioned between the assets as follows:

Land	£14,000
Goodwill	£3,500
Stock-in-trade	£4,000

Under section 34 (4), the stock-in-trade can be disregarded for the purpose of certification, and the instrument certified at £20,000, provided the stock is excluded from the conveyance (*i.e.* is transferred by delivery).

Note. If the land is conveyed separately for £14,000, the conveyance cannot be certified at £15,000, for the sale of the goodwill forms one transaction with the sale of the land.

The relief given by section 34 (4) is valuable inasmuch that it enables the parties to deal with the stock in the agreement (as they must, for tax purposes) [77] without incurring heavy liability for stamp duty.

3. CALCULATION OF THE CONSIDERATION FOR PURPOSES OF DUTY

28-27 The *ad valorem* duty payable under Head (1) in § 28-01 is not on the value of the property conveyed but on the " amount or value of the consideration for the sale." [78] This is not necessarily the consideration stated in the instrument. Thus if land is acquired under compulsory powers and the payment to the vendor includes a sum for compensation for damage by severance or injurious affection, duty is charged on the total figure, even though no reference to the compensation payment is made in the conveyance of the land.

But under the Finance Act 1900, s. 10, where a conveyance on sale is made for any consideration in respect whereof it is chargeable with *ad valorem* duty, and in further consideration of a covenant by the purchaser to make (or of his having previously made) any substantial improvement of or addition to the property conveyed to him, or of any covenant relating to the subject-matter of the conveyance, no duty is chargeable in respect of such further consideration.

There are cases where the assessment of *ad valorem* conveyance or transfer duty presents special problems. Some of these must now be considered.

(a) *Sales and Leases of Building Plots and Houses in the Course of Erection*

28-28 It is a common transaction for a person to purchase or to take a lease of land under an arrangement that the vendor or lessor will (by himself or his nominee) erect a house or other building on the land. The question then arises whether the cost of the house or building is to be treated as part of the cost of the land for stamp duty purposes.

If the building is completed before the date of the contract for the sale (or lease) of the land, the cost of the building is part of the cost of the land [79]; and if the land is conveyed (or leased) before the building is begun, the cost of the building is not part of the cost of the land. [80] So much seems clear from the cases. Where, however, at the date of the contract no house has

---

[77] *Ante,* §§ 2-34 *et seq.*
[78] Head (1); *ante,* § 28-01.
[79] *M'Innes* v. *I.R.C.,* 1934 S.C. 424.
[80] *Kimbers* v. *I.R.C.* [1936] 1 K.B. 132; (*post,* § 28-30); *Paul* v. *I.R.C.* (1936) 15 A.T.C. 57.

been erected (or a house has been partly erected) and at the date of the conveyance (or lease) a house has been wholly (or partly) erected, the position (as appears from a statement issued by the Commissioners in August 1957) is as follows [81]:

28-29   " The Board have taken legal advice concerning the stamp duty chargeable on conveyances or leases of building plots in cases where at the date of the contract for sale or lease no house has been erected or a house has been partly erected on the site which constitues or is included in the subject-matter of the sale or lease, and at the date of the conveyance or lease a house has been wholly or partly erected on the site.

The Board are advised that the law is as follows:

    (i) Subject to what is said under paragraph (iv) below, if under the contract for the sale or lease the purchaser or lessee is entitled to a conveyance or lease of the land in consideration only of the purchase price or rent of the site, the *ad valorem* duty on the conveyance or lease will be determined only by the amount of the purchase price or rent, although it may have been agreed that a house is to be built on the site at the expense of the purchaser or lessee.

       In such a case, the concurrent existence of a contract with the vendor or lessor or any other person for the building of a house on the site will not increase the stamp duty chargeable on the conveyance or lease.

    (ii) If under the contract the purchaser or lessee is not entitled to a conveyance or lease until a house has been built on the site at his expense and if the house is to be built by the vendor or lessor or by his agent or nominee, the payment of the building price by the purchaser or lessee will be part of the consideration for the conveyance or lease and the building price will be liable to *ad valorem* duty accordingly.

       (If the house is to be built by a person who is not the vendor or lessor or his agent or nominee, the payment of the building price will not form part of the consideration for the sale or lease except in so far as paragraph (iv) below applies.)

    (iii) When the position is as in paragraph (ii) above, and a purchaser or lessee not entitled to a conveyance or lease until a house has been erected at his expense in fact obtains a conveyance or lease when the house has been only partly erected, *ad valorem* duty is payable on the conveyance or lease on the proportionate amount of the building price attributable to the partial erection of the house computed as to the date of the conveyance or lease.

    (iv)   (a) If, at the date of the contract, a house has been wholly or partly erected by the vendor or lessor or by his agent or nominee or by a builder not employed by the purchaser or lessee, it normally forms part of the subject-matter of the sale or lease and the consideration or apportioned consideration for that building (as existing at the date of the contract) is accordingly liable to *ad valorem* duty.

       (b) If, at the date of the contract, a house has been wholly or partly erected by the purchaser or lessee or by any person on his behalf the consideration or apportioned consideration for the house wholly or partly erected will not normally form part of the consideration for the sale or lease and accordingly will not be liable to *ad valorem* duty.

       (c) This paragraph is subject to what is said in paragraphs (ii) and (iii) above.

    (v) The contract referred to above may be contained in more than one instrument or it may be partly written and partly verbal. It includes any contractual arrangement between the parties.

---

[81] (1957) L.S.G., p. 450.

These observations explain, so far as is possible in general terms, the view of the law at present adopted by the Board, but they have not, of course, the force of law, and are promulgated merely with the object of assisting the taxpayer. The Board are not bound by them, and the circumstances of any particular case may call for special consideration.''

Certificates of value

28-30   The test for determining whether a purchase of land and a contract to build form part of one larger transaction or series is the same as the test for determining whether the cost of the building is to be reckoned as part of the cost of the land in assessing the *ad valorem* duty.

In *Kimbers* v. *I.R.C.*[82] there was (i) a contract for the sale of land for £x, and (ii) a contemporaneous building contract for £y. The land was conveyed before the building was commenced. The conveyance was held to be properly stamped for £x, and it was not suggested that the conveyance formed one transaction with the building contract.

The matter was in issue in another case from which it emerges that the contracts will be treated as parts of a single transaction if they are so interlinked that, if the purchaser defaults on the building contract, he cannot enforce the contract for the sale of the land.[83]

(b) Special Cases (ss. 55-58)

28-31   The Stamp Act makes special provision for the calculation of the consideration where this consists of foreign currency (s. 6), stock [84] and securities (s. 55), periodic payments (s. 56), a debt (s. 57) or where there is a sub-sale (s. 58). Each of these provisions will now be separately considered.

Foreign currency

28-32   By section 6 of the Stamp Act 1891, where an instrument is chargeable with *ad valorem* duty in respect of any money in any foreign or colonial currency, duty is calculated on its value in British currency at the current rate of exchange on the day of the date of the instrument; and where the instrument contains a statement of the current rate of exchange and is stamped in accordance therewith, it is to be deemed duly stamped unless and until the contrary is shown.

Consideration in stock [84] and securities

28-33   If the consideration, or any part of the consideration, for a conveyance on sale consists of:

(a) any stock or marketable security,[84] the conveyance is to be charged in respect of the value of the stock or security [85];

(b) any security not being a marketable security (*e.g.* a debenture of a private company), the conveyance is to be charged in respect of the

---

[82] [1936] 1 K.B. 132.
[83] *Paul* v. *I.R.C.*   (1936) 15 A.T.C. 57.
[84] See note 6, § 28-02.
[85] S.A. 1891, s. 55 (1). As a consequence of this provision an '' exchange '' of securities constitutes two sales: *J. & P. Coats* v. *I.R.C.* [1897] 2 Q.B. 423 (C.A.).

amount due at the date of the conveyance for principal and interest on the security.[86]

The transfer of the securities themselves, as consideration for the transfer of the other property, will only be subject to the fixed duty of 50p [87] since the other property cannot be regarded as consideration.[85] In (a), the duty must be calculated according to the " average price " on the Stock Exchange at the date of the conveyance.[88] If the conveyance contains a statement of the average price and is stamped in accordance therewith, it is deemed to be duly stamped until the contrary is shown.[89] If there is no average price, as where the shares are unquoted, the Commissioners must assess the value of the stock, etc., on the basis of any recent arm's length dealing or any other available evidence.

If on the formation of a company, property is conveyed in consideration of the issue of shares in the company, the Commissioners assess the *ad valorem* duty on the actual (not the nominal) value of the shares issued, which will be the value of the property conveyed.[90] The rule is the same where the consideration is to be satisfied by the transfer of shares recently issued.

> Thus if property worth £65,000 is sold to a company in consideration of the issue to the vendor of 100 £1 shares (being the whole of the company's nominal capital), the duty is payable on £65,000.[91]

Consideration in periodical payments

28-34   The effect of section 56 of the Stamp Act can be seen from the following table. Where the consideration (or any part of the consideration) for a conveyance on sale consists of the payments referred to in the left hand column, duty is charged on the sums in the right hand column.

	Consideration consisting of:	*Duty is chargeable on:*
s. 56 (1)	Money payable periodically for a definite period not exceeding 20 years, so that the total amount to be paid can be previously ascertained.	The total amount payable.
s. 56 (2)	Money payable periodically for a definite period exceeding 20 years or in perpetuity or for any indefinite period not terminable with life.	The total amount " which will or may, according to the terms of sale, be payable " during the 20 years following the date of the instrument.
s. 56 (3)	Money payable periodically during any life or lives.	The amount which will or may, according to the terms of sale, be payable during the 12 years following the date of the instrument.

---

[86] S.A. 1891, s. 55 (2).   [87] See *post*, § 28-43.
[88] *Ibid.* s. 6 (1).
[89] *Ibid.* s. 6. (2). Consequently a subsequent purchaser cannot object to the conveyance as a document of title: *Re Weir & Pitt's Contract* (1911) 55 S.J. 536.
[90] *Furness Railway Co.* v. *I.R.C.* (1864) 33 L.J.Ex. 173; *Carlyon Estates Ltd.* v. *I.R.C.* (1937) 46 T.C. 413; *John Foster & Sons* v. *I.R.C.* [1894] 1 Q.B. 516 (C.A.); see *post*, § 32-07.
[91] *Carlyon Estates Ltd.* v. *I.R.C.* in note 90, *supra*; *post*, § 32-07.

> *Example:* A conveyance in consideration of a perpetual yearly rentcharge is chargeable with *ad valorem* conveyance or transfer duty under section 56 (2) on the total amount payable during the 20 years after the date of the conveyance.[92]
>
> A conveyance in consideration of a lump sum and a life annuity to the vendor should be stamped on the lump sum and under section 56 (3).[93]

A sum which is payable only on a contingency, such as sufficiency of profits, may nevertheless fall within section 56.[94]

28-35   A grant of a lease in consideration of a rent, or the transfer of part of leasehold property with an apportionment of the liability for the rent, is outside section 56.[95]

28-36   Section 56 (2) was considered in *Western United Investment Co. Ltd.* v. *I.R.C.,*[96] where the facts were as follows:

> On May 9, 1956, W agreed to purchase shares and to pay for them by 125 yearly instalments of £44,000 each. Total £5½ million. The agreement provided (cl. 3) that if W defaulted in payment of any instalment, all the unpaid instalments were to become immediately payable. On June 1, 1956, the transfer of shares to W was executed.

The Revenue contended, *inter alia,* that the transfer was liable to conveyance or transfer duty at £2 per cent. on £5½ million on the ground that, under clause 3, the whole £5½ million " *might* according to the terms of sale " be payable within 20 years. Upjohn J. (at p. 404) rejected this contention:

> " Clause 3 is in a literal sense a term of the sale in that it is an undoubted term of the contract of sale. But it is a term of the contract which only comes into operation if the terms of sale be broken. The terms of sale for the purposes of section 56, in my judgment, are the terms of sale upon which the parties contemplate that the property will be paid for, *i.e.* 125 annual instalments of £44,000. The terms of sale do not, in my judgment, comprehend terms of the contract of sale which come into operation if, but only if, the agreed terms of sale are broken."

The duty assessable was, therefore, only that applicable to the sum of 20 annual instalments.

28-37   *Certificates of value.* It seems that, if property is conveyed in consideration of the payment of (say) £36,000 by 30 annual instalments of £1,200 so that duty is chargeable under section 56 (2) on the total, 20 annual instalments (£24,000), the conveyance can be certified as for a consideration " not exceeding £25,000."

28-38   *Sale of an annuity.* Under section 60 of the Stamp Act 1891, where on the sale of an annuity or other right not before in existence,[97] such annuity or

---

[92] Where at the time of the conveyance, the property conveyed is already subject to a rentcharge or an annuity, s. 56 does not apply. See S.A. 1891, s. 57, *post,* § 28-39, Example (ii).

[93] *Cf. Martin* v. *I.R.C.* (1904) 91 L.T. 453.

[94] See the Contingency Principle, *ante,* § 27-18. A case on s. 56 (2) is *Underground Electric Railways Ltd.* v. *I.R.C.* [1906] A.C. 21.   [95] *Swayne* v. *I.R.C.* [1900] 1 Q.B. 172 (C.A.).

[96] [1958] Ch. 392. For the tax sequel to this case, see *Vestey* v. *I.R.C.* [1962] Ch. 861; *ante,* § 5-27.

[97] See *Great Northern Ry.* v. *I.R.C.* [1901] 1 K.B. 416 at p. 426.

other right is not created by actual grant or conveyance, but is only secured by bond, covenant, contract or otherwise, such instrument is chargeable as a conveyance.

> Thus if A contracts to provide B with £x a year in consideration of a lump sum payment by B of £y, the contract must be stamped as a conveyance on sale, the *ad valorem* duty being assessed on the purchase price, *i.e.,* £y.

The grant of an option for £x may be dutiable as a conveyance on sale under section 60 rather than under section 54.[98] In practice, most life annuities are purchased from insurance companies and are " purchased life annuities " within the taxing Acts.[99] Such annuities are not chargeable under section 60 but are charged at the rate of 5p per £10, or part thereof, of the annuity.[1] Again, section 60 does not apply to a voluntary disposition of an annuity (which formerly attracted bond covenant duty); nor to a transaction whereby a loan is repaid by way of an annuity (which formerly attracted mortgage duty).

Consideration in the form of a debt

28-39   If property is conveyed to any person in consideration (wholly or in part) of a debt due to him, the debt is deemed to be the whole (or part, as the case may be) of the consideration.

> Thus if A accepts Blackacre (worth £14,000) in satisfaction of a debt of £16,000 the conveyance of Blackacre must be stamped on £16,000.

This method of assessing the stamp duty has not escaped criticism: in *Huntington* v. *I.R.C.,*[2] for example, Wright J. suggested that the assessment should be made on a sum not exceeding the value of the property transferred.[3]

If property is conveyed subject either certainly or contingently to the payment or transfer of any money or stock,[4] whether being or constituting a charge or incumbrance upon the property or not, the money or stock is deemed to be the whole (or part, as the case may be) of the consideration.

> *Examples:* (i) If mortgaged property is conveyed for £14,000 duty is assessed on the aggregate amount of the purchase price (£14,000) and the amount of the mortgage debt, including any interest then due, whether the purchaser assumes personal liability for the mortgage debt or not.
>
> (ii) If a fee simple is conveyed subject to an annuity previously charged on the property, duty is assessed on the aggregate of the purchase price and the value of the annuity calculated under section 56, above.
>
> (iii) If on the sale of a business the purchaser agrees to discharge the vendor's debts, whether secured or unsecured, duty is assessed on the aggregate of the purchase price and the amount of the debts.[5]

The effect of this provision in section 57 of the Stamp Act 1891 is that wherever a purchaser assumes a liability of the vendor to a third party (in

---

[98] See *Wm. Cory & Son Ltd.* v. *I.R.C.* [1965] A.C. 1088 and *ante,* § 28-20.

[99] *Ante,* §§ 5-33 *et seq.* (tax).

[1] Under head 3 of bond covenant duty in S.A. 1891, Sched. 1 (as extended by F.A. 1956, s. 38 (1)). This head of charge was not repealed by F.A. 1971, s. 64 (1) (*a*).

[2] [1896] 1 Q.B. 422.

[3] Effect was given to this suggestion in the case of foreclosure orders by the F.A. 1898, s. 6.

[4] See note 6, *ante,* § 28-02.   [5] And see *post,* §§ 29-09 *et seq.*

consequence whereof he will, of course, pay less for the property), the liability must be reckoned as part of the consideration, even if the liability is contingent.

28-40   Liabilities which are inherent in the nature of property conveyed are not, however, within section 57.

> Thus if leasehold property is assigned, the liability to pay the rent is not treated as part of the consideration of the sale [6]; and if partly paid shares are transferred, no duty is in practice claimed in respect of the liability to pay future calls. [7]

Apportionment of consideration

28-41   If property is contracted to be sold for one consideration and is conveyed to a purchaser (or to separate joint purchasers) in parts by different instruments, the consideration must be apportioned as the parties think fit and duty charged accordingly. [8]

28-42   *Sub-sales.* If a person, having contracted to purchase property but not having obtained a conveyance thereof, contracts to sell it to another person to whom the property is immediately conveyed, the conveyance must be charged in respect of the consideration moving from the sub-purchaser (whether it be more or less than the original contract price). [9]

> *Examples:* (i) A contracts to sell property to B for £20,000. B contracts to sell the property to C for £25,000, whereupon A (acting on B's directions) conveys the property direct to C. C must pay duty on £25,000. (B pays no duty, for there is no " conveyance " to him.)
>
> (ii) Facts same as in (i), except that B contracts sub-sales to a number of purchasers of different parts of the property. Each sub-purchaser must pay duty on the consideration moving from him.
>
> It follows that a purchaser who intends to resell the property can avoid stamp duty by avoiding completion. [10]

The Act does not provide for the case where a purchaser, having contracted to purchase property for one undivided consideration, sub-sells part only of the property, so that part is conveyed direct to the sub-purchaser and the remainder to the purchaser. It is now settled, [11] however, that the conveyance to the sub-purchaser must be charged in respect of the consideration moving from him, and that the conveyance of the remainder must be charged on an apportioned part of the original purchase price, and not on the difference between that price and the amount paid by the sub-purchaser.

> *Example:* A contracts to sell two identical properties to B for £20,000. B contracts to sub-sell one property to C for £12,000 and A conveys direct to C. The conveyance to C must be charged on £12,000 and can be certified as " not exceeding £15,000." The conveyance of the other property, although it will acknowledge the receipt of only £8,000, must be charged on £10,000 and, since

---

[6] *Swayne* v. *I.R.C.* [1900] 1 Q.B. 172 (C.A.).   [7] Alpe, *op. cit.*, p. 188.
[8] S.A. 1891, s. 58 (1) and (2).
[9] *Ibid.* s. 58 (4). Strict compliance with this subsection is necessary to take advantage of it; thus it does not apply if the original purchaser obtains a conveyance before contracting to sub-sell: *Fitch Lovell* v. *I.R.C.* [1962] 1 W.L.R. 1325 at pp. 1341-1342.
[10] But see *Escoigne Properties Ltd.* v. *I.R.C.* [1958] A.C. 549; *post*, § 33-10.
[11] *Maples* v. *I.R.C.* [1914] 3 K.B. 303.

it forms part of a larger transaction for £20,000, cannot be certified as " not exceeding £15,000 " but only as " not exceeding £20,000."

Furthermore the Act does not provide for the case where a purchaser, having contracted to purchase property, agrees to transfer it in exchange for the transfer of another property from another person. Here it is considered that, since the only conveyance or transfer is one of exchange and not of sale, no *ad valorem* duty is payable on the original purchase price.

4. HEAD (2): CONVEYANCES LIABLE TO A FIXED DUTY OF 50P

28-43 The second head of charge in § 28-01 levies a fixed duty of 50p on " any conveyance or transfer of any kind not hereinbefore described." The charge extends to

> " Every instrument, and every decree of any court or of any commissioners, whereby any property on any occasion, except a sale or mortgage or voluntary disposition, is transferred to or vested in any person . . ." [12]

excepting, of course, conveyances which are chargeable with duty under **28-44** Head (1). The following are examples of instruments which are chargeable under Head (2):

(1) A conveyance in consideration of marriage or services. These are not conveyances *on sale* because there is no price. A conveyance in consideration of marriage is not dutiable as a voluntary disposition. [13]

(2) A conveyance under which no beneficial interest passes and which is not made on or in contemplation of a sale. [14] A conveyance to a nominee is an example of such a conveyance; but if A agrees to sell land to B who thus acquires an equitable title to the land, the subsequent conveyance to B is a conveyance on sale. [15]

(3) A conveyance for effectuating the appointment of a new trustee [16] or the retirement of a trustee, whether or not a new trustee is appointed. [17]

(4) A transfer by a liquidator of the assets of the company *in specie* to shareholders, in satisfaction of their rights in a winding up; or a transfer by trustees to beneficiaries on a distribution of trust funds.

(5) A conveyance which contains a certificate of value declaring the consideration to be £15,000 or under.

An exchange or partition of property may be dutiable under this head. [18]

5. EXEMPTIONS AND RELIEFS FROM CONVEYANCE OR TRANSFER DUTY

28-45 The General Exemptions from all stamp duties have already been referred to. [19] Other conveyances which are exempt are:

---

[12] S.A. 1891, s. 62, as amended by the F. (1909-10) A. 1910, s. 74.   [13] *Post*, § 30-13.
[14] F.A. 1965, s. 90; see *ante*, § 28-23.
[15] *Oughtred* v. *I.R.C.* [1960] A.C. 206 (H.L.); *ante*, § 28-06.
[16] S.A. 1891, s. 62, proviso.   [17] F.A. 1902, s. 9.
[18] See *post*, § 28-47.   [19] See *ante*, § 27-52.

(1) certain conveyances in connection with the reconstruction and amalgamation of companies [20];

(2) certain conveyances between associated companies [21];

(3) conveyances in consideration of marriage [22];

(4) transfers of shares in building societies, [23] or of local authority stocks [24];

(5) transfers of *loan capital* [25] carrying no conversion rights into shares or other securities, the interest on which does not exceed a reasonable commercial return and does not fall to be determined to any extent by reference to the results of a business or to the value of any property. Also excluded from the exemption is loan capital giving the right to the payment of a premium on redemption which is not reasonably comparable with other such capital listed in the Official List of the Stock Exchange;

(6) any transfer to a stock exchange nominee for the purposes of a stock exchange transaction. [26] There are other special provisions dealing with stock exchange transactions. [27]

Reduced rates

28-46   There are reduced rates of stamp duty on transfers to charities, on transfers of stock or marketable securities to non-residents, on transfers of Commonwealth government stock [28] and on other conveyances (other than conveyances of stock or marketable securities) [29] where the consideration does not exceed £30,000 and a certificate of value is included. [30]

6. EXCHANGE AND PARTITION

28-47   An instrument which effects an exchange of realty for realty (or a partition of realty) attracts a fixed stamp of 50p under the head of charge " Exchange or Excambion " in the Stamp Act 1891; except that if more than £100 is paid for equality, the principal instrument effecting the transaction must be stamped as a conveyance on sale for the sum paid for equality. [31] (The parties can decide for themselves which of the instruments is to be deemed the principal instrument. [32])

> *Examples:* A exchanges his freehold (value £20,000) for B's freehold (value £36,000), A paying £16,000 for equality. The deed of exchange must be

---

[20] *Post*, §§ 33-01 *et seq.*
[21] *Post*, §§ 33-09 *et seq.*
[22] *Ante*, § 28-44.
[23] Building Societies Act 1836, s. 8; Building Societies Act 1874, s. 41.
[24] F.A. 1967, s. 29.
[25] *Ibid.* s. 126. *Loan capital* is defined as any debenture stock, corporation stock or funded debt; or any capital raised by any body corporate or body of persons in the United Kingdom or foreign government which is borrowed or has the character of borrowed money (whether in the form of stock or any other form and whether secured or unsecured). For the meaning of " funded debt " see *Reed International Ltd.* v. *I.R.C.* [1976] A.C. 336; [1975] S.T.C. 427. And see *Agricultural Mortgage Corporation Ltd.* v. *I.R.C.* [1978] S.T.C. 11 (C.A.).
[26] *Ibid.* s. 127 (1).
[27] *Ibid.* s. 127 (2)-(7).
[28] F.A. 1963, s. 62 (2).
[29] F.A. 1958, s. 34 (5) (*b*). Transfer of stock and marketable securities will usually now be exempt within head (5) in § 28-45, *ante*.   [30] *Ante*, § 28-24.
[31] S.A. 1891, s. 73.   [32] *Ibid.* s. 73; s. 61 (2).

stamped on the £16,000 equality money and certified as " not exceeding £20,000." (There will be a duplicate deed bearing the duplicate denoting stamp.)

If £100 or a lesser sum is paid for equality, the instrument bears a 50p stamp under the head of charge " Exchange or Excambion."

An exchange of leasehold for leasehold, or of leasehold for freehold, is outside this head of charge.[33]

Thus in *Littlewoods Mail Order Stores Ltd.* v. *I.R.C.,*[33] a freehold property owned by one company was exchanged for a leasehold property owned by another company. There was no equality money. It was held that the instrument effecting this transaction was not a deed of exchange for the purposes of the Stamp Act; that it was not a conveyance *on sale,* because there was no price in money[34]; but that it was a " conveyance of any kind not hereinbefore described "[35] and attracted a duty of 50p.

28-48   Where equality money is paid in such a case, the instrument is *pro tanto* a conveyance on sale.[36]

If an instrument, though described by the parties as an exchange, effects a transaction of a different nature, it must be stamped accordingly.[37]

Thus if A contracts to sell Blackacre (freehold) to B, and B contracts to sell Whiteacre (freehold) to A, and the two contracts of sale are completed by an instrument which is described as an exchange, the instrument must be stamped as a conveyance on sale.

An opinion of the Controller of Stamps has been given on the following practice, where A has entered into a contract with B to sell A's house for (say) £13,200 and has also entered into a contract with C to buy C's house for (say) £23,200. The transaction is sometimes carried into effect by (1) C conveying his house to A in exchange for A's house and £10,000, and (2) C conveying A's former house to B for £13,200. The Controller's opinion is that in this case the first conveyance would attract duty as a conveyance of C's house for £23,200 and as a conveyance of A's house for £13,200 and that a certificate of value on the footing that £10,000 was paid for equality of exchange would be inappropriate.[38]

28-49   An exchange of stock or securities constitutes a sale for purposes of stamp duty[39] but it may well attract the exemption referred to in § 28-45, (5) *ante.* An exchange which confers substantial benefit on one party may operate as a voluntary disposition.[40]

[33] *Littlewoods Mail Order Stores Ltd.* v. *I.R.C.* [1963] A.C. 135 (H.L.).
[34] *Ante,* § 28-04.
[35] *Ante,* § 28-44.
[36] See *Littlewoods Mail Order Stores Ltd.* v. *I.R.C.* [1963] A.C. 135, *per* Viscount Simonds at p. 151.
[37] *Viscount Portman* v. *I.R.C.* (1956) 35 A.T.C. 349.
[38] (1960) L.S.G., p. 451.
[39] *J. & P. Coats* v. *I.R.C.* [1897] 2 Q.B. 423 (C.A.).
[40] F. (1909-10) A., 1910, s. 74 (5); *post,* § 30-05.

CHAPTER 29

SECTION 59 AND THE SALE OF A BUSINESS

29-01 ON a sale of land, the contract of sale bears no stamp and the subsequent conveyance is stamped *ad valorem*. Payment of the *ad valorem* duty can be avoided if the purchaser dispenses with the conveyance and relies on the equitable title acquired by purchase, but in normal circumstances the purchaser requires the legal estate and a formal conveyance is therefore necessary.[1] But on a sale of goodwill or of an equitable interest in property different considerations arise. In such cases, where the contract is specifically enforceable, the title which the purchaser acquires under the contract is, for all practical purposes, as good as the title which he would acquire under a formal assignment and, indeed, it is the usual practice to

29-02 dispense with a formal assignment. Section 59 of the Stamp Act 1891, however, prevents any loss of stamp duty to the Revenue by providing that any contract or agreement [2] for the sale of

(1) Any equitable estate or interest in any property whatsoever; or

(2) any estate or interest in any property except

   (i) land;

   (ii) property locally situate out of the United Kingdom;

   (iii) goods, wares or merchandise;

   (iv) stock (including shares) or marketable securities [3]; or

   (v) any ship or part of a ship,

shall be charged with the same *ad valorem* duty (to be paid by the purchaser) as if it were an actual conveyance on sale of the property agreed to be sold.[4] A subsequent conveyance or transfer (if any) is not then chargeable with any duty but the Commissioners will, on application, *either* impress a duty paid denoting stamp on the conveyance or transfer *or,* on production of the contract or agreement duly stamped, transfer the *ad valorem* duty to the conveyance.[5]

29-03 A contract or agreement which, though liable to the *ad valorem* duty, bears no stamp (or, if under seal, is stamped 50p) is nevertheless deemed to be duly stamped for all purposes, if a conveyance or transfer is presented for stamping within six months after the first execution of the agreement, or within such longer period as the Commissioners may think reasonable in the circumstances of the case. [6]

---

[1] Law of Property Act 1925, s. 52 (1). In some cases, *e.g.* on the " conversion " of a partnership into a limited company, it may be convenient to dispense with a formal conveyance and leave the legal estate in the former partners. But see *Escoigne Properties Ltd.* v. *I.R.C.* [1958] A.C. 549; *post,* § 33-10.

[2] This does not include an agreement granting an option to purchase: *Wm. Cory & Son Ltd.* v. *I.R.C.* [1965] A.C. 1088 (H.L.), discussed *ante,* § 28-22.

[3] See note 6, *ante,* § 28-02.

[4] For rates of duty, certificates of value, etc., see *ante,* §§ 28-24 *et seq.*

[5] S.A. 1891, s. 59 (3).

[6] *Ibid.* s. 59 (5) as amended by F.A. 1970, Sched. 7, para. 1 (3) (*b*), but there may be a penalty for late stamping: *ante,* § 27-27.

If a contract is stamped *ad valorem* under section 59 and the contract is afterwards rescinded or annulled, or for any other reason is not substantially performed or carried into effect, the Commissioners must return the duty.[7]

EXCEPTIONS TO SECTION 59 OF THE STAMP ACT 1891

29-04 There are three exceptions in section 59 which require special mention.

(1) *Land*

29-05 A contract for the sale of an *equitable* interest in land is within section 59, even if the land is situate outside the United Kingdom.[8] A contract for the sale of a *legal* estate or interest in land is excepted from the section, notwithstanding the equitable title which the purchaser acquires on exchange of contracts.

(2) *Property locally situated outside the United Kingdom*

29-06 It was at one time supposed that intangible property, such as debts, patents and other things in action, could have no " local situation." [9] The earlier cases which supported this view were overruled by the House of Lords in *English, Scottish and Australian Bank Ltd.* v. *I.R.C.,* [10] where it was held that a contract for the sale of debts owed by debtors resident outside the United Kingdom was a contract for the sale of property " locally situate out of the United Kingdom " and was therefore within the exception. It can now be taken as settled that a locality, albeit fictitious, must be imported to all things in action. An agreement for the sale of the goodwill of a business carried on abroad, with customers abroad, has been held to fall within the exception.[11]

(3) *Goods, wares or merchandise*

29-07 An agreement for the sale of the stock-in-trade of a business is subject to no stamp duty. Moreover, stock-in-trade can be included in the sale agreement yet disregarded for the purposes of a certificate of value, if it is excluded from the subsequent transfer.[12]

The interest of an owner under a hire-purchase agreement is not within the exception [13]; though the interest of a pawnbroker in the goods pawned is within it.[14] In practice, the Revenue treat cash in hand and cash in current account (but not cash on deposit) as goods.

---

[7] S.A. 1891, s. 59 (6). Contrast the relief under the Stamp Duties Management Act 1891, *ante*, § 27-51.

[8] *Farmer & Co.* v. *I.R.C.* [1898] 2 Q.B. 141. If the contract was executed outside the United Kingdom, the liability to stamp it in the United Kingdom would not arise until such time (if ever) that it was brought to the United Kingdom: *ante*, § 27-29.

[9] See Sergeant, p. 119.

[10] [1932] A.C. 238.

[11] *I.R.C.* v. *Muller & Co.'s Margarine* [1901] A.C. 217.

[12] *Ante*, § 28-26.

[13] *Drages* v. *I.R.C.* (1927) 46 T.C. 389.

[14] *Riley (Arthur) Ltd.* v. *I.R.C.* (1931) 46 T.C. 402.

PROPERTY WITHIN SECTION 59 OF THE STAMP ACT 1891

29-08 A contract for the sale of any of the following items is clearly caught by section 59 (except where the property is locally situate out of the United Kingdom) and is liable to *ad valorem* conveyance or transfer duty:

(1) *Goodwill.*[15] If A contracts to sell the goodwill of his business and the business premises, the contract is liable to no duty in respect of the premises and to *ad valorem* duty in respect of the goodwill, which must be separately valued for this purpose.[16] In practice, and to save the expense of valuing goodwill, the Commissioners are prepared to stamp the contract *ad valorem* in respect of both the goodwill and the premises. The conveyance is then charged with a fixed duty of 50p and should be adjudicated (or denoted).

The liability for duty in respect of goodwill cannot be avoided by the purchaser taking from the vendor a covenant not to compete; for such a covenant has been held to constitute an agreement for the sale of goodwill, though not so worded.[17]

(2) *Bookdebts.*

(3) *Cash on deposit.* This is a debt due from a bank to its customer.[18] Cash in hand, cash in current account, bills and notes, are in practice treated as falling outside section 59.

(4) *Patents, licences, trade marks, copyrights and " know-how."*

(5) *Benefit of pending contracts.*

(6) *Tenants and trade fixtures on leasehold property.*[19]

(7) *The interest of an owner under a hire-purchase agreement.*[13]

(8) *Equitable interests in freehold and leasehold property.*

STAMP DUTY ON THE PURCHASE OF A BUSINESS

29-09 Where a contract of sale includes items within section 59 and items not caught by the section, the consideration must be apportioned; and the apportionment must be a bona fide apportionment based on the commercial value of the respective properties. If the apportionment is not bona fide, *e.g.* if too large a part of the total consideration is attributed to stock-in-trade or other items transferable by delivery, the Commissioners can assess the transfer of the undervalued items as on a voluntary disposition thereof.[20] An apportionment should be made on Form 22, supplied by the Stamp Office.

Methods of saving duty

29-10 By careful planning, a considerable amount of stamp duty can be saved on the take-over of a business as a going concern. For example:

---

[15] *Benjamin Brooke & Co.* v. *I.R.C.* [1896] 2 Q.B. 356.
[16] *West London Syndicate Ltd.* v. *I.R.C.* [1898] 2 Q.B. 507 (C.A.).
[17] *Eastern National Omnibus Co. Ltd.* v. *I.R.C.* [1939] 1 K.B. 161; *ante*, § 27-06. A bare agreement not to compete in consideration of a money payment is void: *Vancouver Malt, etc.* v. *Vancouver Breweries* [1934] A.C. 181.
[18] *Foley* v. *Hill* (1848) 2 H.L. 28.
[19] Fixtures on freehold property are, of course, part of the freehold and thus within the exceptions to s. 59.   [20] F. (1909-10) A. 1910, s. 74 (5); *post*, § 30-05.

The state of A's business is as follows.

Liabilities	£	*Assets*	£
Secured creditors	9,000	Freehold	20,000
Trade creditors	9,000	Goodwill	4,000
		Stock	9,000
		Bookdebts	8,000
Excess of assets over		Bank: Current A/C	1,000
liabilities	27,000	Bank: Deposit A/C	3,000
	£45,000		£45,000

B will purchase the business for £27,000 and will take over the liability to secured and trade creditors.

The total consideration for stamp duty purposes is:

	£
Purchase price	27,000
Liabilities taken over [21]	18,000
	£45,000

This £45,000 must be apportioned between the assets (as in the account, above).

The sale agreement. Ad valorem duty is payable on the sale agreement (under section 59) on the following items:

	£	
Goodwill	4,000	
Bookdebts	8,000	
Cash on deposit	3,000	
	£15,000	*Ad val.* duty: £300 [22]

The other items attract no duty.

The transfer. The conveyance of the freehold for £20,000 would attract conveyance or transfer duty at £2 per cent. The stock-in-trade and cash in hand would in practice be transferred by delivery, without any instrument of transfer. The duty would thus be on the

	£	
Freehold	20,000	*Ad val.* duty: £400 [22]
Total ad valorem duty:	700	

29-11　　　In order to save duty, the following arrangements should be made:

(1) Cash on deposit (£3,000) should be transferred to current account before the date of agreement. This takes it out of section 59.

(2) There should be no agreement to transfer bookdebts (£8,000). These should be retained by the vendor [23] and, when collected, used to discharge so far as possible the liabilities (which also should so far as possible be retained by the vendor). [23] On the figures given, the vendor should retain the bookdebts (£8,000) plus £1,000 from cash in hand, to discharge the liability to the trade creditors. This achieves a double saving of duty, both in respect of the bookdebts (s. 59) and the liabilities (s. 57).

---

[21] See S.A. 1891, s. 57, *ante*, § 28-39.

[22] No certificate of value can be included in either the sale agreement or the transfer for there is one larger transaction for more than £30,000: *Law Society's Digest*, Opinion 215.

[23] Or, more usually, by the purchaser as agent for the vendor. There may be fiscal disadvantages in excluding bookdebts which should be carefully weighed against the prospective saving of stamp duty. Thus relief from capital gains tax on the transfer of a business to a company is available only where *all* the assets (or all the assets other than cash) are transferred, see *ante*, § 16-13.

If this is done, the property agreed to be taken over will be:

Liabilities	£	Assets	£
Secured creditors	9,000	Freehold	20,000
		Goodwill	4,000
Excess of assets over		Stock	9,000
liabilities	27,000	Bank: Current A/C	3,000
	£36,000		£36,000

29-12   The total consideration for stamp duty purposes is then:

	£
Purchase price	27,000
Liabilities taken over	
(s. 57)	9,000
	£36,000

less		
* Stock	9,000	
* Cash in hand	3,000	
	12,000	
	£24,000	*Ad val.* duty: £240

(*Transferred by delivery, so as to avoid stamp duty.)

Amount of duty saved: £460

The *ad valorem* duty of £240 will be made up as follows:

		£	Stamp
Sale Agreement	Goodwill (s. 59)	4,000	40
Transfer	Freehold	20,000	200
			£240

A certificate of value not exceeding £25,000 should be included in both documents since there is one transaction not exceeding that amount.[24] Consequently it has been possible not only to reduce the consideration on which duty is chargeable but also the rate of duty applicable.

The vendor cannot insist on the purchaser taking a conveyance of the freehold and an assignment of goodwill in one instrument: nor can the vendor object if the purchaser does not require a written assignment of goodwill.[25]

---

[24] *Law Society's Digest*, Opinion 215.
[25] *Op. cit.*, Opinion 159.

CHAPTER 30

VOLUNTARY DISPOSITIONS AND SETTLEMENTS

1. DUTY ON " VOLUNTARY DISPOSITIONS "

30-01 No *ad valorem* duty was imposed on voluntary dispositions by the Stamp Act 1891.[1] A voluntary conveyance or transfer was subject only to a fixed duty of 10s. under the head " Conveyance or transfer of any kind not hereinbefore described." [2] Then, by the Finance (1909-10) Act 1910, s. 74 (1), it was provided that

> " Any conveyance or transfer operating as a voluntary disposition *inter vivos* shall be chargeable with the like stamp duty as if it were a conveyance or transfer on sale, with the substitution in each case of the value of the property conveyed or transferred for the amount or value of the consideration for the sale."

It has been suggested that this duty was levied to compensate the Crown for the loss of estate duty occasioned by the increase in the number of voluntary dispositions after the Finance Act 1894.[3]

Rates of duty and certificates of value

30-02 It will be noted that there is no separate duty entitled " voluntary disposition duty " or the like: section 74 makes the voluntary dispositions to which it applies (including most voluntary settlements [4]) liable to conveyance or transfer duty. The rates of duty are thus the same as on a conveyance on sale and there are the same reduced rates where a certificate of value is included.[5] If the value of the gifted property is not known when the instrument is prepared, the Commissioners will accept a " truncated certificate " merely stating that " the transaction hereby effected does not form part of a larger transaction or of a series of transactions." [6] The appropriate scale of duty is then applied on adjudication when the value of the property has been ascertained. The principles which determine whether a certificate of value can be included in the instrument are similar to those already discussed in connection with conveyances on sale [7]; that is, that where there are contemporaneous transfers of property by one transferor to one transferee, these must be taken to form part of a larger transaction or series if there is any degree of interdependence or linkage between them. If a person makes gifts to different donees simultaneously, as when a father gives properties worth £12,000 each to each of his three children, each gift forms a separate transaction and a " not exceeding £15,000 " certificate may be included.

---

[1] Except of certain Canadian and Colonial Stock.   [2] *Ante*, § 28-43.
[3] MacNaghten J. in *Anderson* v. *I.R.C.* [1939] 1 K.B. 341 at p. 345.
[4] *Baker* v. *I.R.C.* [1923] 1 K.B. 323; affirmed [1924] A.C. 270.
[5] *Ante*, §§ 28-24 *et seq.*
[6] [1954] C.L.Y. para. 3190. Where a full certificate is used, it should refer to the " property conveyed or transferred " and not to the " consideration "; *cf. ante*, § 28-24.
[7] *Ante*, § 28-25.

The provisions of section 34 (4) of the Finance Act 1958, by which a contract for the sale of goods, wares or merchandise may be disregarded in certain circumstances,[8] do not apply to voluntary dispositions.

Instruments liable to the duty

30-03   To be liable to duty under section 74 (1) of the Finance (1909-10) Act 1910, an instrument must be a " conveyance or transfer " and must operate as a voluntary disposition. Each of these requirements must be considered separately:

30-04   (1) *" Conveyance or transfer. "* The definitions of these terms in sections 54 and 62 of the Stamp Act 1891 (with which section 74 of the 1910 Act must be construed as one),[9] have already been discussed, and it will be recalled that a very wide range of instruments, not merely formal conveyances, fall within the definitions.[10] The following instruments have been held to be dutiable as voluntary conveyances:

   (a) A release by a life tenant of his life interest, having the effect of accelerating or bringing into operation interests which would not otherwise have existed.[11]
   (b) An appointment in exercise of a general power.[12] (An appointment under a special power may likewise operate as a conveyance within section 74, but will usually not operate as a voluntary disposition.[13])
   (c) A voluntary declaration of trust.[14]
   (d) A distribution *in specie* by a company not in liquidation to its shareholders.[15] (A distribution by a company in liquidation is exempt from duty under section 74 (6) as a conveyance in which no beneficial interest passes.[16])

30-05   (2) *Operating as a voluntary disposition.* A conveyance for *some* consideration may nevertheless operate as a voluntary disposition. This is because, by section 74 (5) of the Finance (1909-10) Act 1910, every conveyance or transfer (not being a disposition made in favour of a purchaser or incumbrancer or other person in good faith and for valuable consideration) will be deemed to operate as a voluntary disposition *inter vivos,* and (except where marriage is the consideration) the consideration for any conveyance or transfer will not for this purpose be deemed to be valuable consideration where the Commissioners are of opinion that by reason of the inadequacy of the sum paid as consideration or other circumstances, the conveyance or transfer confers a substantial benefit on the person to whom the property is conveyed or transferred.

---

[8] *Ante,* § 28-26.   [9] F. (1909-10) A. 1910, s. 96 (5).
[10] *Ante,* § 28-03.
[11] *Platt's Trustees* v. *I.R.C.* (1953) 46 T.C. 418 and *Thorn* v. *I.R.C.* [1976] S.T.C. 208. It would seem that the release of any equitable beneficial interest, whether in favour of another beneficiary or the owner of the legal estate, constitutes a voluntary conveyance.
[12] *Stanyforth* v. *I.R.C.* [1930] A.C. 339; *Fuller and Shrimpton* v. *I.R.C.* [1950] 2 All E.R. 976.
[13] This is by virtue of exemption 2 (d), *post,* § 30-13.
[14] *Martin* v. *I.C.R.* (1930) 46 T.C. 397.
[15] *Associated British Engineering Co. Ltd.* v. *I.R.C.* [1951] 1 K.B. 15; *Wigan Coal and Iron Co. Ltd.* v. *I.R.C.* [1945] 1 All E.R. 392.   [16] Exemption (2) (c), *post,* § 30-13.

Thus if A conveys Blackacre (worth £20,000) to B for £12,000, the instrument will be treated as a voluntary disposition of property worth £20,000.

The Commissioners do not have to establish that the transaction was *intended* to confer a substantial benefit on the purchaser but simply that it does confer such a benefit. Thus the section will apply where the vendor has simply made a " bad bargain."[17] It is not clear what are the " other circumstances " which may lead the Commissioners to invoke the aid of the section.[18]

How duty is assessed

30-06 Section 74 (1) of the 1910 Act provides that the duty on voluntary dispositions shall be charged on " the value of the property transferred." It is thus necessary to assume a hypothetical sale of the gifted property in the open market, account being taken in valuing the property of any interest reserved to the donor or settlor after the disposition and of any interest which the donor had in the property before the disposition. The leading authority on this matter is *Stanyforth* v. *I.R.C.,*[19] where the facts were as follows:

A deed was executed effecting a partial resettlement of family estates. The deed was executed under a joint power of revocation and new appointment contained in previous dispositions of the estates, and the deed itself contained a power of revocation and new appointment.

The House of Lords held that the overriding power of revocation should be taken into account in assessing the value of the property settled.

Method of saving duty

30-07 In reliance on the *Stanyforth* decision it was assumed that a considerable saving of stamp duty could be effected in all voluntary dispositions by including therein an overriding power of revocation, and the following device for settling property came to be widely used:

(1) A deed was executed by which the property was settled in the ordinary way, except that the settlor reserved to himself a power to revoke the trusts thereby declared, and re-appoint the property to himself or some other person.

(2) The deed was presented for adjudication and stamped 10s.[20]

(3) After adjudication a deed of release was executed by which the settlor released the power of revocation. This was stamped 10s.

30-08 The Finance Act 1965 introduced a provision coming into force on August 1, 1965, which was designed to restrain the use of the device. For the purposes of section 74 of the Finance (1909-10) Act 1910 the value of property conveyed or transferred by an instrument chargeable as a voluntary

---

[17] See *Lap Shun Textiles Industrial Co. Ltd.* v. *Collector of Stamp Revenue* [1976] S.T.C. 83, a case on the identical provision in the Hong Kong Stamp Ordinance.

[18] See *Baker* v. *I.R.C.* [1924] A.C. 270, where s. 74 (5) was discussed and *Lap Shun Textiles Industrial Co. Ltd.* v. *Collector of Stamp Revenue* [1976] S.T.C. 83.

[19] [1930] A.C. 339 (H.L.).

[20] *Stanyforth* v. *I.R.C.* [1930] A.C. 339 (H.L.).

disposition must be determined without regard to any power (whether or not contained in the instrument) on the exercise of which the property, or any part of or any interest in, the property, may be revested in the person from whom it was conveyed or transferred or in any person on his behalf.[21] In order to protect bona fide revocable settlements, the Act provides that if on a claim made to the Commissioners not later than two years after the making or execution of the instrument it is shown to their satisfaction that the power referred to has been exercised in relation to the property, and the property or any property representing it has been re-conveyed or re-transferred in whole or in part in consequence of that exercise the Commissioners will repay the duty so far as it exceeds the duty which would have been payable (apart from the Act) if the instrument had operated to convey or transfer only such property (if any) as is not so re-conveyed or re-transferred.[22] No interest is payable on duty thus repaid.

30-09 *Gift of property subject to a mortgage.*[23] On a voluntary disposition of property subject to a mortgage, duty is assessed as follows:

(1) If there is no covenant by the grantee to pay the mortgage debt, duty is payable on the value of the property transferred *less* the amount of the mortgage debt, *i.e.* on the value of the equity of redemption.

(2) If there is such a covenant, the instrument is treated *either as a voluntary disposition of the equity of redemption or* as a conveyance on sale in consideration of the mortgage debt, whichever yields the higher duty.

30-10 *Gift of mortgage.* In *Anderson* v. *I.R.C.,*[24] A transferred a mortgage to a hospital by way of gift. It was held that duty could be levied under one of two alternative heads of charge, either (a) as a transfer of mortgage,[25] or (b) as a voluntary disposition, and that the Crown could levy duty under (b), since this yielded the higher duty. If A had, instead, given cash to the hospital to enable it to purchase the mortgage from him, the instrument transferring the mortgage would now be completely exempt from duty.[25]

30-11 *Gifts of life policies.* If a life policy is assigned by way of gift, duty is in practice accepted on the surrender value, although the market value may be more.[26]

Adjudication

30-12 A voluntary conveyance is among the list of instruments of which adjudication is obligatory and the instrument is not duly stamped without

---

[21] F.A. 1965, s. 90 (5) (6) (7). The Act also requires the Commissioners to disregard in assessing duty any annuity reserved out of the property or any part of it, or any life or other interest so reserved, being an interest which is subject to forfeiture: *ibid.* s. 90 (5).

[22] *Ibid.* s. 90 (5).

[23] See S.A. 1891, s. 57; discussed *ante*, § 28-39.

[24] [1939] 1 K.B. 341.

[25] Mortgage duty was abolished as from August 1, 1971, by F.A. 1971, s. 64 (1) (c); *ante*, §§ 27-07 and 27-53.

[26] Alpe, *op. cit.*, p. 208.

adjudication.[27] Registrars of companies are, however, permitted to register transfers of quoted shares and debentures without the adjudication stamp, if they are stamped in accordance with the quoted value at the date of the instrument.[28]

Exemptions

30-13 The General Exemptions from all stamp duties have already been noted.[29] The exemption and reduced rates applicable to conveyances on sale [30] apply also to voluntary dispositions.

Other exemptions are as follows:

(1) A conveyance or transfer in consideration of marriage.[31]

(2) A conveyance or transfer [32]

   (a) made for nominal consideration to secure the repayment of an advance or loan; or

   (b) to effectuate the appointment of a new trustee on the retirement of a trustee, whether the trust is express or implied; or

   (c) under which no beneficial interest passes in the property conveyed or transferred [33] ; or

   (d) made to a beneficiary by a trustee or other person in a fiduciary capacity under any trust, whether expressed or implied.

(3) A disentailing assurance not limiting any new estate other than an estate in fee simple in the person disentailing the property.[34]

(4) A conveyance or transfer operating as a voluntary disposition of property to a body of persons incorporated by a special Act, if that body is by its Act precluded from dividing any profit among its members and the property conveyed is to be held for the purposes of an open space or for the purposes of its preservation for the benefit of the nation.[35]

(5) A disclaimer of a gift or legacy before acceptance.[36] " Disclaimer is simply the rejection of a proffered gift and operates by way of avoidance. The person disclaiming has no say in what happens to the gift. It is not a transfer of property at all and attracts no *ad valorem* duty." [37]

In *Re Robb's Contract*,[38] it was held that the instruments exempt from *ad valorem* duty under (2) and (3), above, were nevertheless liable to adjudication by virtue of section 74 (2); but this decision was nullified by section 44 of the Finance Act 1942, which amended the 1910 Act accordingly.[39]

---

[27] F. (1909-10) A. 1910, s. 74 (2); *ante*, §§ 27-41 *et seq.*

[28] Alpe, *op cit.*, p. 210. S.A. 1891, s. 17, imposes a fine for registering an instrument not duly stamped, but the Commissioners have wide powers to remit or mitigate fines. See *Conybear* v. *British Briquettes* [1937] 4 All E.R. 191.   [29] *Ante*, § 27-52.

[30] *Ante*, § 28-24.

[31] F. (1909-10) A. 1910, s. 74 (5); F.A. 1963, s. 64; *ante*, § 28-44; but the restrictions in F.A. 1968, s. 36 do not apply to stamp duty.   [32] *Ibid.* s. 74 (6).

[33] *Ante*, § 28-44.   [34] F. (1909-10) A. 1910, s. 74 (6).

[35] *Ibid.* s. 74 (1), proviso. Gifts to the National Trust fall within this exemption.

[36] Sergeant, p. 160.

[37] Monroe, *Stamp Duties*, 5th ed., para. 79. But it will attract a 50p deed stamp if under seal. But *cf.* the estate duty case of *Re Stratton's Disclaimer* [1958] Ch. 42 (C.A.).

[38] [1941] 1 Ch. 463 (C.A.).   [39] F. (1909-10) A. 1910, s. 74 (6), as amended.

2. SETTLEMENT DUTY AND UNIT TRUSTS

30-14   The charge to stamp duty under the heading " Settlement " in the Stamp Act 1891 was abolished as from August 1, 1962, by section 30 of the Finance Act 1962. Prior to its abolition it had applied to:

(a) marriage settlements;
(b) voluntary settlements where property was transferred without an instrument chargeable as a voluntary disposition (*e.g.* settlements of cash, bearer securities or renounced shares); or
(c) instruments which otherwise escaped duty (*e.g.* a transfer of government stock or funds).[40]

Such settlements now escape stamp duty entirely.

30-15   Section 30 of the Finance Act 1962 added a new head of charge to the Schedule to the Stamp Act 1891 as follows:

> Unit Trust Instrument. Any trust instrument of a unit trust scheme (within the meaning of the Finance Act 1946, ss. 53-57):
>
> For every £100 (or fractional part of £100) of the amount or value of the property subject to the trusts created or recorded by the instrument ... 25p

A unit trust scheme is widely defined in the Finance Act 1946 to mean any arrangements made for the purpose, or having the effect, of providing, for persons having funds available for investment, facilities for the participation by them, as beneficiaries under a trust, in any profits or income arising from the acquisition, holding, management or disposal of any property whatsoever.[41]

It will be recalled that the units (including sub-units) [41] are " stock " for the purposes of stamp duty.[42]

3. VOLUNTARY SETTLEMENTS AND METHODS OF SAVING STAMP DUTY

30-16   It was observed in the earlier part of this chapter that most voluntary settlements are chargeable with conveyance or transfer duty as voluntary dispositions, and that settlement duty (which was abolished in the case of instruments made or executed after August 1, 1962) was chargeable only on those settlements of definite sums of money, stock or securities which, for some reason, escaped the former duty. This is a convenient place to consider the incidence of stamp duty on the types of settlement most frequently encountered in practice, and to summarise the methods commonly used to save stamp duty.

(1) *Settlements of land*

30-17   Every settlement of a legal estate in land made *inter vivos* after 1925 must be effected by two deeds, a principal vesting deed and a trust instrument [43]

---

[40] See, *e.g. Ansell* v. *I.R.C.* [1929] 1 K.B. 608.
[41] *Ibid.* s. 51 (1). This definition was extended by the F.A. 1963, s. 65.
[42] *Ante*, § 28-02, note 6. The characteristics of " stock " are usefully listed in Monroe's *Stamp Duties*, 5th ed., para. 272.
[43] Settled Land Act 1925, ss. 4 and 5.

and the trust instrument is required to bear any *ad valorem* duty which may be payable in respect of the settlement. [44]

> Thus the trust instrument bears *ad valorem* conveyance or transfer duty at the rate applicable to the value of the property settled; and the vesting deed is stamped 50p.

Where the settlement is created by the will of a testator who dies after 1925, the will is treated as the trust instrument (and attracts no stamp duty). The personal representatives vest the legal estate in the tenant for life or statutory owners by a vesting instrument, which may be either a vesting assent (which usually attracts no stamp duty) [45] or a vesting deed (which bears a 50p stamp).

(2) *Settlements of land on trust for sale*

30-18   It is the usual practice, where such settlements are created *inter vivos* to use two instruments, as in the case of settlements of land. The stamp requirements are then the same.

(3) *Settlements of stocks, shares and securities*

30-19   Voluntary settlements of stocks, shares and securities are usually effected by two instruments corresponding to the vesting deed (by which the stocks, etc., are transferred to the trustees) and the trust instrument (which declares the beneficial interests). The instrument which transfers the beneficial interest is chargeable with conveyance or transfer duty as a voluntary disposition.

The usual sequence of events is as follows:

(1) Transfer the stocks, etc., to the trustees. The transfer is stamped 50p under head (2) of conveyance or transfer duty as an instrument under which no beneficial interest passes. [46]

(2) Execute the trust instrument. Upon execution, the beneficial title passes from the settlor to the beneficiaries. Stamp with *ad valorem* conveyance or transfer duty as a voluntary disposition, on the value of the property transferred.

If this sequence is reversed, [47] the transfer ought strictly to bear the *ad valorem* stamp.

30-20   *Methods of saving duty.* In each of the three cases referred to in paras. (1)-(3), above, where the settlement is chargeable with conveyance or transfer duty as a voluntary disposition, duty could formerly be saved by the use of the scheme based on *Stanyforth* v. *I.R.C.,* [48] which is outlined above but this device was restrained by the Act of 1965. [49] Duty can be avoided in the case of shares by making the settlement orally. [50]

---

[44] Settled Land Act 1925, s. 4 (3) (*e*).
[45] *Ante*, § 28-13.
[46] *Ante*, § 28-44. And see *Grey* v. *I.R.C.* [1960] A.C. 1.
[47] See *Ansell* v. *I.R.C.* [1929] 1 K.B. 608.
[48] [1930] A.C. 339 (H.L.).
[49] *Ante*, § 30-08.
[50] But see *Oughtred* v. *I.R.C.* [1960] A.C. 206, *ante*, § 28-06; and *Grey* v. *I.R.C.* [1960] A.C. 1, *ante*, § 28-08.

(4) *Settlements of property of which the title passes by delivery*

30-21   Where the property to be settled is cash, bearer securities, renounced shares or chattels, the legal and equitable title therein can be transferred without the use of any written instrument of transfer and without, therefore, any instrument which is dutiable as a voluntary disposition. The property in question should be transferred to the trustees *after* the settlement is executed. Such instruments were subject to settlement duty prior to August 1, 1962. Settlement duty could be saved if the settlor first settled only (say) £100 (duty 25p) and later added to the settled fund by drawing cheques in favour of the trustees. Although settlement duty has been abolished, the practice of settling a nominal sum and thereafter making additions to the settled fund is widespread.

CHAPTER 31

LEASE DUTY

31-01 LEASES of land are chargeable under the head " Lease or Tack " in the Stamp Act 1891.[1] The Act contains no definition of " lease " which must be taken to have the meaning ascribed to it under the general law. The instrument must therefore (a) confer a right to exclusive possession (b) for a period that is definite or capable of definition. These requirements of the general law are fully discussed in the standard works on the law of property[2]; but with regard to stamp duty, the following points should be noticed:

(1) An instrument which takes effect as a *licence,* even though described as a lease, is not subject to lease duty. A mere licence in consideration of periodical payments now attracts no duty whatsoever.[3] Whether an instrument takes effect as a licence or lease depends on the substance of the transaction and not merely on the form of the instrument.[4]

(2) Lease duty applies only to leases of " lands, tenements or heritable subjects." A hiring of chattels in consideration of periodical payments, even if described as a lease, is outside the charge; nor would it have attracted bond covenant duty.[5] A lease of incorporeal hereditaments, including sporting rights, is within the charge.

The head of charge

31-02   The general scheme of the Stamp Act 1891 is to charge fixed duties on certain short-term leases at low rents, and *ad valorem* duties on leases for more than a year and on periodic tenancies. Considerable changes were made by the Finance Act 1963. The sub-heads of charge are as follows:

(1) Lease for any definite term less than a year:

(a) of a furnished dwelling-house or apartment where the rent for such terms exceeds £250 [6] .... £1 [7]

(b) of any lands, except or otherwise than as aforesaid........................... Same as on a lease for a year at the rent reserved for the definite term.

(2) Lease for any other definite term, or for any indefinite term:

(a) where there is a " premium " moving either to the lessor or to any other person: *ad valorem* duty is charged on the premium. (See " Duty on the premium ": below.)

---

[1] Sched. 1. " Tack " is the Scottish equivalent of " Lease."

[2] Cheshire's *Modern Law of Real Property,* 11th ed., pp. 366-371.

[3] Prior to August 1, 1971, such an instrument would have attracted bond covenant duty. That duty was abolished by F.A. 1971, s. 64 (1) (*a*).

[4] See *Addiscombe Garden Estates Ltd.* v. *Crabbe* [1958] 1 Q.B. 513 (C.A.).

[5] F.A. 1958, s. 35 (1). See note 3, *supra.*

[6] *Ibid.* s. 56 (1).

[7] *Ibid.* s. 56 (2) as amended by F.A. 1974, Sched. 11, para. 10, and F.A. 1972, s. 125 (3). Note that stamp duty on a furnished letting might be saved by making the term one year less one day.

    (b) where the consideration, or any part thereof, is any rent: *ad valorem* duty is charged on the rent.
      (See " Duty on the rent ": below.)

  (3) Leases of any other kind not hereinbefore described [8]:

      If no " premium "; term not over 35 years or indefinite; and rent not exceeding the rate (or average rate) of £100 per annum
                Fixed duty of £2. [9]

31-03 *Meaning of " premium."* In each of the above sub-heads of charge, the word " premium " is used; but this word does not appear in the Act and is merely a convenient abbreviation for the phrase " consideration, moving either to the lessor or to any other person, [10] consisting of money, stock [11] or security other than rent " which is used in the Act. The usual such consideration is the lump sum premium but the phrase used in the Act includes, for example, a fixed sum payable by the tenant in lieu of decorating whether such sum be payable at the beginning or at the end of the term. Again, where the tenant undertakes to bear the lessor's solicitors' costs, such costs are " consideration " within the Act, but it is the practice of the Commissioners to ignore them. [12]

31-04 *Duty on the premium.* Where a premium is payable, the *ad valorem* duty thereon under sub-head (2) is as on a conveyance on sale for the same amount. [13] Reduced rates apply where a certificate of value is included in the lease, provided the rent (or the average rent) does not exceed £150 per annum. [14] The usual form of the certificate is as follows:

    " It is hereby certified that the transaction hereby effected does not form part of a larger transaction or of a series of transactions in respect of which the amount or value, or the aggregate amount or value, of the consideration other than rent exceeds [£15,000, £20,000, £25,000 or £30,000, as the case may be]."

Ad valorem duty is payable on the premium whether it is payable to the lessor or to any other person. [15]

    Thus if T takes a lease of land from L in consideration of a premium payable to B, a builder, duty is payable on the premium even though B is not a party to the lease. [16] The amount of the premium should be stated in the lease. [17]

Leases of building plots and houses in the course of erection, and the question whether a certificate of value can be included, have already been discussed. [18]

---

  [8] A mining lease for royalties would attract duty under head (4). A lease at a fixed rent plus a royalty is charged both on the fixed rent and on the royalty.

  [9] F.A. 1963, s. 56 (2) as amended by F.A. 1974, Sched. 11, para. 10. Such leases may be dutiable, in appropriate cases, as voluntary dispositions: *ante,* § 30-05.

  [10] These words would cover, for instance, consideration paid to a builder who was not the lessor.

  [11] Defined in S.A. 1891, s. 122 (1); and see note 6, *ante,* § 28-02.

  [12] (1959) L.S.G., p. 95.

  [13] See *ante,* § 28-01.

  [14] F.A. 1972, s. 125 (2).

  [15] See sub-head (2) (a), *ante,* § 31-02.

  [16] *Cf. Att.-Gen.* v. *Brown* (1849) 3 Ex. 662. In the common case, T is the builder's nominee under a building agreement and L is the ground landlord granting the lease by direction of the builder.

  [17] See S.A. 1891, s. 5; *ante,* § 27-32.

  [18] *Ante,* § 28-28.

31-05   *Duty on the rent.*[19] The *ad valorem* duty on the rent, under sub-head (2), is as follows:

    (a) Term not exceeding seven years or indefinite:

          Rent not exceeding £250 per annum . . . .   nil

          Rent exceeding £250 per annum . . . .   50p per £50 or part thereof.

    (b) Term exceeding seven years but not 35 years   £1 per £50 or part thereof.

    (c) Term exceeding 35 years but not 100 years . . . .   £6 per £50 or part thereof.

    (d) Term exceeding 100 years . . . .   £12 per £50 or part thereof.

There is a sliding scale for (b), (c) and (d) where the rent does not exceed £250 per annum.[19]

31-06   In 1891, a lease for life or for a term determinable on marriage would have fallen under (a), but such leases now take effect as leases for 90 years determinable after the death (or marriage) of the lessee [20] and fall, therefore, under (c). It seems that the only leases for an " indefinite term " are periodic tenancies. A lease for a fixed term and thereafter on a periodic basis until determined is to be treated as a lease for a definite term plus a further period until the earliest date when the lease can be determined.[21] The following are leases for a definite term:

    (i) A lease for a fixed term, with an option to renew for a further term. This should be stamped as a lease for the original term only,[22] no additional duty being attracted by virtue of the option.[23] If, however, the option is exercised, the instrument exercising the option should be stamped as an agreement for a lease.[24]

    (ii) A lease for a fixed term liable to earlier determination on notice.[25]

31-07   Where the rent is progressive, it must be averaged over the term for the purpose of assessing the duty.

    Example: Land is leased for seven years at a rent of £150 per annum for two years; £300 per annum for the next two years; and £400 per annum for the remaining three years. The average rental is £300.

A lease for inadequate or for no consideration may attract duty as a voluntary disposition under the Finance (1909-10) Act 1910, s. 74 (5).[26]

An instrument increasing the rent reserved under another instrument duly stamped as a lease is itself dutiable as a lease or tack in consideration of the additional rent payable [27] but no additional duty would appear to be payable on the sum paid by the landlord to secure such additional rent.

---

[19] For details, see F.A. 1963, Sched. 11, Part II, and F.A. 1974, Sched. 11, para. 10 (3). For the charge on conditional or contingent rent, see *Coventry City Council* v. *I.R.C.* [1958] S.T.C. 151: see § 27-18.

[20] Law of Property Act 1925, s. 149 (6). See also *Earl of Mount Edgcumbe* v. *I.R.C.* [1911] 2 K.B. 24.

[21] F.A. 1963, s. 56 (3).

[22] *Hand* v. *Hall* (1877) 2 Ex.D. 355 (lease for less than three years with option to tenant to remain for a further three-and-a-half years. *Held*, to create a term for less than three years).

[23] See *ante*, § 27-12.

[24] *Post*, § 31-08.

[25] *Earl of Mount Edgcumbe* v. *I.R.C.* [1911] 2 K.B. 24.   [26] *Ante*, § 30-05.

[27] S.A. 1891, s. 77 (5). See *Gable Construction Co. Ltd.* v. *I.R.C.* [1968] 1 W.L.R. 1426.

Agreement for a lease

31-08   An agreement for a lease, provided the agreement is specifically enforceable and is registered as an estate contract, is almost as good as a lease, at all events so far as the original lessee is concerned.[28] The Stamp Act, however, contains provisions which prevent loss of stamp duty by the use of agreements for leases. Section 75 (1) provides that an agreement for a lease for any term not exceeding 35 years or for any indefinite term [29] shall be charged as if it were an actual lease for the term and consideration mentioned in the agreement. Any lease subsequently made in conformity with such an agreement bears only a 5p stamp (or 50p if under seal), provided the agreement is duly stamped,[30] and a duty paid denoting stamp.[31] This section does not apply to agreements for leases for a definite term exceeding 35 years, which therefore attract only a 50p deed stamp, if under seal.

The Stamp Act contains no provisions for the recovery of the duty if the agreement is afterwards rescinded or annulled.[32] Relief may, however, be available in some cases under the Stamp Duties Management Act 1891.[33]

Other matters

31-09   (1) *Service charges, etc.* Charges made by a lessor for heating, lighting, cleaning or other services (*e.g.* porterage, lifts, etc.) attract stamp duty as follows:

    (a) If reserved as rent, they attract lease duty;

    (b) if they are fixed contributions payable under covenant only they attract no duty.[34]

If the charges cannot be ascertained in advance, no *ad valorem* duty is payable.[35]

31-10   (2) *Penal rents.* Where a lease contains a provision for a penal rent, or an increased rent in the nature of a penal rent (*e.g.* in the event of a breach of covenant by the lessee), no duty is payable in respect of such provision.[36] Similarly, no duty is payable in respect of the surrender or abandonment of an existing lease of the same premises.[36]

31-11   (3) *Covenants to improve the demised premises.* A lease for a consideration which attracts *ad valorem* duty and in further consideration either

    (a) of a covenant by the lessee to make (or of his having previously made) any substantial improvement of or addition to the demised property; or

---

[28] For a discussion on this subject, see Cheshire's *Modern Law of Real Property*, 11th ed., pp. 373 *et seq.*
[29] See F.A. 1963, s. 56 (1) and the text to note 22, *ante*, § 31-06.
[30] S.A. 1891, s. 75 (2), amended by F.A. 1970, s. 32 and Sched. 7, para. 14.
[31] *Ante*, § 27-40.
[32] *Cf.* S.A. 1891, s. 59 (6), *ante*, § 29-03.
[33] *Ante*, § 27-51.
[34] Prior to August 1, 1971, they attracted bond covenant duty.
[35] *Ante*, § 27-20. But a fixed duty of £2 is charged: see (1962) L.S.G., p. 44.
[36] S.A. 1891, s. 77 (1).

(b) of any covenant relating to the matter of the lease, attracts no further duty in respect of (a) or (b).[37]

31-12 (4) *Instruments withdrawing a notice to quit.* Where notice to determine a tenancy is given and is subsequently withdrawn by agreement between the parties, the instrument withdrawing the notice operates as an agreement for a new tenancy and must be stamped accordingly.[38]

Method of stamping leases

31-13 Leases must bear an impressed stamp.
For the stamping of duplicates and counterparts, see *ante,* § 27-39.
For the produced stamp, see *ante,* § 27-45.

---

[37] S.A. 1891, s. 77 (2), as amended by Revenue Act 1909, s. 8. Contrast F.A. 1900, s. 10, *ante,* § 28-27.
[38] *Freeman* v. *Evans* [1922] 1 Ch. 36 (C.A.).

CHAPTER 32

SHARE CAPITAL, BEARER INSTRUMENTS AND COMPOSITIONS

32-01 CAPITAL duty under section 112 or section 113 of the Stamp Act 1891 (on statements relating to nominal share capital of limited companies) was abolished as from August 1, 1973.[1] The duties on loan capital [2] under section 8 of the Finance Act 1899 and marketable securities [3] under Schedule 1 to the Stamp Act 1891 were abolished with effect from January 1, 1973.[4] Thus there is no longer any charge to stamp duty on the creation and issue of any such securities which are also now exempt from duty under the headings " Conveyance or Transfer " or " Voluntary Dispositions " by virtue of section 126 of the Finance Act 1976.[5] There is, however, a new charge to duty which takes the place of the former share capital duty and is effective from August 1, 1973. This charge is found in sections 47 and 48 of, and Schedule 19 to, the Finance Act 1973 and conforms with the United Kingdom's obligations under an EEC directive. This head of charge is now considered.

1. CHARGEABLE TRANSACTIONS OF CAPITAL COMPANIES

32-02 Under section 47 of the Finance Act 1973, stamp duty at the rate of £1 for every £100 (or fraction of £100) is payable on the statement required when a qualifying *capital company* undertakes a *chargeable transaction*.

Capital company

A capital company is:
 (1) a limited liability company or limited partnership incorporated in the United Kingdom [6];
 (2) a company incorporated according to the law of another member state of the EEC [7];
 (3) any other corporation or body of persons whose shares or assets can be dealt in on a Stock Exchange within the EEC [8]; or
 (4) any other corporation or body of persons operating for profit

---

[1] F.A. 1973, s. 49 (1) (*a*). The similar duty under the Limited Partnerships Act 1907, s. 11 is likewise abolished from that date: F.A. 1973, s. 49 (1) (*b*).

[2] Loan capital is defined in F.A. 1899, s. 8 (5), as: " any debenture stock, . . . corporation stock . . . or funded debt, by whatever name known, or any capital raised by any . . . corporation, company, or body of persons formed or established in the United Kingdom, which is borrowed, or has the character of borrowed money, whether it is in the form of stock or in any other form, and whether the loan thereof is secured by a mortgage, marketable security or other instrument, or is unsecured but does not include . . . any overdraft at the bank or other loan raised for a merely temporary purpose for a period not exceeding 12 months. . . ." This definition is, in effect, preserved by F.A. 1973, s. 49 (9).

[3] The expression " marketable security " is defined in S.A. 1891, s. 122 as " a security of such a description as to be capable of being sold in any stock market in the United Kingdom."

[4] F.A. 1973, s. 49 (2) and (3).

[5] See § 28-45, *ante*.

[6] F.A. 1973, s. 48 (1) (*a*) and (*b*).

[7] *Ibid*. s. 48 (1) (*c*).

[8] *Ibid*. s. 48 (1) (*d*).

537

whose members have the right to dispose of their shares to third parties without prior authorisation [9] and who have limited liability. [10]

A unit trust [11] (whether authorised or not) is not a capital company. Nor does an unlimited company, whether having a share capital or not, fall within the above definitions.

The charge under section 47 of the Finance Act 1973 only applies if the capital company has its place of effective management in Great Britain or its registered office in Great Britain (but in the latter case only if its place of effective management is outside the EEC). [12]

Chargeable transactions

32-03   The transactions giving rise to this charge are set out in paragraph 1 of Schedule 19 to the Finance Act 1973 and are as follows:

(1) *Formation* of a capital company. [13] Duty is charged as follows:

(a) If the formation is the consequence of the conversion of a corporation or body of persons into a capital company the duty is charged on the actual value [14] of the net assets of that company immediately after the conversion. [15]

(b) In all other cases duty is charged on the actual value [14] of net assets of any kind contributed by the members. [16]

If, however, in either event, the value of those assets is less than the nominal value of the shares at the relevant time duty is charged on that nominal value. [17] The charge does not extend to the conversion of a capital company into a different type of capital company or to the alteration of a company's memorandum or articles. [18]

32-04   (2) *Increase in capital* by the contribution of assets of any kind. [19] The chargeable event takes place when share capital is *issued* but does not, of course, extend to a bonus issue. There is a similar charge where assets are contributed in return for rights similar to those attaching to shares. [20] Again the charge is on either the actual value of net assets contributed or the nominal value of the shares whichever is the greater. [21] The charge applies to the conversion of loan stock into share capital and the issue of shares in satisfaction of a debt owed by the company. [22]

32-05   (3) *Conversion of an unlimited company to a limited company.* [23] Since an unlimited company is not a capital company its conversion to limited

---

[9] Presumably these words refer to the normal restrictions on transfer in private companies.

[10] F.A. 1973, s. 48 (1) (*e*).

[11] *Ante*, § 30-15 and see F.A. 1965, s. 38. F.A. 1972, s. 112 and Prevention of Fraud (Investments) Act 1958, s. 26 (1).

[12] F.A. 1973, s. 47 (1).

[13] *Ibid*. Sched. 19, para. 1 (*a*).

[14] Presumably this imports the same concept as market value.

[15] F.A. 1973, Sched. 19, para. 4 (2).

[16] *Ibid*. Sched. 19, para. 4 (1).

[17] *Ibid*. Sched. 19, para. 7 (1).

[18] *Ibid*. Sched. 19, para. 2 (1) (*b*).

[19] *Ibid*. Sched. 19, para. 1 (*b*).

[20] *Ibid*. Sched. 19, para. 1 (*c*).

[21] *Ibid*. Sched. 19, paras. 4 (1), 7 (1) (*a*) and 11 (schemes of arrangement).

[22] *Ibid*. Sched. 19, para. 2 (2).

[23] *Ibid*. Sched. 19, para. 1 (*d*).

liability is a chargeable event. This head of charge likewise extends to an increase in the amount contributed by a limited partner. The charge is on the net assets of the company immediately before the transaction (or a part thereof that represents the share in the company's net assets that has become unlimited).[24]

32-06   (4) *Transfer to Great Britain of the place of effective management or registered office* of a capital company unless that company is subject to a similar charge to duty (*i.e.* as that contained in section 47) in another Member State of the EEC.[25] The charge is on either the actual value of net assets belonging to the company at the time of the chargeable transaction or the nominal value of its shares at that time whichever is the greater.[26] Furthermore there is an alternative charge, which lies within the discretion of the Commissioners, in that they may assess duty on the basis of the actual value of the shares in the company at the time of the chargeable transaction.[27]

32-07 *Relief from conveyance or transfer duty* [28]

If the chargeable transaction falls within either (1) or (2) above and assets are conveyed or transferred to the capital company in consideration of the issue of shares in that capital company, no conveyance or transfer duty is payable on the conveyance or transfer of such assets other than on:

   (i) stock or securities,[29] or
   (ii) the whole or any part of an undertaking, or
   (iii) any estate or interest in land.

These exceptions would appear to have the effect of denying relief in virtually all circumstances. The only circumstances in which the relief would appear to apply would be on a conveyance or transfer of assets (other than those within (i) and (iii) above) not constituting part of an undertaking but, apart from this provision, subject to conveyance or transfer duty.[30] Examples would be the transfer of such things as know-how, patents, copyrights or trademarks in consideration of the issue of shares.

32-08 *Stamping*

A statement containing prescribed particulars of the chargeable transaction must be delivered within one month of the date of that transaction.[31] This statement must be delivered to the Registrar of Companies where the transaction is [32]:

   (1) the formation of a limited liability company under the Companies Act 1948;

---

[24] F.A. 1973, Sched. 19, para. 5.
[25] This appears to be the effect of *ibid.* Sched. 19, para. 1 (*e*)-(*h*).
[26] *Ibid.* Sched. 19, paras. 6 (1) and 7 (2).
[27] *Ibid.* Sched. 19, para. 6 (2).
[28] *Ibid.* Sched. 19, para. 13.
[29] Such transfers will now, however, be generally exempt under the provision discussed in § 28-45 (5), *ante.*
[30] *Cf. Baytrust Holdings Ltd.* v. *I.R.C.* [1971] 1 W.L.R. 1333, *post,* § 33-04, note 11.
[31] F.A. 1973, s. 47 (1).
[32] *Ibid.* s. 47 (2).

(2) an allotment of shares in respect of which a return must be delivered under section 52 (1) of that Act;

(3) a registration or change in contribution or liability of a limited partnership under section 8 or 9 of the Limited Partnerships Act 1907.

In the case of all other chargeable transactions the statement must be delivered to the Commissioners. It is this statement that bears the duty payable. Duty is charged at the rate of £1 per £100 (or fraction of £100) [33] and failure to comply with these provisions leads to a fine of 5 per cent. per month of the duty chargeable. [34]

Exemptions from duty

32-09   (1) *An increase in capital following a reduction.* [35] An increase in issued capital is exempt from duty if it follows within four years of a reduction in nominal capital but only if that reduction was " as a result of losses sustained." [36] The exemption is applied to any number of increases during this four-year period but only to the extent of the amount of the reduction attributable to the losses.

32-10   (2) *Groups of companies.* Paragraph 10 of Schedule 19 to the Finance Act 1973 replaces the exemption from capital duty (but not conveyance or transfer duty) contained in section 55 of the Finance Act 1927. [37] The conditions for obtaining relief are as follows:

(a) The capital company is effectively managed or registered in a country within the EEC.

(b) There is a chargeable transaction whereby a capital company acquires:

(i) 75 per cent. of the issued share capital of another capital company, [38] or

(ii) the whole or any part of the undertaking of another capital company. [38]

(c) At least 90 per cent. of the consideration must consist of shares issued [39] by the acquiring company either, in case (i) above, to the shareholders in the acquired company in exchange for their shares [40] or, in case (ii) above, to the acquired company or its shareholders.

(d) Any balance of consideration other than shares must consist wholly of cash.

---

[33] F.A. 1973, s. 47 (5).   [34] *Ibid.* s. 47 (7).

[35] *Ibid.* Sched. 19, para. 9.

[36] It is difficult to see how these words can apply to the ordinary reduction of capital under Companies Act 1948, s. 66.

[37] See *post*, §§ 33-01 *et seq.*

[38] The relief also applies where the *acquired* company is not a capital company within the definition in § 32-02, *ante*, but is a corporation or body of persons treated as a capital company in another EEC Member State: F.A. 1976, s. 128.

[39] The consideration shares must be registered in the names of the acquired company or its shareholders: *Oswald Tillotson Ltd.* v. *I.R.C.* [1933] 1 K.B. 134 (C.A.).

[40] The Commissioners are of the view that the vendors must be the registered holders of the shares in the acquired company and that the mere renunciation of renounceable letters of allotment cannot constitute part of a transaction of " exchange "; this is of considerable importance in transactions where F.A. 1927, s. 55 does not apply so as to confer exemption from *ad valorem* conveyance or transfer duty.

If the transaction is within (b) (i) above the exemption is lost if, within the period of five years [41] after the chargeable transaction, the acquiring company

(a) ceases to retain 75 per cent. of the acquired company's shares, or
(b) disposes of any of the shares in the acquired company which it held immediately after the occurrence of the chargeable transaction.

In either event any transfer is to be disregarded if it is itself an exempt transaction or is effected in the course of winding up the acquiring company. If the exemption is lost by virtue of these provisions duty is payable within one month of the event that led to the exemption being lost and the provisions relating to fines apply accordingly.

2. BEARER INSTRUMENTS

32-11   Section 59 of the Finance Act 1963 [42] introduced into the Stamp Act 1891 a new head of charge on bearer instruments. The charge is imposed on the instruments listed in the left-hand column of the following table and the amount of duty is shown in the right-hand column:

(1) Inland bearer instrument (other than deposit certificate for overseas stock).	Duty of an amount equal to three times the transfer duty. [43]
(2) Overseas bearer instrument (other than deposit certificate for overseas stock or bearer instrument by usage).	Duty of an amount equal to twice the transfer duty. [43]
(3) Instruments excepted from paragraph (1) or (2) of this heading.	Duty of 10p [44] for every £50 or part of £50 of the market value.
(4) Inland or overseas bearer instrument given in substitution for a like instrument duly stamped *ad valorem* (whether under this heading or not).	Duty of 10p. [44]

Exemptions

32-12   (1) Instrument constituting, or used for transferring, stock which is exempt from all stamp duties on transfer by virtue of General Exemption (1) in the First Schedule to the Stamp Act 1891 [45] or of any other enactment.

(2) Bearer letter of allotment, bearer letter of rights, scrip, scrip certificate to bearer or other similar instrument to bearer where the letter, scrip, certificate or instrument is required to be surrendered not later than six months after issue.

---

[41] This provision is more restrictive than that which existed under F.A. 1927, s. 55 (1) (A) but otherwise the conditions for obtaining relief are less stringent. These provisions will, however, have little practical effect: see *post*, §§ 33-01 *et seq.*

[42] Amended by F.A. 1970, s. 32 and Sched. 7, para. 6 (2) (3), as from August 1, 1970.

[43] This means the duty which would be chargeable under the heading " Conveyance or Transfer on sale " in respect of an instrument in writing transferring the stock constituted by or transferable by means of the inland or overseas bearer instrument in question for a consideration equal to the market value of that stock: F.A. 1963, s. 59 (3).

[44] See F.A. 1964, Sched. 11, para. 2.

[45] See *ante*, § 27-51, para. (a).

(3) Renounceable letter of allotment, letter of rights or other similar instrument where the rights under the letter or instrument are renounceable not later than six months after the issue of the letter or instrument.

(4) No duty is chargeable on the issue on or after August 1, 1967, of any instrument which relates to stock expressed in the currency of a territory outside the scheduled territories, or on the transfer on or after that date of the stock constituted by, or transferable by means of, any such instrument.[46]

Definitions

32-13   The instruments referred to in the left-hand column of the table (above) are defined as follows:

(a) " Inland bearer instrument " means [47] any of the following instruments issued by or on behalf of any company or body of persons corporate or unincorporate formed or established in the United Kingdom, that is to say:

(i) any marketable security [48] transferable by delivery;

(ii) any share warrant or stock certificate to bearer and any instrument to bearer (by whatever name called) having the like effect as such a warrant or certificate;

(iii) any deposit certificate to bearer;

(iv) any other instrument to bearer by means of which any stock can be transferred.

(b) " Overseas bearer instrument " means [47] an instrument issued otherwise than by or on behalf of any such company or body of persons as is mentioned in paragraph (a) above, being an instrument described in sub-paragraphs (i) to (iv) of that paragraph or a bearer instrument by usage.

(c) " Deposit certificate " means [47] an instrument acknowledging the deposit of stock and entitling the bearer to rights (whether expressed as units or otherwise) in or in relation to the stock deposited or equivalent stock; and " deposit certificate for overseas stock " means a deposit certificate in respect of stock of any one company or body of persons not being such a company or body as is mentioned in paragraph (a) above.

(d) " Bearer instrument by usage " [47] means an instrument not described in sub-paragraphs (i) to (iv), above, which is used for the purpose of transferring the right to any stock, being an instrument delivery of which is treated by usage as sufficient for the purpose of a sale on the market, whether that delivery constitutes a legal transfer or not."

(e) " Stock " [49] includes securities, and references to stock include references to any interest in, or in any fraction of, stock or in any dividends or other rights arising out of stock and any right to an allotment of or to subscribe for stock; " transfer " includes negotiation, and " transferable,"

---

[46] See F.A. 1967, s. 30, for details.
[47] F.A. 1963, s. 59 (2).
[48] Defined *ante*, § 32-01, note 3.
[49] F.A. 1963, s. 59 (4).

" transferred " and " transferring " are to be construed accordingly; and a bearer instrument by usage used for the purpose of transferring the right to any stock is to be treated as transferring that stock on delivery of the instrument, and as issued by the person by whom or on whose behalf it was first issued, whether or not it was then capable of being used for transferring the right to the stock without execution by the holder.

Payment of duty

32-14 The duty payable under the head " Bearer Instrument " is chargeable *on issue* in the case of:

(a) any instrument issued in Great Britain; and
(b) any instrument issued by or on behalf of a company or body of persons corporate or unincorporate formed or established in Great Britain, not being a foreign loan security;

and " foreign loan security " means a security issued outside the United Kingdom in respect of a loan which is expressed in a currency other than sterling and is neither offered for subscription in the United Kingdom nor offered for subscription with a view to an offer for sale in the United Kingdom of securities in respect of the loan.[50]

In cases not covered by the previous paragraph, the duty is chargeable *on transfer* in Great Britain of the stock constituted by or transferable by means of the instrument, if—had the transfer *not* been effected by an instrument which was not a bearer instrument—the instrument would have been chargeable as a conveyance on sale.[51]

Ascertainment of market value

32-15 Where an instrument is chargeable *on issue*, the market value of the stock constituted by or transferable by means of that instrument is to be taken for the purposes of section 59 of the Finance Act 1963 to be:

(a) Where the stock was offered for public subscription (whether in registered or in bearer form) within 12 months before the issue of the instrument, the amount subscribed for the stock;
(b) in any other case, the value of the stock on the first day within one month after the issue of the instrument on which stock of that description is dealt in on a stock exchange in the United Kingdom or, if stock of that description is not so dealt in, the value of the stock immediately after the issue of the instrument.[52]

Where an instrument is chargeable *on transfer* of the stock constituted by or transferable by means of that instrument, the market value of that stock is to be taken to be the value of that stock:

---

[50] F.A. 1963, s. 60 (1). The instrument must be produced to the Commissioners before issue and must bear a particular stamp denoting this. Within six weeks after issue (or such longer time as the Commissioners allow) a statement must be delivered to the Commissioners and duty paid on delivery thereof. There are penalties for non-compliance: *ibid*. s. 60 (3) (4) and (7).

[51] *Ibid*. s. 60 (2). As to method of stamping and penalties for transferring instruments not duly stamped, see *ibid*. s. 60 (5) (6) and (7).

[52] *Ibid*. s. 61 (1).

(a) in the case of a transfer pursuant to a contract of sale, on the date when the contract is made;

(b) in any other case, on the day preceding that on which the instrument is presented to the Commissioners for stamping, or, if it is not so presented, on the date of the transfer.[53]

3. COMPOSITIONS

32-16   The Stamp Act 1891 and later Acts contained provisions by which certain bodies might, if they wished, compound for the duty payable on transfers of their stock. Transfers covered by the composition were then exempt from duty. Such compositions were of two types: (1) the once for all composition under section 65 of the Finance Act 1971 and (2) composition by periodical payments. With the general abolition of transfer duty on loan capital (see § 28-45 (5), *ante*) all such composition provisions have now ceased to have effect.[54]

---

[53] F.A. 1963, s. 61 (2).
[54] See F.A. 1976, s. 126 (4).

CHAPTER 33

COMPANIES

1. RELIEFS ON RECONSTRUCTION AND AMALGAMATION

33-01 IF, in connection with [1] a scheme for the reconstruction of a company or companies or the amalgamation of any companies, certain conditions are shown to exist, reliefs from (i) capital duty under section 47 of the Finance Act 1973 and (ii) conveyance or transfer duty are available under paragraph 10 of Schedule 19 to the Finance Act 1973 [2] and section 55 of the Finance Act 1927 respectively. The conditions for obtaining relief are, in general, more stringent under section 55 than under paragraph 10 and consequently, since both reliefs will normally be desired, this section will concentrate on the former.

33-02 The terms " reconstruction " and " amalgamation " are not defined in the Act, nor have they any precise legal meaning [3]; but the following are examples of the type of scheme to which section 55 may apply:

(1) A new company is formed (or the share capital of an existing company is increased) for the purpose of acquiring the undertaking of an existing company in consideration of the allotment of shares in the new company either (a) to the existing company, [4] or (b) to the shareholders of the existing company. [5] Relief is available only if not less than 90 per cent. of the consideration for the undertaking is in shares of the new company (see below).

(2) A new company is formed (or the share capital of an existing company is increased) for the purpose of acquiring the shares of an existing company. This is an " exchange of shares." Relief is available only if not less than 90 per cent. of the consideration for the shares is in shares of the new company and not less than 90 per cent. of the issued shares of the existing company is acquired (see below).

(3) A new company is formed (or the share capital of an existing company is increased) for the purpose of acquiring the undertaking of two existing companies. This is an " amalgamation."

---

[1] These words determine the ambit of the relief and were considered by the Court of Appeal in *Clarke Chapman-John Thompson Ltd.* v. *I.R.C.* [1976] Ch. 91; [1975] S.T.C. 567. In that case a company first acquired the shares in another (which transaction constituted an amalgamation) and then subsequently proposed the substitution of the debentures and loan stocks of its newly acquired subsidiary by similar stocks in itself; *held* that, on the facts, this subsequent transaction was " in connection with " the amalgamation and therefore exempt.

[2] See *ante*, § 32-10.

[3] See generally, *Buckley on the Companies Acts*, 13th ed., p. 586.

[4] In this case, the existing company becomes an investment-holding company.

[5] This is a " reconstruction." Usually the existing company will be in voluntary liquidation and the sale of its undertaking will be a sale by the liquidator. See *Brooklands Selangor Ltd.* v. *I.R.C.* [1970] 1 W.L.R. 429 (scheme for partition of assets between two groups of shareholders held not to be a reconstruction—no substantial identity between business and persons interested in new and old company).

33-03   There are two features common to all these schemes:

(a) The formation of a new company or an increase in the share capital of an existing company. This normally attracts capital duty.[6]

(b) The transfer of the undertaking of an existing company (or of its shares) in consideration of an allotment to the transferor of shares in another company. This normally attracts conveyance or transfer duty.[7]

If it were not for the reliefs granted by section 55 of the Finance Act 1927 and paragraph 10 of Schedule 19 to the Finance Act 1973 the reconstruction of a company or the amalgamation of companies would be a costly process. These sections enable the process to be carried out with a considerable saving, sometimes a total saving, of *ad valorem* stamp duty.

General conditions of relief

33-04   Relief is granted only if three conditions are satisfied:

(1) A company (hereafter called " the take-over company ") is incorporated, or the share capital of a company is increased, with a view to the acquisition either of the undertaking (or part of the undertaking) or of not less than 90 per cent. of the share capital of a particular existing company.[8] The " undertaking " denotes the business or enterprise undertaken by a company: hence a mere sale of assets is not a sale of part of the undertaking.[9] It is a necessary condition of relief that the memorandum of association of the take-over company (or the resolution of increase) should state that one of the objects of the company (or the purpose of the resolution, as the case may be) is to acquire the undertaking of or shares in the existing company.[10] The memorandum or resolution must, therefore, be drafted with this condition in mind.

(2) The consideration for the acquisition (except such part as consists in the transfer to or discharge by the take-over company of liabilities of the existing company) must consist as to not less than 90 per cent. thereof:

(a) where an undertaking is to be acquired, in the issue of shares in the take-over company to the existing company or its shareholders; or

(b) where shares are to be acquired, in the issue of shares in the

---

[6] *Ante*, §§ 32-03 and 32-04.

[7] *Ante*, § 28-33. An exchange of shares for shares is a conveyance on sale for purposes of stamp duty, not an exchange: *J. & P. Coats Ltd.* v. *I.R.C.* [1897] 2 Q.B. 423 (C.A.).

[8] F.A. 1927, s. 55 (1) (*b*). Both companies must be incorporated in England or Scotland: *Nestlé Co. Ltd.* v. *I.R.C.* [1953] Ch. 395. An unlimited company is " a particular existing company ": *Chelsea Land Development Co. Ltd.* v. *I.R.C.* [1978] S.T.C. 221 (C.A.).

[9] *Baytrust Holdings Ltd.* v. *I.R.C.* [1971] 1 W.L.R. 1333 at p. 1353H. " A greengrocer's business is no doubt to sell fruit, but the pound of apples which you buy can hardly be described as a purchase of part of the greengrocer's business ": Plowman J. at p. 1354A.

[10] F.A. 1927, s. 55 (3). However this requirement would not appear to be necessary on the issue of previously authorised capital.

take-over company to the shareholders of the existing company in exchange for their shares. [11]

The requirements in (a) and (b) that there should be an *issue* of shares is only satisfied by actual registration of the existing company or its shareholders as holders of those shares. No relief is given if shares in the take-over company are allotted to the shareholders of the existing company on renounceable letters of allotment and these shareholders renounce shares of a value exceeding 10 per cent. of the purchase consideration to outside purchasers [12]; nor even if shares in the take-over company are registered in the names of nominees as trustees for the registered holders. [13] Further, the person to whom the shares are issued must at the time of issue become the beneficial owner of the shares—a condition which is not satisfied if the person is not free to deal with them as he wishes, *e.g.* by reason of some prior commitment to transfer the shares to another person. [14] Thus, if, as part of the scheme, the shares are issued subject to an option to purchase for a cash consideration the relief will not be available whether or not the option is exercised. [15] In effect the shares subject to such a cash option are simply regarded as conferring a right to receive cash.

(3) On an exchange of shares, relief is available only if the take-over company acquires not less than 90 per cent. of the issued shares of the existing company. If, therefore, the take-over company already owns more than 10 per cent. of the existing company's shares, no relief can be obtained. [16] If, when a claim for relief is made, all the necessary conditions of relief are satisfied except the condition that not less than 90 per cent. of the issued share capital of the existing company should be acquired, the Commissioners may repay the duty if the requisite percentage is acquired within the period of six months specified in the Act. [17]

33-05   *Relief from conveyance or transfer duty.* [18] Where the general conditions of relief referred to above are satisfied, no conveyance or transfer duty is payable on any instrument transferring the undertaking or shares or assigning the debts [19] of the existing company. This relief is not, however, available unless the following further conditions are satisfied:

(1) The instrument must be adjudicated; and

---

[11] F.A. 1927, s. 55 (1) (c). In *Central and District Properties Ltd.* v. *I.R.C.* [1966] 1 W.L.R. 1015 (C.A. and H.L.) the question for decision was whether certain rights given to preference shareholders of the existing company by a third party were part of the " consideration for the acquisition " and the meaning of these words was discussed.

[12] *Oswald Tillotson* v. *I.R.C.* [1933] 1 K.B. 134 (C.A.).

[13] *Ibid. per* Finlay J. The Court of Appeal left the point open, but support for this view of Finlay J. can be found in *Murex* v. *I.R.C.* [1933] 1 K.B. 173.

[14] *Baytrust Holdings Ltd.* v. *I.R.C.* [1971] 1 W.L.R. 1333 at pp. 1354D *et seq.*

[15] *Crane Fruehauf Ltd.* v. *I.R.C.* [1975] 1 All E.R. 429; [1975] S.T.C. 51.

[16] *Lever Bros.* v. *I.R.C.* [1938] 2 K.B. 518.

[17] F.A. 1927, s. 55 (7).

[18] F.A. 1927, s. 55 (1) (B).

[19] No relief is given in respect of debts incurred less than two years before relief under the section is claimed, except in the case of debts due to banks or to trade creditors: F.A. 1927, s. 55 (1) (B), proviso (c).

(2) the instrument must be executed within 12 months from the date of registration of (or the date of the resolution for increase by) the take-over company or it must be made to effect a conveyance or transfer pursuant to an agreement filed with the Registrar of Companies within that period.[20]

For the purpose of relief from conveyance or transfer duty, a company which in connection with [21] a scheme of reconstruction or amalgamation issues any unissued share capital is treated as if it had increased its nominal share capital.[22]

A conveyance or transfer which is exempt from duty under section 55 is liable to a fixed duty of 50p under Head (2) of conveyance or transfer duty.[23]

33-06   *Relief from capital duty.*[24] The chargeable transaction, consisting of the formation of a company or an increase in share capital will be exempt if the conditions already considered [24] are satisfied.

Loss of relief

33-07   Where a claim for relief from conveyance or transfer duty is made under section 55 of the Finance Act 1927, the Commissioners have power to require (and usually insist upon) the delivery to them of a statutory declaration made by a solicitor concerned in the scheme of reconstruction or amalgamation that the provisions of the section have been complied with. The Commissioners may also require further evidence.[25] If a claim for relief is allowed, the relief will be lost and the amount of duty remitted will be immediately payable with interest at 5 per cent. per annum in the following cases [26]:

(a) where any declaration or other evidence in support of the claim was untrue in any material particular or the conditions for relief were not satisfied;

(b) where shares in the take-over company have been issued to the existing company in consideration of the acquisition and the existing company ceases within two years to be the beneficial owner of the shares so issued to it, otherwise than in consequence of reconstruction, amalgamation or liquidation. The two-year period is reckoned from the date of incorporation of the take-over company (or of the resolution for increase of capital, as the case may be) [27];

Thus if B Ltd. acquires the undertaking of A Ltd. in consideration of shares issued to A Ltd., the relief from transfer duty given to B Ltd. will be lost if A Ltd. disposes of *any* [28] of the shares within the two-year period. B Ltd. must therefore take appropriate undertakings from A Ltd.

---

[20] See Companies Act 1948, s. 52.
[21] For the meaning of the words " in connection with " see *Clarke Chapman-John Thompson Ltd.* v. *I.R.C.* [1976] Ch. 91; [1975] S.T.C. 567 (C.A.) referred to at § 33-01, note 1, *ante.*
[22] F.A. 1927, s. 55 (2).
[23] *Ante,* § 28-43.
[24] *Ante,* § 32-10.
[25] F.A. 1927, s. 55 (5).
[26] *Ibid.* s. 55 (6).
[27] If the transaction did not require any increase in nominal capital, but simply the issue of previously unissued shares, the Commissioners still regard the date of incorporation or resolution as appropriate and not the date of issue: see F.A. 1927, s. 55 (2) and (6) (*b*).
[28] A Ltd. must therefore retain every share: *Att.-Gen.* v. *London Stadiums* [1950] 1 K.B. 387 (C.A.).

(c) where shares in the existing company have been acquired by the take-over company and the take-over company ceases within two years to be the beneficial owner of the shares so acquired, otherwise than in consequence of reconstruction, amalgamation or liquidation. The two-year period is reckoned as in (b), above.

Thus if B Ltd. acquires (say) 95 per cent. of the shares of A Ltd. and gets the reliefs under section 55 and paragraph 10 of Schedule 19, B Ltd. will lose the reliefs if it disposes of *any* [28] of the shares within the two-year period.

It will be observed that if the take-over company issues shares to the shareholders of the existing company, section 55 imposes no obligation on *those* shareholders to retain shares issued to them. They may, therefore, dispose of them without loss of reliefs.

33-08   The relief from capital duty will be lost if, within the period of *five years* from the transaction the take-over company ceases to retain 75 per cent. of the existing company's shares or disposes of any of the shares it held in that company immediately after the transaction. [29]

2. TRANSFERS BETWEEN ASSOCIATED COMPANIES

33-09   Relief from conveyance or transfer duty is given under section 42 of the Finance Act 1930 on an instrument by which one company transfers property to an associated company where the association is so close that the transfer is virtually a mere change in nominal ownership. It is apparently not necessary in this case that the companies should be incorporated in England or Scotland [30]; nor need the transfer be in connection with a scheme for reconstruction or amalgamation. Relief under section 42 is frequently sought in connection with schemes of reconstruction to which section 55 of the Finance Act 1927 and paragraph 10 of Schedule 19 to the Finance Act 1973 do not apply. No relief is available in the case of instruments executed before August 1, 1967, if either company is an unlimited company.

Conditions of relief

33-10   To obtain relief under section 42 of the Finance Act 1930 it must be shown to the satisfaction of the Commissioners of Inland Revenue [31]:

(a) That the effect of the instrument is to convey or transfer a beneficial interest in property from one body corporate to another; and

(b) That the bodies in question are " associated," that is to say, either

(i) one of such bodies is beneficial owner of not less than 90 per cent. of the issued share capital of the other (*i.e.* transfers between parent and subsidiary); or

---

[29] See § 32-10, *ante.*
[30] *Nestlé Co. Ltd.* v. *I.R.C.* [1953] Ch. 395 at p. 399. Contrast the relief under F.A. 1927, s. 55, above.
[31] F.A. 1930, s. 42, as amended by F.A. 1967, s. 27 (2), in the case of instruments executed on or after August 1, 1967. Or, on appeal, to the satisfaction of the court: *Leigh Spinners Ltd.* v. *I.R.C.* (1956) 46 T.C. 425 at p. 434.

(ii) not less than 90 per cent. of the issued share capital of each of the bodies is in the beneficial ownership of a third such body (*i.e.* transfers between subsidiaries of the same parent company).[32]

The ownership referred to is ownership directly or through another body corporate or other bodies corporate, or partly directly and partly through another body corporate or other bodies corporate.[33] The relief will not apply if one of the companies is in liquidation since its shares and assets will be held on trust for its creditors and members.[34]

The instrument must be adjudicated.[35]

Condition (a) was considered in *Escoigne Properties Ltd.* v. *I.R.C.,*[36] where the facts were as follows:

> X agreed to sell property to A Ltd. but no conveyance was executed. X thus became a constructive trustee for A Ltd. A Ltd. later agreed to sell the property to B Ltd. (its wholly owned subsidiary) whereupon X conveyed the property to B Ltd. by direction of A Ltd. *Held*, that B Ltd. was not entitled to relief under section 42.

Condition (b) requires that the body in question should be " beneficial owner " of not less than 90 per cent. of the issued share capital of the other body. If a company owns shares which an outsider (not an associated company) has a contractual right to acquire, the company is not " beneficial owner," whether the contract be conditional[37] or unconditional.[38] Furthermore, it may be that on the grant of a simple option to purchase a shareholder ceases to be " beneficial owner." [39] The words " 90 per cent. of the issued share capital " refer to nominal, not actual, value.[40]

Further conditions of relief

33-11   After the Finance Act 1930, an ingenious device came into use by which duty-free transfers could be made between companies which were not associated. This device involved the formation of a " dummy-bridge company " and the use (and abuse) of the relieving provisions in section 42.[41] Section 50 of the Finance Act 1938 was designed to prevent the use of this device. That section was substituted as respects instruments executed on or after August 1, 1967, by section 27 (3) of the Finance Act 1967, which requires that the claimant for relief under section 42 must satisfy the Commissioners that the instrument in respect of which relief is claimed was

---

[32] F.A. 1930, s. 42 (2), substituted by F.A. 1967, s. 27 (2).

[33] F.A. 1930, s. 42 (3), substituted by F.A. 1967, s. 27 (2). F.A. 1938, Sched. 4, Pt. I, is to be applied for the purposes of determining the amount of capital held through other bodies corporate, with the substitution of references to issued share capital for references to ordinary share capital.

[34] *I.R.C.* v. *Olive Mill Ltd.* (1963) 41 T.C. 77.

[35] F.A. 1930, s. 42 (1), proviso. See *ante*, § 27-41.

[36] [1958] A.C. 549.

[37] *Leigh Spinners Ltd.* v. *I.R.C.* (1956) 46 T.C. 425.

[38] *Parway Estates Ltd.* v. *I.R.C.* (1958) 45 T.C. 112 (C.A.). And see *Holmleigh (Holdings) Ltd.* v. *I.R.C.* (1958) 46 T.C. 435; *Wood Preservation Ltd.* v. *Prior* (1968) 45 T.C. 112 and *Baytrust Holdings Ltd.* v. *I.R.C.* [1971] 1 W.L.R. 1333 at p. 1354.

[39] See Sergeant at p. 234 and the cases there cited.

[40] *Canada Safeway Ltd.* v. *I.R.C.* [1973] Ch. 374.

[41] See Lord Denning in *Escoigne Properties Ltd.* v. *I.R.C.* [1958] A.C. 549, at pp. 567–568.

not executed in pursuance of or in connection with an arrangement [42] under which either:

(a) The consideration, or any part of the consideration, for the conveyance or transfer was to be provided or received directly or indirectly, by a person other than a body corporate which at the time of the execution of the instrument was associated with either the transferor or the transferee (meaning, respectively, the body from whom and the body to whom the beneficial interest was conveyed or transferred); or

(b) The said interest was previously conveyed or transferred, directly or indirectly, by such a person; or

(c) The transferor and the transferee were to cease to be associated by reason of a change in the percentage of the issued share capital of the transferee in the beneficial ownership of the transferor or a third body corporate.

Without prejudice to the generality of paragraph (a) above, an arrangement is to be treated as within that paragraph if it is one whereunder the transferor or the transferee, or a body corporate associated with either, was to be enabled to provide any of the consideration, or was to part with any of it, by or in consequence of the carrying out of a transaction or transactions involving, or any of them involving, a payment or other disposition by a person other than a body corporate so associated.

33-12   It is the practice of the Commissioners, in claims for relief under section 42, to require a statutory declaration from a solicitor concerned in the transaction as to the matters on which they require to be satisfied.

> In *Shop and Store Developments Ltd.* v. *I.R.C.,*[43] a company transferred properties to its wholly owned subsidiary company for a price which was satisfied by the issue, credited as fully paid, of shares in the subsidiary company, such shares being issued on renounceable letters of allotment. Immediately following the issue of these shares the company renounced some of them to an issuing house for cash and it was admitted that all these transactions were part of an arrangement. *Held*, that the " consideration " in section 50 of the Finance Act 1938 (of which paragraph (a) above is an amended version) denoted the consideration received by the company for its properties and that *this* was provided by the subsidiary company and not by the issuing house, accordingly the conveyances to the subsidiary company were exempt from *ad valorem* duty.

In consequence of this decision, section 50 of the Finance Act 1938 was replaced by section 27 (3) of the Finance Act 1967. The conveyance in the *Shop and Store* case would not now be exempt, because paragraph (a), above, would apply by reason of the words " or received." [44]

---

[42] As to " arrangement," see the income tax case of *Crossland* v. *Hawkins* [1961] Ch. 537; 39 T.C. 493 (C.A.).

[43] [1967] A.C. 472 (H.L.).

[44] Similarly, if a company wishing to sell property to an outsider conveys that property to a wholly owned subsidiary of the vendor company, leaving the purchase price unpaid, and then sells the shares of the subsidiary company to the outsider, paragraph (a) applies. See *Curzon Offices Ltd.* v. *I.R.C.* [1944] 1 All E.R. 606 and *cf. Times Newspapers Ltd.* v. *I.R.C.* [1973] Ch. 155.

33-13   The provisions of the Finance Act 1938, corresponding to paragraph (b), above, were considered in *Littlewoods Mail Order Stores Ltd.* v. *I.R.C.,*[45] where the facts which are relevant to the present discussion were as follows:

> In 1947, L had granted a 99-year lease of premises to A Ltd. (Littlewoods) at a rent of £23,444 per annum. The lease had about 80 years to run. An ingenious scheme was devised by which the subsidiary of A Ltd. would acquire the freehold of the premises by payment of a rent of £42,450 per annum over a period of about 22 years. On six successive days various instruments were executed of which the first two were as follows:
>
> (i) December 8: L granted to A Ltd. a lease for 22 years and 10 days at £6 per annum. This operated as a surrender of the existing 99-year lease.
> (ii) December 9: A Ltd. assigned the new lease to B Ltd., its wholly owned subsidiary.

It was held that the transaction in (i), namely, the grant of the new lease by L, was a " conveyance " and that the instrument in (ii) was executed in connection with an arrangement under which the beneficial interest in the property (*i.e.* the new leasehold term) was " previously conveyed . . . directly or indirectly " by, a non-associated company. The exemption from duty on conveyances between parent and subsidiary did not, therefore, apply.

Consideration provided by outsiders

33-14   If a company conveys property to its subsidiary and the purchase price is to be provided by an outsider, clearly no relief is available because the requirement in (a) above is not satisfied. What, however, is the position if the outsider merely loans the purchase price or guarantees its payment? Can such a person be said to have " provided " the consideration " directly or indirectly "?

> In *Curzon Offices* v. *I.R.C.,*[46] A Ltd. transferred property to B Ltd., its wholly owned subsidiary, under an arrangement by which (i) an outsider, X Ltd., not associated with A Ltd. or B Ltd., was to guarantee a bank advance to enable B Ltd. to pay part of the purchase price, and (ii) part of the purchase price was to be left on mortgage. X Ltd., was to acquire the whole of the issued share capital of B Ltd. on the day after the transfer.

The relief from stamp duty was refused to B Ltd. because X Ltd. had (so it was held) provided part of the consideration. It was not, however, decided in this case that the guarantee of the advance by X Ltd. would of itself constitute a provision of consideration; nor was it suggested that the bank advance constituted such a provision. Part of the purchase price remained on mortgage and if A Ltd. called upon B Ltd. to pay off the mortgage, then either (a) X Ltd. would provide it directly out of its own resources, *i.e.* under its guarantee; or (b) X Ltd. would provide the money out of the resources of B Ltd., its wholly owned subsidiary, thereby diminishing the value of X Ltd.'s own shares in B Ltd. and indirectly providing part of the consideration.

---

[45] [1963] A.C. 135 (H.L.). In *Escoigne Properties Ltd.* v. *I.R.C.* [1958] A.C. 549, the House of Lords held unanimously that paragraph (b) applied on the facts stated *ante*, § 33-10.
[46] [1944] 1 All E.R. 163; 606 (C.A.); 22 A.T.C. 406.

CHAPTER 34

MISCELLANEOUS COMMERCIAL DOCUMENTS

1. POLICIES OF INSURANCE

34-01 THE stamp duty on policies of insurance has been greatly simplified by section 30 of the Finance Act 1959, as amended by section 32 of the Finance Act 1970. Now, duty is leviable under a single charge:

(a) *Policies of life insurance*

34-02 The expression " policy of life insurance " is defined in the Stamp Act 1891 as

> " a policy of insurance upon any life or lives or upon any event or contingency relating to or depending upon any life or lives except a policy of insurance . . . for any payment agreed to be made upon the death of any person only from accident or violence or otherwise than from a natural cause." [1]

Thus the ordinary endowment policy is included, *i.e.* the policy which provides for payment of the sum assured on survival to a certain age or date; but the accident policy is excluded. In some cases, an indorsement on a policy may operate as a separate policy, on a principle already discussed. [2] A policy which is taken out under the Married Women's Property Act 1882, s. 11, is within the section and attracts no further duty by reason of the endorsement that it is for the benefit of wife or children; but if it contains a declaration of trust, it will attract additional duty as a declaration of trust.

34-03 *Rates of duty.* Duty is levied under the head of charge " Policy of Life Insurance " in the Stamp Act 1891. [3] The duty is an *ad valorem* duty reckoned on the amount of the " amount insured." Bonuses are not taken into account in calculating the " amount insured " unless there is a guaranteed minimum. [4] The rates of duty on life policies are as follows:

Where the amount insured exceeds £50 but does not exceed £1,000	5p for every £100 or part of £100 of the amount insured.
Where the amount insured exceeds £1,000 . .	50p for every £1,000 or part of £1,000 of the amount insured.

These rates are subject to an exception made by section 47 of the Finance Act 1966, which levies a maximum duty of 5p [5] on a policy of life assurance if the period of cover does not exceed two years and the policy contains no provision whereby it might become available for a period exceeding two years. The purpose of this exception is to enable insurance companies to

---

[1] . S.A. 1891, s. 98 (1), as amended.
[2] See *ante*, § 27-14.
[3] A new head of charge was substituted by F.A. 1970, s. 33 and Sched. 7, para. 17.
[4] See the Contingency Principle, *ante*, § 27-18.
[5] F.A. 1970, s. 33 and Sched. 7, para. 17 (2).

issue short-term life policies (as distinct from accident policies) to travellers without any *ad valorem* stamp duty.

A policy of life insurance which is made solely in connection with the re-insurance of a risk to which a policy duly stamped under the heading " policy of life insurance " relates is chargeable with duty under that heading only if it is under seal, with a maximum charge of 50p.[6]

(b) *Policies of insurance, other than life assurance*

34-04   This head of charge has now been abolished.[7]

2. LETTERS OR POWERS OF ATTORNEY, ETC.

34-05   The stamp duty under head " Letter or Power of Attorney, and Commission, Mandate, or other instrument in the nature thereof " is 50p, except where the head of charge provides for a smaller duty as, for example, in the following cases:

(a) *An instrument providing for the receipt of the dividends or interest of any stock.* The duty is 5p if made for the receipt of one payment only; otherwise 25p. But if the instrument goes further than to provide for the receipt of money as, for example, where it authorises the attorney to sue or to appoint another attorney, the duty is 50p.

(b) *An instrument providing for the receipt of any money (or any bill or note for money) not exceeding £20 or any periodical payments not exceeding the annual sum of £10.* The duty is 25p.

A power of attorney is not charged with duty more than once by reason only that more than one person is named as donor or donee of the powers conferred thereby or that the powers relate to more than one matter.[8]

Exemptions

34-06   There are a number of exemptions from duty under this head, of which two require some mention:

(a) An order, request, or direction under hand only from the proprietor of any stock to any company (or to any officer of any company or to any banker) to pay the dividends or interest arising from the stock to any person therein named.[9]

(b) A special proxy for one meeting only, including its adjournment. It seems that the exemption applies even if the date of the meeting is not stated in the proxy at time of signing. However a proxy related not only to adjournments but also to any new meeting convened to consider the same or certain stated matters is not within this exception.[10]

A general proxy and a special proxy for more than one meeting are not exempt and are therefore liable to a 50p duty.

---

[6] F.A. 1970, Sched. 7, para. 17 (3).   [7] *Ibid.* Sched. 7, para. 1 (2) (*b*).

[8] F.A. 1927, s. 56.

[9] But such a mandate may be dutiable as, *e.g.* an assignment: *Re Kent and Sussex Sawmills Ltd.* [1947] Ch. 177.

[10] See *Marx* v. *Estates and General Investments Ltd.* [1976] 1 W.L.R. 380; [1975] S.T.C. 671.

PART 4

VALUE ADDED TAX

Chapter 35

VALUE ADDED TAX

1. Introduction

35-01   VAT came into operation on April 1, 1973, on which date both selective employment tax and purchase tax ceased to have effect. The other indirect taxes (the excise duties on drink, tobacco, matches, lighters and hydrocarbon oils) remain, with VAT being charged in addition thereto.[1] Another tax, known as car tax, which is assessable on the wholesale value of cars manufactured or registered in the United Kingdom, also came into operation on April 1, 1973. This chapter is solely concerned with the principles of VAT.

The main provisions relating to VAT are set out in the Finance Act 1972 as amended by section 14 and Schedule 6 to the Finance Act 1977, with effect from January 1, 1978,[2] and in orders and regulations made thereunder. The law stated in this chapter is that applying from January 1, 1978, and material differences between the old and new provisions are noted in the text and footnotes thereto.[3] The tax is under the care and management of the Commissioners of Customs and Excise.[4] Tax is charged at three rates depending on the classification of the goods or services supplied *viz.* the zero rate, the standard rate of 8 per cent. and the higher rate of 12½ per cent. The Treasury may, by order, increase or decrease the two positive *rates* of tax by a percentage not exceeding 25 per cent.[5] The tax is deemed to form part of the consideration for the supply, *i.e.* the standard rate is two-twenty-sevenths and the higher rate is one-ninth of the consideration. Thus a taxable person is given no right to charge an amount of VAT on any supply but must ensure that the consideration to which he is contractually entitled has been computed so as to take account of the liability.[6]

35-02   VAT is a tax on the final consumption of goods or services which is collected by instalments. The tax is charged on the " value added " by a taxable person at each stage in the process of production. In practical terms the " value added " is the profit (including wages) of the taxable person computed on an invoice basis. Thus, in effect, the instalment of tax due at each stage is the amount chargeable on the difference between the cost of

---

[1] See F.A. 1973, s. 1 and F.A. 1974, s. 1. As from September 6, 1976 an excise duty on cider was also introduced: F.A. 1976, s. 2.

[2] References to statutory provisions in this chapter are references to the Finance Act 1972 as amended by section 14 and Schedule 6 to the Finance Act 1977, except where otherwise stated.

[3] For a statement of the law unamended by the Finance Act 1977 reference should be made to the 10th edition of this book, Chap. 35. All previous orders and regulations remain in force subject, of course, to future amendment: F.A. 1977, Sched. 6, para. 32.

[4] In this chapter simply referred to as the Commissioners.

[5] s. 9 (1), (3) and (4) and F. (No. 2) A. 1975, ss. 17 and 20.

[6] s. 10 (2). *Contractual* rights are automatically adjusted on a change in the rate or upon the introduction or abolition of the tax, unless the contract otherwise provides (see s. 42). This provision would not, however, affect contracts governed by foreign law or, *e.g.* the rights of a trustee to remuneration.

acquisition and the proceeds of sale. Whenever a taxable person supplies goods or services to another taxable person he charges him the basic cost of the goods or services plus the amount of VAT thereon, and must give him a tax invoice showing the amount of these items. A taxable person will thus have taxable " inputs " (the supplies to him) and taxable " outputs " (the supplies by him), and he must account to the Commissioners for the difference between his " input tax " and his " output tax " (or, if the former exceeds the latter, he can reclaim the excess). The tax is not borne by the taxable person: he simply passes the burden on by adding the amount of the tax to his bill so as to form part of the contractual consideration for his supply. The ultimate non-business consumer bears the tax since he cannot deduct it as an " input. " A simple example, with tax at the standard rate, may illustrate the principle:

> B is a cabinet maker who, in a particular accounting period, purchases timber from A at a basic price of £1,250 and fittings from C at a basic price of £250. In the same period B sells finished cabinets to D, a retailer, at a basic price of £6,250. The position as regards B would then be as follows:

	£ BASIC		£ VAT
Payments (Input):			
Timber	1,250	+	100
Fittings	250	+	20
	1,500	+	120
Sales (Output)	6,250	+	500

> B would then account to the Commissioners for £380.

In theory the £380 represents the tax on B's " added value " (his profit and the wages paid). However, it will be seen that the timber and fittings do not have to be used in construction of the particular cabinets sold in the particular period. There is a simple balancing of output invoices for the period against input invoices for the period. Plainly there may be many other taxable inputs for the period the tax on which may be deducted, for example accountancy and legal services, telephone bills, stationery and equipment purchased. There is a simple balancing of invoices for the period. This is called the " tax from tax " system (that is the deduction of " input tax " from " output tax ").

This system applies to taxable persons throughout the process of production. On the final sale to a non-business consumer the VAT is added to the basic price but a tax invoice is not given. Thus, in the above example, D (the retailer) will have received an invoice of £6,250 (basic) plus £500 (VAT). In the same period he may have sold goods (whether the cabinets or not) for a basic price of £15,000 to which he would have added VAT of £1,200. From that £1,200 he may deduct all his taxable inputs (including the £500) and only has to account to the Commissioners for the difference. The position is the same, of course, for A and C.

It will be seen from this process that the final consumer of a cabinet has effectively borne a tax of 8 per cent. on its retail price although that tax has been collected at various stages (and in various accounting periods) from the taxable persons concerned in its production and sale.

Exemption

35-03   There are two kinds of exemption from the tax:

(1) exemption for particular kinds of goods or services supplied,[7] and

(2) exemption for a person with a taxable turn-over of less than £10,000 who is not required to register as a taxable person.[8]

However, exemption is something of a misnomer. An exempt person must absorb the VAT on the goods and services paid for by him for the purposes of his business. There is no deduction of input tax against output tax. Consequently, exemption has a hidden tax effect and is most disadvantageous where the person supplies goods or services to a taxable person since the hidden tax cannot be passed on.

Zero Rating

35-04   If the supply of goods or services is zero rated the supply by a taxable person (that is his output) is not chargeable to tax at 8 per cent. or 12½ per cent. but at a zero rate.[9] Consequently such a person is able to reclaim all the tax that he has suffered on his inputs. One of the main advantages of VAT is that exports are zero rated and are therefore subjected to no tax whatsoever. All the elements of tax suffered by an exporter can be identified under the invoice system and therefore all the tax directly or indirectly suffered in the production of exports can be reclaimed.

2. THE SCOPE OF THE CHARGE

There are two heads of charge:

A. Taxable Supply

35-05   *Tax is chargeable on the taxable supply of goods or services in the United Kingdom by a taxable person in the course or furtherance of any business carried on by him and shall be payable by him.*[10]

Taxable supply means any supply of goods or services in the United Kingdom other than an exempt supply.[11] Thus the term simply excludes the exemptions set out in Schedule 5 and these are considered later.[12] Thus for the moment we consider the meaning of the following terms:

(1) *Goods or services,*

(2) *Supply,*

(3) *In the United Kingdom,*

(4) *In the course or furtherance of a business,* and

(5) *A taxable person.*

---

[7] s. 13 and Sched. 5, *post*, §§ 35-18 *et seq.*

[8] s. 4 and Sched. 1, *post*, §§ 35-15 *et seq.* The exemption limit was raised from £7,500 to £10,000 with effect from April 12, 1978, by F.A. 1978, s. 11.

[9] s. 12 and Sched. 4, *post*, §§ 35-27 *et seq.*

[10] s. 2 (as amended by F.A. 1977, Sched. 6, para. 1).

[11] s. 2 (2) (as inserted by F.A. 1977, Sched. 6, para. 1).

[12] *Post*, §§ 35-18 *et seq.*

(1) *Goods or services*

35-06   There is no definition of goods in the Act although certain matters are to be treated as a supply of goods. Tax applies to the supply of both new and secondhand goods. Presumably the term " goods " covers all tangible movables but not choses in action.[13] A transfer of the whole property in goods is a supply of goods but a transfer of an undivided share or of possession (*i.e.* any bailment, hiring or letting) is a supply of services [14] (unless that transfer of possession is under an agreement for the sale of goods or an agreement which contemplates that the whole property in the goods will pass in the future, *e.g.* a hire-purchase transaction).[15] The following are deemed to be a supply of goods:

(a) The supply of any form of power, heat, refrigeration or ventilation,[16] and

(b) The granting, assignment or surrender of a major interest in land. A major interest in land means the fee simple or a tenancy for a term certain exceeding 21 years.[17]

The Act further provides that a person applying a treatment or process to another person's goods is treated as supplying goods and not services.[18] This would apply, for example, to a tailor but not to a cleaner. Subject to this, section 6 (2) (*b*) [19] provides that:

" anything which is not a supply of goods but is done for a consideration (including, if so done, the granting, assignment or surrender of any right) is a supply of services. "

Thus although leases for less than 21 years and choses in action are not treated as goods, any dealing with them would appear to be a supply of services.[20] Section 6 (2) (*b*) is of considerable importance in determining the description of any particular supply. In any contractual situation a person simply receives a bundle of rights under the contract. If, on analysing those rights, they are referable to the supply of particular goods or services those goods or services will constitute the supply.[21] Otherwise the supply will constitute the service of granting a right *simpliciter.* Plainly work done for a fee is a supply of services but a service gratuitously given is not subject to the charge. If both goods and services are supplied in return for a subscription (*i.e.* the facilities or advantages of membership within section 45 (2) (*a*) [22] includes both) the supply must be apportioned. Consequently a

---

[13] *Cf.* Sale of Goods Act 1893, s. 62 (1).

[14] Sched. 2, para. 1 (1) (as inserted by F.A. 1977, Sched. 6, para. 14).

[15] Sched. 2, para. 1 (2) (as inserted by F.A. 1977, Sched. 6, para. 14).

[16] Sched. 2, para. 3 (as inserted by F.A. 1977, Sched. 6, para. 14). This is the ground for claiming that VAT is a tax on " the air we breathe."

[17] s. 46 (1) (as inserted by F.A. 1977, Sched. 6, para. 19 (*a*)). This provision and the last are based on the EEC directives and are strange notions within the concept of English law. A major interest in land is brought within the scope of the charge so that its grant, after the construction of a building, may be zero rated: *post,* § 35-31.

[18] Sched. 2, para. 2 (as inserted by F.A. 1977, Sched. 6, para. 14). The tax is only chargeable on the " service charge ": *post,* § 35-50.

[19] As inserted by F.A. 1977, Sched. 6, para. 1.

[20] They are, however, exempt: Sched. 5, groups 1 and 5: *post,* §§ 35-19, 35-23.

[21] See *British Railway Board* v. *Customs and Excise Commissioners* [1977] 1 W.L.R. 588, a case concerning the fixed part of a " two part tariff " which, the Court of Appeal held, constituted part of the consideration paid for transport which is zero rated by virtue of Sched. 4, Group 10, item 4: see *post,* § 35-33; *cf. Customs and Excise Commissioners* v. *Scott* [1978] S.T.C. 191.   [22] *Post,* § 35-14.

part of the supply may fall to be zero rated as constituting, for example, a supply of books whilst the remainder will be taxable at the standard rate, being a supply of services not zero rated.[23] The Treasury has power to make orders treating any transaction as a supply of goods, or of services or of neither. This power has been used so that exchanges for reconditioned goods shall be treated as a supply of services with the effect that tax is only charged on the payment for the exchange and not the full value of the reconditioned article.[24] Likewise certain supplies have been brought entirely outside the scope of the tax by making them supplies of neither goods nor services.[25] They are:

(a) the supply by finance houses or insurance companies (after repossession under finance agreements, etc.) of used cars, motor cycles and caravans and works of art,

(b) certain transactions in trading stamps, and

(c) transfer of a separate business as a going concern from one taxable person to another or from a non-taxable person to any other person.

The distinction between goods and services may be important since an importation or a gift of goods (but not of services) may be chargeable and the factors determining the time of supply are different.[26]

(2) Supply

35-07   Supply includes all forms of supply, *e.g.* sale, hire-purchase, exchange or part-exchange but, normally, nothing is a " supply " unless it is done for a consideration.[27] One exception to this rule is where goods, but not services, forming part of the assets of a business are transferred unless the transaction is a gift made in the course or furtherance of the business and the cost of the goods was less than £10 (*e.g.* a retirement present to an employee) or a gift of a sample to a customer or potential customer.[28] The kind of " free gifts " given on the purchase of another item, for example free glasses given with the purchase of petrol, are not within the scope of these words. The petrol supplied plus the glass would both be treated as supplied for the price payable for the petrol.

35-08   VAT is payable on the service charges made under simple hiring arrangements. Prior to April 1, 1975, VAT was charged at a reduced rate on television rentals where the television had been supplied on hire prior to April 1, 1973.[29] The relief was given so as to offset the purchase tax originally suffered. This relief applied to no other goods and has now ceased altogether so that such rentals are now chargeable at the higher rate unless they are paid under contracts entered into prior to April 16, 1975, when they are taxed at the standard rate.[30]

---

[23] See *Customs and Excise Commissioners* v. *The Automobile Association* [1974] 1 W.L.R. 1447.
[24] VAT (Special Provisions) Order 1977, art. 13.
[25] (a) *Ibid.* arts. 10 and 11; (b) Sched. 3, para. 6, and VAT (Treatment of Transactions) (No. 1) Order 1973; and (c) VAT (Special Provisions) Order 1977, art. 12.
[26] *Post*, § 35-49.
[27] Sched. 6, para. 2 (as inserted by F.A. 1977, Sched. 6, para. 1).
[28] Sched. 2, para. 5 (1) and (2) (as inserted by F.A. 1977, Sched. 6, para. 1).
[29] s. 48.   [30] See *post*, § 35-41.

35-09   *Secondhand goods.* VAT applies to the supply of secondhand goods but there are provisions in section 14 whereby the Treasury has power to reduce the amount chargeable. An ordinary person selling or trading in his own car would not add on VAT since he is not making a supply in the course or furtherance of a business. However if the normal principles were not modified a dealer would have to add on VAT to the sale price. The Treasury has made orders restricting the amount chargeable to the dealer's margin and not the sale price with respect to the secondhand car trade, boats and outboard motors, and the markets in works of art and antiques.[31] There are similar provisions as regards the supply of secondhand caravans and motor cycles.

35-10   A taxable person is deemed to have supplied all goods which were acquired or produced by him in the course or furtherance of his business[32] if:

  (a) the goods are put to any private use or use other than for the purposes of the business or he appropriates them for his own personal use or that of any other person,[33] or
  (b) they are sold by a judgment creditor or mortgagee exercising a power of sale,[34] or
  (c) he ceases to be a taxable person, unless the business is transferred as a going concern to, or is carried on by, a taxable person.[35]

Thus there is a charge to VAT under this latter provision on all the goods of a business when that business discontinues unless it is carried on by another taxable person. In the latter case, although prima facie within the charge of the tax, the transaction is specially excluded from its scope.[36]

35-10A   *The reverse charge.*[37] Where a taxable person *receives*[38] a supply of certain services from a person who belongs[39] outside the United Kingdom he is treated as both receiving and making that supply in the course or furtherance of his business. Thus he may claim credit for the amount of input tax equal to the tax that would have been chargeable on the supply had it been made in the United Kingdom but must also account for the same amount as output tax as if he had made the supply himself. Where the taxable person makes only taxable supplies the two items will cancel each other out but where he is partially exempt[40] a proportion of the deemed input tax will be irrecoverable. In effect, therefore, these provisions create a

---

[31] VAT (Cars) Order 1977 and VAT (Special Provisions) Order 1977, arts. 4, 5 and 7.
[32] He is charged as if the goods had been disposed of at their market value: s. 10 (3).
[33] Sched. 2, para. 5 (3) and (4) (as inserted by F.A. 1977, Sched. 6, para. 14).
[34] Sched. 2, para. 6 (as inserted by F.A. 1977, Sched. 6, para. 14).
[35] Sched. 2, para. 7 (as inserted by F.A. 1977, Sched. 6, para. 14) and the other exceptions therein mentioned; see VAT (Special Provisions) Order 1977, art. 12, *ante*, § 35-06.
[36] s. 45 (5) and (6) (as inserted by F.A. 1977, Sched. 6, para. 13) brings it prima facie within the charge but VAT (Special Provisions) Order 1977, art. 12, specifically excludes it.
[37] s. 8B and Sched. 3A (as inserted by F.A. 1977, Sched. 6, paras. 3 and 14 with effect from January 1, 1978).
[38] Where he has business establishments both within and outside the United Kingdom the supply is deemed to be received at the establishment where the supply is most directly used.
[39] See *post*, § 35-12.
[40] See *post*, § 35-57.

partial tax on the importation of services. The services to which they apply are set out in Schedule 2A to the Act and, in brief, are as follows:

    (a) Transfers and assignments of copyright, patents, licences, trademarks and similar rights;

    (b) Advertising services;

    (c) Services of consultants, engineers, lawyers, accountants, etc. (but excluding any services relating to land);

    (d) Refraining from pursuing any business activities;

    (e) Banking, financial and insurance services;

    (f) The supply of staff;

    (g) Procuring any of the above.

35-11   *Self-Supply.* An exempt person suffers a hidden tax on goods and services supplied to him for the purposes of his business. The same applies to a partially exempt person as regards that part of his business. To reduce this effect he might decide to produce such goods or services himself. To prevent this form of unfair competition the Treasury is given power to treat such self-supplies as taxable on their open market value.[41] Such orders have been made in respect of stationery and motor cars, etc.[42]

(3) *In the United Kingdom*

35-12   Subject to the reverse charge mentioned above [43] if the goods or services are not supplied in the United Kingdom there is no charge to VAT and sections 8 (goods) and 8A (services) of the Act set out principles for determining the place of supply. Goods are treated as supplied in the United Kingdom if they are in the United Kingdom, even if their supply involves their removal from the United Kingdom.[44] The provisions regarding services are more complicated. Services are generally deemed to be supplied in the country where the supplier *belongs* and the following rules apply in determining where a person belongs [45]:

    (a) the country where he has a business establishment [46] provided he has no such establishment elsewhere; or

    (b) the country which is his usual place of residence [47] if he has no business establishment anywhere; or

    (c) where he has business establishments in more than one country the country in which is the establishment with which the service is most directly concerned.

However where the service relates to land it is deemed to be supplied in the country where the land is.[48] Thus the travel agent, barrister, solicitor or accountant, with his sole business establishment in the United Kingdom, would be prima facie liable to VAT on services rendered to overseas clients.

---

[41] s. 6 (5) (as restated by F.A. 1977, Sched. 6, para. 1).

[42] See VAT (Cars) Order 1977 and VAT (Special Provisions) Order 1977, art. 14.

[43] See *ante*, § 35-10A.   [44] s. 8 (2) and (3).

[45] s. 8A (3) (as inserted by F.A. 1977, Sched. 6, para. 3).

[46] A branch or agency constitutes a business establishment: s. 8A (4) (*a*).

[47] " Usual place of residence " in the case of a body corporate means where it is legally constituted.

[48] This rule is to be implemented by Treasury Order under s. 8A (5) and see VAT (Consolidation) Order 1978 substituting Sched. 4, Group 9, item 1, *post* § 35-32.

Where he has such an establishment in the United Kingdom but also another outside he must determine the establishment with which the service is most directly concerned and if this is the United Kingdom the supply is within the prima facie charge to tax. Such services however will normally be zero rated.[49] Since the Isle of Man has also adopted VAT it can, in effect, be regarded as part of the United Kingdom for the purposes of the tax.[50]

(4) *In the course or furtherance of a business*

35-13   Section 45 (1) provides that the term " business " includes any trade, profession or vocation. This follows the wording of Schedule D, Cases I and II, but the provision would not appear to have the extended meaning of " adventure or concern in the nature of trade." [51] Thus the isolated transaction that may be taxable under Case I will not bring the taxpayer within the scope of VAT.[52] However this definition is *inclusive* and is therefore not restricted to traders, etc. that are subject to income tax. Thus an investment business such as the purchase, development and letting of a building would be a business for the purposes of VAT.[53] Further, it is not necessary that an activity should be carried on for the purpose of making a profit so as to constitute a business.[54] Section 45 (4) provides that where a person accepts any office in the course or furtherance of a trade or profession, any services supplied by him as holder of the office shall be treated as supplied in the course or furtherance of a business carried on by him.[55] The provision would seem to cover the case of an accountant who was an auditor and a solicitor who was a company registrar.[56] It would not, however, apply in the case of a practising solicitor or any other taxable person who took up a part time *employment*. Anyone remunerated wholly by salary and taxable under Schedule E is not, of course, subject to VAT.

35-14   Certain other matters are deemed to be the carrying on of a business under section 45 (2):

(a) The provision by a club, association or organisation (for a subscription or other consideration) of the facilities or advantages available to its members. Such associations, for example sports clubs, are not subject to income tax or corporation tax by virtue of the mutuality principle [57] but they will be subject to VAT on subscriptions received and goods sold.[58] There is an exception for bodies having objects in the public domain being of a political, religious, philanthropic, philosophical or patriotic nature provided

---

[49] *Post*, § 35-32.
[50] See VAT (United Kingdom and Isle of Man) (Consolidation) Order 1978.
[51] *Cf.* I.C.T.A. 1970, s. 526 (5).   [52] See *ante*, §§ 2-05 *et seq.*
[53] The definition does not, however, extend to a person building a house for his own occupation: see *R. A. Archer* [1974] V.A.T.T.R. 1, although such persons are now entitled to a refund of tax on the goods used in such construction: F.A. 1975, s. 3.
[54] *Customs and Excise Commissioners* v. *Morrison's Academy* [1978] S.T.C. 1.
[55] Prior to January 1, 1978, the holders of public offices (*e.g.* a commissioner for oaths) were excluded from the application of these words.
[56] See *I.R.C.* v. *Brander and Cruickshank* [1971] 1 W.L.R. 212; 46 T.C. 574. *Ante*, § 3-03.
[57] *Ante*, §§ 2-16 *et seq.*
[58] Subject to the £10,000 registration limit, *post*, § 35-15. This provision has been held to apply to the Club Cricket Conference in providing the facilities of a fixture bureau and an umpires' panel (see [1973] V.A.T.T.R. 53); and see *Royal Highland and Agricultural Society of Scotland* [1976] V.A.T.T.R. 38.

the subscriptions paid to them obtain no facility or advantage other than the right to participate in the management of the body or receive reports on its activities. Thus a distinction must be drawn between subscriptions which are, in reality, donations or contributions towards the furtherance of the aims of an association or charity (which would not be taxable) and subscriptions paid for securing something substantial for the subscriber in return (which would be taxable). Subscriptions to, and the ordinary activities of, trade unions and professional associations are exempt [59] but the taxable supplies of trade union clubs are subject to the tax.

    (b) The admission, for a consideration, of persons to any premises. This applies to theatres, cinemas, funfairs, casinos and the like.

These provisions would apply to fund-raising businesses or activities run by charities (as opposed to transactions carried out in furtherance of the charitable purpose).[60]

In the course or furtherance of a business.[61] The words " or furtherance " have been added with effect from January 1, 1978. This is to make it clear that any purchases or sales subsidiary to the main purpose of the business fall within the scope of the tax. Thus a professional person, for example, disposing of (or appropriating to personal use on retirement) some of his office furniture is making a supply which attracts tax albeit that he is not in business to sell furniture. Also, as from January 1, 1978, it has been provided that the disposal of the whole of the business or anything done in connection with its termination is deemed to be in the course or furtherance of the business.[62]

(5) *Taxable persons*

35-15   A person who makes, or who intends to make, taxable supplies is a taxable person while he is or is required to be registered under Schedule 1 to the Act.[63] A person is liable to be registered:

    (i) After the end of any quarter, if the value of his taxable supplies in the period of one, two, three or four quarters then ending has exceeded the following amounts:

        (a) First quarter   £3,500
        (b) Second quarter   £6,000
        (c) Third quarter   £8,500
        (d) Fourth quarter   £10,000

---

[59] Sched. 5, Group 9, as inserted by VAT (Consolidation) Order 1978: see § 35-26A. Prior to January 1, 1978, such professional associations had a right to elect to be treated as taxable or exempt. Now such bodies, if falling within the terms of the order, will be exempt and therefore unable to recover the tax on their inputs.

[60] However on the introduction of the tax the Chancellor of the Exchequer stated that favourable consideration would be given to the registration of local branches of charities so that they could come within the exemption limits.

[61] s. 2 (1) (as inserted by F.A. 1977, Sched. 6, para. 1) and see *ante*, § 35-10.

[62] s. 45 (5) and (6) (as inserted by F.A. 1977, Sched. 6, para. 13) and see the excluding provisions where the business is sold (rather than simply discontinued) in VAT (Special Provisions) Order 1977, art. 12, *ante*, §§ 35-06 and 35-10.

[63] s. 2 (2) (as restated by F.A. 1977, Sched. 6, para. 1). The figures stated are those inserted by F.A. 1978, s. 11 (1), with effect from April 12, 1978.

If, however, his taxable supplies exceed the amount applicable for a period of less than a year he will not be liable to be registered if the Commissioners are satisfied that his taxable supplies for the whole year will not exceed £10,000. [64]

(ii) At any time if there are reasonable grounds for believing that his taxable supplies in the period of one year beginning at that or any later time will exceed £10,000. [65]

Registration applies to all the business activities carried on by the particular person: he is not entitled to separate registration in respect of separate businesses. [66] Further it appears that he is not entitled to separate registration in respect of a business carried on by him as trustee from that carried on by him personally. [67] This is because the charge to tax under section 2 of the Act is laid on a taxable person and it therefore encompasses all taxable supplies made by him in whatever capacity, and regardless of the fact that the supplies made in respect of any one business carried on by him may amount to less than £10,000 per annum. Since a taxable person makes only one return this provision has the consequence that he may deduct the inputs of one business from the outputs of another.

The same provisions, however, do not apply for de-registration. A person only ceases to be liable to be registered:

(i) After the end of any quarter

    (a) if he has been registered for the whole of the two years then ending and the value of his taxable supplies in each year has been £8,500 or less, or

    (b) the value of his taxable supplies in each of the quarters comprised in those years has been £2,500 or less,

(ii) at any time, if the Commissioners are satisfied that the value of his taxable supplies in the period of one year then beginning will be £8,500 or less, [68] and

(iii) on his giving notice within 10 days of the date that he ceases to make taxable supplies. [69]

The Commissioners may cancel the registration of any person who has ceased to be liable to be registered. [70]

35-16   A person who makes or intends to make taxable supplies, but who is not liable to be registered, may if he so requests, and the Commissioners think fit, be treated as being so liable. [71] Since exemption has the hidden tax effect already noted such a person might wish to be registered so as to obtain relief for his inputs. A person who sells direct to the public would usually not desire to do this, but persons selling goods or providing services to a taxable

[64] Sched. 1, para. 1 (*a*).
[65] Sched. 1, para. 1 (*b*).
[66] See *Customs and Excise Commissioners* v. *Glassborow* [1975] Q.B. 465 and *post*, § 35-64.
[67] See *Customs and Excise Commissioners* v. *British Railways Board* [1976] 1 W.L.R. 1036; [1976] S.T.C. 359.
[68] Sched. 1, para. 2.
[69] Sched. 1, para. 8.
[70] F.A. 1978, s. 11 (3), inserting a new Sched. 1, para. 10A.
[71] Sched. 1, para. 11. An appeal lies from the Commissioners' decision: F.A. 1978, s. 11 (4).

person would be in a better position if they registered. It is difficult to envisage a wholesaler with taxable supplies of under £10,000. However, as the legislation stands, a barrister would appear to be in this position. A barrister supplies services to the solicitor instructing him and not the lay client. If he is a taxable person he may deduct the tax on his inputs, for example his telephone bills and his purchases of stationery and office furniture, from the output tax added to his fees. The latter tax will then be an input which the solicitor can deduct from the tax chargeable on the final total fee to the client. If the barrister is not a taxable person he will have to absorb his inputs or charge a higher fee whilst the solicitor will have to pay VAT on the total of his own and the barrister's services with no corresponding deductible input.[72]

B. Importation

35-17 *Tax on the importation of goods shall be charged and payable as if it were a duty of customs* [73]

This applies to the importation of goods by any persons (whether taxable or not). At the time that goods are removed from customs bond both import duty and VAT become payable. The value of the goods on which VAT is payable is determined as follows:

(1) If the goods are imported at a price in money payable as on a transfer of the property and for no other consideration, the value is an amount equal to the price plus import duties payable and the cost of freight and insurance to the place of importation.[74]

(2) Where (1) above does not apply the value is the open market value of the goods as determined in accordance with the appropriate Community legislation plus (so far as not already included) import duties and the cost of freight and insurance.[75]

The open market value of the goods is their value on the date when they come out of customs bond into the United Kingdom. Any sale of the goods whilst they remain in bond will not attract VAT. The Treasury have power to grant relief in whole or in part from VAT on the importation of goods so as to give effect to international agreements.[76] The Commissioners have power to make provision for the remitting or repaying of VAT in whole or in part on goods which have previously been exported [77] or on goods that are to be re-exported.[78]

---

[72] Costs incurred by a solicitor, in providing his services to the client, although charged as disbursements, form part of his inputs and therefore, when charged to the client attract tax at the standard rate as being in respect of legal services albeit that the costs themselves may have been exempt or zero rated: *Rowe and Maw* v. *Customs and Excise Commissioners* [1975] S.T.C. 340.

[73] s. 2 (4) (as restated by F.A. 1977, Sched. 6, para. 1).

[74] s. 11 (2) (as inserted by F.A. 1977, Sched. 6, para. 4).

[75] s. 11 (3) (as inserted by *ibid.*). Both these provisions differ from the previous terms of s. 11 in the fact that they provide machinery for determining value on the eventual abolition of customs duties in the Community.

[76] s. 16 (1). See VAT (Imported Goods) Relief (No. 1) Order 1973.

[77] s. 16 (2). See VAT (General) Regulations 1977, regs. 39, 40 and 41. Broadly the provisions cover reimportation of goods by non-taxable persons, the importation of cars that had suffered purchase tax or VAT, or works of art that had been exported prior to April 1, 1973, or had been exported by a non-taxable person after that date.

[78] s. 16 (3).

The Commissioners have also made regulations postponing the payment of the tax on importation where goods are imported by a taxable person.[79] Since the amount of the tax will be an input in the taxable person's computation he is allowed to take the goods without immediately paying the tax, and must account for the tax at the end of his accounting period.

3. EXEMPTIONS

35-18 Those matters that are not to be treated as a taxable supply are set out in Schedule 5 to the Act and the Treasury has power to vary that Schedule by order.[80] The exemptions are as follows:

35-19 (1) *Land.* This group consists of the grant, assignment or surrender of any interest in or right over land or of any licence to occupy land.[81] Thus sales of land and rents will not attract VAT. The exemption does not apply to the provision of hotel or holiday accommodation, facilities for camping in tents or caravans, parking facilities, game and fishing rights, rights to fell timber, storage and mooring facilities for ships and aircraft and the provision of space to an exhibitor at an exhibition. Certain supplies of land fall to be zero rated.[82]

35-20 (2) *Insurance.* This group consists of the provision of any kind of insurance or re-insurance and insurance brokerage.[83]

35-21 (3) *Postal Services.* This group consists of the conveyance of postal packets (other than telegrams) and services connected therewith. The telephone service is not exempt.

35-22 (4) *Betting, Gaming and Lotteries.* This group consists of the placing of bets, the playing of games of chance and the granting of a right to take part in a lottery. These activities are presently subject to the betting and gaming duties. There is no exemption, however, in respect of admission fees, fees paid to take part in a game, club subscriptions or sums paid for the use of a gaming machine. If such fees or subscriptions are paid to a gaming club it will only be partially exempt.[84] Amusements and facilities provided at such places as fairgrounds are not exempt.[85]

35-23 (5) *Finance.* This group consists of any dealings with money,[86] securities for money, foreign exchange and the granting of credit. The exemption

---

[79] s. 18. See VAT (General) Regulations 1977, regs. 33–36.

[80] The full list of exemptions is now to be found in VAT (Consolidation) Order 1978.

[81] An agreement conferring a franchise to sell goods at a particular place may still constitute a licence to occupy land: *British Airports Authority* v. *Customs and Excise Commissioners* [1977] 1 W.L.R. 302: on the other hand a subscription paid to a sports club (where the members own the land in common) is not paid for an interest in land but for the facilities provided by the club: *Trewby* v. *Customs and Excise Commissioners* [1976] 1 W.L.R. 932; [1976] S.T.C. 122. The difference turns on the analysis of the legal rights conferred under the agreement: *British Railways Board* v. *Customs and Excise Commissioners* [1977] 1 W.L.R. 588.

[82] *Post,* § 35-31.

[83] Some supplies of insurance are zero rated, see *post,* § 35-32.

[84] *Post,* § 35-57.

[85] Where a " gaming machine " is operated the consideration for and the value of the supply made are determined by special rules: see F. (No. 2) A. 1975, s. 21.

[86] This would include the assignment of a chose in action.

applies to the services of money and mortgage brokers (except in respect of the issue of Exchange securities such as certificates of deposit [87]) but not stockbrokers. Stockjobbers, however, are exempt. A credit facility separately charged for, would fall within this exemption. Likewise, any dealings in discounts as a separate business. The exemption only applies to the money transactions of banks and their advisory services are subject to the tax. In such cases the provisions relating to partial exemption will apply. [88]

35-24   (6) *Education.* This applies to the provision of education (and goods and services incidental thereto to the persons receiving the education) by schools and universities and similar non-profit-making entities. [88a] The Commissioners consider that the provision of meals in such institutions is so incidental, and the tribunal has held the same in the case of car parking facilities. [89] The exemption is extended to the provision of facilities by a youth club, but this would not cover the provision of accommodation and meals by, for example, the Youth Hostels Association.

35-25   (7) *Health.* This group consists of the supply of services (and the supply of goods in connection therewith) by registered medical practitioners, dentists, opticians, nurses, midwives, hearing aid dispensers and ancillary persons. Thus the supply of spectacles is exempt if they are supplied as part of the service of the optician, for example, after an eye test. The supply of services (but not of goods) by a chemist is also exempt. The exemption also applies to the provisions of care or medical or surgical treatment (and the supply of goods in connection therewith) in a hospital or other registered or exempted institution such as a registered private nursing home.

35-26   (8) *Burial and Cremation.* The services of undertakers are exempt though coffins and headstones are not.

35-26A   (9) *Trade Unions and Professional Bodies.* The supply to its members of services (and goods connected therewith) referable to its aims and available only in return for subscriptions by trade unions or professional associations. The exemption does not extend to social activities undertaken by such bodies.

4. ZERO RATING

35-27   If a supply of goods or services is zero rated no tax is payable on the supply and the taxable person is able to reclaim the tax on his inputs. Thus the purchaser acquires them completely free of VAT. The supplies of goods and

---

[87] See *Customs and Excise Commissioners* v. *Guy Butler (International) Ltd.* [1977] Q.B. 377 (C.A.).

[88] *Post,* § 35-57.

[88a] See *Church of Scientology of California* [1977] V.A.T.T.R. 278.

[89] *Re R. A. Archer (No.5)* [1975] V.A.T.T.R. 1. Now that the scope of the tax extends to supplies in the course *or furtherance* of a business it would seem that educational establishments will be prima facie chargeable to VAT in respect of disposals of goods, etc., that they no longer require for the purposes of their business.

services that are zero rated are set out in section 12 of and Schedule 4 to the Act. Section 12 (6) provides that a supply of goods is zero rated if they have been exported or are used as stores on a voyage or flight terminating outside the United Kingdom.[90] The other matters to be zero rated are set out in Schedule 4, which the Treasury can vary by order.[91] They are as follows:

35-28   (1) *Food.* A sale of food, animal feeding stuffs, seeds and live animals of a kind generally used as food for human consumption (but not alcohol, pet foods, sweets, chocolates, crisps, etc.[92]) is zero rated. A supply of food in the course of catering, however, is not zero rated. Broadly speaking the distinction is between the purchase of food and the purchase of a meal. The Schedule states that " a supply of anything in the course of catering includes any supply of it for consumption on the premises on which it is supplied." It should be noted that this definition is merely inclusive. However the tribunal has held, on two occasions,[93] that a supply of food for consumption on the spot, for example, from a mobile van or stall, is not zero rated. Shops supplying food either to be taken away or for consumption on the premises, for example, a fish and chip shop, have to determine the proportions of their supplies made in this way or charge differing prices.

(2) *Sewerage Services and Water* other than distilled water, deionised water or bottled waters, for example soda water.

35-29   (3) *Books,*[94] brochures, pamphlets, leaflets, newspapers, music, maps and other articles supplied with them and not separately accounted for. Zero rating is not extended to any charge made for the delivery of such items.

(4) *Talking Books for the Blind and Handicapped and Wireless Sets for the Blind.* This group covers specially adapted magnetic tape and tape-recorders supplied to the Royal National Institute for the Blind, the National Listening Library or other similar charities. It also covers the supply of a radio to a charity for gratuitous loan to the blind.

35-30   (5) *Newspaper Advertisements.* This group consists of the preparation and publication of such advertisements and the supply of services for that purpose, for example advertising agents. Other advertisements such as television and poster advertisements are not zero rated.

(6) *News Services,* excluding the supply of photographs.[95]

(7) *Fuel and Power.*[96] Coal, electricity, heat and air conditioning are

---

[90] After January 1, 1978 the letting of goods is deemed to constitute a supply of services; therefore the Commissioners are empowered to make regulations zero rating such lettings if they are satisfied that the goods have been exported during the period of the letting, etc.

[91] s. 12 (4). The full list of items zero rated is now to be found in VAT (Consolidation) Order 1978.

[92] See Sched. 4, Group 1 and VAT (Consolidation) Order 1978.

[93] See *James* MAN/76/169 and *Spragge* LON/77/108 both, as yet, unreported.

[94] The question of whether these words extend to the supply of a binder for a loose-leaf work has come before the Tribunal no less than four times. The result of these cases appears to be that if the binder is supplied separately it does not fall to be zero rated: see *Re Marshall Cavendish Ltd.* [1973] V.A.T.T.R. 65.

[95] A news clipping service is not zero rated: *Re Newsclip (U.K.) Ltd.* [1975] V.A.T.T.R. 67.

[96] See VAT (Consolidation) Order 1978.

zero rated as is domestic heating oil, but petrol and oil used in road vehicles is subject to tax at the higher rate.

35-31   (8) *Construction of Buildings, etc.* This group consists of:

(a) The granting, by a person constructing a building,[97] of a major interest in, or in any part of, the building or its site. If a taxable person owning a site arranges for the construction thereon of a building and subsequently sells the freehold or grants a lease in excess of 21 years (whether at a rack rent or not) the whole of his input tax attributable thereto (including the fees of architects and surveyors etc.) will be deductible.

(b) The supply of services in the course of construction, alteration or demolition of any buildings or of any civil engineering work other than the services of an architect or surveyor, etc. A building is altered if it is made different in some respect, without changing the whole building for a new one.[98] Such supplies made within the garden or grounds of a private dwelling (such as a swimming pool or tennis court) are not zero rated.[99]

(c) The supply by a person supplying services,[1] of materials in connection with those services. Input tax on " luxury fittings," however, is disallowed.[2]

Work of repair or maintenance is not zero rated. Zero rating now applies regardless of the fact that the supplier is a sub-contractor supplying to a main contractor.[3] A supply of a prefabricated building (such as a garage) to a non-taxable customer who then erects it is not zero rated but if the supplier erects it, it is.[4] There are provisions whereby a person constructing a building for his own occupation (and therefore not making taxable supplies) can recover the tax suffered.[5]

35-32   (9) *International Services.*[6] This group zero rates the following services supplied by persons belonging in the United Kingdom:

(a) The supply of services relating to foreign land. This extends to architectural and surveying services and possibly conveyancing.

(b) The letting on hire of goods which are exported.

---

[97] The provision also applies where the interest is granted by someone on the builder's behalf, *e.g.* trustees for a building partnership: VAT (Construction of Buildings, etc.) Order 1975, now VAT (Consolidation) Order 1978, Group 8, Note 1.

[98] *Re M. Gumbrell and Dodson Bros.* [1973] V.A.T.T.R. 171 at p. 176. The installation of a sauna bath may or may not amount to an alteration depending on the manner and circumstances of its installation: *Re Nordic Saunas Ltd.* [1974] V.A.T.T.R. 40.

[99] VAT (Consolidation) Order 1978, Sched. 4, Group 8, Note 2 (b).

[1] *Ibid.* Sched. 4, Group 8, item 3.

[2] s. 3 (6), *post*, § 35-56; VAT (Special Provisions) Order 1977, art. 8; and see *F. Booker Builders and Contractors Ltd.* [1977] V.A.T.T.R. 203.

[3] VAT (Consolidation) Order 1978, Sched. 4, Group 8, superseding VAT (Construction of Buildings etc.) (No. 2) Order 1975.

[4] VAT (Consolidation) Order 1978, Sched. 1, Group 8, Note 2 (c) prevents a supplier who does not do the installation himself from " employing " his customer to do it on his behalf and therby converting a standard rated supply into a zero rated one.

[5] F.A. 1972, s. 15A (as inserted by F.A. 1975, s. 3) and VAT (" Do-It-Yourself " Builders) (Relief) Regulations 1975.

[6] VAT (Consolidation) Order 1978, Sched. 4, Group 9, with effect from January 1, 1978.

(c) The supply of services relating to cultural, artistic, sporting and entertaining activities where those services are performed outside the United Kingdom.

(d) The supply of services relating to the valuation of goods and work on goods where the services are performed abroad.

(e) The supply of any services comprised in Schedule 2A [7] where such supply is received by a person who belongs in another Member State of the Community for the purposes of a business carried on by him.

(f) The supply of any services comprised in Schedule 2A [7] (excluding insurance) and the supply of insurance and re-insurance by authorised insurers [8] when it is made to a person who belongs outside the Community (and whether received by him for the purposes of a business or not).

(g) The supply of certain types of insurance in connection with the carriage of passengers and of goods for export to or from a place outside the Community.

(h) The supply by the Export Credits Guarantee Department (or another person making a similar supply) of insurance in connection with the export of goods.

(i) The supply of financial services primarily falling within Schedule 5, Group 5 [9] where those services are related to the export of goods or the transhipment of goods whose ultimate destination is outside the Community.

(j) The supply to a foreigner of work carried out on goods acquired within or imported to the United Kingdom, and then exported.

(k) The supply of services in procuring for another any export of goods or any of the services within (a)–(f) and (j) above or any supply of goods or services made outside the United Kingdom.

35-33   (10) *Transport.* [10] This applies (broadly) to the supply, chartering, letting on hire, repair or maintenance of ships and aircraft (excluding yachts and air-taxis), transport of passengers, [11] pilotage, salvage and ancillary services. Travel agents would be included though they would have to make an apportionment in respect of a supply of services including both transport and accommodation, for example package deal holidays. Taxis are not zero rated.

35-34   (11) *Caravans and Houseboats.* This group applies to caravans exceeding the size limits for use on roads, that is, to caravans that can only be used as homes, not necessarily to all those that are so used, and to houseboats, designed or adapted as homes and incapable of self-propulsion.

---

[7] For the full list of these services see *ante*, § 35-10A.

[8] Sched. 4, Group 9, item 6, and see VAT (Consolidation) Order 1978, Sched. 5, Group 2.

[9] See *ante*, § 35-23.

[10] With effect from January 1, 1978, this group was amended: see now VAT (Consolidation) Order 1978, Sched. 4, Group 10. The amendments are minor, mainly to take account of the fact that, after that date, a hiring of goods is treated as a supply of services rather than goods.

[11] In *British Railways Board* v. *Customs and Excise Commissioner* [1977] 1 W.L.R. 588 the question arose as to whether a payment securing a right to cheap fares was itself consideration for the supply of transport; the Court of Appeal held that it represented the first part of a two part tariff paid for the supply of transport and therefore fell to be zero rated.

(12) *Gold*.

(13) *Bank Notes*.

35-35   (14) *Drugs, Medicines, Medical and Surgical Appliances etc.* This group consists of the supply of such goods by a chemist on a doctor's or dentist's prescription; and the general supply to the chronically sick and disabled of invalid beds, commodes, chair lifts, hoists, etc.

35-36   (15) *Imports, Exports, etc.* This group consists of a supply of goods whilst in customs bond, a transfer by a taxable person of goods or services to his other place of business outside the United Kingdom and the supply to an overseas body in connection with a defence project. [12]

35-37   (16) *Charities*. This group covers the supply of new and used goods donated to and sold by a charity established for the relief of distress except where those goods are donated from the stock in trade of a taxable person and the cost to that person exceeded £10. The export of goods by a charity is also zero rated. [13]

35-38   (17) *Clothing and Footwear*. This covers articles *designed* as clothing and footwear for young children and not suitable for older persons. [14] There is no definition of young children. It also covers protective boots and helmets for industrial use and crash helmets.

5. THE HIGHER RATE

35-39   Originally VAT had only two rates: the positive rate of 10 per cent. (and now 8 per cent.) and the zero rate just considered. The former is now called the standard rate and a higher rate was introduced with effect from May 1, 1975, by section 17 of the Finance (No. 2) Act 1975, on the supplies set out in Schedule 7 to that Act. The Treasury can, by order, vary or add to the supplies set out in that Schedule. [15] The higher rate was originally 25 per cent. but this has now been reduced to 12½ per cent. with effect from April 12, 1976, by section 17 of the Finance Act 1976. In summary the supplies subject to the higher rate are as follows:

35-40   (1) *Domestic appliances*. This group includes electrical goods of a kind suitable [16] for domestic use (other than cooking, heating and lighting, or telephones, tools, clocks, watches, mechanical lighters, hearing aids or parts of such goods), electrical or motor mowers, refrigerators and freezers, and all accessories and parts of such goods (other than nuts, bolts, hinges, batteries, plugs, bulbs and wheels etc.). Also subject to the higher rate

---

[12] See VAT (Consolidation) Order 1978, Sched. 4, Group 15.
[13] *Ibid.* Group 16.
[14] *Ibid.* Group 17, item 1.
[15] See VAT (Higher Rate) Order 1975, and the Schedule, as amended, set out in VAT (Consolidation) Order 1978.
[16] As to the meaning of " suitability " in this context, see *Customs and Excise Commissioners* v. *Mechanical Services* [1978] 1 W.L.R. 56; [1977] S.T.C. 485.

within this group are services supplied in the installation, alteration, testing, repair or maintenance of such items together with goods supplied in connection therewith.

35-41   (2) *Radio and Television sets, etc.* This group extends essentially to the supply (*i.e.* sale, rental, etc.) of radios, televisions, gramophones or tape recorders, electronic musical instruments and all parts and accessories (*e.g.* aerials) to the same. Rental payments under contracts of hire entered into prior to April 16, 1975, are excluded and are only taxable at the standard rate. Again the installation, alteration, testing, repair or maintenance of such goods together with goods supplied in connection therewith are also made subject to the higher rate.

35-42   (3) *Boats and Aircraft.* Items specified under this heading are boats under 15 tons or those designed or adapted for use for recreation or pleasure; aircraft under 8,000 kilograms or, if of greater weight, those designed or adapted for use for recreation or pleasure; hovercraft so designed or adapted; and parts or accessories (being outboard motors and engines, generators, sails, automatic pilots and steering gear, and trailers and trolleys) to such goods. Certain radio equipment designed for distress calls at sea, navigational aids, and compasses, echo sounders and radar sets are excluded.[17] The alteration, testing, repair or maintenance of boats and their parts and accessories together with the supply of materials in connection therewith are also covered. Finally the heading is also extended to the making of any arrangements for the supply of such goods.

35-43   (4) *Caravans.* This group covers the supply of (or of parts of), the making of arrangements for such a supply, and the alteration, repair or maintenance of caravans suitable for use as trailers with an unladen weight of less than 2,030 kilograms or of caravan units designed to be mounted and carried on motor vehicles. This group does not include the letting or hire of a caravan on a specified site as holiday accommodation for a period not exceeding 28 days.

35-44   (5) *Photographic Equipment, Binoculars, etc.* This covers the supply and installation, alteration, testing, repair or maintenance (together with goods supplied in connection therewith) of cameras, developing and printing apparatus, etc., film, binoculars and all accessories and parts of such goods.

35-45   (6) *Furs.* This group covers all fur skin, rugs made of fur skin and clothing made wholly or partly of fur skin except headgear, gloves, footwear, buttons, belts and buckles or any garment merely trimmed with fur (unless the trimming has a greater area than one-fifth of the whole garment or exceeds the cost of the rest of the garment). Also subject to the higher rate is the application of any process or treatment (*i.e.* alterations but not cleaning) to such goods and the storage of such goods.

---

[17] See note 15, *ante.*

35-46   (7) *Jewellery, Goldsmiths' and Silversmiths' Wares, etc.* This group covers such goods made wholly or partly from precious metal, precious or semi-precious stones, real or cultured pearls. It also extends to the stones themselves (except uncut diamonds and diamond powder or dust), real or cultured pearls and jade and articles of jade. Also covered is the design, valuation or application of any process or treatment to any such goods together with any other goods supplied in connection therewith.

35-47   (8) *Petrol, etc.* This group covers the supply of light oil (other than as fuel for lighters), petrol substitute and power methylated spirits but not, of course, domestic heating oil which is zero rated.[18]

35-48   There is also a provision whereby any person applying or causing to be applied any treatment or process whereby a boat (over 15 tons), an aircraft (over 8,000 kilograms) or a hovercraft is adapted for use for recreation or pleasure, or jewellery etc. is produced, is chargeable to tax as if the supply had been a sale for full consideration of the resultant goods.[19] This ensures that the higher rate of tax is payable on the total value of the object rather than the service charge of the adaptor.

6. COMPUTATION

35-49   (1) *Time of Supply*

The basic tax points are:

(i) *Goods:* (a) the time of removal from the supplier's premises,[20] or (b) if the goods are not to be removed, the time when they are made available,[21] or (c) if they are taken on approval or sale or return, the time when it is certain that the supply has taken place, but that time is not to be later than 12 months after removal.[22]

(ii) *Services:* the time when the services are performed.[23] If a service is performed over a period it is considered that this time would be the completion of the service.

If a tax invoice is given, or a payment (unless the case is within (i) (c) above) is made in respect of the supply prior to these times, the earlier time is the tax point.[24] If a tax invoice is given within 14 days after the times referred to in (i) and (ii) above, or such longer period as the Commissioners may specify, then the time when the invoice is given is the tax point, unless the taxable person elects to adhere to the basic rules of delivery and performance.[25] Thus in ordinary cases it will be the tax invoice that is the tax point. This is sensible since such an invoice represents money in the recipient's hands as an input, but it would have been much simpler to have

---

[18] See *ante*, § 35-30.
[19] F. (No. 2) A. 1975, s. 18.
[20] s. 7 (2) (*a*).
[21] s. 7 (2) (*b*).
[22] s. 7 (2) (*c*).
[23] s. 7 (3). The services of a barrister or advocate are treated as performed on the date when his fee is received or a tax invoice is issued, whichever is the earlier, or the day when he ceases to practise: VAT (General) Regulations 1977, reg. 20.
[24] s. 7 (4). The supply is only treated as having been made to the extent covered by the invoice or payment.
[25] s. 7 (5) and see F. (No. 2) A. 1975, s. 19.

made the tax invoice or payment, whichever was the earlier, the sole determinant.

If the whole or part of a consideration is determined or payable periodically or at the end of any period or is determined at the time when goods are appropriated for any purpose the Commissioners may, by regulations, determine the tax point.[26] This provision applies mainly to hiring arrangements where the tax will be chargeable on the service charge.[27] All such service charges payable after July 31, 1974, are within the ambit of the charge whether or not the goods or services were supplied prior to the introduction of the tax.[28] Where the consideration for the supply of services is not ascertainable at the time when they are performed (as is often the case with royalties) then a further supply is deemed to take place whenever a payment is received or a tax invoice issued.[29] Provision is also made for the determination of the date of supply where services are supplied continuously and the supplier gives a tax invoice covering a period not exceeding one year.[30]

A special relief in respect of bad debts has now been introduced by section 12 of the Finance Act 1978 and regulations made thereunder.[31] The taxable person is only entitled to a refund where his debtor is insolvent (*i.e.* has been adjudged bankrupt or, if a company, is the subject of a creditors' voluntary winding up or is being wound up under a court order). He must prove in the insolvency (the amount of refund being any deficiency), the value of his supply must not have exceeded its open market value and, if a supply of goods, the property therein must have passed to the purchaser.

(2) *The Value of Supply*

35-50   If the supply is for a consideration in money that consideration minus the amount of the tax is the value of the supply.[32] Thus, where the supply is standard rated, the tax amounts to two-twenty-sevenths (with a VAT rate of 8 per cent.) of the consideration for the supply and where the supply is taxable at the higher rate this proportion is one-ninth.[33] If the supply is not for a consideration or is for a consideration not consisting or not wholly consisting of money the value of the supply is its open market value less the amount of the tax chargeable.[34] This rule would apply to exchanges of goods but not gifts since it is elsewhere provided [35] that the value of the supply of a gift of goods is to be the cost of the goods to the person making the supply.[36] If the cost of the goods does not exceed £10 there is no charge

---

[26] s. 7 (8) as amended by F.A. 1977, Sched. 6, para. 2 and VAT (General) Regulations 1977, regs. 14, 18 and 19.

[27] For the position as regards televisions hired prior to April 1, 1973, see *ante*, § 35-08.

[28] F.A. 1974, s. 5, and *Customs and Excise Commissioners* v. *Thorn Electrical Industries Ltd.* [1975] 1 W.L.R. 1661; [1975] S.T.C. 617 (H.L.).

[29] VAT (General) Regulations 1977, reg. 19.   [30] *Ibid.* reg. 18 (2).

[31] It applies where the debtor becomes insolvent after October 1, 1978: F.A. 1978, s. 12 (6), and see VAT (Bad Debt Relief) Regulations 1978.

[32] s. 10 (2).

[33] s. 9 (1) as amended by F. (No. 2) A. 1975, s. 17, and F.A. 1976, s. 14.

[34] s. 10 (3) and (5), and see *Davies* v. *Customs and Excise Commissioners* [1975] 1 W.L.R. 204; [1975] S.T.C. 28 for the effect of this provision where the ordinary price is discounted under a cheque trading arrangement: it would appear that tax is chargeable on the full, and not the discounted, price.

[35] Sched. 3, paras. 7 and 8 (as amended by F.A. 1977, Sched. 6, para. 14).

[36] Thus the rule in *Sharkey* v. *Wernher* [1956] A.C. 58, *ante*, § 2-46, has not been applied.

on the gift.[37] This latter provision might cover the gift of, for example, a watch to a retiring employee. Furthermore, if parts were supplied free under a guarantee there would be no charge to VAT since this would have been covered by the original charge on the purchase of the machine or motor, etc. These provisions do not apply to gifts of services since they are not subject to the tax.[38]

35-51   If goods are sold (or imported) under terms that allow for a cash discount the value of the supply is the lower sum even though the purchaser fails to pay within the specified time and subsequently pays the higher amount.[39] If quantity discounts are given there will be an adjustment at the end of the period as appropriate. The value of the supply on a credit sale is the cash price for the goods disregarding the interest element. If goods are sent out in returnable containers, for example a bottle on which a deposit is paid, the value of the container, or the deposit, is not taken into account in determining the value of the supply unless the container is not returned. The value of the supply under hiring arrangements is the amount of the service charge.[40]

35-52   The consideration given for such things as book or record tokens is disregarded except to the extent (if any) that it exceeds the amount stated on the token.[41]

35-53   If a taxable person carries on his business or part of it by supplying goods to a number of exempt persons for sale by retail, the Commissioners may give directions securing that the value of the supply made by him shall be equal to the price at which the goods are sold by retail.[42] This provision will cover direct selling through domestic outlets, for example, the sale by an exempt person at a coffee morning. The object is to raise the price that attracts VAT from the wholesale price to the retail price. The provision will only apply to business organisations adopting this course and not, for example, to charity coffee mornings.

35-54   Where hotel or similar accommodation is provided for a period exceeding four weeks the value of so much of the supply as is in excess of four weeks shall be reduced to such part thereof as is attributable to facilities other than the right to occupy the accommodation.[43] However the value of the supply cannot be reduced below 20 per cent. This provision is to give a corresponding benefit to hotel dwellers as is given to house dwellers.[44]

---

[37] Sched. 2, para. 5 (2) (as inserted by F.A. 1977, Sched. 6, para. 14).
[38] Unless the Treasury make an order specifying that the gratuitous supply of a particular service shall be treated as a taxable supply: see s. 6 (4) (as inserted by F.A. 1977, Sched. 6, para. 1). However during the Committee stage of the Finance Bill 1977 it was stated that there was no present intention to invoke this provision and, so far, it has not been invoked.
[39] Sched. 3, paras. 4 and 5 (as inserted by F.A. 1977, Sched. 6, para. 14).
[40] See s. 7 (8) (as amended by F.A. 1977, Sched. 6, para. 2) and VAT (General) Regulations 1977, regs. 14, 18 and 19.
[41] Sched. 3, para. 6 (as restated by F.A. 1977, Sched. 6, para. 14).
[42] Sched. 3, para. 3 (as restated by F.A. 1977, Sched. 6, para. 14).
[43] Sched. 3, para. 9 (as restated by F.A. 1977, Sched. 6, para. 14).
[44] Rents are exempt under Sched. 5, Group 1, *ante*, § 35-19.

35-55 There is also an anti-avoidance provision whereby the Commissioners may serve a notice on a taxable person directing that the value of his supplies is not less than their open market value.[45] The provision would apply where a taxable person sells (or imports) goods to an exempt person and the price is artificially depressed in view of the relationship between the two.

(3) *Calculation*

35-56 Having determined the value of a taxable supply the taxable person adds on VAT at the appropriate rate and charges his customer the total amount. If his customer is also a taxable person he must give him a tax invoice showing the amounts of these items.[46] Although this tax is now made technically due at the moment of supply [47] it is accounted for by returns made for each accounting period in which the taxable person may take credit for the input tax suffered by him. Thus the total amount of tax payable on the taxable supplies made by him, in an accounting period, is called output tax. From this he may deduct input tax, that is the tax (at whatever rate) he has paid on the supply of goods or services used or to be used for the purpose of any business carried on by him or tax paid on the importation of goods for the same purpose.[48] He then accounts to the Commissioners for the difference or, if the input tax exceeds the output tax, claims a repayment.[49] The Treasury have power to make orders disallowing the deduction of input tax in cases specified in such an order.[50] This has been done as regards business cars, entertainment expenses and luxury fittings such as washing machines, fitted carpets, televisions and cookers in zero rated buildings. If goods or services are supplied to a taxable person and are used partly for business purposes and partly for other purposes the supply is apportioned so that only the part referable to his business use is allowed as an input tax credit.[51]

35-57 *Partial Exemption.* In the ordinary case a taxable person will be able to deduct all his input tax, but, if some of his supplies of goods or services are exempt, there will have to be an apportionment.[52] Examples of such persons are chemists or banks. For this purpose there are provisions whereby exempt supplies can be disregarded if they do not exceed a stated amount.[53] The system of apportionment is not laid down in the Act but is

---

[45] Sched. 3, paras. 1 and 2 (as restated by F.A. 1977, Sched. 6, para. 14). However the taxpayer appears to be allowed at least one bite of the cherry.

[46] s. 30 (2); see VAT (General) Regulations 1977, regs. 8–11.

[47] s. 2 (3) and ss. 3 and 4 (as inserted by F.A. 1977, Sched. 6, para. 1).

[48] s. 3 (3) (as amended by F.A. 1977, Sched. 6, para. 1). It should be noticed that as from January 1, 1978, the words " used or to be used " have been added although it is not considered that this represents a significant change from the previous provision.

[49] s. 3 (5) (as amended by F.A. 1977, Sched. 6, para. 1). If he so desires the taxable person may have his input tax credit held over to a subsequent period: s. 3 (6).

[50] s. 3 (9) (as restated by F.A. 1977, Sched. 6, para. 1); VAT (Special Provisions) Order 1977, arts. 8 and 9.   [51] s. 3 (4) (as inserted by F.A. 1977, Sched. 6, para. 1).

[52] s. 4 (as inserted by F.A. 1977, Sched. 6, para. 1), and see VAT (General) Regulations 1977, regs. 23–29. The procedure works by first provisionally attributing a proportion for any accounting period and then making subsequent adjustments (unless the difference is less than 10 per cent. or £10, whichever is the greater): s. 4 (3) (as inserted by F.A. 1977, Sched. 6, para. 1).

[53] See VAT (General) Regulations 1977, reg. 27, under which exempt supplies will be disregarded if less than £100 per month or 5 per cent. of the value of all supplies, whichever was the greater.

left to regulations made by the Commissioners.[54] Two basic methods have been adopted: (i) an apportionment calculated on the percentage of the taxable person's total supplies that constitute taxable outputs including items zero rated, and (2) the deduction of all input tax on the purchase of goods subsequently sold by him in the same state together with a proportion of the input tax on other items. The Commissioners will allow other methods if it can be shown that they achieve a fair attribution.

(4) *Refund of Tax*

35-58   (i) Section 15 provides that certain bodies can claim a refund of tax on goods or services supplied to them or goods imported by them for the purpose of their non-business activities. For the purpose of their business activities the normal input/output mechanism operates. Consequently these bodies will only suffer tax on supplies to them or importations by them for the purpose of an exempt business carried on by them. However, where, in the opinion of the Commissioners, their exempt supplies represent an insignificant proportion of the whole, the whole of the tax may be refunded. The bodies to which this provision applies are local authorities, various statutory undertakings providing similar services, police authorities, the London Transport Executive, the B.B.C. and Independent Television News Limited.

35-59   (ii) Under section 28 the Commissioners have power to give refunds of tax to exempt traders on their purchases of machinery or plant.

(iii) Under section 5 [55] the Commissioners may provide for the repayment of tax (generally through United Kingdom agents) to persons carrying on business in a member state of the Community other than the United Kingdom if such tax would be input tax of theirs if they were taxable persons in the United Kingdom. This reimbursement procedure can be extended to persons outside the Community under any Community Directive.

(5) *Income Tax and Corporation Tax*

35-60   There are no express provisions in the Act dealing with the deduction of VAT under Schedule D, Cases I and II, for income tax and corporation tax purposes. Money expended wholly and exclusively for the purposes of a trade or profession is deductible.[56] If the taxpayer is a taxable person for VAT he would not take the tax into account at all. This is because he actually suffers no tax by virtue of the input/output system. However if he is exempt or partially exempt (and then only in respect of the inputs that are not deductible for VAT purposes) he is able to claim the total price (including VAT) of the goods or services purchased. In such a case he is the ultimate consumer and the tax will have been part of the price of the goods or services.

---

[54] *Supra*, n. 52.
[55] As inserted by F.A. 1977, Sched. 6, para. 1, with effect from January 1, 1978.
[56] See *ante*, §§ 2-57 *et seq.*

7. SPECIAL CASES

35-61   (1) *The Crown.*[57] VAT applies to any taxable supplies made by the Crown by way of business. The Treasury have power to subject supplies by government departments to VAT if those supplies appear to be similar to supplies made by other persons in the course of carrying on a business.

35-62   (2) *Local Authorities.*[58] Local authorities making taxable supplies must register even though the value of their supplies is less than £10,000.

35-63   (3) *Groups of Companies.*[59] Any supply of goods or services by one member of a group to another is to be disregarded and any taxable supplies made outside the group shall be treated as made by the representative member. Two or more companies are to be treated as a group if one of them controls each of the others, one person controls all of them or two or more individuals carrying on a business in partnership control all of them. A company controls another for this purpose if it is empowered to do so by statute, such as a public corporation, or has control within the meaning of the Companies Act 1948, s. 154, that is, that it holds over 50 per cent. of the nominal share capital, controls the composition of the board of directors or is itself the holding company of a company which has such control. An application specifying the company that is to be the representative member must be made to the Commissioners for these grouping provisions to apply. Such an application can be made on behalf of only part of a group. Once the application is made the registration limit of £10,000 would be determined by reference to the external transactions of the group as a whole. Thus in certain circumstances it may be beneficial not to apply for group treatment. There is joint and several liability for the tax due from the representative member. Applications may be made to add a new member to the group, remove a member, to treat another member as the representative member or to discharge the group notice.

If a company carries on business in various divisions the registration may, if the company applies and the Commissioners see fit, be in the names of those divisions.[60]

35-64   (4) *Partnerships.*[61] Partnerships are to be registered in the partnership name and no account is to be taken of a change of partners. If two partnerships comprise exactly the same persons there can only be one registration.[62] The liability to pay the tax is governed by section 9 of the Partnership Act 1890, but if a person is only a partner for part of a period his liability is only to be such proportion of the firm's liability as may be just.

---

[57] s. 19.
[58] s. 20.
[59] s. 21.
[60] s. 23. The Commissioners are of the view that this provision does not apply to partially exempt companies.
[61] s. 22.
[62] See *Customs and Excise Commissioners* v. *Glassborow* [1975] Q.B. 465, and *ante*, § 35-15.

35-65   (5) *Agents.*[63] Where a person who is accountable for any tax is not resident in the United Kingdom the Commissioners may serve a notice on any resident person, who is his agent, substituting him for the accountable person. However a person does not necessarily become another's agent for this purpose by merely being his accountant.

35-66   (6) *Terminal Markets.*[64] For the markets in futures there is a " tax free " ring for sales and purchases and no tax will be chargeable unless or until the goods are delivered. Consequently these activities have been zero rated.

8. Collection and Enforcement

35-67   The Commissioners have a general power to make regulations requiring the tax to be paid by reference to such periods (" prescribed accounting periods " which are of three months' duration) at such time and in such manner as they shall determine.[65] In particular the regulations may prescribe the form of accounts and returns and the requirements relating to tax invoices that have to be given with (or within a prescribed time after [66]) every taxable supply to a taxable person.[67] Every taxable person must keep such records as the Commissioners may require for a period of up to three years.[68] If a taxable person fails to make the required returns the Commissioners may make an estimated assessment.[69]

Tax due from any person is recoverable as a debt due to the Crown.[70] In such proceedings a certificate of the Commissioners to the effect that a person was or was not registered, that a return was not made or that tax was not paid is prima facie evidence of those facts.[71]

35-68   *Security.* The Commissioners have power to require a taxable person, as a condition of his supplying goods or services under a taxable supply, to give security for the payment of any tax which may become due from him.[72] Furthermore when making a repayment of or allowance for any input tax to any person they may require him to produce documents and give security.[73] It is thought that these powers are only used in cases involving an exceptional repayment of input tax and the security required is a bond.

35-69   *Information.* The Commissioners have power to require taxable persons to furnish them with information and produce documents.[74] Taxable persons supplying services can only be required to give information relating to the consideration for the supply and the name and address of the person

---

[63] s. 24.
[64] s. 26; and VAT (Terminal Markets) Order 1973.
[65] ss. 3 (1) and 30 (as amended by F.A. 1977, Sched. 6, paras. 1 and 9); see VAT (General) Regulations 1977.
[66] See s. 30 (2A) (as inserted by F.A. 1977, Sched. 6, para. 9).
[67] s. 30; see VAT (General) Regulations 1977.
[68] s. 34.
[69] s. 31.
[70] s. 33; see *Customs and Excise Commissioners* v. *Holvey* [1978] 2 W.L.R. 155; [1978] S.T.C. 187.
[71] s. 39.
[72] s. 32 (2).
[73] s. 32 (1).
[74] s. 35.

to whom it is made.[75] Thus the professional man cannot be required to disclose confidential information. There is also power to take samples.[76]

35-70 *Entry and Search.* There are wide powers of entry to business premises for persons acting under the authority of the Commissioners so that a series of spot checks can be anticipated.[77] If there are reasonable grounds to suspect that an offence in connection with the tax has been committed a magistrate may issue a warrant authorising the entry and search of premises and a person acting under that warrant may seize and remove any documents or other things found on the premises reasonably required for evidence, and may search any person found there whom he reasonably believes has committed or is about to commit an offence.[78]

35-71 *Offences.* The fraudulent evasion of the tax is a criminal offence subject to a penalty of £1,000 or three times the amount of the tax, whichever is the greater, or imprisonment for a term not exceeding two years, or both.[79] There are similar penalties for false statements or documents.[80] Where a person's conduct *must have* involved the commission by him of one or more of these offences, then, whether or not the particulars of that offence or those offences are known, he shall be guilty of an offence and subject to the usual penalties.[81] This latter provision is of an unusual nature, but it merely seems to place the onus of proof on the taxable person for matters that are solely within his knowledge. The safeguard is that the court must be satisfied that he *must have* committed an offence.

35-72 *Tribunals.* There are special VAT tribunals to hear appeals under the Act.[82] Before an appeal can be heard the proper returns must have been made and the amount of any output tax in dispute deposited with the Commissioners unless the tribunal directs otherwise. There is a power to award costs. These tribunals are the sole arbiters of fact but an appeal lies to the High Court on questions of law. Many of the disputes relate to the classification of a particular supply, *i.e.* whether it is taxable or zero rated or exempt. It has now been determined that this question turns on analysing the legal rights of the parties to the transaction and therefore, once the primary facts have been established, this question of classification is purely one of law.[83]

---

[75] s. 35 (3).
[76] s. 36.
[77] s. 37 (1) and (2).
[78] s. 37 (3).
[79] s. 38 (1).
[80] s. 38 (2).
[81] s. 38 (3).
[82] s. 40.
[83] *British Railways Board* v. *Customs and Excise Commissioners* [1977] 1 W.L.R. 588 (C.A.), overruling on this point the decision of the Divisional Court in *Customs and Excise Commissioners* v. *The Automobile Association* [1974] 1 W.L.R. 1447.

PART 5

TAX PLANNING

" We seem to have travelled a long way from the general and salutary rule that the subject is not to be taxed except by plain words. But I must recognise that plain words are seldom adequate to anticipate and forestall the multiplicity of ingenious schemes which are constantly being devised to evade taxation. Parliament is very properly determined to prevent this kind of tax evasion, and if the courts find it impossible to give very wide meanings to general phrases the only alternative may be for Parliament to do as some other countries have done and introduce legislation of a more sweeping character, which will put the ordinary well-intentioned person at much greater risk than is created by a wide interpretation of such provisions as those which we are now considering."

Per LORD REID in *Greenberg* v. *I.R.C.* (1971) 47 T.C. at p. 272.

" Such a situation would be obviously unjust. If it be correct, it is clear that something has gone seriously wrong with the enactments or the case law or with both. It must be disturbing to the citizen if such a situation can arise. Such an injustice is not in the interests of anyone—certainly not of the Revenue, since injustice causes evasion. Each year there is an adjustment of the mechanism of taxation wherever that is necessary to ensure that ingenious schemes of avoidance shall not succeed. There is a corresponding duty to adjust the mechanism where it is found to be creating a clear injustice."

LORD PEARCE in *Pook* v. *Owen* [1970] A.C. 244 at p. 257; 45 T.C. 571 at p. 591D.

" I wish at the outset to make this general observation. The question in every estate duty case is whether the Crown demonstrates that the circumstances fall within the ambit of a relevant charging provision. The fact that a settlement is drawn with a view to avoiding particular charging provisions is neither reprehensible, nor a proper ground for inclination to a conclusion that it ought to come within those or some other charging provisions. It is not right to label something a ' device ' and then strain to see that it fails. The question remains that which I have stated. These principles equally apply to cases in which ingenuity in avoiding a charge to estate duty is not confined to the framing of the original settlement, but extends to subsequent transactions. If by an adjustment or variation of beneficial interests a small group can avoid contributing, say, £100,000 to the Crown out of their own pockets, they are well entitled to do so. If any moral criticism could be levelled at them, then the consciences of the judges of the Chancery Division, in the exercise of their discretionary jurisdiction under the Variation of Trusts Act 1958, would be in a sorry state."

RUSSELL L.J. in *Re Ralli's Settlements* [1965] Ch. 286 at p. 327.

CHAPTER 36

INTRODUCTION

36-01 THE first four parts of this book have been devoted to a statement of the fundamental principles of income and capital gains taxation, capital transfer tax, value added tax and stamp duties. In the part that follows some aspects of these subjects are considered in relation to problems of tax planning; that is, the arranging of a client's affairs with a view to minimising the burden of taxation in its various forms. The words " tax " and " taxation " are used in this part of the book to refer to all forms of taxation, including capital transfer tax and stamp duties.

36-02 All forms of taxation are imposed by Parliament: there is no rule of common law or of equity which makes a person liable to tax. " Tax is the creature of statute." The function of the court in relation to all statutes is to interpret their meaning and " the fundamental rule of interpretation to which all others are subordinate is that a statute is to be expounded according to the intent of them that made it." [1] This intention must be discovered from the actual words used in the statute, taking the statute as a whole and the words in the context in which they appear [2]; and in this respect, no distinction is made between taxing statutes and other statutes. Where the meaning of the words is clear, the court will not allow speeches made during the course of parliamentary debates, reports of Royal Commissions or official circulars to be admitted in evidence as an aid to interpretation. [3] Furthermore, where the words are clear, the court must give effect to them, however inconvenient or undesirable the result may be. [4] Where an Act of Parliament contains a provision which imposes a charge to tax (called a " charging section "), the section will be strictly construed in the sense that the taxpayer will be given the benefit of any doubt as to the scope of the charge: clear words must be used to create a liability to tax. [5] This emphasis on the letter of the law was explained by Rowlatt J. as follows:

> " In a taxing Act one has to look merely at what is clearly said. There is no room for any intendment. There is no equity about a tax. There is no presumption as to a tax. Nothing is to be read in, nothing is to be implied. One can only look fairly at the language used." [6]

Lord Cairns stated the rule as follows:

> " If the person sought to be taxed comes within the letter of the law he must be taxed, however great the hardship may appear to the judicial mind to be. On the other hand, if the Crown, seeking to recover the tax, cannot bring the

---

[1] Maxwell, *The Interpretation of Statutes*, 11th ed., p. 1.
[2] *Colquhoun* v. *Brooks* (1889) 14 App.Cas. 493; 2 T.C. 490.
[3] *Assam Railways and Trading Co.* v. *I.R.C.* [1935] A.C. 445; but see *Escoigne Properties Ltd.* v. *I.R.C.* [1958] A.C. 549, *per* Lord Denning at p. 566.
[4] *Re Robb's Contract* [1941] Ch. 463 (C.A.). This decision was nullified by F.A. 1942, s. 44, which amended the F. (1909–10) A. 1910, s. 74 (6).
[5] *Russell* v. *Scott* [1948] A.C. 422 at p. 433; 30 T.C. 375 at p. 424, *per* Lord Simons.
[6] *Cape Brandy Syndicate* v. *I.R.C.* [1921] 1 K.B. 64 at p. 71; 12 T.C. 358 at p. 366.

subject within the letter of the law, the subject is free, however apparently within the spirit of the law the case might otherwise appear to be.'' [7]

and in *Hochstrasser* v. *Mayes*, Viscount Simonds said [8]:

" It is for the Crown, seeking to tax the subject, to prove that the tax is exigible, not for the subject to prove that his case falls within exceptions which are not expressed in the Statute but arbitrarily inferred from it.''

Form and substance

36-03   Before a taxing statute can be applied in relation to any given transaction, the Revenue (or the court) must first ascertain the effect of the transaction as between the parties; that is, the rights and obligations created by the transaction must be determined in accordance with general principles of law. An important case which illustrates this point is *I.R.C.* v. *Duke of Westminster,* [9] where the facts were as follows:

Deeds of covenant were executed by the Duke in favour of employees. The deed provided that the payments were to be without prejudice to any claim for remuneration to which the employee might thereafter be entitled but it was understood by the employee that he was not expected to make any such claim so long as the amount received under the covenant and any other payments he received equalled his current salary.

The Revenue contended that although the transaction was in the *form* of a grant of an annuity or annual payment, in *substance* the transaction was an agreement by the employee to continue in service at his normal salary. This contention was rejected by the Court of Appeal and the House of Lords. Lord Tomlin stated the position as follows [10]:

". . . it is said that in revenue cases there is a doctrine that the court may ignore the legal position and regard what is called ' the substance of the matter,' and that here the substance of the matter is that the annuitant was serving the Duke for something equal to his former salary or wages, and that therefore, while he is so serving, the annuity must be treated as salary or wages. This supposed doctrine . . . seems to rest for its support upon a misunderstanding of language used in some earlier cases. The sooner this misunderstanding is dispelled and the supposed doctrine given its quietus, the better it will be for all concerned. . . . Every man is entitled if he can to order his affairs so as that the tax attaching under the appropriate Acts is less than it otherwise would be. If he succeeds in ordering them so as to secure this result, then, however unappreciative the Commissioners of Inland Revenue or his fellow taxpayers may be of his ingenuity, he cannot be compelled to pay an increased tax. This so-called doctrine of the ' substance ' seems to me to be nothing more than an attempt to make a man pay notwithstanding that he has so ordered his affairs that the amount of tax sought from him is not legally claimable.''

Lord Russell of Killowen said this [11]:

" If all that is meant by the doctrine is that having once ascertained the legal rights of the parties you may disregard mere nomenclature and decide the

[7] *Partington* v. *Att.-Gen.* (1869) L.R. 4 H.L. 100 at p. 122.
[8] (1959) 38 T.C. 673 at p. 706. See also *I.R.C.* v. *Reinhold* (1953) 34 T.C. 389; and Russell L.J. in *Re Ralli's Settlement* [1965] Ch. 286 at p. 327 (C.A.).
[9] [1936] A.C. 1; 19 T.C. 490. For recent reaffirmations of the principle in this case see *I.R.C.* v. *Europa Oil (N.Z.) Ltd.* [1971] A.C. 760 *per* Lord Wilberforce at p. 771; *Floor* v. *Davis* [1978] S.T.C. 436 (C.A.) at pp. 441 and 447.
[10] [1936] A.C. 1 at pp. 19–20; 19 T.C. 490 at p. 520.
[11] *Ibid.* at pp. 25 and 524, respectively.

question of taxability or non-taxability in accordance with the legal rights, well and good. . . . If, on the other hand, the doctrine means that you may brush aside deeds, disregard the legal rights and liabilities arising under a contract between parties, and decide the question of taxability or non-taxability upon the footing of the rights and liabilities of the parties being different from what in law they are, then I entirely dissent from such a doctrine."

The language used by the parties to a transaction is not conclusive as to the nature of their legal relationship.[12] On the other hand, the nature of the transaction may be determined by the form selected by the parties [13] or even by the stamp which the instrument bears.[14]

Tax planning

36-04 Much nonsense is talked about tax avoidance. Politicians, unaware of its real nature, speak of it as a social evil to be legislated against. Others speak of avoidance as if it were a game of chess played annually with the Revenue. In fact, avoidance is a natural consequence of the fact that there is often more than one way of achieving the same result. This can be demonstrated by two contrasting examples. A father, with a high income, wishes to make an allowance to his unmarried son, aged 18, who has no income. He can make a voluntary allowance; alternatively, he can covenant by deed to make the allowance. In the first case the father gets no tax relief on the payments he makes but the son pays no tax, since a voluntary allowance is not " income." In the second case the father gets relief from tax at the basic rate (but not at the higher rates [15]), provided the covenant is to run for a period which might exceed six years and is irrevocable [16]; the son has a taxable income (and will suffer basic rate income tax by deduction: see §§ 5-30 *et seq.*) but will be able to reclaim from the Revenue so much of the tax suffered by deduction as exceeds his true liability, taking into account the single person's allowance and the lower-rate tax band. Thus in 1978–79 a son (with no other income) who was paid £1,735 under an appropriately drafted deed of covenant, and who suffered tax at 33 per cent. on this amount by way of deduction would be able to reclaim £985 (the single person's allowance) at 33 per cent. (£325·05) plus £750 (the limit of the lower rate band) at 8 per cent. (£60)—a total reclaim of £385·05. Anything in excess of £1,735 would suffer tax at the basic rate.[17] Thus there will be an overall saving or " avoidance " of tax resulting from the father's alienation of income to his son.

36-05 These two simple contrasting examples show that " avoidance " may be no more than the result of choosing one of two equally acceptable methods of achieving a desired result. In the world of commerce the transactions are often more complex and the range of alternative methods is much wider; if one method is used, the tax is £x, and for another it is £y (or even £ nil), and

---

[12] *I.R.C.* v. *Wesleyan and General Assurance Society* [1948] 1 All E.R. 555 at p. 557; 30 T.C. 11 at p. 24 (H.L.); *per* Viscount Simon.
[13] *Ruskin Investments* v. *Copeman* [1943] 1 All E.R. 378.
[14] *Re McArdle* [1951] Ch. 669.
[15] *Ante,* §§ 10-04 *et seq.*
[16] *Ante,* § 10-19.
[17] *Ante,* § 10-11 and § 8-69 Computations C and D.

the terms " tax avoidance " or " tax planning " conveniently describe the techniques by which the lawyer and accountant can so arrange a client's affairs as to achieve a reduction in the amount of tax he would otherwise have to pay. This is an important function, for the burden of tax is nowadays so great that taxation must be regarded as one of the major costs of production; and enterprising and productive schemes are often made possible only by intelligent tax planning. In other cases legislation is so hasty and ill-conceived, essential reforms are so long delayed,[18] or the consequences of legislation—unforeseen by ill-informed or non-commercially-minded legislators—are so immoral, that taxpayers have to rely on the concoction of highly artificial schemes to avoid what would otherwise be a manifestly unjust or even absurd result. The comments of Lord Reid in a recent case could often be made of sections of Finance Acts:

> " I have suggested what may be a possible meaning but if I am wrong about that I would not shrink from holding that the subsection is so obscure that no meaning can be given to it. I would rather do that than seek by twisting and contorting the words to give to the subsection an improbable meaning. Draftsmen as well as Homer can nod, and Parliament is so accustomed to obscure drafting in Finance Bills that no one may have noticed the defects in this subsection." [19]

---

[18] Consider, *e.g.* I.C.T.A. 1970, s. 451 (*ante*, §§ 10-30 *et seq.*), and the remarks of Lord MacDermott in *Potts' Executors* v. *I.R.C.* [1951] A.C. 443 at p. 466; 32 T.C. 211 at p. 236; see also *I.R.C.* v. *De Vigier* (1964) 42 T.C. 25 (H.L.); *Bates* v. *I.R.C.* [1968] A.C. 483; 44 T.C. 225 (H.L.).

[19] *Associated Newspapers Group Ltd.* v. *Fleming* (1972) 48 T.C. 382, commenting on F.A. 1965, s. 15 (9) *ante*, § 2-72.

CHAPTER 37

GIFTS, SETTLEMENTS AND WILLS

1. OUTRIGHT GIFTS

37-01 AN outright gift may now give rise to a number of different charges to tax, all of which have been considered in detail elsewhere in this book. An outright gift is a disposal for the purposes of the tax on capital gains and a charge to tax may arise unless the gift is exempt from the charge.[1] The donor is treated as disposing of, and the donee as acquiring, the gifted asset at its market value at the time of the gift. The charge to tax falls on the donor; but there are provisions under which the donee can be assessed, subject to his right, if he pays the tax, to recover an equal amount from the donor or his personal representatives.[2]

37-02 An outright gift is also a voluntary disposition for the purposes of stamp duty and may give rise to *ad valorem* duty payable by the donor.[3]

37-03 An outright gift is also a transfer of value and a liability to capital transfer tax will arise unless the gift is exempt or the property is excluded property. Capital transfer tax is payable on the amount by which the donor's estate is reduced in value in consequence of the gift so that if the donor pays the capital transfer tax himself otherwise than out of the gifted property, capital transfer tax will be payable on the sum of the gift and the tax, *i.e.* on the grossed up amount, as explained in Chapter 20. Both capital gains tax and capital transfer tax may be payable on a lifetime transfer—the former on any gain that is treated as accruing on the deemed disposal at market value (see § 16-18) and the latter tax on the diminution in the value of the transferor's estate; but capital gains tax and stamp duty payable by the transferor are left out of account in reckoning this diminution.[4] If the donor dies within three years of the gift, more capital transfer tax will be payable. Grossing up is avoided and capital transfer tax saved if, in the case of a gift of cash, the donor deducts the amount of the capital transfer tax from the gift and accounts for this to the Revenue; or if the donor obtains an undertaking from the donee to pay the tax; or if, no such undertaking having been given, the donee in fact pays the tax when it falls due, whether he pays it out of his own resources or out of later exempt gifts made by the donor. Capital transfer tax is charged in such a way that later gifts are more expensive in terms of tax than earlier gifts, so the order in which gifts are made may require special consideration, especially if some gifts are settled and others not.[5] A father who, for example, decides to give each of his four children £30,000 on their eighteenth birthdays will find that the gifts get progressively more expensive in terms of capital transfer tax.

---

[1] *Ante*, § 16-18.
[2] F.A. 1965, Sched. 7, para. 19.
[3] *Ante*, §§ 30-01 *et seq.*
[4] *Ante*, §§ 20-06 *et seq.*
[5] *Ante*, § 22-64A.

37-04   Although gifts made *inter vivos* attract capital gains tax and capital transfer tax on the lifetime scale (if the donor survives three years), gifts on death attract no capital gains tax but capital transfer tax at the higher scale. In some cases it will pay to make the gift on death and not *inter vivos*.

Although transfers between husband and wife are in many cases exempt from both capital transfer tax and capital gains tax, it may not be good tax planning for a wealthy husband to transfer property to his equally wealthy wife; for this will merely increase the tax payable on her death. Some equalisation of estates is sensible when the marriage is satisfactory but, once equalisation is achieved, transfers to children and/or grandchildren may be worthy of consideration. When the intended beneficiary is destined for a course of higher education, special attention should be given to the possible effect of any income or capital settlement on the beneficiary's entitlement to a local authority grant, *e.g.* a maintenance grant for a course of university study.[5a]

37-05   If the gifted property is trading stock of the donor's trade, the donor may incur liability to tax through the operation of the rule in *Sharkey* v. *Wernher*.[6] No charge to capital gains tax will arise in such a case but a charge to capital transfer tax may arise.

Gifts to directors or employees may be taxable under the rules of Schedule E as emoluments of an office or employment.[7]

2. INCOME SETTLEMENTS

37-06   Income settlements, such as " seven year covenants," are a useful means of alienating income from one taxpayer to another. If A, having an income of £10,000, covenants to pay £1,000 to B, the covenanted amount becomes income of B (charged at the basic rate by deduction at source, because A will in fact pay B £1,000 less tax at the basic rate and is treated as such, with the consequence that B can reclaim from the Revenue the amount of overpaid tax. A secures tax relief at the basic rate in the manner described in §§ 5-33 *et seq*. See § 8-69, Computations C and D.

37-07   The gross amount payable under an income settlement is no longer deductible in computing the liability of the covenantor to higher rate income tax, except [8] in the cases of:

(1) annual payments made under a partnership agreement to or for the benefit of a former member, or to the widow or dependants of a deceased former member of the partnership, being payments made under a liability incurred for full consideration;

(2) certain annual payments applied in acquiring a business; and

(3) certain payments made by one party to a marriage to the other, after the dissolution or annulment of the marriage or while they are separated: see Chapter 38.

[5a] See The Local Education Authority Awards Regulations 1978 (S.I. 1978 No. 1097).
[6] *Ante*, § 2-46.   [7] *Ante*, § 3-09.
[8] See I.C.T.A. 1970, s. 457; *ante*, §§ 10-17 *et seq*.

37-08   Income settlements continue to be useful in tax planning where the
covenantee's income is not fully absorbed by personal reliefs, or where the
covenantee is exempt from income tax (as in the case of a charity), provided
the covenant is so drafted as not to cause the income to be treated as the
income of the covenantor under one or other of the provisions considered in
§§ 10-04 *et seq*. The settlement must be for a period which might exceed six
years and must not be " revocable " in the extended income tax sense.[9]
Further, the covenantor must have sufficient income taxed at the basic rate
for section 52 of the Taxes Act 1970 to apply and for section 53 of that Act
not to apply. The phasing out of child tax allowances makes covenants a
sensible method whereby a parent can provide for a child undergoing
university education, where the parent's income disqualifies him from
obtaining a local authority grant.

3. CAPITAL SETTLEMENTS

37-09   A capital settlement is a settlement of income-producing property, often for
the benefit of the settlor's children and/or remoter issue. For the purposes
of capital transfer tax, capital settlements are classified according to the
trusts on which the settled property is held. The legislation distinguishes
(i) settled property in which there is a beneficial interest in possession;
(ii) settled property in which there is no beneficial interest in possession; and
(iii) settled property held on special trusts, such as trusts for accumulation
and maintenance. It will be convenient under this heading to mention
briefly some considerations which will affect the use of each type of
settlement in the future and the extent to which settlements made before the
introduction of capital transfer tax should now be dismantled. Their use in
connection with arrangements made on separation and divorce is
considered in Chapter 38.

A. *Settled property in which there is a beneficial interest in possession*

1. *Use in the future*

37-10   Settlements were made long before any form of taxation existed and there
will continue to be numerous occasions when individuals will wish to
distribute their wealth so as to delay the vesting of capital and, meanwhile,
to confer limited interests in income, whether by way of life interest or
annuity. It will be remembered that, in addition to capital gains tax, capital
transfer tax is now payable on the making of a settlement (and not only if
the settlor fails to survive seven years, as was the case with estate duty) and
that the legislation treats each holder of an interest in possession as the
beneficial owner of the fund in which his interest subsists. Capital transfer
tax is accordingly payable on the termination, or deemed termination, of
each interest in possession, for however short a time that interest endures
(subject only to quick succession relief).[10] Hence, in drafting this kind of
settlement, a succession of interests in possession should be avoided; and

---

[9] See *ante*, § 10-26.
[10] See *ante*, §§ 22-14 *et seq*.

instead of annuities being charged on settled property, they should where possible be secured by personal covenant or purchased.

2. *Past settlements*

37-11   The introduction of capital transfer tax has made it desirable to review all settlements made beforehand in order to determine what tax has to be provided for in the future and by what means it can be raised. It should be remembered that a reversionary interest is generally excluded property and that such an interest can be extinguished before it vests in possession without any charge to tax. Such an interest should be extinguished where its duration is likely to be short or where the combination of a low income yield and a high capital fund will produce overburdensome tax. Where the settlement was made before March 27, 1974, the charge to tax which would have arisen if the settlor had died within seven years and estate duty had not been abolished is preserved by section 22 (5) (*a*) of the Finance Act 1975.

B. *Settled property in which there is no interest in possession*

1. *Use in the future*

37-12   The discretionary settlement is the commonest form of settlement which falls under this head. Plainly, there will continue to be cases when this form of settlement alone meets the requirements of a particular client but it is thought that, in future, they are unlikely to assume a major role in tax planning. More capital transfer tax will in many cases be payable by the settlor and the trustees than would have been payable if the settlor had retained the funds and made direct gifts *inter vivos*. A study of the example in § 22-57 makes this clear: the £80,000 contributed by S is taxed at 12·03 per cent. when the settlement is made and distributions up to this amount are also taxed at 12·03 per cent. It should be kept in mind that capital distributions have to be grossed up, except when the beneficiary bears the tax: see § 22-45. Discretionary settlements were frequently used for the holding of assets intended to be preserved intact, *e.g.* agricultural property or shares in closely held companies. The periodic charge (§ 22-49) may in such cases put trustees in the embarrassing position of having tax to pay but no funds wherewith to pay it.

2. *Past settlements*

37-13   The general observations in § 37-11, above, apply equally to this form of settlement. There are transitional arrangements in paragraph 14 of Schedule 5 to the Finance Act 1975 (*ante*, § 22-62) which enable discretionary settlements to be determined before 1980 at reduced rates of capital transfer tax and it is thought that many trustees will desire to take advantage of these provisions. Where beneficiaries are resident and domiciled outside the United Kingdom, reinvestment of the trust funds in exempt government securities may be appropriate: see § 19-26.

C. Accumulation and maintenance settlements

37-14 " Accumulation and maintenance settlement " conveniently describes a settlement under which the capital is destined to vest in a person or persons contingently on attaining a specified age. Section 31 of the Trustee Act 1925 applies to English settlements of this type with the consequence that beneficiaries become entitled to the income (and therefore acquire an interest in possession) on attaining the age of 18 years, before which time the income can either be applied for the maintenance, education or benefit of the beneficiary or beneficiaries, or accumulated. Capital transfer tax (and capital gains tax) is payable on the creation of such a settlement but paragraph 15 of Schedule 5 to the Finance Act 1975 (*ante*, § 22-68) prevents any further charge to capital transfer tax arising when the beneficiary's interest in capital vests in possession. Note that it is not necessary for the purposes of paragraph 15 that the interest in *capital* should vest when or before the beneficiary attains the age of 25 years; it is sufficient if his interest in *income* so vests.[11] Such a settlement has the further advantage that income which is accumulated attracts no higher rate income tax but only income tax at the basic rate plus investment income surcharge of 15 per cent., *i.e.* 48 per cent. in 1978–79. Income which is applied for a child's maintenance, education or benefit is treated as the child's income (and can be reduced by personal reliefs), except where the settlor is the child's parent and the child is under 18 years and unmarried, when the income is treated as the parent's income. Settlements of this kind will continue to be widely used in tax planning as a means of saving for children.

4. WILLS

37-15 There are many problems of a revenue nature which arise during the course of advising clients about to make their wills. Before advice can be given, an inventory should first be made of the client's estate and its value estimated. The amount of capital transfer tax likely to be payable on death should be estimated. The client's wishes as to the disposition of each item of property can then be considered in relation to the tax payable and the funds available to meet it. Against this background the client may wish to consider (i) the extent to which the burden of capital transfer tax might be reduced, *e.g.* by *inter vivos* dispositions; and (ii) ways and means of funding the payment of capital transfer tax, *e.g.* by insurance policies. Where the will is deficient in tax-planning terms, there is a two-year period after the death during which it might be possible to put matters right without adverse capital gains tax (see § 16-20A) or capital transfer tax (see § 19-63) consequences.

The consequences of making gifts " free of tax " or " free of duty " are considered in §§ 24-17 *et seq.*

The exemptions from capital transfer tax have been considered in detail in Chapter 19 but the following general comments are relevant in the present context:

---

[11] This view has been confirmed in an Inland Revenue Press Release in [1975] S.T.I. 469.

37-16   (1) The exemption for transfers between spouses (§ 19-02) enables one spouse to transfer an absolute or limited interest in property to the other, either *inter vivos* or by will, free of the tax. If a husband (H) gives property to his wife (W) absolutely or for life, and H dies first, no capital transfer tax is payable on H's death on the property given to W; but capital transfer tax is payable on W's death, whether she has a life interest or an absolute interest in the property. The abolition of the old " surviving spouse exemption " has now removed the need to give the surviving spouse only a limited interest, such as a life interest.

Where husband and wife are comfortably off and there are children, it is obviously desirable that the husband should not transfer more property to the wife than she needs, for to do so will aggravate the wife's own tax position. Often in such a case it is desirable for each spouse to make a will leaving property not needed by the other to their children.

37-17   (2) The exemption for transfers not exceeding £2,000 in each year (§ 19-07) is useful as a means of dissipating an estate in annual stages. The exemption may also be useful to fund the payment of capital transfer tax on a transfer of value previously made to the payee, *e.g.* where the tax is payable by instalments.

37-18   (3) The " normal expenditure out of income " exemption (§ 19-11) can be used to fund the payment of premiums on a policy which the payer has effected for the benefit of a third person, *e.g.* to enable that person to pay capital transfer tax on the payer's death.

37-19   (4) A marriage is a convenient opportunity to make tax-free transfers of a limited amount (see § 19-15).

37-20   (5) Investment in exempt Government securities may be a useful method of saving capital transfer tax for persons neither domiciled nor ordinarily resident in the United Kingdom or for trustees holding property on trust for such persons (§ 19-26).

CHAPTER 38

ASPECTS OF MATRIMONIAL FINANCE

1. THE TAXATION OF HUSBAND AND WIFE
WHEN LIVING TOGETHER

38-01 IT was explained in § 8-23 that the separate incomes of husband and wife
are generally aggregated for the purpose of determining the total tax
payable. By section 37 of the Income and Corporation Taxes Act 1970, a
woman's income chargeable to income tax, so far as it is income for a year
of assessment or part of a year of assessment during which she is a married
woman living with her husband, is deemed for tax purposes to be his income
and not to be her income. By way of exception to this general rule, husband
and wife can jointly elect for the wife's earnings (as defined) to be charged
to tax separately from their other income: see § 8-29. This exception was
introduced to " encourage " wives with an earning capacity to resume, or
continue, work. Care should be taken before making such an election since,
from the wife's *earned* income, there have to be deducted her reliefs, *e.g.*
interest or annuities paid by her. Her investment income is, however,
treated as her husband's income. Problems may therefore arise if her reliefs
exceed her earned income. This right of election should not be confused
with the separate provision, discussed in § 8-26, under which either husband
or wife may apply to be separately *assessed*. An application for a separate
assessment does not alter the total amount of tax payable by the two
spouses: its only effect is that each spouse is liable for his or her own tax.
Section 39 of the Income and Corporation Taxes Act 1970 provides for the
same reliefs and allowances to apply as if there were no separate assessment.
It also provides for the allocation of the reliefs and allowances between
husband and wife. The reliefs and allowances available to spouses are
discussed in §§ 8-42 *et seq.*

38-02 The exemption from capital gains tax on disposals between husband and
wife applies only to disposals made in a year of assessment during which the
woman is a married woman living with her husband: see § 16-17. Hence
disposals made after separation may not be exempt from capital gains tax,
subject to the concession referred to in § 38-21 below.

38-03 Transfers between spouses are normally exempt from capital transfer tax
if made while the marriage subsists, whether or not the spouses are living
together: see § 19-02.

What constitutes living together

38-04 A married woman is treated for tax purposes as " living with her
husband " unless either:
    (a) they are separated under an order of a court of competent
        jurisdiction or by deed of separation; or

(b) they are in fact separated in such circumstances that the separation is likely to be permanent.

The Revenue treat the separation as likely to be permanent if the parties have been living apart for one year. For the position where one spouse is resident, outside or absent from the United Kingdom, see § 8-23.

2. SEPARATION

38-05 If, throughout a year of assessment, husband and wife are not living together (see § 38-04), the income of each of them is separately charged and separately assessed to tax. The man is entitled to the personal relief appropriate to a married man if he wholly maintains his wife and is *not* entitled to deduct any sum paid for her maintenance in computing his total income. Accordingly, if husband and wife are separated and the wife is wholly maintained out of payments made by the husband on a voluntary basis, he is entitled to the personal relief appropriate to a married man. If he maintains her under a court order or under an enforceable agreement, he is entitled to the personal relief appropriate to a single man: see § 8-42.

As regards capital gains tax and capital transfer tax, see § 38-02 and § 38-03, above.

Periodical payments

38-06 Where husband and wife live separately, the husband will normally provide for his wife and children by means of periodical payments; and he may do so either voluntarily or under an enforceable agreement.

38-07 Where voluntary payments are made, the payee incurs no tax liability (because voluntary payments are not " income ") and the payer gets no tax relief on the payments. A husband making voluntary payments continues to be entitled to the personal relief appropriate to a married man: see § 8-42. The payments are exempt from capital transfer tax under the exemption discussed in § 19-02.

38-08 Where payments are made under an enforceable agreement, whether an agreement *inter partes* or a deed poll, and whether orally or in writing, periodical payments are annual payments within Case III of Schedule D: see § 5-04. If the husband agrees to pay his wife (say) £100 a month, the husband deducts tax at the basic rate (33 per cent. in 1978–79, as explained in §§ 5-30 *et seq.*) and thus actually pays £67 monthly. The wife thus " suffers " tax at the basic rate by deduction at source. If by reason of her reliefs and allowances the wife is not liable to tax at so high a rate, she can recover the difference from the Revenue by means of a repayment claim. Conversely, if she has other income, the grossed up amount of the periodical payments (£100 monthly) is brought into the computation of her total income as explained in § 8-18. Note that maintenance payments (as defined) are not investment income: see § 8-05. The husband may deduct the gross amount payable to his wife in computing his total income and so obtain relief from income tax at the higher rates: see §§ 8-31 *et seq*. Because of this he is entitled only to the personal allowance appropriate to a single person: see § 8-42. See § 8-69, Computations C and D.

Agreements for a net sum

38-09 The example in § 38-08 illustrates the position where the agreement provides for a gross sum of £100 monthly. The disadvantage of expressing a periodical payment as a gross sum is that the net amount will decrease if the basic rate of tax increases. It is often more convenient for a net sum to be specified which will remain constant whether or not the basic rate changes. The husband may, for example, agree to pay his wife such a sum as after deduction of tax at the basic rate will leave her with £67 monthly. If the basic rate is 33 per cent., this represents a gross income of £100. If the basic rate is 50 per cent., it represents a gross income of £132. Where the formula " such a sum as after deduction of tax " is used, this means tax at the basic rate and not tax at the higher rate or investment income surcharge: the reference to " deduction " can refer only to tax at the basic rate because tax at the other rates cannot be suffered by deduction.

Agreements to meet expenses

38-10 The parties to an agreement may wish to include a provision under which the husband is to meet the expense of keeping the matrimonial home or of educating the children. If the husband pays the bills he is entitled to no tax relief on expenditure so incurred because payment of bills does not put his wife in receipt of an income. (This would be so even if he were bound by a court order to pay the bills: the obligation would be as to the *application* of his income and not its disposition.) If, on the other hand, the husband agrees to pay his wife such a sum as after deduction of tax at the basic rate will provide her with an amount equal to the amount of the expenses, which she then bears out of the income so provided, the husband is entitled to tax relief on the grossed up amount of the sums paid.

Mortgage interest

38-10A Mortgage interest is eligible for tax relief if the mortgaged property is the only or main residence of the borrower or of his separated spouse; but the relief is available only on loans up to £25,000: see § 8-60A. Thus if after separation the wife continues to occupy the matrimonial home on which the husband has borrowed (say) £20,000, the husband's borrowing limit for the purchase of a residence for his own occupation is £5,000. Where the former matrimonial home is owned in equal shares and there is a joint mortgage, the husband's tax position will be alleviated if his wife covenants in the separation agreement to pay (say) half the mortgage interest and the husband agrees to provide her with an amount of income equal to the interest so paid. This, in the example, would increase the husband's borrowing limit (with tax relief) from £5,000 to £15,000; and he would also obtain tax relief on the amount paid to his wife.

Provision for children

38-11   Where under a separation or similar agreement a husband agrees to make a periodical payment to his child, the amount so paid is deemed to be income of the husband if at the time of payment the child is unmarried and under the age of 18 years: see § 10-23. Where, however, the child is either married or has attained the age of 18 years, the appropriate amount is treated as income of the child and the father is entitled to tax relief.

Agreements to consent to divorce

38-12   Separating spouses may wish to have included in a separation agreement a provision that if one spouse petitions for divorce after two years of separation, the other will consent to a decree being granted for the purposes of section 1 (2) (*d*) of the Matrimonial Causes Act 1973. It is arguable that such a clause would enable a husband to terminate his obligations to make periodical payments under the agreement so as to make the agreement " a revocable settlement " within section 445 of the Income and Corporation Taxes Act 1970 and thus deprive the husband of tax relief on payments made thereunder: see § 10-26.

Maintenance orders and small maintenance orders

38-13   Periodical payments made to a wife under a maintenance order are treated in the same way as periodical payments made to a wife under an enforceable agreement, except that there are special provisions which apply to " small maintenance payments ": see § 5-05.

3. DIVORCE ETC.

Orders for periodical payments

38-14   The court has wide powers under Part II of the Matrimonial Causes Act 1973 to make orders for periodical payments (secured or unsecured) in cases of divorce, nullity or judicial separation and also in cases of neglect to maintain.

38-15   A court order, not being an " agreement " within section 106 (2) of the Taxes Management Act 1970 may lawfully provide for a " tax free " sum (see § 5-48). An order to pay £x " free of tax " means an order to pay such a sum as after deduction of tax at the basic rate will leave £x, *i.e.* the amount stated is treated as the net amount. Where no reference to tax is made in the order, the amount stated is the gross amount.

38-16   Payments made under a court order which do not exceed £21 weekly or £91 monthly are " small maintenance payments " and are made without deduction of tax: see § 5-05. Where the payments are not small maintenance payments the tax position of the payer and payee respectively are as stated in §§ 38-08 *et seq.*

38-17   Some of the problems which arise where there is a foreign element in the transaction have been referred to in § 5-43.

Whose income?

38-18   A court order which directs payment to be made *direct* to any individual is treated by the Revenue as *not* being a settlement to which the provisions of section 437 of the Income and Corporation Taxes Act 1970 apply; see § 10-09.[1] Thus if an order provides for periodical payments to be made to a child, the payments are treated as income of the child and not as income of any other person. If, however, periodical payments are ordered to be made to the wife for the maintenance of the child, the payments are income of the wife.[2] Where the order is for payments to be made to the child, there may be an exchange of letters between petitioner and respondent as to the form compliance with the order should take, *e.g.* that payments should be made into a bank account in the mother's name, out of which she will pay school fees, etc. If by some such arrangement the father agrees to pay the school fees himself, the sums paid may nevertheless be income of the child for tax purposes.

38-19   A single person's allowance is currently £985 so an order for payments up to this amount can be made in favour of a child without making the child liable for any tax (assuming this is the child's only income). Although child relief is reduced by the amount by which the child's income exceeds £115 (see § 8-47) this loss of relief becomes insignificant as child relief is phased out and is replaced by tax-free child benefit. Nevertheless, some care is needed in deciding whether or not the order should be made to the child direct or to the parent.[3]

Capital provision

38-20   Part II of the Matrimonial Causes Act 1973 empowers the court to order a lump sum provision in favour of a party to the marriage or a child of the family or to make a property adjustment order directing, for example, the transfer of the matrimonial home from husband to wife, or the making of a settlement, or the variation of an existing settlement. The taxes on capital gains and capital transfers have to be kept in mind when considering orders of this kind.

38-21   As regards capital gains tax, it will be remembered that the exemption which applies to transfers between spouses does not apply in years of assessment following the year in which the parties separate: see § 16-17. There is, however, a limited concession which applies only to the matrimonial home. Where as a result of a breakdown of the marriage one spouse ceases to occupy his or her matrimonial home and subsequently as part of a financial settlement disposes of the home, or an interest in it, to the other spouse (or, if the transfer is after divorce, ex-spouse), the home may be regarded for the purposes of section 29 of the Finance Act 1965 (exemption or relief from capital gains tax on an individual's main

---

[1] See *Yates* v. *Starkey* [1951] Ch. 465; 32 T.C. 38.
[2] *Stevens* v. *Tirard* [1940] 1 K.B. 204; 23 T.C. 321 (C.A.).
[3] See " Children's Maintenance—Tax and Welfare Benefit Advantages of Direct Payments " by J. E. Adams, LL.B., in the *Law Society Gazette*, vol. 72, number 26 at p. 750.

residence: see § 16-41) as continuing to be a residence of the transferring spouse from the date his (or her) occupation ceases until the date of transfer, provided that it has throughout this period been the other spouse's only or main residence. Thus where a married couple separate and the husband leaves the matrimonial home while still owning it, the usual capital gains tax exemption or relief will be given on the subsequent transfer to the wife, provided she has continued to live in the house and the husband has not elected that some other house should be treated as his main residence for this period.[4]

38-22   As regards capital transfer tax, transfers between spouses, *i.e.* prior to decree absolute, are exempt from the tax: see § 19-02. Transfers of property made after decree absolute may qualify for exemption from capital transfer tax under the exemption discussed in § 19-10. Dispositions in favour of a child of the family may be exempt from capital transfer tax under the exemption discussed in § 19-55.

Settlements

38-23   Where there are young children, the court may order that the wife be permitted to remain in occupation of the matrimonial home for a specified period, that it be then sold and that the proceeds of sale be then divided in specified proportions. An order in this form creates a " settlement " for the purposes of capital transfer tax and capital gains tax. Under the settlement the wife has an " interest in possession " as explained in § 22-14. The transfer into settlement in such case is exempt from capital transfer tax under the exemption discussed in § 19-55 and from capital gains tax under the concession referred to in § 38-21. On the termination of the wife's interest in possession, no capital transfer tax is payable in respect of so much of the settled property as reverts to the settlor husband (see § 22-27). It is thought that the exemption in § 19-55 applies to that part of the settled property which passes to the wife. The husband is liable to capital gains tax on any increase in the value of the matrimonial home between the date of the transfer into settlement and the deferred sale.

---

[4] Inland Revenue Press Release of October 22, 1973, quoted in [1973] S.T.I. 450.

CHAPTER 39

PROBLEMS RELATED TO
OFFICES AND EMPLOYMENTS

1. GENERAL MATTERS

39-01　THE taxation of emoluments under Schedule E has been considered.[1] At the outset it was pointed out that a difficult question sometimes arises, in the case of individuals who undertake a number of different engagements at the same time, whether each engagement constitutes a different office or employment or whether they together constitute a single profession or vocation.[2] Where claims for expenses are concerned, the rules of Schedule D are more favourable to the taxpayer than the rules of Schedule E and it is sometimes practicable so to arrange matters that an individual is brought under Schedule D; but it should not be assumed that Schedule D is always to be preferred. The " golden-handshake " provisions of Schedule E [3] are more favourable to the taxpayer than the corresponding rules of Schedule D [4]; and the rules of Schedule E provide more opportunity than is sometimes realised for tax-free " fringe-benefits." [5]

39-02　Normal remuneration paid to directors and employees of trading concerns is deductible in computing profits for tax purposes. Excessive remuneration may be disallowed.[6] Pensions and salary which are, in reality, annual payments, may be taxed as such.[7] The Revenue tend to restrict the amount of directors' remuneration allowable by way of management expenses, especially in the case of companies with pure investment income.[8]

39-03　In the case of directors and employees with £7,500 a year or more in 1978–79 (£8,500 in 1979–80) the statutory provisions relating to expenses allowances and benefits in kind must be carefully watched.[9]

39-04　Considerable care is required in drafting service agreements for directors, especially where these contain provisions for pensions or other retirement benefits. It is not always appreciated that a service agreement providing retirement benefits for a single director may be a " retirement benefits scheme " to which the provisions of section 23 of the Finance Act 1970 apply.[10] This may result in a wholly unexpected tax liability. A service agreement which is a vehicle for providing a pension for a director's widow in circumstances where the prosperity of the company is in no way enhanced may be *ultra vires* and void.[11]

---

[1] *Ante,* Chap. 3.
[3] *Ante,* §§ 3-24 *et seq.*
[5] *Ante,* §§ 3-14 *et seq.*
[7] *Ante,* § 5-04.
[8] *Ante,* § 6-32.
[9] *Ante,* §§ 3-40 *et seq.* The figure of £5,000 was increased from £2,000 for 1975–76 and subsequent years: F.A. 1974, s. 18.
[10] *Ante,* §§ 3-30 *et seq.*

[2] *Ante,* § 3-03.
[4] *Ante,* §§ 2-25 *et seq.*
[6] *Ante,* § 2-59.

[11] *Re W. & M. Roith Ltd.* [1967] 1 W.L.R. 432.

39-05   A payment which is made in connection with the termination of an office or employment, and which is not otherwise chargeable to tax, is chargeable to tax under Schedule E by virtue of section 187 of the Income and Corporation Taxes Act 1970, subject to an exemption from tax for the first £10,000.[12] A payment which is chargeable to tax apart from the section does not qualify for this exemption. The question whether such a payment is deductible depends, in the case of a trading company, on the general principles applicable to Schedule D expenses and, in particular, on whether the payment is made wholly and exclusively for the purposes of the company's trade.[13] A payment made by way of compensation to an employee who is wrongfully dismissed will be allowed as a deduction if there is a genuine pre-estimate of the damage he suffers; and even where the employee could be rightly dismissed, a sum paid to secure his voluntary retirement might be allowed.[14] Where the shares of the person to be compensated are being acquired, the compensation will be disallowed if it represents consideration for the shares or a disguised dividend.[15]

39-06   If an award of damages by the court is based on income which has been lost to the claimant and that income would have been taxable if received by the claimant, the court will take tax into account in assessing damages under the rule in *Gourley's* case.[16] Tax will not be taken into account by the court if the sum awarded is itself chargeable to tax. Thus in an action for damages for wrongful dismissal, the *Gourley* principle applies in the case of an award of less than £10,000 [17]; and where the award exceeds £10,000, it applies to the tax-free £10,000.[18]

39-07   Stock option or incentive schemes for directors and employees have now generally ceased to be effective as a means of providing benefits free of Schedule E tax.[19]

2. APPROVED PENSION SCHEMES

39-08   Many of the income tax and capital transfer tax problems which arise where a pension scheme exists have been discussed elsewhere in this book. These problems can be summarised as follows:

(1) Problems which concern the employer [20]:

  (a) Whether annual contributions made by the employer are deductible in computing profits under Schedule D.
  (b) Whether an initial contribution to establish the pension fund is similarly deductible.
  (c) Whether the income of the pension fund is subject to tax.
  (d) Whether pensions are deductible in computing profits.

---

[12] *Ante*, §§ 3-25 *et seq.*   [13] *Ante*, §§ 2-51 *et seq.* Note especially § 2-66.
[14] See *Mitchell* v. *B. W. Noble Ltd.*, *ante*, § 2-55.
[15] See *ante*, § 2-66.
[16] *British Transport Commission* v. *Gourley* [1956] A.C. 185 (H.L.). For a statement of the conditions to be satisfied, see *London & Thames Haven Oil Wharves Ltd.* v. *Attwooll* (1966) 43 T.C. 491 (C.A.) at p. 515; and see *Raja's Commercial College* v. *Gian Singh & Co. Ltd.* [1976] S.T.C. 282 (J.C.).
[17] *Parsons* v. *B.N.M. Laboratories* [1964] 1 Q.B. 95.
[18] *Bold* v. *Brough, Nicholson & Hall Ltd.* [1964] 1 W.L.R. 201.
[19] See §§ 3-18 *et seq.*   [20] Discussed *ante*, § 2-78.

(2) Problems which concern employees [21]:
- (a) Whether the employee's contributions are deductible in computing emoluments under Schedule E.
- (b) Whether contributions of the employer are to be treated as additional emoluments of the employee.
- (c) Whether pensions are taxable.
- (d) Whether benefits paid on the death of the employee are subject to capital transfer tax.

It is generally to the advantage of the employer and the employees that the pension scheme should be approved by the Commissioners of Inland Revenue and the main types of approved scheme are now considered. The setting up of pension schemes and matters relating to them is nowadays a matter for pension specialists, and only a brief outline of the subject is given in this book.

Approved retirement benefits schemes

39-09   Under section 19 of the Finance Act 1970 the Board are under an obligation to approve a retirement benefits scheme provided the following conditions are satisfied:

- (a) The scheme is bona fide established for the sole purpose of providing " relevant benefits " [22] payable to the employee or to his widow, children, dependants or personal representatives;
- (b) The scheme is recognised by the employer and employees to whom it relates and every employee who is, or has a right to be, a member of the scheme has been given written particulars of all essential features of the scheme which concern him;
- (c) There is a person resident in the United Kingdom responsible for discharging the duties imposed on the administrator of the scheme under the Act;
- (d) The employer is a contributor to the scheme;
- (e) The scheme is established in connection with some trade or undertaking carried on in the United Kingdom by a person resident in the United Kingdom;
- (f) In no circumstances, whether during the subsistence of the scheme or later, can any employee's contributions under the scheme be repaid.

The requirement that, when the employer is a company, service rendered by a person while he is a controlling director shall be left out of account, no longer applies. [23]

39-10   There are certain other conditions which must be satisfied in practice: broadly speaking, (i) contributions by the employee should not exceed 15 per cent. of his salary; (ii) the benefits payable to the employee must consist only of benefits payable on or after retirement at a specified age not earlier than 60 or later than 70, or on earlier retirement through incapacity;

---

[21] Discussed *ante*, §§ 3-28 *et seq.*
[22] Defined F.A. 1970, s. 26 (1).
[23] F.A. 1973, s. 15.

(iii) the aggregate value of the relevant benefits payable on or after retirement after 40 or more years' service must not exceed two-thirds of his final remuneration; and (iv) the lump sum benefits payable on or after retirement must not exceed three-eightieths of his final remuneration for each year of service up to a maximum of 40 (the overall limit for 40 years' service being, therefore, 120/80ths).

There are provisions whereby the Revenue have a discretion to approve a scheme even if it does not satisfy one or more of the prescribed conditions.[24]

If an employer pays a sum to provide benefits for any employee pursuant to a retirement benefits scheme, that sum is deemed to be income of the employee assessable under Schedule E (if not otherwise chargeable to income tax as income of the employee). Where the retirement benefits scheme is approved, the employee is exempted from this charge to tax.

However, to obtain the maximum tax benefits, the scheme should be an " exempt approved scheme." Under the provisions of section 21 of the Finance Act 1970, an " exempt approved scheme " is one which is approved and which is established under irrevocable trusts.

39-11   Where the retirement benefit scheme is an " exempt approved scheme " the consequences are as follows:

(a) The investment income of the fund is exempt from tax, and capital gains on the disposal of investments are not chargeable gains for the purposes of capital gains tax.

(b) The employer's contributions to the fund are deductible in computing profits: ordinary annual contributions being deductible in the year when they are paid and other contributions being treated as the Board direct. An initial contribution to establish a pension fund will normally be spread over a period of not more than 10 years.

(c) Employees' contributions (if they are " ordinary annual contributions "[25]) are deductible in computing emoluments under Schedule E in the year when they are paid; no allowance is given under section 19 or 20 of the Taxes Act 1970 in respect of any payments which qualify for relief under section 21 of the Finance Act 1970 (s. 21 (5)).

(d) An annuity paid out of the fund to a person residing in the United Kingdom will be treated as an emolument falling under Schedule E to which P.A.Y.E. will apply instead of as an annual payment under section 53 of the Income and Corporation Taxes Act 1970.[26]

39-12   Where contributions are returned to the employee (as, for when he leaves the employment), they are taxed at one-half of the basic rate in the year of repayment, the administrator of the fund being charged to tax under

---

[24] F.A. 1973, s. 20.
[25] " Back contributions " are not " ordinary annual contributions ": *Kneen* v. *Ashton* [1950] 1 All E.R. 982; 31 T.C. 343.
[26] F.A. 1970, Sched. 5, Pt. II, para. 1.

Case VI of Schedule D on that amount. [27] Where contributions are repaid to the employer (as on a winding up of the pension fund), if the scheme relates to a trade, profession or vocation carried on by the employer the repaid contributions are treated as a receipt of the trade, etc., and if the scheme does not relate to a trade, profession or vocation, they are assessed on the employer under Case VI of Schedule D. [28]

Retirement annuities

39-14 [29] Before the Finance Act 1956, self-employed persons, controlling-directors of controlled companies and employees who were not in pensionable employment were unable to provide for their old age out of untaxed income, as were employees who were members of an approved pension scheme. The Finance Act 1956 introduced provisions by which an individual could make arrangements to secure a retirement annuity, either from an insurance company or through a professional body, and obtain a measure of tax relief in respect of the premiums or contributions paid by him. These provisions (as extended by s. 20 of and Sched. 2 to the Finance Act 1971) are now in sections 226–229 of the Income and Corporation Taxes Act 1970.

39-15   Section 226 of the Income and Corporation Taxes Act 1970 gives tax relief to an individual chargeable to income tax in respect of relevant earnings (as defined) from any trade, profession, vocation, office or employment who pays a premium or other consideration (called " a qualifying premium ") under an annuity contract approved by the Board as having for its main object the provision for the individual of a life annuity in old age or under a contract approved under section 226A of the Act. Section 226A allows the Board to approve (a) a contract the main object of which is the provision of an annuity for the wife or husband of the individual, or for any one or more dependants of the individual and (b) a contract the sole object of which is the provision of a lump sum on the death of the individual before he attains the age of 75, being a lump sum payable to his personal representatives. A number of conditions have to be satisfied before approval will be granted. Approval can in some cases be obtained for a retirement annuity contract which enables the individual to transfer the value of his accrued benefits to another life office. [30]

Under section 227 (1) of the Income and Corporation Taxes Act 1970, relief is given in respect of a qualifying premium paid by an individual only on a claim being made for the purpose and, where relief is given, the amount of the premium may be deducted from or set off against the *relevant earnings* (as defined [31]) of the individual for the year of assessment in which the premium is paid. There are provisions for carry forward in the event of an insufficiency of relevant earnings in any one year.

There are limits to the tax relief which is obtainable. Generally, the

---

[27] F.A. 1970, Sched. 5, Pt. II, para. 2.
[28] *Ibid.* para. 4.
[29] The last paragraph was numbered 39–12.
[30] F.A. 1978, s. 26.
[31] I.C.T.A. 1970, s. 227 (4).

amount which may be deducted in respect of a contract (including a contract approved under section 226A) must not exceed £3,000 [32] or 15 per cent. of the individual's *net relevant earnings* (as defined [33]) for the year. Not more than £1,000 [34] or 5 per cent. of the individual's net relevant earnings for the year may be deducted in respect of a contract approved under section 226A.

Approval will be given for a contract which gives the individual the right to receive, by way of commutation of part of the annuity payable to him, a lump sum not exceeding three times the annual amount of the remaining part of the annuity.

---

[32] Increased from £2,250 in and from 1977–78 by F.A. 1977, s. 27.

[33] I.C.T.A. 1970, s. 227 (5). Charges on income must be deducted from relevant income for the purposes of computing net relevant earnings.

[34] Increased from £750 in and from 1977–78 by F.A. 1977, s. 27.

CHAPTER 40

TAX AVOIDANCE

40-01 PART XVII (ss. 460–496) of the Income and Corporation Taxes Act 1970, is entitled Tax Avoidance. Many of the anti-avoidance provisions contained in Part XVII have been mentioned earlier in this book including—

(1) A group of sections (ss. 478–481) designed to prevent avoidance of United Kingdom tax by transferring assets abroad [1];

(2) A section (s. 482) which makes it a criminal offence without the consent of the Treasury *inter alia* for a body corporate resident in the United Kingdom to cease to be so resident or for the trade or business, or part of the trade or business, of a United Kingdom resident company to be transferred to a person not so resident [2];

(3) Sections (ss. 483–484) designed to prevent avoidance of tax by the sale of " tax loss companies " [3];

(4) Sections (ss. 485–486) to prevent avoidance of tax by transactions between associated companies, such as sales at an undervalue or overvalue [4]; and

(5) A section (s. 491) restricting the amount of rent which is deductible in the case of certain sale and lease-back transactions. [5]

(6) A section (s. 496) entitled " transactions associated with loans or credit " which, *inter alia*, deals with " disguised interest."

In this chapter, three groups of the remaining anti-avoidance provisions in Part XVII of the 1970 Act are considered, the topics dealt with being those which are of such importance in practice as to merit special mention; but nothing more than a bare outline of the relevant provisions is attempted.

1. CANCELLATION OF TAX ADVANTAGES: SECTION 460

40-02 Section 460 of the Income and Corporation Taxes Act 1970 (formerly section 28 of the Finance Act 1960), applies where in certain circumstances stated in the section and in consequence of a transaction in securities or of the combined effect of two or more such transactions, a person is in a position to obtain, or has obtained, a tax advantage. Tax advantage includes the avoidance of a possible assessment to tax. The section does not apply if the person in question shows that the transaction or transactions were carried out either for bona fide commercial reasons or in the ordinary course of making or managing investments *and* that none of them had as their main object, or one of their main objects, to enable tax advantages to be obtained. [6] Further, the section does not apply if the transaction or

---

[1] *Ante*, § 7-26.
[2] *Ante*, § 7-22.
[3] *Ante*, § 14-30.
[4] *Ante*, § 2-44.
[5] *Ante*, § 2-62.
[6] I.C.T.A. 1970, s. 460 (1). For a case falling within this exemption, see *I.R.C.* v. *Brebner* [1967] 2 A.C. 18; 43 T.C. 705 (H.L.). In that case the extraction of cash from the company in a non-taxable form was an

transactions in securities were carried out and any change in the nature of any activities carried on by a person, being a change necessary in order that the tax advantage should be obtainable, was effected before April 5, 1960. [7]

Procedure

40-03   The procedure under section 460 is initiated by the service by the Board of a notice under subsection (6), notifying the person in question that the Board have reason to believe that the section might apply to him in respect of a transaction or transactions specified in the notice. The person in question may, on receipt of the notice under subsection (6), make a statutory declaration to the effect that the section does not apply to him stating the facts and the circumstances upon which his opinion is based. The declaration must be made within 30 days of the issue of the notice [8] but, in practice, the Board may agree within the period of 30 days to accept a declaration some days after the period of 30 days has expired. Where several notices are served on shareholders of the same company in respect of the same transaction, it is common practice to deliver a principal declaration by one shareholder together with supporting declarations by the other shareholders. On receipt of the declaration, the Board may decide to take no further action in the matter; but if they decide otherwise, they must send the declaration to the Tribunal constituted under the section together with a certificate stating that the Board see reason to take further action in the matter. [9] In addition, the Board may send to the Tribunal a counter-statement replying (in effect) to the taxpayer's declaration. [9] Proceedings before the Tribunal are in private and the taxpayer has no opportunity at this stage of seeing or commenting on the counter-statement. [10] The function of the Tribunal is to determine from the statutory declaration and any counter-statement whether or not there is a prima facie case for proceeding in the matter and it may reasonably be assumed in all save the most unusual cases that a prima facie case for proceeding will be found. If the Tribunal finds a prima facie case for proceeding (or if no statutory declaration is made within the time specified), the Board serve a further notice under subsection (3) of section 460 which, for the first time, specifies the manner in which it is proposed to counteract the tax advantage. A person to whom a subsection (3) notice is given may within 30 days thereafter give notice of appeal to the Special Commissioners on the ground that section 460 does not apply and/or that the adjustments proposed to be made are inappropriate. [11] Proceedings before the Special Commissioners are conducted in the same way as ordinary appeals against an assessment. If the appellant or the Revenue is dissatisfied with the decision of the Special Commissioners, the dissatisfied party may require the case to be reheard by the Tribunal. [11] Proceedings before the Tribunal are conducted in

---

integral part of a commercial scheme. See also *Goodwin* v. *I.R.C.* [1976] 1 W.L.R. 191; S.T.C. 28 (H.L.). *Cf. Hague* v. *I.R.C.* (1968) 44 T.C. 619 (C.A.); *I.R.C.* v. *Horrocks* (1968) 44 T.C. 645; *Hasloch* v. *I.R.C.* (1971) 47 T.C. 50.
    [7] I.C.T.A. 1970, s. 460 (1), proviso. See *Greenberg* v. *I.R.C.* [1972] A.C. 109; 47 T.C. 240.
    [8] *Ibid*. s. 460 (6).
    [9] *Ibid*. s. 460 (7).
    [10] See *Wiseman* v. *Borneman* [1971] A.C. 297 (H.L.).
    [11] I.C.T.A. 1970, s. 462 (2).

substantially the same way as are proceedings before the Special Commissioners. There is a right of appeal by way of Case Stated on a point of law to the High Court from the Special Commissioners or from a rehearing by the Tribunal.[12]

Conditions for the operation of the section

40-04   Three conditions [13] must exist before section 460 of the Income and Corporation Taxes Act 1970 applies. First, there must be a transaction or transactions in securities. Secondly, the person in question must be in a position to obtain, or have obtained, a tax advantage in consequence of the transaction in securities or of the combined effect of two or more such transactions. Thirdly, the tax advantage must be obtained in one of the circumstances mentioned in section 461. Each of these three conditions requires separate consideration.

40-05   (1) *Transaction in securities.* The phrase " transaction in securities " is defined [14] as including transactions, of whatever description, relating to securities, and in particular:

(i) the purchase, sale or exchange of securities;

(ii) the issuing or securing the issue of, or applying or subscribing for, new securities;

(iii) the altering, or securing the alteration of, the rights attached to securities.

40-06   In *I.R.C.* v. *Parker* [15] it was held that the particular instances referred to in (i), (ii) and (iii) do not in any way restrict the meaning to be given to the general words which precede them and that the redemption of debentures was accordingly a transaction in securities. Where shares are sold for cash the act of payment by the purchaser is a transaction in securities; and a payment of a dividend may also be such a transaction.[16]

40-07   Section 460 (2) provides that

" . . . for the purposes of this chapter a tax advantage obtained or obtainable by a person shall be deemed to be obtained or obtainable by him in consequence of a transaction in securities or of the combined effect of two or more such transactions, if it is obtained or obtainable in consequence of the combined effect of the transaction or transactions and of the liquidation of a company."

40-08   This subsection is aimed at various types of company reconstruction. Suppose that A Limited carries on a business, has distributable reserves of £100,000 and has cash or other liquid assets of the same amount. The shareholders of A Limited form a new company, B Limited, and A Limited (or its liquidator) sells the business of A Limited to B Limited in consideration of an allotment of shares in B Limited credited as fully paid

---

[12] I.C.T.A. 1970, s. 462 (3).   [13] *Ibid*. s. 460 (1).
[14] *Ibid*. s. 467 (1). Securities includes shares and stock and (generally) the interest of a member in a company not limited by shares: *ibid*. s. 467 (1).
[15] [1966] A.C. 141; 43 T.C. 396 (H.L.); for the facts, see *post*, § 40-09.
[16] See *Greenberg* v. *I.R.C.* [1972] A.C. 109; 47 T.C. 240 (H.L.).

up. The cash or liquid assets are left in A Limited, which then goes into liquidation. In such circumstances section 460 applies and the shareholders of A Limited are treated as if the assets received by them in the liquidation of A Limited (less the amount of cash subscribed for the shares and excluding the shares in B Limited) represented the net amount of a dividend.[17] It is assumed in the example that the shareholders in both companies are the same and hold their shares in the same proportions. A notice under section 460 would probably not be issued to a shareholder of A Limited who had no shares in B Limited.

In *I.R.C.* v. *Joiner*,[18] a members' voluntary liquidation was preceded by a liquidation agreement, the purpose of which was to vary the shareholders' rights to receive surplus assets in a liquidation in such a way that the taxpayer could both continue to carry on the business of the company and receive surplus cash. The liquidation agreement was held to constitute a transaction in securities and the tax advantage to be the combined effect of that transaction and the liquidation.

40-08A *Liquidation.* At one time it was supposed that the liquidation of a company was not a transaction in securities because it involves no alteration of the rights attached to securities: it merely gives effect to pre-existing rights. But since the decision of the House of Lords in the *Greenberg*[19] case, in which some of their Lordships expressed the view that a payment of a dividend might be a transaction in securities, the Revenue have been advised that a distribution to a shareholder in the liquidation of a company is a transaction in securities. In 1960 an assurance was given to the House of Commons[20] that an ordinary liquidation was outside section 460 and, on March 21, 1973, Mr. John Nott assured the House " that the Inland Revenue have not sought and will not seek to apply the provisions of section 460 of the Income and Corporation Taxes Act 1970 to ordinary liquidations." In answer to a further parliamentary question asked on April 19, 1973, Mr. John Nott said that the Inland Revenue

> " do not propose any change of practice in relation to an ordinary liquidation, that is to say the bona fide winding up of a business as a distinct entity, whether the business with its concomitant goodwill then comes to an end or is taken over by some other concern which is under substantially different control. On the other hand the Inland Revenue would not regard as ' ordinary ' a liquidation which is part of a scheme of reconstruction which enables the old business to be carried on as before with substantially the same shareholders, directly or indirectly, in control. Section 460 does not of course apply where a taxpayer can show that the transaction or transactions were carried out for bona fide commercial reasons or in the ordinary course of making or managing investments and that the main object or one of the main objects was the obtaining of a tax advantage."

A further " explanation " of the official practice was given to the Standing Committee dealing with the Finance Bill 1973 on May 16, 1973.[21]

---

[17] For the computation of liability, see *post*, §§ 40-13 *et seq.*
[18] (1975) 50 T.C. 449; [1975] S.T.C. 657 (H.L.).
[19] See note 16, above.
[20] *Hansard*, May 25, 1960, col. 511.
[21] (1973) S.T.I. 263.

The effect of the Revenue's statements appears to be that every distribution in every liquidation will be regarded as falling within section 460 unless the taxpayer can satisfy the Board (or the Special Commissioners on appeal) that the distribution formed part of a transaction carried out for bona fide commercial reasons etc.; but having regard to the decisions in *Hague* and *Horrocks* [22] it seems unlikely that the " bona fide commercial test " could ever be satisfied in regard to most voluntary liquidations. In the author's opinion no liquidation or reduction of capital should now be carried out in any circumstances without prior clearance under section 464 of the Act.

In *I.R.C.* v. *Joiner,* [23] Goulding J. and the House of Lords declined to decide in the Revenue's favour the point which was forcefully argued by the Crown that, since the *Greenberg* case, every distribution in a liquidation is a " transaction in securities " for the purposes of section 460. The *Joiner* case was decided against the taxpayer on the narrower ground referred to in § 40-08. If section 460 applies to ordinary liquidations, the statutory provision in section 460 (2) (see *ante,* § 40-07), which was introduced by way of amendment by section 25 (5) of the Finance Act 1962, is otiose and it is difficult to see why it was not omitted from the consolidation amendments made by the Finance Act 1969. Viscount Dilhorne and Lord Diplock expressed firm opinions in the *Joiner* case that the liquidation of a company could not itself be regarded as a transaction in securities.

40-09   (2) *Tax advantage.* The phrase " tax advantage " is defined [24] as meaning a relief or increased relief from, or repayment or increased repayment of, tax, or the avoidance or reduction of an assessment to tax or the avoidance of a possible assessment thereto, whether the avoidance or reduction is effected by receipts accruing in such a way that the recipient does not pay or bear tax on them, or by a deduction in computing profits or gains.

> In *I.R.C.* v. *Parker,* [25] a company in May 1953 capitalised £35,002 of its accumulated profits and applied the same in paying up in full at par debentures which were duly issued to the members. The debentures conferred no charge on any of the company's assets nor did they carry interest. It was a condition of the issue of the debentures that the company might at any time after the death of the registered holder or after the expiration of seven years from the date of the debentures, whichever was earlier, give notice of its intention to pay off the debentures on the expiration of six months from the giving of the notice. In July 1960 the company gave notice of intention to redeem the debentures which were duly redeemed in January 1961. A notice was duly served on a debenture holder under section 460 (then section 28 of the Finance Act 1960), and the Revenue contended that the amount repaid to the debenture holder should be treated for the purposes of the section as if it represented the net amount of a dividend.

The House of Lords held, by a majority, that section 460 applied. The debenture holder received in a capital form (*i.e.* by way of redemption of his debenture) moneys which, apart from the capitalisation in 1953, would have been available for distribution by way of dividend; a possible assessment to

---

[22] See *ante,* § 40-02, note 6.
[23] [1973] S.T.C. 224 (Goulding J.) and (1975) 50 T.C. 449; [1975] S.T.C. 657 (H.L.).
[24] I.C.T.A. 1970, s. 466 (1).   [25] [1966] A.C. 141; 43 T.C. 396 (H.L.).

surtax was thereby avoided and a tax advantage was obtained. Further, it was held (by a majority) that the tax advantage was obtained in 1961 when the debentures were redeemed and not in 1953 when the profits were capitalised and the taxpayer received a mere acknowledgment of indebtedness which could be redeemed at the company's discretion.

40-10   In *I.R.C.* v. *Cleary*, [26] the taxpayers had 50 per cent. each of the shares of two companies, A Limited and B Limited. B Limited had a balance on profit and loss account of £180,000 of which £130,000 was represented by cash at the bank. The taxpayers sold their shares in A Limited to B Limited for £121,000 in cash (being their market value). The Revenue contended that the taxpayers had secured a tax advantage by receiving from B Limited as the price for their shares assets which were available for distribution by way of dividend and that they had thereby avoided surtax on £121,000 grossed up at the standard rate of tax. The House of Lords unanimously upheld the Revenue's contention.

It will be observed that the definition of " tax advantage " includes the avoidance of a *possible* assessment to tax. The point of the *Cleary* case was that B Limited had paid out cash which, in view of the amount of the revenue reserve, could have been distributed by way of dividend; so the shareholders avoided a possible assessment to surtax. In fact, however, the revenue reserve of B Limited was unaffected by the transactions in securities: all that happened was that a sum of cash in the balance sheet of B Limited was replaced by shares in A Limited. On a subsequent distribution of assets by B Limited, whether in cash or *in specie,* a further liability to tax would arise until the revenue reserve of £180,000 was exhausted. It is difficult in these circumstances to see what tax advantage was secured by the transactions in the *Cleary* case. In a recent case it has been suggested that a person secures a tax advantage if there is any conceivable way in which the transaction could have been carried out more expensively in tax terms. [27]

40-11   (3) *The prescribed circumstances.* Section 461 prescribes five circumstances in which the section applies. Paragraphs A, B and C are aimed at dividend-stripping transactions of various types and are not further considered. The circumstance mentioned in paragraph D is:

" That in connection with the distribution of profits of a company to which this paragraph applies, [28] the person in question so receives as is mentioned in paragraph C (1) above such a consideration as is therein mentioned."

The consideration referred to is a consideration which either—

" (i) is, or represents the value of, assets which are (or apart from anything done by the company in question [29] would have been) available for distribution by way of dividend, [30] or (ii) is received in respect of future receipts

---

[26] [1968] A.C. 766; 44 T.C. 399 (H.L.).

[27] *Anysz* v. *I.R.C., Manolescue* v. *I.R.C.* [1978] S.T.C. 296. See also *Williams* v. *I.R.C.* [1978] S.T.C. 379.

[28] The paragraph applies to (a) any company under the control of not more than five persons, and (b) any other company which does not satisfy the condition that its shares or stock or some class thereof (disregarding debenture stock, preferred shares or preferred stock), are authorised to be dealt in on a stock exchange in the United Kingdom, and are so dealt in (regularly or from time to time); but the paragraph does not apply to a company under the control of one or more companies to which the section does not apply.

[29] *e.g.* a capitalisation of reserves.

[30] This means assets *legally* available for distribution, not assets which are available in a commercial sense: *I.R.C.* v. *Brown* (1971) 47 T.C. 217 (C.A.).

of the company, or (iii) is, or represents the value of, trading stock of the company, and the said person so receives the consideration that he does not pay or bear tax on it as income."

This paragraph was held to apply in the *Parker* [31] and *Cleary* [32] cases. In the *Parker* [33] case the debenture holder had in 1962, on redemption of his debentures, received a consideration representing the value of assets which, but for the capitalisation in 1953, would have been available for distribution by way of dividend; and he received it " in connection with the distribution of profits." The word " distribution " in this context includes application in discharge of liabilities. In the *Cleary* [34] case, the payment of cash by B Limited was a transfer of assets and was therefore a distribution of profits in the sense in which those words are expanded by section 467 (2).

40-12   Paragraph E of section 461 prescribes the circumstance

" That in connection with the transfer directly or indirectly of assets of a company to which paragraph D applies [35] to another such company, or in connection with any transaction in securities in which two or more companies to which paragraph D applies are concerned, the person in question receives non-taxable consideration [36] which is or represents the value of assets available for distribution [36] by such a company and which consists of any share capital or any security (as defined by section 237 (5) of this Act) issued by such a company."

So far as this paragraph related to share capital other than redeemable share capital, it does not apply unless and except to the extent that the share capital is repaid (in a winding up or otherwise). [37] The following are examples of cases to which paragraph E would apply. A Limited which carries on a business has cash or other liquid assets which the shareholders wish to extract. A new company (B Limited) is incorporated to which A Limited transfers its business in consideration of an allotment of ordinary shares and its liquid assets in consideration of debentures or redeemable preference shares. A Limited is then liquidated. Similarly, if the assets of an existing company are " hived off " into a number of newly formed subsidiary companies for a consideration which includes debentures or redeemable preference shares in a subsidiary company, paragraph E will apply to any distribution of such debentures or redeemable preference shares to members of the existing company; but it will not apply to distributions of ordinary shares.

Computation of liability

40-13   In relation to transactions carried out before May 3, 1966, the tax advantage to be counteracted under section 460 was measured by determining what liability to surtax would have been incurred if the person in question had received the amount he in fact received as the net amount of a dividend. There was no income tax liability because, under the pre-corporation tax system, shareholders were not liable to income tax on dividends received from United Kingdom companies.

---

[31] [1966] A.C. 141; 43 T.C. 396 (H.L.); facts, *ante*, § 40-09.
[32] [1968] A.C. 766; 44 T.C. 399 (H.L.); facts, *ante*, § 40-10.   [33] See note 31, above.
[34] See note 32, above.   [35] See note 28 above.
[36] Defined in I.C.T.A. 1970, s. 461 (3).   [37] I.C.T.A. 1970, s. 461, para. E (2).

The position was changed when corporation tax was introduced and dividends were made chargeable to Schedule F income tax, the amount of such tax being borne by the company. Section 466 (2) of the Income and Corporation Taxes Act 1970, provided that, for the purposes of the definition of tax advantage, it should be assumed that a person who might have received from the company any dividend or other distribution (as defined for the purposes of the Corporation Tax Acts [38]) would have borne the income tax chargeable under Schedule F which the company would have had to account for under section 232 (2) [39] of the 1970 Act in respect of the distribution.

Under the imputation system the tax advantage to be counteracted where a member of a company receives an amount otherwise than by way of dividend is the tax that would have been payable by the member had the company made a non-qualifying distribution of an amount equal to the sum received by the member. Thus, if X receives £10,000 in a liquidation or in a " *Cleary* situation " (see § 40-10), X avoids Schedule F income tax on £10,000. There is no tax credit to be added to the £10,000: see § 14-60. If, however, X is to be treated as receiving *income*, it would be right to treat the company as distributing income. Thus if the company had distributed £10,000 by way of dividend, it would have accounted for advance corporation tax and obtained credit in its corporation tax computation; and there are provisions to enable the Board to treat advance corporation tax as having been paid where it is just and reasonable in the circumstances that it should do so. [40]

Return of sums paid by subscribers

40-14   The assets to which paragraphs C, D and E apply " do not include assets which (while of a description which under the law of the country in which the company is incorporated is available for distribution by way of dividend) are shown to represent a return of sums paid by subscribers on the issue of securities." [41] Thus section 460 does not apply to assets representing capital (*e.g.* a share premium account) even though such assets are distributable by way of dividend under the relevant foreign law.

Clearances

40-15   There is a procedure whereby particulars of a proposed transaction may be sent to the Board and the Board asked to give a clearance for the transaction. [42] In cases where a clearance is refused, it has been the general practice of the Board not to enter into any correspondence with the taxpayer or to allow any interviews. In June 1978 the Deputy Chairman of the Board of Inland Revenue announced that, for a trial period of 12 months, an indication of the main grounds for refusing an application for clearance would be given where possible, provided the applicant had given full reasons for the transaction. [43] No appeal lies against a refusal to give a

---

[38] *Ante*, §§ 14-33 *et seq*.
[39] *Ante*, §§ 14-33 *et seq*.
[40] See generally the amendments in F.A. 1973, Sched. 11.
[41] I.C.T.A. 1970, s. 461, para. C (2).
[42] See I.C.T.A. 1970, s. 464.
[43] See S.T.I. (1978), p. 277.

clearance. Section 460, as interpreted by decisions of the House of Lords, has become a monstrous provision and the manner in which the section has been administered has given cause for concern. It is hoped that the position will improve following the announcement of June 1978. Applications for clearance under section 464 have to be submitted at the same time as applications under section 40 or 41 of the Finance Act 1977 (see § 40-32).

2. ARTIFICIAL TRANSACTIONS IN LAND: SECTIONS 488–490

40-16   Section 488 of the Income and Corporation Taxes Act 1970, was enacted " to prevent the avoidance of tax by persons concerned with land or the development of land." Its purpose, expressed in general terms, is to tax as income all *quasi*-dealing profits derived directly or indirectly by the exploitation of land or any interest in land. The marginal note refers to " artificial " transactions in land but this is something of a trap: there is nothing " artificial " in selling shares in a land-owning company, yet this is the very type of transaction to which the section might apply. Section 488 (2) provides that the section applies whenever—

(*a*) land, or any property deriving its value from land (including (*i*) any shareholding in a company, or any partnership interest, or any interest in settled property, deriving its value directly or indirectly from land, and (*ii*) any option, consent or embargo affecting the disposition of land [44]), is acquired with the sole or main object of realising a gain from disposing of the land, or

(*b*) land is held as trading stock, or

(*c*) land is developed with the sole or main object of realising a gain from·disposing of the land when developed,[45]

and any gain of a capital nature [46] is obtained from the disposal of the land in the circumstances next mentioned.

40-17   The section applies to a disposal " by the person acquiring, holding or developing the land, or by any connected person." [47] A company is connected with another person, if that person has control of it or if that person and persons connected with him together have control of it,[48] and any two or more persons acting together to secure or exercise control of a company are treated in relation to that company as connected with one another [49]; so that, for example, section 488 will apply where a company owns land to which (*a*), (*b*) or (*c*) in § 40-16 applies and shares in the company are sold by a person connected with the company, *e.g.* any of the shareholders of a closely controlled company. The section will not apply to sales of shares by members of a quoted company, merely by reason of the company's ownership of land falling within (*a*), (*b*) or (*c*). The section also

---

[44] I.C.T.A. 1970, s. 488 (12).
[45] See *ante*, § 2-11A.
[46] A gain is of a " capital nature " if, apart from the section, it is not chargeable as income. The section does not apply to a gain realised before April 15, 1969: *ibid*. s. 488 (14). And see footnote 54, below.
[47] I.C.T.A. 1970, s. 488 (2). The question whether a person is connected with another is to be determined in accordance with section 533 of the Act: *ibid*. s. 488 (12). See § 16-18A.
[48] *Ibid*. s. 533 (6).   [49] *Ibid*. s. 533 (7).

applies " where any arrangement or scheme is effected as respects the land which enables a gain to be realised by any indirect method, or by any series of transactions, by any person who is a party to, or concerned in, the arrangement or scheme." [50] Thus it would apply if land was disposed of by, for example, the method employed in the case of *Associated London Properties Ltd.* v. *Henriksen.* [51]

40-18   Briefly, where the section applies, the gain (determined in accordance with the section) is treated as income chargeable to tax under Case VI of Schedule D. [52] The section applies to all persons, whether resident in the United Kingdom or not, if all or any part of the land in question is situated in the United Kingdom. [53]

40-19   There is an exemption from the section where a company holds land as trading stock and there is a disposal of shares in that company; but the exemption applies only where all land held by the company is disposed of in the normal course of its trade so as to procure that all opportunity of profit in respect of the land arises to the company. [54] This is an exceedingly badly drafted provision and it is by no means clear how it will operate in practice.

> Suppose that A Ltd. is a property dealing company owning two trading assets, Blackacre and Whiteacre. X and Y, who are brothers, together own the whole of the issued capital of A Ltd. On the sale of the shares, X and Y (if not dealers in shares) would be assessed to tax under Case VI of Schedule D by virtue of section 488 (2). But if subsquently A Ltd. sold Blackacre *and* Whiteacre in the normal course of trade and for full market value, section 488 would cease to apply with the consequence (apparently) that X and Y would be entitled to recover the tax paid by them under Case VI.

It is not clear what the position is if the sale by the company occurs more than six years after the year of assessment in which the sale of the shares takes place. *Quaere* whether X and Y can claim repayment and are assessable to capital gains tax. The practical answer may be that X and Y should take a covenant from the purchaser of the shares to procure that the company will dispose of all its trading stock in the ordinary course of its trade within a period not exceeding six years from the time of the agreement.

40-20   There is a procedure of limited value by which, in certain circumstances, a person who considers that paragraph (*a*) or paragraph (*c*) of section 488 (2), set out in § 40-16, might apply to him can seek a clearance from the Inspector. [55] A clearance under section 488 will in practice preclude an assessment under Case I of Schedule D.

3. SALES OF INCOME DERIVED FROM THE PERSONAL ACTIVITIES OF AN INDIVIDUAL: SECTIONS 487 AND 489

40-21   Schemes of an elaborate nature have existed for some years to enable high tax payers, especially entertainers, to " capitalise " their future earnings.

---

[50] *Ibid.* s. 488 (2). See also *ibid.* s. 489.
[52] I.C.T.A. 1970, s. 488 (3), (6)–(8).
[54] *Ibid.* s. 488 (10).
[51] (1944) 26 T.C. 46: see *ante*, § 2-13.
[53] I.C.T.A. 1970, s. 488 (13).
[55] See *ibid.* s. 488 (11).

Briefly, the individual would form a company, subscribe for shares, and enter into a contract giving the company the benefit of his services for a specified period for a salary. He would then sell the shares in the company to a public non-close company, often in consideration for the issue of loan stock redeemable over a period of years and related in some way to the company's earnings. The Finance Act 1969, contained provisions for taxing under Case VI of Schedule D, as income, the capital amounts received in such circumstances but, as is so frequently the case with anti-avoidance legislation, the relevant provisions are expressed in such wide terms as to include transactions far removed in concept from the transaction which is legislated against. The provisions of the 1969 Act are now in section 487 of the Income and Corporation Taxes Act 1970, which is expressed to apply where—

40-22   (a) transactions or arrangements are effected or made to exploit the earning capacity of an individual in any occupation by putting some other person in the position to enjoy all or any part of the profits or gains or other income, or of the receipts, derived from the individual's activities in that occupation, or anything derived directly or indirectly from any such income or receipts, and

(b) as part of, or in connection with, or in consequence of, the transactions or arrangements any capital amount [56] is obtained by the individual for himself or for any other person, and

(c) the main object, or one of the main objects, of the transactions or arrangements was the avoidance or reduction of liability to income tax.

40-23   In the conventional scheme at which the section was aimed, the individual's service agreement with the company provided for a salary which, even if substantial, was very much less than the expected earning capacity of the individual; and in that sense the service agreement was an arrangement by which the company was able to " exploit " the earning capacity of the individual it employed. It is thought that paragraph (a) in § 40-22 would not apply in a case where an individual was employed at a full commercial rate.

40-24   The section provides that references to any occupation are references " to any activities of any of the kinds pursued in any profession or vocation, irrespective of whether the individual is engaged in a profession or vocation, or is employed by or holds office under some other person." [57] In the case of the conventional scheme at which the section was aimed, the individual was commonly an entertainer pursuing a vocation who, prior to the implementation of the scheme, had been charged to tax under Case II of Schedule D; but the section is made to apply to a person who, while pursuing " Case II activities," had chosen from the start to do so as a director or employee of a company.

---

[56] " Capital amount " means any amount in money or money's worth, which apart from ss. 487–488 does not fall to be included in any computation of income for purposes of the Tax Acts, and other expressions including the word " capital " are to be construed accordingly: *ibid*. s. 489 (13). *Quaere* whether unremitted emoluments earned wholly outside the United Kingdom fall within this definition.
[57] I.C.T.A. 1970, s. 487 (3).

40-25   Section 487 (4) provides that the section shall not apply to a capital amount obtained from the disposal (a) of assets (including any goodwill) of a profession or vocation, or a share in a partnership which is carrying on a profession or vocation, or (b) of shares in a company, so far as the value of what is disposed of, at the time of disposal, is attributable to the value of the profession or vocation as a going concern, or as the case may be to the value of the company's business, as a going concern. Thus the section will not ordinarily apply if, for example, a solicitor sells his partnership share for a capital sum. It is provided, however, that if the value of the profession, vocation or business as a going concern is derived to a material extent from prospective income or receipts derived directly or indirectly from the individual's activities in the occupation, and for which, when all capital amounts are disregarded, the individual will not have received full consideration, whether as a partner in a partnership or as an employee or otherwise, section 487 (4) should not exempt the part of the capital amount so derived.

40-26   Where the section applies, the capital amount is treated for all the purposes of the Income Tax Acts as earned income of the individual which arises when the capital amount is receivable, and which is chargeable to tax under Case VI of Schedule D.[58] An amount is not regarded as receivable by a person until that person can effectively enjoy or dispose of it.[59] The section does not apply as respects a capital amount receivable before April 15, 1969.[60]

40-27   The section applies to all persons, whether resident in the United Kingdom or not, if the occupation of the individual is carried on wholly or partly in the United Kingdom.[61]

4. ASPECTS OF CAPITAL GAINS TAX AVOIDANCE

There are a number of provisions in the legislation relating to capital gains tax by which tax liability is deferred in what may loosely be called " paper for paper " transactions. Many of these provisions have been used in the past in schemes of tax avoidance and the Finance Act 1977 contains anti-avoidance provisions. Some of these are now considered.

Share exchanges

40-28   Assume that X owns 30 per cent. of the issued share capital of Company A. Company B offers to acquire X's shares in Company A and to issue shares in Company B in exchange. X accepts the offer. This transaction involves a disposal by X for money's worth but paragraph 6 of Schedule 7 to the Finance Act 1965, as amended, treats the two companies as if they were the same company and the exchange as if it were a re-organisation of that company's share capital. The effect of this is that the transaction is not treated as involving any disposal of the shares in Company A owned by X or any acquisition of the new holding in Company B; instead, the original

[58] I.C.T.A. 1970, s. 487 (2).
[60] *Ibid.* s. 487 (8).
[59] *Ibid.* s. 489 (13).
[61] *Ibid.* s. 487 (7).

shares and the new holding are treated as the same asset, acquired as the original shares were acquired. This means that X is to be treated for capital gains tax purposes as having acquired the shares in Company B at the time when, and at the price for which, he purchased the shares in Company A. Hence any gain (or loss) which has accrued in respect of X's holding of shares in Company A is deferred or " rolled over " until X makes a disposal of the shares in Company B.

Paragraph 6 of Schedule 7 was capable of being misused in the following way. Assume, as before, that X owns 30 per cent. of the issued share capital of Company A for which X has been offered £10,000 in cash by Company P. The shares in Company A cost X £1,000; hence a sale from X to Company P will give rise to a chargeable gain of (say) £9,000 ignoring expenses. In order to defer this charge, X procures the incorporation outside the United Kingdom of Company B. Company B offers to acquire X's shares in Company A in exchange for an issue of shares in Company B. As explained above, X can " roll over " his gain on this disposal. If Company B immediately sells its shares in Company A to Company P, no chargeable gain accrues in Company B because the expense incurred by Company B in acquiring the shares in Company A will equal their market value at the time Company B acquired them. Hence X will have secured the cash in Company B (from which it might be borrowed) and, provided X retains the shares in Company B until his death, the gain of £9,000 will escape capital gains tax.[62]

Schemes of reconstruction or amalgamation

40-29   The following is an example of an amalgamation of assets. Company A owns a portfolio of investments which Company P wishes to acquire, issuing its own shares (or units, if Company P is an authorised unit trust) in exchange. Company A arranges to go into members' voluntary liquidation and its members enter into an agreement with the liquidator, *e.g.* under section 287 of the Companies Act 1948, that the liquidator will transfer the assets of Company A (after satisfying liabilities) to Company P and that the members of Company A will accept in the liquidation, in satisfaction of their rights as members, shares issued by Company P. This is a scheme of amalgamation. Two questions arise which affect the charge to tax on capital gains: (i) Is the transfer of assets from Company A to Company P exempt from tax by reason of section 267 (1) of the Income and Corporation Taxes Act 1970? This section applies where, *inter alia,* any scheme of reconstruction or amalgamation[63] involves the transfer of the whole or part of a company's business to another company and the transferor company receives no part of the consideration for the transfer (otherwise than by the transferee company taking over the whole or part of the

---

[62] For a similar scheme, see *Floor* v. *Davis* [1978] S.T.C. 436 (C.A.).

[63] Difficulty frequently arises in practice in determining what is, or is not, a scheme of reconstruction. Schemes of partition are so regarded for capital gains tax purposes: see Inland Revenue Press Release of October 16, 1975, in [1975] S.T.I. 484; but this seems inconsistent with stamp duty cases: see, *e.g. Brooklands Selangor Ltd.* v. *I.R.C.* [1970] 1 W.L.R. 429 in § 33-02 and *Baytrust Holdings Ltd.* v. *I.R.C.* [1971] 1 W.L.R. 1333. Since there is now a clearance procedure requiring the Board to determine what is or is not a scheme of reconstruction, it is to be hoped that the Capital Gains Tax and Stamp Duty Departments of the Inland Revenue will sing in unison.

liabilities of the business); (ii) Can the members of Company A defer any liability to capital gains tax on their holdings in Company A under paragraph 7 of Schedule 7 to the Finance Act 1965? This paragraph refers to the case where, under any arrangement between a company and the persons holding shares in or debentures of the company or any class of such shares or debentures, being an arrangement entered into for the purposes of or in connection with the scheme or reconstruction or amalgamation,[63] another company issues shares or debentures to those persons in respect of and in proportion to (or as nearly as may be in proportion to) their holdings of the first-mentioned shares or debentures. Where this paragraph applies, the transaction is treated as if it were a share exchange: see § 40-28.

The transaction in the last example involves an element of tax avoidance. The alternative and simpler procedure would have been for Company A to go into members' voluntary liquidation and to distribute its assets in the form of cash to enable its shareholders to re-invest in Company P; but this transaction would have involved two liabilities to capital gains tax, one on the company and the other on its members. The scheme mitigates this dual liability.

Avoidance provisions: Finance Act 1977, ss. 40–41

40-30   Sections 40 (2) and 41 (1) of the Finance Act 1977 now provide that neither paragraph 6 of Schedule 7 (share exchanges) nor paragraph 7 of Schedule 7 and section 267 of the 1970 Act (reconstructions and amalgamations) shall apply unless the transaction in question is effected for bona fide commercial reasons and does not form part of a scheme or arrangements of which the main purpose, or one of the main purposes, is avoidance of liability to capital gains tax or corporation tax or, in the case of section 267, income tax. However, section 40 (2) is not to affect the operation of paragraph 6 or 7 (a) in any case where the person to whom the shares or debentures are issued does not hold more than 5 per cent. of, or of any class of, the shares in or debentures of the acquired company or (b) in any case where, before the issue is made, the Board have on the application of *either company* notified the applicant that the Board are satisfied that the exchange, reconstruction or amalgamation [63] will be effected for bona fide commercial reasons and will not form part of any such scheme or arrangements as are there mentioned.[64] The sections apply when the issue or transfer takes place after April 19, 1977.[65]

Applications for clearance [66]

40-31   Applications for clearance under section 40 or 41 of the Finance Act 1977 have to be in writing and to contain particulars of the operations to be effected. The Board has 30 days within which to require the applicant to furnish further particulars for the purpose of enabling the Board to make their decision (such period being further extended if further particulars are

---

[64] F.A. 1977, s. 40 (3). As to recovery of unpaid tax, see *ibid*. s. 40 (8) and the new I.C.T.A. 1970, s. 267 (3B) and (3C).
[65] *Ibid*. ss. 40 (10) and 41 (2).
[66] *Ibid*. s. 40 (3)–(7).

required). The Board have to notify their decision to the applicant within 30 days of receiving the application or, if they require further particulars, within 30 days of the notice requiring such particulars being complied with. If the Board are not satisfied that the transaction will be effected for bona fide commercial reasons, etc., or do not notify their decision within the time specified, the applicant may require the matter to be referred to the Special Commissioners. An application for clearance under the section is void if it does not fully and accurately disclose all facts and considerations material for the decision.

40-32   An Inland Revenue Press Release on April 19, 1977,[67] requires that applications for clearance under section 40 or 41 of the Finance Act 1977 should be made separately from (but cross-referenced to) any clearances or consents being sought under sections 464 (§ 40-15), 482 (§ 7-24) or 488 (§ 40-20) in respect of the same scheme. The applications are required to give full particulars of the proposed scheme and of all companies directly involved, the tax districts and references to which the company's accounts are submitted; and they must be accompanied by copies of accounts for the last two years for which accounts have been prepared.

Value shifting

40-33   There have been a number of schemes for shifting value out of shares into other shares owned by the same person, or a person connected with him; and often such schemes have been designed with a view to the disposal of the shares from which value has passed, so as to give rise to an allowable loss capable of being set off against chargeable gains made elsewhere. The object of many such schemes is to " manufacture " artificial losses. Assume, for example, that X subscribes £10,000 for the whole of the share capital of Company A. Company A then applies the £10,000 in subscribing for (say) 40 per cent. of the share capital of Company B. Company Y owns the remaining 60 per cent. of Company B. The immediate effect of the investment by Company A is to reduce the value of X's shares in Company A and to increase the value of the shares held by Company Y. Thus a sale of the Company A shares by X would produce an immediate loss, which could be utilised if chargeable gains had accrued to X in respect of some other transaction. X or members of his family might own shares in Company Y.

40-34   Section 43 of the Finance Act 1977 is couched in wide terms and is expressed to have effect as respects the disposal of an asset if a scheme has been effected or arrangements have been made (whether before or after the disposal) whereby—

(a) The value of the asset has been materially reduced; and

(b) a tax free benefit has been or will be conferred—

(i) on the person making the disposal or a person with whom he is connected; or

---

[67] [1977] S.T.I. 88.

(ii) on any other person, except where it is shown that avoidance of tax was not the main purpose or one of the main purposes of the scheme or arrangements in question.

A *benefit* is to be treated as conferred on a person if he becomes entitled to any money or money's worth or the value of any asset in which he has an interest is increased or he is wholly or partly relieved from any liability to which he is subject; and a benefit is treated as *tax-free* unless it is required, on the occasion on which it is conferred on the person in question, to be brought into account in computing his income, profits or gains for the purposes of income tax, capital gains tax or corporation tax. Where the section applies, any allowable loss or chargeable gain accruing on the disposal is to be calculated as if the consideration for the disposal were increased by such amount as appears to the Inspector, or on appeal the Commissioners concerned, to be just and reasonable having regard to the scheme or arrangements and the tax free benefit in question. There are provisions to prevent a double charge to tax on a later disposal. The section does not apply to disposals by personal representatives to legatees, disposals between husband and wife or disposals within a group of companies; nor does it apply if, for example, a parent company selling a subsidiary withdraws surplus cash in the form of a dividend prior to the sale of the subsidiary. The section applies where the disposal and reduction in value are after March 29, 1977. The section contains no provision for obtaining clearance in advance of the transaction being implemented.

INDEX